The Civilization of the American Indian Series

The Quiché Mayas of Utatlán

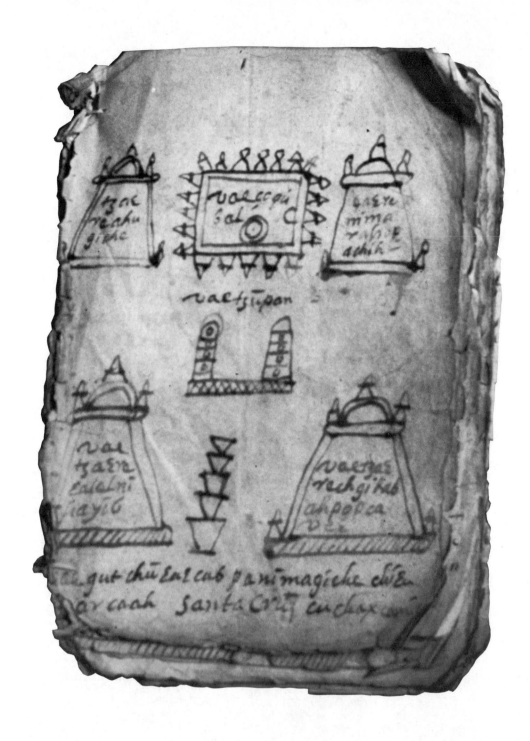

A native pictorial view of Utatlán,
prepared in conjunction with the *Título Totonicapán*, A.D. 1554.

The
Quiché Mayas
of Utatlán

The Evolution of a
Highland Guatemala Kingdom

By Robert M. Carmack

UNIVERSITY OF OKLAHOMA PRESS : NORMAN

By Robert M. Carmack

Quichean Civilization: The Ethnohistoric, Ethnographic, and Archaeological Sources (Berkeley, Calif., 1973)
La formación del Reino Quiché segun la arqueología y etnología (with John Fox and Russell Stewart) (Guatemala City, 1975)
Archaeology and Ethnohistory of the Central Quiché (editor, with D. T. Wallace) (Albany, N.Y., 1977)
Historia social de los Quichés (Guatemala City, 1979)
The Quiché Mayas of Utatlán: The Evolution of a Highland Guatemala Kingdom (Norman, 1981)

Library of Congress Cataloging in Publication Data

Carmack, Robert M   1934–
    The Quiché Mayas of Utatlán.

    (The Civilization of the American Indian series; 155)
    Bibliography: p. 409
    Includes index.
    1. Quichés. 2. Guatemala—History—To 1821.
I. Title. II. Series: Civilization of the American
Indian series; 155.
F1465.2.Q5C267   972.81'01   80–5241

To my family

Gladys and Cecil
Carmen and Harold
Adele, Curtis, Matthew
Philip, Laura, and Tommy

CONTENTS

Contents

ILLUSTRATIONS

MAPS AND DRAWINGS

Maps and Drawings

TABLES

PREFACE

For a number of years my own research has focused on the Quichés of Guatemala. It began with a doctoral dissertation in which I attempted to summarize and evaluate the documentary sources available for reconstructing pre-Hispanic Quiché culture. I continued that work for another six years after the dissertation was completed, consulting most of the world's archives with Quiché holdings. In addition I searched many Quiché community archives for old papers. The result of that work was a book on the Quiché sources, in which I summarized, described, and evaluated the contents of the most important documentary sources for studying Quiché culture (Carmack 1973). That research was a critical first step in preparing the present book, which is based primarily on the documentary sources.

While working on the dissertation, I became aware of the importance of survivals of Quiché culture among present-day peasants in highland Guatemala. An ethnographic study of a Quiché-speaking community seemed essential, and for a year (1966–67) and later for six months (in 1970) I carried out ethnographic investigations in Santiago Momostenango. From that work I learned to speak Quiché, and with this invaluable tool I began translating and interpreting the ancient native chronicles. Momostenango also opened up a world of traditional Quiché cultural forms not sufficiently clear in the documentary sources: lineage organization, customary law, ritual associated with the earth deity, the ancestors, the calendric fates, rural territorial divisions, traditional stratification, and authority allocation. I began visiting other Quiché communities, gathering comparative data on traditional culture. I carried on some ethnographic surveying in conjunction with work for the Peace Corps, some as part of an ethnology summer field school held in Quiché in 1973 and some as part of studies related to the earthquake damages in 1976. The reader will discover that many details about ancient Quiché culture in this book derive from my ethnographic experience in the highlands.

In the dissertation I used archaeological data gathered from site reports and from brief visits to some of the Quiché sites. The sites provided a sense of reality about the pre-Hispanic Quichés not easily captured from the documents alone. I became convinced of the importance of archaeological data for the study of the pre-Hispanic Quichés and began surveying Quiché sites in the highlands with the aid of graduate archaeology students. To locate the sites we made use of information contained in the early documents and Quiché-speaking native informants who led us to the sites. In the summer of 1973 an all-out effort was made to locate the most important Quiché sites mentioned in the documents, especially in the central area. The result of that work was a doctoral dissertation by John Fox (1975), comparing the settlement pattern of about one hundred Quiché sites. For the fifteen historically identified sites that we located in the Quiché basin, we prepared a small book (Carmack, Fox, and Stewart 1975) summarizing the development of Quiché culture as revealed by surface archaeology.

Beginning in 1972 and continuing in 1973 and 1974, archaeologists of SUNY at Albany began excavations at Utatlán and related sites. I have worked closely with them in the planning and direction of this work, since we believed that historical data might provide particularly interesting excavational questions and also details helpful in interpreting artifacts. I have followed the results of their work, and I include many of their data in this book. In a sense I attempt to summarize their work up to this point, for beginning in 1977 major new excavations were undertaken in the area.

Further to prepare for this book, I translated from the original Spanish and Quiché documents all passages containing references to pre-Hispanic Utatlán. There were over one hundred pages of translations, attesting to the extensive documentation on the community. Unfortunately, during a visit to Guatemala City in 1976 these translations were stolen along with other papers before copies could be made. I have not attempted to duplicate the work; rather, I went back to the originals to write this book. Unless otherwise specified, all translations in the book are mine, taken directly from the Spanish or Quiché texts. I had intended to include the translated texts as appendices; instead the reader must turn to the published editions to check my interpretation of them.

Many years ago John Lloyd Stephens commented that Santa Cruz del Quiché would be an ideal place in which to live and study the language and history of the Quichés, "for here they still exist in many respects an unchanged people, cherishing the usages and customs of their ancestors" (1841, p. 191). While I realize that Santa Cruz is no longer the traditional community it was in the days of Stephens, nevertheless I decided to live there while writing this book. That made it possible to check many details about Utatlán history and culture on location. For example, I studied old maps and drawings of Utatlán at the site itself, traced the boundaries and location of ancient territorial divisions with natives living in those areas, discovered colonial- and republican-period documents in private hands, interviewed aged natives on their past customs and traditions, and observed at first hand the geographic and ecological conditions of the Quiché area. I have not deemed it necessary to cite all the specific sources of this kind in the book, but the reader is assured that much detail and background information was obtained in this fashion. The great French historian Marc Block argued that the student of history had best learn as much as he can about the social life of a people as it is today if he hopes to understand how it was in the past. That is good advice, and I believe that my account of the Utatlán community was greatly enriched by the eight months' residence in Santa Cruz del Quiché.

Those Guatemalans, especially Quiché Indians, who have most richly contributed to this book are too numerous to be named—and too removed from the cares of a scholar's world to appreciate the gesture. Almost without exception the Quiché Indians of the western highlands of Guatemala have been generous to me with their time, talents, and knowledge. The understanding of Quiché culture that they gave me is the foundation upon which this book was built. That is true despite the historical nature of the book. This fact has been an object lesson to me about the essential importance of ethnographic knowledge for any historical work. I gladly recognize that and pay homage to those living souls who helped give life to those who have gone on, the *santos ánimas*.

As mentioned above, two Quiché communities have been the loci of much of the research that went into this book: Santiago Momostenango and Santa Cruz del Quiché. Authorities in these two towns provided me with official permission to conduct my research. It is not possible to name them all, though I would be remiss if I did not mention the former alcalde of Momostenango, Roberto Pérez Zárate, and his *oficial cuarto*, Santiago Guix. They more than anyone else opened the community for my research, and I thank them. In Santa Cruz del Quiché it was Alcalde Carlos Alonzo Samayoa who paved the way for my work in that town. I hope my small contribution to Quiché "history" will be counted as still another worthy *obra* left behind by Don Carlos.

Cooperation from officials at the national level in Guatemala was equally forthcoming. Luís Luján Muños, past director of the Instituto de Antropología e Historia, never failed me in all the years I depended upon his authorization and support. I consider him a true friend. Many other staff members of the institute could be mentioned, as well as authorities from the Instituto Nacional Indigenista, the Archivo General de Centroamerica, the

Seminario de Integración Social Guatemalteca, the Ministerio de Educación Pública, and the Universidad de San Carlos. It would not be fair to mention their names, for invariably some would be left out. I thank them all collectively.

I am greatly indebted to those agencies and institutions that have generously provided financial support for my Quiché studies. They include the National Science Foundation, the National Endowment for the Humanities, the Social Science Research Council, the National Geographic Society, the American Philosophical Society, the Wenner Gren Foundation, the State University of New York Research Foundation, and the Department of Anthropology of the State University of New York at Albany. Combined ethnohistoric and archaeological research is expensive, and the above agencies made it possible for me.

Many graduate students from the State University of New York at Albany contributed to the information and to the enthusiasm that went into the preparation of this book. I want particularly to thank John W. Fox, Russell E. and Florence Stewart, John Weeks, and Steve Marqusee for contributions from the archaeological side. Ethnological support has come from Barbara Tedlock, Stewart Stearns, Garrett Cook, Nancy Black, Laurel Bossen, and Duncan Earle. I have benefited from the linguistic contributions of James Mondloch, and also of Chris DeCormier, whose untimely death has been a great personal loss to me.

Finally, I acknowledge the continuing support in many forms from the Department of Anthropology of the State University of New York at Albany. I have received constant stimulation from my "Mesoamericanist" colleagues there, Lyle Campbell, Peter Furst, Dean Snow and Dwight Wallace, as well as friendly and intellectually stimulating encouragement from other colleagues in the department. The university also provided me with a sabbatical leave, during which time most of the actual writing of the book was done. No scholar ever appreciated a sabbatical leave more than I did that one, and I thank those who made it possible.

State University of New York   ROBERT M. CARMACK
Albany

The Quiché Mayas of Utatlán

1
INTRODUCTION

THIS BOOK IS ABOUT THE QUICHÉS, a people who created a powerful Maya kingdom in the highlands of Guatemala shortly before the Spanish conquest. From their political center at Utatlán they controlled much of what is now Guatemala. Their accomplishments made them the primary object of the Spanish conquest in central America.

The name Quiché derives from the language that was spoken at Utatlán and in most of the kingdom's provinces. The Quiché language belongs to the Quichean branch of the Maya family, its closest relatives being Cakchiquel, Tzutujil, and Sacapultec (Campbell 1977). Quiché was spoken elegantly at Utatlán and was the lingua franca of the kingdom and probably the marketing language of the highlands. The people also used the Nahua language at Utatlán and elsewhere in the kingdom, especially in dealings with Pacific Coast peoples and other Mesoamerican peoples.

The Quichés' tradition, as recorded in their chronicles, states that they came from Toltec stock in Mexico. The traditions tell of a legendary migration to the mountains of Quiché and the subsequent conquest of local peoples. After the native communities on the plains had been completely subjugated, the Quichés built a large town there and called it Utatlán.

The Quiché kingdom at Utatlán was ostensibly a confederacy formed by three original peoples, the Quichés proper (Nima Quichés), the Tamubs, and the Ilocabs. Each confederate unit had its own town, known anciently as K'umarcaaj (Utatlán), Pismachi, and Pilocab. The three towns were united in one community, which in this book is referred to as Utatlán. Their tripartite rule was firmly established over the peoples of the plains, who were pulled into the nuclear community. They also rapidly expanded their rule to the far corners of the highlands and much of the Pacific coastal area as well (Fig. 1.1). This expansion was carried out at the expense of competing political groups, who are known to us by the languages they spoke: the Cakchiquels, Tzutujils, the Mams, the Ixils, the Pokomams, and the Pipils.

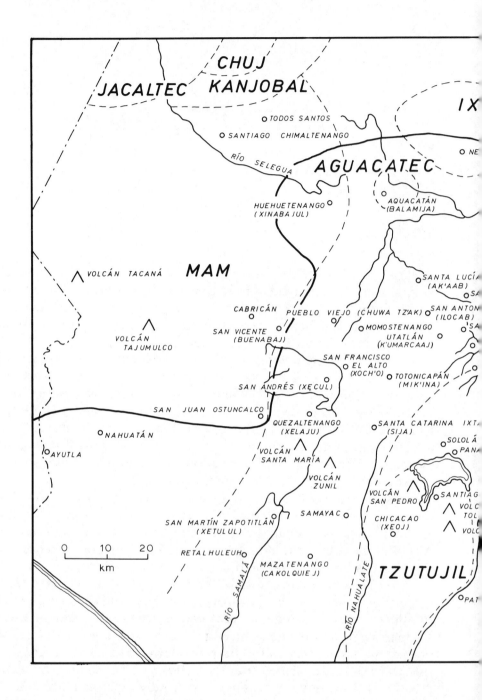

Fig. 1.1.

The political and linguistic boundaries of the pre-Hispanic Quiché state, ca. 1450. Modified from Miles 1957.

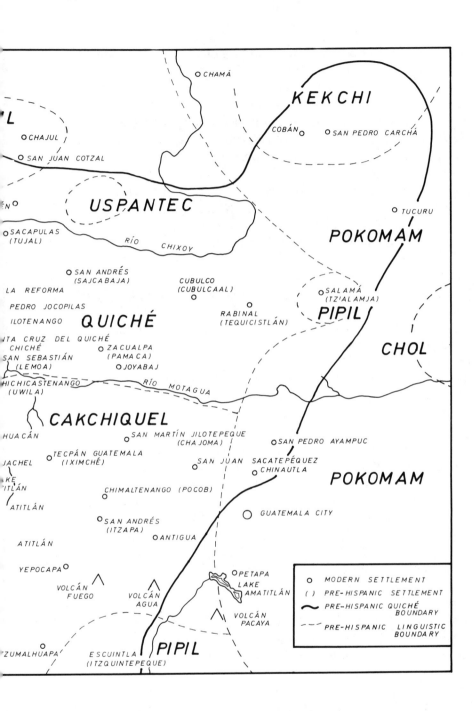

CHAMÁ

KEKCHI

'L

CHAJUL

SAN JUAN COTZAL

COBÁN   SAN PEDRO CARCHÁ

N

USPANTEC

TUCURU

SACAPULAS
(TUJAL)

RÍO   CHIXOY

POKOMAM

SAN ANDRÉS
(SAJCABAJA)

CUBULCO
(CUBULCAAL)

SALAMÁ
(TZ'ALAMJA)

LA REFORMA

PEDRO JOCOPILAS

ILOTENANGO

QUICHÉ

RABINAL
(TEQUICISTLÁN)

PIPIL

TA CRUZ DEL QUICHÉ
CHICHÉ

SAN SEBASTIÁN
(LEMOA)

ZACUALPA
(PAMACA)

JOYABAJ

CHOL

HICHICASTENANGO
(UWILA)

RÍO   MOTAGUA

CAKCHIQUEL

HUACÁN

SAN MARTÍN JILOTEPEQUE
(CHAJOMA)

SAN PEDRO AYAMPUC

JACHEL

TECPÁN GUATEMALA
(IXIMCHÉ)

SAN JUAN   SACATEPÉQUEZ
CHINAUTLA

POKOMAM

KE
ITLÁN

CHIMALTENANGO (POCOB)

ATITLÁN

SAN ANDRÉS
(ITZAPA)

GUATEMALA CITY

ANTIGUA

ATITLÁN

YEPOCAPA

PETAPA
LAKE
AMATITLÁN

VOLCÁN
FUEGO

VOLCÁN
AGUA

VOLCÁN
PACAYA

ZUMALHUAPA

ESCUINTLA
(ITZQUINTEPEQUE)

PIPIL

○   MODERN SETTLEMENT

( )   PRE-HISPANIC SETTLEMENT

〜   PRE-HISPANIC QUICHÉ
        BOUNDARY

---   PRE-HISPANIC   LINGUISTIC
        BOUNDARY

In the process of building a far-flung conquest state, the Quichés gained the ascendancy in the confederacy over the Tamubs and the Ilocabs. Eventually the Ilocabs challenged them militarily, were defeated, and after that became totally subordinate to the Quichés of Utatlán. The Tamubs continued to share in state government but gradually lost influence. The dominant position of the Quichés allows us to refer to the three groups collectively as the Quichés and to their tripartite community as Utatlán. Though the Quichés referred to their chief town as K'umarcaaj, it was also called by its Nahua name, Utatlán, within broader Mesoamerican contexts. I have chosen to use the Nahua name in this book to emphasize the close relationship between the Quichés and other Mesoamerican peoples.

The basic patterns of Quiché culture at Utatlán are known: a preoccupation with military conquest, commoner-aristocrat social ranking, human sacrifice, segmentary lineage organization, quadripartite political rule, a variant of Mixteca-Puebla arts and crafts, dualism and cardinal-point orientation in religious symbolism, ritual calendrics, heroic history. These patterns show that the Quichés were full participants in the Mesoamerican culture tradition. They shared all its main features (Kirchhoff 1952) and combined its two major cultural streams, the Mexican (specifically Epi-Toltec) and the Mayan (specifically highland Quichean). The Quiché culture was based on a great civilized tradition with almost three thousand years of history. To understand the Quichés is to understand Mesoamerican civilization in the broad sense.

This book, then, is about Quiché culture as it was expressed at Utatlán. It also includes the cultural forms of the rural zone in the central Quiché basin surrounding the three towns. The study has been restricted to the central area partly to facilitate the integration of data from the *Popol Vuh* and other documentary sources with the archaeological data of the Utatlán sites. These sites have been the object of intensive investigation by archaeologists of the State University of New York at Albany (SUNY at Albany), and their data are highly complementary with the documentary sources on the Utatlán community. I have attempted to take advantage of that complementarity in writing this book.

The central area is also a fairly well defined ecological zone, often referred to in this book as the Quiché basin or plateau. Early in Quiché history the basin defined the extent of state territory, and even later, after boundaries had been extended to distant provinces, the central area continued to constitute the core sustaining area. The local population was organized into coordinated territorial divisions and integrated into affairs of state. In contrast, the provinces were much less tightly integrated into the state and remained culturally diverse. It will be shown that the Utatlán community alone, without the provinces, is worthy of our full attention and that it manifests the important cultural characteristics of the Quiché state as a whole.

In 1524, Pedro de Alvarado and a small band of Spanish forces invaded the kingdom of Utatlán. The Quichés sent their bravest warriors against the Spaniards, led by Tecum, the king's grandson. In a decisive battle near present-day Quezaltenango, the Quichés were ignominiously defeated, and Tecum was killed. Utatlán easily fell after that, and Quiché culture began changing radically. This book, finally, is also about the "decline" of Utatlán culture, a topic no less interesting because it was forced from the outside. Possibly more of Quiché culture has survived among the rural inhabitants of the area than has that of any of the other great kingdoms of Mesoamerica. These survivals will be of interest, especially as they help us reconstruct the pre-Hispanic culture of the Quichés at Utatlán.

The ethnohistoric sources containing references to Utatlán are relatively extensive compared with those of other pre-Hispanic communities in Mesoamerica. No doubt that is due to Utatlán's position as the most important politicoreligious center in pre-Conquest Guatemala and perhaps in all of Central America. Utatlán was famous, and the native chroniclers and Spanish officials and priests had much to say about it. Utatlán, in fact, is one of the best-documented archaeological sites in all of Mesoamerica, the Aztec center of Tenochtitlán, Mayapán, and possibly some Mixtec sites being its closest rivals.

The native chronicles are the most important ethnohistoric source for the study of the Utatlán community. In a careful analysis of the relevant passages about Utatlán in the native Quiché and Cakchiquel texts, my objective has been to reconstruct to the extent possible the native view of the community. The Spanish accounts add details not found in the chronicles and generally provide a more pragmatic, secular view of the community. The two sources of data are felicitously complementary.

Undoubtedly the *Popol Vuh* is the most important single source for the study of Utatlán. Though I shall refer to it as a chronicle, as is well known, its historical parts are perhaps less important than its mythological and ritual content. Both have specific relevance for Utatlán. I believe the document to have been written at Utatlán (Santa Cruz del Quiché) by Quiché lords shortly after A.D. 1560,[1] though it was later found by Fray Francisco Ximénez in Chichicastenango. Recently I discovered a previously unknown Quiché document at Totonicapán that contains a summary of the historical part of the *Popol Vuh* (Carmack 1975). It was written at Utatlán by descendants of the

---

[1] All dates in this book are A.D. unless otherwise indicated.

rulers of that community, and is almost identical in language with the *Popol Vuh*. This is an important verification of the Utatlán origin of the *Popol Vuh*, though the document adds little new information to that great book. The *Popol Vuh* itself provides us with the "official" view of the Utatlán community as seen by its leading resident rulers (Edmonson 1969).

A close rival to the *Popol Vuh* in importance for the ethnohistory of Utatlán is a Tamub *título* (Recinos 1957). I recently found a second version of that document at Totonicapán, identical in text except for different land boundaries in the last section. The Totonicapán version pushes back the composition date of the *Título Tamub* to at least the 1560s. After several years of working with the *título*, I have determined that it contains by far our most extensive account of the political geography of the Utatlán community as seen by the Quichés themselves. It is also our best source on lineage organization at Utatlán.

After the *Popol Vuh* and the *Título Tamub*, next in importance for the study of Utatlán is a set of chronicles written on behalf of Quiché princes one step below the royal lines of the community. I shall refer to these documents as the *Títulos Nijaib, C'oyoi, Totonicapán*, and *Yax* (Carmack, 1973). The Totonicapán and Yax *títulos* were also part of the Totonicapán discovery mentioned above. The *Título Totonicapán* is especially important for the study of Utatlán now that we have the original Quiché text. Each one of these "second-line" documents contains penetrating, if brief, accounts of the Utatlán community. Two of them provide us with "maps," highly stylized drawings of buildings at Utatlán as they were remembered by people who had lived there before the Conquest.

The Cakchiquel chronicles have a special value for the study of Utatlán. They provide us with an interested but partly independent view of the community. Certainly the Cakchiquels understood the Quiché community and were more willing than the Quiché chroniclers to reveal some of its more disruptive elements. The Cakchiquels were also more history-oriented than the Quichés, so that some of our most intricate details of Quiché history come from Cakchiquel sources. The most important Cakchiquel documents are *The Annals of the Cakchiquels* (Villacorta 1934) and the *Títulos Xpantzay* (Recinos 1957*a, b, c*).

The Spanish sources of first-order importance are eyewitness accounts by officials of the Spanish government, both political and religious. Accounts by the conquistador Pedro de Alvarado and the judges Alonso de Zorita and Tomás López Medel are brief but highly perceptive. More extensive, though mostly based on secondhand information, are accounts prepared by Friars Bartolomé de las Casas and Pedro de Betanzos. Both of these sources are rich in their description of the sociopolitical organization of the Utatlán community, though they present very different interpretations of the community.

Almost as important as the accounts of Las Casas or Betanzos is the one written by the seventeenth-century Guatemalan creole Francisco Antonio de Fuentes y Guzmán. He came in possession of a detailed map of Utatlán prepared by the Tamub Quichés in the sixteenth century. Unfortunately he failed to include the map in his book (though he left a blank page for it), and his account is exaggerated in some places. Nevertheless, I now believe that his descriptions of the buildings and places in the Utatlán community are authentic and deserve our close attention.

Fuentes y Guzmán was "archaeological" in the sense that he referred specifically to buildings still standing in his day at Utatlán and other sites. Similar though less detailed "archaeological" accounts were written by other colonial scholars—for example, Martín Alfonso Tovilla (1635) and Ximénez (ca. 1700). Apparently as late as the times in which they wrote, native traditions remained about the identity and functions of some of the buildings of Utatlán. The descriptions of the site from the nineteenth and twentieth centuries can be considered archaeological reports, though Robert Wauchope's test excavations in the 1940s were the first "scientific" archaeology carried out there. I treat all archaeological reports about Utatlán as primary historical data on the material culture of the community and attempt to integrate them with the other historical documents. A fuller discussion of the archaeological sources will be found in chapter 8.

Various "secondary" documentary sources contain scattered, highly selective information about the Utatlán community. They include tributary and later national censuses, colonial histories (such as Ximénez's), land-dispute documents and titles, Quiché and Cakchiquel dictionaries, travel accounts by visitors to Quiché, and others. While such sources have limited value for reconstructing the pre-Hispanic Utatlán community, they provide crucial insight into the process by which that community changed and adapted after the Conquest. Their importance will be especially evident in chapter 8, where the decline of the community is sketched.

In connection with sources it should be remembered that at the present time about 100,000 Quiché-speaking natives live in the area. Descendants of the original inhabitants of the community, they retain many of the ancient place names and practice some of the old cultural forms. Ethnographic studies in the area, therefore, constitute still another important source for studying the Utatlán community. Of special utility are the several studies of cultural life at Chichicastenango made during the 1930s. Similarly important is Ricardo Falla's recent dissertation on culture at San Antonio Ilotenango. There is still no adequate ethnography of Santa Cruz del Quiché, though several students and I have made ethnographic surveys in the municipality during the past few years. Much more research of this kind is needed, and two ethnographic studies are in progress in the central Quiché area. Ethnographic data were especially useful in preparing the chapters detailing the ecology of the central area and the decline of the Utatlán community, and they provided interpretative detail for the other chapters as well.

It should be obvious that the term "ethnohistory" is being used broadly in this book. The primary data for the book come from the ancient chronicles, but all available archaeological and ethnographic data have been incorporated where relevant. The reconstruction of the pre-Hispanic Utatlán community and the process of its development and decline have been my primary goals, while the methods and sources used have been secondary considerations. The basic problem of the book is clearly historical in nature, and that was a decisive factor in my decision to refer to the study as ethnohistory. It is my hope that archaeologists, ethnologists, historians, and other students of the Quiché Mayas will find the account useful and relevant to their own studies.

This book does not contain a reconstruction of pre-Hispanic Utatlán culture in the traditional ethnohistoric or ethnographic sense. The reader will find no systematic treatment of Quiché economics, kinship, political organization, art, religion, or language. That more holistic task must be reserved for the future and another volume on Quiché culture.

There is much groundwork to be laid before an ethnography of Quiché culture can be written. The documentary sources need better translations and more exegesis. First-approximation analyses of Utatlán functional systems (economics, kinship, and so on), based on a comparative study of the chronicles and Spanish sources, need to be undertaken. It is also hoped that additional chronicles will be found, especially ones that might shed more light on social life at Utatlán during the last years of its independent existence. Intensive archaeological work began at Utatlán and related sites in March, 1977, and is continuing. This research should provide enough data on Utatlán material culture to establish better functional relations between artifact and social life in the community. Undoubtedly many more examples of Utatlán art will be uncovered, including painted frescoes. They will be invaluable for reconstructing Utatlán symbolism, to judge from the mural paintings already discovered at the site. Further, linguists are finally beginning to understand the grammatical and semantic structure of the Quiché language. The first steps in comparing the structure of modern Quiché with the language of Utatlán and other pre-Hispanic communities have been taken, and well-qualified specialists plan to continue that work. Thus it is clear that Quiché research in the next few years will yield rich data for construction of a holistic view of pre-Hispanic Quiché culture. I hope to participate in that cultural construction at the appropriate time.

For now my emphasis in this book is on process—the development and change of the Utatlán community. In chapter 2, "The Questions," I set out the major questions to be examined. The general theoretical questions are laid out for the reader, and the contribution of past students of the Quichés is summarized. This somewhat long second part of chapter 2 is necessary because of the relative unfamiliarity of Quiché studies. It is important for the reader to understand that first-rate scholars have studied Quiché development and that in this book I have built on many of their ideas.

In chapter 3, "Origins," I provide an account of the events and processes leading to the formation of the Utatlán community. Historical studies of the documents, Quichean languages, and archaeology are combined in this chapter in order to reconstruct the antecedents of central Quiché society. The prototypic political system in the mountains north of the central Quiché plains, which later developed into the Utatlán "kingdom," is also described.

In chapter 4, "Ecology," the Utatlán community is placed in its physical setting. This chapter permits us to understand more fully the limitations and potential for development resulting from Utatlán's material environment. The account is an attempt to reconstruct the Quichés' own view of the physical world around them and to identify the natural resources of the central area. Much of the information in this chapter is still preliminary, and more specialized research is needed before we can truly understand the ecological "underpinnings" of Utatlán.

Chapter 5, "Utatlán History," contains a brief historical overview of Utatlán, especially its major political events. I deemed this chapter essential because I believe that historical events both reflect and influence developmental processes in society. This is seen especially clearly in the "revolution" at Utatlán during the reign of Q'uik'ab, described in chapter 5. At that time new political relations were established that significantly altered the Utatlán community.

In chapter 6, "Social Structure," I deal especially with those overarching features that characterized all levels and sectors of the Utatlán community: horizontal stratification, lineage organization, territorial divisions, and authority. While the reconstruction may appear overly static, there is nevertheless at least an implicit stress on the dynamic, developmental aspect of Utatlán society. In a slightly different form the contents of this chapter were published in an earlier monograph (Carmack and Wallace 1977).

In the discussion on "Symbolics," chapter 7, I confine myself to the Quichés' own view of their community. This is in keeping with the over-all theme of the book, which centers on the archaeological site of Utatlán and its interpretation through use of documents. Ritual, myth, and art, as well as political symbolism, are brought together in the chapter. Contrasts drawn between town and rural symbolism will give the reader some feeling for changing symbols through time.

Chapter 8, "Settlement Patterns," relies heavily on archaeological research. There is perhaps less original research of my own in this chapter, though I have been closely associated with all the recent archaeological work at Utatlán (but not with the actual excavations). Much of the information is widely scattered in field notes, reports, and all-but-inaccessible publications. One of the purposes of this chapter and the next is to bring together the various sources in convenient summary form. In chapter 8, I define settlement patterns primarily in physical terms, after which I try to provide symbolic interpretations either from archaeological inference or from data in the documents.

Chapter 9, "The Buildings of Utatlán," also relies heavily on archaeological data. The detailed studies by Dwight Wallace (1977) of buildings at Utatlán have been an invaluable source for this chapter. The reader should be aware that for very few ancient communities is it possible to combine historical detail with building remains to the degree that it has been done in this chapter. One of the interesting results for such "historical archaeology" is the discovery that the two sets of data do not always fit perfectly together; indeed, they sometimes clash. This raises the possibility of a dialectic relation between ideal and actual, and a basis for social change.

Chapter 10, "After the Fall," provides documentation for the disintegration of the Utatlán community beginning with the Conquest. Nevertheless, the emphasis in the chapter is on cultural continuity, for the student discovers that a remarkable syncretism between native and Hispanic cultures took place in the Quiché area. This brief chapter does not do justice to the rich historical materials available for studying post-Conquest Utatlán culture, and a more thorough study is needed.

Chapter 11, "Survivals," contains a summary of native cultural patterns that have survived into the twentieth century. Bringing the study of the Utatlán community down to modern times makes it possible to exploit the rich ethnographic studies of recent years. It also provides the reader with an up-to-date account of the natives' condition, something too often neglected in ethnohistoric accounts.

In chapter 12, "Conclusions," I summarize what this study tells us about the development of the Utatlán community. In particular I address questions raised in chapter 2 and take up comparable studies that appear to shed light on Quiché development. It is my hope that my effort to generalize from the Quiché study will help make the book a useful contribution to general studies of cultural evolution. I want to emphasize, however, that I believe the descriptive material assembled in this book on Utatlán has value per se. One of my goals has been to reconstruct as accurately and thoroughly as possible the history, general structural features, and accomplishments of the Quichés of Utatlán. For that reason every chapter contains considerable cultural detail, as well as general comments about development and process.

Thus by design the book is both descriptive and analytical. The approach is characteristic of ethnological studies, and I make no apologies for it. I am confident that in years to come students of the Quichés will improve on both the descriptive and the analytical accounts. It is also my hope that this book will be an essential starting point for their work.

2
THE QUESTIONS

T HE QUICHÉS HAVE BEEN THE SUBJECT of many different kinds of studies by scholars of Maya culture, history, and archaeology. Most attention has, of course, focused on the *Popol Vuh*, though the ruins of Utatlán and the cultural traditionalism of Chichicastenango have also attracted researchers. Nevertheless, we still lack an adequate reconstruction of pre-Hispanic Quiché culture and an analysis of its development. The latter topic would seem logically to precede the cultural reconstruction and provide the necessary context for it. That is, before analyzing the internal structure and substance of Quiché culture, we need to know what kind of "species" it was and the adaptive processes by which it took on its special characteristics. This is the approach of cultural evolution, and it constitutes the broad framework for this book.

Cultural process or evolution has become perhaps the dominant problem orientation of anthropology and the closest thing to a paradigm in the field (Kuhn 1962). It requires that we examine change in the functional systems of culture, as well as the internal and external factors that trigger such changes. Thus it subsumes the functionalist, culture-historical, and even ecological approaches of the past (White 1945; Harris 1965). The problem of cultural evolution directs us to clarify the adaptive mechanisms responsible for systematic changes and the material and social factors to which they are responding.

The Quichés of Utatlán are a particularly appropriate case for the study of cultural evolution. Evidence indicates that Quiché culture underwent fundamental change over a known period of time. The rich documentary sources on the Quichés refer not only to the origins and decline of the Utatlán community but also to its internal development processes during its climax years. Conflicts and other historical events related in the chronicles provide a window for viewing the broad social processes taking place within Quiché culture.

We have access to the archaeological remains of the earliest, the intermediate, and the latest Quiché sites. While preservation is not particularly good, surface features and excavated forms provide invaluable insight into changes in Quiché culture, especially with respect to its material conditions. In few other cultures is it possible to compare the archaeological remains of settlements of known historical relationship and thus examine directly the developmental process. For example, a comparison between the sites of Chuitinamit (Jakawitz, later Chitinamit) and Utatlán provides a dramatic view of development from early to late Quiché culture.

The persistence of native speakers and aspects of Utatlán culture down to the present day further aids the study of Quiché cultural evolution. Survival of language and other symbolic forms enables us to understand ancient Quiché communication systems in elaborate detail, which is not possible with historical (documentary and archaeological) sources alone. These systems, of course, have undergone change, but they tend to be more resistant to change than other less-well-integrated features of a community. It may be added that changes in Quiché culture brought by post-Hispanic influences can tell us much about the nature of the pre-Hispanic cultural adaptation. What had to be done to break down the Utatlán community reveals something about what had been done to build it up.

Evolutionary studies are often classified as either specific or general, depending on whether the changes being investigated occur in a particular culture or in generally similar types of cultures (Sahlins and Service 1960). The study of specific evolution is patently historical, a tracing of the changing structure of a culture through time; its methods are strongly inductive. The study of general evolution tends to be ahistorical, for it traces major structural transformations regardless of genetic or temporal connections between cultures; its methods are highly deductive. In practice evolutionary studies increasingly include both specific and general perspectives. Instances of specific cultural evolution are used to test the deductive statements of general evolution, while the latter provide hypotheses for studying the former (Harris 1965). As described by one evolutionist (Flannery 1972), cultural evolution always involves both general and specific processes. Evolving cultures experience general changes, such as specialization and centralization, while the adaptive mechanisms responsible for the changes are specific to each case. This method leads us away from the futile search for single prime movers to a multivariate approach, in which different material, social, symbolic, and historical factors, alone or together, are seen as potential "causes" of cultural development.

The Quiché case would again seem to be ideal for working within a multivariate evolutionary approach. The variety of data sources available should allow us not only to reconstruct the general developmental processes of Quiché culture but also to specify the selective factors and adaptive mechanisms at work. It will be possible to avoid the tendency noted in a review of studies on the origin of the traditional state (Service 1975) to assign material factors a primary causal role when archaeological data are used and sociopolitical factors when ethnohistoric data are the basic source. The Quiché case will permit us to make meaningful choices among selective factors, since substantial data are available on changes in such traditionally important evolutionary "prime" movers as agricultural technology, demography, trade, political centralization, kinship and territorial organization, warfare, and stratification and such communication systems as language, writing, calendrics, religious ideologies, and the arts.

Because in this evolutionary approach the stress is on adaptive factors that influenced the evolution of the Utatlán community, the study tends to emphasize specific rather than general evolution. That is consistent with my belief that general statements about cultural evolution in Mesoamerica have too often been accepted without adequate testing in actual historical cases. General cultural processes (such as centralization) are often insufficiently detailed or are assumed without testing. Specific adaptive mechanisms tend to be applied too widely, often without solid supporting evidence or consideration of other possible mechanisms. I have sought, therefore, a balance between specific factors of Quiché cultural development and general questions of Mesoamerican evolution. The reader will find the latter questions implicit in the discussions of, among others, political centralization (chapter 6), the integration of settlement pattern symbolics (chapter 7), comparisons between early and late Quiché sites (chapter 8), and the differentiation of rural territories on ecological grounds (chapter 4). A more specific discussion of their relevance for the Quichés is found in the conclusions (chapter 12).

As befitting a study of specific evolution, I include extensive cultural and historical detail, showing that it is necessary for a meaningful interpretation of Quiché evolution. In addition I intend the detail to serve as a small contribution toward the ethnography of Quiché culture so sorely needed. It may cause the reader to lose the evolutionary thread from time to time, but it is my hope that the understanding of Quiché culture that is gained will be sufficient compensation for the loss in clarity of theoretical argument.

EARLY STUDIES OF QUICHÉ CULTURE

It will be useful to summarize briefly prior studies of the Quichés of Utatlán. So that the summary will conform to the problem set out above, I look at only those features that have to do with the origin, development, and decline of the Utatlán community. This limitation is necessary because the literature on the Quichés is voluminous, especially that dealing with the *Popol Vuh*. I focus on those studies that have been most influential, though brief comments about lesser contributions are made. For a fuller treatment of this topic, the reader may consult my study of the Quiché sources (Carmack 1973).

The Sixteenth Century

Some of the most important sixteenth-century Spanish interpretations of the Quichés are lost. We are missing an early treatise by the Dominican missionary Domingo de Vico and one by early Franciscan priests. According to Ximénez (1967, p. 5), Vico believed that the Quichés were descended from the lost tribes of Israel and that they had preserved many biblical traditions. Apparently that was the general view of the Spaniards, especially the missionaries, and they taught it to the Quichés themselves. It appears in all the important native chronicles written during the sixteenth century.

The most influential early interpretation of Quiché culture was that of Bartolomé de las Casas (1909, pp. 615ff.), the Dominican who labored in Guatemala during the first half of the sixteenth century. He specifically referred to the "kingdom of Utatlán" and to its founding by four brothers who came from "the provinces of New Spain [Mexico]." He claimed that when the brothers went to the Utatlán area there were few inhabitants, and they settled it without resistance. He said that they called the land Calcatum (a name I fail to find in the other sources), which he believed tied the Quichés to biblical lands. Las Casas went on to say that the oldest of the four brothers was timid and that the second gained the leadership role. Later the second brother constituted his two sons as successors, the second son to become the elect when the first entered office. This act initiated the Quiché form of political succession. Later, Las Casas continued, the Quichés became a populous group and conquered the other peoples of the highlands within a radius of fifteen leagues around Utatlán. They became the supreme power of the area and retained that position down to the Conquest.

Las Casas also outlined the Quichés' "prehistory." He mentioned their belief in several creation attempts, a great flood survived by only a few persons, and the subsequent development of patriarchal succession from those survivors. He made no attempt to connect these religious events with the founding of the Utatlán "kingdom."

Las Casas thought that Utatlán culture was comparable to the ancient civilizations of the Old World. He called it a monarchy, with a supreme ruler and a governing council. He lauded the Quichés' books, calendar, fixed laws, merchandising, marriage customs, military capabilities, and complex rituals. Human sacrifice and cannibalism showed them to be barbarians, but no worse than the ancient peoples of the Old World. Besides, he wrote,

17

many features of their religion were worthy of praise: the good order of their ritual celebrations, the special priests, the elaborate fasts, the confessions, the thoughtful prayers, and so on.

Las Casas's interpretation of the Quichés was remarkably accurate and free of prejudice. Although we cannot accept his belief that there were biblical parallels in Quiché history and culture, the analysis that follows largely supports his position.

Alonso de Zorita (1941, p. 202), a mid-sixteenth-century judge in Guatemala, reported having seen a book from Utatlán containing an eight-hundred-year history. Obviously, like Las Casas, he believed Quiché culture to be of great antiquity. Unfortunately he did not elaborate on his views.

Fray Pedro de Betanzos, another early missionary in Guatemala, gave a rather different interpretation of Utatlán from that of his contemporary Las Casas. He was aware that the Quichés came to Utatlán "from other parts," led on the journey by their gods, but he did not comment on that part of their history (Carrasco 1967, pp. 255–59). Betanzos claimed that the Quichés were more powerful and prosperous than their neighbors because they were "more warlike." But, he said, they lost much of their power when an Utatlán tyrant was overthrown and killed by subject peoples, who then became independent. Thus at the time of the Conquest the Quichés of Quezaltenango, Totonicapán, and Ixtahuacán were said to have gone into battle against the Spaniards without bothering to inform the rulers of Utatlán.

Betanzos did not view Utatlán as a monarchy. Authority, he said, was held by lineages rather than by the whole town, and there were at least four rulers of equal authority at Utatlán. Outside towns were not subject to them but were confederates who honored them and gave them gifts only out of respect for lineage ties. Utatlán was a Mecca, where the gods had been first established, but not a ruling town. The Quichés were no more powerful than the kingdoms of Guatemala or Atitlán, which were completely independent of them.

Later in this book, in chapter 6, it will be shown that Betanzos grasped some important aspects of the Quiché political system. His view of specific features of Utatlán development is not supported by the evidence, however. He was probably a spokesman for the Spanish officials who opposed Las Casas, and that may explain some of the distortions in his interpretation of the Quichés.

The Colonial Period

Among colonial interpretations of Utatlán culture the two most important were expressed by the creole official Francisco Antonio de Fuentes y Guzmán and the Spanish priest Ximénez. Both wrote around the turn of the seventeenth century, and both had access to important sixteenth-century native chronicles. Fuentes y Guzmán was a friend of the Franciscans and the conquistadors, while Ximénez was a Dominican and a friend of the natives. Curiously, both tended to exaggerate the accomplishments of the Quichés of Utatlán, Fuentes y Guzmán to magnify the Conquest and Ximénez to give more meaning to the work of the Dominicans who labored in Quiché.

Other colonial writers who commented on Quiché culture include Fray Antonio de Remesal (1932), Fray Juan de Torquemada (1943), Fray Francisco Vázquez (1937–44), the anonymous Dominican author of the *Isagoge histórica apologética* (1935), and the anonymous author of the *Crónica franciscana* (Carmack 1973). Remesal was not particularly interested in the natives, but he nevertheless provided a few important documents on the conquest of the Quichés. He argued that the Quichés were subject to the Aztecs before the Conquest. Torquemada based his account of the Quichés on that of Las Casas and provided no interpretation. He believed that Utatlán compared favorably with the Mexican cultures in numbers of people, large buildings, and nucleation (1943, 1:311). Vázquez is disappointing for, though he had original native chronicles in his possession, he failed to interpret them. His account of the religious conversion of the natives was given almost entirely from the Spanish viewpoint. He did give the correct etymology of the name Guatemala, stating that it came from the Nahua word *cuauhtemallan* ("tree of white sap"). The anonymous author of the *Isagoge* gave an elaborate account of the conquest of the Quichés, based on sources already known from other writings. He had, however, documents that provided a few new facts about the conversion of Utatlán princes to Roman Catholic ways. The anonymous author of the *Crónica franciscana* (Carmack 1973, pp. 193–94) apparently provided the Franciscan view of Utatlán history that Vázquez avoided— possibly Vázquez was deferring to the *Crónica* on that point. The viewpoint expressed in the *Crónica* has come down to us indirectly through the writings of Fuentes y Guzmán and Brasseur de Bourbourg (see below).

Fuentes y Guzmán's rambling volumes (1932–33) contain many individual interpretations of Utatlán cultural features. Some of the interpretations contradict one another, partly because he used several different native chronicles, as well as early Spanish sources (such as the *Crónica franciscana*). Nevertheless, his over-all view of the Quichés can be reconstructed. Fuentes y Guzmán was convinced that the Quichés were Toltecs who went to Guatemala as part of the same migrations that led to the founding of the Mexican empires. He emphatically rejected the view that the Quichés might have been subject to the Mexicans, however, suggesting instead that the Mexicans came from the Quichés. He accepted the Franciscan view that the Toltecs had migrated from Babylon and found confirmation in the native sources. He also thought that the native skin color, the hair, and the sparse beards, as well as the languages and the pyramids, confirmed the Old World origin.

According to Fuentes y Guzmán, the Quichés' forefathers were the younger brothers of Toltecs who conquered the Chiapas, Verapaz, and Mam-Pokomam areas. The Quichés went to Guatemala, which, because it had the best lands, allowed them to dominate the Toltecs from the other three regions. They developed the potential to raise an army of 1,400,000 warriors. At first the Quichés devoted themselves exclusively to war and conquest, but later they turned their efforts to exploiting the riches of the land and to making their "cities and towns" opulent. Fuentes y Guzmán ascribed to particular Quiché rulers the custom of succession by a chain of three elect sons, the discovery and use of cotton and cacao, the belief in "idols," and the introduction of human sacrifice.

Fuentes y Guzmán believed that there had been two thousand years of dynastic rule at Utatlán. He combined native accounts about the coming of the forefathers with other traditions in an effort to reconstruct that dynasty. The resulting list of twenty-two rulers is a potpourri of political groups (Tamub, Ilocab, and Nima Quiché), founding fathers (Balam Quitze, Balam Ak'ab, and so on), political offices (*ajpop*), places (Cacubraxechechim and Iximché), and legendary figures (Acxopil and Junajpu). The list has no validity, though a few of the names were in fact rulers at Utatlán.

Fuentes y Guzmán believed that Pismachi was founded before Utatlán and that Utatlán was the city from which the Quichés maximally expanded their empire. He was confused, however, about when that occurred and under whose reign. He tied to Utatlán a Franciscan tradition (*Crónica franciscana*) that told of a powerful Quiché ruler named Acxopil who controlled the empire from Utatlán. Acxopil made his two sons, Jiutemal and Acxicuat, rulers over the Cakchiquels and the Tzutujils and later established them as elect successors to his throne. Dynastic squabbles between subsequent elect successors led to a split among the three kingdoms. Fuentes y Guzmán described long fraternal wars among the groups lasting down to the Conquest. Even news of the approaching Spaniards failed to unite them.

The Quiché king at the time of the Conquest, said to have been Tecum, led an army of 72,000 warriors out of the city to meet the Spaniards. By the time the main military encounter took place, the army had expanded to 172,000. Fuentes y Guzmán went on to describe the encounter in dramatic prose based on conquerors' accounts and native chronicles. Each battle was glorious, and both the natives and the Spaniards fought valiantly. Two years after Utatlán was destroyed, the Quichés rebelled against the Spanish overlords. They were again defeated in a great battle near Quezaltenango, where their leader Xequechul, along with Sinacan, the Cakchiquel leader, were taken captives.

Fuentes y Guzmán believed that the Quichés were highly civilized and politically advanced, and thus could have been dominated only by a superior culture (the Spanish). He contrasted the Quichés with "savages" living in the mountains and lowlands surrounding Utatlán. The key to Quiché development was the formation of a pure nobility guarded carefully by strict endogamy: "The part of the Indians who are nobles and principals are very capable, with an excellent gift for governing." Even porters and household servants had to be of noble birth, according to this creole writer. He lamented that the mixture in his time of Indians with blacks and mestizos had corrupted the Quichés and caused them to lose the best elements of their culture.

Fuentes y Guzmán claimed that the Quiché had an aristocratic monarchy, with councilors also from the noble class. There was a strict code of laws that gave "order to the Republic." He emphasized that aristocratic inheritance of office was combined with the requirement that holders of high office must first gain experience in lesser positions. If they did not perform well, they did not rise in command.

Nothing showed the sophistication of Utatlán culture more clearly than the ruins of its "city," according to Fuentes y Guzmán. He described a huge town, like a medieval city, basing his description on a native map in his possession and his own visit to the site. The town had had great forts, palaces, or castles of several stories with doors and walls; a seminary that had been attended by five thousand princesses; and warriors, artisans, serfs, and slaves of many kinds in residence. On the outskirts of the city were the houses of the lords, and the rural lands of the commoners stretched out in all directions.

For Fuentes y Guzmán a major blight on the otherwise glorious Quiché culture was its polytheism. The Quichés believed in many gods: of water, wind, maize, fertility, sickness, "each thing." He explained this phenomenon as a rather simple confusion: A king's son had died, leaving the king disconsolate. To comfort him, his vassals made a figure in the likeness of the son. It gladdened the king, who passed it to his descendants, and in that way idols evolved. Eventually they became so numerous that they no longer fit in the temples and had to be placed in caves, on mountaintops, and in canyons. The pernicious practice of idolatry became so entrenched that it continued in Fuentes y Guzmán's own time. He thought that it explained the destitute condition of the natives around him.

Despite the many Quiché gods, Fuentes y Guzmán affirmed that they had only "one common god," Xbalanque. He blamed most of the barbarities in Quiché religion, especially the human sacrifices, on the native priests. According to him they had deceived everybody, old and young, and made their subjects follow them in their debauchery.

The interpretations of Fuentes y Guzmán have been widely accepted, and are influential to this day in Guatemala. In fact, they contain grains of truth, though many errors and his creole prejudices make it difficult to recover them. Certainly his chronology and dynastic reconstructions are hopelessly wrong. He greatly exaggerated the aristocratic nature of Quiché culture. He grossly oversimplified the process of cultural development. And, as will be seen in the archaeology chapters of this book, his account of the ruins of Utatlán requires substantial modification. Still his attempt to analyze Quiché culture is admirable, and the sheer scope of his study requires that his view be taken into account.

Francisco Ximénez (1929; 1967) lived for several years among Quiché natives, spoke their language, and was able to base his interpretation of Quiché culture on personal ethnographic observations. The *Popol Vuh*, which he discovered in Chichicastenango, was his sole native documentary source. He noted that the native dances performed at Chichicastenango in his time were claimed to have originally come "from there where the sun goes up." Ximénez apparently believed that the Quichés had come from biblical lands, and he accepted the possibility that Saint Thomas had visited them. This topic was not of much interest to him, however, and he interpreted the Quiché tradition of a return visit to the East simply as a visit to the Nicaragua area. He also realized that there was some connection between the Quichés' eastern origin and the Mexican cultures but felt that the Quichés were older than the Aztecs and probably gave rise to them.

Ximénez correctly understood that the forefathers of the Quichés (Balam Quitze and so on) were not really the first created men, as stated in the *Popol Vuh*, but were rather the beginning of "royal descent." He accepted the dynastic list of the *Popol Vuh*, rejecting Fuentes y Guzmán's long list. Fuentes y Guzmán had erred, he said, because he could not read the native documents in his possession and because those documents did not contain the true ruling dynasty of Utatlán (which was to be found only in the *Popol Vuh*). Ximénez interpreted the thirteen Quiché rulers listed in the *Popol Vuh* as generations, and, assigning forty years to each generation, fixed the beginning date for the "kingdom" at 1054.

In Ximénez's historical reconstruction Pismachi was founded by C'ocawib, the second king. K'ucumatz-C'otuja, the fifth king, founded K'umarcaaj. By the time of the eighth king the kingdom included the Pacific Coast; the Lake Atitlán, Cakchiquel, and Sacatepéquez areas; Verapaz; the Quiché area; and the Tzotzil and Tzendal areas of Chiapas. During that reign the Cakchiquels became independent of the Quichés because "they wanted the command." During the tenth reign (Waxaki C'aam) the events portrayed in the Quiché Winak dance took place. Oxib Quej–Belejeb Tzi' (Three Deer and Nine Dog), the thirteenth king, was ruling at the time of the Conquest. Ximénez was mistaken in assigning a generation to each succession, and he failed to realize that the two names given for each succession referred to two separate rulers rather than one.

Ximénez found Fuentes y Guzmán's account of the Conquest unsatisfactory, and he corrected both its emphasis (which glorified the conquistadors) and several specific errors. He argued that the claim that Pedro de Alvarado himself had killed the Quiché general Tecum had no basis in fact. He cited a tradition held by the Argueta family of Totonicapán that they had killed Tecum and kept a lance with dried blood on it said to be "the blood of that eagle." Fuentes y Guzmán's account of the burning of Utatlán was particularly offensive to Ximénez. He did not think that opposition of the Quiché rulers to the conquistadors should be called "treason and perfidy," since they were defending their kingdom against an attacking force with superior arms. He also rejected Fuentes y Guzmán's innuendo that the Quiché king might have had the opportunity to hear the Gospel and be baptized before being burned. Ximénez further rejected the claim that the Quichés had joined the Cakchiquels in the 1526 revolt against the Spaniards. He correctly argued that Xequechul was a Cakchiquel, not a Quiché, chief.

Like Fuentes y Guzmán, Ximénez approved of the aristocratic basis of Quiché government, noting that it was a monarchy with a council of nobles. Political succession was from father to son, Ximénez said, not the father–brother–son succession claimed by writers before him. Ximénez deplored the sorry condition in his day of the descendants of the ancient nobility at Utatlán, who, contrary to statements by Fuentes y Guzmán, represented the one "correct line." Ximénez made a sharp distinction between the nobility living in town (*tinamit*) and the commoner class scattered in hamlets (*amak'*). The ancient organizational pattern of commoners still existed in his day, and Ximénez was able to describe it. He found an order and justice in the rural organization that was as worthy of praise as was the aristocratic government of the ancient towns.

Ximénez was particularly impressed by the Quiché language, which he claimed to know better than anyone else did in his time. He believed it to be the mother language of all the others—Cakchiquel Tzutujil, Pokomam, Chol, Tzotzil, and so on. He called it the "most ordered of the world," with its monosyllables and perfect declensions. He concluded that it had come from the "Adamic tongue."

Quiché religion manifested many elements of Christianity, but in Ximénez's view these elements were only half truths planted by Satan. A trinity was present in Quiché religion, disguised in the form of a duality of twin creator (Tzakol-Bitol), engenderer (Alom-C'ajolom), and metamorphic animal (Wuch-Utiw) deities. Satan insidiously planted the belief that the trinity (or Quiché duality) was dependent upon an old woman (Xmucane) and that demons associated with hell (Xibalba) influenced man. Quiché religion was superficial, Ximénez said. The natives were interested in external features—dancing, drinking, and loud, beating music—rather than correct theology. In this they were like "children with beards."

Ximénez found so much of traditional Quiché culture still practiced in his day that he failed to appreciate sufficiently how much of the elite culture had been lost. His missionary zeal also caused him to misinterpret slightly Quiché beliefs and practices: he saw them as closer to Christian forms than they really were. He was further limited in his view by relying too heavily on the *Popol Vuh*, and that dependence especially distorted his reconstruction of Quiché history (as seen, for example, in his dynastic list). Despite these limitations his interpretation of Utatlán culture was far more accurate than that of Fuentes y Guzmán, and many of his interpretative points are valid.

NINETEENTH-CENTURY STUDIES

In the interpretation of Quiché culture the dominant figure of the nineteenth century was Abbé Charles Étienne Brasseur de Bourbourg. That learned French ecclesiastic lived in Rabinal near mid-century and traveled widely in the Quiché area. He obtained copies of most of the important native and Spanish chronicles and made himself the unrivaled expert of his time on Quiché history and culture. Most subsequent writers of the nineteenth century closely followed his interpretations, particularly such historians as José Milla, Hubert Howe Bancroft, and J. Antonio Villacorta. The writings of Daniel G. Brinton and Otto Stoll have been less influential than those of Brasseur, but they too represent independent nineteenth-century interpretations of Quiché culture.

The Brasseur Tradition

Brasseur (1857; 1861) rejected the traditional view that the Quichés had come from the Old World or were descendants of biblical peoples. He derived them from the Nahuas, a powerful race of people who anciently settled both central Mexico and Guatemala. The connecting link was the Quiché god K'ucumatz, the Feathered Serpent, who was Quetzalcoatl of central Mexico. K'ucumatz settled in Tamoanchan, the Xicalango area (the Gulf Coast of Mexico), and from there the Quiché ancestors migrated to the Guatemalan highlands. Brasseur was the first student of the Quichés to locate correctly their original homeland, although, as we shall see, he was confused about the rest of the migration story.

Brasseur believed that the Nahuas had been preceded in highland Guatemala by a mysterious race of people who founded a powerful kingdom called Xibalba. His reconstruction of events associated with Xibalba was based on the mythic tales recorded in the *Popol Vuh*. These tales, which describe an underworld filled with lords and messengers of the dead, were taken literally by Brasseur. He argued that the death lords were actual rulers of a past kingdom and that their messengers were military chiefs. The heroes of the tales, Junajpu and Xbalanque, along with their brothers and parents, were said to have been ancient Nahuas making contact with the ancient kingdom. The pregnancy of Xquic', the daughter of a death lord, was interpreted as an expression of intermarriage between the two peoples.

The heart of the old Xibalba kingdom was the lowlands, according to Brasseur, and Palenque was its capital. That is why the Quiché documents refer to Xibalba as being on the north, below Cobán. The kingdom extended across the entire Guatemalan and Chiapas highlands and down into the eastern part of Central America. Later, after the Nahuas had successfully challenged the power of Xibalba, the political center of gravity shifted to Guatemala, where Xbalanque formed a new capital at Utatlán (said to have been formerly settled by the Mams and other peoples).

A later wave of Nahuas migrated to the highlands from the area near the old Xibalba capital, Palenque. For some unexplained reason Brasseur thought that the Tamubs and the Ilocabs were already established powers in the highlands so that only the Quichés came with this migration. Thus, like Fuentes y Guzmán before him, Brasseur believed the first rulers to have been Tamubs (C'opichoch and others) and that only gradually did the Quiché house of Cawek gain political superiority.

Brasseur was the first scholar to identify the early Guatemalan home of the Quichés with the mountains just north of present-day Santa Cruz del Quiché. He thought that the area was much larger than it actually was, however, and he claimed that their chief town, Jakawitz, was north of Rabinal. He compared the social life of the Quichés during their early history in the mountains with that of the "savages" of North America and of the Chichimecs of northern Mexico.

Brasseur's account of the development of the Quiché kingdom at Pismachi closely followed that of Fuentes y Guzmán, for both of them took their ideas from the lost *Crónica franciscana*. Brasseur recited the story of Acxopil, the Quiché ruler, and his two sons, Xiuhtemal and Acxoquauh, who ruled over the Cakchiquels and the Tzutujils respectively. This arrangement gave rise to three somewhat independent groups, who joined together for war against other peoples but formed no unified political system.

Brasseur's reconstruction of the Quichés' ruling dynasty shows only slight improvement over Ximénez's previous effort. Brasseur could not correlate Acxopil and his sons with the list of rulers given in the native documents. While he recognized that the paired rulers of the documents were separate persons, he erroneously stated that the kings' assistants could succeed to the supreme position. Like Ximénez, he gave the dynasty a greater antiquity than it warranted, claiming that it dated from the eleventh century, though he correctly dated the reign of Q'uik'ab to the fifteenth century.

The historical events mentioned in the native chronicles were subjected to speculative elaboration and explanation by Brasseur. Thus the Ilocab revolt against King C'otuja was said to have resulted from the supposed ancient and prior domination of the Quiché area by the Ilocabs. A later king, K'ucumatz, was portrayed as a Solomon, healing through his wise policies a pervasive schism infecting Quiché society. K'ucumatz supposedly gave the aristocratic lords provincial "fiefs," thereby blunting their ambitions. He "rebuilt" the town of Utatlán, including the old temple of Xbalanque, which he then dedicated to Tojil. Another temple, which had a shrine with an oracle stone, was supposedly also built at this time. It reminded Brasseur of Arabian Mecca shrines. By such tactics K'ucumatz was said to have won over the traditional vassals, as well as peoples from Chiapas, Lake Atitlán, and other places in the highlands. In Brasseur's fantasy weaving, K'ucumatz took over the ancient kingdom of Xibalba and lived part of each year at Palenque. Brasseur identified K'ucumatz with Junajpu, the inventor of cotton and chocolate drink.

Also fantastic was Brasseur's interpretation of the "revolution" that occurred at Utatlán during the reign of Q'uik'ab. He claimed that the revolt took place because Q'uik'ab had removed feudal rights from second-level lords and had tried to become the sole authority of the kingdom. He had done this by requiring provincial lords to reside at Utatlán and by creating a new caste of "captains" to serve him. This awakened the "egalitarian spirit" of the commoners, who commissioned a group of men to go before the king on their behalf. Brasseur referred to these men as "fathers of national liberty for the Quichés," though no such group is even mentioned in the source he used (*The Annals of the Cakchiquels*). In an equally erroneous interpretation of his sources Brasseur claimed that the members of this commission were executed by Q'uik'ab. According to Brasseur the people rose up in anger, killing all the men, women, and children of the ruling houses except the king and his sons, who escaped. The rebellious people gathered at Xebalax and Xekamak' "to plan the new constitution." Later the king was forced to confirm the rebellious leaders in their new positions of authority over the new "nation."

The revolution at Utatlán led to the separation of the Cakchiquels from the kingdom and later the peoples of Chiapas, Huehuetenango, Sacapulas, and Rabinal; the Tzutujils of the lake; and the Quichés of Quezaltenango. From then on these former subjects dominated the historical scene, and that is why, Brasseur reasoned, the native sources were silent on the last period of Quiché history. Like others before him Brasseur confused the son of the

Quiché king at Conquest time with Tecum, the "general" who led the Quiché forces against the Spaniards outside Quezaltenango.

Brasseur was for many years the only scholar to understand that Pismachi, Utatlán, and Pilocab were within the same canyon system, west of present Santa Cruz del Quiché. Nevertheless, he gave the much-inflated figure of 300,000 for the resident population of the "city" Utatlán. He was unable to identify the ancient rural zones surrounding the three towns and misidentified many places outside the central Quiché area (for instance, he misidentified the Quiché name for Momostenango—Chuwa Tz'ak—as Antigua Guatemala).

It is apparent that Brasseur viewed Quiché culture from a developmental perspective. He saw it starting out simply, like the cultures of the tribal societies of North America. Then it became a monarchy, administered by aristocratic families holding "seigneurial fiefs." It developed into an absolutist monarchy, controlled by a despotic king and his elite military caste. Then, after experiencing a "bourgeois" revolution, it slipped back to the simple feudal monarchy of earlier times (Brasseur did not elaborate on this last phase). Clearly Brasseur's interpretation is too secular and shows signs of having been strongly influenced by ideas derived from the French Revolution. This is most evident in his grossly inaccurate account of the revolt at Utatlán.

Brasseur's weighty influence on later students of the Quichés stems from his precocious control of the Mexican and Quiché native sources and his dramatic, if fanciful, portrayal of native history. He came closer than anyone before him to placing the Quichés in their proper place and time, though, as we have seen, he committed many errors in this regard. He brought Quiché history to life by making it appear to parallel European history more closely than it did. His most speculative interpretation—that Xibalba was an ancient kingdom rather than the mythical underworld of the dead—particularly warped the views of subsequent students. It might be noted too that Brasseur showed relatively little interest in the decline of Quiché culture or the condition of the natives among whom he taught and lived in the nineteenth century.

José Milla's history of Central America (1937), written in 1879, contains an extensive account of Quiché history and culture. Most of his interpretation follows Brasseur and adds little to our understanding of the Quichés. Thus, for example, he accepted Brasseur's speculation that Quiché myths about Xibalba, the underworld, referred to an ancient Central American empire. Perhaps his most valuable contribution consisted of a few clarifications regarding the Conquest. He argued that in alliance with the natives of Soconusco the Quichés offered resistance to Alvarado in Mexico even before the Spanish forces reached Guatemala. He rejected Fuentes y Guzmán's outlandish military figures—72,000 warriors leaving Utatlán during the Conquest—noting that Germany's late-nineteenth-century army of one million men required a total population of 41 million people. He cited proof that Alvarado did indeed burn the Utatlán rulers, contrary to what some writers had argued. Milla praised Quiché culture, though he thought it inferior to the European culture of the Spaniards, lacking a true legal code, iron tools, the best cereals (wheat and barley, among others), large domesticated animals, wool, and good means of transportation. And, of course, the Quichés practiced human sacrifice and a form of idolatry.

In Bancroft's famous history of the Americas he included a long account of the Quichés and related peoples (1886, pp. 620ff.). Though his narration is stirring, it represents no essential improvement over previous interpretations of the Quichés. He followed Fuentes y Guzmán closely—for example, in his exaggerated population figures—and so missed some of the advances made by Ximénez. He was also taken in by Brasseur's theory about a pre-Quiché Xibalba empire in Guatemala, which he tied in with the great Maya ruins of the lowlands. Like Milla he clarified a few details about the conquest of Utatlán. He confirmed that the Quiché rulers were burned by Alvarado before they heard the Gospel preached and after an attempt had been made to get gold from them.

Though writing in the twentieth century, Antonio Villacorta (1927; 1938) offered a view of the Quichés that was largely derived from Brasseur's and other nineteenth-century interpretations. He accepted Brasseur's idea that Quiché history involved a series of ancient migrations, the first group encountering the remnants of the old "Xibalba peoples." According to him both Nahua and Maya sources went into the formation of Quiché culture. The Nahuas, he said, migrated originally from North America and the Mayas from Africa (the *Popol Vuh* mentions "black" people). Like those before him, Villacorta assigned far too large a territory to the Quiché kingdom. He said that it extended from Tehuantepec on the west to Lacandón country on the north, to the whole Pacific coast on the south, and to the Guatemala Valley on the east. His reconstruction of the Quiché dynasty was no improvement over past efforts, and he continued to date its beginnings in the eleventh century. Villacorta was inconsistent about the level of development attained by Quiché culture, stating in one place that it was the "model of the most important monarchies of pre-Columbian America" and in another that it was like that of feudal Europe. He claimed that the Quichés were monotheistic, although they had various gods at Utatlán. He called the Quichés' language, calendric, and writing systems highly advanced. He said that, like all the other great civilizations of the past, Egyptian, Assyrian, Greek, and Roman, the Quichés made astounding accomplishments, only to disappear.

Rafael Girard (1952; 1966) has carried the Brasseur tradition down to the present. He outdoes the Frenchman in interpreting *Popol Vuh* myth as history, finding four stages of unilinear evolution (patrilineal, matrilineal, grandmother rule, and patriarchal). He derives the Quichés from the Toltecs and says that when they migrated to Guatemala in the tenth century they were only "returning to their primordial country." Girard includes in his writings some useful data on native ritual forms, but his interpretations of Quiché cultural development are without foundation.

The German Tradition

The German ethnologist Karl Scherzer initiated an interest in the Quichés among German-speaking scholars. He visited Guatemala in 1854 and later published the *Popol Vuh* (1857) and a description of religion in the Quiché-speaking community Santa Catarina Ixtahuacán (1856). He made little attempt, however, to interpret Quiché culture for German readers (Ximénez 1967, footnotes; Scherzer 1854).

The real forefather of German studies of the Quichés was Otto Stoll, a medical doctor who visited Guatemala between the years 1878 and 1883. Although he provided interesting ethnographic details about surviving Quiché culture (1886), his major contribution was in synthesis and analysis. Of special importance is his *Ethnology of the Indian Tribes of Guatemala* (1889), in which he attempted a complete reconstruction of ancient Quiché cultural patterns. For now our interest will be on the developmental aspects of that excellent study.

Stoll was a cautious scholar. With respect to Quiché origins he was willing to assert only that they came from somewhere in the "East" and that they had ties with both the Mayas of Yucatán and the Nahuas of Mexico. Stoll claimed that their closest linguistic affiliation was with the peoples of Chiapas, Tabasco, and Yucatán. He was perhaps the first scholar to distinguish correctly between Nahua words used for Quiché names and places that existed before the Conquest and those that were applied after the Conquest. The pre-Conquest names proved that the Quichés were culturally connected in some way with the Nahua peoples.

Stoll saw Quiché society in rather flexible terms. A lord (*ajaw*) was only a chief of a land estate, like the Aztec *calpullec* ("ward head"). There was no general term for a commoner, he (incorrectly) thought, because such a person could easily move into the lordly class. He believed that there was a class of noble officials situated between the ruling class and the commoner chiefs. The Quiché ruler was not a monarch or despot but more like a "responsible state official." He could be deposed by his kinsmen in alliance with lords and commoners.

Stoll ascribed a strong "folk" component in Quiché culture. The main social unit was the *chinamit*, a group of kinsmen living within the same land area. It was the Quiché Big House, or sublineage, and was equivalent to the Aztec *calpulli*. Similarly, Quiché religion was a "nature" religion. There were sky gods and underworld gods, but they were all paralleled by zoological and botanical deities. Man, nature, and deity were physically unified.

It is not possible to summarize briefly Stoll's elaborate synthesis of Quiché culture. It is surprisingly sophisticated and concisely argued. He lacked many of the sources now available, but his study was easily the most judicious interpretation of Quiché culture up to his time. Its major weakness, perhaps, was his tendency to see Quiché culture as more similar to Aztec culture than it really was. Also he did not always distinguish between the Quiché and other pre-Hispanic cultures of highland Guatemala.

German interest in the Quichés was continued by the great Eduard Seler, best known for his ethnological studies of Mexican culture. Seler (1960) was able to identify the original homeland of the Quiché ancestors with the Tabasco region. He also noted an ancient trade route from there to the Guatemalan highlands by which the Quichés were connected with Toltec "merchants." Other references by Seler to the Quiché were designed to connect them with the Mexican documentary traditions. For example, he suggested that Cama Sotz (Death Bat) mentioned in the *Popol Vuh* might be identified with a bat god in the *Codex Borgia*. The latter deity was associated with the sun deity, human sacrifice, and the east cardinal direction.

The Anglo-American Tradition

An Anglo-American tradition of Quiché studies can be said to have begun with Daniel G. Brinton, the Philadelphia anthropologist (1881; 1885; 1891; 1893; 1896). His interpretation of Quiché culture was based entirely on philological and ethnological studies of the native documents. A sophisticated scholar, he was versed in the important ethnological literature of his day. He totally rejected Brasseur's use of myth as the "apotheosis of history." The idea that Xibalba was an ancient kingdom was for Brinton an idea "so unsupported as to justify the humorous flings which have so often been cast at antiquaries" (1891, p. 292). His approach to Quiché culture was broad and careful and framed in a humanistic secularism. His careful methods seem modern even by today's standards.

Brinton explained Quiché origins in naturalistic terms. He rejected all theories about lost tribes and continents, relying instead on the Bering Strait theory. In his view Asiatics had slowly infiltrated the New World during the Ice Age, and after many millennia in the north the ancestors of the Quichés made their way down the shore of the Gulf of Mexico and from there into the highlands of Guatemala. Brinton did not lend his scholarship to the specific details of this migration. Once in place the Quichés became part of general

Maya culture, characterized by small, fragmented states, patrilineal clans, and excellence in arts (architecture, calendrics, and writing).

Though Brinton believed, incorrectly, that the *Popol Vuh* was not written until the seventeenth century, nevertheless, he judged it to be "one of the most valuable monuments of ancient American literature" and said that its "substantial authenticity cannot be doubted" (1891, p. 158). He commented that, once the book's considerable amount of Christian influence was excised—for example, the good-evil theme in the Xibalba story—it was an excellent example of early man's "intuition of reason." He found themes in it that paralleled those of many other American Indian groups, for example, the concepts of an earthly paradise, a flood, the soul in bones.

Brinton argued that advances in religious development came from "great men who cultivated in themselves a purer faith [and left] unforgotten models of noble qualities" (1891, p. 338). He listed Quetzalcoatl as such a great man, whose influence presumably carried over to the Quichés.

Language and myth were Brinton's primary interests, and his major contributions to Quiché studies were in those fields. He gave reasonable etymologies for the major Quiché deities and calendar units and clarified some important metaphorical associations. For example, he glossed the Quiché sky god, Jurakan, as the First Great One (Lightning), and Cabrakan as the Second Great One (Earthquake). Perhaps because of the excesses of his predecessors, Brinton was reluctant to acknowledge Nahua influence on Quiché language and myth. Despite many obvious Nahua borrowings by the Quichés, he claimed that "the Maya and Nahuatl stocks were distinct in origin, different in character, and only similar by reason of that general similarity which of necessity arose from the two nations being subject to like surroundings, and in nearly the same stage of progress" (1881, p. 645).

As important as any specific substantive contribution was Brinton's careful, logical approach to the subject. After Brinton it would be difficult to speculate about Quiché myths in the manner of Brasseur and others.

Lewis Spence, the British scholar of comparative myth, was in the Brinton tradition. He too studied the Quichés through their chronicles, referring to the *Popol Vuh* as a source of unequaled importance for understanding pre-Columbian mythology (Spence 1908).

Spence was more willing to speculate than Brinton was, arguing that the original American Indian migrations from Asia and later movements into Mesoamerica were adumbrated in the migration story of the *Popol Vuh*. The Quichés, he said, came from the Toltecs, a connection most clearly seen in K'ucumatz, the same personage as the Mexican god Quetzalcoatl. Quiché myths also revealed some broad American Indian themes, such as the belief in a great brooding bird who hovered over the primeval waters in the creation of the earth. Even the Quiché migration story was said to contain

North American Indian mythic elements, with its mystical homeland, crossing of waters, and groups of four.

It is worth mentioning that the Anglo-American tradition early involved a serious concern with the archaeological remains of Utatlán. Alfred Maudslay visited the site in 1887 and compared it (1899) with statements made in the documentary sources. He found the site much smaller and simpler than the ancient chroniclers (especially Fuentes y Guzmán) had led their readers to believe it was. He concluded that the Quichés were rather simple warring tribes compared with the lowland Mayas, with their highly advanced, artistic civilization. Maudslay's account will be discussed in greater detail in later chapters, but it can be noted here that he underestimated the extent and complexity of the Utatlán towns in their pre-Hispanic structure. His correction of Fuentes y Guzmán's excesses was a step forward, nonetheless.

TWENTIETH-CENTURY STUDIES

The numbers of persons studying the Quichés have greatly increased in the present century. Major contributors to an understanding of Quiché cultural development remain few, however. I judge the most important of those to be Leonhard Schultze-Jena, Robert Wauchope, and Adrián Recinos. Consistent with the specialization that characterizes modern cultural studies, these three scholars made contributions mainly in their special fields: Schultze-Jena in ethnography, Wauchope in archaeology, and Recinos in ethnohistory. Others who have contributed will be briefly mentioned in connection with these three specialists.

Ethnography

The work of Leonhard Schultze-Jena can be seen as a continuation of the German tradition begun by Scherzer and Stoll. In Guatemala that tradition was strongly ethnographic from the beginning, and the trend was continued after Stoll by the geographer-ethnographer Franz Termer. Termer (1957) recorded a few details about surviving Quiché culture in the central area but generally contributed little to the interpretation of Quiché culture per se.

Schultze-Jena (1933; 1947) gathered many ethnographic texts in the Quiché community of Chichicastenango and analyzed them for cultural content. Later (1944) he translated the *Popol Vuh* into German and summarized his findings about Quiché culture. Despite some criticism of the manner in which he combined ethnographic data from two communities (Chichicastenango and Momostenango) and of errors in his understanding of the structure of the Quiché language, Schultze-Jena's work is of high quality.

Perhaps Schultze-Jena's main ethnographic contribution was his demonstration that much of the ancient Quiché language, shamanistic ritual, rural social structure, and beliefs about the forces of nature and time had survived into the present century. Specifically he documented the use of the 260-day calendar, with its names, associated fates, and functions. He clearly explained how divination by *tzité* beans was carried out. He reconstructed the rural pattern of alternate ritual service and the language and symbols accompanying it. With these and many other patterns he demonstrated that a powerful rural component existed alongside the more elite features of ancient Quiché culture. Many cultural patterns that had formerly been known only through documentary references or incomplete descriptions for the first time were described in detail by Schultze-Jena and related to other features of Quiché culture.

Schultze-Jena's study of Quiché culture through the *Popol Vuh* is somewhat disappointing. He made relatively little effort to link the contents of that great book with the cultural patterns he had discovered at Chichicastenango. Nor was he able to identify places mentioned in the book. He was more concerned about providing a linguistically accurate translation of the *Popol Vuh* than about reconstructing Quiché culture.

Schultze-Jena was a careful scholar not given to speculation. He was content, for example, to discuss Quiché origins largely in the terms given in the *Popol Vuh*. He nevertheless demonstrated convincingly a fundamental relationship between Quiché and Aztec, or Mexican, cultures. Like many before him he connected Nacxit, the lord of the East, with Aztec tradition, and placed the lord "possibly" in the Tabasco area. He was the first, to my knowledge, to derive the names of the old Quiché creator-diviners, Xpiyacoc and Xmucane, from the Nahua names for the otiose gods, Cipactonal and Oxomoco. He also fruitfully discussed the relationship between the Quiché gods K'ucumatz and Jurakan, and the Nahua gods Quetzalcoatl and Tezcatlipoca.

Schultze-Jena was at his best in describing the social structure of the Quichés. He grasped its fundamental military orientation and subtle stratificational distinctions. For example, his definition of the *rajpop achij* official, "title of a class of dignitaries of young princes in Quiché nobility," is accurate (see chapter 6). He cautiously perceived in Quiché mythology ancient astral themes. Thus the descent of Junajpu and Xbalanque to the underworld was seen to symbolize the struggle between the sun (light) and the moon (darkness).

Despite the shortcomings mentioned above, Schultze-Jena left us with a largely "demythologized" view of Quiché culture. He performed a task that he warned had to be done before Quiché history and culture could be fruitfully reconstructed: he analyzed the sources for their correct linguistic and semantic relationships.

Two other important ethnographic studies, also in Chichicastenango, were those by Ruth Bunzel and Sol Tax. Bunzel (1952) worked mainly through a single informant and gave only a partial view of culture in that community. Nevertheless, her informant knew traditional culture, and we learn much about native ritual, calendrics, rural social organization, and agricultural practices. Bunzel's perceptive analysis of her data greatly enhances the importance of the work. This is especially evident in her interpretation of the ritual "process," the religious beliefs, and the structure of rural power.

Tax (1947) spent only six months in Chichicastenango but provided interesting, if somewhat disorganized, insights into Quiché belief and ritual. His major contribution, however, lies in the statistical studies he made of land tenure and family structure in the rural area and items traded at the town market. Some of the specific findings about traditional Quiché culture of both Bunzel and Tax are summarized in chapter 12.

A study by Ricardo Falla (1975), a Jesuit priest, in the community of San Antonio Ilotenango is also important. He is the first ethnographer to work in the Quiché area who correctly describes the patrilineal-descent system of the rural Quichés. He also obtained information on the year-bearer and "leap-year" system of the Quiché calendar employed in the central area.

Archaeology

Early in the twentieth century Samuel Lothrop (1933; 1936) surveyed sites in the Quiché area, though his main area of concentration was around Lake Atitlán. He cited Fuentes y Guzmán's account of wars between the Tzutujils and the Quichés of Utatlán, claiming that they took place during the last archaeological phase in the lake area. He correlated that phase with the site of Chuitinamit, near present-day Santiago Atitlán, and a white-on-red ceramic ware. He also visited Utatlán and made surface observations of the site. Red-on-white ware found at the site suggested to him that Utatlán shared the same late phase he had discovered at the lake. He correlated the nine plaster layers visible in the central plaza of Utatlán with the fifty-two-year renewal cycle of the Aztecs. He used that cycle to date the first layers in the central plaza as twelfth century. There is no evidence that the Quichés used the fifty-two-year cycle, and, as will be seen in later chapters, the twelfth-century date is too early for Utatlán.

The dominant figure in Utatlán archaeology has been Robert Wauchope, of the Middle American Research Institute, Tulane University. He excavated the Zacualpa site, which closely neighbors Utatlán, and worked out a cultural sequence that tied in with Quiché history (1947; 1948). Wauchope was undecided whether the Quichés were to be correlated with the Early (Tohil) or the Late Postclassic (Yaqui) phase of Zacualpa. The Yaqui phase at the site was expressed only by a few cremation urns, leading Wauchope to postulate that they had been left there at the time of the Conquest by Aztec warriors who accompanied the conquistadors. This left the Tohil phase, marked by the appearance of effigy plumbate vessels, to be correlated with the arrival of the Quichés at Zacualpa. Using dynastic genealogy to work back to the coming of the Quiché forefathers, Wauchope dated the beginning of the Tohil phase at somewhere around 1250 to 1300. He went on to tie this date with the long-count dating system of the Classic lowland Mayas, arguing that his findings supported Thompson's correlation.

Wauchope later tested the hypotheses derived from his work at Zacualpa by sinking exploratory test pits at Utatlán. The results of that work (1949; 1970) showed that Quiché culture could be correlated with the white-on-red ceramic phase found at several other late sites in the highlands. He found no ceramic ware of the Tohil phase at Utatlán, the logical conclusion being that Quiché culture corresponded with his Yaqui rather than Tohil phase. Wauchope was slow to accept the finding, but he eventually came around to that view (1970, p. 174; 1975).

Wauchope's reconstruction of the ruling dynasty at Utatlán represents considerable advancement over the work of his predecessors. He clarified the following points: (1) a change in ruler was not necessarily equivalent to a change in generation; (2) the length of the average generation should be calculated at far fewer than forty years (he used a twenty-year figure); (3) the beginning part of the dynasty was abbreviated in the *Popol Vuh* but could be corrected by the *Título Totonicapán*; (4) the precise chronology of *The Annals of the Cakchiquels* could be used to cross-date the Quiché dynasty; and (5) through a study of Quiché history the average generation figure should be shortened or lengthened to give more accuracy to the reconstruction. Wauchope arrived at the following chronological data: 220 years of Quiché rule, eleven generations of succession, a dynastic-origin date of 1303, and a founding date for Utatlán of about 1433. Though it is possible to quibble with Wauchope on fine points, his reconstruction was basically correct (compare my chronology in chapter 5).

Wauchope was the first to interpret successfully Quiché cultural development on the basis of archaeological information. Though he concerned himself mostly with chronological questions, he made other important interpretations. He showed, for example, that cremation was practiced by the Quichés, that they had metallurgy, and that they built palacelike structures with painted murals. From his reconstruction of the Quiché dynasty he concluded that warfare resulted in early deaths of many rulers and that there was a flexible succession pattern. Most important, Wauchope (1975, pp. 60ff.) showed that the coming of the Quichés was manifested by a radical change in archaeological patterns. The Yaqui phase brought far more changes in ceramics, architecture, and artistic styles than had occurred during the preceding Classic and Early Postclassic periods. As he stated, "If ever there was a time in Guatemalan highland prehistory when, one would suspect, a racially new ethnic group entered the country and dominated local populations, I think that [the Late Postclassic] would be it" (1975, p. 64).

Sir J. Eric S. Thompson attempted to fit the Quichés into his synthesis of southern Maya archaeological history (1943; 1954). He correctly identified them with "Mexican" influences that reached the highlands in the Postclassic period (after 987), but he was uncertain whether they belonged to the Mexican Period (987–1204) or the Mexican Absorption Period (1204–1524). The strong Tula traditions of the Quichés led him to postulate that Quiché culture had its beginnings in the Mexican (Tohil) Period, and he associated Utatlán with other sites of that period, such as Tajumulco, Zaculeu, and Zacualpa. He also thought that the wars between the Quichés and the Tzutujils took place during the early period. As will be shown later, both Utatlán and the wars belong to the later period (his Mexican Absorption Period).

Thompson realized that later Quiché history given in the chronicles took place during the Late Postclassic, or Yaqui, Period. He saw the main thrust of Quiché history as the expansion of the Quichés (and the Cakchiquels) into the Pacific lowlands, at the expense of the Tzutujils and the Pipils. He also correctly correlated Quiché culture with specific archaeological features: postplumbate pottery, evidences of cremation, evidences of metallurgy, and Mexican architectural features, such as divided stairways.

Thompson's later Putun theory (1970, pp. 3–47) showed his continued unwillingness to differentiate clearly between the Early and the Late Postclassic periods. He argued that Putun merchants from the Tabasco-Veracruz region dominated the lowland Maya area from 850 to 1500 and were responsible for the "Mexican" features that characterized the Maya culture during that period. Since highland Guatemala received Mexican influence similar to that in Yucatán and the Petén lowlands, Thompson might well have applied his Putun theory to the Quichés. For some reason he did not. I shall test its application to the Quichés in chapter 3.

Thompson (1960; 1970) demonstrated the fundamentally Mayan framework of Quiché culture by comparing Quiché linguistic and cultural forms with those of other Maya groups. He found the twenty day names of the Quichés to be similar to those of other Maya groups, though the relationship is indirect in some instances; for example, Quej (Deer), a Quiché day name, corresponds with Manik, a Yucatecan black deity, since "there is a widespread connection between gods of the deer and black features." Other correlations between Maya and Quiché cultural patterns suggested by Thompson include the sexual drama of the sky and the earth, whose intercourse brings life; the notion that if Xbalanque is the moon she should be feminine; the equivalence between the rain gods of the lowlands (the Chacs) and the mountain gods (Juyup Tak'aj) of the highlands, both of which are closely associated with snakes; the association of the jaguar with the underworld, darkness, and the starry night; and many parallels in mythic themes. Many of Thompson's suggestions about Quiché culture continue to merit our careful consideration.

Recent syntheses of highland Guatemala archaeology have included some interpretation of Utatlán and the Quichés. Michael Coe (1961a; 1963; 1967) emphasizes their militaristic and "Mexican" features and connects them with the Toltec diaspora of the eleventh century. Though this dating is too early, Coe correctly dates the conquests of Q'uik'ab in the Pacific coastal region to the fifteenth century (see chapter 5 below). Ledyard Smith (1955) assigned sites like Utatlán to the Protohistoric Period (Late Postclassic, 1200 to 1524), noting their location on defensive hilltops. Such sites reveal "Mexican" architectural features, the most important of which are twin temples on a single platform, altar platforms and shrines, double stairways, batter at the bases of superstructures, enclosed ball courts, round structures, and balustrades with vertical upper zones. Many of these so-called Mexican features date back to Classic times in the Guatemalan highlands, while lowland Maya features are almost absent from the area. Robert Rands and Robert Smith (1965) filled out the ceramic picture by defining the marker for the Protohistoric in Guatemala as white-on-red ware, often called fortress white-on-red because of its almost universal occurrence at hilltop sites like Utatlán. A red-and-black-on-white polychrome ware (Chinautla), moldmade ladle censers, and thin micaceous jars and dishes are other markers.

Stephan de Borhegyi (1965) attempted an exhaustive reconstruction of cultural development in highland Guatemala based on the archaeological sources. Though he failed to differentiate clearly between the Early and the Late Postclassic periods and erroneously connected the Quichés' ancestors with Early Postclassic developments, his synthesis is valuable. Borhegyi correctly identified the original homeland of the Quiché forefathers as the ethnically mixed region of the Gulf Coast (he refers to the people there as Nonoalca-Pipil-Toltec-Chichimecs). The migrants to Guatemala founded hilltop sites similar to medieval European castles, which in time "became not only places of refuge and festive gatherings but also the administrative and commercial capitals of the warring highland Maya nationality groups." Thus he linked the Quichés to the transformation of highland peoples from theocratic and folk societies to more politically conscious military kingdoms or "nations."

Borhegyi ascribed to the Quichés and related groups many Mexican cultural traits that appear in Postclassic archaeology. Some of the specific traits probably came into the area before the arrival of the Quichés, but others may indeed have been brought in by them. Among these were the practice of cremation rather than inhumation, the cult of sacred bundles, new ball-court rules and paraphernalia, the use of *comales* to make tortillas, leaf-shaped bifacial points for spear-throwers and arrows, and anthropomorphic censers representing such Mexican gods as Quetzalcoatl, Xipe, and Morning Star. Other traits mentioned by Borhegyi—metallurgy, Mixteca-Puebla tripod censers, and trade with Mexico—were more likely aspects of Mexican influence that reached the area before the Quiché migrations. Borhegyi's study reminds us that changes introduced by the Quichés were part of a Mexicanization of highland culture that had been going on for at least two centuries before they came onto the scene.

Ethnohistory

Work on the Quiché documentary sources during the first half of the twentieth century was dominated by the late Guatemalan scholar and statesman Adrián Recinos. As Guatemalan ambassador to Washington, D.C., Recinos gained access to Quiché-language manuscript holdings in libraries in the United States. He became the first scholar since Brasseur to control both the native chronicles and the ancient dictionaries and grammars. Armed with those sources, an acute mind, and enthusiasm for his work, Recinos set about translating the Quiché chronicles. Among these documents were the *Popol Vuh* and five other major Quiché chronicles (1950; 1953; 1957). In his introductions and footnotes to those documents he offered his view of Quiché cultural development. The present discussion will focus on that view rather than on the translations themselves (see Carmack 1973, pp. 23–43).

Recinos was aware of the Toltec contribution to Quiché culture but believed it to be only a "superficial layer" covering a more fundamental Maya core. Though he somewhat naïvely traced Maya influence to Yucatán, his demonstration of Maya cultural patterns in Quiché culture is convincing. Some examples of the Maya elements he found are the prominence of the hunter (*ajpú*) as leader, the monkey as patron of artisanry, Xibalba as the place of phantasms, the belief in magical transformations, the deer as symbol of departure, and the mat as symbol of authority. Most of the Mexican elements he mentioned had been pointed out by others before him, especially Brasseur. Nevertheless, his list of Mexican parallels is valid and shows that he knew the Mexican sources.

Recinos's reconstruction of the geographic features of Quiché origins was also accurate, more so than most previous attempts. He traced the Quiché Tula tradition to northern Mexico and understood that it did not refer to Quiché migrations per se. He correctly located the departure place for the "Guatemalan tribes," as he referred to them, in the Tabasco area. This was an intermediate area where Nahuas of the north mingled with Mayas of the south. He recognized several places in that area mentioned in the Quiché chronicles: Coatzacoalco, Xicalango, Nonoalca, and Olmeca. The Quiché tradition, he thought, tied in with the Toltec legend in which Quetzalcoatl left central Mexico, traveled to the Tabasco area (called Tlapallan), and from there founded political dynasties at Chichén Itzá and Mayapán, as well as in Chiapas and Guatemala. This occurred toward the end of the tenth century, the approximate time the Quiché ancestors migrated to the highlands. Thus Recinos thought that Nacxit of the Quiché documents was Quetzalcoatl or a successor using his name. It will be shown later that Recinos's dating of Quiché origins is two centuries too early and that no direct tie with Quetzalcoatl existed.

Recinos explained the origins of the Maya component of Quiché culture less satisfactorily. He argued that the inhabitants of the Quiché area encountered by the Toltec migrants were descendants of the Old Empire Maya people from the central lowlands (especially the Petén), who fled there when that empire collapsed. Though Recinos emphatically rejected some of the earlier attempts to interpret Quiché myth as history, he believed that the Quichés had retained knowledge of the Old Empire. Thus he noted that Xibalba, the mythic world of the dead, was definitely associated with the northern lowlands in the minds of the Quichés. The road leading there started in Verapaz around Carcha and its nearby caves and then dropped down to Xibalba. The Ajtzás (People of the Itzá) and Ajtucurs (People of the Owl), associated with Xibalba in the Quiché tradition, proved that Verapaz (known anciently as the Owl Place) and the Petén (where the Itzás lived) were the location of both Xibalba and the Old Empire. It should be noted that there is no evidence that Quiché peoples ever participated in Classic lowland Maya culture or that remnants of that society migrated to the highlands after its dissolution.

Recinos added little to our understanding of subsequent Quiché history. He followed Brasseur in believing that Jakawitz was north of Rabinal and speculated that it might have been the archaeological site of Chipal. He made no new identifications of places in the central Quiché area. His dynastic list generally followed the *Popol Vuh*, although he was one of the first to note that it was truncated in some places (as shown by the Totonicapán document), and so may have been longer than formerly thought. Because he erroneously believed that each Quiché ruler and his son represented a single "generation" of rule, he accepted Ximénez's estimate of forty years a generation. That caused him to take Quiché dynasty back to the eleventh century and so correlate it with his reconstruction of tenth- and eleventh-century Toltec migrations.

In Recinos we finally get the correct boundaries of the Quiché state under Q'uik'ab. Quiché territory included most of what is now central and western

Guatemala, as well as the Pacific coast to Soconusco. The Chiapas area, the northern lowlands, and the eastern part of present-day Guatemala were all outside its bounds. With respect to post-Q'uik'ab history, Recinos accepted Ximénez's speculation that the "Quiché Winak" dance portrayed historical events from the time of the third-to-last Quiché ruler, though there is no evidence to support it. Recinos may have been the first student of the Quichés to distinguish between the Tecum who was the son of the ruler burned to death by Alvarado and the Tecum who was killed in the battlefield outside Quezaltenango.

Recinos did not analyze the development of the Quichés in a systematic way. He appears to have assumed that Quiché culture was sophisticated and advanced, much like the other cultures of ancient Mexico and Central America. He referred to Utatlán as the most important town in Central America at the time of the Conquest and to the *Popol Vuh* as "the most lively and significant" literary work of indigenous Americans. Though the Quiché language may not have been a principal language of the world, as Ximénez had asserted, Recinos found it elegant, highly evolved, rich in vocabulary, and flexible in structure. Quiché culture reflected the two great traditions of the past, the Toltec and the ancient Maya. The central position of the Quichés in aboriginal history led Recinos to argue that Quauhtemallan, the original Nahua name for Guatemala, was a translation of Q'uiche' (Many Trees), and was applied to the entire highland area where the Quichés ruled. As the Franciscan priests noted in early colonial years, the name actually was the Nahua word for Iximché, the Cakchiquel capital.

Recinos certainly moved Quiché studies forward, and he effectively built upon the work of many before him. He had an essentially correct view of Utatlán and the Quichés, though he did not address such topics as internal social structure, political geography, Utatlán archaeology, and the post-Conquest Quichés. Perhaps his greatest contribution was in demonstrating the important Maya component in Quiché culture. He was strong "philolog-ically," and only recently have modern linguistic studies of the Quichés begun to surpass his lexical and semantic comparisons of Quiché with other Maya languages.

Recinos's studies of the chronicles brought ethnohistoric research on the Quichés into the modern era. Of the many scholars who have carried on since Recinos, Nicholson, Miles, Carrasco, and Edmonson should be briefly mentioned.

H. B. Nicholson (1957) found evidence of definite Toltec cultural traditions in the Quiché sources. Chief among these were Quichés' claims that they came from Tula (which Nicholson suggests might have been a secondary Toltec center in Tabasco or Yucatán), visited with Nacxit of the East (a successor to Quetzalcoatl in the Tabasco area), had a famous ruler named

Quetzalcoatl—or K'ucumatz in Quiché (who was a different person from the Toltec priest-ruler but whose life was recast so as to conform to that famous Toltec). The god Tojil was called Yolcoatl Quetzalcoatl, probably the "night-wind" deity, known in Mexico as Ehecatl. But the Quiché deity K'ucumatz may also be identified with the creator god and fructifier of ancient Mexico called Ehecatl-Quetzalcoatl. Later (1976) Nicholson high-lighted some of the main cultural differences between the Quichés and the peoples of central Mexico. Compared with central Mexicans, the Quichés can be characterized by their kinship orientation, emphasis on political legitima-tion, parochial view of history, use of dynastic rather than year counts, and predilection for dance dramas and the dawn ceremony. He doubts that much accurate history before the fourteenth century can be obtained from the native chronicles.

Suzanna Miles briefly compared Quiché culture with other highland Guatemalan cultures, especially the Pokomam (1952; 1957; 1965). She found that Quiché month names do not correspond with those of the Pokomams or the lowland Mayas. Rather they share several features with central Mexican calendars. Further, Quiché year-bearers follow the highland Ik rather than the lowland Kan pattern. Their gods can be identified with Mexican deities too, while the Pokomam deities were notably lowland in derivation. Simi-larly, the lowland Maya Omaha-type kinship system contrasts with the "modified descriptive system" of the Quichés. Only the Quichés had a hereditary "class" of rulers, other highland groups having little more than a "hereditary lineage power structure." Miles was uncertain about the nature of Mexican influence on Quiché culture, though she seems to have believed that it came indirectly from intergroup trade and marriage with the Pacific Coast Pipils and the central Mexicans. Mexican contact was probably more direct than she supposed and about a century earlier than the 1300 date she assigned to it.

Pedro Carrasco, while best known for his ethnohistoric reconstruction of central Mexican cultures, has used the early sources to clarify features of Quiché social structure (1959; 1964; 1967*a*, *b*). He argued that the basic Quiché social unit, called *chinamit* in the sources, was functionally similar to the Aztec *calpulli*. Both were territorial units important in landholding, rights to political office, and ceremonial presentation. They differed in that the Quiché units were internally organized as patrilineal-descent groups while the Aztec units were ambilateral or cognatic groups. In other studies Car-rasco reconstructed the naming system of the Quichés and related groups (patrilineal names were dominant as in Yucatán, though individual and calendric names similar to those of central Mexico were also used), their system of landed serfs (resettled conquered peoples called Nimak Achí, Big Men), and the nature of the "elect" ruler (*ajpop c'amja*, an official who,

41

according to Carrasco, exercised power "during the childhood of the successor to the ruler").

Ethnohistoric studies of the Quichés have been carried forward in recent years by Munro Edmonson (1964; 1965; 1971). He has emphasized the lineage structure of Quiché society, with its inherent divisive tendencies. He believes that calendric associations were dominant in Quiché ideology and has worked out intriguing if somewhat speculative correlations among calendric days, lineage units, and ritual dances. Thus Edmonson associates the nineteenth calendar day, Cawok, with the Cawek lineage and the Rabinal Achi dance. Many other interpretations of esoteric Quiché symbols are attempted by Edmonson, and some of them represent advances over previous work; for example the *c'o* prefix of rulers is given the meaning "head" or "chief," the deity Awilix is identified with the moon goddess, and certain Quiché authority insignia are derived from icons of central Mexico.

Perhaps Edmonson's major contribution is his demonstration of the literary nature of Quiché writings, especially the *Popol Vuh*. He has shown that the Quichés frequently wrote in couplets, employing an antiphonal literary device. Edmonson found evidence that glyphic texts were used in some instances, oral poetry then providing the basis for interpreting the texts. While one might argue that not all Quiché literature is poetic and that his allusions to glyphic texts are based on speculative evidence, the extensive use of the antiphonal technique would seem to be demonstrated.

Edmonson apparently believes the culture of the Quichés to have been somewhat schismatic and kinship-structured compared with that of other Mesoamerican peoples. He maintains that the Quichés were "subjected to considerable Mexican influence" while Yucatecan Maya influence was negligible. More than other students before him Edmonson has pointed to important Mam influence on the Quichés, the result of their extensive contacts with that group. He has suggested (1976) that the name of the greatest Quiché ruler, Q'uik'ab, was of Mam derivation. These and other provocative suggestions require careful linguistic and historical testing.

3
ORIGINS

THIS BOOK IS ABOUT THE PEOPLE who lived in the Utatlán community, their culture, and the settlements they built. It is also about the development of that culture—how it was created and adapted to the surroundings. The latter subject requires that we look at the antecedents of Utatlán. Fortunately considerable information is available on this topic, thanks to the native chronicles and the recent discovery of all the major archaeological sites of the early Quichés. In the account to follow, the archaeological and ethnohistoric data will be brought together in a brief synthesis of what the Quichés were like before they settled on the plains of the Quiché basin.

The Quiché history may have relevance for understanding a question that has long concerned students of the Mayas: What caused the collapse of the classic Maya civilization? As with the classic lowland Mayas, it will be shown that the indigenous settlements of the central Quiché plains were suddenly abandoned and that a radically new cultural era was ushered in. For the Quichés it will be documented that this was the result of the entry into the area of small bands of warlords who established tiny strongholds in the mountains a few miles from the plains. Without the information contained in the documentary sources and the aid of living descendants of the natives of the area, we would not know of the invaders, nor would we understand the cause of the abandonment of the plains sites. The lowland Maya case may be parallel; at least the idea is worth testing. For now it is enough to note that the reconstruction of early Quiché culture has implications beyond providing answers to developmental questions about the community of Utatlán.

THE ORIGIN OF THE QUICHÉ FOREFATHERS

The rulers of Utatlán retained a knowledge of their forefathers through the sacred books they kept. According to the sources the original founders of the Quiché political system came from faraway "Mexico." In some of the chronicles, especially the *Popol Vuh* and *The Annals of the Cakchiquels*, the narration of this primordial migration appears to have been taken directly from poems, tales, and songs recorded in the old books. They are more than mere traditions and deserve serious consideration as historical fact.

Several years ago, in 1968, I offered the argument, based on a study of the origin accounts in the chronicles, that the Quiché forefathers were Chontal-Nahua speakers from the Tabasco-Veracruz area (Fig. 3.1). They came as small military bands, commissioned originally at Epi-Toltec centers (places of Toltec influence after the fall of Tula) in the Gulf Coast area for purposes of conquest and political control. They built small defensive centers in the Quiché mountains, the most notable of which was called Jakawitz. From there they began terrorizing the surrounding peoples through warfare and human sacrifice. They were superior to the local peoples in military technology and organization, introducing such weapons as the atlatl (spear thrower); the copper hatchet; the macana (an obsidian-blade sword); a hard, round shield; and cotton-quilted armor. Gradually they established an Epi-Toltec state, complete with a ruling line back to Quetzalcoatl (called Nacxit in the sources), sacred Toltec icons (jaguar claws, tobacco gourds, heron feathers, and so on), tributary provinces, ritual human sacrifice, monumental buildings with "Toltec" architecture (slope-and-batter balustrades, I-shaped ball courts, small altars in front of temples, painted stucco panels, and so on), and nucleated towns with urban characteristics. Entry into the Quiché area by these warlords can be correlated with the Late Postclassic (or Protohistoric) phase of highland Guatemala archaeology, and dated from about 1250. A chronology based on the dynastic genealogies of the chronicles confirmed this beginning date. Thus I concluded in that study that the origins of the Quichés of Utatlán were to be associated with the Late Postclassic archaeology of highland Guatemala and not with the Early Postclassic as had been previously argued (Thompson 1943; Wauchope 1948; Borhegyi 1965).

Long experience in such matters has taught anthropologists to be skeptical of migration tales. Often they turn out to be myths that serve to rationalize the occupation of a territory or a connection with some prestigious authority source. Mythic elements are certainly associated with the Quiché origin story—for example, the biblical tale of the parting of the Red Sea is woven into it—but fundamentally it appears to be historical. Research carried out since the time I wrote about Quiché origins has generally supported the story as narrated in the chronicles.

Many general features of the Gulf Coast homeland were correctly described in the documents. It was said to be a place near the sea with many rivers and lagoons on which people traveled in boats. Fishermen lived there, as well as farmers, who grew such lowland crops as cacao, *zapotes*, and

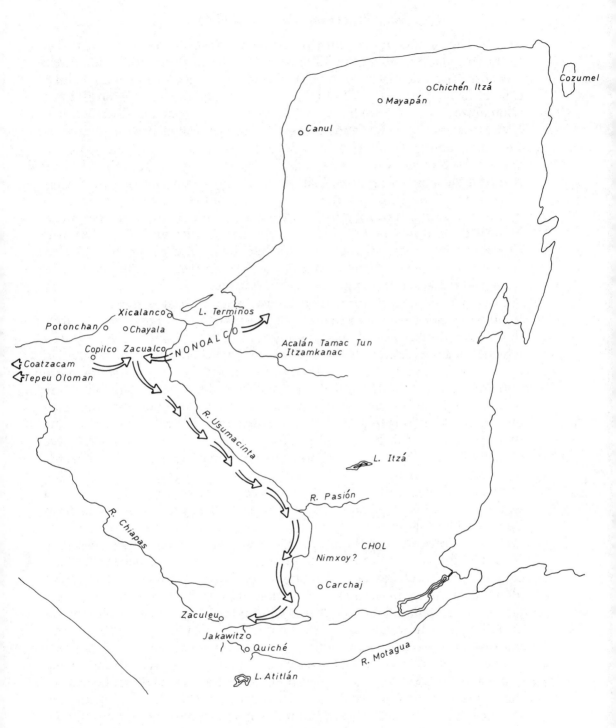

Fig. 3.1.   The origin of the Quiché forefathers. Modified from Carmack 1968.

pataxte. The documents also provide the names of several peoples and places in the original homeland, and almost every one of these can be identified with pre-Hispanic places in the Gulf Coast area. They include Cayala (also called Chayala), a town of Chontal speakers near Potonchan; Tepeu (Tepew) Oloman, a town of the Olmecs who lived just west of the Coatzacoalcos River; Coatzacam, a marketing center of Nahua speakers beside the river of the same name; Teozacuancu and Atzocopih, apparently the Chontal-speaking settlement Copilco-Zacualco in Tabasco; Nonoualcat, the Mexican name for the lands of Tabasco, Campeche, and Yucatán; Zuiwa, a place west of Yucatán surrounded by water, which may be an old name for Xicalango, a Nahua-speaking trading port; and Tulan, the Tollan or Tlapallan of Nonoalco mentioned by the Mexican chroniclers, which until about 1200 was probably the great settlement of Chichén Itzá. One of the first Quiché settlements in the highlands, Amak' Tan (or Tam) was also the name of a territory (Tamac Tun) along the Río Candelaria.

Obviously the Quiché forefathers knew the Gulf Coast well, which makes it hard to deny their claim that they came from there. Furthermore, they describe in precise terms their sufferings during the journey and the route by which they traveled from the Gulf Coast to Quiché. On the way they had to hunt deer and rabbits for food, though, we are told, they took some maize with them. It was cold, and the nights were dark. Years later they still remembered the howling of the animals at night and the privations they endured on their long trek. Both the *Popol Vuh* and the *Título Totonicapán* state that the first places they came to after leaving the homeland area were Nimxoy and Carcha. These are known places in the Verapaz region, indicating that the Quiché forefathers entered the highlands by way of the Usumacinta River route. Next they arrived at Chixpach, Chiq'uiche, and Chipixab, in or near the San Andrés Sajcabaja Valley. This suggests that from Verapaz they followed the Río Negro west, using the Río Agua Caliente branch to drop down to the San Andrés Basin. From this area they passed by Mount Mamaj and entered the mountains, where they established their first settlements: Patojil, Pawilix, Jakawitz, Amak' Tan, and Uquin C'at. We have identified all these places near a tiny mountain valley about ten kilometers northeast of Utatlán, known today as Chujuyup. Within one hundred years of settling the Chujuyup Valley, the people from the Gulf were able to move onto the Quiché plains below, where they founded the Utatlán communities.

Research on the cultures of the Gulf Coast by Thompson (1970) and Rathje and Sabloff (1975*a, b*) sheds important light on the reasons for and nature of the migrations to Guatemala from that area by the Quiché forefathers. During the Postclassic Period the Gulf Coast was a frontier zone between the highly dynamic Mexican cultures on the west and the creative Mayan cultures on the east. The Gulf Coast peoples absorbed cultural elements from both sources and became intermediaries between the two cultural worlds. They specialized in trade, taking advantage of their strategic position between highland and lowland ecological zones. Using both water and land routes, they traveled great distances to exchange goods at various ports of trade in the Maya area, such as Yucatán, Cozumel, and Nito. For example, they integrated Cozumel into a trading network that included Chichén Itzá. Later, about 1250, when Mayapán replaced Chichén Itzá as the main trading center in Yucatán, Cozumel reached the peak of its development by being tied in with that great center.

Thompson likened these Gulf Coast peoples to the Macedonians of the Old World, creating an "empire" out of seagoing trade and warfare. He called them the Putuns, after their main town, Potonchan, near the mouth of the Grijalva River. He credited them with having controlled areas distant from their heartland over a long period of time. Besides the supposed Putun control at Chichén Itzá, Mayapán, and Cozumel already mentioned, Thompson linked them with changes at Late Classic Maya sites along the Usumacinta and Pasión rivers (for example, Seibal and Altar de Sacrificios) and with such Late Postclassic political groups as the Acaláns of the Candelaria River, and the Itzás of Lake Petén. At all these places the defining characteristics of Putun presence were an emphasis on trade, syncretic Mexican-Mayan cultural features (in language, art, and ritual), political rule by fours, and the prominence of the moon (Ixchel), the feathered serpent (Kukulchan), and north star (Ik' Chawa) gods.

Thompson's Putun theory provides a ready explanation for the migration of the Quiché forefathers from the Gulf Coast to the Guatemalan highlands. According to this view they would be seen as colonists sent to the area to control important highland resources—such as jade, obsidian, salt, and metals—and so to promote the highland-lowland exchange in which the trading ports of the Gulf Coast specialized. However plausible this explanation may seem in the light of studies on the Putuns, it does not adequately explain the Quiché case. There is no solid evidence that the Quiché forefathers were traders or that they ever instituted long-distance exchange between the Quiché highlands and the Gulf Coast.

Rather than as Putun merchants, the Quiché forefathers appear in the sources as aggressive warlords. They were warriors within the Toltec tradition who conquered in order to obtain sacrificial victims to feed the sun and simultaneously to gain tributes with which to feed themselves. Their social ideology was strongly aristocratic: the militarily strong were successful because they were in the service of deity, and as servants of deity they were deity also. Their descent lines had to be kept pure, a condition that they believed made them superior to other peoples and thus gave them the right to rule. As befitting rulers, they were to live higher than and separate from other peoples. Special foods, clothes, ornaments, utensils, language, and elaborate residences would symbolize their high status.

This form of exploitative militarism had ancient roots in Mesoamerica but especially flourished within Toltec culture. It reached the Gulf Coast perhaps most strongly from Chichén Itzá, the main center of Toltec influence in Yucatán during the Early Postclassic Period (800–1200). The history of the Gulf Coast reveals that many groups there came under Toltec influence, but the trading environment, with its requirement of political neutrality (Chapman 1957; Rathje and Sabloff 1975a), was not congenial to the imperialistic approach to political organization. Highly militarized Gulf Coast groups, such as the "mercenaries" at Canul (Yucatán), and the Itzás of Chichén Itzá and later Lake Petén, employed the militaristic Toltec approach outside the coastal area. The fall of Chichén Itzá about 1200 created a political vacuum in the northern Maya area, which appears to have stimulated several Epi-Toltec imperialistic drives. Mayapán represents one such drive, and the Quiché warlords probably represent another.

Thus it was as Epi-Toltec warlords, rather than as Putun merchants, that the forefathers of the Quichés migrated to the Guatemala highlands. They essentially stated as much in the chronicles. We are told that they went to Tulan, Chichén Itzá, or some other Toltec center (perhaps Mayapán), where they were commanded:

"Go, my sons and daughters. I will give you your riches and your rule, your power and your majesty, your royal canopy and throne. They will pay tribute to you in the form of shields, bows, quetzal feathers, and lime, as well as jade, metals, green and blue feathers; and they will give you writings, scrolls, calendars, and cacao. The enemy peoples will pay these to you in tribute, and they will be yours. You will be favored, and this will make you happy. I will not give you this rule, but those peoples will be your tributaries. In truth, great will be your glory. . . . Do not sleep, and you will conquer, my sons and daughters. [*Annals*]

The ideology expressed here is the old Toltec one of empire expansion. By the time the Quiché forefathers ventured forth, however, there was no empire. They went as Epi-Toltec lords to found their own conquest state, and though contact with the old Tulan center might be maintained, their relationship would henceforth be one of political equals. Indeed, the *Relación de Yucatán* (Roys 1943, p. 58) states that rulers all the way from Guatemala, Chiapas, and Mexico came to the Toltec center Chichén Itzá, but only to bring "tokens of peace and friendship."

Though the Quiché forefathers may not have been Putun merchants, they shared with the Putuns cultural forms characteristic of the Gulf Coast. Like most other peoples there they appear to have been bilingual. The chronicles make it clear that the Quiché forefathers spoke a Maya language and that they also knew a Nahua dialect. They refer to the Tepeu Olomans as their "brothers and kinsmen" and state that they were "Yaqui," that is, Nahua speakers. Sahagún (1961, 10:187–88) claimed that the Olmecs spoke a non-Nahua language, though "many spoke Nahuatl." Wigberto Jiménez Moreno (1942, pp. 125–28) suggested that they may have been Nahuatized Popoloca-Mixtec speakers. More likely it was Chontal Maya, the main language of the Gulf Coast, that was spoken in the Quiché homeland. Like so many other peoples of the area, the Quiché forefathers were probably Nahuatized Chontal speakers.

Whatever language they spoke, it apparently was not Quiché. Once in the highlands they ran into language problems. They recorded this in their history: "The speech of . . . [the forefathers] is different. Oh! We have given up our speech! What have we done! We are lost. How were we deceived? We had only one speech when we arrived there in Tulán; we were created and educated in the same way. It is not good what we have done" (*Popol Vuh*). But Chontal was part of a language group (Cholan) with mutually intelligible languages stretching all the way from the Gulf Coast to the highlands of Guatemala. Apparently the Quichés' forefathers encountered other Cholan speakers with whom they could communicate: "Certainly their language was difficult; only the barbarians understood their tongue. . . . Those of Chol Amak' were astonished when we spoke to them in their language; they were frightened, but they replied to us with fair words" (*Annals*). It would seem that the Quiché forefathers made contact with some of the Chol speakers who had once inhabited the eastern part of the Guatemalan highlands. Since this language was similar to Chontal, they could communicate with them.

Many of the forefathers' names, as well as names of early places, objects, and institutions, do not appear to be Quiché. As I suggested several years ago, perhaps they are Chontal. For example, such ancestral names as Balam Quitze and Majucutaj have been assigned the unlikely Quiché etymologies Jaguar of Sweet Laughter and Not Brushed (Ximénez 1929, p. 172). Though we lack early Chontal dictionaries, the closely related Yucatecan-language dictionaries (Motul 1929) seem to provide more reasonable etymologies: Balam Quite (Forest Jaguar), Majuctaj (One Who Does Not Stay; Traveler), and Eke Balam (Black Jaguar, a god in Yucatán) (Recinos 1953, p. 176). Other Quiché ancestral names, such as C'opichoch and C'ochojlan, contain basic Maya roots, as well as the familiar *ch* phone of Chontal. Similarly, the early Quiché settlements Jakawitz and Amak' Tan do not translate easily into Quiché but have familiar Yucatecan roots: *witz* is the Yucatecan word for "mountain," and we have already seen that Amak' Tan was the name of a place near the Río Candelaria. Another word from the chronicles that does not appear to be Quiché, *ajcajb*, is a title used to refer to the priestly aspect of the forefathers. In Yucatecan *balamil caj* means "the priests of the town."

Many other words associated with the forefathers appear not to derive from the Quiché language. They deserve more linguistic analysis than they have received. Lyle R. Campbell (1976), who has begun examining the Quiché chronicles with such questions in mind, detects a fairly large number of "Cholan" loans into Quiché. Though he suggests that most of the words diffused into Quiché much earlier than the time of the Quiché forefathers, some of them may have been brought in late with these immigrants. One example from his list, *chol k'ij* ("calendar"), is specifically mentioned in the documents as the name for something that the forefathers brought with them from the homeland. As suggested above, there may be many other examples of this kind.

The Nahuatization of the Quiché forefathers is much easier to document from the chronicles. They used many Nahua words for military and ritual matters: *tinamit* ("fortified town"), *tepewal* ("dominion or power"), *achcayupil* ("cotton armor"), *chalamicat* ("priest"), *tacaxepual* ("calendar month for receiving tributes and flaying sacrificial victims"). Many of the names of early ruling lines were Nahua also: Acxopil, Istayul, Cipac, Tepepul, and so on. The forefathers knew an archaic Nahua dialect, for the *tl* and *o* phones of the later Aztec dialect were rendered as *t* and *u*. In a linguistic study of Nahua loans into Quiché, Campbell (1970) found that Nahua words in Quiché derive from dialects of the Gulf Coast. Besides the *t* and *u* features, Nahua words in the Quiché chronicles share with the Gulf Coast dialects the patterns of changing *iwi* to *i* (Nahuatl *xiwitl*, "jade," becomes *xit*), and *cwaw* to *co* (Nahuatl *cwawtli*, "eagle," becomes *cot*). Campbell also discovered that many Nahua loans in the Quiché language have to do with domestic and everyday economic activities, not just warfare and ritual. Possibly some of these Nahua terms predate the coming of the forefathers from the Gulf Coast (see below).

The chronicles associate several customary practices with the Quiché forefathers that are similar to ones described for the Gulf Coast area. For example, under different names the main coastal deities were worshiped by the Quiché warlords. Tojil, the chief deity of the early forefathers, is identified in the *Popol Vuh* as Yolcuat-Quitzalcuat. This is the Nahua form of Kukulchan, a major deity of the Gulf Coast. The second-most-important early Quiché deity was called Awilix, a name that appears to be an abbreviated form of C'abawil Ixchel (Edmonson 1965). Like the Gulf Coast peoples the Quichés associated this goddess with the moon. Jakawitz, the third major deity of the Quiché forefathers, was possibly related to the merchant deity of the Gulf Coast peoples. The *Popol Vuh* informs us that bees and wasps were the symbol of this god, just as they represented the merchant deity of the coastal peoples.

The Gulf Coast peoples' custom of defining political rule in terms of fours was strictly observed by the Quiché forefathers. Each group of warlords was said to number four, though in at least one instance, that of the Ilocabs, five leaders have been identified. Other similarities in the customs of the two peoples include the use of a four-hundred-day calendric unit, the importance of the bow and of the copper hatchet, and the prominence of the "bloody-skin" icon (Carmack 1968, pp. 69–70).

The list of similarities in what the chronicles say about the Quiché forefathers and what we know about early Gulf Coast customs is impressive, considering our limited knowledge of the latter area. Even less is known about Gulf Coast archaeology, at least for the Postclassic Period, in which we are interested here (Coe 1965, p. 713). Nevertheless, Fox (1975, pp. 75ff.) has noted some parallels between the archaeology of the Chujuyup area, where the Quiché forefathers first settled, and Postclassic archaeological sites near the Río Candelaria described by E. Willis Andrews (1943, pp. 45–47). In both areas the sites consist of small plazas placed on leveled neighboring hilltops. The plaza in each area has single temples facing a ball court across opposite sides of the plaza and long structures placed along the other sides of the plaza in perpendicular relationship to the first two structures. Unfortunately, these features are general and perhaps could be found at other sites in Mesoamerica during the Late Postclassic Period.

At one early Quiché site, Oquin, a temple and platform were carved out of the bedrock. John W. Fox (1975) argues that the Quiché forefathers were unfamiliar with stone-block construction and that it took some time for them to adapt to the new conditions of the area. In this regard it is worthy of note that stone is scarce along the Gulf Coast and much of the construction there was of brick. It would appear that the Quiché forefathers continued the old Gulf Coast building techniques for a while after arriving in the highlands.

We know little about the ceramics of the early Quichés. The fine, highly diagnostic orange wares of the Gulf Coast have not been found at the early Quiché sites, except for a few fine orange sherds found at Patojil. Fox (1975, p. 77) explains this by noting that the Quiché forefathers came without women, obtaining wives from the native groups of the Quiché area, who apparently produced their own ceramic wares, using local materials and techniques. The chronicles, however, indicate that a few of the warlords brought their wives with them. Excavations at the early Quiché sites may yet turn up ceramic types similar to those of the Gulf Coast.

Taken together, the language, documentary, and archaeological evidence supports the idea of a Gulf Coast origin for the ancestral fathers of the Utatlán rulers. They appear to have been warlords, imbued with the Epi-Toltec goals of empire building through conquest, the sustainment of cosmological gods through human sacrifice, and the establishment of an aristocratic way of life for themselves. We now turn to the peoples whom they encountered upon their arrival in the Quiché mountains.

NATIVES OF THE QUICHÉ AREA

It should be clear from the above discussion that the migration of the Quiché forefathers did not involve large numbers of people. They came as small bands of mostly male, mobile, tightly organized military lineages. They encountered an indigenous population that no doubt far outnumbered them. It has long been recognized that the native peoples already spoke the Quiché language (Thompson 1950, p. 16; Goubaud Carrera 1949) and that the incoming warlords eventually assimilated to their language. By and large, however, the natives were subjugated by the Quiché forefathers and thereby lost most of their native political organization and elite cultural patterns. In contrast, the peasants, the rural component of the native society, probably retained much of their ancient social life.

The chronicles concentrate on the history of the ruling lines of Utatlán. They have relatively little to say about the native peoples whom they subordinated as servants and vassals. Linguistic studies can tell us something about the pre-Quiché natives, but our primary source of information must be archaeology. Unfortunately, as yet no pre-Quiché site has been excavated in the area. We have only survey data, and the following account relies heavily on Russell E. Stewart's brief 1973 survey (Stewart 1976; Carmack, Fox, and Stewart 1975; see also Gruhn and Bryan 1976).

The main features of pre-Quiché culture revealed by archaeology can be briefly summarized as follows: (1) communities were predominantly provincial and outside the main currents of innovation occurring elsewhere in Mesoamerica; (2) social life was stable, little basic change having taken place for some five hundred years preceding the entry of the Quiché forefathers; (3) the population was large but mostly rural and scattered more or less evenly over the flat and upland zones of the Quiché basin; (4) small chiefdoms, each generally confined to a single plateau, constituted the highest level of political integration; (5) warfare and defense were secondary to ritual in the relations within and among chiefdoms; and (6) after a short period during which the culture brought in by the Quiché forefathers overlapped with native culture, the latter was largely replaced by the new forms, which became dominant in the whole area.

From at least the cessation of Teotihuacán influence in highland Guatemala (ca. 600–700) until the coming of the Quiché forefathers (ca. 1200), the native peoples of the Quiché basin appear to have lived in relative isolation. Settlements consisted of small, open plazas placed in linear series; buildings were apparently constructed without cut stone or exterior plaster. As far as we can tell, architectural forms were simple, consisting of square temple mounds and a few rectangular buildings. Ceramic forms were simple too and do not appear to have changed dramatically over a long period of time. The diagnostic wares are red-on-buff and red-and-brown wares with punctate and wavy-line incisions. The few examples of carved-stone statuary that have been found are crude, the anthropomorphic forms being barely detectable. One statue (from Panajxit) of better quality was carved in the form of a person with an animal draped over his back. Still by Mesoamerican standards it was crude, like pieces from Central America rather than from Mayan or Mexican sources.

The situation in the Quiché basin was in sharp contrast to that of other areas in the Guatemalan highlands, some of them close by. Fox (1975, pp. 28ff.) has documented the influence of hybrid Mexican-Mayan cultural forms during the Late Classic Period (ca. 700–900) in the highland basins of Sajcabaja (La Laguna), Sacapulas (Xolchun), and Aguacatán (Chalchitan). Classic Maya influence is evident in the architecture and ceramics at such Late Classic highland sites as Zacualpa, Zaculeu, and Lililla (Sajcabaja). These same sites, along with others, such as Pantzac (Sajcabaja), Chalchitan, and Chuitinamit (Sacapulas), came under Toltec influence during the Early Postclassic Period (ca. 900–1200). Some of the rather specific "Toltec" architectural features that appear at these sites are enclosed plazas; long, colonnaded structures; use of *talud y tablero* designs; central temples with inset terraces and four stairways; round structures; and double stairways. New ceramics are equally diagnostic of Toltec influence: effigy plumbate wares (Tohil), Mixtec censers, effigy-foot tripod bowls, and fine orange wares.

A comparison of the archaeology of the Quiché area and nearby highlands leads to the conclusion that native culture was much more a local development at Quiché than it was elsewhere. Pre-Quiché sites show few signs of either Classic Maya or Toltec influence, at least from the surface. There are no carved stelae, and the sherd or two of polychrome wares suggest the weakness of Maya influence. Similarly the lack of enclosed plazas and effigy plumbate pots suggests the absence of Toltec influence. One result of Quiché provincialism was that relatively few traditional cultural patterns survived the onset of the Late Postclassic Period. This contrasts with other nearby areas, such as Sacapulas or Huehuetenango, where pre-Quiché cultural patterns continued to dominate down to the Conquest. Nevertheless, even at Quiché a few early features survived in the new culture initiated by the Quiché forefathers. Two persisting features mentioned by Stewart are the linear arrangement of plazas and helix and concentric-circle designs painted on polychrome ceramics.

Recent analysis of the Quiché language and its relationship to the other Mesoamerican languages (Kaufman 1974, 1976; Campbell 1976) is consistent with the archaeological view just presented (see Fig. 3. 2). Quiché is closely related to other highland Guatemala languages. In fact, comparison of all the Maya languages (Kaufman 1964) demonstrates that from an early time native speakers of the area shared in a general Maya cultural substratum that included agriculture, nucleated settlements, markets and crafts, and many ideas about deity, magic, and ritual. By 700, Quichean was already a separate language of the central highlands, and Quiché was a "dialect" spoken in the central Quiché area somewhat in isolation from the other Quichean dialects (Sacapultec, Cakchiquel, Tzutujil, and Sipacapec). Terrence Kaufman (1976) states that at that time Quiché was the most independent dialect of this language, though it did have some contact with Sacapultec.

We have seen a similar cultural independence in the archaeology, suggesting that the other Quichean speakers shared greater language contact because they participated more actively than the Quichés in the mainstream of Mesoamerican cultural development. Nevertheless, that may have been the period when some of the Cholan words diffused into the Quiché language—it is assumed that the Classic Mayas (300–900) spoke a Cholan language. It should be noted, however, that the Cholan terms found in Quiché are few and are mostly names of plants and animals (fish, snakes, trees, and so on). This is again consistent with the cultural isolation of the native Quiché people suggested by the archaeology.

Quiché had become a separate language by 1000 and was almost the sole language of the Quiché basin when the migrants arrived in 1200 (Cakchiquel was probably still spoken in the southern zone). After many centuries of relative isolation the Quiché language must have been intimately adjusted to the community forms so long dominant in the area. The new lords of the land found it necessary to introduce many Nahua words into Quiché in order to make operational the Epi-Toltec institutions they soon established among the natives. A few of the Nahua loans may have diffused into the Quiché language before the arrival of the Quiché forefathers, but as yet it has not been possible to distinguish them from later borrowings. The vast majority, however, came from the Gulf Coast (Campbell 1976), and were used in referring to Epi-Toltec military practices and weapons, political offices and symbols, human-sacrifice ritual, monumental buildings, and social units of an urban character. These words certainly enriched the Quiché vocabulary, and their appearance correlates with the emergence of the more complex archaeological sites that replaced the pre-Quiché sites at that time. Nevertheless, the Quiché language retained its basic structure, and the invaders were ultimately forced to adopt it as the language of their new community. Paradoxically, they eventually became identified by the name of the native language of the area, though the Utatlán lords themselves always used the name Quiché to refer to their territory rather than to their language.

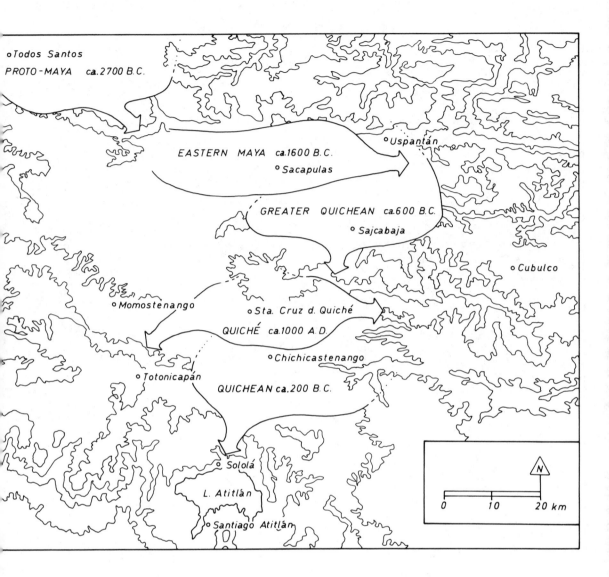

Fig. 3.2. The history of the central Quiché languages. From IGN, map, 1:250,000.

55

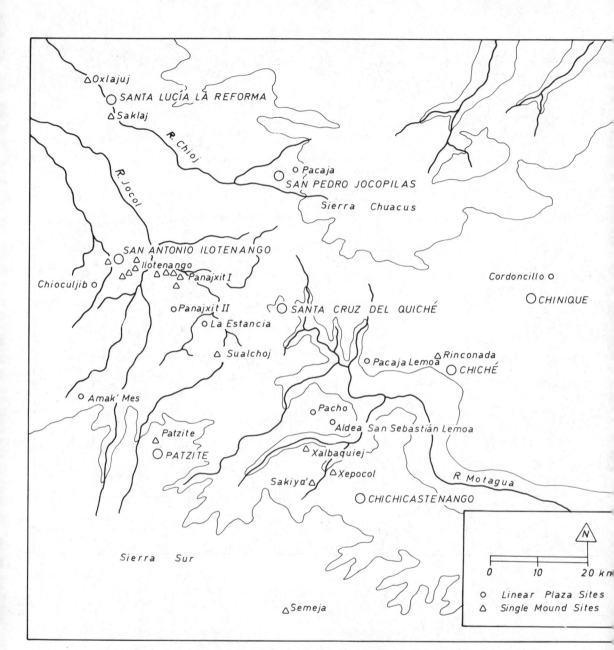

Fig. 3.3. Pre-Quiché archaeological sites. Modified from Carmack, Fox, and Stewart 1975.

The use of Nahua words to refer to complex sociopolitical institutions points to a fairly low level of political integration among the pre-Quiché natives of the area. The archaeology shows the same thing. Stewart found about nine linear plaza pre-Quiché sites, all on plateaus of the basin floor (see Fig. 3.3). The largest of these sites (Pakaja Lemoa) consisted of only eight buildings, indicating the small size of these settlements. Many more single-mound sites were found scattered around the plaza sites, though most of them are higher—on ridgetops, hillside terraces, or hills.

The small size of the latter sites precludes their being residential ones. Stewart argues that they were ritual shrines of individual rural lineages, which were integrated at a higher level by the small administrative centers represented by the plaza sites. This form of integration characterizes traditional rural zones of the Quiché area even today. For example, the canton San Sebastián Lemoa has a small administrative center where the peasants gather to worship in the Catholic chapel, carry out weekly marketing activities in a tiny plaza, and bring lineage disputes before the presiding elders and elected officials in the small courthouse. The center itself has had an extremely small population (about forty persons in 1950), and most of the ritual and political leaders of the canton live elsewhere. The rest of the people are scattered over the land, living near their *milpas*. They are organized along lineage lines, each lineage (*alaxic*) having its own head (*c'amal be*) who leads them in ritual at a small lineage altar (*warabal ja*). Several lineages together make up a hamlet (*calpul*), which also has a head (chosen from the leading lineage), and a special altar for ritual (*nima mesa*). Hamlet altars are placed on prominent hills and are visited by shamans from the other hamlets of Lemoa. The most important altars together form a cross whose end points are roughly at the cardinal directions. These altars are part of a ritual symbolism that integrates the four directions, the lineages, the calendar dates, and good and bad fates (see Fig. 3.4). In the Lemoa-type organization the strongest political integration is at the lineage and hamlet level, the canton level functioning only on special occasions. The Lemoa people are also presently under the authority of the municipal officials of Santa Cruz del Quiché, and this relationship is rapidly eroding the traditional organization at the canton level.

A comparison between Lemoa and pre-Quiché archaeological sites suggests many similarities. The linear-plaza sites, like the Lemoa center, must have functioned to provide primarily ritual but also adjudicative and marketing opportunities. The more impressive monumental architecture of the pre-Quiché sites suggests that leadership there, in contrast to the egalitarian arrangement of traditional Lemoa, was provided by an elite corps of resident officials. The Lemoa data further suggest that the hamlet unit rather than the lineage was associated with the single-mound sites. The tiny lineage

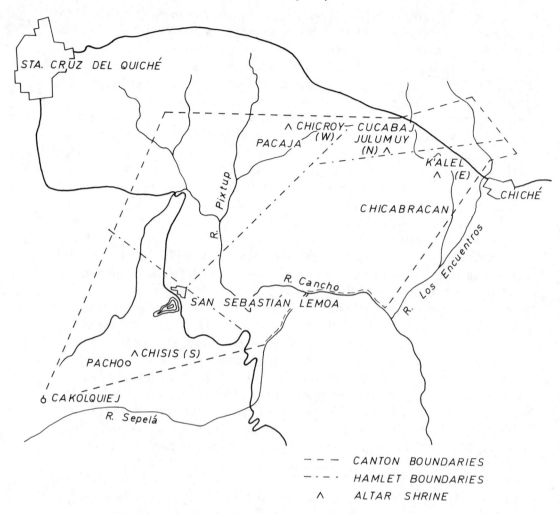

Fig. 3.4. Canton San Sebastián Lemoa. From IGN, map, 1:50,000.

altars would scarcely have been noted in the archaeological survey, while hamlet altars, like the single-mound sites, are fairly large and situated on prominent hills. The Lemoa data suggest that they may have been arranged according to sacred spatial orientations. The pre-Quiché pattern differs from the Lemoa situation in that there was apparently no over-all administrative center similar to Santa Cruz del Quiché.

The main pre-Quiché plaza sites are situated on the unprotected plains of the Quiché basin and lack large-scale defensive fortifications. This suggests that warfare was somewhat limited in Quiché before the arrival of the Gulf

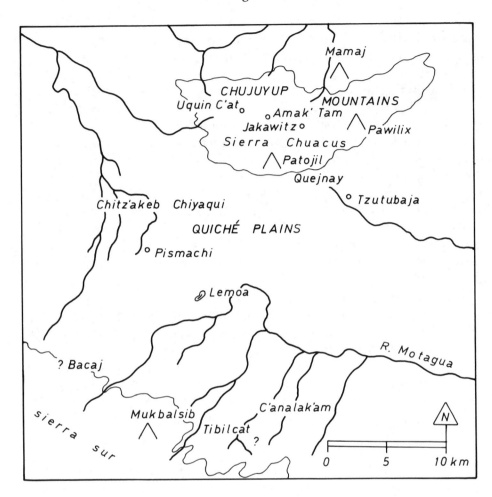

Fig. 3.5. Wukamak peoples conquered by the Quichés of Jakawitz. Modified from
IGN, map, 1:250,000.

Coast warlords. As might be expected, the military capability of the native
culture was of great interest to the Quiché forefathers, and much of the
information about native peoples in the chronicles relates to this subject.
Though the view of those peoples given us by the Quiché "historians" is no
doubt highly distorted, it is uniquely valuable as an eyewitness account of
what their forefathers encountered when they came to the area.

The general term used in the chronicles to refer to the native peoples is
Wuk Amak' (Seven Settlements). To the Quichés, *amak'* signified a rural
lineage population or settlement, the opposite of *tinamit*, or town. The native

peoples are never described as town dwellers, which indicates that the invaders found a largely rural settlement pattern. The term *wuk'* ("seven") was applied metaphorically rather than literally and meant diverse or confederated rural peoples. The sources intimate that the native peoples were capable of uniting in loose unions of political groups to combat a common enemy. For this reason the appellative *wuk amak'* took on a meaning something like "the enemy" for the Quiché forefathers.

The chronicles mention the names of many political groups into which the native peoples were divided: C'analak'am (People of the Strong-spirited Banner), Tibilcat (People of the Well), Chitz'akeb Chiyaqui (People of the Mexican Buildings), Tz'utubaja (House of Maize Flower), Bacaj (Curly People), Uxab (Powerful Ones), Rotzjaib (House of Spots), Q'uibaja (House of Diligent Workers), Quebatzunjai (House of Maize Grinders), Quejnay (Deer House). Most of these groups lived in central Quiché (the Uxabs and Rotzjaibs were from the Rabinal valley on the east), and appear to have been independent political units (see Fig. 3.5).

There were apparently many cultural variations among the native groups. Two of them had Nahua names (Tibilcat and Chiyaqui), suggesting some kind of Toltec or Epi-Toltec identity. The Chiyaqui group occupied a fortified structure and had an impressive idol (C'axc'ol), while the Quejnay group lived in simple deerskin houses in the forest. There are references to lords (*ajawab*) with their followers (such as Tzutubaja and his people), warriors (*achijab*), fishermen (*chajcar*), and humble mountain people (*q'uechelajil winak*). As might be expected, the best-organized and most-sophisticated groups (such as the Chiyaquis, the Uxabs, and the Tzutubajas) occupied the flattest zones of the Quiché area.

The native peoples were both willing and able to engage the encroaching warlords in warfare. One confederation of native groups planned and carried out an attack on the main fortified settlement (Jakawitz) of the Quiché forefathers. Another group defended its territory from the top of a prominent mountain (Mukbalsib). The weapons used by the natives, according to Quiché sources, were bows, shields, and lances. What most impressed the Quiché forefathers was how elaborately the native warriors were adorned. It is specifically stated that they had crowns (*yachwach*) and lances (*ch'amiab*) adorned with metal. Acts of war were engaged in according to the divinatory fates of the calendar; for example, the attack on Jakawitz was specified for the day Cawok. Behind the story of the natives who sent maidens to tempt the Quiché forefathers at a bathing place (see *Popol Vuh*) was a belief that the desecration of the moral or ritual status of warriors would destroy their capacity to make war effectively.

The view of native culture that emerges from the chronicles is one of highly ritualized and ornate patterns. Everywhere the warlords went they met persons gifted with magical powers and icons: the sacred stone (*cwal abaj*) of Tzutubaja, the Bacaj transformers (*jalebal*), the dancing (*xajoj*) Pokomam, the stone cult (*c'abawilanic abaj cwal*) near Chik'ojom. The invaders were impressed with all of this and apparently attempted to assimilate much of it. Thus we find that whenever the Quiché warlords were successful in battle against the native peoples they credited their victory to magical powers. The political reality was different, however. The ceremonialized warfare of the natives was no match for the efficient war-making organization of invaders. The following account from *The Annals of the Cakchiquels* epitomizes the plight of the native peoples before the aggressive militarism of the Quiché forefathers:

Then [the warlords] met up with the Nimpokom and Raxchich, . . . who exhibited within sight all their presents and performed their dances. Their presents consisted of female deer and birds, hunted down and caught in traps. The warlords observed them from afar, and then sent in the weasel to spy on them; they also sent the C'oxajil and C'obakil [natives] to perform their magical transformations. . . . At last the signal from the weasel was given, consisting of the beat of a gourd drum and sound of a flute. "Now we will go," they said. "Their power is great, and there are many of them. They are performing a magnificent dance." Then [the leaders of the warlords] commanded their companions to put on their fighting equipment and prepare to enter the battle. They armed themselves with bows, shields, and adornments, and showed themselves before the enemy. The enemy people were struck with terror, and were overcome and killed. [My translation]

This story, repeated many times, spelled the demise of the native political system and the destruction of much of its culture. We must depend on the archaeology of the future to provide more of the details of their communities. The cultural forms the invaders brought from the Gulf Coast were radically different from anything that had previously existed in the Quiché, even if here and there important cultural elements of the past were syncretized into the newly emerging Quiché community.

SOCIOCULTURAL PATTERNS OF THE QUICHÉ FOREFATHERS

Much of the initial military success of the warlords who came to the Quiché mountains resulted from a flexible system of political confederacy. This organization was similar to the segmentary lineage system that has been described for other native societies of the world (Service 1962; Sahlins 1961). Within this system lineages unite or divide along genealogical lines into larger or smaller groups according to the size of the enemy or the task confronting them. The basic unit of such a system is the lineage, with its brotherhood of men occupying the same territory, sharing obligations of wife giving, collective labor, mutual defense, ritual, and honor. Thus, in describing early Quiché social structure, it is appropriate to begin with the lineage.

Lineage

The lineage of the early Quichés was called *amak'*, a term designating a group of people related through descent and living within a defined territory. The same term was used to refer to the native peoples (*wuk amak'*), apparently in recognition of the simple lineage structure of their settlements. As we shall see, however, the Quiché lineages had special characteristics that gave them an advantage over the native peoples.

The peoples of invading warlord lineages bore names that may have been in some way totemic: Q'uiche' (Forest People), Tamub (Drummer), Ilocab (Seer), Cakchiquel (Red Staff People), Rabinal (Spinner, Flyer), Tzutujil (Maize Flower People), and Tepew Yaqui (Mighty Mexican). The Q'uichés, as forest people, were hunters and leaders in warfare. The Ilocabs were "seers," perhaps in the sense of scouts, and were placed in outpost positions. The Tamubs were drummers who called the lineages together. The red staff of the Cakchiquels, taken from a tree outside Tulan, was the symbol of war; they were warriors. The Tepew Yaquis were "mighty" in Toltec ritual and were thus priests. The Tzutujils were farmers, and the Rabinals were flying-pole warrior-dancers. As for most other peoples of antiquity their names were important and had some influence on the role they played in the larger alliances. Except for Tzutujil, the names suggest the importance of military action in lineage affairs.

An even more important identifying symbol of the ancient lineage was its patron deity. Like the lineage names the deities were associated with the forces of nature and thus had totemic powers. Tojil, the god of the Q'uiché, Tamub, Ilocab, and Rabinal lineages was identified with thunder and lightning storms. Quitzalcuat (Quetzalcoatl), the Feathered Serpent, was the Tepew Yaqui deity, and was associated with clouds and water. The patron god of the Cakchiquels was Tak'aj (or Chimalcan), a serpent and symbol of the low parts of the earth. The Tzutujils' patron deity was Sakibuk (Steam), a substance that was both water and air. Clearly these patron deities linked their respective lineages with the great forces of the world—sky and earth, light and dark, male and female, rectangular and round, water and steam or clouds. The position of a given lineage in ritual relations between the lineages depended on which force its deity symbolized, whether sky or earth, male or female, and so on.

The mythic charter of the lineages centered on the founding fathers who came from the east (the Gulf Coast). Though no claim was made that they were descended from gods, the fathers were venerated for having gone to

Tulan and having been commissioned by the Toltec lord himself, Nacxit. Like all other powerful Toltecs the forefathers were magical transformers, or *naguales*, as the Quichés called them. The founding fathers of the Q'uiché lineage, for example, defeated the native peoples by transforming themselves into jaguars, eagles, and bees, which attacked the enemy. The Cakchiquel founder Jakawitz (Fire Mountain), was transformed into a cloud serpent to calm Lake Atitlán. The essence of this magical power brought from the east was somehow enclosed within the sacred bundle (*pizom c'ac'al*), and was kept by the founding fathers and their successors. The contents of the bundles, known only to those leaders, were probably quartz crystals, snakeskins, and clothing for the idols.

As lineage heads the forefathers combined in their persons both priestly and political functions. The two functions reinforced one another, the sacred power of ritual legitimizing political authority and political conquests adding to the leaders' charisma. In their priestly aspect they were known as "sacrificers" (*ajq'uixb, ajcajb*), for they offered to the patron deities their own blood and the blood and skins (*tzum silisib*) of animals and human beings. They led the way in all lineage rituals, the most dramatic of which was the reception of the Morning Star (Ikok'ij) on top of sacred mountains. After the star finally appeared, heralding the coming of the sun, the lineage priest burned sacred incense (*pom*), and led his brotherhood in song and dance. Most ritual was closely linked to warfare.

In his political aspect the lineage head was "the one who leads the way" (*c'amal be*). Originally this term referred to those forefathers who had led the way from the Gulf Coast to the Quiché mountains. Later these lineage heads literally led their groups along the paths to council meetings or rituals and, most important, in war. They were also expected to give counsel and advice to lineage brothers, applying a strict military law (*pixab*) derived from the Toltec ancestors.

Conflict over the position of lineage head was avoided by strict adherence to patrilineal inheritance. The position was patriarchal, older sons succeeding their fathers. There was some tendency for lineage heads to take on the name of the founding father, for all his magical power, sacred symbols, authority, and bloodline were assumed by the new leader. Even the essence of the founding mother was taken on; thus these leaders became known as the "grandmothers and grandfathers" (*atit, mam*), or "mothers and fathers" (*chuch, kajaw*). Patrilineal descent was strictly maintained, not only for succession to leadership but for membership in the lineage as well. Failure to produce male offspring resulted in the termination of a lineage, as occurred in a Q'uiché sublineage whose founder (Iq'ui Balam) died without children. Similarly, a strict exogamy prevailed, and women who married into the lineage retained outsider status. They were referred to as *c'ulel* ("enemies"),

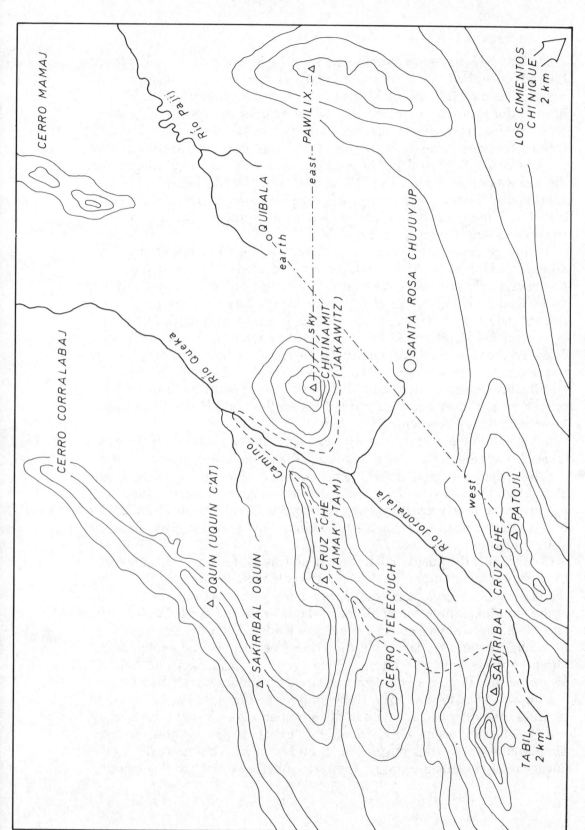

Fig. 3.6. The early Quiché zone of Chujuyup (Jakawitz). From Fox 1975.

suggesting that they were often obtained through war or conquest.

Each lineage occupied a territory whose location was agreed upon by the warlords who first entered the Quiché area. The territories were mountainous and highly defensible. Undoubtedly the rugged nature of the terrain in the Chujuyup area was the main reason why the warlords settled in that particular place. Each lineage occupied a section of land that included mountain peaks, a major skirt extending downward from those peaks, and a patch of flatland in the lower basins. On top of the mountain peak each lineage constructed an altar for its patron deity and surrounded it with small buildings where ritual activities could be carried out. At these shrines, for example, the ritual of the morning star (Sakiribal) was dramatically performed. Downslope, on narrow, level zones surrounded by canyons, each lineage built its political center (*tinamit*). Here the lineage house, the altar and temple for the patron deity, and the residence of the lineage head were built. The lineage houses were long structures with back benches where the lineage head and elders made decisions for the group. The temples were architecturally "Toltec" in style and appropriately positioned and decorated according to the natural force symbolized by each god. The residences for the families of the lineage heads were apparently modest structures placed on terraces alongside the public section of the settlement. Agriculture within the lineage territory was probably carried out mainly in the flatlands below. The territories were selected more for their strategic position in defense and attack than for agricultural potential, and most food was provided by the surrounding native peoples as they successively came under the control of Q'uiche lineages.

Through the chronicles and with guidance from indigenous informants it has been possible to locate most of the ancient lineage territories with their associated mountain shrines and political centers (Carmack, Fox, and Stewart 1975). The Ilocab and Tamub lineages occupied two skirts of the Telec'uch mountain separated by a river canyon (see Fig. 3.6). The ruins of their small political centers (Uquín C'at, Amak' Tam) have been found about midway down these two ridges of land. Sites with remnants of shrines to their patron deity have been discovered on the peaks of the mountain above. They are still known by the old name, Sakiribal (Dawning). The Q'uiché lineage occupied the Chujuyup Valley just to the east. Its lineage political center, Jakawitz, was placed on a high hill at the western edge of the valley, while the shrine to the patron deity was placed on a high peak (Patojil) above the valley on the south. The Cakchiquel and Rabinal lineage territories were on the southern and eastern borders of the central Quiché area (Fig. 3.7). The Cakchiquels occupied territory in the mountains above Chichicastenango, but the specific sites of their political center, Bitol Amak', and mountain shrine, Paraxone, have not yet been identified. Rabinal territory was situated in the mountains above Joyabaj; the combined political center and shrine (Tzamaneb), is also still unidentified.

The various characteristics of the early Quiché lineage combined to make it a superb military unit. It united a group of men in bonds of brotherhood and strict discipline under a well-established authority structure. These spartan groups were grounded in the most advanced techniques of warfare known at the time and a fanatic religious drive to establish their rule over the natives. Though few in number compared with the masses of natives in the plains surrounding them, their tiny mountain ridges and peaks provided them with an impregnable defense. Further they were in a position to raid the less-well-defended native settlements and quickly retreat to their mountain strongholds.

Despite the military prowess of these ancient lineages, individually they would have been insufficient for the conquest of the Quiché area. That required higher levels of political organization, a topic to which we now turn.

Confederacy

The chronicles indicate that the lineages that came to the Quiché mountains maintained alliances with other Epi-Toltec groups who settled in adjacent areas of the highlands. These included groups from the Lake Atitlán, Sacapulas, Huehuetenango, Aguacatán, and other areas. These alliances probably consisted of recognition of their common origins and cultural heritage and an agreement not to interfere with their respective zones of influence. There were also gift exchanges, possibly including wives, and probably a certain amount of mutual respect for their deities. It is likely that the wives of the Quiché lineage heads at first came mostly from other Epi-Toltec groups.

It is possible that the Quiché lineages could call on the aid of Epi-Toltecs from other areas in times of extreme difficulty, though our sources provide no direct evidence of this. What seems evident is that the *pax fraternitis* established by the various groups provided controlled spheres of influence in which smaller lineage confederacies could successfully carry out military operations. Years later, after the invaders had become well established on the Quiché plains, the old Epi-Toltec alliances finally broke down. But in the early days, when balances of power between invaders and native peoples were uncertain, the alliances served a useful purpose.

Our sources indicate that a smaller, somewhat tighter alliance was forged between the lineages that emigrated to the central Quiché region of the highlands. We are told that the Q'uiché, Cakchiquel, Rabinal, and Tzutujil lineages united on a mountain called Chipixab (on the border between San Andrés Sajcabaja and San Bartolomé Jocotenango) and divided the central territory among themselves (Fig. 3.7). The Q'uichés were given the northern part of the region, including the central Quiché plains. The Tzutujils had the

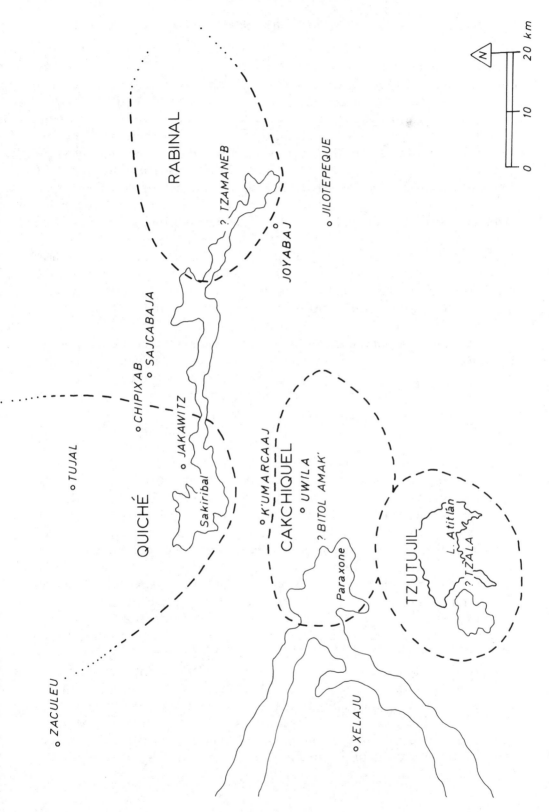

Fig. 3.7. The early Quichean confederacy. Modified from IGN, Mapa Hipsométrica.

southern part of the region around Lake Atitlán. These two lineage groups were dominant in the confederacy, for, as expressed in their mythic charter, they had arrived first at Tulan. The Cakchiquels were assigned a middle section between these two, and set up home base in the southern part of what is today Chichicastenango. They were clearly subordinate to the Q'uichés, for, according to the mythic charter of the confederacy, the Cakchiquels were the last ones to be allowed into Tulan. They were warriors rather than leaders, and were made to follow behind and carry the gear of the Quiché forefathers. The Rabinals were assigned the eastern part of the region and established a base of operations in the mountains overlooking the Rabinal basin. The Rabinals, like the Cakchiquels, appear to have been lower-status warriors.

The "Quichean confederacy," as we may call this alliance, did not involve much coordinated activity. There is no evidence that the Quichés and the Tzutujils ever combined their lineages for military action; rather, they were allies in the sense that they did not interfere with each other's spheres of influence. They celebrated the same rituals, such as the Dawning (Sakiribal) of the morning star, and apparently attended each other's rites of accession to lineage office. Through exchanges of women they established affinal ties. Years later, even after the Quichés and Tzutujils had become major political powers and bitter rivals, some of the old marital and ritual exchanges continued (see chapter 6).

Relations among the other three members of the confederacy were much closer. The Cakchiquels played a major role in the Quichés' conquest of the plains. They combined their forces with those of the Quichés on many occasions in opposing the native armies, especially in the Chichicastenango area. They even fought alongside the Q'uiché and Rabinal lineages in defeating the Pokomams of the Rabinal basin. The close relations between the Quichés and the Cakchiquels had a kinship basis. K'akawitz, the Cakchiquels' founding father, traced descent from a branch of the Q'uiché line (Recinos 1957, pp. 135, 147). Apparently this was a secondary-descent line (that is, through younger sons or wives from non-Toltec lineages), and thus the Cakchiquels were subject to the authority of the Q'uiché patriarchs.

The Rabinals were probably related to the Q'uichés in a similar way, though we lack specific information on the point. Conquests in the Rabinal area were directed by Quiché leaders, the Rabinals apparently serving as military auxiliaries. Like the Cakchiquel lineages, Rabinal lineages may have come from secondary Q'uiché lines. One of these lines, Smalej, provided a descent link between the Rabinal and Cakchiquel lineages. There is evidence that both the Rabinals and the Cakchiquels took wives from the Tzutujils, thus giving them kinship ties with the fourth member of the confederacy. In the Cakchiquel version of this relationship (Villacorta 1934, pp. 210–12), the

Cakchiquels and the Tzutujils entered into an agreement to share the resources of Lake Atitlán. They sealed the pact by exchanging wives, each lineage giving its sisters (*rana'*) and becoming mothers' brothers (*ikan*) to the other. The lake symbolized the alliance, and was called *coon* ("vagina"); as they shared the lake, so too they shared (the vaginas of) their women.

The idea of a quadripartite organization was central to the Quichean confederacy, an Epi-Toltec idea brought from the east. Apparently the idea involved the assignment of confederate units to the four directions. This gave the confederacy "worldwide" coverage and ritual balance. In military terms this may have been a useful idea, for it divided the region to be conquered into smaller units and placed the four confederate groups in strategic positions with respect to the native peoples. It was a difficult organization to maintain, however, as illustrated by the limited relations between the Quichés and the Tzutujils. Nevertheless, there is evidence that it was the dominant organizational framework for the Quiché political system in pre-Utatlán times.

The difficulties of a decentralized confederacy were recognized by the Quichés. Language differences increased among the member units. The "folk" explanation by the Quichés was that the groups had different patron deities. The Rabinals spoke only a slightly different language from that of the Quichés because their god, Jun Toj (One Thunder, a calendar name), was almost identical with the Quiché god Tojil. In contrast, differences in the Cakchiquel and Tzutujil languages increased because their gods were so different from Tojil—the Cakchiquel god is given as Chimalcan, and that of the Tzutujils is not even named. Up to a point these differences could be fused into a symbolic system of contrasts and did not disrupt the ideological integration of the confederacy. The sky gods of the Quichés and the Rabinals (Tojil, and Jun Toj) on the north were balanced by the earth goddesses of the Cakchiquels and the Tzutujils (Tak'aj and Sakibuk, the gods of the plains and the lake) on the south.

The erosion of a common language was a progressive problem for the confederacy as each group became influenced by the native peoples of the area. This brought other cultural differences and eventually political independence. Fox (1975, 1977) presents archaeological evidence that the Tzutujils, the Rabinals, and the Cakchiquels adopted the architectural and settlement patterns of the people among whom they lived. These patterns, along with religious and linguistic differences, made the confederacy increasingly difficult to maintain. Still it was not totally disrupted until after the Quiché state had been firmly established at Utatlán.

The prototype for the political system that later developed at Utatlán was an even smaller confederacy of three Quiché lineages, the Q'uiché, the Tamub, and the Ilocabs. They formed bonds of much greater social and cultural unity than those of the larger Quichean alliance. They claimed to be derived from the same descent line, they spoke the same language, they had the same patron deity, they occupied the same territorial zone, and they held roughly the same political rank. Our sources indicate that this Quiché confederacy took on important military, ritual, kinship, and administrative functions in the pre-Utatlán period. Its development is perhaps best symbolized by the emergence of a single administrative center at Jakawitz, the old Q'uiche lineage town (Fig. 3.6). The chronicles indicate (Recinos 1957, p. 38) that this was the place where the officials of the three lineage settlements, the *utzam chinamital* and *aj tz'alam* ("heads and guards of the walls"), acceded to office. There they were seated on the sacred chairs and benches, isolated and "refreshed" with a cold wind-and-water bath, censed with tobacco smoke, and finally given the lion and jaguar bones of authority. These elaborate investiture ceremonies established Jakawitz as the political center of the confederacy.

The archaeological remains of Jakawitz, known as Chitinamit (Carmack, Fox, and Stewart 1975), reveal that six lineage houses were constructed there, presumably four for the Q'uiche sublineages and one each for the Tamub and Ilocab confederates (Fig. 3.8). There were two temples, one of them probably having been dedicated to Jakawitz, the god of the original Q'uiche sublineage after which the settlement was named. The other temple was dedicated to Tojil, the patron of the confederacy. Jakawitz is the only confederacy settlement that had a ball court, which suggests that this highly important ritual building was shared by the three confederate members. The town was also fortified far more extensively than was any other Quiché settlement in the area, with defensive bulwarks (*caxtun*), palisaded walls (*tz'alam ch'ut*), and walled terraces (*quejbej rij*). Obviously the settlement was meant to be a place into which the confederate members could retreat in the face of a common enemy.

The establishment of a confederacy center at Jakawitz indicates that the Q'uiché lineage had gained leadership advantage over the Tamubs and the Ilocabs in the alliance. It also shows that within the Q'uiché lineage the third sublineage, founded by the warlord Majucutaj, provided that leadership. According to the chronicles, Majucutaj excelled over his older brothers in the conduct of war and in this way became their leader. His sublineage took on the name Ajaw Q'uiché (Lord of the Quichés) in recognition that it provided the chiefs of the confederacy.

It is clear from the case of the Ajaw Q'uiché sublineage that the sublineages of the three Quiché lineages were playing increasingly specialized roles in lineage and confederacy affairs. Internal lineage segmentation and coalition provided different combinations of alliance that could be used to carry out the many tasks of varying importance confronting the confederacy. Thus the

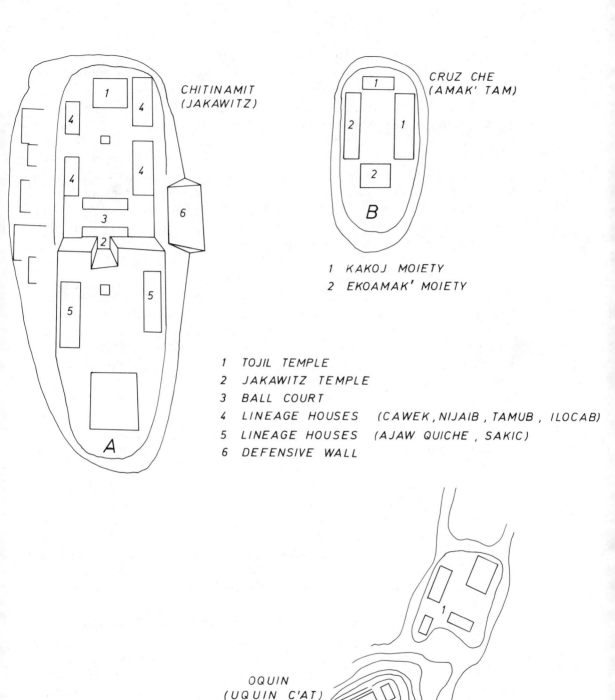

CHITINAMIT
(JAKAWITZ)

CRUZ CHE
(AMAK' TAM)

1 KAKOJ MOIETY
2 EKOAMAK' MOIETY

1 TOJIL TEMPLE
2 JAKAWITZ TEMPLE
3 BALL COURT
4 LINEAGE HOUSES (CAWEK, NIJAIB, TAMUB, ILOCAB)
5 LINEAGE HOUSES (AJAW QUICHE, SAKIC)
6 DEFENSIVE WALL

OQUIN
(UQUIN C'AT)

1 SIC'A PLAZA
2 WANIJA PLAZA

Fig. 3.8.   Early Quiché townsites. From Carmack, Fox, and Stewart 1975.

Q'uiché lineage segmented into four sublineages, though it was necessary to graft in a new line to replace one that died out. The names of the sublineages perhaps suggest the special functions that they were taking on: Ajaw Q'uiché (Lord of the Quichés), Cawek (from *cawik ja*, "two-storied house"), Nijaib (from *nim ja*, "big house"), Sakic (from *sakic*, "lot casting"). As we have noted, the Ajaw Q'uiché lineage provided leadership at Jakawitz. The Cawek and Nijaib lineage names apparently refer to buildings that were under their control, a tall (ritual) structure of the Caweks and a long (lineage) house of the Nijaibs. This is probably a reference to buildings at Patojil, where the Caweks carried out the cult to the lineage patron deity Tojil. Our sources indicate that at Patojil they shared a lineage house with the Nijaibs; presumably the controlling rights of the building belonged to the Nijaibs. The Sakic was a new sublineage adopted into the old Iq'ui Balam line, and its name suggests that the replacement was chosen by lot casting.

These sublineages may have provided the cardinal-point directional symbolism so essential to the ritual well-being of this Epi-Toltec confederacy. The settlements of the four sublineages were situated approximately at the cardinal points, and their respective temples may have faced the four directions (Fig. 3.6). Jakawitz, the Ajaw Q'uiché center, was on the north, its temple facing south. Patojil of the Caweks was on the west, and its temple faced east. Pawilix, the Nijaib center, was on the east, its temple perhaps facing west (the site has not yet been mapped). I believe the Sakic sublineage center to be the Los Cimientos site in Chinique, which would make it the southern point of the rough cross formed by these four settlements. The temple there, Nic'aj Tak'aj, is virtually destroyed, but it appears to have faced west. A secondary symbolic balance achieved by the settlements of these four Q'uiche sublineages was the union of male-female, and mountain-plains principles. The sky god Tojil was placed far above the mountain god Jakawitz, while the sky goddess Awilix was similarly placed above the plains goddess Nic'aj Tak'aj. This arrangement associated the male principle with the east and the female with the west. As will be seen in the chapters to follow, an attempt was made to retain these ritual orientations at Utatlán.

The Q'uiché sublineages had individual ritual and political functions in the confederacy, while collectively their role was one of leadership in both war and ritual. The Tamubs and Ilocabs, as suggested by their names, performed the auxiliary services of military communication (*tamub*, "drummer") and intelligence (*ilocab*, "seer," or "scout"). The Cakchiquels were part of the Quiché confederacy, I believe, but as a subordinate cadre of warriors rather than an allied lineage. Thus the ideal of confederating lineages into quadri-partite organizations was not realized within the Quiché alliance. It is likely that the four Q'uiché sublineages performed the important function of symbolizing the unity of four in one and the sacred cardinal directions for the entire confederacy. In contrast the political centers of the three lineages did not symbolize the four sacred directions; rather they were placed on a horizontal line from west (Ilocab) to east (Q'uiché). The river system in this area, which also runs west to east, suggests a possible secondary symbolic positioning of the three lineages. The western section of the river was called *joronalaja* ("cold water"), while the eastern section was *mik'inaja'* ("hot water"). This associated the Quichés with hot water and presumably fire and power. The Ilocabs were perhaps associated with cold water and thus lesser power. The Tamubs were in between.

Though the documents refer to four original Tamub lineage ancestors (C'opichoch, C'ochojlan, C'ok'anawil, and Majquinalo), their significant internal lineage subdivision was in halves. The names of these sublineages (or moieties), Ekoamak' (Lineage of Messengers) and Kakoj (Swindler), suggest the special roles they played in the confederacy. Members of the Ekoamak' lineage perhaps served as carriers or messengers for the chiefs at Jakawitz, a task that they probably performed in conjunction with trading activities ("swindling"). The Tamubs may have been specialized traders, for we are told that during this early period they marketed with the people around them. Bunchgrass, honey, firewood, and *jocotes* are mentioned as goods sold by the Tamub people.

The Tamub lineage center, Amak' Tam, was about half the size of Jakawitz, the main confederacy center (Fig. 3.8). It may have been a communication and marketing center because it is situated on the road leading to the Tabil Valley, which is the main passageway to the Quiché plains below. The site has been identified at Cruz Che (Carmack, Fox, and Stewart 1975, pp. 66–70), but excavations would be required to determine whether or not it had a market. The moiety subdivisions of the lineage were represented at the site by the east- and west-facing temples and lineage houses on opposite north and south sides of the plaza. Presumably these paired temples and lineage houses were occupied by the Ekoamak' and Kakoj sublineages of the Tamubs.

Five Ilocab ancestors are named in the chronicles (Chiyatoj, Chiyatz'iquin, Yolchitum, Yolchiramak', and Ch'ipel Canmuk'el), but it is uncertain whether sublineages existed for all five during this early period. Two early sublineages mentioned in the *Título Totonicapán* are the Sic'a (Announcer) and Wanija (Juanija, from *wanij ja*, "lineage of strikers or hitters"). These names point to a military function for the Ilocab sublineages, a suggestion supported by the frontier location of the territory of this lineage. The main Ilocab settlement, Uquin C'at, was situated west of Jakawitz, on the border of the hostile native peoples of the Quiché basin. The remains of that settlement consist of a linear series of small sites placed along a narrow ridge that drops about three hundred meters from south to north (Fig. 3.8). The dispersed pattern of the sites and their defensible location would seem to correlate well with the documented outpost role for the Ilocab lineage in the confederacy. The largest of the sites forms a plaza at the lowest point along the ridge; like the Tamub center it is small. Just above it on the south are a temple mound and a rectangular structure, both carved out of schistose stone outcropping there. Over all, the sites suggest that the Ilocab sublineages were rather loosely coordinated and heterogeneous in their settlement patterns. The two most important sublineages, occupying the lowest sites, were possibly the Sic'a and the Wanija. They were apparently military specialists guarding the western flank of the Quiché confederacy.

In summary, leadership for the confederacy came from the Q'uiché lineage, trade and communication from the Tamub lineage, and outer defense from the Ilocab lineage. Internal sublineages of these three components provided specialized functions for the confederacy: ritual, scouting, trading, administration, fighting, guarding, and so on. The four Q'uiché sublineages spatially expressed the symbolism of the important cardinal-point orientation. Perhaps they also entered into marital, ritual, and military alliances with the moietal divisions of the Tamubs and the two primary sublineages of the Ilocabs. Thus through lineage coalition and segmentation, combined with incipient lineage specialization, the Quiché confederation marshaled sufficient power to subdue the native political systems of the area. In the process the alliance began taking on the characteristics of a centralized political system. By the time they left the Chujuyup area for the plains, the Quichés were appropriately referring to their government as a "state" (*ajawarem*).

4
ECOLOGY

THE PURPOSE OF THIS CHAPTER is to place the Quichés of Utatlán in space and to associate them with the ecological factors that influenced the development of their culture. Special attention must be given to Quiché agriculture, since the Quiché "kingdom," like all ancient states, was agrarian; power derived directly from the ability to control land and its production. In societies in which large numbers of rural peoples are warriors, as in the Quiché society, an agrarian structure is particularly important because it must support the warriors as well as the town elite. Thus factors closely related to agricultural productivity dominate the contents of this chapter.

The Quichés endearingly referred to their lands as "the mountains and plains" and mentioned the canyons that set apart each town. In their chronicles and other writings they left us a dramatic account of how they viewed their environment and interacted with it. That ethnoecological viewpoint is the subject of the first section of this chapter. Not only does it tell us what the Quichés thought was important in their natural setting, but also it tells us much about the specific features of that setting. Many features that once formed part of the Quichés' ecology have been altered or eliminated in the years since the Conquest, but a reconstruction of that ecology from the documentary sources allows us to recover much that was lost.

While it is true that ecological conditions have changed through the years, it is also true that many features of the natural environment have persisted into modern times. Thus we have a unique opportunity to investigate an important aspect of Utatlán culture at first hand. In the second section of the chapter I turn to modern geographic and ethnographic studies of central Quiché ecology. Recourse to such data can be unsettling for the ethnohistorian, because the documents dramatize for him how much a culture can change over time. Indeed, much has happened to alter the environment and composition of the resident population since Utatlán flourished as an independent community. Furthermore, data available on ecological conditions in

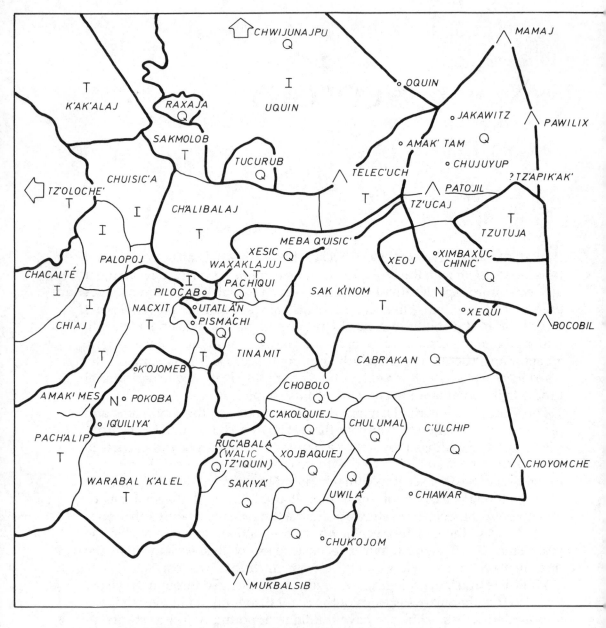

Q   NIMA QUICHE
T   TAMUB
I   ILOCAB   ▬▬ CALPUL GROUP BOUNDARY
N   NIJAIB   ⌒ INDIVIDUAL CALPUL BOUNDARY

Fig. 4.1.   The *calpul* boundaries of the central Quiché area. Based on IGN, maps,
1:50,000.

76

the area in recent times are sparse, especially for the years before 1950, when conditions were less markedly affected by the drastic changes brought on by modernization. I have tried to use modern data with caution. Facts are lacking on some strategic points, but studies on Quiché ecology, partly under my direction, are now under way, and they should improve our understanding of this subject in the coming years.

The last section of the chapter provides a comparison between the view of Quiché ecology that emerges from a study of the native sources and the one that emerges from direct observations. I am not as much interested in which of the two is more accurate, or the significance of their contradictions, as I am in combining them to obtain a more nearly complete picture of ecology in the Utatlán area. It will be discovered, in fact, that the two data sources match up very well, though the Quichés greatly elaborated on the sacred meanings of many natural features in their environment.

A final caveat is in order. I have concentrated in this chapter on the ecological conditions of the central Quiché area to the exclusion of provincial regions subject to the Quiché state. Those regions formed part of the ecological system within which the Quichés carried out their social life at Utatlán. I have investigated these wider relations in another context (Carmack 1965), and Fox (1975) has looked at them from an archaeological perspective. Despite their importance, in this chapter I am interested in the immediate environment that directly and continuously influenced the Utatlán community. It is clear that the central area was the main sustaining unit of Utatlán and that its residents became tightly integrated into the Utatán community. It is likely, in fact, that the expansion of the Quichés into distant regions was closely linked with changing ecological conditions in the central area. The analysis to follow should help us to determine what those conditions were.

ETHNOECOLOGY

We turn first to the Quichés' own view of their environment, particularly those aspects that they incorporated into their cultural system. The chronicles provide most of our data for this reconstruction, especially the *Popol Vuh* and the main Tamub *título*. I have also used a few later sources, including my own ethnographic field notes, but only where it is certain that the traditional native viewpoint is expressed. It should be noted that much more ethnoecological information could be obtained by more thoroughly culling the old dictionaries and working with contemporary traditional natives of the central Quiché.

General View

The Quichés conceptualized their world as extending in four directions: toward the earth, toward the sky, toward where the sun comes up, and toward where the sun goes down (Villacorta 1962, pp. 17, 223). This three-dimensional model of the world was also simplified for conceptualizing horizontal space, the sky being associated with the north, the earth with the south, and the two phases of the sun with the east and west. World roads were thought to course in the cardinal directions, each road bearing the color associated with its direction: red for east, white for west, black for north, and yellow for south (Villacorta 1962, p. 98). These colors and directions were associated with different geographic conditions: red (east) was the direction of heat (and power), white (west) was cold, yellow (south) was vegetation, and black (north) was infertility and sickness.

The Quichés apparently did not apply this model directly to the central area, and it does not particularly fit the general ecological conditions there (for example, east-west ecological differences are not pronounced). The Quichés' conceptual world, in fact, was geographically much larger than the central area, incorporating such distant places as Tula in Mexico, the caves of Alta Verapaz, and the volcanoes of the southern axis. Evidence suggests that the central area per se was conceptualized more in social than in ecological terms (see chapter 6). Nevertheless, small territorial divisions within the area were viewed as squares extending in the cardinal directions, the symbolic corners (*retal*) being formed by prominent mountains (Recinos 1957, p. 62). There must have been many such divisions, some larger than others, like boxes within boxes. Perhaps most of the central area formed one large box, with symbolic corners at, say, Mounts Mamaj (north), Iquilija (west), María Tecum (south), and Bocobil (east). This is only a hypothetical reconstruction, however; there is no direct evidence for it in the sources.

The highland character of the central area was firmly fixed in the Quichés' view of their habitat. They continually referred to it in the chronicles as "the mountains and plains" (*juyubal, tak'ajal*). In their creation account (Villacorta 1962, pp. 19, 24), it is a highland world that comes into existence. The earth is made up of mountains and plains, rocks, canyons, rivers, and lakes. The vegetation consists of dense forests of pine and cypress, bunchgrass, vines and bushes (*c'aam, tucan*), and fertile plains of green and gold (Villacorta 1962, p. 161). The fauna is highland too; rattlesnakes, vipers, lizards, frogs, coyotes, deer, peccaries, opossums, *pisotes* (coatis), rats, bats, and such insects as ants, mosquitos, lice, fireflies, wasps, and bees. The wet and dry seasons of the highlands are reflected in the creation story. The creator deities form balanced pairs associated with rain and sun: the lightning god (Jurakan) versus the sun god (Cakix), the sky god (C'ux Caj) versus the earth god (C'ux Uleu), and the water god (K'ukumatz) versus the god of light (Tepew) (Villacorta 1962, pp. 20 ff.)

The highland ecology shows up in certain geographical features repeatedly mentioned in the chronicles. The following features seem to have been the most significant for the Quichés.

1. *Mountains (juyup)*.   The Quichés referred to mountains as big and little and red, black, and white; surrounded by canyons and rock cliffs; shrouded in mists; visited by thunder and lightning; frequented by snakes, jaguars, lions, and coyotes; and covered with trees or treeless. Mountains were places on which to build towns, settle rural peoples, fight wars, observe the movement of astral bodies, hide idols, perform sacrifices, divide up the lands, accede to political office, and hunt game animals and birds. As noted above, mountains marked the symbolic corners of important territorial units. They also memorialized important historical and ritual events, as suggested by such mountains as Ancestors (Mamaj), where the ancestors passed upon entering the central Quiché area (*Título Totonicapán* n.d., p. 10); Dawning (Sakiribal), where the morning star was first commemorated (*Título Totonicapán* n.d., p. 18v.); Council (Chipixab), where the forefathers counseled together (Villacorta 1962, p. 253); Burial (Puquimulu), where the ancestors were buried (Recinos 1967, p. 60); and many others. The one native map of the central area preserved for us (Carmack 1973, p. 12) portrays the southern mountains as its most prominent natural feature. A mountain setting was so fixed in the Quichés' view that when they described Canaan and other biblical places of the Old World they could think of them only as mountains (*Título Totonicapán* n.d., p. 5).

2. *Trees (Che')*.   The Quichés called the central area Paq'uiché (Place of Many Trees). Indeed, trees figure prominently in their history and description of the area. The original creation story placed trees and forests (*q'uechelaj*) there, cypresses and pines being mentioned specifically (Villacorta 1962, pp. 19, 24, 26). The forests were said to be dense, covered with moss and vines (Villacorta 1962, p. 262; *Título Totonicapán* n.d., p. 9). Trees had to be felled to plant maize (Villacorta 1962, pp. 137ff.; 1934, p. 216) and to provide timber and firewood (Recinos 1957, p. 62; Villacorta 1962, p. 195). Many products were taken from trees: resins, bark, and branches for offerings; pitch for lighting; logs for buildings and hollow drums; and wood for carving "dolls," furniture (benches and chairs), tools, and weapons.

Certain trees played special roles in Quiché mythology: the nance, which provided food for the demigod Seven Macaw; the gourd tree in the underworld, containing the head of Junjunajpu; the tree that grew tall and isolated One Batz and One Chowen; and the tree that gave off a red sap that looked like blood (Villacorta 1962, pp. 53, 63, 105, 129, 114). Densely wooded places were sacred, and the Quichés bled themselves and left other offerings there

(Las Casas 1909, p. 470). It is not surprising, then, to find trees memorialized in many Quiché place-names: Piled Wood, Willow Tree, Broad-leafed Tree (K'anak'), Carbon, Tied Tree, Curved Tree, Cypress, Oak, Dense Trees, Thick Trees, The Tree. One of the month names of the ecologically based solar calendar was Che' (Trees, see below).

3. *Roads (Be).* It was noted above that the Quichés viewed the world as traversed by great colored roads that crossed, forming the symbol of the world directions. At road crossings human sacrifices were performed (López Medel n.d.), and men bled themselves (Las Casas 1909, p. 470). We are told that men and gods traveled on paths along rivers and over mountains (Villacorta 1962, p. 25). In their prayers to the gods the Quichés asked that their journeys might be without accident (Villacorta 1962, p. 358). Traveling on the roads was a sacred act, and roadside shrines permitted the people to sanctify it (Las Casas 1909, p. 470). Great roads inside and leading to the towns were used for spectacular processions (Recinos 1957, p. 108). The Quiché underworld, the place of the dead, was reached by a black road fraught with hardship and danger (Villacorta 1962, pp. 98ff.). Life too was thought of as a road, a verdant road (*raxa be*) if it was peaceful and good (Villacorta 1962, p. 358).

4. *Deer (Quej).* Large mammals such as jaguars, lions, weasels, coyotes, and dogs are mentioned frequently in the sources, but deer received the most attention. The deer "lifeway" was well known: "Thou, deer, wilt sleep in the roads and canyons, and inhabit the bunchgrass, bushes, and forests; thou wilt multiply and travel about on all four legs" (Villacorta 1962, p. 27). Deer hoofprints were studied and carefully tracked (Villacorta 1962, p. 283). Deer were hunted and butchered (*Título Totonicapán* n.d., p. 20v.). They were given in offerings to the deities (Villacorta 1962, p. 275). Their skins were removed and used as offerings to the gods and as dance costumes (Villacorta 1962, p. 282; *Título Totonicapán* n.d., p. 27v.). Deerskins were used for other purposes: clothing, houses, and ball-playing gear (Villacorta 1934, p. 202; 1962, p. 92). Many places in the Quiché area were named in honor of the deer; Deer Wash, Deer Is Shot, Doe, Deer Crossing, and Deer Head. The Quichés celebrated the movements and lifeway of the deer in one of their favorite dances (De León n.d., p. 167; Chinchilla 1963).

5. *Snakes (Cumatz).* Snakes are mentioned frequently in the chronicles. They were said to have been created to serve, along with other animals, as guardians of the earth (Villacorta 1962, p. 26). The Quichés found them ubiquitous in the mountains of their first home (Villacorta 1962, p. 259) and down on the plains where they built their towns (Recinos 1957, p. 44). The

most commonly mentioned snakes are the rattler (*sochoch*) and the yellow viper (*k'anti*) (Villacorta 1962, p. 26), but others also appear in the documents (Recinos 1953, p. 145). Snakes were associated with the rains that follow the summer solstice (De Leon n.d., p. 89), and were caught and danced with in ceremonies preceding the rainy season (Termer 1957). The importance of snakes in the Quiché view of the world caused them to identify strongly with the biblical story of Moses in Egypt, in which the magicians changed staffs into snakes (*Título Totonicapán* n.d., p. 5v.).

6. *Birds (Tz'iquin)*. The "biogram" of birds, according to the Quichés, was as follows: "You big and little birds are to make your homes on top of the trees and bushes; there you are to multiply, on the branches of the trees and bushes" (Villacorta 1962, p. 27). The birds most frequently mentioned in the sources are hawks, eagles, owls, parakeets, parrots, crows, vultures, quail, doves, hummingbirds, bluebirds (*raxon*), macaws, and gulls (*azacuanes*). The Quichés were preoccupied with the predation of eagles and hawks (Villacorta 1962, pp. 42, 156); the special cry of owls, hawks, and parakeets (Recinos 1953, pp. 145, 155, 198); and the close association between darkness and owls (Villacorta 1962, p. 94; 1934; Recinos 1950, p. 57), vultures and the dawn (Villacorta 1962, p. 186), and crows and parakeets and corn (Villacorta 1962, pp. 186, 217). Birds were hunted and trapped (Villacorta 1962, pp. 81, 156). They were a prized food given as gifts (*Título Totonicapán* n.d., p. 24). Their feathers were used for adornment, especially those of the eagle, the bluebird, and the quetzal (*Título Totonicapán* n.d., p. 30v.). Birds were memorialized in dances, such as the Hummingbird Dance, (De León n.d., p. 169), the "Macaw" (Carmack 1973, p. 292), and the Owl Dance (Recinos 1953, p. 167). Quiché place-names reflect the importance accorded to birds: Young Bird, Eggs, Green Feathers, Feathered Stone, Bluebird, Hummingbird River, Vulture Mountain. The most important ceremonial month in the solar calendar was T'ziquin K'ij (Bird Days) (Carmack 1973, p. 295).

7. *Maize (Ixim)*. Many plants of great significance to the Quichés are mentioned in the chronicles, especially white flowers, mushrooms, reeds, bunchgrass, maguey, tobacco, and various weeds and bushes. But it was the maize plant that was the most important to them, and not only for its food value (see below). Maize kernels were used along with *tzité* beans for divination, apparently by female shamans in particular (Villacorta 1962, pp. 37, 41). Yellow and white maize grains were the main ingredients from which man was created (Villacorta 1962, p. 219). Maize kernels were also associated in some special way with teeth (Villacorta 1962, p. 60). The Quiché solar calendar was geared to the production of maize, and its monthly divisions were named accordingly (see below). And maize was memorialized in the names

of several places in the central area: Planting, Milpas, Maize Food, Planted Fields, Maize Grinders, Old Maize. Maize was discovered in the original homeland of the Quiché forefathers (Villacorta 1934, p. 184), and the two were closely associated. The Quichés equated the homeland with the biblical paradise because of its verdure and golden maize fields (*raxalaj, k'analaj*) (*Título Totonicapán* n.d., p. 7v.).

Other ecological features might be listed. Rain, wind, mud, crabs, flying insects, jaguars, quetzal birds, rabbits, rivers, lakes, bats, and volcanoes are frequently mentioned in the documents. The features described above, however, received special emphasis in the native sources. It should be noted that some of the specific items mentioned in the chronicles are not indigenous to the central Quiché area. The items can usually be distinguished either because they are said to have come from the outside or because they are associated with mythical beings and places. For example, the macaw and the red-dragon tree do not occur naturally in the Quiché area, and in the chronicles they are directly associated with mythological places. Apparently mythological space was expressed by referring to ecological conditions different from those of the Quiché area. The forbidden fruit of the biblical paradise was *tulul*, the *zapote*, not found in the Quiché area. Many other tropical fruits were associated with the paradisiacal east (*Título Totonicapán* n.d., pp. 3, 4; Villacorta 1962, p. 218).

The Quichés, in fact, specified the east as the source of some of their important material items. Among these were lion and jaguar claws, seashells, parrot and heron feathers, tobacco, three varieties of incense, and black and yellow minerals, used for painting the body (Recinos 1953, pp. 197, 220–22). Frequently listed in the chronicles are objects the Quichés claimed to have received from tributaries outside the central area: metals, precious stones (including jade), quetzal and other tropical bird feathers, flowered garlands, cacao and *pataxté* (an inferior cacao), gourds, salt, fish, turtles and crabs, and woven cloths (Villacorta 1962, p. 361; 1934, p. 186; Recinos 1957, pp. 78–84, 106, 174). Obsidian stone (*chay*) is not listed as a tribute item, but its close association with the mythic underworld and eastern homeland (Recinos 1953, p. 124; 1950, p. 49) points to its external source in the minds of the Quichés.

A most important feature of the Quichés' view of their world was its animatistic character. All things were alive and capable of acting upon all other things. The belief in an animating essence common to people, animals, plants, and physical objects resulted in a world in which these elements were interrelated. The natural elements were personified, and people and gods were closely tied to animals, plants, and natural forces. The howling of jaguars or lions in the mountains could be interpreted as either the animals themselves or the priest-leaders symbolically linked with them (Villacorta 1962, p. 283). Powerful men could transform themselves into the animals magically related to them (Villacorta 1962, pp. 297, 340). Natural elements linked to people in this way were known as *naguales*, and their fates were closely tied with those of the people with whom they were associated. From modern survivals (Tax 1947, pp. 472–76) we know that animals not easily caught, and therefore, not easily harmed, usually served as *naguales*. The particular *nagual* animals and persons linked to them were thought to have common characteristics: dogs and promiscuous men, coyotes and thieves, *zopilotes* ("buzzards") and homely women, and so on. The whole system of beliefs was totemism writ large, and it significantly affected the way the Quichés interacted with their environment.

Animatism was so universal among the Quichés that it becomes difficult to interpret ecological conditions from their totemic beliefs. We have the famous passage in the *Popol Vuh* (Villacorta 1962, pp. 42–45) in which all the domestic objects are given life and voice to speak: bowls, jars, grinding stones, dogs, turkey hens. When they try to escape, the trees and holes of the earth come to life and stop them. Nevertheless, some totemic relations were clearly of prime importance to the Quichés, as indicated by the complexity of their interrelations and the frequency with which they are mentioned in the sources. It can be assumed that such relationships tell us something about what the Quichés thought was most important in their environment. The following totemic relationships were worked out with that goal in mind.

The Quichés appear to have ranked totemic fauna by size and type, mammals being the highest, large birds next, followed by smaller animals, insects, and plants. Thus the three ranked Quiché ancestors, Balam Quitze, Balam Ak'ab, and Majucutaj were totemically related to the jaguar (mammal), eagle (bird), and wasp (insect), respectively (Villacorta 1962, p. 296). Faunal associations with the demigods reveal the same pattern. The hero-twins Junajpu and Xbalanque were linked to large mammals, such as the deer, the coyote, the peccary, and the *pisote*; smaller animals, birds, and plants were associated with lesser characters: the crab with Cabrakan, bats with death messengers, wasps with the four hundred children of Seven Macaw, the gourd tree with Junjunajpu, and the *tzité* tree with the otiose ancestor Xpiyacoc (Villacorta 1962, pp. 47ff.) Tiny spirits (*saki c'oxol*), lords of the dead, and lower classes of people in Quiché society were associated with the earth, whose totems were such low-ranked animals as crabs and snakes (Villacorta 1962, pp. 16, 72; Recinos 1950, p. 65; 1957, p. 44). The unfortunate half brothers of the hero-twins, Jun Batz and Jun Chowen, along with an intermediate class of artisans, were totemically related to monkeys. Since the monkey was not present in the Quiché area, its totemic association was with low-ranked woods and trees (Villacorta 1962, p. 130).

These faunal forms, totemically linked to human and deified powers in ranked order, were further associated with the natural elements. This association also tied men and their gods to these forces and provided a totemic basis for influencing them. Presumably the rank order of such relationships said something about the importance the Quichés attached to the various natural forces. Thus the largest mammals (the jaguar, deer, peccary, and opossum) were consistently associated with the sun, daylight, and heat. The next-largest mammals (the coyote, wildcat, and *pisote*) were associated with night, darkness, and cold (Recinos 1953, p. 82; Villacorta 1934, p. 216). Birds (the eagle, quetzal, and vulture) and the bat (*sotz*, classified as a bird by the Quichés) were associated with night and death and secondarily with rain (for the eagle, Villacorta 1962, p. 296; De León n.d., p. 180; for the quetzal, De León n.d., p. 69; Villacorta 1934, p. 196; for the vulture, Villacorta 1962, p. 186; Recinos 1957, p. 132; for the bat, Villacorta 1962, p. 244; 1934, p. 184). Flying insects (wasps, butterflies, and flies) were also associated with rain and rain clouds (Schultze-Jena 1947; De León n.d.). Apparently insects were classified with the birds, at least in some ethnoecological contexts.

A number of plant totems—mushrooms, anise, bark, branches from trees, copal, reeds, *tzité* beans, and gourds—were closely associated with the earth and its fertility (Recinos 1953, pp. 202–203; Villacorta 1934, p. 216; 1962, pp. 37–39). Maize, of course, was a totem of the earth, almost personifying its green-and-yellow vegetal growth (Villacorta 1962, pp. 217–18; *Título Totonicapán* n.d., p. 7v.). It was an anomalous totem, however, since it was totemic for man himself. Correspondingly, maize was associated with more powerful beings, Xmucane and female spirits (Villacorta 1962, pp. 37, 121). Obsidian stones were also totemically connected with the earth, perhaps through a metaphorical association with mushrooms (Carmack n.d.; Villacorta 1934, p. 216).

The basic totemic relationships described above were extended by the Quichés to include astral associations. The most important astral bodies and their totemic connections were (1) the sun (K'ij) with light and heat and large mammals; (2) the moon (Ic') with darkness and cold and smaller mammals; (3) Venus (Ikok'ij) with rain and birds, especially the quetzal; (4) the Pleiades (Motz) with rain and insects; (5) lightning (Cakulja') with earth vegetation, stones, and mushrooms (*Título Totonicapán* n.d., p. 7v.; Villacorta 1962). There were other astral associations, but these are the ones stressed in the native sources (see chapter 7).

While the Quichés do not appear to have been as concerned with time cycles as other Maya groups were, nevertheless there are strong calendrical associations with the ecological relationships described above. The solar calendar was almost a blueprint of how the Quichés viewed the relationship between agriculture and other features in the environment. It will be discussed below in connection with maize production. The sacred calendar (*chol k'ij*) was composed of twenty day names permutated with thirteen numbers, forming a cycle of 260 days. It took in wider environmental factors than the solar calendar did, but more indirectly, no doubt because the Quichés' version of the 260-day calendar was closely related to equivalent calendars in Guatemala and other parts of Mesoamerica. It was a less direct reflection of local ecological conditions than the solar calendar was, though, as we shall see, it bears traces of important ecological influence from the central Quiché area.

According to Ximénez (1929, pp. 101–102), Lehmann (1911), and Brinton (1893), the twenty day names of the Quichés were Imox (Envy, Fish), Ik' (wind), Akbal (Night, House), C'at (Net for Carrying Maize, Lizard), Can (Serpent, the K'anti), Came (Bite, Death), Quej (Deer), K'anel (Rabbit, Yellow Maize), Toj (Thunderstorm, Straw), Tz'i' (Dog), Batz (Monkey, Thread), E (Tooth Maize), Aj (Young Maize, Cane), Balam (Jaguar), Tz'iquin (Bird), Ajmac (Owl, Sinner), Noj (Resin, Weather), Tijax (Flint Knife, Clawing), Cawok (Rain and Thunder), and Junajpu (Chief, Hunter). These day names were combined with the thirteen numbers to form the 260 days of the sacred Quiché calendar.

Ecological factors seem to be associated with at least seventeen of the day names. Of these six have to do with animals (snake, deer, rabbit, dog, monkey, and jaguar), two with birds (bird and owl), four with plants (net of maize, yellow maize, young maize, and "tooth maize"), and three with weather (thunderstorm, weather, and rain). One other name is metaphorically associated with animals (Junajpu, Deer), and another with weather (Tijax, Lightning). The ecological emphases these associations represent may be general, but they also correspond well with the Quichés' ethnological view as reconstructed from other kinds of information.

Exploitation of Resources

The Quichés mentioned many technologies that they used to exploit the resources of their environment, ranging from the simple gathering of plants to complex metallurgical practices. We can do little more than list the technologies, since details are largely lacking.

Some of the natural products from the central area that were utilized without major processing include bunchgrass for roofing; feathers for adornment, honey, and incense (Recinos 1957, p. 38); fruits (avocados and *jocotes*) (*Título Totonicapán* n.d., pp. 19v, 23); lakes as reflecting mirrors (*Título Totonicapán* n.d., p. 30v.); animal excrement for whitening wood (Villacorta 1934, p. 218); pupae of insects cooked as food (Recinos 1957, p. 26; Brasseur 1972, p. 408; Carmack 1973, p. 279); tobacco for smoking; wild-bird eggs

(Berendt n.d.); and springs and rivers for washing and bathing and for drinking water (Villacorta 1962, pp. 286, 289, 148; 1934, p. 216). Of course, the Quichés used many other resources of these kinds.

The sources list other products whose utilization required at least limited processing. One of the most important products was wood. Trees provided house posts, firewood, pitch for torches, and wood for carving and for tools (Villacorta 1962, pp. 39, 63, 101; Recinos 1957, p. 62). Trees were felled with hatchets (*ikaj*) (Villacorta 1962, pp. 138). Closely associated with tree cutting was firemaking, for which the Quichés used the fire drill (Villacorta 1962, pp. 81, 242; *Título Totonicapán* n.d., p. 9v.).

The Quichés were hunters. Their hunting weapons included blowguns for killing birds (Villacorta 1962, pp. 81, 156), traps for catching birds and small animals (Villacorta 1934, p. 202; Carmack 1973, p. 274), and, apparently, the bows and arrows and spear throwers for deer and other large game (*Título Totonicapán* n.d., p. 20v.). They wore animal skins as camouflage while hunting large game (*Título Totonicapán* n.d., p. 30v.). The Quichés also fished, but they gave us no details about the techniques they employed (*Título Totonicapán* n.d., p. 25v.; Villacorta 1962, p. 288).

The extraction of a few resources is briefly mentioned in the native sources: resins (Villacorta 1963, p. 274; Recinos 1953, p. 202; 1957, p. 38), salt (Carmack 1973, p. 280), and lime (Villacorta 1962, pp. 82, 326). We are told that lime (*chun*) was worked into cement for building construction and that a finer lime (*sajcab*) was made into a white paint or wash (Villacorta 1962, pp. 325–26; Recinos 1957, p. 42; Carmack 1973, p. 273). Strangely, the Quichés did not mention quarrying stone or using it to build their town structures. Nor is there reference to extracting obsidian or other kinds of stone for making tools, for the reason that those materials are absent from the Quiché area.

References to many common manufacturing techniques are found in the sources. They include the manufacture of mats, nets, bark clothing, maguey-fiber cloth, cotton cloth, pottery, leather goods, and wooden tools (Villacorta 1962; *Título Totonicapán* n.d., , p. 27v.; Recinos 1957, pp. 54–66). Such goods were differentiated from "elite" goods, which were manufactured by special artisans under the tutelage of patron gods (see chapter 6). The crafts specified as elite in the *Popol Vuh* are the carving of wood (*tz'alam*) and precious stones (*cuwal, yamanic*), stone knapping (*chut, cot*), decorating of ceramic (*raxa lak*) and gourd (*raxa sel*) wares, copal (*k'ol*) production, painting or writing (*tz'iba*), and metallurgy (*toltecat*) (Villacorta 1962, pp. 16, 37, 136). It was pointed out above that some of the resources used in the elite crafts came from outside Quiché, but the sources make it clear that the residents of Utatlán performed the craftsmanship.

Food production and preparation are widely mentioned in the native chronicles. Wild game, for example, was cooked and consumed by the

Quichés, especially the elite. The game specifically referred to are deer, peccary, rabbits, fish, and birds (Villacorta 1962, p. 125; *Título Totonicapán* n.d., pp. 20v., 23, 25v.). Dogs and turkeys were raised for food (Villacorta 1962, p. 43; Carmack 1973, p. 368; Recinos 1953, p. 96).

By far the most important food product was maize, and the main Quiché terms for food (*echa wa*) were almost synonymous with the word for prepared maize (Villacorta 1962, pp. 120–21). Grinding maize on stone *metates* was a constant feature of domestic life (Villacorta 1962, pp. 43, 147). The resulting maize mass was made into tamales (*sub*), both stuffed and unstuffed, and gruels (*atol*) (Villacorta 1962, p. 147; 1934, p. 232; *Título Totonicapán* n.d., p. 23). Chili and beans were eaten along with maize products, the former as a sauce (*cutum ic'*) (Villacorta 1962, pp. 145, 147). Maize was fermented into a beverage (*qui'a'*) and was mixed in chocolate drinks (Villacorta 1962, pp. 70, 146, 334; *Título Totonicapán* n.d., p. 24). Other fermented beverages were made from fruits, maguey, and honey (Las Casas 1909, p. 469).

The production of maize receives considerable attention in the native sources. Milpa farming (*abix, awan*) is the only technology described (Villacorta 1962, pp. 119–21, 136–45; 1934, p. 216). Hill and mountain lands near the farmers' houses were cleared of trees and brush, the work being done with the hatchet (*ikaj*) and a kind of hoe (*xoquem*). The cut vegetation was allowed to dry and then burned. The soil was turned with a digging stick (*mixquina*). Two problems accompanied milpa growing: weeds grew back, and birds ate the sprouting plants. The old grandmother (Xmucane) and her female helpers were guardians of the growing crop (Ximénez n.d.; Villacorta 1962, p. 121). The ears of corn (*jal*) were gathered in nets and taken to the houses for storage.

The Quiché solar calendar was closely adapted to the milpa cycle in the central area. The names of the months of that calendar and their ecological associations provide a graphic view of maize production as the Quichés practiced it.

It should be noted that, because of the considerable variations among solar calendars throughout the highlands, the reconstructed calendar below, while based on the available sources, is not certain in every detail (Berendt n.d.; Basseta n.d.; Villacorta and Rodas 1927, pp. 147–51; Recinos 1950, pp. 33–34; Recinos 1953, p. 114; Ximénez 1929, pp. 101–102; De León n.d., pp. 66–67). In Table 4.1 are listed the eighteen 20-day units and 5 extra days at the end, followed by the Quichés' ecological associations with each unit. What I believe to be the appropriate correspondence of each unit with our calendar is also given.

The Quiché year began in early March (Carmack n.d.; Falla 1975), or possibly late February (Ximénez 1929, p. 101). If Tequexepual was the first "month," as seems likely, then the other months followed the chronological

Table 4.1. **The Quiché Solar Calendar and Calendric Correspondence**

Number	Twenty-Day Unit	Ecological Association	Calendric Correspondence
1	Tequexepual	Plant milpas, begin year	March 10–29
2	Q'uibapop	Forty days' rain, insects	March 30–April 18
3	Sak	White flowers, rain, insects	April 19–May 8
4	Ch'ab	Planting, muddy soil	May 9–28
5	Jun Bix K'ij	First song to the sun	May 29–June 17
6	Nabe Mam	First old man, bad for planting	June 18–July 7
7	Ucab Mam	Second old man; same	July 8–27
8	Nabe Liquinca	Muddy and soft	July 28–August 16
9	Ucab Liquinca	Same; first cutting	August 17–September 6
10	Nabe Pach	Casting, hatching	September 7–26
11	Ucab Pach	Same	September 27–October 16
12	Tz'ici Lakam	Sprouts	October 17–November 5
13	Tz'iquin K'ij	Birds	November 6–25
14	Cakam	Hot, red clouds	November 26–December 16
15	Nabe Sij	Dry, burning; white flowers	December 16–January 4
16	Ucab Sij	Same; plant in mountains	January 5–24
17	Rox Sij	Same	January 25–February 13
18	Che'	Trees; cold	February 14–March 5
	Batam (Tz'ap K'ij)	Five unlucky days	March 6–10

sequence given above, and the five "closing days" (Batam, or Tz'ap K'ij) were the last part of February or early March. The ancient "monthly" ecological associations tell us how the Quichés felt about the seasons and agricultural cycle of the central area, as the following comments indicate.

We are specifically told that Tequexepual (March) began the year and the planting. This planting must have been minor, for the main planting season was in the fourth month, Ch'ab (May). Perhaps the more important association for Tequexepual was the tribute collection that was carried out during the month (Villacorta 1934, p. 188). That season, coming at the end of the preceding cycle and just before the new main planting, would have been an appropriate time for tribute goods to come in.

Planting began in Ch'ab, a period of mud and thus rains. The two Mams, which began near the summer solstice (De León n.d., p. 69), were too late for planting and so were thought to be ill-fated old men.

The associations for the "months" Liquinca, Pach, and Lakam seem to have been important features of the main part of the rainy season (August to November): mud and water, clearing of weeds, and hatching of birds(?). The dry season (November and December) brought sprouting corn tassels, the augur of birds flying south (De León n.d., p. 180), and heat around harvesttime. Significantly, the Quichés held their major ritual celebration in Tz'iquin K'ij (November), just before the harvest (*Título Totonicapán* n.d., p. 27v.; Carmack 1973, p. 295).

The first months of the new year (by the present calendar) were a time when white flowers (*sij*) grew in the maize fields, dried weeds and stalks from the past crops were burned, and planting began in the mountain areas. Appropriately, the lull before the new year was to begin, unpredictable February, was foreboding, cold, and connected with the five unlucky days that closed the year. These days were associated with Batam, a god of the underworld.

Resources and products were carried on foot in the Quiché area. The tumpline (*patan*) and the pack (*coc*) were used for carrying on the back such items as firewood, pottery, maize, and stone (Villacorta 1962, pp. 92, 237; Recinos 1957, p. 160). The pack consisted of a cage for fragile goods or a box for unbreakable objects. It was tied to the tumpline, which had a leather strap that went over the forehead. Known today as *cacasté*, this pack is still used by Quiché peasants of Guatemala (Brasseur 1972, p. 400). There is little mention in the native sources of goods being moved about, except for special tribute items brought in from the outside, such as metal, precious stones, feathers, salt, cacao, and gourds.

Markets for the central area are never specifically mentioned, though we are told of some buying and selling of maize foods, fruits, honey, feathers, incense, and bunchgrass (Villacorta 1934, p. 232; Recinos 1957, p. 38; *Título Totonicapán* n.d., p. 19v.). Nevertheless, early Spanish writers citing native sources (Las Casas 1909, p. 623; Fuentes y Guzmán 1932–33, 7:427) indicate that markets (*c'aybal*) were important in the central area.

Internal Variation

The natives described an environment with considerable variation, and though a substantial component of the variation derived from provinces outside the central area, some of it was internal. Perhaps the main internal distinction the Quichés drew was between the zone in which they first settled and the later zone around Utatlán. Many smaller ecological distinctions can also be detected in the sources.

The zone of initial occupation by the Quiché forefathers was a "wilderness" in the minds of the Quichés, a place of mountains and forests. They referred to its bushes and canyons (*tucan*, *ciwan*), trees and vines (*che'*, *c'aam*) (Recinos 1957, p. 28–32; *Título Totonicapán* n.d., p.9). Mountains of all kinds are mentioned, and the names of many of the most prominent are still in use.

Most of the mountains were covered with thick forests of pine and other trees, which in turn were enveloped with mosses and vines (Villacorta 1962, p. 262). Mountain lions, coyotes, deer, and jaguars roamed the forests, while rattlers and vipers slithered through the bushes (*Título Totonicapán* n.d., p. 10v.; Villacorta 1962, pp. 259, 266). Craggy cliffs were the home of eagles, the trees were a haven for noisy parakeets and bluebirds, while quail ran along the ground and vultures soared in the skies (Villacorta 1962, pp. 262, 274; Recinos 1957, p. 132). References to streams of clouds, mists, and fog, as well as to wind and cold, indicate that the zone had a high elevation (*Título Totonicapán* n.d., p. 21; Carmack 1973, pp. 274–75). The Quichés made astronomical observations, especially of the sun's cycle, from the top of the mountains. Observations of the morning star from the mountaintops led the Quichés to name the zone the Dawning Mountains (Sakiribal Juyup).

Native imagery of the flatlands where the Quichés founded Utatlán tended to be focused on the towns, with their dramatic buildings of mortar and stone (Villacorta 1962, pp. 331, 333; Recinos 1957, p. 46). The most important feature of the zone was a chain of "canyon towns" (*ciwan tinamit*), by which expression we are to understand that the towns were surrounded by steep canyons (Villacorta 1962, pp. 329, 347). A native map portrays the zone as flat, with rivers coursing through it from south to north (Carmack 1973, p. 12). An early post-Hispanic document refers to it as the "Valley of Santa Cruz and Santa Elena" (Carmack 1973, p. 365). In general, animals were not associated with the zone, except for snakes (Recinos 1957, p. 44). It was a place with "dry weeds," "old reeds," "open fields," "planting," "milpa," and the like. Compared with the magical and mysterious early mountain homeland, the Utatlán zone seems to have been political and secular in the Quiché perspective (see chapter 7).

The Quichés were fully aware that even their second zone of occupation was not all plains. In fact, they never referred to it as merely "plains" (*tak'aj*) but always as "mountains and plains" (*juyup tak'aj*). As the lands surrounding Utatlán became subdivided into many political jurisdictions, the ecological character of each unit was noted. The units were called *calpules*, the Mexica term for territorial divisions. *Calpul* names usually epitomized some basic ecological feature. The lists of the *calpul* units in the chronicles contain such names as the following: Scattered Settlement (Amak' Tam), Cleared Place (Ch'alibalaj), Flowering Maize (Tzutuja), White Jocote (Sak K'inom), Round Hills (Sakmolob), Toltec Ruler (Nacxit, a place of milpas), Dark Mountain (Ak'ab Juyup), Cleared Place (Pach'alib), Brushed Settlement (Amak' Mes), Lord's Sleeping Place (Warabal K'alel), Willow Trees (Tz'oloche') Oxidation Place (Chulumal), Young Bird (Ruc'abala, or Walic Tz'iquin), White River (Sakiya'), Deer Wash (Xojbaquiej), Straight Town (Coloquic Tinamit), Logs (Chitemaj), Many Milpas (Waxaklajuj Patiqui), Prickly Plant (Uwila'), Twin Mountains (Cabrakan), Round Lake (Chobolo), Deer Shot with Sling (C'akolquiej), Neighbors (C'ulchip), Enclosed Fire (Tz'apik'ak'), Corner (Tz'ucaj), Middle of the Plains (Ximbaxuc Chinic'),

Tobacco (Meba Q'uisic'), Blow Gunner Mountain (Chwijunajpu), Green House (Raxaja), Owls (Tucurub), Log Drums (K'ojomeb), Shield River (Pokoba), Condiment River (Iquiliya'), Guava (Sak' K'inom), Maguey (Xequi), and Avocados (Xeoj) (Recinos 1957, pp. 54–60, 71–73; Villacorta 1962, p. 347; Carmack 1937, pp. 302–303).

According to Quiché political geography the rural *calpules* were grouped into four great divisions corresponding to the four major political units of the Utatlán community, Nima Quiché, Tamub, Ilocab, and Nijaib. There is some evidence in the documentary sources that the four divisions were associated with the cardinal directions (see Fig. 4.1). Presumably the Quiché also recognized general ecological differences among the divisions, though that is not explicitly stated in the sources.

Demography

References to population size in the Quiché sources are general and vague. We are told that the original Quiché ancestors were few at first but that they greatly multiplied later and eventually became numerous at Utatlán (Villacorta 1962, pp. 268, 300, 336, 339). The only actual population figures given are in connection with war. Early in Quiché history an army of men indigenous to the area was said to have numbered between 16,000 and 24,000 (Villacorta 1962, p. 307). That would suggest a maximum indigenous population of 80,000 to 120,000, assuming that 2 out of 10 persons were warriors (Veblen 1975, p. 311; cf. Milla 1937, pp. 225–26). The figure was obviously inflated to glorify the Quichés' victory over their enemies and should not be taken literally.

A more literal demographic statement by the Cakchiquels tells us that the Quichés raised an army of 8,000 to 16,000 men to fight their forces (Villacorta 1934, p. 238). That would indicate a maximum population of 40,000 to 80,000 people, though we are uncertain about the precise area in which they lived. For the major battle with the Spaniards, according to Quiché sources, they raised an army of 8,000 to 10,000 men (Carmack 1973, p. 282; Recinos 1957, p. 86). This army appears to have been recruited exclusively from the central Quiché area, suggesting a maximum population there of about 50,000 people.

The Quichés were silent about population declines, but the more historically oriented Cakchiquels indicate that the Quichés lost many people in wars, including most of the 8,000 to 16,000 warriors who attacked the Cakchiquels on the above-mentioned occasion (Villacorta 1934, pp. 240, 254, 256). The Cakchiquels also tell of infectious diseases striking down large numbers of people shortly before the Conquest (Villacorta 1934, pp. 256–58). The Quichés do not indicate whether they were plagued with the same diseases, though that is likely. References in the *Popol Vuh* (Villacorta 1962, pp. 90, 91) to demon messengers of sickness and disease suggest that death from disease was common and probably leveled the population at Quiché. Death was said to result from such syndromes as bleeding, body swelling, leg sores, jaundice, wasting away to the bone, strokes, and vomiting of blood (Villacorta 1962, pp. 90–92; Recinos 1953, pp. 116–17). It appears that lethal diseases were a serious problem in the Quiché area before the arrival of the Spaniards.

The Quichés were virtually silent on population differences between the towns (*tinamit*) and the rural areas (*amak'*). They stated simply that the families of town lords were constantly multiplying and that the rural peoples were numerous (Villacorta 1962, pp. 334, 336). Within Quiché ethnoecology, it would appear, demographic factors were of limited interest.

ETHNOGRAPHIC ECOLOGY

It is possible to approach the ecology of the central Quiché area directly, since many features of the environment have persisted down to the present and can be observed. In the following account I focus on present-day ecological conditions, especially those related to traditional native exploitation of resources. A few colonial and early republican documentary sources will be used, but most of the information comes from modern ethnographic and geographic studies. Of particular importance are the several ethnographic studies of Chichicastenango in the 1930s (Tax 1947; Bunzel 1952; Schultze-Jena 1947; Rodas y Rodas 1938), from which I have tried to extrapolate cautiously for the central area. Other data come from the 1950 national census, which was perhaps Guatemala's first reasonably accurate census. It was carried out before the sweeping changes that have come to the area in the past twenty-five years, brought about by chemical fertilizers, improved health care, extensive bus transportation, and rural developmental programs. The National Forestry Institute (INAFOR) has prepared a series of useful ecological maps of the area. The maps are based on aerial photographs and fieldwork by the institute staff. Finally, several graduate students of SUNY at Albany have gathered "geographic" data in the area, and I have personally visited all parts of the area to observe present-day ecological conditions firsthand.

General Conditions

A creole official in the seventeenth century, Fuentes y Guzmán (1932–33, 7:412), described the Quiché area in the following terms: It is a land of mountains and canyons, with a cold, cloudy climate; there are no fish and few game animals; though there are many poisonous snakes, they rarely bite man, and the land is free of noxious insects; there is no irrigation, because the rivers are too deep and rapid; the area produces great surpluses of maize, beans, and chili peppers; busy traders exchange these food surpluses for cacao, fish, and other products of the coast.

McBryde (1947), who studied the Quiché area in the 1930s, classified it with the interior trough country of Guatemala. Geologically part of an old volcanic zone, it is an eroded area of lava and ash north of a more recent volcanic axis that runs the length of the Central American highlands. Temperatures in the coldest month fall to between −3° and 18° C (27° to 65° F.), and 40 to 80 inches of rain fall in the summer between May and October. The natural vegetation consists of pine and oak, and the area is rich in native cultigens. Among the food plants that McBryde listed as native to the area are maize, several varieties of beans (*Phaseolus*), varieties of squash (*Cucurbita*), *huisquil* (chayote) and other green vegetables, gourds, chilies, small red potatoes, tomatoes, tobacco, maguey, avocados, and *jocotes*. McBryde observed that the milpa horticulture of the area had a fairly short growing season of seven to eight months and gave moderately good yields (see below). He also observed that, despite limited nonagricultural resources—there are no obsidian, major limestone outcroppings, lime, salt, stone for *metates*, or special fibers—trading was extensive. Alternate-day markets allowed merchants to visit regular markets at Chichicastenango, Santa Cruz, Chiché, Chinique, and Chiquimula. The surplus agricultural products of the area were exchanged for outside goods.

More recent studies of the area confirm earlier views and add further information about conditions in general in the central area (Fig. 4.2). Maps prepared by the National Geographic Institute (IGN) and INAFOR show that Utatlán was situated on a highland plateau between the Sierra Madre volcanic axis on the south and the Sierra Chuacus on the north. West of the site the plateau continues for many kilometers, beyond Ilotenango becoming a country of ridges, hills, and tiny valleys. East of Utatlán the plateau also extends many kilometers, eventually dropping off sharply into the Motagua River basin (IGN 1960, maps 1, 4; 1961, maps 2, 3). It is important to understand that the ancient Utatlán community occupied territories both on the central plains and along the ridges and elevations of the Sierra Madre and the Sierra Chuacus. These gave it rather precise boundaries on the north and south, but east and west, on the plateau, its boundaries were arbitrary. On the west the community extended to the Río Sajcolaj, which today separates Chiquimula and Momostenango. On the plateau on the east the community line was even more arbitrary, apparently consisting of the prominent hills that today separate Chinique and Chichicastenango from Zacualpa.

The central plateau is broken in many places by river canyons, though in the zone nearest Utatlán the land divisions are still large and flat (IGN 1961, map 2; INAFOR, map, "Inclinación de tierras"). Some of the rivers run east and west and facilitate communication in those directions. Other rivers provide passage through the mountain chains on the north and south, especially the southeast-flowing branches, which feed the Río Motagua, and northwest rivers, which become part of the Río Negro–Usumacinta system.

The unusual topography of the Utatlán area has made it a traditional crossroads for major land routes. About 140 years ago John Lloyd Stephens (1841, p. 188) was shown a point just outside Santa Cruz where four roads crossed, "which led and . . . are still open to Mexico, Tecpan Guatimala, Los Altos, and Vera Paz." Most of the old road system is still in use. It includes (1) a main north–south route from Lake Atitlán through Chichicastenango, Santa Cruz, and San Pedro to points north; (2) a main east–west route, from Totonicapán through San Antonio, Santa Cruz, and Chinique to points east; (3) important routes from Santa Cruz and Chichicastenango through Patzite and on to Totonicapán; and (4) a route from Santa Cruz to Chujuyup and on to San Andrés Sajcabaja.

The Utatlán area has been referred to as the "central plains" and described as part of the largest temperate zone in Guatemala, with moderate and stable conditions (Simmons et al. 1959, p. 589). Situated at the somewhat intermediate elevation of 1,500 to 2,000 meters, the area enjoys regular wet and dry seasons, relatively constant warm days and cool nights, and a uniform natural forest covering. The flooding of the lowland zones and the frosts and freezes of higher mountain zones are generally absent. In modern times the immunity of the area from natural disasters, except for earthquakes (the area is at the extreme end of a major fault), attests to the moderate geographic conditions.

Nevertheless, the normal climatic cycle produces easily observable changes, and the natives respond to them. Bunzel (1952, pp. 46–48) found that the natives did not like April, a hot, sultry month preceding the rains, and that their rituals during that month were somber. They liked the period from May to July, the early months of steady but not heavy rains, and the rituals of those months were gay. The heavy rains of August through October, bringing fog, cold, and gray skies, depressed the natives. They tended to stay in their houses and mope. The dry months from November through March brought clear, cool weather and blooming flowers. The people were gay at this time, filled the markets, and visited other towns. As we shall see, this cycle of attitudes also relates closely to the milpa cycle.

Exploitation of Resources

Game animals have been virtually eliminated from the central Quiché area. I have never seen a deer in the area, though stragglers are reported from time to time. Even rabbits are scarce, as are quail and other edible birds. Today the most commonly seen animals are coyotes, snakes, squirrels, and the ubiqui-

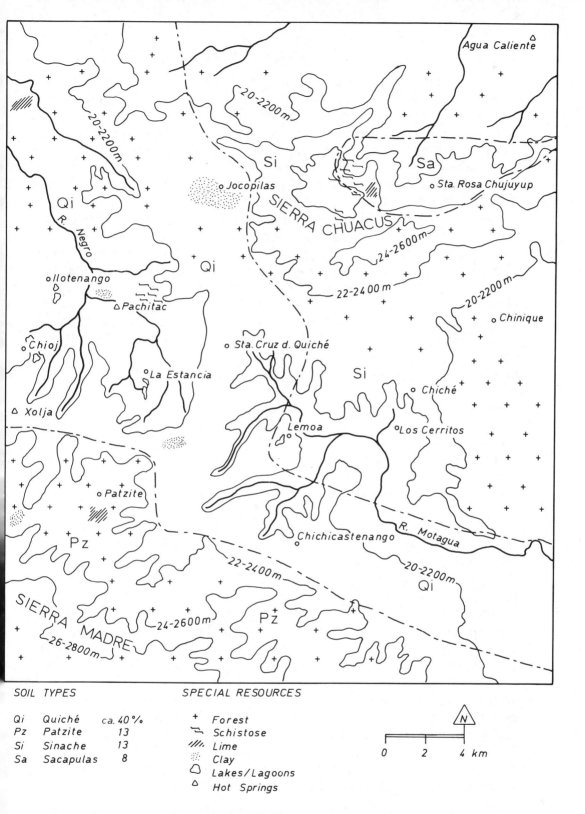

SOIL TYPES

Qi	Quiché	ca. 40%
Pz	Patzite	13
Si	Sinache	13
Sa	Sacapulas	8

SPECIAL RESOURCES

+ Forest
⌐ Schistose
/// Lime
⣿ Clay
△ Lakes/Lagoons
△ Hot Springs

0   2   4 km

Fig. 4.2. Ecological factors in the central Quiché area. Modified from Carmack, Fox, and Stewart 1975.

tous rats and mice (Tax 1947, pp. 472ff.). Bluebirds can still be spotted from time to time in the mountains, but only buzzards, doves, and hummingbirds seem very common. The one native-domesticated animal in the area is the turkey, and it is overshadowed by the European chicken. European pigs, sheep, and cattle raised in small numbers supply most of the meat eaten by the Quiché people.

The Quiché area is extensively cultivated today, and the central plains are denuded of trees. In the hilly country patches of forest are preserved, however, and in the canyons and mountains the forests remain dense. The traditional farmers preserve sections of forest in order to obtain firewood and leaves for fertilizer (Bunzel 1952, p. 6; Brunius and Whitehead n.d.). Veblen (1975) thinks that the Quichés are exceptional in this regard and that the practice accounts for the extensive forests that survive in the western region of the highlands.

Apple and peach orchards have become an important feature of food production in the Quiché area, but that is a recent development. Native fruits consist of large numbers of avocados and a few *jocotes*, *anonas* (a fruit), guavas, and *matasanos* ("custard apple") (Bunzel 1952, p. 43; Tax 1947, p. 295).

As in times past, milpa culture today dominates food production in the Quiché. The staple crops continue to be maize, beans, squash, and other traditional vegetables. Irrigation is lacking except for a few terraced plots watered by hand in a technique that has slowly moved into the area from the Lake Atitlán region in recent years. Quiché milpa production is thus dry farming and depends on the natural fertility of the soils and the regular annual rainfall.

The soils of the central area, formed from volcanic ash, are generally well drained and deep and have a good natural fertility (Simmons et al. 1959). They have the capacity to retain humidity but are susceptible to erosion and the loss of organic material because of a hard outer layer. In the Simmons classification "Quiché," "Patzite," and "Sinache" soils make up 60 to 70 percent of the soils in the central area. They are common to the highlands and are capable of rendering good return on traditional milpa horticulture if erosion has not progressed too far. To be most effective, a one-to-one fallow-cultivation schedule should be followed. Unfortunately, land is now so scarce that it is no longer fallowed in most places, and as a consequence soil fertility is low, and erosion has become extensive. The southwestern part of Chiché, for example, is now a wasteland of eroded hill country. As recently as the 1930s milpa lands were adequately fallowed, production was high, and food was "cheap and plentiful" (Bunzel 1952, p. 43). Today lands are rarely left fallow, and yields are good only if chemical fertilizers are applied. Food is expensive and in short supply locally.

Ecology

The traditional milpa cycle of the Quiché area can be reconstructed from modern ethnographic studies (Stearns n.d.; Mantz n.d.; Falla 1975; Bunzel 1952, pp. 48–59; Tax 1947, p. 230). It can be divided into the following periods or cycles:

January–March.   This is the season for turning the soil and chopping the past year's corn stalks (*mucupatzan*). I have seen digging sticks used for this purpose, obviously a survival of ancient practices. Planting may begin this early in the mountainous zones, and a small second crop of short maize is harvested.

March–April.   Dried maize stalks and weeds, if any, are burned at this time. Planting in higher elevations continues. A special planting (*jumba*) in low, moist plots takes place on the plateau.

May.   This is the main planting season (*awex*). Small mounds are prepared with hoes, and five grains of maize along with beans and squash are planted in holes punched with a stick. This is done just after the rains begin and the soil is moist. Maize seeds are selected from the best ears stored in house attics especially for that purpose. There are four varieties of creole seeds: a durable white; a cold-resistant yellow; a large, tight-grained yellow; and a small yellow-blue. The yellow variety is preferred, but a short-season white may also be planted at this time. The yellow and white seeds are never planted together because it is believed that they will "mate."

June–September.   This is the time when the milpa must be weeded (*josoj*) and mounds built up around the cornstalks to prevent them from bending with the wind and rain. There are three or four cleanings, usually in the middle of June, July, August, and September. Today chemical fertilizers are added at these times. Beans that were planted with the maize seeds have sprouted and are allowed to wind around the maize stalks. They help protect the maize, the natives say, as the woman supports the man. Small crosses and animal figures are placed in milpas to protect the maize. Some squashes are harvested during this period.

September–November.   This is an early harvest season when some maize, squashes, and potatoes are taken from the fields. A second crop of short maize is planted. Late-maturing maize stalks are doubled over to prevent them from breaking in the winds and rains.

November–December.   This is the main harvest season (*jach*), which may extend into January at higher elevations. The crops are brought from the

97

fields in nets, seeds are set aside for next year's planting, and the maize ears are hung on rafter poles for storing.

Milpa farming in the central plains usually does not involve fallowing, and this appears to have been the case for many years. No doubt that is possible because of the good volcanic soils there, but it means that production has been decreasing through time in areas where fertilizers are not applied. Traditionally in the mountain areas milpa fields were left fallow "for many years" (Bunzel 1952, p. 16). The mountains are today the poorest zones, for the natives cannot afford to buy fertilizers. Their yields are down too, because fallowing has been shortened or even eliminated, owing to the scarcity of land.

Serious plant diseases also reduce yields of maize and, to an ever-greater extent, beans. Several varieties of beetles, worms, and weevils (*xpakpan, lem, xajut, pok'*) have become uncontrollable on traditional milpa farms in the central area. Hail, heavy rains, strong winds, and drought also affect crop yields, and are considered by the natives to be "diseases" along with plant insects.

Maize yields from *individual* fields aided by fertilizers are between 11 and 33 quintals (1,100 to 3,300 pounds—1 quintal equals about 100 pounds) per manzana (about 1.7 acres) (Stearns n.d.). Yields were about the same in the 1930s without fertilizers (McBryde 1947, p. 81; Tax 1947, p. 231; Termer 1957, p. 75). Production figures from the 1950 census give a rough idea of *over-all* yields in the area at a time when land was less intensively cultivated and chemical fertilizers were unknown. Over-all yields for maize were 8 to 9 quintals a manzana, and total maize production for the central area in 1950 was approximately 160,000 quintals. That yield would have supported only about 23,000 people (at 7 quintals a person a year) (Falla 1975). Since the 1950 population of the central area supported by maize was much higher—perhaps double that (see below)—it seems likely that our production data are on the low side.

Maize yields in pre-Hispanic times were probably higher than they are today. Soils were less depleted, and individual fields probably yielded 20 to 50 quintals a manzana. Nevertheless, over-all yields may have approximated those of the 1930s because the total amount of land in production was probably smaller. A pre-Hispanic population figure of 50,000 based on maize production seems reasonable, but the inadequate data make this figure little more than a guess for now.

Maize is the staple food of the native diet. It is made into tamales (*sub*), solid cakes synonymous with food (*wa*). Tortillas (*lej*) are also prepared, and green ears of maize (*aj*) are roasted and eaten. Coffee is the main drink, though atol (*k'or*), a gruel of maize and water, is the traditional drink and is still relied on by the poor. A special *atol* is prepared by grinding maize cake into flour and combining it with water, spices, cacao, and a special spice called *sapuyul*. The drink is then heated in a pot and swirled with a round instrument until the cacao cream rises to the top.

The traditional way of preparing beans (*quinak'*), black or red, is to boil them, adding a red spice called *pulic'*. Fried beans have become popular, but that is a Latin innovation, and the poorer natives cannot always afford the lard needed to prepare them in this fashion.

Vegetables are eaten with maize and beans; they consist of *ayote* and *chilacayote* squashes (*mukun*, *k'ok'*), huisquil, potatoes, tomatoes, and European vegetables (especially onions, carrots, and cabbage). A chili sauce (*c'atan ic'*) is another indispensable element in the native diet (Bunzel 1952, pp. 40–43; Tax 1947, pp. 224–28).

Maguey (*qui*) is found widely in the central area, but it is not cultivated, nor is any kind of food or drink extracted from it today. It is used mainly as a boundary marker, and on a limited scale its fibers are extracted for making baskets and nets (McBryde 1947, map 17). Some local residents have mistakenly postulated that the name Quiché derives from the maguey plant: *qui* ("sweet"), *che'* ("tree"). As discussed under "Trees" above, the correct etymology is quite different.

The central Quiché is not particularly rich in special resources. It lacks such traditionally important resources as salt, precious stones, feathers, obsidian, flint, cacao, and metals. The area is, however, well endowed with materials for construction, pottery making, and basket weaving.

It has already been pointed out that trees are abundant and that even today large stands of pine, oak, and cypress remain in the mountainous and canyon zones. Branches are cut for firewood to heat homes, and small trees provide poles for houses. Timber remains an important resource in the eastern part and in the southwest corner, around Chimenté (Totonicapán).

The subsurface of most of the central plains is pumice. It was used extensively as fill for the buildings at Utatlán. It is rarely used today, however. McBryde (1947, map 18) claimed that there are no large limestone outcroppings in the Quiché area, but J. F. Guillemin (personal communication) stated that small quarries are readily available. The tower of the department building was constructed of limestone from a nearby quarry (not from stone taken from Utatlán, as is widely believed). Limestone is not exploited today. Schistose is abundant in the Sierra Chuacus north of the plains. It was used as a stone facing at some pre-Utatlán sites but is not exploited today.

There are two kinds of lime in the Quiché area. The thick, rocklike lime suitable for making mortar and cement is confined to a site in the southwestern part of Chiquimula. It is brought to Santa Cruz through the local market system. It is also used in soaking maize kernels to remove the outer shell before the kernels are ground. The other, thinner form of lime, called *sajcab* in

Quiché, is suitable for making stucco and whitewash. There are good deposits in Patzité and Santa Lucía la Reforma. *Sajcab* is used by the inhabitants to make a whitewash for houses and public buildings.

Two major clay deposits occur in the central area, one near San Pedro Jocopilas and the other in Chimenté. Other small deposits occur near Utatlán at Pachitac and Xatinab and in the western part of Chiquimula in Tzakibala. The clay from these sources, still used to make pottery by traditional methods (see below), appears to be virtually inexhaustible.

A chain of lakes or lagoons extends along an east–west axis through the center of the central plains. The two largest lakes lie next to San Antonio and the Lemoa hamlet. Remnants of smaller lagoons can be seen on the plateau below San Antonio; on the Panajxit, La Estancia, and Xatinab plateaus near Utatlán; and on the tableland southeast of Chiché. These small bodies of water may have been much larger in pre-Hispanic times, and some of them may have held fish and crustaceans. Natives from Lemoa traditionally ate an amphibian from the lake (*nurutuk*) (Tax 1947, p. 207). Today they catch fish from the lake, but the fish are stocked. The several lagoons are minor sources of reeds, aquatic birds, water for construction (such as making adobes), and for drinking (especially today for cattle).

It has already been noted that many rivers flow through the Quiché plains. They too are sources of drinking water, though most of them lie at the bottoms of deep canyons, and transporting the water is difficult. The central area is also rich in fresh-water springs, and populations have always been clustered around them. For example, there are springs near the canyon edge at both Jakawitz and Utatlán, the first and last capitals of the Quichés. Other well-known springs are in the Chujuyup Mountains near Aguacate, on the eastern tableland close to present-day Chiché, and in Chimenté.

Hot springs are important to the Quichés as bathing and medicinal places. The most important hot springs are at Pachitac, near Santa Cruz; Xolja', near Chimenté; Patzam, north of Chiquimula; and Agua Caliente, in the northern part of Chujuyup.

A striking consequence of the lack of specialized resources in the Quiché is the limited traditional artisanry practiced by the natives. The only crafts that stand out are pottery making at San Pedro Jocopilas and Chimenté, and weaving at Chichicastenango. Both crafts are the work of women, and the methods and products are traditionally ordinary. There is some mat making in Chiniqué, copal production in Chiquimula (and other places), and *ocote* production in Chichicastenango, but on a small scale. Documentary sources from the colonial period do not mention other crafts that might have disappeared later, though they indicate that weaving by women was more widespread at one time (AGC, *A*1, 1587–10,231).

Pottery making at Jocopilas and Chimenté is performed by a traditional process (Conte n.d.; Tax 1947, pp. 60–63). The women gather clay from the deposits, grind it into a fine powder, mix it with water, and work it into a soft mass. The mass is placed on a saucer, which is spun as rolls of clay are added. The shape of the vessel is molded with the fingers and a corncob and finally smoothed with leather and cloth strips. Designs and adornments are pinched and scratched on with the fingers, and the vessels are dried in the sun. They are later fired face down over firewood and sherds, straw having been added to cover the outsides of the vessels. After firing, the vessels may be "cured" with lime and maize. The whole process takes only three hours. The vessels most commonly produced are water jars, pitchers, cooking pots, griddles (*comales*), and bowls. Braziers and colanders (*pichachas*) are made by the same process.

Traditional weaving at Chichicastenango was intricate. Later it became fancy to satisfy the growing tourist industry (Bunzel 1952, pp. 60ff.; Conte n.d.; Tax 1947, pp. 254ff.). In former times cotton from the coast was spun into thread and colored with natural dyes. Now weavers largely use manufactured dyed cotton or wool thread. The handloom (*tzul*) has a backstrap (*ik' wuquim*) that fits around the woman's waist, the other end being tied to a tree or other stable object. Huipils (blouses), sashes, ribbons, and other small articles of clothing are made on these looms, while women's skirts, men's woolen suits, and blankets are made by men on European foot looms. Hand weaving has been almost totally lost in the Quiché except in Chichicastenango.

Despite the limited native crafts of the Quiché area, traditional markets flourish. There is a major regional market at Chichicastenango, and important markets flourish at Santa Cruz, Chiché, and Chiquimula. The small markets at Jocopilas and Ilotenango are recent (Fallas 1975), as is the larger market at Chiché. The Chinique market has a fairly long history (Maudslay 1899), but it has always been very small.

The traditional markets at Santa Cruz and Chichicastenango have depended on surplus maize, beans, potatoes, turkeys, eggs, and firewood to be exchanged for such outside products as pottery from Chimenté and Jocopilas, lime from Chiquimula, grinding stones from Naguala, painted gourds from Rabinal, ropes and nets from Cobán, mats from Lake Atitlán, wooden furniture from Totonicapán, fish from the Tapachula area, salt from the Pacific Coast, chili from Sajcabaja, and incense from Sacapulas. The situation is greatly complicated today, with the special weaving at Chichicastenango, hat making at Santa Cruz, European vegetable produce from the lake area, and so on. The Chichicastenango market, strongly rooted in the past, is clearly the dominant one. Since the colonial period traveling merchants based in Chichicastenango have gone to all parts of Guatemala to supply the central area. As recently as 1917 maize was still sold by boxloads rather than by weight (McBryde 1947, p. 248).

Internal Variation

Compared with other areas of highland Guatemala—such as the Lake Atitlán basin—the central Quiché does not manifest much ecological variation. Nevertheless, the data reveal some obvious differences, and these should be mentioned for the influence they may have had on the pre-Hispanic Utatlán community.

An obvious ecological contrast exists between the mountainous zone of Chujuyup within the Chuacus Range and the central plains below on the south (the mountains in the southern part of Chichicastenango provide a similar contrast with the plains). As seen in chapter 3, this small, mountainous zone was the early habitat of the Quichés. That zone is far inferior to the central plains in economic potential and correlates with the dramatic cultural development of the Quichés after they moved from the mountains to the Utatlán plains.

The Chujuyup zone is extremely mountainous, making communication difficult. The main egress from the basin is northeast by way of a branch of the Río Negro, which cuts through the mountains in that direction. In contrast the central plains have open roads both eastward and westward and good river-valley passages in nearly all directions.

The soils of the Chujuyup area are Sacapulas type (Simmons et al. 1959), sandy and infertile, in contrast to the predominantly Quiché soils of the central plains, which are much more arable.

The few agricultural-production figures available (Stearns n.d.) suggest that productivity is higher in the central plains than in the Chujuyup area, even though the plains have been under more or less continuous cultivation. Some Chujuyup farmers rent lands on the plains because their own fields cannot support them. An exception to the general low fertility of Chujuyup lands is the Agua Caliente River valley, in the northeastern tip of the area; ownership of the valley was long disputed with San Andrés Sajcabaja, however, and may not have been part of the original Utatlán community.

Chujuyup is also poorer than the central plains in other resources. There is good timber, but stone is mostly schistose rather than limestone. The good clay and lime deposits and the lakes of the central plains are lacking. Population is sparse too, with perhaps one-half to one-third the density level of the plains.

The people of Chujuyup have a long tradition of independence and several times in this century have been allowed to establish a municipal government separate from that of Santa Cruz. They have their own small market and their own ritual dances. Significantly, the resources and population of the area have been too limited to support this independence continuously (Brunius and Whitehead n.d.).

In summary, a comparison of the ecologies of the Chujuyup and central plains zones suggests that early Quiché development in Chujuyup must have been restrained by the limited potential of the area. Once the Quichés moved onto the Utatlán plains, however, their potential for cultural development greatly expanded.

The land-use maps of the National Forestry Institute reveal additional variations within the rural zones of the Quiché area with respect to flatness of land, soil fertility, agricultural potential, and other ecological factors (IN-AFOR, *Uso potencial de tierras*). Using these maps and other data gathered in the field (Stearns n.d.; Carmack 1974), I have worked out a series of ecological "zones" for the rural area of Quiché. They may be termed flat, hilly, and mountain zones.

1. *Flat zones* have long stretches of level lands; fertile volcanic soils; high agricultural production, requiring no fallowing (*barbecho*); and large, dense populations often living in nucleated centers.

2. *Hilly zones* are characterized by a broken topography of rolling hills or eroded ridges and valleys, which are usually somewhat colder than the flat, lower zones; soils are less fertile than those of the flatlands, partly because of erosion; agricultural production is about half that of the flat zones and requires some fallowing; populations are large but not as dense or as nucleated as those of the flat zones.

3. *Mountain zones* are broken into rugged peaks, mountain skirts, steep canyons, and tiny meadows and valleys; the temperature is colder, and the soils less fertile; agriculture is not productive and requires continuous fallowing for swidden; and populations are much smaller, less dense, and more dispersed than those of the other two zones.

I emphasize that this simple classification only approximates the ecological variations in the rural part of the central Quiché area today. The fit for earlier times would be even looser. Nevertheless, it is suggestive. For example, the largest and most numerous flat zones fall within the boundaries of Santa Cruz del Quiché. Ilotenango also has relatively extensive flatlands, but soils there are not as fertile. Municipalities like Chichicastenango, Jocopilas, and Chinique have a few tiny flat zones, but mostly their country is hilly and mountainous. Patzite, Santa Lucía la Reforma, and Chiquimula are almost completely hilly or mountainous. These ecological considerations influence the economic capacities of these several communities, just as they must have influenced the rural territorial divisions (*calpules*) of the ancient Utatlán community.

It should be possible to characterize ecologically the many rural divisions, or cantons, of the central area today. No doubt cantonal differences in resources provide the basis for a subtle economic and political ranking among them. I do not have the data to define that presumed rank order, and it would probably have limited relevance anyway for the pre-Hispanic period because of the extensive outside influences now reaching even the most distant cantons. A simplified version of the scheme will be applied to the ancient rural territorial divisions in the final section of this chapter.

Demography

The present-day population of central Quiché is large and dense. As of the 1974 census there were over 100,000 inhabitants—a density of more than 90 persons per square kilometer. That is far beyond the support capacity of the land, given traditional farming techniques, and thousands of natives must engage in artisanry or migrant farming to survive (see chapter 11).

Population figures from the 1950 census are probably somewhat closer to the natural carrying capacity of the land. The census was taken before the introduction of modern agricultural methods (especially the use of fertilizers) and health practices, and most of the people were able to sustain themselves from the land. Furthermore, there is some evidence that the population had partly stabilized, or at least was growing at a modest rate compared with that of recent times. Thus in the first national census of 1893 the population of the Quiché totaled about 55,000, representing a density of approximately 37 persons per square kilometer. Another 8,000 persons were added by 1926, and by the census of 1940 there were about 78,000 people, or a density of 52 persons per square kilometer. There was little change in the next ten years; the Quiché area population crept up to about 81,000 and a density of 54 per square kilometer. That figure, however, exceeded the maximum population that the area could support by traditional farming methods. Since voluntary migration to the coast had begun, these figures are roughly consistent with the reconstruction above—that some 50,000 people might have lived in the area, an estimate based on maize-production potentials. Thus the maximum potential was probably reached and overtaxed during the first half of the twentieth century.

Though the population of Quiché may not have reached its maximum potential before the Conquest, the earliest Spanish sources suggest that it had. Alvarado (1946), the conqueror of Utatlán, observed that the land "is temporate and healthy, and populated with crowded towns; and this city is well constructed and marvelously strong, and has many large breadlands [milpas] and many peoples sheltered within it." Las Casas, one of the first Spanish priests to visit the area, reported that there were large "settlements" in Guatemala before the Conquest, some of which rivaled those in Mexico in size (1909, p. 114). He maintained that "the kingdom of Guatemala and other similar parts of that land" had towns and cities with a thousand houses (1909, pp. 157–58). Including the houses within four or five leagues around the towns, there were as many as ten thousand houses in some territories. Even settlements scattered over the mountains and valleys had ten to fifteen thousand inhabitants. Utatlán, as the largest political group in Guatemala (Las Casas 1909, p. 615), surely had more inhabitants than the ten to fifteen thousand of a more rural territory. These claims by the first visitors to Utatlán make the postulated fifty thousand population for the entire Quiché area seem reasonable.

Ideally the population of the Quiché area could be reconstructed by using census data obtained through the centuries and working back to the Conquest. I have attempted to do this, as shown in Table 4.2, using the limited census data available.

For the present discussion the most important figures in Table 4.2 are those for circa 1524 and 1550. They certainly are the most controversial. A comparison of various censuses from the mid-sixteenth century to the 1570s reveals that they were based on the same 1549 (Cerrato) census. That census was notoriously inaccurate, but it is all we have for the early years. I have added another 100 tribute payers to the Santa Cruz figures in order to take into account the indigenes who paid tribute to native chiefs rather than to the crown. Since figures from 1550 are lacking altogether for San Pedro Jocopilas, I have estimated 100 tributaries for that town. It is uncertain whether I have correctly identified San Antonio Ilotenango in the census lists (apparently called there Ocotenango). Obviously the estimated 1,000 tributaries for the central area is subject to considerable error. Nevertheless, it is somewhat supported by a 1569 census (*CDI* 1925, p. 180), which gives 1,500 tribute payers for a somewhat larger Quiché zone administered by the Dominicans (the zone was called Sacapulas in those early days). No one is quite sure what conversion factor should be used to go from tribute payers to total number of persons. In the early years it was probably higher than the factor 5 that I use, because extended families were prevalent, and chiefs were not factored in. Later the Spaniards pared down the family units, and accordingly I drop the factor to 4 for the post–sixteenth-century colonial period.

It might be objected that my estimate of a 75 to 90 percent population loss between contact and 1550 is too high. In the one case in highland Guatemala (Santiago Atitlán) where we have figures for both the pre-Conquest and the 1550 periods, there was a drop from 12,000 to about 5,000 inhabitants, a 60

Table 4.2 **The Population of Quiché Towns, 1524–1974**

Town	1524[a]	Ca. 1550[b]	Ca. 1650[c]	Ca. 1750[c]	1893[d]	1950[e]	1974[f]
				Year			
Santa Cruz (including Lemoa)	5,600–14,000	1,400 (280 tr.)	576 (144 tr.)	804 (221 tr.)	13,914	19,881	35,147
San Pedro	2,000–5,000	500 (100 tr.)	280 (70 tr.)	300 (75 tr.)	3,305	6,196	11,431
San Antonio	1,000–2,500	250 (50 tr.)	568 (142 tr.)	436 (109 tr.)	2,061	4,156	7,124
Chichicastenango	8,000–20,000	2,000 (400 tr.)	2,660 (665 tr.)	1,484 (370 tr.)	16,239	27,693	45,733
Chiquimula	3,200–8,000	800 (160 tr.)	1,640 (400 tr.?)	572 (143 tr.)	12,350	10,015	15,161
Patzite					736	1,289	2,324
Chiché					5,692	6,221	10,974
Chinique					2,780	2,963	4,353
Santa Lucía						2,912	5,895
Totals	19,800–48,000	4,950	5,720	3,600	54,690	81,400	138,140

[a]Reconstructed from the 1550 figures, estimating a 75–90 percent decline in population during the first 25 years.

[b]Based on the censuses of 1549 (AGI Guatemala, 128) and 1555 (AGC A3, 2797–40,466). Tr. = tribute payer. Each piece of cloth, chicken, or *xiquipil* of cacao is equivalent to 1 tribute payer.

[c]Based on various censuses in the Archivo General de Centroamérica. Estimates for this time period are based on 4 persons to 1 tribute payer.

[d]Based on the first Guatemalan national census. San Sebastián Lemoa is combined with Santa Cruz. Patzite, Chiché, and Chinique had become independent towns.

[e]Based on the 1950 Guatemalan national census. Santa Lucía la Reforma had become an independent town.

[f]Based on the 1974 Guatemalan national census.

percent decline (Paez Betancor and Arboleda 1965; Macleod 1973, p. 131). Veblen found evidence of a population decline of 80 to 90 percent in nearby Totonicapán (1975, pp. 333ff.). Utatlán suffered greater ravages from the Spanish conquest than either of those two towns, and so a loss of 75 to 90 percent of its inhabitants seems a reasonable estimate.

I suspect that the tribute-payer figure (280) for mid-sixteenth century Santa Cruz is significantly deficient and that the figure was actually closer to the 1,000 to 1,400 characteristic of other major highland towns. Either the data are deficient, or population loss was drastic. In either case the estimate of 48,000 based on 90 percent decline for the central Quiché at contact is the likely figure and may even be a conservative one. Las Casas claimed that major pre-Hispanic towns and their rural zones had up to 10,000 houses each. Five persons per household, undoubtedly a conservative figure for the aboriginal state, would give 50,000 people, a total very close to that estimated for Utatlán with a 90 percent population loss. It will be recalled that this total agrees with population estimates given above from other sources.

With respect to nucleation it should be noted that the population of the central Quiché today, despite its great size, is predominantly rural (see chapter 11). In 1950, when ecological conditions were largely unchanged, population was widely dispersed. Ninety percent of the inhabitants lived in the rural area. Population had been even more predominantly rural in the preceding centuries, according to the sources (see chapter 10). This dispersed settlement pattern can be correlated with the agrarian nature of the Quiché economy and the relative unimportance of craftsmanship. It will be argued below that the pre-Hispanic population was considerably more nucleated.

SUMMARY

There is a good fit between the natives' view of their environment, as revealed by the chronicles, and the view in the ethnographic and geographic studies of the area in recent times. Nevertheless, some interesting differences appear in the data. Both the similarities and the differences deserve comment.

The apparent failure of the ancient Quichés to view the central area as a closed, clearly bounded unit was consistent with the rather open topography that characterizes the area. The boundaries of the Utatlán community were arbitrary at least in part, only the northern and southern mountain ranges providing natural boundaries.

The mountains, plains, forests, and fertile maize fields that define the central area today were clearly perceived by the Quichés. They also, however, described animal life that must have been far more abundant and important than it is today. The cacophony of howling jaguars, mountain lions, and coyotes and of screaming parakeets, bluejays, and eagles has been largely silenced. Deer no longer roam the forests and canyons as they once did, and the multitudinous snakes have been reduced to but a few seen on rare occasions. Obviously, too, the forests have been drastically reduced in size and density. This change in ecology has greatly altered Quiché culture, which is perhaps most dramatically revealed by the disintegration of the ancient totemic view of the world (though it has not been entirely lost; see Tax 1947, pp. 471ff.).

It is clear that many of the natural resources and simple crafts through which they were exploited anciently were abandoned in the years following the Conquest. The highly select hand-loom weaving and simple pottery making found today in the Quiché area scarcely give an idea of the wide variety of techniques practiced anciently. Gone are mat-making, woodcarving, leatherworking, hunting, trapping, skinning, feather-plucking, and other crafts. The ancient elite crafts—metallurgy, stone carving, gourd decorating, and ornate pottery making—have disappeared without a trace.The equivalents of these crafts are now practiced exclusively in the towns, either by Latins or by indigenes acculturated to Latin ways.

Only milpa horticulture has persisted in its basic form as an important production process. In recent years it too has begun to change radically as chemical fertilizers, new seed varieties, insecticides, and other modern practices are introduced. Until recently milpa techniques were similar to those described in the chronicles. The ancient solar calendar still matches up well with the milpa cycle recorded by modern ethnographers. Then, as today, it began in March, when the Quiché farmers planted a fast-maturing maize and prepared to plant the regular maize crop. The main planting was (and is) in May, when the rains began. The two-to-three-week break in the rains in July or August, now called *canícula* ("dog days"), seems to have corresponded to the ancient Liquinca periods, the time of major ritual celebrations (Carmack 1973, p. 292). Similarly, the end of the rainy season corresponded to Tz'iquin K'ij, also a period of ritual celebration in ancient times; today it corresponds with the All Saints' Day celebration. The natives of Quiché still associate December (Cakam in the ancient calendar) with heat and colors, as well as with the harvest season. Finally, the first months of the modern year are the time for burning the fields and planting in the mountainous zones, just as they were anciently.

Ethnographic studies of milpa horticulture reveal that *barbecho* cultivation involves no fallowing on the plains, where it provides yields greater than can be obtained from swidden cultivation in canyons or on mountain slopes. Except for some possible references in the solar calendar, the ancient Quichés did not differentiate the two forms of milpa cultivation in their writings.

Traditional foods of the modern Quiché natives are almost identical to those described in the ancient sources. Maize in the form of a tamale was the staple, and was eaten with boiled beans, squashes, and chili sauce. *Atol* (maize gruel) was the usual drink; on ritual occasions it was combined with cacao and other spices. The common people of today eat little meat, as was the case anciently. The meat now comes from domesticated pigs and cattle, while anciently it came mostly from wild game. Latin-produced distilled liquor and moonshine made from sugarcane have replaced the fermented maize, maguey, and fruit drinks of the ancient Quichés. It is apparent that drinking habits today are closely linked with the natives' marginal position in society and are probably radically different from those of aboriginal times.

Modern studies reveal a present-day market system that is more extensive and important than that suggested for the ancient Quichés in the chronicles. Today the market is based mostly on the agricultural surpluses of the area, which are exchanged for important resources and goods from outside (grinding stones, furniture, and so on). Anciently food surpluses were perhaps largely taken in tributes by the town elites, but a highly varied craftsmanship must have provided a strong basis for market exchanges. Though information on the subject in the chronicles is scarce, present-day patterns indicate that marketing was an ancient and important activity in the Quiché area. Long-distance traveling was involved, too, as shown by the traditional merchant "class" of Chichicastenango.

The ancient Quichés certainly were aware of ecological differences in the mountainous and the plains zones of their territory, but they stressed aspects different from what one might expect. Rather than emphasizing the relative economic importance of the two zones, as is commonly done today, the Quichés associated the plains with power and secular work and the mountains with magic and sacred ritual. The surprisingly few references to the central plains in the chronicles mostly have to do with the mortar-and-stone towns. In contrast, the ritually important mountains and totemic animals that abounded there were topics of much commentary by the Quichés. It is unlikely that the Quichés were unaware of the importance of the plains, the center of their political system, but the mountains, as their early home, were more "magical" and thus more interesting to talk about.

The ancient Quichés considered ecological differences among their rural territorial divisions (*calpules*) to be highly significant, as revealed by the names of the divisions, which often reflected key ecological factors. Most of the some forty ancient *calpules* can be identified with modern rural cantons and hamlets, and their ecologies can be observed at first hand. Some understanding of the variations among *calpules* can be gained from Table 4.3. The table contains a reconstruction of ancient *calpul* ecologies based on land documents, INAFOR land-use maps, ethnographic observations, and demographic features taken from figures provided by the 1950 national census. The estimates are rough and subject to error. It was especially difficult to

Table 4.3. **Ecological and Population Data for the Quiché** *Calpules*

Group	Calpul	Ecological Zone	Total Population	Population Density per Square Kilometer
Tamub	Amak' Tam	Mountain; dispersed population	1,010	85
	Tzutuja	Mountain, with some hilly	450	20
	Sak K'inom	Hilly south, some mountain north; nucleated population south	1,500	71
	Ch'alibalaj	Hilly, mixed with mountain	720	25
	Sakmolob	Hilly north, mixed mountain south; some nucleation north	1,890	59
	Nacxit	Flat, with good productivity; dispersed population	1,690	99
	Amak' Mes	Hilly, with some mountain; dispersed population	580	72
	Warabal K'alel	Mountain, with some hilly; dispersed population	1,110	74
	K'ak'alaj	Hilly mixed with mountain; some nucleation	1,150	22
	Pach'alib	Mountain, mixed with hilly; dispersed population	2,000	84
	Tz'oloche	Mountain mixed with hilly areas; some nucleation of population	7,000	150
Ilocab	Uquin	Mountain; dispersed population	2,760	32
	Chuwisic'a	Hilly; dispersed population	590	53
	Palopoj	Some flat, mostly hilly; some nucleation	880	110
	Chiaj	Hilly; some nucleation	1,130	103
	Chacalté	Hilly north, mountain south; dispersed population	610	86
Nijaib	Southwest	Mountain; dispersed population	645	81
	Northeast	Mountain; dispersed population	300	37

determine total areas of the various *calpules*, and this uncertainty naturally affects the reconstructed population sizes and densities. The rural divisions are listed by their ancient group and individual names.

Most of the ancient territories were either hilly or mountainous, and, of course, this is true of the central area today. A few *calpules* dominated the flatlands, and they were near important towns (as is the case today). The political implications of this variation will be discussed in chapter 6.

Table 4.3. *Continued*

Group	Calpul	Ecological Zone	Total Population	Population Density per Square Kilometer
Nima Quiché	Chulumal	Flat, good agriculture; some hilly; dispersed population	1,000	200
	Ruc'abala (Walic) Tz'iquín	Hilly; dispersed population	500	125
	Sakiya'	Hilly north, mountain south; some nucleation of population north	770	72
	Xojbaquiej	Mixed hilly and mountain; dispersed population	940	117
	Uwila	Flat, some hilly, mountain south; nucleated population north	1,850	116
	Tinamit	Flat, becomes hilly south; nucleated population	4,100	255
	Pachiqui	Flat, becomes hilly north and west; nucleated population, dispersed north	780	130
	Chobolo	Hilly; dispersed population	40	13
	C'akolquiej	Hilly; dispersed population	880	220
	Cabrakan	Hilly; some nucleation of population east	1,230	50
	C'ulchip	Hilly, now badly eroded; dispersed population	870	44
	Chinique	Flat, with hilly margins and surrounding mountain; central nucleation but dispersed outside	1,100	50
	Tz'ucaj	Hilly, with valley; dispersed population	160	25
	Meba Q'uisic'	Mountain north, hilly south; dispersed population	1,520	253
	Chujuyup	Hilly, surrounded by mountain; central nucleation of population	2,080	55
	Tucurub	Hilly; dispersed except for town nucleation	550	183
	Raxaja	Mountain with small hilly area; dispersed population	50	25
	Chwijunajpu	Mountain; ?	?	?

My reconstruction of population densities for the different *calpules* is probably too high, no doubt because I have reconstructed the ancient territories smaller than they actually were. Nevertheless, the error probably applies generally to the *calpules*, and the figures should indicate *relative* densities. The figures, though approximate, suggest that the *calpules* varied widely in the number and density of people who could be supported by the land. They range from several thousand to fewer than one hundred persons, and density ratios vary as much as ten to one. Even today former Nima Quiché territories produce 83,000 quintals of maize annually, compared with 21,000 quintals produced by former Tamub and 23,000 produced by former Ilocab territories. The Quiché lands produce about 9 quintals a manzana, while the Tamub and Ilocab lands produce only 5 and 3 quintals respectively. Such estimates, gross though they may be, permit us to appreciate the strategic importance that control over different rural zones of the central area might have had for ancient political divisions.

Our information on aboriginal Quiché demography is disappointing. The Quichés themselves did not give us exact figures for the most part, though they considered their population to be large. That may be significant, since they were acquainted with other truly populous groups, such as the Aztecs and Gulf Coast merchant towns. The first Spaniards who went to the area confirmed the natives' view, comparing the Quiché area with central Mexico in population size and density. Several lines of evidence converge to suggest an aboriginal population of at least fifty thousand for the central area and a density of more than forty persons per square kilometer. Better documentary sources will be needed, however, before this estimate can be stated with assurance.

The strongly rural character of settlements in the Quiché until recent times would seem to argue against much pre-Hispanic nucleation; nevertheless, the post-Conquest situation may be misleading in this regard. Alvarado specifically stated that there was a large population *within* Utatlán at the time of the Conquest, and Las Casas spoke of towns with nucleated populations of a thousand households (1909, p. 157). Furthermore, there is some evidence that other towns outside Quiché, such as Iximché, Atitlán, and Xeluju, perhaps had nuclear populations of several thousand (MacLeod 1973; Carmack 1968; Guillemin 1967). It would be surprising if Utatlán, the greatest town of the highlands, turned out to have been smaller. Archaeological remains in the area point to the urban character of Utatlán, indicating that at least four towns were compacted together (see chapter 8). It will also be documented later (chapter 6) that large numbers of craftsmen, merchants, warriors, and officials lived at nuclear Utatlán.

As with total population for the area, more archival and archaeological research is needed before the urban population of the Utatlán towns can be estimated with accuracy. I would not be surprised, however, if it were found that the four nuclear Utatlán towns together had a population of ten to twenty thousand and that the surrounding rural zones had the approximately fifty thousand people estimated above.

The early Chujuyup homeland of the Quiché forefathers. The twin-peaked Mount Mamaj can be seen in the distance. (*Unless otherwise noted, all photographs were taken by the author.*)

The two mountain ridges west of Chujuyup on which the Ilocab and Tamub groups established their main settlements.

Río Joronalaja, which separated the Tamubs from the Caweks in early times.

The Amak' Tam settlement, perched on top of a heavily cultivated ridge in Canton Cruz Che, Santa Cruz del Quiché.

The largest mound at the Amak' Tam site, with a milpa planted in the ancient plaza.

The site of the ancient Uquin C'at settlement, now a boundary marker between San Pedro Jocopilas and San Bartolomé Jocotenango.

The crest of the mountains dividing the Quiché plains and Chujuyup. The wooded peak is the site of ancient Patojil.

Badly disturbed archaeological remains of the Patojil site.

The northern side of Mount Jakawitz (Chitinamit), partly cleared of pine trees.

Mounds at the Chitinamit site, which, along with the ancient court, are now in cultivation.

The Quiché plains seen from the Chuacus Mountains on the north. The continental divide can be seen in the distance.

The rolling plains east of Pakaman, extending in the direction of Chichicastenango.

The plains just east of Utatlán. The elevated hill in the background is the Resguardo (Atalaya) site. *Photograph by Dwight T. Wallace.*

The deep canyons surrounding the Utatlán plateau. Utatlán can be seen as a heavily forested feature on the right.

5
HISTORY

It will be useful to outline the major sociopolitical events that took place in the Utatlán community and to specify as accurately as possible their chronology. Such history is valuable per se and also provides data for the reconstruction of Quiché cultural development in the chapters to follow.

Quiché history has been the subject of considerable interest (see chapter 2). Disagreements among authors on important historical matters abound, and it is tempting to discuss those issues in detail. I shall resist that temptation, however. My focus will be on those historical events most closely tied to the initiation of social and symbolic structural features at Utatlán. I attempted to give only enough historical context to understand those features, rather than a detailed account of the events themselves. In several instances I provided my own interpretation of complex historical issues, but I do not discuss the way these interpretations might relate to the arguments of others. Some discussion of that kind will be given in the conclusions to the book.

Before describing the events of Quiché history, I will summarize the problems of chronology related to that history. The chronology worked out below provides the framework for the remainder of the chapter.

CHRONOLOGY

Unfortunately, our sources lack absolute dates for the major events that took place in the Utatlán community. A few scattered 260-day calendar dates are recorded in the chronicles, such as the day on which the Spaniards arrived in Guatemala. Without a zero reference point, however, these dates are chronologically useless.

Only *The Annals of the Cakchiquels* describe the use of a long-count system with a zero point. The zero point can be correlated with an internal dispute that occurred at Iximché in 1493 and so is useful for dating events very late in Quiché history (Recinos 1950, pp. 32–37). The few dates mentioned in the

Annals for events taking place at Utatlán before the 1493 zero point provide no absolute chronology because elapsed time is not given. The Cakchiquel long count differs from the Classic Maya long count in that the Cakchiquel Tun (called Juna' in Cakchiquel) had a value of 400 rather than 360 days.

Undoubtedly the Quichés at Utatlán used a long-count dating system similar to that of the Cakchiquels. Analogy with the Cakchiquel system makes it probable that it was vigesimal. The sources suggest that the day units were ones (*k'ij*), twenties (*winak*), four hundreds (*junab*), and eight thousands (*may*). Zorita, a sixteenth-century judge in Guatemala, claimed to have seen a Quiché codex at Utatlán with a history stretching back eight hundred years. Apparently the Quiché long-count system was lost with the destruction of such books. The Cakchiquels, who were, perhaps, slightly more secular in their outlook than the Quichés of Utatlán, revived the system after the Conquest.

One secondary Quiché chronicle, a Nijaib *tíitulo*, states without explanation that some of the earliest Quiché conquests originating in Utatlán took place in 1300 (Recinos 1957, p. 76). It is also stated there that a much later series of conquests ended in 1501. In another Nijaib *título* (Recinos 1957, p. 84) it is claimed that Moctezuma warned the Quichés of the coming of the Spaniards in the year 1512. We do not know the basis for such dates, but they were probably post hoc projections made after the Conquest. As we shall see below, the 1300 date for Utatlán is too early.

An ethnohistorically based chronology for the Utatlán community is possible through a reconstruction of the genealogical and political successions recorded in the major chronicles. A single term, *le*, is often used to refer both to generations and to political successions, and this practice has caused problems in chronological reconstruction. Generation and political succession did not correspond to one another, since not only sons but also brothers and other kinsmen succeeded rulers in office. Thus care must be taken to distinguish between references to one and the other. Further, contradictions exist among the documents with respect to generations and political successions. I am convinced that some of the early Quiché chroniclers themselves sometimes contradicted themselves in the same chronicle. Nevertheless, a careful comparative study of the sources reveals that such contradictions are fewer than appear on the surface. Of course, it must also be remembered that alteration of genealogy for political purposes is a general phenomenon in traditional societies like that of Utatlán.

I have relied primarily on generation data for my chronological reconstruction. Basing my estimates on data for the Aztecs and other traditional peoples, I use an average of twenty-five years for each generation (compare Wauchope's twenty years [1949]). The use of an average value, taken with the above-mentioned contradictions, means that any ethnohistorically based

Table 5.1. **Dynastic Generations, 1225–1524**

Generations	Rulers	Dates	Events
1	Balam Quitze	1225–50	Migrates from east
2	C'oc'oja	1250–75	
3	E, Tz'iquin	1275–1300	Conquers Rabinal area
4	Ajcan	1300–25	
5	C'ocaib	1325–50	Returns to east
6	C'onache	1350–75	Rules at Pismachi
7	C'otuja	1375–1400	Killed while living at Pismachi
8	K'ucumatz	1400–25	Founds K'umarcaaj
9	Q'uik'ab	1425–75	Lives long life at K'umarcaaj
10	Eight C'aam	1475–1500	Cakchiquels revolt
11	Three Quej	1500–24	Spaniards arrive at K'umarcaaj

chronology is subject to error. I do not think the errors are greater than plus or minus fifty years, however, and these variations are probably mostly concentrated in the pre-Utatlán phase of Quiché history.

Of special importance for Utatlán chronology is the original Quiché text of the *Título Totonicapán* (n.d.). It contains the most nearly complete dynastic genealogy of all the Quiché chronicles. New information found there required that I add another generation to my earlier reconstruction of ten generations for the leading Quiché lineage of Utatlán (Carmack 1966). K'ucumatz is listed as the son of C'otuja and the father of Q'uik'ab. Though C'otuja is also called K'ucumatz, I have nevertheless added an extra generation. I warn that the authors of the *título* may have been confused and that these two rulers may have been one person, as I have argued earlier (1968).

Working back from Three Quej, the ruler at the time of the Conquest in 1524, to the founding generation of Balam Quitze, we arrive at a date of about 1225 for the beginning of the Quiché ruling line of Utatlán. This includes a fifty-year generation period for Q'uik'ab, the most famous Quiché ruler of Utatlán. Q'uik'ab apparently lived a very long life. My estimate may be conservative, partly because of the Quichés' tendency to foreshorten genealogies in the distant past, and I would not object to moving the founding date back to 1200. This reconstruction would date the settling of Pismachi in the fifth generation at about 1325. K'umarcaaj was founded during the eighth generation, in about 1400. Evidence from the *Título Tamub* suggests that the companion site of Utatlán, called Pilocab (Chisalin), was founded around the same time as K'umarcaaj. Thus the Utatlán community, with its several centers, had an occupation of less than two hundred years, and the Quiché political dynasty a reign of some three hundred years.

Corroboration of these reconstructed dates comes from cross ties with the more chronologically oriented *Annals*. The ninth-generation Quiché ruler, Q'uik'ab, whom I date at about 1475, had died a few years before 1493, when the Cakchiquels initiated their long-count dating system. The famous Quiché ruler C'otuja, who reigned about 1375–1400 according to the above reconstruction, was a contemporary of Cakchiquel rulers who can be dated to about 1385 in the Cakchiquel genealogy (Wauchope 1949). It might be noted in this context that the founding of the Cakchiquel sites around Uwila (Chichicastenango) and Iximché (Tecpán) would date to 1450 and 1470, respectively, according to this reconstruction.

A reconstruction of Quiché chronology based on dynastic generations (see discussion below) appears in Table 5.1. This reconstructed chronology will be used for the summary to be given of the most important sociopolitical events occurring in the Utatlán community.

PRE-UTATLÁN HISTORY

Some of the major historical events which took place while the Quiché forefathers lived in the Chujuyup Mountains will first be summarized. The origin of the Quiché forefathers has already been discussed (see Figs. 3.5 to 3.7).

The precise chronology of events which followed upon the arrival of the Quiché forefathers from the Gulf Coast cannot be worked out from the sources; apparently the people who wrote the chronicles did not have that information themselves. Thus the order of events described below may not be precise.

The subjugation of the native peoples was a major preoccupation of the Quiché forefathers. The *Título Totonicapán* states that two main battles occurred before the founding of Pismachi, one at Jakawitz and the other at places in the Quiché basin called Chiq'uix and Chich'at. The *Popol Vuh* refers only to the battle at Jakawitz. The Zapotitlán *título* states that the Utatlán area was explored and conquered first, and later the Rabinal area. The *Annals* present the conquest of the native peoples as a series of battles and political arrangements. According to that source, many peoples submitted peacefully to the Quiché warriors, offering to be wife givers and tribute-paying vassals (*ikan*).

The battle for Jakawitz was decisive, according to Quiché historical tradition. As recorded in the *Popol Vuh* and the *Título Totonicapán*, the fighting was associated with the story of the maidens tempting the forefathers at the bathing place. It is impossible to know what historical facts, if any, are enclosed in that myth, though the location where the events supposedly took place is a hot spring (Chimik'ina') north of Chujuyup.

The description of the battle itself is wrapped in mythic elements. For example, while the native warriors slept outside Jakawitz before the fighting began, the Quichés used magic to strip them of their eyebrows and whiskers, as well as the metal of their pendants, headdresses, and staffs. Similarly incredible was the ease with which the Quichés deceived their enemies with wooden dolls placed along the walls of Jakawitz. And when the Quichés released bees and wasps from their gourd containers, they miraculously headed straight for the enemy warriors, who were completely overcome by them.

Despite the mythic elements the battle at Jakawitz is clearly historical. It took place at the Quiché confederacy center, where the Quichés had gathered for protection. We are told how defensive walls and a moat were built in anticipation of the battle. Upon arriving, the enemy warriors came to a place below the site called Xetinamit, today a hamlet still known by that name. The specific names of the native peoples involved are given— Rotzjayib, Uxab, Q'uibaja, Bacaj, Quebatzunja—as are the weapons they brought—*ch'ab*, *pocob*, *cawutal* ("bow and arrows, shield, adornments")— and the day on which they attacked, *Cawok* (Rain). We are informed that Quiché women also participated in the fighting and that the weapons used, in addition to the magical wasps and bees, were *atlatls*, hatchets, and wooden clubs. The outcome of the fighting is clearly reported: the native peoples were humiliated, uncountable numbers of them died, and those who survived submitted to tribute obligations (*patan*). This victory by the first fathers and mothers (*chuch*, *kajaw*) of the Quichés was remembered years later with much joy, for it symbolized the conquest of "all the native peoples."

The Cakchiquels, as the main military arm of the Quichés down in the Quiché basin, briefly described several other encounters with native peoples. Apparently very early the Quichés conquered the peoples living along the southeastern face of the mountain divide above Jakawitz. At places like Ximbaxuc (now a hamlet of Chinique), Paoj (Aguacate, a hamlet of Santa Cruz), and Cakjay (Sajcabaja?) they subdued the native people who hunted and gathered the products of the forest in that area. The indigenes were patrons of the deer (*ajquej*), and lived in deerskin houses (*quejnay*). They became Quiché vassals (*ikan*), giving wives and paying such tribute items as deer, honey, and maguey-twine products (sandals, traps, and nets). The C'oyoi lineage of the Quichés was created from this vassal relationship. In this general area too, the Quichés met a native lord named Tzutuja, who governed a people living around present-day Chinique. Tzutuja surrendered to the Quichés, pleading not to be killed, and, indeed, his life was spared. He was accepted into the Q'uiché lineage as a substitute (*uc'axel*) for the Iq'ui Balam sublineage, which had died out.

Tzutuja fought with the Quichés in a major battle against the native peoples of C'analakam and Tibilcat in the mountains south of present Chichicastenango (Chich'at, Chiq'uix?). The *Título Totonicapán* (n.d.) informs us that the fighting started when two native hunters discovered the remains of butchered deer in their territory. They reported it to their leaders, and in the fighting that followed, the Quiché peoples living in the area were forced to send messengers to Jakawitz asking for help. Warriors were dispatched from Jakawitz, and their Cakchiquel vassals were also brought in. The main battle took place at Mount Mukbalsib, where most of the enemy peoples were killed. Two of them escaped, we are told (Villacorta 1934, p. 216), one of them fleeing to Jakawitz. He was taken in and fed, and later a Cakchiquel lineage was created out of the remnants of this people (the Tibilcats).

The conquest of the Rabinal basin by the Quichés was said to have occurred as follows:

> They fought at night; they would go at night to kill the enemy people who were scattered and disorganized. To frighten them they would take on the form of demon tigers and lions, flying at night in the air, giving off fire from their mouths, and in this way did them great damage. In this manner they were frightened, and the land of Rabinal was subjected. And they made them understand that they were the sons of Tzakol Bitol, . . . [and later] a fortified town was established in Rabinal. [Recinos 1953, p. 249]

Cakchiquel warriors participated in the fighting against the native peoples in this area, who, we are told, were Pokomams. We are also informed that the rulers of the Cubulco area, the Ikomak'i, fell under Quiché control during this early period. The Tzotzil lineage of the Cakchiquels derived from the Ikomak'i peoples.

There must have been many more important battles and other kinds of hostile encounters, but our sources tell us only of these few. Nevertheless, the pattern is clear, and the ultimate outcome appears invariably to have favored the new lords from the east over the native peoples.

After the death of the forefathers who had come from the Gulf Coast, it was decided that ambassadors should return for a visit with Nacxit, the "great lord and judge of many kingdoms." Apparently it was felt that a fresh Epi-Toltec legitimation was needed because of the deaths of the original warlords. Toltec affiliation was necessary to maintain the position of political superiority the leading lineages of the confederacy had assumed. Further, the confederacy had become complex, with internal lineage specialization and many vassals allied in various ways. The authority structure needed to be expanded, and the experienced state-building Toltecs (probably Gulf Coast Epi-Toltecs or Mayapán rulers by this time) were the most likely source for new offices, titles, and insignia.

Representatives from the three main lineages of the confederacy were sent. Among them were C'ocaib and C'ocawib, direct descendants of the elder Q'uiche lineage father, Balam Quitze. According to the *Título Totonica-pán*, C'ocaib took an eastern route, and C'ocawib a western route. Possibly C'ocaib descended along the course of the Usumacinta River, while C'ocawib traveled the Grijalva River valley. For some reason C'ocawib could not find the lake of their original homeland, and returned to Jakawitz a failure. There he impregnated C'ocaib's wife, Tzipitawar (Without Water). The Tamubs (Recinos 1957, p. 44) claimed that she was from their lineage. When C'ocaib finally returned to Jakawitz and asked his wife to whom the child belonged, he was told that it was his. C'ocaib was pleased and named the child Balam C'onache (Jaguar, Chief in My Likeness). He vowed that the child would receive his office and authority.

C'ocaib had been successful in his visit to the east and brought back many new symbols of state (*retal ajawarem*). Most important among these was the office of *ajpop* ("chief"), to be supported by the *ajpop c'amja* ("assistant chief") and many other high offices (see chapter 6 for their names). The legitimacy of these offices was backed by a host of sacred Epi-Toltec icons: feathered canopies, bone flutes, black and yellow mineral stones, lion and jaguar hooves, and others. C'ocaib was made the *ajpop* and his brother, C'ocawib, became *ajpop c'amja*. The other offices were also assumed by lords of the three lineages at Jakawitz. Not long afterward, when Balam C'onaché, the son of C'ocaib, acceded to his father's office, the Quichés moved their town down to the plains at Pismachi.

Though the chronicles differ considerably on the early genealogy of the main Quiché lineages, it is possible to reconstruct at least the line which gave rise to the *ajpops* of Utatlán. An attempt will be made also to estimate from the lineage genealogy the time the Quiché forefathers spent in the Chujuyup area.

The *Popol Vuh* states that Balam Quitze, one of the forefathers who came from the east, was succeeded by his sons C'oacaib and C'ocawib, the lords who returned to the east. The *Totonicapán* and *Zapotitlán títulos*, however, clarify for us that there were three generations of descendants between Balam Quitze and C'ocaib. The sons of Balam Quitze were C'oc'oja and C'oraxonamak', who in turn engendered E and Tz'iquín. E engendered Ajcan, who fathered C'ocaib and C'ocawib. These two brothers were the first *ajpop* and *ajpop c'amja*. As mentioned above, C'ocawib engendered C'onache through an adulterous union, and C'onache became perhaps the first *ajpop* at Pismachi. C'ocaib had five legitimate sons, Quejnay, C'oyoi, Xmayquej, Cakamal, Rochoc'oy. Apparently all of them lived at Pismachi at least part of their lives.

The above reconstruction provides four generations of Q'uiche lineage

Table 5.2. **Pre-Utatlán Genealogies of the Cawek Q'uiche and Tamub Lineages**

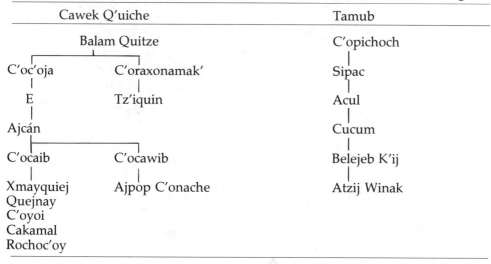

Cawek Q'uiche		Tamub
Balam Quitze		C'opichoch
C'oc'oja	C'oraxonamak'	Sipac
E	Tz'iquin	Acul
Ajcán		Cucum
C'ocaib	C'ocawib	Belejeb K'ij
Xmayquiej Quejnay C'oyoi Cakamal Rochoc'oy	Ajpop C'onache	Atzij Winak

heads subsequent to the original fathers and before the founding of Pismachi on the plains. At twenty-five years for each generation this represents approximately 100 to 125 years of residence in the Chujuyup Mountains. That is consistent with statements in the chronicles that the Quichés spent "several twenty-year periods" at Jakawitz.

The genealogy of the ruling line within the Tamub lineage confirms the accuracy of the Quiché successions reconstructed above. According to one of the Tamub *títulos* (Recinos 1957, pp. 28ff.), the lords who returned to the east were five generations removed from the founding fathers. From first to fifth generation the line was as follows: C'opichoch, Sipac, Acul, Cucum, and Belejeb K'ij. All these men were said to have lived in the "bushes and canyons" (*patucan, paciwan*), before the founding of Utatlán. Belejeb K'ij and Aj Walikom, the Tamub ambassadors to the east, are reported to have been contemporaries with C'ocaib, and to have been born in the same bushes and canyons. It is after their return that the Tamubs finally settled "here at Quiché," on the Utatlán plateau.

The complete pre-Utatlán genealogies of the two lineages is shown in Table 5.2.

THE FOUNDING OF THE UTATLÁN TOWNS

The chronicles describe a long migration that the Quichés supposedly took when they left their former habitation zone in the mountains of Chujuyup

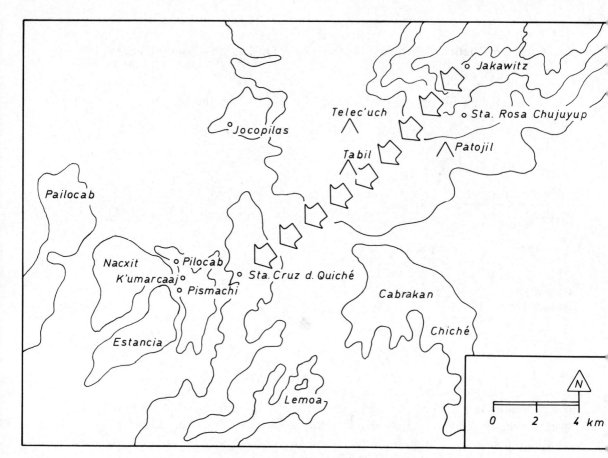

Fig. 5.1.   The transfer of the Quichés from Chujuyup to the Utatlán area. Based on
IGN, map, 1:250,000.

(with its capital at Jakawitz), going from place to place until they settled at
Pismachi (Fig. 5.1). Most of the stopping places mentioned are in the rural
zones surrounding Utatlán, and should be interpreted as settlements that
came under Quiché domination. The "migrations" appear to be descriptive
of the kinds of relations the Quichés established with the native peoples.
There are references to intermarriage, adoration of local deities, lineage
adoption, construction of fortified buildings, presentation of sacred icons,
and so on. The *Título Tamub* makes the important observation that K'umarcaaj was one of the places that early became subject to the Quichés. There, we
are told, the two lineages Cawek and Nijaib, which had formerly been united
in one big house (lineage house) at Patojil, were now divided into two

separate big houses. This was done at an elevated site called Q'uilak and Puquimulu.

It was at a place called Pismachi (Beard) that the Quichés built their defensive town. We are not told why that particular place was selected, though the *Título Totonicapán* associates it with a third round of warfare (the other two having been at Jakawitz and Chiq'uix-Chich'at). The *Título Tamub* refers to the place as Pismachi C'ajol (Bearded Son) and states that the rattlesnake and the yellow-mouth snake were its totems (*naguales*). The same document states that the messengers who returned to the east for new symbols of power and government were not born at Pismachi but lived there after their return. The other sources are vague on this point, though they are all in agreement that Pismachi was founded after the trip to the east (probably in the early years of the fourteenth century).

In Pismachi all the sacred symbols from the east were displayed: the canopies, deer hooves, jaguar claws, small chairs and benches, drums, rattles, feathers of rare birds (quetzals, herons, parrots). The new offices such as *ajpop, ajpop c'amja, k'alel,* and *atzij winak,* were bestowed in elaborate ceremony at Pismachi. The old, sacred rituals were initiated—such as waiting for the coming of the great star Venus (Ik'ok'ij), which precedes the sun. They danced the monkey, macaw, and shield dances and began great drinking and gift-giving festivities as part of marriage exchanges. According to a document which Fuentes y Guzmán (1932–33, 7:39lff.) had in his possession, the Quichés also "saw three suns in one day" at Pismachi. Without further information it is difficult even to speculate on the meaning of this astronomic event.

For the Quichés the founding of the town and the celebration of those important rituals marked the beginning of their "kingdom" (*ajawarem*). We are told in the *Título Tamub* (1957) that before that time they were known as "the sons of the eagle, sons of the dawn" (*walic cot, walic sak*) but that that name was lost when they became a kingdom. The three confederate groups, the Nima Quichés, the Tamubs, and the Ilocabs, were settled in the same town at Pismachi. C'onache, the sixth-generation ruler of the leading Nima Quiché lineage, was recognized by all three groups as their *ajpop*. However, it was his cousin once removed (his father's brother's son's son), C'otuja, who became the first powerful *ajpop* at Pismachi.

Pismachi soon became rife with conflict between the resident lineages and the confederate units. One issue must have been the legitimacy of the ruler, C'onache. As described earlier, C'onache was an illegitimate son of C'ocaib, the first Quiché *ajpop*. There must have been conflict over this, and, even though the details are not given, C'onache's line was dropped to second place: it became the Istayul lineage with rights to the *ajpop c'amja* office. C'ocaib's legitimate son Xmayquej perhaps won the rights to the *ajpop* office, and later his son took that office at Pismachi. Since there were four other eligible sons, not to mention the other lineages vying for power, the political struggle for office must have been intense.

There were other controversial issues at Pismachi: who had the right to marry whom, who was to share wealth and rank, and so on. Apparently because of these conflicts the Ilocabs left Pismachi under the leadership of the lord Chibul Cwi (Recinos 1957, p. 44). He settled them at a place called Mukwitz Chilocab (Burial Mountain of the Ilocabs, as the place became known later). For the same reason, perhaps, the Nima Quichés were dispersing too. They began occupying K'umarcaaj (Place of Old Reeds), Panq'uib (Dry Place), and Panpacay (Place of the Palm) on the plains adjacent to Pismachi.

During the time of K'ucumatz the Quichés moved their political center to K'umarcaaj, where their vassals built a new town. Apparently the Tamubs remained as the sole inhabitants of Pismachi. That the Quichés almost immediately divided their three lineages into nine and later twenty-four confirms their claim that conflict between the different groups led them to make the move. By about 1400, K'umarcaaj had been added to Pismachi and Mukwitz as part of the growing community of Quiché. Apparently, Panq'uib and Panpacay were smaller appendages to those three towns.

THE REIGN OF C'OTUJA AND K'UCUMATZ

It is difficult to distinguish between the events that occurred during the life of C'otuja and those in the time of K'ucumatz. As noted above, there is confusion in the documents about whether they were one or two rulers. The *Título Totonicapán* is the only chronicle to distinguish them, and even it refers to the first ruler as both C'otuja and K'ucumatz. The distinctions made between them below are based primarily on chronological grounds, and thus should be viewed as tentative for now.

C'otuja and K'ucumatz greatly expanded the Quiché kingdom centered first at Pismachi and then at K'umarcaaj. An early rival to their expansion plans was Tepew, "Lord of the Cauke" (Villacorta 1934, p. 218). I believe that Tepew was K'ucumatz (Carmack 1965; Fig. 5.2) and that Tepew's town, Custum Chixnal, was Pismachi. All the peoples paid tribute to Tepew, we are told by the Cakchiquels. The Xajil Cakchiquel lords, Two Noj and Two Batz, were tribute collectors for him among the Tzutujils of Lake Atitlán. As humble servants they entered his presence and dwelled in his town. They also participated in councils with the Ikomak'i of Cubulco, presumably allies of Tepew. The *Annals* tell a delightful story about these two tribute collectors, who took wives from among the Tzutujils and then worried that it would anger Tepew. They hid in a cave, and were coaxed out only after their kinsmen assured them that messengers would be sent to Tepew to assuage his anger. Tepew received them joyously.

These two Cakchiquel lords, as allies of C'otuja-K'ucumatz at Pismachi, took on the Quiché offices of *ajpop* and *ajpop c'amja* for the Xajil lineage. They fought in the Quiché armies, and as those armies were increasingly successful, their prestige among the Quichés grew. The Cakchiquels and Quichés of Pismachi began exchanging wives. The Cakchiquels were definitely the inferiors in the exchange, becoming the "younger brothers" of the Quichés. In great celebrations they would carry their women and liquor to Pismachi, where the marriages were consummated (Recinos 1957, pp. 132ff., 160).

If I am correct in identifying C'otuja-K'ucumatz with the Acxopil mentioned in documents used by Fuentes y Guzmán (Carmack 1968), then it would seem that C'otuja made his son Xiutemal ruler over the Cakchiquels at this time. Another son, Acxicuah, was given charge of the Tzutujils. Unfortunately, these are Nahua names, and it has not been possible to equate them with any Quiché or Cakchiquel rulers mentioned in the native chronicles.

The main Cakchiquel political center during this early period was Mukbalsib Bitol Amak' (Place of Smoky Mist, the Created Settlement), a site in southwestern Chichicastenango.

C'otuja seems to have used marriage effectively for political purposes. He initiated a marriage alliance with the Tzutujils of Malaj (near present-day Tolimán), taking the ruler's daughter Xlem as his wife. The Malaj Tzutujils became his vassals, some of them being his own maternal offspring (*oliaj*). Like the Cakchiquels they were given Quiché political titles and became warriors for C'otuja. Most of the coastal peoples were forced into vassalage by these coastal warriors. Even the Tzutujils of Atitlán felt the force of this new element on the coast. Two "Mexican" warriors of the Tzutujils, Welpan and Xucutzin, were taken prisoners and brought before C'otuja at Pismachi (*Título Totonicapán* n.d.).

The Ilocabs became alarmed by the growing power of C'otuja and decided to challenge the Quichés at Pismachi. The leaders of the revolt were two *pop c'amja* ("mat assistants"), named Rokche Taom and Four Aj Tumacaj. They tried to turn C'otuja against his assistant Istayul and vice versa. When that did not work, they attacked the Quiché lords as they bathed in a canyon (Pachitak?). The Ilocab rebels were countered by Quiché warriors and roundly defeated. Many prisoners were taken and sacrificed before the gods "in payment of their wrong." Others were kept as slaves. The Quichés claimed that this began human sacrifice at Pismachi and instilled great fear in all the other peoples (*Popol Vuh*, Villacorta 1962; *Título Totonicapán* n.d.).

K'ucumatz, the son of C'otuja and founder of K'umarcaaj, was the Quichés' greatest magical transformer. It was reputed that he could change himself into snakes, eagles, jaguars, and blood. He could rise to the sky or drop into the underworld (Xibalba) (Villacorta 1962, pp. 340ff.).

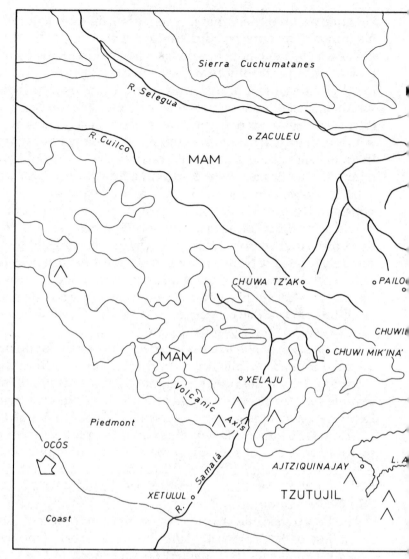

Fig. 5.2.   Sites referred to in the history of Utatlán.
Based on IGN, map, 1:250,000.

132

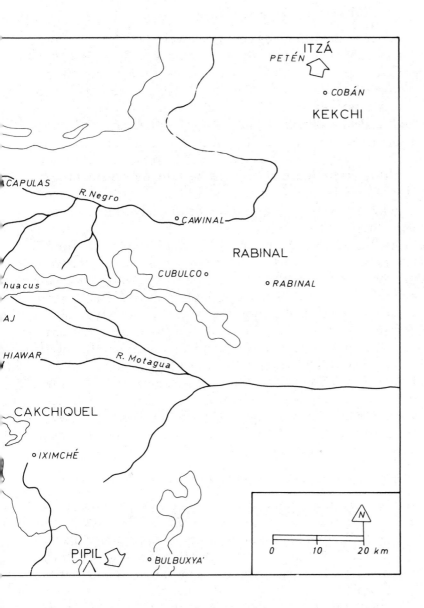

K'ucumatz greatly expanded the kingdom northward through conquest. According to a remarkable account left us by the Cakchiquels (*Título Xpantzay*), Cakchiquel warriors provided his most important military strength in the conquest of the people of C'oja (Mask Lineage) near Sacapulas (?). K'ucumatz trained the Cakchiquel warriors and gave them weapons. A camp (*warabal*) was established outside Utatlán, and from there the warriors left for the campaign. As the Cakchiquels told the story, the fearful Quichés turned back, and it was left to the Cakchiquel warriors to fight the enemy. They triumphed and brought back many prisoners to be sacrificed. They presented them as food to the Quiché deities (*c'axtoc'*) Tojil and Awilix. In anger the Cakchiquels asked the deities why they had been deceived by the Quiché people.

One aftermath of the battle, apparently, was that K'ucumatz sent his daughter to marry the lord of C'oja, Tecum Sic'om, presumably in order to stabilize his domination over the area. Tecum killed her, and K'ucumatz vowed to take revenge—to eat the "insides" of his son-in-law. He gathered his army again, including the Cakchiquels, arrogantly claiming that he would need only four hundred warriors to finish off the C'ojas. The army fasted and then ate roasted meat at their camp and left for the north. On the expedition K'ucumatz was killed in battle. In a touching narrative the Cakchiquels told how a hunchback was sent to K'umarcaaj to inform K'ucumatz's wife of her husband's death. He was to go directly to the lady (*xokojaw*) and tell her; if she was not in, he was to wait for her outside town where she went to weave each day. In this way word of K'ucumatz's death reached K'umarcaaj (Recinos 1957, pp. 134–39).

EVENTS IN THE LIFE OF Q'UIK'AB

One of the Xpantzay *títulos* states that Q'uik'ab was "gathered" on the edge of a river and had no father or mother (Recinos 1957, p. 163). Perhaps this was a play on words, for "gathered" (*sic'om*) was the name of the C'oja lord who had killed his father. The other sources make it clear that Q'uik'ab was the son of K'ucumatz and that he was magical like his father. It is said that a hunchback announced his birth.

With the death of his father Q'uik'ab began planning to avenge him. He met with his Cakchiquel allies in night councils at K'umarcaaj and finally persuaded them to fight with him. In the presence of all the warriors of Utatlán he vowed to destroy C'oja and gather the bones of his father. Finally, two years after his father's death, he left with his force, assisted by the *ajpop c'amja* and his closest kinsmen, Tecum and Tepepul. The Cakchiquels claimed that they again were first in battle and that the Quichés hid during the fighting.

The attackers left their camp outside C'oja at dawn and overran the town.

While it was still dark, they killed Tecum Sic'om and took his young son captive. Q'uik'ab found his father's bones first off and gathered them in a bundle. Then the warriors seized the large supply of jade and metal the C'ojas had stored in their town. Many enemy lords (we are told that there were thirteen) were killed, and many vassals were tied and taken prisoner to K'umarcaaj. There, as the Quichés expressed it, the vassals died, "not of sickness but of their skulls being broken open." Several towns and peoples were conquered during the campaign, including Cumatz and Tujal in Sacapulas and the Mams around Zaculeu (Recinos 1957, pp. pp. 140–47).

Q'uik'ab was an active military campaigner, and during his rule the Quiché kingdom was expanded to its ultimate limits. It extended all the way to the Cobán area, where precious stones, feathers, and metals were taken as spoils. Contact was even made with the Itzás farther north (Recinos 1957, p. 104). The Rabinal people, under their lord Talmalin, became subject to the Quichés, partly through their kinship ties with Q'uik'ab's Cakchiquel vassals (Recinos 1957, p. 146).

On the west the peoples of the entire Quezaltenango area were made tributaries, and the boundaries on the coast were extended to the Río Ocós, on the border with Soconusco (present-day coastal Chiapas). On the east the Quichés' rivals at Sajcabaja, Caukeb and Cubulco (Ikomak'ib), were subjects, thus linking up the Rabinal province with the central zone.

Q'uik'ab initiated a large-scale colonization program for the conquered areas. The rural peoples surrounding Utatlán were reorganized, and the warriors were called into councils at K'umarcaaj. The "first vassals," from secondary-descent lines, were elevated in rank on top of Xebalax, Xekamak', and Chulimal mountains. They were given the rank of *achij* ("soldier") and the offices of *ajpop* and *k'alel* within the rank. They were then commissioned to go to the provinces of the kingdom and supervise the construction of towns there. They were to live in those defensive towns, supported by local vassals, in order to maintain the kingdom intact (Villacorta 1962, pp. 349–52).

In great ceremonies the colonists were counseled (*pixabaj*) by Q'uik'ab and the rulers of K'umarcaaj in words that have been preserved for us: "You, our valiant watchmen, go do battle with the [enemy] towns and hamlets; go take them by the armpits and sacrifice them. . . . Go, our older brothers, do not cry, do not be sad. . . . Go and trample them, make yourselves valiant warriors and watchful guardians" (*Título C'oyoi*). We are told that the rulers were sad. They cried and placed their hands on the warriors' heads, and they embraced one another.

In this way many groups, both within K'umarcaaj, Pismachi, and Pilocab and from the outside hamlets, left for the distant provinces. A reorganization of the greater Utatlán community was occurring, as more and more peoples were brought into participation in the affairs of state. At this time, too, the

Cakchiquels were made a more integral part of Q'uik'ab's growing kingdom. He ordered them to build a colonial town at Chiawar Tz'upitak'aj (Fortified Plains of Milpa), where they could protect the eastern flank of the kingdom. The Cakchiquels became a regular component of the "thirteen groups of warriors at K'umarcaaj." They fought under Q'uik'ab's command and helped extend the eastern boundaries along the Motagua River basin, and southward through the Antigua Valley (Bulbuxiya') to Escuintla (Atacat) (Villacorta 1934, pp. 226–30).

Subsequent events demonstrated that Q'uik'ab had overextended himself. In about 1470 a revolt erupted against him that became the most far-reaching event in Quiché history, except, of course, the Spanish conquest. The *Popol Vuh* passes over the crisis without comment, but it is recorded in detail in the *Annals* and in the *Título Totonicapán*. The latter document informs us that the revolt took place during a great celebration held at K'umarcaaj on the thirteenth month of the year, Tz'iquín K'ij. Representatives of the most important peoples of the highlands came to the sacred city with their rulers, priests, warriors, and deities (icons). Besides the Tamubs and the Ilocabs also present were the Lord Talmalin from Rabinal, the various Cakchiquel groups, peoples from the Sacapulas area, the Aguacatecs, and the several Tzutujil groups.

An extraordinary scene took place, as recorded in the *Título Totonicapán*. In the presence of the rulers the lords who had been responsible for the death of C'otuja dressed up in skins and hunting attire and danced with the deities of the various groups. Then, starting with the son of an *ajpop* the Quichés gave sacrificial offerings to Tojil. The scene was followed by a bloody attack against Q'uik'ab and other high officials of his lineage.

The *Annals* explain that the instigators of the revolt were Q'uik'ab's own vassal warriors and his sons, Tata Yac (Father Mountain Cat) and Ajitza ("he of the Itzá"). The vassals were jealous of Q'uik'ab's serfs, who apparently had more privileges than they did. The vassals specifically mentioned their desire to travel freely on the roads. Q'uik'ab's sons, perhaps the offspring of foreign wives (Mams and Itzás), desired the jade, metals, slaves, power and wealth of their father. In the attack many of the highest-ranked serfs as well as Cakchiquel warriors were killed. A number of high-ranked Cawek lords also died. The warriors even tried to kill Q'uik'ab himself, but he was saved because he was staying at Panpetak (Place of Entry) under the protection of loyal sons (Villacorta 1934, pp. 230–33).

It is probable that the revolt was the same event referred to by Fray Betanzos, who wrote:

In times past, before the coming of the Spaniards to these provinces, there was a lord at Utatlán with counternatural and abominable vices; and the people not being able to suffer him, complained to the other towns; and these counseled among themselves and went to Utatlán to carry out justice against that lord, and killed him and elected another [ruler] in his place. [Carrazgo 1967*a*]

Perhaps Q'uik'ab's military and sacrificial excesses were the "vices" remembered by Betanzos's informants, though that judgment certainly was not held by all the highland peoples (see below). The story suggests that the visiting peoples aided the Quiché warriors and princes in their revolt against Q'uik'ab and his lineage. The statement that the ruler was killed would be simply an error in fact, though as we have seen, an attempt was made to kill Q'uik'ab.

As a result of the revolt Q'uik'ab was forced to give the warriors high rank and rights over the common people. He was also forced to share his wealth with his sons. The Cakchiquels who recorded the event stated that Q'uik'ab became deeply bitter. We are told that the power and respect of the Quichés at K'umarcaaj was lost because of the revolt. The validity of these observations was quickly confirmed by another conflict, which soon broke out at K'umarcaaj.

According to the Cakchiquels' version of the event (Villacorta 1934, pp. 232–36), the crisis was caused when a Cakchiquel woman (Nimpam Ixcacauw) selling maize foods at K'umarcaaj was set upon by one of the newly elevated Quiché warriors who tried to take the food from her. Q'uik'ab took quick, decisive action against the man, hanging him from a tree to be tortured. This action outraged the soldiers, who wanted to kill the woman in retribution. When the Cakchiquels refused to hand her over, the soldiers tried to persuade Q'uik'ab that the Cakchiquels were seeking to subordinate their authority and should be attacked. The bitter Q'uik'ab not only refused to accede to their wishes but went by night to warn the Cakchiquels of the danger to them. Calling them his "sons and brothers", he lamented that the newly elevated men would no longer obey him. He referred to the soldiers as "penises and feces," and advised the Cakchiquels to abandon a town so disrespectful and divisive as K'umarcaaj had become.

The Cakchiquels left K'umarcaaj, and also Chiawar, settling at Iximché (Maize Tree). They praised Q'uik'ab as a wise and magical ruler, while saying that the warriors at K'umarcaaj were seeking glory only through warfare. The Cakchiquels claimed that many peoples came to offer obeisance to them, since the power of the Quichés had been broken. Q'uik'ab died, they said, during the reign of thirteen Tzij and twelve Tijax (ca. 1475). After that the Cakchiquels began fortifying their town against the hostile Quichés.

CONTINUOUS WARFARE

The long, involved wars between the Quichés and the Tzutujils, which were described by Fuentes y Guzmán (1932–33, 7, pp. 37ff.) and which students such as Thompson (1943) have ascribed to early Quiché history, I believe to have taken place after the time of Q'uik'ab (1475–1524). The Cakchiquel sources make it clear that they too were engaged in almost continuous warfare with the Quichés after Q'uik'ab's death. These wars suggest that the Quichés of Utatlán were in a holding operation, trying by military means to maintain the fragmenting remnants of the kingdom achieved by Q'uik'ab and his predecessors. No doubt the community of Utatlán became considerably more secularized and militarized during this last phase of its history.

War with the Cakchiquels (Villacorta 1934, pp. 238–41) began shortly after the death of Q'uik'ab, during the reign of his successor, Tepepul, and the *ajpop c'amja* (the latter official also from the Istayul sublineage). A cold spell struck Iximché in the fifth month of the year Uchum, and the Cakchiquels experienced a famine. A man from the town informed the Quichés at K'umarcaaj of the Cakchiquels' plight. Under the leadership of Tepepul, the Quichés made preparations to attack the Cakchiquels. For a year K'umarcaaj was in ferment, as the lords and warriors prepared for war. Peoples from the surrounding rural hamlets were recruited until an army of over 16,000 warriors was gathered (*Annals*). They were resplendent in their war outfits. Their hair was cut and adorned with feathers, and their weapons and shields were decorated with feathers, metal, and stones. In the lead were men carrying conch shells, drums, and flutes to sound the call and provide magical power. In the rear came Tepepul and the Istayul, accompanying the image of their god Tojil. In this formation they left K'umarcaaj for Iximché.

A spy had preceded them to Iximché, and the Cakchiquels were prepared to meet them. In the frantic fighting that ensued outside Iximché, the Quichés suffered a devastating defeat. Tepepul and the *ajpop c'amja* were taken prisoner and forced to hand over the image of their god. Uncounted numbers of soldiers and officers—the latter sons and grandsons of lords— were killed. The victory dramatically increased the power of the Cakchiquels of Iximché vis à vis the Quichés at Utatlán.

The Quichés never again directly challenged the Cakchiquels at their power center, though many other battles were fought along the borders between the two. One conflict arose in 1493, when the Tukuchés, a faction at Iximché, revolted, were cast out, and joined the Quichés at K'umarcaaj (Villacorta 1934, pp. 246–50). They were made vassals of the Quichés, but were eventually driven out, probably for insubordination. They fled to the old Cakchiquel colonial town Chiawar, where they attacked the Quichés. After 1511 there was more or less continuous warfare between the Cakchiquels and the Quichés. In one of the battles (1517), Yaxonquic', the son of The Quiché ruler (Ajpop Tuj, possibly Seven Noj) was killed, along with many lesser warriors (Villacorta 1934, p. 256). Finally, in 1522 peace came to the two peoples, apparently through an agreement made by their respective rulers, Three Quej and Nine C'at.

The prolonged wars between the Quichés and the Tzutujils, which Fuentes y Guzmán extracted from two early Ixtahuacán chronicles (Carmack 1973, pp. 71–79), cannot be dated with certainty. His account refers to three "Quiché kings" during the period of the war whose names are actually those of the founding warlords (Balam Ak'ab, Majucotaj, and I'qui Balam). The Nijaib *títulos* also refer to the post-Q'uik'ab rulers of Utatlán by these titles without revealing their actual names. The fourth ruler mentioned by Fuentes y Guzmán is Q'uik'ab, whose name was often assumed by Utatlán rulers who late in Quiché history succeeded that great leader. Most likely the wars took place during the reigns of Tecum and Eight C'aam (Eight Vine, a Nahua calendar name rendered in Quiché), around 1485 to 1500. Eight C'aam's *ajpop c'amja* was called Q'uik'ab, according to the *Popol Vuh*, and might be the same Q'uik'ab referred to in Fuentes y Guzmán's account.

The cause of the war was a traditional Quiché *causus belli*: capture of a royal bride (Fuentes y Guzmán 1932–33, 7:37ff.). The daughter and the niece of the Quiché ruler, Ixcun Socil and Esel Ixpua, were induced by Tzutujil and Ilocab lords to abandon the palace at Utatlán, scaling the walls of the town by night. When news of their disappearance reached Aticotal, the girls' aunt and chief guardian, she informed the ruler. He was so upset that he, upon meeting a porter in the patio, killed him with a lance. He ordered all those who were in charge of the girls taken prisoner and later killed. Spies and "explorers" were dispatched to track down the girls, and they quickly reported back that the girls had been taken to the Tzutujil town Ajtziquinajay (the site of present Chuitinamit, Atitlán).

The Quiché ruler sent messengers throughout the kingdom, convoking at Utatlán a great council of all his chiefs and leaders. The native sources apparently recorded his words, which were translated into Fuentes y Guzmán's flowery Spanish as follows:

My faithful vassals and captains, you already know of the disgrace which has befallen me; nor will you be ignorant of my natural suffering because of a perfidious daughter and infamous niece, and the offense to my honor because of a kinswoman not only a traitor to her own blood, but a stain on her kinsmen. This calls for bloody vengeance, and for this reason I have called you together. Well known in the towns and hamlets are my great military feats against your arms, as general for my father, Balam Quiché. Although this effeminate servant, the king of the Tzutujil, is equal to me in blood, for this treasonous action he has become lowered in esteem. With this wrong, if you do not oppose the insolent act of that servant, the Quiché will be infamous. . . . I am resolved to raise a large army to fight a bloody war against him, without reserving my person in any way. . . . It is necessary that all the chiefs, lords, and captains that hear my voice gather their people, taking charge of all their equipment and weapons, and be ready for war at this court of Utatlan within 20 days. . . . I give you my royal word that I will reward those who are outstanding in war with honors and favors. So, go and announce the war in all my kingdom, that we may quickly carry out these plans. [Fuentes y Guzmán 1932–33, 7:39–40]

Within twenty days warriors from all over the kingdom had set up camp in the fields outside Utatlán. Each squadron of warriors could be distinguished by its banners and insignia, surrounding the cotton-cloth tents of their officers. The ruler of Utatlán and his chiefs and counselors came from the town to inspect and count the warriors. Within the confines of the town many victims were offered to the gods. At the conclusion of these rites the army left for Atitlán. Besides the units mentioned above, there were musicians to play the conch shells, flutes, and drums. A multitude of carriers took food and weapons. In the center of the squadron was the ruler himself, carried on a litter. He wore a crown decorated with gold and precious stones, and his chest was covered with crystals. He was attended by his Momostecan shield bearer and fanner and an elite guard of warriors.

No attempt will be made here to recount the complicated battles described by Fuentes y Guzmán. The Quichés won some important victories, and we are told that metals, cloth, and other spoils were taken to the storehouses of Utatlán. The Quiché rulers rewarded their officers and soldiers from these spoils and "exalted many of them to positions of great dignity and estimation." Perhaps the most strategic gain from the war was the Pipils' concession of free access through their territory for Quiché and Cakchiquel soldiers and merchants. This concession was largely won by the Cakchiquels, who temporarily were thrown on the side of the Quichés when their traditional enemies the Pipils formed an alliance with the Tzutujils.

Besides the Pipils, the Tzutujils managed to recruit as allies such Quiché-dominated peoples as the Ilocabs, the coastal Quichés of Zapotitlán, and the Mams. So allied, they were the military match of the Quichés, who suffered huge losses in the war. According to Fuentes y Guzmán, thousands of warriors were killed in battle, among them many lords and officers. The Utatlán ruler himself was killed when he was knocked from his litter while directing the fighting in a zone south of Lake Atitlán. His body was recovered by Quiché warriors and taken back to Utatlán, where his death was mourned. One of the Xpantzay *títulos* informs us (Recinos 1957, p. 149) that the son of Q'uik'ab was killed by the Tzutujils. He may have been the Quiché ruler mentioned by Fuentes y Guzmán. Possibly it was Tecum, the successor to Tepepul, for Tecum was a son of Q'uik'ab, according to the *Título Totonicapán*. Such an identification would reinforce the suggestion that the Tzutujil wars took place during the last years of the fifteenth century.

Other major military expeditions that appear to have been carried out toward the end of the fifteenth century are recorded in Nijaib *títulos*. Significantly, in these wars the military encounters involved peoples who for the most part had previously been under Quiché control. The Quichés were attempting to respond to revolts in different parts of the kingdom but, as we have seen, with only partial success.

In one expedition (Recinos 1957, pp. 79–84) representatives of the four major lineages at K'umarcaaj returned to the western coastal area formerly conquered by Q'uik'ab. This time they pushed on past the Río Ocós to Ayutla, Tapachula, and Mazatlán in Soconusco. They extorted from the inhabitants cacao, fish, cloth, gold, feathers, and precious stones to take back to K'umarcaaj. When the lords of Tapachula (Tapaltecat) refused to pay such tributes, two of them (Quep and Jucatzin—the names of the Tzutujil warriors taken before C'otuja; see above) were carried off as prisoners.

As the triumphant military force neared Lake Atitlán on the return march, they dispatched messengers to K'umarcaaj to notify the rulers of their arrival two days hence. They went on to Chuwila (Chichicastenango) the last day and finally arrived outside K'umarcaaj. The chiefs of the major lineages went out to meet them, accompanied by vassals, armed with weapons and organized into banner-waving squadrons, all to the sound of drums. The conquering heroes were led into the town, where they reported their deeds to the rulers. The spoils they had won were turned over to the stewards responsible for storing them. We are told that from then on the conquered peoples began coming to K'umarcaaj without fail to pay their tributes.

Another military expedition was directed against the peoples of Rabinal and Cubulco, who apparently had shaken off their subordination to the Quichés (Recinos 1957, pp. 104–108). The Quiché warriors seized salt, gourds, cacao, and metals and took many prisoners. All these spoils they took back to K'umarcaaj, where the Quiché rulers held a seven-day celebration. As on earlier such occasions the rulers of the major lineages went out to meet the returning warriors. They formed a grand procession from the hill called Ujulutil (Shining Place), led by the lords and military officers and followed by warriors, lancers, bowmen, and shield bearers.

Inside the walls of the town the conquerors reported to the rulers of each lineage and deposited the spoils with the stewards (Tepew and K'ucumatz). At the court of the ruler the captive lords of Rabinal were judged, and their tributes set. They were allowed to return to Rabinal, but their vassals were ordered to return to K'umarcaaj regularly to pay tribute.

A final expedition (Recinos 1957, pp. 108–12) took the Quiché warriors to the Río Negro, where they seized precious stones from such towns as Cawinal and Tujal (Sacapulas). They moved on to Momostenango, finally returning to K'umarcaaj in 1501. This was familiar territory to the Quichés, but at each place they met resistance from their rebellious subjects. Rebellion apparently had become endemic in the Quiché kingdom.

MEXICA INFLUENCE AT UTATLÁN

The final years before the Spanish conquest at Utatlán were dominated by Mexicas (Aztecs), who encroached on Quiché affairs. This subject has been a controversial one in Guatemala since the seventeenth century, when the Dominican priest Antonio de Remesal (1932) wrote that twenty-three years before the Conquest, in 1501, the peoples of Guatemala became subject to the Aztecs under Ahuitzotl. We are now in a position to understand more clearly Remesal's statement.

From Aztec history we know that Mexica merchants (*pochteca*) were operating in Soconusco during the same period the Quiché warriors were extending Utatlán control to Ayutla, Tapachula, and Mazatlán. Undoubtedly there was contact between the two peoples, as suggested by the Mexicas' knowledge of a "rich and powerful nation" among the mountains and along the rivers of Guatemala (a description found in Tezozomoc). It is even possible that the Quichés instigated the infamous Soconuscan ambush of Mexican merchants a few years before 1500, though we have no record of it in any of the sources. At any rate, under Ahuitzotl in about 1500 the Mexicas conquered the Soconuscan peoples and incorporated the province in their empire. Both Ayutla and Mazatlán were taken from the Quichés and submitted to the heavy tribute obligations the Mexicas imposed on them (consisting particularly of cacao, feathers, and jaguar skins).

According to a Pipil document used by Fuentes y Guzmán (1932–33, 6:47–48), Ahuitzotl sent "some of his people . . . disguised as merchants and officials" into the southern coastal territory of the Quichés. Clearly this is a reference to the Pochtecas, who regularly preceded the Mexica armies into an area, where they served as spies while ostensibly engaging in trade. In 1501, it would seem, the Pochtecas visited Utatlán, were later cordially received at Iximché, and finally returned to Utatlán. There, we are told, the "great chief or lord of that region [Utatlán] ordered them to leave his court within one day, and the entire jurisdiction of his kingdom within twenty suns" (Fuentes y Guzmán 1932–33, 6:47). The Quiché ruler, probably Seven Noj (Seven Season, a calendar name), felt powerful enough to contend with the Mexicas, who were far from their home base and must have been few in number.

By 1510 the situation had changed. In that year, according to the Cakchiquels at Iximché, "the Yaquis of Culuacan arrived, the messengers of the king Modeczumatzin, king of Mexico" (Villacorta 1934, p. 254). At Utatlán the Mexica emissaries demanded tribute, and the weakened Quichés agreed to pay it. We are told in a Nijaib *título* that in that year the Quichés began paying tributes in quetzal feathers, gold, precious stones, cacao, and cloth. From a pictorial that I found at Momostenango we learn that Moctezuma later paternalized his domination of the Quichés by giving two of his daughters in marriage to the "Quiché lord before whom the tributes were brought at our Quiché center of Utatlán" (Carmack 1973, p. 371).

Subordination to the Mexicas brought peace to the Quichés, and "for many years they made no new conquests." Shortly before the Conquest, at a date surely later than the year 1512 recorded in the Nijaib *título* (Recinos 1957, p. 84), Moctezuma sent messengers (named for Uitzitzil, Hummingbird, the Mexica patron deity) to warn the Quichés of the impending Spanish invasion. Other details of the event were recorded in a Xecul document used by Fuentes y Guzmán (1932–33, 8:161–64). After the Mexica messengers left Utatlán, the Quiché ruler (said to have been Q'uik'ab) called four young diviners to determine the course of action to be taken. The diviners shot their arrows at a huge stone, and when the stone was not damaged, they predicted that the Quichés were doomed to defeat. The ruler then called for the priests, who confirmed the prognostication. Nevertheless, we are told, at Utatlán banners of war were raised, drums sounded, and preparations were made to meet the Spaniards in battle as commanded by Moctezuma.

The more or less continuous presence of Mexica representatives at Utatlán, including women from the court of Tenochtitlán, must have added a strong "international" flavor to the town. Evidence from the Conquest period indicates that K'umarcaaj, Iximché, and other towns, such as Xetulul (Zapotitlán), became known in Mexico by their Nahua names (Cortés 1961, pp. 267–68). Utatlán (Place of Reeds) was the name used in Mexico as a close translation of K'umarcaaj (Place of Old Reeds), Cuauhtemallan (Guatemala) was the name the Mexicas used to refer to Iximché. The Tlaxcalan warriors who accompanied Alvarado to Guatemala represented (Anonymous 1963) Iximché with an eagle pictograph, apparently as a rebus for *cuauh* ("eagle"). But *cuauh* can also be glossed as "wood" or "tree," which suggests that Cuauhtemallan was actually the Nahua translation of Iximché (Maize Tree; cf. Vásquez's *palo de leche*).

It is clear, then, that strong Mexica influence at K'umarcaaj in the years preceding the Conquest had to some extent Nahuatized the town. Before the Spanairds ever saw the place, it was known in Mesoamerican circles as Utatlán.

THE SPANISH CONQUEST OF UTATLÁN

As noted above, the Mexicas kept the Quichés at Utatlán informed about the movements of the Spaniards in Mexico. What the Quichés heard must have been disturbing, and even their own diviners predicted that they were coming into bad times. At about the same time that the Spaniards attacked the Mexicas, a terrible plague struck the Cakchiquels at Iximché and possibly the inhabitants of Utatlán as well (Villacorta 1934, pp. 256–59). The Cakchiquels capitulated to the psychological warfare and in 1520 sent messengers to Cortés offering to become his subjects. They also told him about their enemies the Quichés and asked him to intervene on their behalf. Cortés sent messengers back to Utatlán, offering his friendship in exchange for their peaceful submission. He also told them to cease their hostilities against the Cakchiquels. We do not know the Quichés' reply to Cortés, but it must have been a negative one.

The rulers of Utatlán began a campaign to enlist the aid of all the peoples of Guatemala to present a common resistance force against the Spaniards. They even approached the Cakchiquels and the Tzutujils, but both peoples rejected the plea. Many others, however, rallied around the Quiché ruler (probably Seven Noj), as proved by the events of the Conquest. Shortly before the actual Spanish invasion, according to sources used by Fuentes y Guzmán (1932–33, 7:390), the Utatlán ruler died. His successor was probably Three Quej (Three Deer), and his assistant was Nine Tz'i (Nine Dog).

In 1523, Alvarado left for Guatemala with 135 horsemen; 120 foot soldiers; 400 Mexica, Tlaxcaltec, and Cholultec auxiliaries; and four artillery pieces. From Soconusco they again made contact with the Cakchiquels of Iximché, who sent back tribute goods and promises of military assistance. Throughout the conquest of the Quichés, beginning with the Spaniards' departure from Soconusco and ending with the fall of Utatlán, the Utatlán rulers were kept informed of the Spaniards' activities by a well-organized system of spies and messengers. Alvarado tells us that he captured three Quiché spies near Zapotitlán (San Martín) and sent them to Utatlán to demand the peaceful capitulation of the Quichés (Fig. 5.3). The Utatlán rulers refused even to respond to the conquistadors' demand (Alvarado 1946).

As the Spaniards entered the Quezaltenango valley, Utatlán's involvement in the conflict rapidly expanded. K'alel Atzij Winak Tieran, the chief of Xelaju' (Quezaltenango), sent a military messenger to the ruler of K'umarcaaj, telling him of the Spaniards' arrival (Recinos 1957, p. 85). The ruler's grandson, Tecum, a powerful captain living at Tzijbachaj (Totonicapán), was sent for. He went to K'umarcaaj, where for seven days he was ritually carried about the town on a litter, draped in feathers and precious stones. He was ceremonially painted and censed, while the lords performed war dances. Tecum's military attire consisted of green feathers covering his arms and legs; mirrors on his chest, forehead, and back; and a crown of gold and precious stones. With this magical attire Tecum could reportedly fly in the air and see both ahead and behind. Finally Tecum was sent to meet the Spaniards in Quezaltenango Valley. He left accompanied by 39 flag bearers, including his personal ensign, Q'uik'ab Cawisimaj; many captains and "sergeants"; and 8,400 warriors (Carmack 1973, pp. 301–303).

The details of the battle at Pinal, south of Quezaltenango, are well known

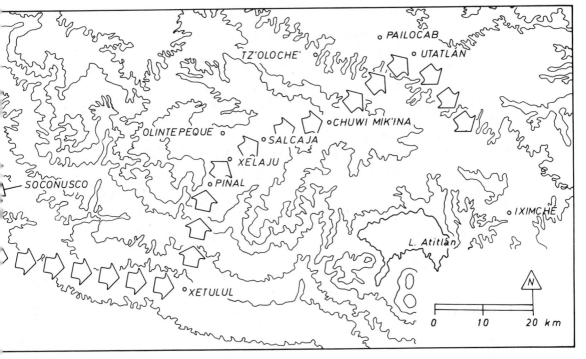

Fig. 5.3. The Spanish conquest of the Quichés. Based on IGN, map, 1:250,000.

and will not be repeated here. The slain Tecum was singled out by Alvarado (1946) as "one of the four lords of that city of Utatlán who had come as captain general of all the land." After suffering several defeats and the loss of many warriors in battles with the Spaniards, the Utatlán rulers sent messengers to Alvarado offering peace. They asked to be pardoned for their hostility and promised to obey the Spaniards. Alvarado and his forces were invited to Utatlán, which, the messengers said, was larger than Quezaltenango and more suitable for providing the Spaniards' needs.

The Spaniards arrived at Utatlán in the spring of 1524, entering the town by way of the narrow, man-made causeway that connected it with the surrounding plains. Alvarado became suspicious of the causeway, for it gave the appearance of having been purposely cut away and was surrounded by canyons posted with warriors. His concern grew when he saw the narrow, well-paved streets, on which it would be difficult to maneuver horses. He noted the absence of women or commoners inside the town and the lords' preoccupation with their own councils. Díaz del Castillo (1933), using sources that were later lost, wrote that Quezaltec warriors who had joined forces with the Spaniards informed Alvarado that the Quichés planned to burn the Spaniards inside the town that night. Whether or not that was true, Alvarado feared an attack by the Quichés inside the town, where his horses would be ineffective.

He sent soldiers to secure the causeway and, using the excuse that the horses needed to be exercised each evening, left the town with his forces. By a verbal deception he managed to apprehend the ruler and several other Utatlán lords. As they were being tied up and taken to the plains outside town, Quiché warriors in the surrounding canyons began shooting at the Spaniards, using bows and arrows, lances, and slings. One Spaniard was hit, lost his footing, and fell dead into a canyon.

On the plains outside Utatlán the lords were given a hasty trial, interrupted with demands for gold. One of the lords "confessed" to the alleged plot to burn the Spaniards and was set free. The rest were tied to posts and burned (Anonymous 1934). Three Quej and Nine Tz'i', the *ajpop* and *ajpop c'amja*, were killed along with other lords. Some of the captured leaders were kept as hostages, among them Tecum and Tepepul, the sons of the executed rulers. Later, in an attempt to pacify the community, Alvarado appointed them as administrators of Utatlán under his personal rule.

Alvarado next began a campaign to subdue the greater Utatlán community, which by this time was entirely under arms. He dispatched messengers to Iximché, asking for warriors from among the Cakchiquels. By their own testimony (Villacorta 1934, p. 262) the Cakchiquels sent an initial force of 2,000 men, and warriors went to Utatlán on two later occasions. Alvarado (1946) stated that the Cakchiquels sent him 4,000 warriors in all. For seven or eight days the Spaniards battled the Quichés near Utatlán, killing many of them and putting others in chains as slaves. When at last the Utatlán lords capitulated, offering to obey the Spaniards and pay tribute, Alvarado ordered them to return to their houses in the zones surrounding the town. (An interesting footnote to this campaign is that Leonora, the daughter of Pedro de Alvarado and his Tlaxcalan wife, was born in the camp just outside Utatlán. She was perhaps Guatemala's first *mestiza* [Recinos 1958].)

The various events associated with the fall of Utatlán, taken largely from Spanish sources, are confirmed by the *Annals* and an isolated Quiché source (Anonymous 1935). The latter was written by Diego Reynoso, the old Popol Winak of the Quichés, who in the 1530s was taken by the first bishop of Guatemala to the Spanish capital to learn to read and write in Quiché. In the margins of a religious book he wrote that "during the *Cuaresma* captain Tonatiu came to make war here at Quiché. The town was burned, and the kingdom and tribute were taken over. The peoples no longer came to pay tribute to our grandfathers and fathers at Quiché." Utatlán was burned and leveled in an effort to prevent the Quichés from reoccupying it. The town was later reoccupied, nevertheless, and the same bishop blessed it, giving it the name Santa Cruz, probably because it had been conquered during the holy days of Easter (see chapter 9 for the subsequent history of Utatlán).

6
SOCIAL STRUCTURE

The social structure of the Utatlán community is the feature perhaps most clearly and extensively revealed by the ethnohistoric sources. Nevertheless, it should be made clear that, in general, I describe only the normative aspects of Utatlán social structure (sometimes referred to as "mechanical structure" in the anthropological literature). Since it is the social component most readily available in the sources, it can be more reliably summarized than can the more dynamic political divisions (the "statistical structure"). A focus on the normative structure is consistent with my attempt in this book to present the Quichés' view of their community.

As will be seen below, the social structure of Utatlán was a complicated integration of rank, descent, territoriality, hierarchy, and four-part sections. These principles will be discussed as a series of contrasts between caste and class stratification, segmentary lineages and territorial divisions, and political centralization and decentralization.

CASTE AND CLASS STRATIFICATION

The over-all stratification of the community is schematically summarized in Table 6.1 (Carmack 1976a). This simplified scheme will be elaborated upon in the discussion to follow. It should be noted that I use terminology borrowed from other historical situations, especially feudal Europe. I believe that these terms give a proper connotation to Quiché social structure, as long as they are not taken too literally. The particular meaning for each term in the Quiché case will be given in the text, and the reader is asked to adhere to those definitions rather than their meanings in some other context.

Lords and Vassals

The fundamental stratification at Utatlán was a caste division between the lords, called *ajawab* (Saenz 1940), and their vassals, the *al c'ajol*. The lords

Table 6.1. **Castes and Classes at Utatlán**

Castes	Classes
Ajawab (lords)	*Achij* (warriors)
Al c'ajol (vassals)	*Ajbeyom* (merchants)
Munib (slaves)	*Ajtoltecat* (artisans)
	Nimak achi (serfs)

were patrilineal descendants of the original warlords who came from the east and therefore claimed Toltec descent. Their forefathers were created by the majestic Toltec deities Tepew and K'ucumatz (Quetzalcoatl). The vassals, though not created separately, were perhaps more closely associated with the procreative deities, Alom and C'ajolom (Engenderors; Villacorta 1962, p. 20). They were said to be the "children" (*al c'ajol*) of the lords who were born outside the noble patrilines. Some of them, in fact, were probably fathered by lords with secondary commoner and slave wives. Others, however, were conquered commoners who became subject to the Quiché lords, while still others were dissident peoples from neighboring towns who took refuge with the Quichés at Utatlán.

The social contrasts between the lords and the vassals were all-inclusive (Carmack 1976a). The lords occupied the political, religious, and military offices of state, while the vassals performed the physical labor of building, providing food and offerings, and fighting for the lords. The lords were sacred, surrounded by royal emblems: feathers, gold ornaments, jade and other precious stones, and jaguar and lion claws. They were linked to the gods and temples through ritual participation. The vassals were secular, kept away from contact with the royal emblems and patron gods. The lords received tribute to support their subsistence and ostentatious living. The vassals paid tribute and also provided their own humble subsistence. The lords lived in elaborate palaces, within the walls of the town. The vassals lived in the rural zones, in simple mud-and-pole huts roofed with straw. The lords dressed in fine cloth woven from multicolored cotton threads. The vassals were expected to dress in henequen cloth (Estrada 1955, p. 73). Similarly, braided hair and the use of metal earplugs and quetzal feathers as adornments were restricted to the lords.

Even the postmortal state of the two strata differed. There was a tendency to immortalize the lords, and some of the most important rulers were said to have disappeared without leaving notice whether or not they "tasted death." Las Casas (1909, p. 630) reported that high-ranked lords were burned and their bones gathered into bundles, which were kept in stone or wooden boxes to be worshiped like gods. The vassals were the servants of deity, fit only to make sacrificial offerings to the gods. We know from modern ethnographic studies (Carmack n.d.; Bunzel 1952) that no attempt was made to preserve the bodies or memories of deceased commoners. The body of the vassal was food for the earth, while the essence of the deceased was believed to enter the air and clouds, where it would coalesce with the other dead, to be carried to and fro with the winds. The individual lost his personal identity, returning to the earth and sky from which he had never been far removed.

Thus the traditional caste features of economic complementarity, ideas of ritual contamination, and political domination characterized relations between lords and vassals at Utatlán. Also castelike was the endogamous marriage patterns of the two strata. While the lords could have secondary commoner wives, legitimate wives had to be "ladies" (*xok'ojaw*) (Las Casas 1909, pp. 624–25). Typically, ladies from outside Utatlán were preferred as wives, probably for political reasons. There are references in the documents to Utatlán rulers who took wives from the Tzutujils, Cakchiquels, Ilocabs, Tamubs, Quejnays, Mams, Mexicas, and possibly Itzas. The vassals, in contrast, married only other vassals who lived in the same community.

The respective caste statuses of the lords and vassals were firmly established in law (Las Casas 1909, pp. 616–17; Fuentes y Guzmán 1932–33, 7:388–89). Some of the laws directly maintained the inequalities between the castes. For example, there were laws against fleeing from vassalage or influencing a vassal to disobey his lord. The tribute vassals were to pay their lords was fixed by law, both in amount and in frequency (probably every eighty days in most cases). Other laws, though not directly establishing the caste relationship, maintained it indirectly. Thus witchcraft was punished by death from burning, no doubt because it was a challenge to the priests of the lordly caste. From ethnographic studies of modern-day Quiché peasants we know that witchcraft is the universal rural means of competing for women, lands, and favors. Any law against witchcraft, therefore, would have been prejudicial to the vassals of the rural zones. The documents further reveal that magical practices engaged in by the lords were interpreted not as witchcraft but as displays of "power and might" (*tepewal, pus nawal*). Other laws prejudicial to the vassals were those against fornication (because they were enforced by the lords), losing or breakage of the goods of another (usually by vassals working for lords), sexual relations with slaves (owner-lords were exempt from this law), and adultery with a lady (though both lords and vassals theoretically received the death penalty for this act, the punishment for vassals was an ignominious casting into the canyon).

Slaves

The slaves formed the bottom stratum of the Utatlán caste structure. A well-developed slave vocabulary in the documents attests to their impor-

tance and antiquity in the Utatlán community. The general term *munib*
("slaves, captives") referred to male and female domestic servants of the
lords and, in a few cases, of vassals. Probably every lord at Utatlán had at
least a few domestic slaves. They did the grinding, cooking, food serving,
washing, wood gathering, and errand running for the lords' households.
Some slaves attained a certain freedom of action, and the word *munib* carried
the connotation of "those who are disobedient, who will not do what they
are told" (Vico n.d.).

Slavery at Utatlán was a complex institution, for slaves were recruited in
different ways, and could be in various phases of servitude. Captives in war
were *cana* ("those who are won"; Vico n.d.), in analogy with deer and other
animals taken in the hunt. Some of them would have to be given as offerings
to the war deity, just as offerings would be made to the patron of animals
after a successful hunt. The captives who were carried off to Utatlán were
called *teleche* ("dragged from one place to another"; Saenz 1940). Even the
Ilocab Quichés who tried to overpower the ruler (C'otuja) at Utatlán were
taken to the town as *teleche* (Villacorta 1962, pp. 328–29).

Once in town, the prisoners were destined either to be sacrificed or to
become domestic slaves (*munib*). A term used in the sources to refer to slaves,
tz'i' ("dogs") probably was reserved for those captives who were to be
sacrificed. The dog was the other offering besides human beings, believed to
be of supreme value to the Quiché deities. Generally, only captive lords were
sacrificed, while vassal prisoners were relegated to slavery (*munil*). The
cadavers of sacrificed lords were eaten, and in this way their sacred power
could be assimilated by the lords of Utatlán. Their decapitated heads were
impaled on the *tzumpan* ("skull rack altar"; *Título Totonicapán* n.d.; Las Casas
1909, p. 468).

In addition to originating from vassal prisoners, domestic slaves were
criminals made slaves as punishment, poor vassals sold into slavery by their
kinsmen or lords, vassals who married slaves, slaves bought on the open
market, and children born of slaves (Las Casas 1909, 616–18). Apparently
those who were sold into slavery, married slaves, or were enslaved because
of crimes came from the same poor sector of vassals. They were known as
winakitz ("bad or lowly people"). Those born into slavery carried the additional opprobrium of *alabitz* ("those of bad birth"; Coto n.d.; Vico n.d.; Saenz
1940).

Domestic slaves had a few rights under law and could legally marry one
another. Fornication or adultery with them was prohibited, and the latter
crime could be severely punished. Nevertheless, their masters had virtually
absolute rights over them, including sexual access to unmarried slave wom-
en. Further, slaves could be sacrificed at any time, though special victims
were often purchased for that purpose. Slaves were also sacrificed upon the

deaths of their lords, to serve as retainers for the afterlife, and during the many rituals of the ceremonial cycle. For the major ceremonies the slaves who were to be sacrificed were released under guard to wander in the town, eating at the various palaces and residences, and generally being treated with kindness and generosity. Then on the day of the celebration they were gathered together and carried by the hair to the temple precincts, where their hearts were cut out and offered to the gods. They were not eaten, but their decapitated heads were probably impaled on the *tzumpan*.

Had the stratification of Utatlán consisted only of the lord, vassal, and slave castes, social conditions might have been stable. In fact, however, they were not, because new, specialized ranks of people were constantly being created by the changing fortunes of the community. Inasmuch as these ranks were not well institutionalized under Quiché law and were derived from specialized productive and occupational activities, they can be viewed within a social-class framework. As incipient classes these groups challenged the favored positions of the castes and so were a source of conflict within the Utatlán community. Probably because they were a threat to the privileged order, the chronicles have few references to them. I shall begin with a description of the three "middle" sectors mentioned in the sources: the warriors, the merchants, and the artisans.

Warriors

There can be little doubt that a military life was the highest calling the Utatlán lord could have. From the ruler down, the lords participated actively in the Quiché wars. Some of the rulers themselves died in battle, along with many of their sons and other close kinsmen. Even as late as the founding of K'umarcaaj (ca. 1400), all political titles (*ajpop, k'alel,* and so on) were simultaneously administrative and military in function. The vassals served as foot soldiers for the lords, without title. Apparently as a result of the large number of military campaigns and the prodigious success of the Quiché armies, some of the vassal leaders became specialized warriors. Known as *achij* ("the men"), they finally challenged the lords of Utatlán, aided by dissident Quiché princes (see chapter 5). The authors of the *Popol Vuh*, who try to downplay the violent aspects of the challenge, explain that these warriors were "the first of the vassals." This implies that they were the heads of the vassal lineages and the leaders directly under the authority of the military lords.

The lords were forced to create a new military rank, which they called *achij* ("military") and to formalize it as part of the lord stratum. The graded titles of the lords (*ajpop, k'alel, utzám*) were given to these new military officers, always in conjunction with the descriptive rank, *achij* (Villacorta 1962, p. 351). This rank was given not only to socially climbing vassals but also to the younger and peripheral kinsmen of the lords. For example, Tecum, the grandson of the Utatlán ruler Oxib Quej, held the title and rank of *rajop achij* ("military chief," or "captain"; (*Título Totonicapán* n.d.; Carmack 1973, p. 302). Along with the titles came some of the symbols of lordly caste, particularly the sacred benches and chairs upon which they sat during council meetings. The newly entitled vassals were given the privilege of residing near the town so that they could attend the military councils. They took up the crafts, including stone carving, painting, and metallurgy (Villacorta 1934, p. 240). They also won increased authority over the vassals, probably providing a new form of mediation between the rural commoners and the town lords. For the first time they were sent outside the Utatlán area to serve as petty rulers of subject peoples.

The Cakchiquel sources, which are the clearest on this point, reveal that the emergence of this military class radically altered the old caste structure at Utatlán. Even so, the lordly caste did hold on at Utatlán, and the town never became as secular and military as Iximché, the Cakchiquel capital.

Merchants

The crisis at Utatlán that led to new military titles for some of the vassals may also have involved the merchants. One of the issues of the revolt, according to the Cakchiquel source (Villacorta 1934, pp. 230–32), was the vassals' desire for free travel on the roads. Furthermore, the facts surrounding a second conflict, centered upon the Cakchiquel woman who was selling tortillas at Utatlán (see chapter 5), suggest that the newly titled warriors wanted to control the market. Unfortunately, there is no direct evidence in the sources tying the vassal warriors to the merchants. In fact, in the chronicles there are few references at all to the merchants, and I have had to rely mostly on Spanish sources, especially the dictionaries, to reconstruct their position in Utatlán stratification. Apparently the merchants of Utatlán shared a similar low prestige with the Pochtecas of the Aztecs and other merchant peoples of the ancient world, and so received little recognition in the Quiché histories.

Las Casas (1909, p. 623) tells us that the merchants of highland Guatemala, like the vassals, were obligated to pay tributes. From the goods they gained in trade they paid a part in tribute to the lords of the town where they obtained them and a part to the lords of their own town of origin. We learn that the merchants used by the Dominican friars to send messages to Verapaz (Remesal 1932, pp. 184ff.) would stay with lords of the towns in which they traded. After paying their required tribute, they would eat and even engage in recreation with the lords "in accordance with the prestige of each merchant." That they held a privileged status is also suggested by the fact that they could read and write the painted codices and play the musical instruments of the lords.

The merchants traveled several times each year to buy and sell in the different markets of the highlands. They especially traded for rare goods, such as salt, cacao, feathers, and metal objects. They must have been wealthy, for one of the names used to refer to them, *ajbeyom*, meant both "merchant" and "rich man" (Coto n.d.; Basseta n.d.; Saenz 1940), as well as "one who comes and goes." Another name for them, *yacol* (Coto n.d.), was also used to refer to men who served the tables of lords. Perhaps the coming and going of these servants, carrying food for the table, was seen in analogy with the merchants, traveling from town to town with their rich treasures. The native sources reveal that three Utatlán lords bore the *yacol* title and may have been merchants, though other evidence suggests that they were ritual specialists associated with ceremonial banquets (Villacorta 1962, pp. 336–37; Recinos 1957, pp. 48–54).

It would seem that the merchants were a "class" somewhere between the vassals and the lords, at least in most cases. They paid tribute but had free access to the roads and direct association with the lords. Whether or not they formed a social group of their own, with a patron deity, we cannot say from the information available. We are not told where they resided, though the fact that they were welcome in the palaces of lords suggests that some of them might have had houses within the town. Most of them probably lived near the main market, either within the town or in the "suburbs" just outside.

Vassals were part-time buyers and sellers at local markets. In contrast with the long-distance traveling merchants, they were simple *ajc'ay* ("sellers"; Coto n.d.). Perhaps most of their transactions were worth less than twenty cacao beans (*q'uex*, "sales when the goods are worth less than twenty cacao beans"). The merchant sales would have been much larger in value, or *lok'* ("sales worth twenty cacao beans and above"). The instance of the Cakchiquel woman selling tortillas in Utatlán reminds us that, even more than today (McBryde 1947), commoner women did much of the buying and selling in the local markets.

Artisans

Another middle group at Utatlán was formed by the artisans. They were neither lords nor vassals but made up a specialized ethnic group with its own organization and monkey patron deity. The artisans are described by the Spaniards (Las Casas 1909, p. 624) as "ingenious craftsmen in painting, featherwork, carving, metallurgy, and the like." They sold at least some of their products at the market and apparently paid tribute in kind to the lords.

Besides the lords, the artisans are the only social group mentioned by name in the *Popol Vuh* (Villacorta 1962, pp. 37, 88). They are referred to by the prefix *aj* ("he of") followed by the craft specialty. *Ajtoltecat* ("toltec craftsmen") may have been a general term for them; it suggests a Mexica ethnic identity. Perhaps only major centers such as Utatlán had resident "Mexican" artisans, since they are not mentioned in discussions of other Quiché towns.

The artisans lacked the rank of *ajaw* ("lord") and sold goods in the markets, which would seem to place them outside the noble stratum. Some of them were from the warrior class (*achij*), which included the younger sons and kinsmen of lords occupying high office. Avocation may have been a factor in determining whether or not a young lord would practice a craft. The Tamub *títulos* (Recinos 1957, pp. 48ff.) make it clear that there were specialized craftsmen within lesser lordly lineages. Ladies were artisans, too, especially in the art of weaving. As we know from Las Casas and modern ethnography, the vassals engaged in weaving, pottery making, and other minor arts part time, trading their wares in the local markets. Apparently the goods produced by the specialized artisans circulated in a different cycle from those of the vassals, the one cycle in the hands of lords, the other in the hands of commoners.

Unfortunately, the sources are mute on the sociopolitical role the specialized artisans played as a group in Utatlán social life. They may have been closely tied to the merchants, though it is more likely that they were tightly controlled by the lords of the town. We are not even sure about where they resided, but a location near the town seems likely. Recent archaeological work in the zone just outside Utatlán has shed new light on the artisans (see chapter 7) and suggests that archaeology may help clarify the position of this middle class in the Utatlán community.

Serfs

One of the most interesting developments at Utatlán late in its history was the emergence of a growing class of rural laborers who were to some extent partly in competition with the vassals. Las Casas (1909, p. 625) describes them as "married slaves" who worked the lands of the lords and paid them a "tribute of crops, firewood, and pine resin for torches." Like the serfs of Mexico (*mayeques*), they were inherited as families with the land. Whereas the vassals paid tribute from their own lands or rent from lands loaned to them by lords, the serfs were completely beholden to the Utatlán lords for the land they worked.

The serfs at Utatlán were called *nimak achi* ("big people"), a misleading name that for many years hid from scholars their true significance in Quiché society. They were people who "had been captured in war, and were afterwards made vassals and neighbors" (Carrasco 1967a, p. 263). Presumably among the original resident captives were important men, and for that reason the name *nimak achi* was applied to this category of people. Given the tremendous number of conquests by the Quichés of Utatlán, the number of serfs must have increased dramatically through the years. No doubt they became extremely useful to the lords, for, unlike the vassals, they lacked local connections with land and kinsmen through which they could resist being manipulated.

Gradually more and more responsibility and tasks were given to the serfs. Though their main work probably remained agricultural, they were also used as trusted warriors, carriers of tribute and trade goods, and guards of valuable land and properties (Carmack 1973, p. 386). The lords paternalized their relations with them, and some serfs became well respected and even privileged. They were allowed to form lineages and sometimes were given status similar to that of the vassals within the estates of the lords. They may even have been allowed to retain their own languages and customs, and through endogamy to become internal ethnic groups at Utatlán.

The serfs became a threat to the vassals as the old caste structure was eroded. The vassals resented the lords' favoritism toward the serfs (because they were more easily controlled), who occupied many of the agricultural lands as they fell into the hands of lords and who were given some freedom of movement (as carriers and quasi-traders). Eventually the vassals revolted, and we are told that many of the serfs' leaders were killed (Villacorta 1934, pp. 230f.). They were far from eradicated from Utatlán society, however. Three centuries after the Conquest the descendants of Utatlán rulers still had *nimak achi* living on lands the descendants had inherited from their forefathers (Carrasco 1967a; Contreras 1965; see also chapter 9 of this book).

SEGMENTARY LINEAGES

The patrilineal-descent group was an integral component of Utatlán social structure. The lords of the Utatlán community were affiliated with descent groups whose patrilines (*c'ajolaxel*) could be traced back to the original forefathers who came to the mountains above Utatlán (Villacorta 1962, pp. 217ff.; *Título Totonicapán* n.d.). Genealogical lines were carefully recorded, for they provided the lords with their claimed Toltec origins and served as a means of excluding the vassals from the upper level of society. Nevertheless, genealogies were altered to conform to lineage-group realities, though usually some record of the actual relationships was retained. The Sakic lineage, for example, which was adopted into the genealogical position of the fourth Nima Quiché line, enjoyed full legal status at Pismachí and K'umarcaaj (*Título Totonicapán* n.d.; Villacorta 1962, p. 337). Similarly, the C'ocawib line was moved up into the position occupied by the C'ocaib line when the latter fell into illegitimacy. Other examples of genealogical changes included the adoption into the Cawek lineage of the Tepew Yaqui line, derived from a

Mexican source, and the Quejnay line, an indigenous line from the Chinique area. The Nijaib line added Tamub (Yacolatam) and Ilocab (Yeoltux) lines to its lineage.

Principal Lineages

By the time of the Conquest there were twenty-four "principal" lineages (primary-lineage units) at Utatlán, twenty-two at Pismachí, and eighteen at Mukwitz Pilocab (Recinos 1957, p. 46; Villacorta 1962, pp. 365–71). These figures indicate a rapid expansion of the original three Quiché, two Tamub, and five Ilocab sublineages founded by the warlords in the mountains. They also show an increase in the number of lords at Utatlán and also indicate that the Quichés had assimilated local ruling lines into their lineage structure.

Throughout the history of Utatlán the principal patrilineages of the lords retained their important function of regulating marriage and kinship relations. The lineages were strictly exogamous, and their members were united as brothers and sisters, fathers and fathers' sisters, and children. Substantial bride-price expenses were shared by the members of the lineage, and through marriage the kinsmen of different lineages became allied. In other ways too the lineages tended to act together as a cohesive group.

The patrilineages of the lords became increasingly important as units in the Quiché political system of Utatlán. Each principal lineage was associated with a political office and was named for that office. The head of the lineage was the actual occupant of the political position. The rank and importance of the offices gave rank to the lineages, though prior genealogical position had a predetermining influence on which office a given lineage obtained. For example, the Cawek principal lineages, already ranked high because their founding father (Balam Quitze) was the oldest warlord, gained control of the office of *ajpop* ("chief"), the highest-ranked position of the Quiché political system. The expansion of political offices at Utatlán and the competition for those offices explain in part the rapid segmentation and increase in number of principal lineages at Utatlán. Another cause of segmentation was disagreement over marriage arrangements, for a lineage placed rigid restrictions on where wives could be obtained, as well as heavy obligations for aiding in bride-price payments (Villacorta 1962, pp. 330–31).

Major Lineages

In segmentary-lineage fashion, prior-generation patrilineal ties were remembered, and the various principal lineages could be coalesced into larger lineage units based on those ties. For the Nima Quichés of Utatlán, quadripartite groupings, which we may refer to as "major" lineages, were of special importance. The major lineages consisted of nine Cawek, nine Nijaib, four Ajaw Quiché, and two Sakic lineages each (Villacorta 1962, pp. 336–37;

Título Totonicapán n.d.). The Tamubs of Pismachi and the Ilocabs of Mukwitz formed similar major-lineage divisions. The Tamubs had four major lineages, consisting of five C'opichoch, eight Majquinalo, four C'ochojlan, and four C'ok'anawil principal lineages (Recinos 1957, pp. 44ff.). The Ilocabs had five major lineages, the Rokche, Cajib Aj, Sic'a, Xuwanija, and Wukmil; the exact number of principal lineages for each is unknown (Carmack 1973, p. 287ff.).

For the Tamubs even more significant than the major lineages were moietal divisions based on the union of the C'opichoch with C'ochojlan major lineages (the Ekoamak' moiety), and Majquinalo with C'ok'anawil (the Kakoj moiety). A moiety grouping was not pronounced in the Nima Quiché lineages of Utatlán, though the Caweks and Ajaw Quichés apparently formed one moiety and the Nijaib and Sakic another in some contexts. We lack information about whether or not the Ilocabs united their lineages along moietal lines, though references to five sublineages during the pre-Utatlán period, and to five major lineages later suggest that they did not.

It should be noted that the major and the moietal lineage divisions bore ancestral rather than political names. An exception was the Nima Quiché major lineage Ajaw Quiché (Lord of the Quichés). This name appears to be a political title retained from an earlier time when that lineage ruled at Jakawitz. The ancestral names for major lineages and the political titles for principal lineages suggest functional differences between the two lineage divisions of the Quichés at Utatlán. The higher-level lineage divisions had especially important ritual functions (to be described later). Nevertheless, the major lineages of the Quichés provided the framework for the quadripartite political rule at Utatlán (see "Minimal Lineages" below) and for the structure of the "colonies" (*calpules*) under their jurisdiction. Similarly, the moieties of the Tamubs provided the basis for a dualistically organized central government and colonial rule for that group. It is also highly probable—the sources are unclear on this point—that the higher-level lineage segments functioned in marriage exchanges. Both major lineages and moieties of the Nima Quichés and Tamubs were apparently exogamous, and alliances with outside-descent units were probably established by these segments. This marital function might explain the use of genealogical names for these higher-level lineage divisions, since precise kinship connection would be critical in establishing the lines of exogamy.

Minimal Lineages

Below the principal lineages, the lords were organized into even smaller units, which might be termed "minimal" lineages. Most of our information about the minimal lineages derives from the Tamub sources (Recinos 1957, pp. 48ff.), though we have enough data for the Nima Quichés to know that their situation was similar. While some of the principal lineages had no minimal-lineage divisions and others had several, there were about two to three for each principal lineage. Most of the minimal lineages appear to have consisted of short patrilines within which it was common to inherit the names of ancestors (mostly those of grandfathers). Nevertheless, the occurrence of several Nima Quiché lineage names in the Tamub minimal-lineage list (Istayul, Menchu, Cutec, Quewek, Sakimox, and C'otuja) makes it seem likely that minimal lineages sometimes derived from matrilines as well—for example the children of Nima Quiché fathers and Tamub mothers formed Tamub minimal lineages. We can conclude that cognatic tendencies were operating at the minimal-lineage level of the Utatlán community.

Most of the minimal lineages have names suggesting low-level political, ritual, military, and economic functions. Clearly the minimal lineages of a principal lineage made up the main staff of that group's chief political officer. The names of the Tamub minimal lineages are highly informative in this regard (Recinos 1957, pp. 48–56): Bracelet Keeper, Messenger, Chief Carrier, Gourd (Maker), Council Debater, Blood Sacrificer, Chief of the Sweat Bath, Guardian of the Orphaned (Young) Men, Councilman, War Dancer, War Leader, Guardian of the Wall, Metalworker, Helper, Painter, Son of the Councilman, Rattler, Son of the Council Transformer (Balam), Lone Councilman, Banquet Servant (or Merchant), Ambassador to Foreign Peoples, Tormentor, Patcher of Metal Objects, Woodcutter, Wood Splitter, Dye Maker, Loom (Maker), Server of Fowl, Toaster, Council Announcer, Flutist, Tribute Collector, Stomach Cramp (?) Speaker, Council Diviner.

The minimal lineages of the higher-ranked principal lineages took on functions of greater political authority and importance. In fact, the Nima Quiché sources (*Título Totonicapán* n.d.; Carmack 1973, pp. 273–306) suggest that minimal lineages frequently competed with principal lineages for office and status. The Ajpop principal lineage of the Caweks, for example, had succeeded in elevating one of its minimal lineages to the status of principal lineage (Ajpop C'amja) and two other minimal lineages to positions of high status in the military structure: Nima Rajpop Achij (Great Military Chief) and Ch'uti Rajpop Achij (Little Military Chief). Certainly the twenty-four principal lineages officially recognized at Utatlán (as well as the twenty-two at Pismachi and the eighteen at Mukwitz Pilocab) were merely those that prevailed at the time of the Conquest. As the chronicles attest, this number fluctuated through time and according to the fortunes of the various lineages and sublineages.

Big Houses

From early in Quiché history the principal lineages were closely identified with the buildings in which they carried out their affairs. Such buildings were called *nim ja* ("big houses") and were expressly used for the ceremonial lecturing, bride-price giving, and eating and drinking associated with marriages between the lineages (*Popol Vuh*, *Título Totonicapán* and *Título Tamub*). Some of the houses were shared by more than one lineage; the Cawek and Nijaub lineages occupied the same big house at Patojil. At Pismachi separate big houses were constructed for the three principal lineages of the Nima Quichés (Villacorta 1962, p. 326).

The big houses became so closely associated with the lineage groups occupying them that the lineages themselves became known as "big houses." The segmentation of the Nima Quiché principal lineages from three at Pismachi to nine and then twenty-four at K'umarcaaj was remembered by the Quichés as the construction of three, nine, and then twenty-four big houses (Villacorta 1962, pp. 326–37). The actual room occupied by a lineage, its size, location, height, and so on, became a major consideration, related to the increasingly political functions the principal lineages took on. Just as the political offices filled by the lineages came to dominate their strictly kinship character, so too did the buildings in which those political activities took place. Sometimes the big houses had names different from those of the lineage units occupying them; for example the big house of the Ajpop lineage was called Cuja; and that of the Ajpop C'amja, Tz'iquin (Villacorta 1962, p. 365).

There is no indication in the chronicles that the major lineages or moieties had big houses independent of the principal lineage houses. They probably did not, since the leaders of the principal lineages were the same as those for the major and moiety divisions. Nevertheless, there are hints in the sources that the big houses of principal lineages of a major lineage or moiety division were grouped together in the same section of the town. In the crowded towns of Utatlán, territorial organization in the form of aggregates of buildings became an integral feature of lineage structure.

Vassal Lineages

Like their lords, the vassals attached to the Utatlán community were organized into patrilineal-descent groups. These groups are not named in the chronicles, though many surnames listed in colonial baptismal records for central Quiché towns (Carmack 1965) probably derive from vassal patrilineages. They appear to be names of ancestors, taken ultimately from animals, rivers, trees, and so on (Carrasco 1964).

The vassal lineages of Utatlán were exogamous like those of the lords, though vassals' wives had to be selected from within the Utatlán community. Adjacent patrilineages probably intermarried, as is still the tendency in traditional Quiché areas. Aged Quiché informants with whom I have spoken claim that in past centuries patrilineages were tied together as wife-exchange units, called *calpules*. Las Casas (1909, p. 625) informs us that, like the lords, vassals engaged in levirate marriages (in which brothers married their deceased brothers' wives) and made multiple bride-price payments. These practices can still be found in modified form in traditional rural zones of Quiché (Carmack n.d.).

The vassals lacked the big houses of the lords. In the chronicles the vassals are described as living dispersed among the canyons and mountains. The term used to refer to their settlements is *amak'*, which, as Ximénez (1929, p. 130) explained, "is a small settlement spread out like the legs of a spider, which is the likeness from which they get that name." He went on to say that they were "hamlets" (*aldeas*) and that they contrasted with the "towns" (*tinamit*) where the lords lived. The families of a lineage resided near their milpas, and this was the reason for their dispersal. Each group had a lineage head who was responsible for representing his group before the lords of the town.

Ximénez (1929) claimed that the same rural organization existed in his day, and I have found it still extant today (Carmack n.d.). Present-day patrilines usually extend back to an ancestor five or six generations in the past. In the Quiché area these patrilineages are referred to as *ojalaxic* ("we who are born [together]"). The lineage head is known as *chuchkajaw* ("mother-father") or *c'amal be* ("leader") and is both a religious and a political leader. These lineages are the primary landholding units of the traditional rural areas, through a complicated form of joint ownership (Falla 1975). Lineage lands are always demarcated by natural boundaries, trees, rocks, bunchgrass, and so on. The lands of each lineage also have sacred spots where altars are built, the most important of which are the *warabal ja* ("sleeping house") for the ancestors and the *winel* ("created") for animals and crops. Though some large lineages form independent hamlets (today called *parajes*), most hamlets consist of two or more lineages tied together through marriage, shared labor, and ritual activities. The ancient hamlets of the Utatlán community, the *amak'*, were probably of similar organization.

It should be clear from the description above that lords and vassals had independent lineages. It is true that the lords referred to the vassals as their "children," but the very terms used, *al c'ajol* ("children in the female *and* male lines") indicate that they were not related through lineage. The idea that the vassals were children of the lords was largely fiction anyway, as we have seen. The vassals were children of the lords in a paternalistic and metaphorical rather than literal sense.

Summary

The segmentary lineage structure of the Quichés at Utatlán can be summarized as shown in Table 6.2.

Table 6.2. **Lineage Structure at Utatlán**

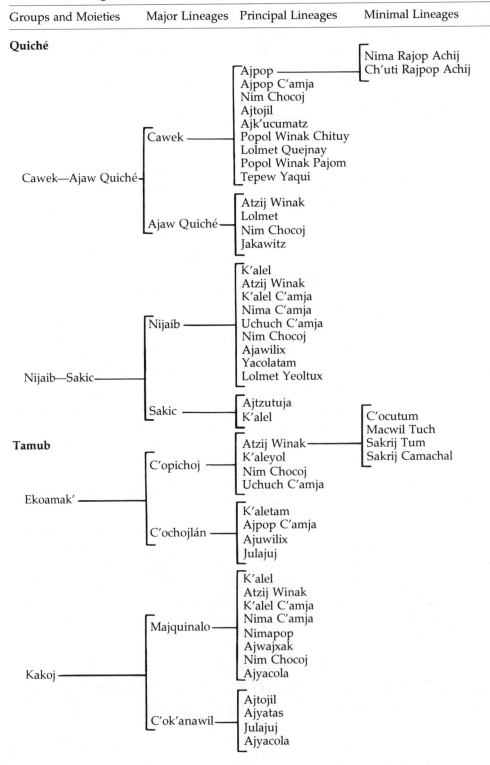

Groups and Moieties	Major Lineages	Principal Lineages	Minimal Lineages

Quiché

Cawek—Ajaw Quiché
- Cawek
  - Ajpop
    - Nima Rajop Achij
    - Ch'uti Rajpop Achij
  - Ajpop C'amja
  - Nim Chocoj
  - Ajtojil
  - Ajk'ucumatz
  - Popol Winak Chituy
  - Lolmet Quejnay
  - Popol Winak Pajom
  - Tepew Yaqui
- Ajaw Quiché
  - Atzij Winak
  - Lolmet
  - Nim Chocoj
  - Jakawitz

Nijaib—Sakic
- Nijaib
  - K'alel
  - Atzij Winak
  - K'alel C'amja
  - Nima C'amja
  - Uchuch C'amja
  - Nim Chocoj
  - Ajawilix
  - Yacolatam
  - Lolmet Yeoltux
- Sakic
  - Ajtzutuja
  - K'alel

Tamub

Ekoamak'
- C'opichoj
  - Atzij Winak
    - C'ocutum
    - Macwil Tuch
    - Sakrij Tum
    - Sakrij Camachal
  - K'aleyol
  - Nim Chocoj
  - Uchuch C'amja
- C'ochojlán
  - K'aletam
  - Ajpop C'amja
  - Ajuwilix
  - Julajuj

Kakoj
- Majquinalo
  - K'alel
  - Atzij Winak
  - K'alel C'amja
  - Nima C'amja
  - Nimapop
  - Ajwajxak
  - Nim Chocoj
  - Ajyacola
- C'ok'anawil
  - Ajtojil
  - Ajyatas
  - Julajuj
  - Ajyacola

Table 6.2. *Continued*

Groups and Moieties	Major Lineages	Principal Lineages	Minimal Lineages

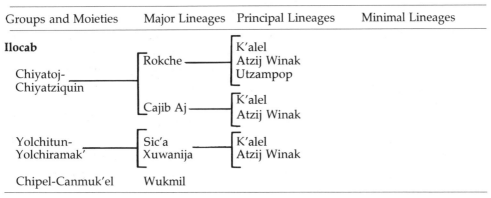

		K'alel	
	Rokche	Atzij Winak	
Chiyatoj-Chiyatziquin		Utzampop	
	Cajib Aj	K'alel	
		Atzij Winak	
Yolchitun-Yolchiramak'	Sic'a / Xuwanija	K'alel	
		Atzij Winak	
Chipel-Canmuk'el	Wukmil		

The chart is incomplete, especially in the minimal lineage column, for many of the minimal lineages are not mentioned in the chronicles. I have selected a few examples to illustrate their relationship to the rest of the segmentative lineage structure.

It might also be noted that the number of Tamub and Ilocab principal lineages does not correspond with the number they are reported to have had. The Tamub chronicles list only twenty principal lineages, though they claim to have had twenty-two. Possibly two that they list as minimal lineages were in the process of achieving principal status. In the case of the Ilocabs, we lack information on any but the leading principal lineages.

Generally it would appear that a group's power could be measured by the number of principal lineages it had. This suggests that the Quichés were more powerful than the Tamubs, who in turn were more powerful than the Ilocabs. Within the Quiché group the Caweks led the Nijaibs, Ajaw Quichés, and Sakics. Among the Tamubs, the Kakoj moiety was probably more powerful than the Ekoamak'. Our scant data suggest that the rank order of power among the Ilocabs was the Rokche, the Cajib Aj, and the Sic'a lineages, followed by the Xuwanija and the Wukmil. Statements in the chronicles indicate these rankings.

The hyphenated names used to denote the Quiché and Ilocab moieties indicate that dualistic structures were not strongly recognized among the two groups. Nevertheless, the chronicles support the theory that these presumed combinations were actualized for some functions within Utatlán social life. For the Tamubs the moietal division was fundamental.

The meanings of some of the principal lineage names listed in Table 6.2 are given below.

TERRITORIAL DIVISIONS

To the integration of the Utatlán community through stratification and lineage organization must be added territory, which by the time of the Conquest was challenging lineage in importance as an integrational mode at Utatlán. As noted above, buildings occupied by the lineages in town became as important symbolically as the lineages themselves; hence the name *nim ja* ("big house") as the general term for lineage. Outside the towns the rural people continued to identify strongly with their lineages (*ojalaxic*), but their relations with the lords of the towns were increasingly based on physical or territorial arrangements. At least two types of territorial organization emerged at Utatlán to integrate town and country, lord and vassal.

Estate (Chinamit)

The first unit which integrated lords and vassals was the *chinamit*, a territorial organization which has been widely confused with the lineage. *Chinamit* is a Nahua word meaning "fenced-in place," and it retained that meaning for the Quichés of Utatlán. The members (*chinamital*) of a given *chinamit* were "all those living within a single territory separated by a wall" (Saenz 1940). An early dictionary (Carrasco 1964, p. 325) defines the members of a *chinamit* as those "called by the name and under (the authority) of one chief, so that anyone who might like to [could] join this lineage and brotherhood of people." Thus the *chinamit* was a territorial unit of people related by virtue of being subject to the same chief. They bore the name of the lineage of their chief, though "they were not necessarily all patrilineal kinsmen" (Carrasco 1964, p. 327). I shall occasionally refer to this unit as an "estate," in analogy with the similarly structured estates of feudal Europe.

According to the *Popol Vuh*, each principal patrilineage of the lords (*nim ja*) ruled over an estate, which therefore bore its name (Villacorta 1962, pp. 336, 366, 369). Thus there were twenty-four estates of the Nima Quichés, usually one for each principal lineage. The Sakic lineage was an exception; it had two estates subject to its single big house (though there were two chiefs, one for each estate). We are told that the vassals in each estate were numerous and were subject to their respective big house, that is, lordly principal lineage. Undoubtedly each estate included several vassal patrilineages. The serfs of the Utatlán community were another component of the estates. Like the vassals they lived in the territorial boundaries of the big house to which they were subject. At Iximché, the Cakchiquel town, one group of serfs had its own estate head and territory (Carrasco 1963), but there is no evidence that the serfs achieved such independence at Utatlán.

The early Spaniards correctly claimed that the *chinamit* structure at Utatlán was like the vassal estates of Spain. Las Casas (1909, p. 616) explained that "there were in this kingdom of Utatlán certain heads of noble lineages and families, with known residences called big houses, as we say the house of Guzman or Mendoza in Spain." In both the Spanish and Quiché estates the rural agricultural serfs and vassals were subject to particular noble lineages residing in the towns. In both cases also these territorial units were the basis for tribute and service obligations, judicial and ritual processes, and recruitment of soldiers to fight with their lords. The administration of the various activities of the Quiché estates was largely assigned to minimal lineages of the big houses, for which there were special officials (see *"Calpul"* below). These officials in turn worked closely with the lineage heads of the vassals. In this fashion lineage and territory were combined at Utatlán.

Just how far beyond the towns of the Utatlán community the estate boundaries extended has been a difficult question to answer from the chronicles. The *Popol Vuh* (Villacorta 1962, pp. 347–49) contains a list of the places of origin of the "representatives of the estates" (*wachinel chinamit*) who were sent to serve as watchmen and guards at Quiché frontier centers. Most of the chronicles contain similar lists of places, which include much of present-day Chichicastenango, Chiché, Chinique, Santa Cruz del Quiché, Patzite, Santa Lucia la Reforma, and Chiquimula. Beyond those places, perhaps, the territories were seen as separate provinces (*ajawarem*), and the subjects there were outside the estate organization.

Calpul

The Tamub *títulos* (Recinos 1957, pp. 54–60; Carmack n.d.) refer to the places from which estate representatives were taken as *calpules*, listing thirteen for the Nima Quichés and eleven for the Tamubs (those of the Ilocab are not given). It is clear that the *calpules* were larger than the estate units and thus were a second territorial organization. The walled-estate territories probably did not extend out to all the *calpules*—for example, all the way to the central part of Chichicastenango. Rather, they were perhaps physically confined to the flatlands surrounding the Utatlán towns. Nevertheless, estate jurisdiction in some fashion reached the *calpules*, providing authority and control over the larger divisions.

The *calpules* appear to have been ancient, traditional territorial units, perhaps going back to the period before the invasion of the central basin by the Quiché forefathers. Originally they may have corresponded to native chiefdoms, and it is possible that even after the Quichés established control over them some local leadership continued to be recognized (see "Rural Settlements" in chapter 7). Most ancient boundaries were probably retained, just as many cantons in the central Quiché area today retain their pre-Conquest boundaries. Socially the *calpul* was a group of intermarrying commoner lineages, and in any given *calpul* might be found vassals from several different estates. *Calpul* is a term still used in the rural zones of the Quiché area. In some places it designates a large territorial division similar to those described in the chronicles (Bunzel 1952; Rodas y Rodas 1938), while in others (such as Chiquimula) it refers to a patrilineal clan (Carmack n.d.).

As a further integration of the rural zone around Utatlán these larger territorial units were under the jurisdiction of the major lineages and moieties of the Utatlán lords. In each Tamub *calpul* territory resided at least one high political official and one military officer from each of the two moieties (Recinos 1957, pp. 54ff.). The Nima Quiché *calpules* were probably similarly organized, except that there were apparently political and military officials from each of the four major lineages: Cawek, Nijaib, Ajaw Quiché, and Sakic (*Título Totonicapán* n.d.). The presence of such officials in these territories suggests that at least incipient town centers may have been built in the *calpul* territories. It may be supposed that they were roughly similar to the traditional canton divisions found today in rural Quiché, with their scattered lineages and tiny town centers.

The *calpul* territories were also grouped into larger zones corresponding to the jurisdictions of the three major towns in Utatlán. The Nima Quichés controlled the *calpules* located generally east of Utatlán; those of the Tamubs were in the southwest, and those of the Ilocabs were in the north (Recinos 1957, pp. 62–67). These large territorial divisions apparently functioned for convenience of political control from the respective towns of the three groups.

In summary, the territorial organization of the Utatlán community consisted of (1) discrete towns (*tinamit*), controlled by the three political divisions of the Quiché state; (2) walled-off small territorial divisions (*chinamit*) surrounding the towns, controlled by the elite principal lineages; and (3) large, cantonlike territories (*calpul*) spread continuously throughout the basin, under the jurisdiction of the three major political groups at Utatlán.

Political Geography

It is possible to place the various territorial divisions described above in their actual geographical setting (see chapter 4). When this is done and account is taken of the resource potential of the various territories, political relations of the Utatlán community stand in relief (see Fig. 4.1).

The dominant Nima Quiché group occupied the largest town (Utatlán), and possibly a second town (Atalaya). Their twenty-four walled estates extended from the entire eastern side of the nuclear zone, although they were probably built up primarily in the flat Pachiquí and Tinamit *calpul* territories. Their many *calpules* included the large, flat plains on the east, the hilly Chichicastenango zone on the southwest, and the mountain valley and slopes to the northeast. They established "colonial" *calpules* within the Ilocab territory northward, as well as zones of serfs within Tamub territories on the west. Newly formed Nijaib *calpules* provided additional Nima Quiché territories within the Tamub zone on the southwest. Thus the political advantage the documents ascribe to the Nima Quichés receives territorial and geographic confirmation. They controlled the largest area, the most people, the richest resources, and the primary avenues of communication.

The Tamub town, Pismachi, south of Utatlán, was considerably smaller than Utatlán. The twenty-two walled estates of the Tamubs extended outward south and west, the major buildup probably occurring in the flat Nacxit *calpul*. Tamub *calpul* territories were discontinuous, as suggested by their grouping into three named aggregates of *calpules*: Amak' Tam on the north, Nacxit on the south and west, and Tz'olojche on the west on the other side of the Ilocabs. The relatively large *calpul* holdings of the Tamubs were probably permitted by the Nima Quichés only because they were so fragmented. The geography of the three territories, except for the Panajxit and Estancia division, was hilly, and less productive than the Nima Quiché lands.

The Ilocab town, Mukwitz Pilocab, was small in comparison to Utatlán, and much smaller in area than Pismachi. The eighteen walled estates of the Ilocabs extended out northwest, and presumably were built up in the flat zones of the Chuisic'a and Palopoj *calpules*. The Ilocabs' *calpul* territory was concentrated in an area north and west of their town. The territory shows signs of having lost lands to the other two groups. The Nima Quichés established *calpules* squarely within the northern Ilocab section and also placed serfs in one section that either was close to or overlapped the southern part of their western zone. The Tamubs drove a wedge of *calpul* territory between the Ilocabs' northern and western sections and took land away from them in the southern part of their western section (at Amak' Mes, and possibly Pach'alip). Ilocab *calpul* terrains were generally rolling hills, though they had some flatlands in the western section. The Ilocabs' territory was clearly geographically inferior to the Nima Quichés', though the Ilocabs may have been the equals of the Tamubs before their territorial losses.

The political advantages derived from geographic control continued to hold long after the Spaniards conquered the Quichés. Modern census figures show that municipalities that inherited Nima Quiché lands (Santa Cruz del Quiché, Chiché, Chinique, and northwestern Chichicastenango) produce almost four times as much maize as municipalities derived from Tamub lands (Chiquimula, Santa Lucia la Reforma, Patzité, and norhtwestern San Pedro Jocopilas) or Ilocab lands (San Antonio Ilotenango and western San Pedro Jocopilas). Not only is this the result of differences in size, but the Nima Quiché lands yield more maize per unit of area. Correspondingly, modern Nima Quiché population sizes and densities are three times those of the Tamubs and six times those of the Ilocabs. Present-day political power in Quiché still follows ancient geographical lines.

Other, less important sociopolitical relationships (see below) also corresponded to geographic positioning. A Cawek and Ilocab alliance was facilitated by the contiguity of their towns, while a similar Tamub and Nijaib alliance (assuming that the latter inhabited the Atalaya town) was correlated to the contiguity of their two towns. Further, alliances between major lineages (such as Cawek and Ajaw Quiché) may have had geographic bases too, but that depended on an estate organization whose territorial boundaries our sources do not permit us to reconstruct. Similarly, control over provinces may have had some correlation with geographic location, but again our sources are too skimpy to permit us to work out the details.

POLITICAL CENTRALIZATION AND DECENTRALIZATION

In the sixteenth century the Spaniards were already debating whether Utatlán had a centralized or a decentralized political system. Las Casas, the Dominican friar, argued that the Utatlán political system was centralized (1909, pp. 615–16). He referred to Utatlán as a "kingdom" and claimed that it was a "monarchy." The Utatlán king, he said, was always succeeded by his sons, brothers, or close kinsmen, according to a system of four graded positions: the king himself, the elect king, and major and minor captains. On the death of the king, he was succeeded by the elect king, while the two captains moved upward in office. Subject to the king were certain officials, like judges, who formed a council to deal with affairs of state. The king had other governors and officials who ruled over the provinces of the kingdom. They were appointed by him, and he could remove them from office for misconduct. In all these offices, from the king down, noble descent was required, but prior administrative experience and capability were also taken into account. The Utatlán king's close kinsmen ruled over Chiquimula (the Tamubs) and Oloquitlán (the Ilocabs). They honored him and aided him in war, but they were not directly subject to his authority. Even the rulers of the Rabinals, Cakchiquels, and Tzutujils had to be confirmed by the Utatlán king at the time of their accession to office. The symbol of the Utatlán king's supremacy in the highlands was that only he wore a nosepiece.

The Franciscan friar Betanzos insisted (Carrasco 1967, pp. 252–57) that authority at Utatlán was highly decentralized. He claimed that, rather than a single ruler, there were four, one from each of the principal lineages of the town: Cawek, Nijaib, Ajaw Quiché, and Sakic. Further, the lords of each of these lineages entered office not through inheritance but by the vote of the members of the lineage from several towns. These rulers had authority only over the people of their lineage, just as the elaborate ceremonies in honor of the lineage gods were attended only by persons of that lineage. Rulers of other towns were not subject to the four rulers of Utatlán, he said. Nevertheless, as close relatives and out of respect for their sacred gods they visited the lords of Utatlán and brought them presents. The lords from these towns also joined in the councils that decided on war or political succession at Utatlán. They could remove an Utatlán ruler from office, and did so on one occasion, killing him and putting another in his place. Again according to Betanzos, the ruler of the Guatemalan (Cakchiquel) and Atitlán (Tzutujil) kingdoms were completely independent of Utatlán.

These two drastically different views of political authority at Utatlán were held by men who had access to reliable information on the subject. Their conflicting claims illustrate how difficult it is to describe in simple terms the political authority at Utatlán. As we shall see, in a sense both views were correct.

Quadripartite Rule

It might be supposed that the king, the king-elect, and the two "captains" referred to by Las Casas were the same rulers whom Betanzos claimed were independent heads of four separate lineages. If that were the case, Las Casas would surely be in error. The heads of the four leading lineages at Utatlán, the Ajpops (Caweks), K'alels (Nijaibs), Atzij Winaks (Ajaw Quichés), and K'alels (Sakics), were independent lines and did not succeed one another. Were they the rulers who Las Casas said succeeded each other and had four, three, two, and one canopies, respectively, over their thrones? I am convinced that Las Casas was not referring to the four lineage heads mentioned by Betanzos. Rather, he was talking about four Cawek lineage officials, whom the *Titulo Totonicapán* (n.d.) gives as *ajpop*, *ajpop c'amja*, *nima rajpop achij*, and *ch'uti rajpop achij*. The same document explains that these were not just lineage positions but important political offices at Utatlán, and that four, three, two, and one sacred canopies, respectively were associated with them. This is consistent with Las Casas's description and confirms the theory that there was an elite succession line to the highest office at Utatlán.

The two *rajpop achij* offices were probably lesser ones, in which Cawek lords proved themselves worthy of the higher positions. We know that Tecum, who died in battle against the Spaniards, was *nima rajpop achij* and, as grandson of the *ajpop*, was in line for that office (Carmack 1973, p. 302). On the other hand, it is doubtful that the so-called elect king, the *ajpop c'amja*, could succeed to the office of *ajpop*. The chronicles make it clear that the Ajpop C'amja lineage had become principal in its own right and separate from the Ajpop lineage. The *ajpop c'amja* was more an assistant than an elect king, and succession to the position was exclusively within the Ajpop C'amja lineage. Possibly the *ch'uti rajpop achij* position also pertained to that lineage and was in the succession line to the "assistant-king" position. This explanation makes plausible Las Casas's claim that there were two fathers and two sons in the succession unit. It was common for sons to succeed their fathers both as *ajpop* (from the *nima rajpop* position) and *ajpop c'amja* (from the *ch'uti rajpop* position). As Las Casas himself said, father-son succession was not always the case, and experience and aptitude could result in brothers or other close relatives succeeding before sons.

If we accept Las Casas's description as modified above, we must still deal with Betanzos's claim that the heads of the other three major lineages at Utatlán were equal in authority to the *ajpop*. In support of Betanzos, the chronicles make it clear that quadripartite rule was an extremely important principle of Utatlán political structure. Usually, when affairs of state are mentioned—such as receiving tribute, conquering warriors, or visiting dignitaries or sending out colonizers—the four rulers of the major lineages are mentioned (Villacorta 1962, pp. 346ff.). Though the personal names of these rulers are sometimes recorded, and sometimes they are called by the names of the founding ancestors, Balam Quitze, Balam Ak'ab, Majucutaj, and Iq'ui Balam (Recinos 1957, pp. 82, 109), usually they are listed by their lineage titles: *ajpop*, *ajpop c'amja*, *k'alel*, and *atzij winak*. As Betanzos indicated, succession to these four offices took place within the respective lineages, and lineage members from other towns participated in the selection. The titles indicate, however, that only three major lineages were involved rather than four: Cawek (*ajpop*, *ajpop c'amja*), Nijaib (*k'alel*), and Ajaw Quiché (*atzij winak*).

So, in a general way, Betanzos was correct in stating that Utatlán rule was oligarchical rather than monarchical. He failed to understand, however, that the major lineages of Utatlán were ranked and that the ranking provided a hierarchical ordering of the four rulers. It is clear from Quiché history that the rank order could change. The Ajaw Quiché lineage, descended from Majucutaj, held the highest rank in pre-Utatlán times, when its town, Jakawitz, was the Quichés' political center. The Caweks gained the top spot at Pismachi, probably during the time of C'otuja (the first powerful *ajpop*). Tzutubaja (Sakic), an outsider, was adopted into the Quiché lineage structure to replace the fourth major lineage, which had previously died out. The Sakics demonstrate the importance of the quadripartite principle, but the failure of this lineage to gain one of the four ruling positions, and its usurpation by the Caweks, shows the even greater importance of rank in the political structure.

In a sense, then, the *ajpop* was a supreme ruler at Utatlán. Only the *ajpop* had the nosepiece and four canopies (Las Casas 1909, pp. 615–16; *Título Totonicapán* n.d.). Only members of his lineage could succeed him, usually sons occupying the next-highest lineage office, *nima rajpop achij*. The *ajpop* claimed the most illustrious dynastic line, and only that line was remembered with historical detail and genealogical accuracy. He was the head of the army, a position for which he had been specifically trained while serving as *nima rajpop achij* ("great military captain"). The *ajpops* of Utatlán usually accompanied their armies in battle, where, surrounded by elite guards and the icons of the gods, they provided the symbol of strength and unity. The *ajpop* also had the power of appointing men to many offices and the first voice in the councils (though not the only one). He undoubtedly symbolized and singly represented, when necessary, the Utatlán political unit as a whole.

The other three "rulers" of Utatlán gave the appearance of providing quadripartite rule, but they were actually assistants to the *ajpop*. The *ajpop c'amja*, although from the Cawek major lineage, represented a lineage line (Istayul) tainted with illegitimacy (Carmack 1966). The rank was substantially below that of the *ajpop*, and the heroes in Quiché history were not from that line. The *ajpop c'amja* was the assistant to the *ajpop*. As the word *c'amja* ("receiving house") suggests, he received visitors and officials in the name of the *ajpop*. Apparently he could represent the *ajpop* when the latter was absent, and, as Carrasco (1967*b*) has shown in another context, he could stand in for the deceased *ajpop* until another was selected; hence he was the "elect."

The *k'alel* came from the Nijaib major lineage. That lineage was below the Caweks, as attested by the secondary importance of their recorded historical exploits compared with those of the Caweks. The *k'alel* was a "courtier" (Saenz 1940) who attended the *ajpop* in public matters as a chief judge and counselor. His role was to explain, question, witness, and denounce and so assist the *ajpop* in making important decisions.

The *atzij winak* ("speaker") was also a counselor to the *ajpop*. Perhaps his role differed from the *k'alel's* in being more legislative than judicial in public functions. The *atzij winak* came from the Ajaw Quiché major lineage, which had dropped in rank from an early leading position to fourth place. As the lineage of power in times past, the counsel of the Ajaw Quiché speakers may have been revered.

Confederated Authority

The structure of the highest authority of the other two groups, the Tamubs at Pismachí and the Ilocabs at Mukwitz, was generally similar to that at Utatlán. The four ruling titles of the Tamubs are given in the chronicles (Recinos 1957, pp. 48ff.; *Título Totonicapán* n.d.) as *ajpop tam*, *k'ale tam*, *k'ale kakoj*, and *atzij winak kakoj*. The first two officials were from the Ekoamak' moiety, the latter two from the Kakoj. There apparently was little hierarchical ranking of these four offices, the emphasis being instead on equal dual rule by the two moieties. The first Ekoamak' official (*ajpop tam*) was originally an Atzij Winak

171

like his Kakoj counterpart and apparently rose in rank only late in Tamub history. It is noteworthy also that both Kakoj officials were from the same major lineage, the fourth major lineage (C'ok'anawil) having no political representation. Thus the Tamubs favored dualistic over quadripartite rule, and the highest Tamub officials were "judges" and "speakers," rather than rulers.

Our information on Ilocab rule at Mukwitz is scarce (*Título Totonicapán* n.d.; Carmack 1973, pp. 287–306). While the Ilocabs were divided into five major lineages (Rokche, Cajib Aj, Sic'a, Xuwanija, and Wukmil), only three of them provided high-level officials. The Rokche, Cajib Aj, and Sic'a lineages had both *k'alel* and *atzij winak* officials. This structure was similar to the Tamubs' (two *k'alel* and two *atzij winak* officials), except that the officials were found within the same major lineages. Further, the chronicles indicate that the Rokché officials were clearly the highest in rank and the Wukmil officials were lower than those of the other three lineages. The Ajpop lineage of the Caweks at Utatlán had intermarried with the Rokche lineage of the Ilocabs. Like the Tamub officials the Ilocab officials were only judges and speakers. They had no chief ruler (*ajpop*), at least not until late in their history.

The above analysis of the highest authorities of the three Quiché groups raises the question of the political relationship between them. Since the chronicles generally confirm Las Casas's account on this point, it is worth quoting in full (1909, p. 616):

> The other two brothers [of the king of Utatlán] had their own rule, but it was different from that of Utatlán because, though they were the lords of their people, they recognized the lords of Utatlán as their superiors. This recognition of superiority was not in giving them tribute, rather only in reverential obedience as one would give to an older brother, and in helping them when they went to war. They had their own rule, and distinct ministers of justice, especially over the towns called Chiquimula and Oloquitlán, which were next to the city of Utatlán.

The reference to the "two brothers" is to the Tamubs and the Ilocabs, whose jurisdictions (*calpules*) included the territories of modern Chiquimula and Ilotenango, respectively (see chapters 9 and 10). There is evidence that at least one Tamub line shared common ancestors (Acul and 9 K'ij) with the Nijaib lineage of the Nima Quichés (Recinos 1957, pp. 30–32; Villacorta 1962, p. 367). Since the original ancestor of that Tamub line (C'opichoch) is nowhere said to have been related to the Nima Quiché founding fathers, it may be assumed that the ancestors shared with the Nijaibs derived from intermarriage between the two groups. As discussed earlier, the Tamubs used maternal as well as paternal ties to establish their lineages in certain cases. The situation was probably similar with the Ilocabs, though we lack specific information on the point. It is also possible that there was a presumed kinship tie between the founding warlords of the three groups, but that is not stated in the chronicles.

The Tamubs, who specifically wrote about their relations with the Nima Quichés, stated (Recinos 1957, p. 46) that they were "one at Quiché," one in territory (*chinamit*), one in town (*tinamit*), and one in government (*ajawarem*). Political rather than kinship relations were stressed, and the Tamubs specifically argued that one group was not above the other in rank at Quiché. Ideally, the Tamubs were correct, and the Quiché political system was a confederacy of the Nima Quichés, Ilocabs, Tamubs, and eventually Nijaibs. Their towns had become one city, their territories were integrated into a single estate of vassal support, their most important decisions were made in joint councils, and their lineages were allied and cross-tied through multiple marriages. In practice, however, Las Casas was correct: the Tamubs and Ilocabs were subordinate to the Nima Quichés. As we have seen, the highest authorities of the Tamubs and Ilocabs were not rulers but judges and speakers who joined with their Nima Quiché equivalents to assist the king (*ajpop*) at the Utatlán court.

Despite the Tamubs' claims, then, they were ranked below the Nima Quichés. They had no ruling lines that could compete in fame or power with the Cawek line of Utatlán. Their own chronicles demonstrate this by repeating Cawek exploits rather than Tamub history. Their inferior rank is shown also by the truncated genealogy they kept and the lineages created from Nima Quiché lines. The Ilocabs were even further down in rank. They lost much of their standing early, when the Rokche and Cajib Aj lineage heads attempted to kill C'otuja at Pismachí. The rebellion was attempted precisely because the *ajpop* had begun to outrank them (*Título Totonicapán* n.d.; Villacorta 1962, pp. 327–30). The Ilocabs suffered a defeat from which they never recovered. Their highest officials were ignominiously sacrificed in public at Utatlán, and many of their vassals became serfs to the Nima Quiché lords. The chronicles suggest that after that time the Ilocabs were carefully watched by the Nima Quichés and kept relatively powerless.

In summary, while "constitutionally" the Quiché political system at the top was a tripartite and ultimately quadripartite confederacy, in terms of power it was a "kingdom" ruled by the *ajpop* of the dominant Cawek lineage. As we have noted, the superiority of the *ajpop* largely derived from his strength as a military leader. Consequently, there was some danger that another lineage or confederate would become militarily more powerful than the *ajpop* and challenge his rule. Both the chronicles and Spanish sources indicate that such rebellions were common problems of the Quiché political system.

Second-Level Authorities

Below the king, according to Las Casas, the Utatlán political structure consisted of a council of "principal men," who were like judges and tribute collectors. Elsewhere in his account (some of which refers to Verapaz but seems to apply to Utatlán as well), Las Casas (1909, pp. 622–23) explains that there were specialists on the council for each activity and that persons experienced in each subject under discussion were brought in to help make council decisions.

The special military captains of the council consisted of men of both lordly and vassal status. War councils were kept secret, and only experienced warriors were brought in to participate. They were assisted by cadres of ensign and logistical officials. The king's central authority over the military is clearly evident: (1) the warriors received their weapons directly from him at the palace, (2) his son had the supreme military position (*nima rajop achij*), and (3) he sometimes personally participated in the fighting.

The council judges heard only serious legal cases, some of them on appeal from provincial chiefs. They frequently called in the leaders of vassal lineages to testify in cases needing clarification. Outside the central court vassal lineage heads served as justices of the peace, assisted by messengers who brought interested parties to the courts. The direct authority of the king in judicial matters is again shown in that the final appeal could be made to him and in his power to appoint even low-level judges and officials "through a certain ceremony, sign, and name particular to those offices" (Las Casas 1909, p. 623). Fuentes y Guzmán (1932–33, 7:426–29), who appears to have used the same priestly document upon which Las Casas based his account, claims that the king met with his supreme justices and the provincial judges for three days during each fifteen-day period. Criminal cases were recorded in writing, some examples of which Fuentes y Guzmán had seen. He further states that the judges and other council members received tribute from their own vassals but that they were also supported by the king. They were fed the first meal of the day in communal kitchens of the court. They were not allowed to receive gifts in payment for their services.

Ritual matters were highly specialized and were in the hands of "a priesthood that was not given to [just] everyone but came through a line as with the tribe of Levi among the Jews" (Las Casas 1909, p. 622). The elite priestly lineages were Mexica (Yaqui Winak), as befitting the keepers of Toltec deities (Villacorta 1962, p. 270). Though they were sometimes referred to by the Maya terms *ajq'uixb* and *ajcajb* ("sacrificers") (Villacorta 1962, pp. 249ff.), the Nahua title *chalamicat* ("priest," from *tlamacazqui*?) was probably the more prestigious term applied to them (Villacorta 1962, p. 285). The priests were in charge of the codices that contained the ritual calendar and divination charts (Las Casas 1909, p. 618). They were called into council to interpret those charts in all matters pertaining to religion and ritual. The high priest was held in great respect, though less than that of the king at Utatlán. The priests in general were greatly respected for their incredible penitences and self-sacrifice rather than through any secular power. Perhaps for this reason two of them, Tepew and K'ucumatz, became the trusted stewards of the state's wealth.

It appears that the priests were the most independent of the king's officials. We are told that warriors could not enter the temples nor sleep in their portals (Las Casas 1909, p. 466). Nevertheless, the king and his assistants were lay priests of a sort, making public prayers on behalf of the people in the temples and playing a central role in the major sacrificial rituals (Villacorta 1962, pp. 353–62). They did so, however, only after much fasting, anointing, and preparation. The full-time priests may have been relatively few, for we are told that the "children and nephews of the lords" served as their assistants.

From the perspective of the chronicles, the Spanish officials portray the levels of officials below the king in somewhat too centralized and integrated terms. They failed to understand—and in this Betanzos was on the right track—that the "heads of lineages and noble families" at Utatlán were the same second-level officials under discussion. That is to say, the *ajpop's* council and officials of state were also independent authorities for their respective lineages. A question to be addressed of the chronicles is how far their authority had been diverted from lineage matters and centralized under the control of the ruler. A related question is the extent to which they had become specialized to carry out the various functions of the political system.

It has already been noted that the list of sixty-four principal lineage heads given in the chronicles (twenty-four Nima Quiché, twenty-two Tamub, and eighteen Ilocab heads) is a chart of what might be considered the council or chief administration of the Utatlán community. The names of these officials and the order in which they are given provide information about their functions and ranking. The special status of chief ruler or king (*ajpop*), assistant ruler (*ajpop c'amja*), judges (*k'alel*), and speakers (*atzij winak*) has already been discussed. The other Nima Quiché officials listed in the *Popol Vuh* (Villacorta 1962, pp. 336–37, 365–70) consisted of six priests (Aj Tojil, K'ucumatz, Tepew, Awilix, Jakawitz, and Tzutubaja); three tribute collectors (*lolmet*); two stewards (Tepew and K'ucumatz); three spokesmen, or town criers (Nim Ch'ocoj); two special counselors (*popol winak*); two other assistants (*uchuch c'amja* and *nima c'amja*), and one banquet director (*yacolatam*).

The diversity of functions represented by these titles shows that, beside any lineage functions they might have had (see below), they were all officials of state. In some cases that is specifically indicated in the chronicles. The Tojil priest, for example, may have been the high priest. He officiated for all the

Quichés at Utatlán, since Tojil was the patron of war for the three "confederates," the Nima Quichés, Tamubs, and Ilocabs. The K'ucumatz priest had a broad jurisdiction too, since that god was probably a major creator deity for the three groups. Further, the priests of Tojil, Awilix, Jakawitz, and Tzutubaja probably formed a united network, officiating at certain rituals affecting the entire community (see chapter 7).

The special counselor for the ball game, *popol winak pajom tzalatz*, administered the ball court on behalf of all the lords at Utatlán (there was only one court in the town, and it had to be shared). Similarly, the stewards, Tepew and K'ucumatz, who were apparently from priestly lineages, received the spoils of conquest from all returning heroes, whether Cawek, Nijaib, or other lineages. As mentioned earlier, such riches were first presented to the *ajpop*, and then turned over to the stewards for storage (Recinos 1957, pp. 83, 106). The three spokesmen, or criers, of the Nima Quichés met together to "create" the proper words for their announcements (Villacorta 1962, p. 371). They were apparently old men, respected as "the fathers of all the Quiché lords."

It is doubtful that there was a well-worked-out rank order for these officials. In general, however, the priests appear to have ranked below the more secular officials. An exception were the Cawek priests (Aj Tojil, Aj K'ucumatz, Tepew Yaqui), but then the lowest-ranked Cawek official probably outranked the highest-ranked officials of the other lineages, excluding, of course, the judges (*k'alel*) and speakers (*atzij winak*) of those lineages.

The Tamub officials were broadly organized like the Nima Quichés', though there were interesting differences (Recinos 1957, pp. 48–56). One difference was that the Tamubs had more priests (seven), one major lineage consisting entirely of priests (Aj Tojil, Aj Yatas, Ajaw Julajuj) and a ritual specialist (Ajaw Yacola). The Tamubs lacked the tribute collectors, special counselors, and stewards of the Nima Quichés, though there were several minimal-lineage officials who exercised these functions. The number of town criers (*nima ch'ocoj*), two rather than three, is consistent with the Tamub moiety system.

Compared with the Nima Quiché officials, Tamub officials seem to have been less well integrated into a central administration and perhaps more oriented to individual lineage affairs. Except for the priests of Tojil and Awilix, the Cawek and Nijaib patron deities, Tamub priests officiated on behalf of relatively obscure lineage rather than community-wide cults. The several tribute collectors and counselors with minimal-lineage rank suggest that they functioned exclusively within their respective lineages rather than for the state. They seem to have shared equal rank with many minimal-lineage officials concerned with nonpolitical matters such as providing firewood, food, baths, artwork, music, divination, and so on. These "offices" were surely a long step removed from the central authority structure of Utatlán.

Third-Level Authorities

As the lineage heads at Utatlán became specialized officers of state, a third level of officials was created to administer the affairs of the lineages and their associated territorial estates (*chinamit*). They were known by the titles formerly held by lineage heads, *utzam chinamital* ("head of the estate members") and *aj tz'alam* ("wall official"), referring to the walls of the estates (Villacorta 1962, pp. 351–52). These officials were put in charge of the administration of tributes, justice, military recruitment, land rentals, and ritual within the lineage estates. They were given the chairs and benches that denoted authority but were not considered officials of state. They were intermediaries between state officials and the vassals and serfs, and so carried some of the stigma (low rank) of the latter.

Late in the history of the Utatlán community this third level of officials became thoroughly militarized. The Utzam Chinamital and Aj Tz'alam were given the military rank of *achij*, and new titles within the military rank were created (*rajpop achij, uk'ale achij*). These offices were filled by young lords and successful vassal warriors (as discussed in the section "Caste and Class Stratification" above). They were under the authority of the principal lineage heads, who were also officers of state, and the *ajpop*. These third-level positions were important training and proving grounds for lords who would later occupy the second- and even first-level offices of state. It was mainly from this third level of officials that the "governors and lieutenants" of the provinces were chosen (Villacorta 1962, pp. 347–49). As noted by Las Casas (1909, p. 616), they were "armed people sent to guard the frontiers," and they could rise in position by serving the lords well in their respective jurisdictions.

It is important to understand that the third-level officials (*achij*) functioned not as individuals but as squadrons made up of officers tied to vassal warriors along military lines. They were captains, lieutenants, and ensigns who personally formed close military bonds with their vassals (Recinos 1957, pp. 102–105). The vassals became their loyal shield bearers (*ajpocob*), lancers (*tzununche*), bowmen (*ajch'ab*), and hand-to-hand fighters (*tz'olaj*). It seems likely that the vassal warriors followed these third-level officials as the latter moved up to the offices of state and even high command. Thus we see that both lineage and military statuses were central to the political structure of Utatlán from top to bottom.

Political Alliances

Las Casas's claim (1909, p. 616) that the Utatlán king "placed, confirmed, approved, and authorized all the lords, rulers, and jurisdictions of the

Table 6.3. **Central Administration at Utatlán**

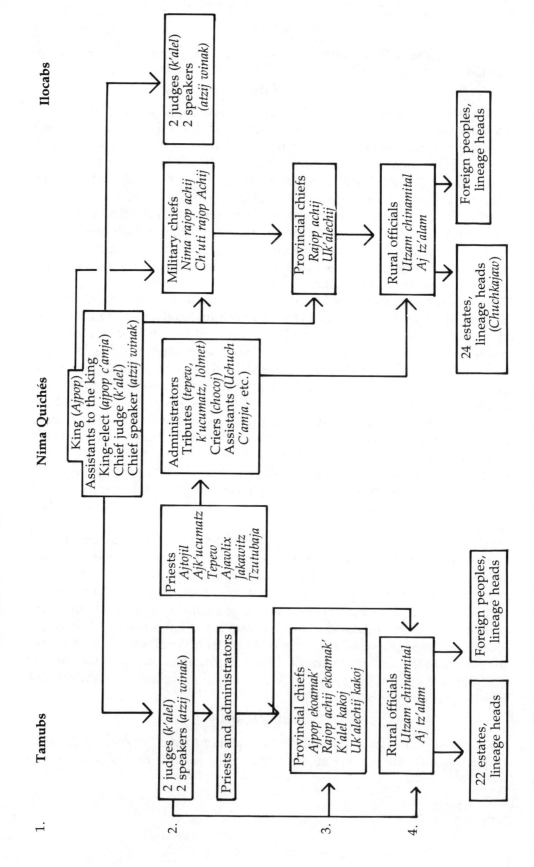

provinces and neighboring kingdoms, such as Tecuciztlán (Rabinal), Guatemala (Cakchiquel), and Atitlán (Tzutujil)" was definitely exaggerated. The *ajpop* exercised that kind of authority only over the Utatlán provinces, as has been explained. Interestingly, Betanzos denied even this provincial authority to the Utatlán rulers, but his description of relations between the Utatlán rulers and the provinces accords well with the kinds of relations the chronicles say existed between Utatlán and other kingdoms (the Rabinal, Cakchiquel, Tzutujil, and other hostile political groups). He states (Carrasco 1967a, p. 257) that people from other towns

came to worship [the gods at Utatlán] because they always had respect for the lords there as kinsmen and friends, to whom they gave presents. The lords of Utatlán did the same, sending messengers with presents for reasons of friendship and kinship. . . . This town of Utatlán was the beginning and foundation of the lineages that came to this country from other parts, and as the head its gods were held in respect, . . . and there the people of the other towns gave great sacrifices and reverence, even though they had other gods and temples in their own towns.

Down to the time of the Conquest the Quichés of Utatlán maintained ritual, kinship, and gift-giving ties with even their most-hated enemies. In this and many other ways described above, the Quichés of Utatlán reveal the ancient character of a political system that had both centralized and decentralized elements.

Summary

This discussion of central administration at Utatlán is summarized schematically in Table 6.3.

It will be noted from Table 6.3 that there were three fundamental levels of authority: (1) the ruling quadruplet body headed by the *ajpop*; (2) the second-level judges, priests, administrators, and military chiefs; and (3) the provincial chiefs and rural officials. Below the central administration were (4) the lineage heads of the rural peoples.

Offsetting the hierarchical structure of the organization were several institutional, or "vertical" divisions: the Nima Quiché, Tamub, and Ilocab divisions of officials; the priests and individual administrators who were independent in relation to other officials on the same level; the authority all first- and second-level officials exercised as lineage heads over the rural officials presiding over the estates.

The fundamental importance of the military officials in the Utatlán administration is seen in the fact that they formed the deepest and best-coordinated hierarchy. The line of authority went from the king to the military chiefs, down to the provincial chiefs, and on down to the rural officials, who were warriors. The king also had direct authority over the provincial chiefs and rural officials. I have shown the arrows within the military hierarchy going both ways, since young men from the royal lineages started out their careers as rural officials, became provincial chiefs (an example being Tecum at the Totonicapán province), later qualified as military chiefs, and finally became either king or his assistant.

The chart shows the officials of the Utatlán administration as more specialized in function than they actually were. It is likely that, except for some of the most important priests and the old criers, all officials served as warriors in time of military crisis. We also have the case of the Tepew and K'ucumatz priests doubling as stewards, and there were probably other, similar overlappings.

As discussed above, the Tamub organization is represented in the chart as less specialized than that of the Nima Quichés. The arrows leading to the provincial chiefs and rural officials indicate that each second-level Tamub official acted primarily as a lineage head in assigning officials to the estates and conquered peoples. Information on the Ilocab organization is too sparse to allow a detailed reconstruction of their administrative pattern.

7
SYMBOLICS

THE DOCUMENTARY SOURCES PROVIDE US with considerable information on the natives' own view of their community. I now attempt to summarize this information as it relates specifically to Utatlán. Since the community's social organization has already been discussed (see chapter 6), in this chapter I focus only on the interpretative and symbolic aspects of that social order. Later it will be useful to compare the settlement ethnosemantics presented here with the archaeological view that emerges from work at the Utatlán sites (see the following two chapters).

The discussion to follow starts with the Quichés' view of the Utatlán community in its broadest features, including a general description of what kind of community the natives believed Utatlán to be. Next I discuss the meaning for the Quichés of the most important buildings of the community. Finally I attempt to reconstruct the symbolic ties the Quichés understood to exist among the various buildings and social divisions at Utatlán.

A GENERAL VIEW OF THE UTATLÁN COMMUNITY

The Quichés made definite distinctions among the settlement per se, the town, and the site it occupied. The site was usually thought of as a "mountain" (*juyup*), though canyons (*ciwan*) and plains (*tak'aj*) are also mentioned as sites where towns were established. Natural features were used to identify the towns: Old Reeds (K'umarcaaj), Moss of Whiskers (Pismachí), Burial Mountain (Mukwitz), Dry Place (Panq'uib), Palms (Panpacay). Some natural features may have had special symbolic significance. Possibly the "old reeds" for which K'umarcaaj was named were equated with the reeds planted in memory of the hero-twins of Quiché mythology, who descended to the underworld (see the *Popol Vuh*).

Modern ethnography among the Quiché teaches us that the sites upon which the towns were built were thought to be aspects of the "mountains and plains" (*juyup tak'aj*) (Carmack 1975; Bunzel 1952). They were parts of Earth, the great deity who gives and takes life and sustenance. The towns, usually built on mountains, must have been generally seen as manifestations of the masculine power of Earth, with its associated militarism, human sacrifice, authority, brightness, and dryness. The plains and river canyons surrounding the towns were manifestations of the feminine forces of Earth, and were associated with domestic work, food and sustenance, procreation, darkness, and water. The plains also brought man close to the underworld, closely linked to the female principle.

The mountains and plains (or rivers), as high and low spots, were sacred points of contact with Earth. These points were guarded by naguals, animal messengers sent to Earth. To the Tamubs (Recinos 1957, p. 42), the naguals of Mount Ismachi were the rattle and coral snakes. They were appropriate naguals because of their dual nature, inhabiting both the interior of the earth (their burrows) and its surface (where they search for food). In form they must have been symbolically masculine (phallic) but feminine (water) in spatial association. To the Nima Quichés, the naguals of Pismachí were four frogs (?; *zt'ul*) (*Título Totonicapán* n.d.). They too were appropriate messengers from Earth, since they frequent both water and land. Their association with water suggests a feminine symbolism for Pismachí from the Nima Quichés' point of view.

The sources do not specify the naguals of Mount K'umarcaaj. References to serpents, eagles, and jaguars in connection with K'ucumatz, the founder of the town, suggest that they were the town's principal naguals (Villacorta 1962, p. 340). The jaguar's association with the inside of the earth as well as its surface, and the eagle's symbolic connection with both sky and earth made them good nagual candidates. They appear to have been strongly masculine symbols. We have no information on the naguals of Mukwitz Ilocab, the other main town of the Utatlán community. As a "burial mountain," it must have been associated with the underworld.

The symbolic associations between the land on which the Utatlán settlements were built and the earth deity, with its masculine, feminine, and nagual manifestations, was probably most strongly held by the indigenous vassals of the rural zones. The lords thought mainly in terms of buildings rather than the lands on which they were constructed. They referred to the political centers as *tinamit*, or, rarely, as *tecpan*, Nahua terms meaning "town" and suggesting both nucleation and defensiveness (Villacorta 1962, pp. 331–32). The *tinamit* contrasted sharply with *amak'* (rural hamlets), dispersed like the legs of the spider (*am*). The imagery of the two terms included contrasts between manufactured objects (*tinamit*) and permanent possessions, such as land (*amak'*).

A perhaps even more important symbolic contrast between the towns and the rural hamlets was the belief held by Utatlán lords that the former were sacred while the latter were profane. This undoubtedly was not the view of the vassals, however, for both mountains and plains were elements of sacred Earth, and the town was perhaps just a particularly powerful manifestation of that deity. But for the lords the town was associated with the most sacred of all symbols, the Mexican Toltecs. These symbols (*retal*) consisted of objects brought back from Tula in the East: deer hooves, tiger claws, sacred bundles, precious feathers, tiny wooden benches and chairs, tobacco gourds, colored stones, special incenses, and painted codices. At another level was the symbolism of Toltec monumental architecture, with its constructions of stone and mortar, whitened with lime coating (*chun sajcab*); buildings with stairways and multiple stories (*xocoxak ja, tanatak ja*); special courts (*k'alibal*) with suspended canopies (*muj*); and, of course, temples housing the gods themselves (Recinos 1957, p. 42; Villacorta 1962, pp. 321–22).

In addition to these physical manifestations of Toltec sacredness, in the towns were performed the special rituals offered to the Toltec gods. Our sources mention great Toltec war dances, marriage exchanges, and succession ceremonies during which the lords were anointed with yellow and black paint. To the Quichés these activities made Utatlán and its companion towns "marvelous," "beloved," and "magical": they transformed the towns into sacred shrines. The Spaniards were told that Utatlán had "the divine cult, . . . the head place respected for its gods, . . . [and that other] peoples came to offer great sacrifices and reverence there, even though they had their own particular gods and temples in their own towns" (Carrasco 1967a, p. 256).

According to Quiché imagery, the towns were sacred sanctuaries for gods and lords. The highest lords rarely left the centers, and when they did venture forth, they were surrounded by the retinues and symbols of the town. Vassals were too profane to frequent the town sanctuaries, so their movements within Utatlán were restricted to such activities as responding to summonses for judicial processing, for receiving weapons, or for viewing the major ceremonies. The lords of Utatlán had stewards and attendants (junior or peripheral nobles) who mediated between them and the vassals. By this means much of the business between the two strata could be conducted outside town and so preserve its sanctity.

Lords who had fought in battle had to be ceremonially purified outside the town before they could enter. They would announce their arrival several days in advance and, after ritual purification, would be met near the entrance and escorted into town by the resident rulers and lords (Recinos 1957, pp. 82, 108). Though some of Utatlán's sacredness undoubtedly was lost when the vassal warriors gained high rank, it remained a sacred city down to the Conquest.

As seen in chapter 6, Utatlán was a composite community. It consisted of (1) the three towns, K'umarcaaj, Pismachi, and Mukwitz, (2) the estates (*chinamit*) of each town, and (3) the larger rural territories (*calpules*) subject to the towns. The entire unit was known as Paq'uiche (Place of the Quichés). Paq'uiche was the heart of the Quiché kingdom, especially in the sense of being the residence of the people who were loyal and provided the core warriors for the Quiché armies. Outside the towns of Paq'uiche were to be found "Quiché men" (*q'uiche winak*), the vassal hillmen (Villacorta 1962, p. 347). They worshiped the same patron god (Tojil) as the townspeople, and could be counted on to guard and fortify (*chajal, k'atey rij*) the town against foreign attack.

A tendency to organize Paq'quiche, the core community, along directional lines is evident in Quiché settlement patterns. The Nima Quiché territories stretched generally south and east; the Tamub territories, south and west; and the Ilocab territories, north and west (Fig. 7.1). Further, sacred shrines and topographic features within the core area were recognized and given symbolic and perhaps directional importance. This is illustrated by the native map of Utatlán in the possession of Fuentes y Guzmán, which included sacred places far beyond the canyons of the town. The map indicates that the Quichés saw the Utatlán area as dotted with mountain shrines, such as Hombros de los Sopilotes (Telec'uch), Mancebo que Ayuda (Tabil?), and Mano Derecha (Ikik'ab?). Similarly, the chronicles mention special elevations in the Quiché area, such as Xebalax-Xekamak' (Below the Place of Our Hamlets) and Chuwiquilak-Chuwipuquimulu (Above the Pottery-making Place–Mound of Earth), where political offices and titles were bestowed (Villacorta 1962, 350; Recinos 1957, p. 40). The various points within the core Quiché area were probably associated with the cardinal directions; there is both ancient and modern evidence for this pattern (Recinos 1957, p. 62; Carmack n.d.).

Possibly the urban centers were more strongly conceptualized in spatial terms than was the rural zone surrounding Utatlán. Pismachi and K'umarcaaj were almost always thought of as being spatially linked towns, and Pilocab, Panq'uib, and Panpacay were also closely linked to them. The Quichés may have come to see these towns as mirroring the spatial universe, with K'umarcaaj in the center, Pismachi on the south, Pilocab on the north, and Panpacay and Panq'uib on the east and west. Panpetak (Entry Place) may have been a settlement (*tinamit*) just east of K'umarcaaj or was possibly another name for either Panpacay or Panq'uib (see chapter 8).

A spatially central position for K'umarcaaj seems assured from general references in the chronicles, but nowhere are the other towns specifically assigned to the directions suggested by their geographical locations. Panpacay and Panq'uib have not even been identified for certain. Our best

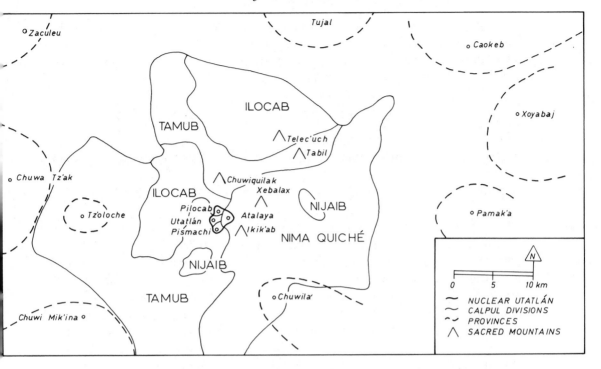

Fig. 7.1.   The spatial arrangement of the central Quiché political units. Based on IGN, map, 1:250,000.

evidence that the Quichés actually viewed the towns as symbolizing the cardinal directions comes from Juan de León (n.d., pp. 18, 19), who claims to have learned of the relationship early in this century from aged informants in Santa Cruz del Quiché. Nevertheless, given the Quichés' tendency to view the world in cardinal-point orientation (as expressed many places in the *Popol Vuh*, for example), I think that it was probably part of the imagery of their nuclear settlements. Nevertheless, it could not have been a strong imagery, or there would be mention of it in the chronicles.

The core community (Paq'uiche) contrasted conceptually with the provinces making up the larger Quiché kingdom. The subjects in the provinces could not be trusted and had to be watched over by faithful warriors from the core area. The provinces, perhaps about thirty in all, were named for the main towns where the Quichés established military rule: Chuwila' (Chichicastenango), Pamak'a (Zacualpa), Caokeb (Sajcabaja), Chuwi Mik'ina' (Totonicapán), Zaculeu (Huehuetenango), Xelaju (Quezaltenango), Chuwa Tz'ak (Momostenango), Tz'olojche (Chiquimula), Sija (Ix-tahuacán), Tujal (Sacapulas), and Xoyabaj (Joyabaj) (Fig. 7.1). The Quichés saw such centers and their associated provinces as sources of tribute support for the core community at Utatlán.

THE SYMBOLISM OF UTATLÁN BUILDINGS

Our sources mention various buildings in Utatlán: temples, altars, lineage houses, palaces, ball courts, defensive walls, streets and plazas, and several lesser constructions. Each of the major construction types will be briefly described in terms of its Quiché symbolism (see also chapter 8).

Temples

As the residences of deities, the Quichés' temples were "houses of the gods" (*cochoch c'abawil*) (Villacorta 1962, p. 333). Apparently because of their large size, they were also spoken of as "the great buildings" (*nimak tz'ak*). Some of them were conceptualized in phallic form, rising up above the town (*chunic'ajal uwi tinamit*) (Villacorta 1962, pp. 333–34). A drawing from the *Título C'oyoi* suggests that phallic and mammary roof shapes were used to portray the sexual symbolism of Utatlán temples (Fig. 7.2). In addition, the names of some temples strongly denoted sacrificial images. For example, the temple of the fourth major lineage, Tzutuja Sakic, was specifically called *cajbaja* ("house of sacrifice," Villacorta 1962, p. 354).

From Las Casas (1909, p. 466) we learn that the temple shrines lacked doors and therefore sometimes the stone (or wood) deity icons were kept hidden in caves and secret places outside town. The high priest used a special sign to signal those times when the icons were to be brought from hiding and placed in the temples. Once he had given the sign, ceremonial music, dances, and acting began.

In front of each icon was an offertory stone. In the Tojil temple it was a large sacrificial stone with a trough in which the victim was placed and with tiny orifices for tying him firmly in place (Fuentes y Guzmán 1932–33, 7:422). After the victim had been struck on the head, the chest was opened with an obsidian knife (called the "hand of God"), and the still-beating heart was extracted. The icon was sprinkled with blood by the high priest; like the Aztecs, the Quichés believed that the blood of the victim was food for the deities. Las Casas (1909, p. 468) suggests that human sacrifice was performed mainly in the temple of Tojil, after which the priests took the blood from the victims to the other icons.

The temples with their icons were sacred (Villacorta 1962, p. 356). Warriors could not go near them without elaborate preparation. The regular and lay priests climbed the stairs to give offerings, but only after the required

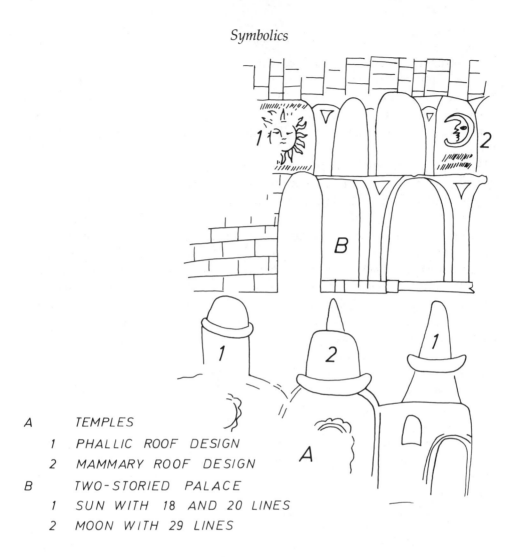

A   TEMPLES
    1   PHALLIC ROOF DESIGN
    2   MAMMARY ROOF DESIGN
B   TWO-STORIED PALACE
    1   SUN WITH 18 AND 20 LINES
    2   MOON WITH 29 LINES

Fig. 7.2. A pictorial of Utatlán from the *Título C'oyoi*. Drawing by J. Weeks.

fasting and continence. In groups of nine, thirteen, and seventeen the lords and officials, acting as priests, humbly offered incense, their own blood, and prayers for the welfare of their vassals, families, and kingdom (Villacorta 1962, pp. 356ff.). These "lay" temple ceremonies were the counterpart of the individual rituals of the vassals, who performed similar rites in thick woods, beside fountains, in caves, on mountaintops, and at road crossings (Las Casas 1909, p. 465). Like the lords, the vassals fasted, kept away from their wives, and blackened their bodies with smoke. On the mountaintops they bled themselves and burned incense day and night. To the vassals the pyramidal temples must have been symbolically equivalent to the mountains and closely associated with the earth. For the lords, however, this association was weak (they never mention it in their writings), and the temples were more accesses to the sky (especially the sun) than contact points with the earth.

The deity icon, generally made of stone, was called by the generic term *c'abawil* ("worshiping"). It had an anthropomorphic shape, but it was more than an image of the deity it represented, for it could manifest itself in human and animal forms. In animatistic fashion, the icons were dressed in beautiful clothes and adorned with gold and precious stones. They were given offerings of animals, plants, incense, and the blood of man (from both self-bleeding and sacrifices). When the offering was placed in the mouth of an icon, it would speak. In exchange for the food the gods instructed the Quichés in such matters as making war to obtain sacrificial victims, building towns in particular locations, and performing special ritual celebrations (Villacorta 1962). It is recorded that even Cakchiquel warriors spoke with the deities of Utatlán, though they demeaningly referred to them as *c'axtoc'* ("deceivers") rather than *c'abawil* (Recinos 1957, p. 136).

We are told little about the identity symbolism of the Utatlán deities. As already mentioned, they could transform themselves into naguals, the jaguar, the eagle, and wasps being prominent examples (*Título Totonicapán* n.d.; Villacorta 1962, p. 244). Their human apparitions were apparently dramatizations by the priests who attended them and spoke for them. There are hints in the sources that the dress of the priests symbolized the deities' naguals and their transformation to human forms. The deities were also closely identified with the forces of nature (Villacorta 1934, p. 196; see also chapter 4). Tojil, a sky god, was associated with thunder and the sun. K'ucumatz was identified with clouds and water. Jakawitz was a mountain deity and strongly phallic (Carmack 1973, p. 294). Awilix is never identified, though indirect evidence points to a symbolic association with the moon (Edmonson 1965). Tzutuja had a special stone (obsidian?) for its icon, which was apparently identified with death and the interior of the earth (*Título Totonicapán* n.d.).

From the prayers the Quichés offered to their deity icons in the Utatlán temples we know that they considered the gods to be the providers of life, sustenance, tranquillity, and military success. They especially venerated the gods for bringing their forefathers from the east and aiding them in the conquest of the natives of the Quiché (Villacorta 1962, pp. 357–59; Las Casas 1909, p. 471).

The temple complex was rather extensive. It had a patio for processions with the deity icon. There were portals where young lords eight years and older slept. These youths kept the braziers of the temple burning, and were trained by priestly assistants in the esoteric customs and ritual of the Toltec heritage. There is indirect evidence that some of the children fell into homosexual practices while living in the temple complex (Las Casas 1909, p. 624). One of the temples had a "seminary" room where the daughters of the lords were educated (Fuentes y Guzmán 1932–33, 7:421). Close to the temples were special rooms for the lords who were serving as lay priests. We are told that they stayed there from dusk to dawn, making prayers and offerings (Villacorta 1962, p. 356). The braziers in those rooms were also kept continuously burning. An adjacent room was set aside for sacrificial victims, where they were well fed and were made intoxicated shortly before they were sacrificed (Las Casas 1909, p. 467). Unfortunately, our sources make no mention of the residences of the regular priests, but they must have been near the rooms used by the noble children and the lay priests.

Altars

As noted above, the temples of Utatlán had altars for receiving priestly offerings, and in the temple of Tojil the altar was a large sacrificial stone. A special altar, called *tzumpan*, is portrayed in the *Título Totonicapán* map (Fig. 7.3). *Tzumpan* is the archaic Nahua word for *tzompantli*, the skull-rack altar of the Aztecs. It apparently is shown in side view on the map, suggesting that it consisted of four vertical posts supporting eight horizontal poles, upon which the skulls were hung. The cross-hatching portrayed on the platform base may represent painted crossbones. The ritual use of the skull-rack altar by the Quichés was described by Las Casas:

They put the heads of the sacrificed victims on some poles above a certain altar dedicated especially to this, where they kept them for some time, after which they were buried. The reason they did this was first and principally so that the idol or god which it represented would remember the sacrifice which had been made in service to him, and thus would be good to them and keep them from any harm. Another reason they gave was that those who saw (the skulls) would contemplate that they had been sacrificed for the common good. Another reason was that when a king or lord succeeded to office he would see it and add to [that religion] rather than take away. Another reason was that their enemies who heard about it would be afraid to attack them, because, if they did, they would certainly be sacrificed. [Las Casas 1909, p. 468; my translation]

Las Casas goes on to explain that the flesh of the victims was ritually eaten by the lords and priests.

A second altar represented in the *Título Totonicapán* is called *soquibal*, ("place of obsidian hatchet or lance," or, metaphorically, "place of injury"). The map suggests that it was a large, square platform, richly adorned with cube-shaped elements along the four sides. A round object on one side of the platform seems to have been functional rather than ornamental. I would suggest that the *soquibal* was sacrificial, similar to the "gladiatorial" altars of the Aztecs. In the Aztec ritual, the sacrificial victims were tied to a round stone that formed part of the altar and given a wooden weapon to fight against warriors armed with obsidian weapons. The round object in the Totonicapán map is probably the stone to which the victim was tied. The reference to the obsidian hatchet or lance (*soc*) (Saenz 1940) suggests the kinds of weapons used by the Quichés against their enemies.

The portrayal of a gladiatorial altar at Utatlán is surprising, because there is no mention of it in the chronicles (at least, none has been recognized as such). Nevertheless, it is possible that traditional sacrificial dances such as the "Rabinal Achi" (Brasseur 1862), "Quiché Winak" (Ximénez 1929), and "Lotz Tun" (Chinchilla 1963) were ritual sacrifices associated with the *soquibal*. All these dances involved the sacrifice of a captive lord by warriors dressed in military attire within a setting that was clearly combative.

From the map in the possession of Fuentes y Guzmán we learn that the palaces of Utatlán had their own altars, ". . . certain shrines that were private to them, so that they lived inside (the palaces) almost in cloistered form." The vassals' houses outside town also had tiny altars, dedicated to the "house-guard" deity (*chajalja*) (Las Casas 1909, p. 369). The altars were placed in the center of the patio or in front of the door. The vassals offered incense, blood, and other gifts on the altar to prevent harm from entering the houses.

Modern ethnography among the Quichés has revealed additional altars in the rural area (Carmack n.d.). Though undoubtedly there have been changes since the Conquest, and there is variation even today from area to area, these modern shrines probably reflect ancient pre-Hispanic patterns. Most of the altars are situated on prominent hills near lineage lands. Not uncommonly a circular area is cleared on top of a hill to serve as the site of an altar to be used by several lineages from the same hamlet. In the center of the area are the communal altars: (1) small, rectangular, houselike stone structures for offering blood, called *mesa mundo* ("earth's table"), and (2) round stone-and-ceramic structures for praying, called *wak ch'ob* ("six groups"). Surrounding the communal altars are the tiny stone-and-ceramic altars of the individual lineages: the *warabal ja* ("sleeping house"), a tiny room where, it is believed, deceased lineage ancestors come and where their descendants make contact with them; and the *winel* ("created"), similarly constructed altars that may be used by one lineage or several of them together. Offerings are made at the *winel* to ensure that the animals and crops of the land will multiply and be plenteous.

The rituals conducted at the various rural altars are determined by the days of the 260-day calendar, with their good and bad fates. These rituals bring the

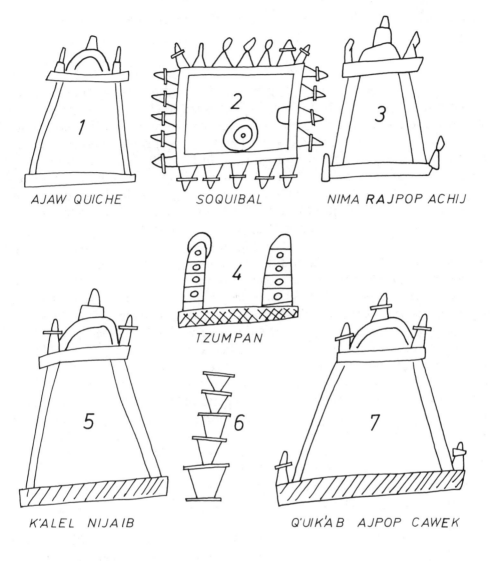

AJAW QUICHE	SOQUIBAL	NIMA RAJPOP ACHIJ

TZUMPAN

K'ALEL NIJAIB	Q'UIK'AB AJPOP CAWEK

7 AJPOP BIG HOUSE
5 NIJAIB BIG HOUSE
3 NIMA RAJPOP ACHIJ BIG HOUSE
1 AJAW QUICHÉ BIG HOUSE
4 SKULL-RACK ALTAR
2 GLADIATORIAL PLATFORM
6 UNKNOWN CONSTRUCTION

Fig. 7.3. A pictorial of Utatlán from the *Título Totonicapán*. Drawing by J. Weeks.

rural Quichés into direct contact with Earth, the provider of almost everything of value to them (Schultze-Jena 1947).

Lineage Houses

The lineage houses, or *nim ja* ("big houses"), are the most frequently mentioned buildings in the chronicles. As discussed in chapter 6, through time they became more administrative than kinship in function. Judicial affairs (*k'atbal tzij*) were particularly associated with the big houses, and even today among the lineages of rural Quiché legal judgments based on traditional procedures are called *nim ja*. The lineage function of exchanging wives continued in the big houses at Utatlán, and the Quiché lords used them as places to debate bride-prices and take food and drink in celebration of important marriages (Villacorta 1962, pp. 334, 336–39).

The question whether or not the big houses were also considered residences for the lineage lords is difficult to answer. The chronicles seem to suggest that the big houses were part of building complexes with different compartments, some of which were residential. This can be illustrated by the highest-ranked Tamub principal lineage, C'ocutum Atzij Winak (Recinos 1957, 48). Its big house was said to be the "council hall" (*popabal c'uchbalib*) of Lord C'ocutum. But the building is described as having a compartment (*tz'ak*) for the house (*rochoch*) of Lord C'ocutum, as well as three other compartments, one of which was simultaneously a residence and a council hall for a minimal-lineage captain (*rajpop achij*). In general, the ideal pattern seems to have been for each complex to have a public administrative building, a residence for the lineage head (an officer of state), and other compartments to serve as both public and residential units for important lineage members. The several compartments were probably connected to the public building in both literal and figurative senses, though some were physically removed; for example, the compartment of one Tamub minimal lineage was "down below the Big House" (Recinos 1957, p. 50).

As the term "big house" suggests, these administrative buildings were large. The four largest structures represented in the Totonicapán map (Fig. 7.3) appear to be big houses, though they are labeled by the general term *tz'ak*, ("buildings"). We are shown a side view of the structures, which gives them pyramidal form. Each structure consists of a base platform with cube adornments, front and back walls, a roof, and a roof "comb" composed of front, back, and central cubes. Banners were placed in front of the base platform near the cubes. The buildings varied in size according to the rank of the sponsoring lineages, the Ajpop being the largest of the big houses at Utatlán.

The big houses apparently were furnished simply. The lords sat on short-legged benches and chairs (*tem, ch'acat*) draped with mats (*Título*

Totonicapán n.d.; Vico n.d.; Carmack 1973, p. 294). There was a seating order that was faithfully maintained. López-Medel (n.d.) informs us that famous and just rulers were buried in the big houses under the locations where they had exercised their administrative duties in life. A fire was kept burning at each big house symbolizing the independence of that lineage from all other lineages (Villacorta 1962, p. 335). It is likely that special Toltec icons and insignia brought from the east were kept inside the big houses by their lineage owners. References in the chronicles to bone-throwing contests among the lineages in disputes over marriages indicate that trophies taken from war captives were also kept in the big houses (Villacorta 1962, p. 334; Brasseur 1862).

Palaces

The residential quarters (*cochoch*) of the rulers of Utatlán, especially of the *ajpop*, became so elaborate that they overshadowed the public component (big house) of a lineage building complex. The sumptuous living of the rulers, with their many attendants, wives, children, and guards, required a labyrinth of chambers, patios, passageways, columns, and stories. The component of the complex devoted to public administration formed a special courtyard (*k'alibal*) (*Título Totonicapán* n.d.), from which steps led to the ruler's throne. Above the throne was the special feathered canopy (Fuentes y Guzmán 1932–33, 7:423). The canopy of the *ajpop* had four tiers, "one over the other, so that the water of each one fell over the other in sequence; a distinguished thing worthy of a great lord, and a great sight and praiseworthy" (Las Casas 1909, p. 616).

The Spaniards were impressed by the grandeur of the Quichés' palaces, referring to them as "castles." Fuentes y Guzmán (1932–33, 7:422ff.) provides an elaborate description of the "palace and castle" of the ruler of Utatlán, based on the native map in his possession. He was confused about the size of the palace, the number of its stories, and what was included within its walls (see the discussion below); nevertheless, his map was unquestionably authentic, and the divisions he described (after allowances for his exaggerations) were probably at least components of palaces.

The palace was built of cut stone, raised to more than one story in some sections. Higher stories were smaller and lighter than the ones below them. The drawing of a "castle" at Utatlán and its associated text in the *Título C'oyoi* (Carmack 1973, pp. 290–91) confirm that the Quiché palaces were multistoried (Fig. 7.2). Apparently the stories (*wikab*) were supported by pillars. It is doubtful, however, that the king's palace at Utatlán had six stories, as claimed by Fuentes y Guzmán. More likely the different levels he describes were separate divisions or sections of one or more palaces, spread horizontally on the same level. Apparently Fuentes y Guzmán became confused by a reference in the map to more than one story and interpreted all the sections of the palaces as levels or stories.

According to Fuentes y Guzmán, the several compartments and divisions of the palace complex (which, in fact, may have been more than one palace) were as follows: (1) quarters used for a militia, with patio for training, kitchens for preparing food, and rooms for manufacturing arms; (2) rooms occupied by the princes and close male relatives of the ruler, assisted by servants and slaves (other kitchens and gardens were connected to this section); (3) the residence of the ruler, with its associated court; (4) the two-storied residence hall of the wives of the ruler, with special rooms for cooking, weaving, mat making, and duck raising for feathers (there were sweatbaths in this section of the palace); (5) the residences of the "princesses" and other female relatives of the ruling lineage (this section had a private passageway that led to one of the temple complexes). As already noted, different sections of the palaces had shrines for carrying out private rituals.

The *Título C'oyoi* drawing (Carmack 1973, p. 290) suggests that the upper stories of the palaces were used for astronomy purposes (Fig. 7.2). These stories had windows (shown as arches in this somewhat syncretic drawing) through which the astral bodies could be observed. In one window of the *C'oyoi* drawing the moon is portrayed in its half phase. Below are twenty-nine lines, which undoubtedly represent the lunar cycle. In the other window the sun is shown full face (the solstice phase?). Above the sun are eighteen lines, and below it an undertermined number of lines (probably twenty). Apparently the solar calendar of eighteen months of twenty days each was correlated with the sun's phases through observations made in the palaces.

The *C'oyoi* drawing reveals certain additional chambers seemingly associated with the palace, which were elaborately adorned with roof combs (Fig. 7.2). They probably represent foreground temples not directly connected to the palace. Nevertheless, they could be portrayals of sepulchers which the lords of Utatlán are reputed to have built on top of their palaces (Tovilla 1960). These tombs were reportedly up to eight persons in height and richly adorned with paintings. In this connection we should remember Las Casas's statement (1909, p. 630) that the cadavers of famous lords and rulers were burned and their bones joined together with gold thread and precious stones to form a kind of "mummy." The tombs of such rulers were held in great veneration, and the people burned incense and made sacrifices to them during important temple ceremonies. Obviously distinctions among palace, tomb, and temple became blurred in the context of such practices.

The interior palace walls were whitewashed and painted with frescos. Tovilla states (1960) that when a lord of Utatlán died "they did not knock down his house, but rewhitened all of it, and ingeniously painted some history of his past exploits. When the king died, they rewhitened all the streets and the palaces inside and out, and painted new histories." Fuentes y Guzmán also mentions frescos and adds that entire rooms were in different colors. The outside walls and cornices were further decorated with stone mosaic work.

It is clear then that the palaces became symbols of the wealth and power of the Quiché rulers at Utatlán. Though important matters of state continued to be carried out within the palace complex, it became the domain where the rulers lived in splendor. There they held "great banquets, in which they ate many birds and much meat, and drank diverse wines." These celebrations were attended by "especially the supreme lord, high priest, and other lords, feasting one day in the house of one, and other days in the houses of the others" (Las Casas 1909, p. 469).

Ball Courts

Las Casas states (1909, p. 466) that each town had a ball court, on the highest parts of which the deity icons were placed, "and there before them the lords and principals played ball in order to give them fiesta." As mentioned earlier, the *popol winak* official of the ruling Cawek lineage was in charge of the ball court at Utatlán, an indication of the importance of the game to the Quichés (Villacorta 1962, p. 336).

The ball court was called *jom tzalatz* ("sunken court with narrow walls") (Saenz 1940). It was swept to keep it free of dust. The rubber ball (*quic'*) was "so hard and light that if you give it a throw to the floor it will bounce two persons high in the air" (Tovilla, 1960). The playing equipment included leather pads (*tzuun*) for the wrists (*bate*), arms (*pachk'ab*), and shoulders (*cawubal*). Special ringed crowns (*yachwach*, *wachsot*) were worn around the head, probably for both protection and adornment (Villacorta 1962, pp. 88, 92). Our sources make no mention of yokes in their lists of playing gear.

The *Popol Vuh* (Villacorta 1962, pp. 88ff.) provides a few details about how the game was played (*chaajic*). It was always a contest between equal units—twos, fours, or larger numbers. Each unit defended its own side (*cabichal*). The players' hands could not be used to throw the ball; rather, it was stroked by the padded parts of the body, especially the wrists. There were rapid exchanges between the competitors, the ball bounding on the floor and rebounding against the walls. Frequently the ball left the court and had to be retrieved. At the top of the side walls were markers the players tried to hit with the ball. Victory came from striking the markers.

The ball game was a diversion for the Quichés at Utatlán, and we are told that they enjoyed playing it. Tovilla (1960) claims that it was also used for political purposes, perhaps providing contests between power factions both inside and outside Utatlán. Its primary function, however, was ritual. The game and court were profoundly symbolic. The ball court was the "road to the underworld of the dead" (*ubeel xibalba*), the "black road" (*k'eka be*) beset with dangerous canyons, thorns, and bloody rivers. It led to *pucbal chaj* ("the place of dust and ashes") the habitat of the buried dead, and a name possibly given to the ball court itself.

As the lords descended to the ball court, they re-created the descent to the underworld of the hero-twins, Junajpu and Xbalanque. The markers were probably representations of the decapitated head of Junajpu (and Junjunajpu?), as in the *Popol Vuh* tale. Like the game played by those heroes, the contest was against death itself. Some blood sacrifice of the losers was probably always part of the game. The ball, *quic'* ("blood"), was the personification of blood. As it bounded underground, it represented Xbalanque, the moon, night, menstrual blood, and the female principle. As it sailed in the air, it represented Junajpu, the sun, light, sacrificial blood, and the male principle. It symbolically united day and night, the underworld and earth's surface, male and female principles. This gave the game a ritual role that was symbolically equivalent to the mythic role played by Xquic' (Blood Woman) in the *Popol Vuh* tales.

Roads and Walls

The Spanish sources describe a complex of causeways, streets, roads, walls, and fortifications for Utatlán. Las Casas (1909, p. 470) tells us that the roads leading away from the town had tiny shrines called *mumuz*, spaced so as to provide resting spots. The travelers would rub their legs with an herb, spit on the herb, and leave it at the shrine. They also left offerings of cotton, cacao, salt, and other goods. The intersection of roads was another sacred place for travelers, who upon arriving would bleed themselves as an offering.

The conquistadors reported (Alvarado 1946) that there were two entrances into Utatlán: a narrow causeway on one side (which had been cut away before the arrival of the Spaniards) and a path of twenty-four steps on the opposite side of town. Fuentes y Guzmán (1932–33, 7:419) explained that over the causeway was a small bridge, wide enough for two men, that was removed each night. The causeway spanned the wide canyon surrounding Utatlán and separated it from the adjacent plains. Underneath the causeway was a swamp. The causeway was further protected by a stone door at the entrance to the town and a huge fortified "castle" on the eastern end. A "gangway" (*portalon*) led from the stone door of the causeway to the main plaza. It was rather long, and we are told that it was defended by young warriors from the noble class quartered there. The stairway of steps on the other side of the canyon was very steep. It too was protected with a stone door and fortification.

Inside the town were many streets and plazas paved with white stucco.

The conquistadors found them so narrow and broken that they could not effectively maneuver on horseback. As Alvarado observed (1946), the construction seemed to be adapted more for defense than for living. Fuentes y Guzmán also mentioned narrow streets leading from the palace to adjacent sections of the town. Some were meant to be private, and the one leading from the "princesses' " quarters to their "seminary" was secret.

During major celebrations the mazelike streets and plazas were filled with people. Before such occasions the streets were swept clean and adorned with pine branches and flowers. The deity icons were carried on litters down the streets and into the plazas, their bearers stopping at selected sites. In coordination with the processions "the musical instruments began to sound, and the songs, dances, farces, and mimicry (were begun), . . . and all with much order and concert" (Las Casas 1909, p. 468).

The natives made little mention of streets and plazas in their chronicles. A single reference in the *Título C'oyoi* (Carmack 1973, pp. 275–76) shows that the Quichés were aware that their town was crowded with streets, multistoried edifices, and rows (*rap*) of buildings. Generally, however, the streets were not thought of independent of the "limestone and white stucco" (*chun*, *sajcab*) constructions that symbolized the political power of the towns. The Quichés placed the emphasis on the ritual and military processions at Utatlán rather than on the streets on which the processions moved. We are told that the socially climbing vassal warriors (*achij*) regularly marched in procession "behind" their leaders at Utatlán (Villacorta 1962, p. 352), and when conquering warriors returned, the lords went out to meet them. In grand procession, the warriors were triumphantly brought back along the road (*beyawoc*) leading to the town (Recinos 1957, p. 108).

The defensive nature of Utatlán is stressed in the chronicles. The *Popol Vuh* (Villacorta 1962, pp. 345–47) tells us that the back side of the canyon and the towns of Utatlán was fortified (*k'atey*) and guarded by the vassal warriors. Several different kinds of walls and fences were constructed: *kejoj* ("walls," probably of stone), *tz'alam* ("wooden plank fences"), *c'oxtun* ("fortified walls, bulwarks"), *ts'apib* ("doors," sometimes of stone), and *chinamit* ("small territorial walls."). All of these were defenses behind which Quiché bowmen could hide while shooting at the enemy. The *c'oxtun* were large stone walls placed at vulnerable points near the canyons. Pismachí was apparently especially well defended with this kind of fortification.

The Spanish sources report that some of the walls were built inside the town itself. Fuentes y Guzmán (1932–33, 7:420) states that there was a high wall of cut stone surrounding the palace. This was probably the same wall that Ximénez (1929) claims surrounded the town center at Utatlán. These walls "were made of stone and mud, and were called *tz'alam c'oxtum*, which means wooden planks and palisade, or wall; and this is the name for all such constructions, because in most places, besides being the house of the idol (for example), it was also like a castle and fort where they defended themselves against the attack of their enemies" (Ximénez 1929, p. 75).

Fuentes y Guzmán's native map of Utatlán listed two additional large fortifications ("castles") at Utatlán, one within the town, and the other outside it. The outside "tower" (*atalaya*) was in front of the narrow causeway, near a branch of the canyon surrounding the town. It had four terraces and warriors stationed there to make it impregnable. The inside "guardhouse" (*resguardo*) was near the entrance to the town. It had five terraces (or divisions?) and was armed with four small "turrets" along its sides. This fort was manned by the "neighboring natives from the town of Chiquimula," who were famed for their fighting capacity.

All the information we have suggests that the Quichés believed their town to be invincible. As we have seen, much of the construction at the site was defensive or had defensive features. Had the circumstances of the Conquest been different, the Spaniards would have found it extremely difficult to penetrate Utatlán.

Other Structures

Our sources mention a few less-important structures at Utatlán. Several of these appeared on the map used by Fuentes y Guzmán, while the others come mainly from Las Casas. Thus, in addition to the buildings already described, Fuentes y Guzmán (1932–33, 7:417ff.) reports the following:

1. A "place of disgrace" was situated between the tower and the town. This may be the public place in the *Título C'oyoi* (Carmack 1973, p. 292) called *ch'ubic'abal*, where "the condemned are whipped." Possibly related to this is a reference in the *Annals* (Villacorta 1934, p. 232) to a tree at Utatlán where transgressors of the law were hanged or otherwise punished (*jec'*).

2. Near the place of disgrace the Quichés maintained a collection of beehives (*akaj*). Transgressors were sent there naked to pay their debts.

3. West of the palace the Quiché lords set aside an area for gardens and trees. The gardeners, probably slaves or serfs, lived next to the plots they tended.

Las Casas tells of two other Utatlán sites. He states (1909, p. 623) that in Verapaz marketplaces were established near the temples and that they had special judges to settle disputes arising over transactions. There was a market at Utatlán, but we are not told where it was. It may have been in the central plaza near the temples or outside the town, possibly near the fortified tower. In another context Las Casas (1909, p. 466) tells of a special "green house" (*raxaja?*) to which the high priest retired during troubled times. There he did penance for up to a year, fasting, bleeding himself, and offering gifts (but not human ones) to the deities. The hut was made of green leaves, which were continually replaced as they dried out. This temporary edifice was built outside the town, near the forests and caves where the deity icons were guarded.

INTEGRATION IN UTATLÁN SYMBOLISM

The symbolic interrelations between the different buildings and sections of Utatlán are poorly defined in the sources available to us. Perhaps, this is partly due to the relatively little information on religion preserved for us by the Spaniards. It probably also reflects the extensive secularism of Utatlán, especially its militarism, which often allowed pragmatic considerations to override symbolic and sacred building arrangements. This point is made emphatic in a section of the *Popol Vuh* that describes the primary activities carried out by the Quiché lords at Utatlán (Villacorta 1962, pp. 353–62). We are told of the lords entering temples in search of favors from the deities. They were followed by the conquered peoples, who came to Utatlán to make ritual offerings, first to Tojil and then to the other deities (*c'abawil*). Confederates and even enemies "worshiped there at Quiché," especially the Tamubs, Ilocabs, Rabinals, Cakchiquels, Tzutujils, and Sacapultecs (Tujaljas, Uchabajas). As if not wanting to give a one-sided picture, the authors of the *Popol Vuh* next inform us that Utatlán was also the place where the peoples came to pay tributes. They went first to Tojil but then appeared before the lords with their jade, metal, precious stones, and other goods. The Quichés finally summed up Utatlán's dual political and ritual functions in these words (Villacorta 1962, p. 360): "They were not just great rulers (*ajawab*), but also great fasters. They had both beloved temples, and beloved government." Just as the deities were sustained by blood and sacrifice, so the lords were sustained by tribute brought to Utatlán.

Political Integration

A source that perhaps overemphasizes the political basis of community at Utatlán is Fuentes y Guzmán (1932–33, 7:415ff.). Since he claims to have based his account on a sixteenth-century native map, it will be worthwhile to examine carefully the relationships he describes. It is usually possible to determine when his account was based on the 1579 map and when it was based on his own observations of the ruined site made in 1672. One source of the confusion in his description derives from the measurements of buildings, which were based on his own calculations and not on the native map. These measurements no doubt were authentic, but they referred to whole sections of the town rather than to specific buildings recorded on the map. Those buildings existed at Utatlán, but Fuentes y Guzmán was hopelessly confused when he tried to identify them with ruins still standing in his day. Once we understand that, it is possible to identify the most important sections of the town as they were remembered by the natives in their sixteenth-century map and interpreted for us by Fuentes y Guzmán.

The map portrayed the area surrounding Utatlán as a highly defensive zone. The canyon encircling the town had been purposely cut, and gave entry into town only by way of the narrow causeway on the east and precipitous steps on the west. Both entryways were protected by elevated fortifications. The giant fortified tower (*atalaya*) just east of town provided further protection for the eastern entrance. Also shown on the map were other, unidentified and fortified structures in the zone that ringed the town.

Information in the native map seems to indicate that the town itself was broadly divided into three sections: eastern, central, and western. The eastern section (188 by 230 steps, according to Fuentes y Guzmán's calculations) was organized primarily for defense. In that section were the large guardhouse (*resguardo*), fortified mounds on four sides. The best soldiers were quartered there, including some "foreigners" (the Chiquimultecos, or Tamubs, are mentioned).

The western section, which Fuentes y Guzmán erroneously identified with the palace alone (it measured 376 by 728 steps), was both residential and administrative. Courts, council rooms, storehouses, armories, and other offices were situated there. Most of the space, however, was taken up by the elaborate residential structures of the lords and attendants' quarters. There the arts of the elite were practiced, such as fine weaving, featherwork, weapon making, and plant husbandry.

The central zone is only briefly mentioned by Fuentes y Guzmán, but it appears to have been the ceremonial precinct. It consisted of a large plaza with a single passageway on the southern side that connected it with both the eastern and the western sections. Its dominant structure was an elevated temple (*sacrificatorio*), built up from four terraces and provided with stairways of about twenty steps each. Also mentioned in this section is a ball court, which stood next to the passageway where it led through the western section.

From the perspective of the map used by Fuentes y Guzmán, Utatlán seems to have been relatively secular. The largest sections were defensive and politico-residential in function. The residences of the lords were protected by several layers of defense, the ceremonial center itself serving as the fortified zone of last resort. Nevertheless, as will be shown below, the buildings of the ceremonial zone were integrated into an elaborate cosmological scheme, which in turn significantly influenced the more pragmatic arrangement of the western residential and political section.

The giant temple (*sacrificatorio*) dominating the ceremonial plaza in the map used by Fuentes y Guzmán was undoubtedly the temple of Tojil. The chronicles indicate that it became the symbolic center of Utatlán. Like a giant phallus or soldier, it projected from the center point high above the town (Villacorta 1962, pp. 333–34). The overriding prominence of Tojil derived from political considerations—he was the patron deity of the Caweks, the ruling military lineage of Utatlán. Even at the Tamub town Pismachi and the Ilocab center Mukwitz, Tojil was the leading deity and must have occupied prominent positions there.

Cosmological Balance

The political centrality of Tojil as patron of the Cawek rulers no doubt blurred the older cosmological balance between Tojil and Awilix, the latter the patron deity of the Nijaib major lineage. As mentioned earlier, these two lineages had shared living quarters before the establishment of Utatlán, and their deities had formed a highly symbolic union of male and female forces. Tojil was the sun, viewed as a young man (*c'ajol*), while Awilix was the moon, a young maiden (*k'apoj*) (*Título Totonicapán* n.d.).

These two deities were associated with complex religious symbolism. As the sun, Tojil ruled the day and represented elements directly related to that astral body. He was the thunder and storm (*toj*) controlled by the sun and the star Ikok'ij that preceded the sun each day. In his Venus aspect Tojil was said to be "Quitzalcuat," the morning-star god of the Mexicans (Villacorta 1962, p. 270). I think it likely that Tojil was also the personification of Junajpu, the older of the hero-twins, who became apotheosized as the sun. In his Junajpu aspect Tojil would be a hunter-warrior (blowgun warrior), patron of the ball game (Junajpu was the player *par excellence*), and lord of human sacrifices (Junajpu had been decapitated by the underworld lords). Junajpu was also the twentieth day of the sacred calendar (Ximénez 1929, pp. 101–102), and so Tojil may have been associated with the highly propitious final position of the twenty-day cycle, and possibly the beginning of the twenty-year units (May). The prayers offered by Quiché lords at Utatlán preserved for us in the chronicles suggest that Jurakan (One Leg), the god of lightning, was still another manifestation of Tojil, at least in some contexts (Villacorta 1962, p. 357). More than any other deity at Utatlán, Tojil was equated with the sky, or, as the Quichés expressed it, "the heart of heaven" (*uc'ux caj*) and "the center of heaven" (*upam caj*).

Awilix, the moon, ruled the night. The *Título Totonicapán* (n.d.) substantiates the statement in the *Popol Vuh* that Xbalanque became the moon and further clarifies that an important aspect of this conqueror of the underworld lords was female. Awilix, therefore, was probably the personification of Xbalanque, which would make her the patroness of the ball game (along with Tojil) and the underworld, with its associated illness and death. Her calendar day was probably Tz'iquin, the fifteenth day of the twenty-day cycle and apparently associated with the moon (Ximénez 1929, p. 101; Thompson 1960).

The cosmological relationship between Tojil and Awilix, as companion lord and lady of day and night, was expressed in building arrangements at Utatlán. Their respective temples were undoubtedly in meaningful spatial association with each other, perhaps oriented to cardinal directions. If such was the case, sun and moon orbits as well as ancient orientations would have positioned Awilix east of Tojil (Carmack, Fox, and Stewart 1975). Tojil would face east, where the sun rises, Awilix west, where the moon was thought to originate (it is the sun in the underworld). Furthermore, the association between sex and elevation in Quiché cosmology placed Tojil toward the sky (*xucat caj*), and Awilix toward the earth (*xucut ulew*). Thus the temple of Tojil must have been elevated above that of Awilix. Additionally, the association between the color yellow and both daylight and the southern direction would place the Tojil temple south relative to Awilix. The association of Awilix with darkness would correlate with a northern position for her. The temples of Tojil and Awilix, patron and patroness of the ball game, probably stood near the ball court and also in close proximity to their respective Cawek and Nijaib big houses. Possibly the nine big houses subject to each of these two ruling lineages were clustered nearby.

Las Casas (1909, p. 468) confirms that there were temples dedicated to the sun and moon deities at Utatlán. He further indicates the existence of deities symbolizing the cardinal directions, each with its altar and temple. The chronicles (*Título Totonicapán* n.d.; Villacorta 1962, p. 223) refer to these gods as the "four corners and sides" (*caj tzuc, caj xucut*). They are listed in the *Título Totonicapán* as the deities of the sky, the earth, the rising sun, and the setting sun (Caj, Ulew, Relibal K'ij, Rakanibal K'ij). The sky and earth—the latter in its underworld aspect—have already been identified with Tojil and Awilix, who also symbolized the rising sun and the setting sun, respectively. But this basic cosmological arrangement was complicated by the deities of the companion lineages of the Caweks and Nijaibs at Utatlán, the Ajaw Quichés and Tzutuja Sakics.

In contrast to the astral associations of the Cawek and Nijaib patron deities, the Ajaw Quiché and Sakic patron deities were primarily earthly. Jakawitz (Open Mountain), the god of the Ajaw Quichés, was a mountain deity. He symbolized the male aspect of the earth and was overtly phallic. In one passage of the *Título C'oyoi* (Carmack 1973, p. 276), Jakawitz is referred to as the "phallic deity" (*runum c'abawil*). The god of the original fourth lineage (Iq'ui Balam), called Nic'aj Tak'aj (Middle of the Plains), symbolized the female, or lower, portions of the earth (Villacorta 1962, p. 238). The Cakchiquels, who retained this deity as their patroness, wrote that her image was a sacred stone, probably of obsidian (Villacorta 1934, pp. 196, 216). Such stones were thought to come from the center of the earth, and so were appropriate icons for Nic'aj Tak'aj, deity of the low parts of the earth. When the lord Tzutuja was substituted for Iq'ui Balam and later gave rise to the Sakic major lineage at Utatlán, Nic'aj Tak'aj appears to have been retained as the patron deity. Like the Cakchiquels, the lord Tzutuja possessed a sacred stone (*cwal abaj*), which served as the icon (*c'abawil*) of the deity of that lineage (*Título Totonicapán* n.d.; Villacorta 1962, p. 354).

The arrangement of the temples dedicated to the mountain and plains deities of the Ajaw Quichés and Sakics must have symbolized in some way their cosmological relationship. Undoubtedly the temple of Jakawitz was high and phallic, like the temple of Tojil. The temple of Nic'aj Tak'aj must have been lower and flatter. The two temples probably also symbolized the points where the sun rose and set on the earth; like Tojil and Awilix they had aspects of the east and west deities of Utatlán. The temple of Jakawitz, male and reaching toward the sky, would greet Tojil on his ascent each day. In a tradition recorded by Juan de León (n.d., pp. 45ff.), Jakawitz (given as Cakwitz by de León) was identified with the sun at its zenith. Presumably Tojil's cosmological association with Jakawitz placed him west (to see the rising sun), while Jakawitz was placed in the skyward, or southern, direction with respect to Tojil. Nic'aj Tak'aj, female and interior of the earth, would meet Awilix each night after the sun had gone to the underworld. While Awilix received the sun as it went into the underworld, Nic'aj Tak'aj must have represented the sun at its nadir, "under" the earth. This would place her north of Awilix, in the direction associated with death and the underworld. Finally, we would expect the temples of Jakawitz and Nic'aj Tak'aj to have been located near the big houses of their respective Ajaw Quiché and Sakic lineages.

At this point it may be recalled that the *Título C'oyoi* drawings (Carmack 1973, pp. 290–91) depict buildings at Utatlán with distinctly sexual adornments (Fig. 7.2). The mammary and phallic roof combs shown there would have been most appropriate for the temples under discussion here. Such constructions would have grandly dramatized the sexual forces suggested by the sources. Unfortunately, the identity of the C'oyoi buildings is not revealed, and other interpretations of the buildings are equally plausible (see the discussion above of the palaces at Utatlán).

In summary, while the temple of Tojil was dominant and central at the ceremonial precinct of Utatlán, it was nevertheless integrated with the Awilix major temple in a complicated cosmological balance. The sacred directions were symbolized: Tojil toward the sky and east, Awilix toward the earth and west. Jakawitz also symbolized the sky and south, and Nic'aj Tak'aj the interior of the earth and north. On the basis of symbolic similarities Tojil was perhaps closely tied to Jakawitz, and Awilix to Nic'aj Tak'aj. This correlates with the proposed moietal arrangement (however weak) between the four major lineages at Utatlán described in chapter 6. The administrative and residential buildings were clustered around the temples of their respective lineage deities.

The positional relationship between Tojil and Awilix symbolically provided an alliance between the opposite forces of male and female, day and night, life and death, war and peace (domestic life). Jakawitz and Nic'aj Tak'aj also conceptually bound together opposites: mountain and plains, male and female, south and north. A more complex symbolic alliance existed between the similar pairs: Tojil and Jakawitz were counterposed to Awilix and Nic'aj Tak'aj. Within this cosmological framework the powerful military, sacrificial, and male principles of Tojil and Jakawitz would stand in balanced opposition to domestic life, illness and death, and female principles of Awilix and Nic'aj Tak'aj. I would judge this last relationship of union and opposition to be expressed strongly in the spatial arrangement of the major ceremonial buildings at Utatlán because it was consistent with the political forces operating in the community.

Unfortunately, any attempt to reconstruct the cosmological scheme of the Utatlán community will be incomplete. For example, our sources do not indicate whether the deities associated with the four directions were also integrated by temporal or calendric principles. Were they, perhaps, identified with the four year-bearers, who were thought to bring different fates to the years over which they presided (Carmack n.d.; Berendt n.d.; Miles 1957). If there was such an association, I would hypothesize that Tojil was linked to the year-bearer Quej (Deer) through Junajpu the hunter, and Awilix to Ik' (Wind, and Sickness). The other two year-bearers would be more difficult to identify, though Noj (Strong, Resin, Weather) would seem to correlate best with Jakawitz, and E (Tooth) with Nic'aj Tak'aj, through that day's association with maize (Recinos 1953, pp. 104, 113). These identifications would associate the four gods with major cycles of time; the time cycles, in turn, would receive directional associations: Quej with the east, Ik' with the west, Noj with the south, and E with the north.

Another question arises over the cosmological position of K'ucumatz, the feathered-serpent deity. As the rain and wind deity (Villacorta 1934, p. 196), he must have had a low, round temple, like temples dedicated to him elsewhere in Mesoamerica. The god's association with clouds and water probably gave it also a feminine symbolism, though one aspect of the masculine Tojil was the Feathered Serpent. The dualistic masculine and feminine characteristics of K'ucumatz may have qualified this deity to serve as a symbolic mediator between Tojil and Awilix (a theory held by Juan de León).

What was Tepew's place in the cosmological scheme? The sources tie K'ucumatz to Tepew, a deity who apparently had his own priestly lineage

(Tepew Yaqui) and temple. Tepew (Powerful, Elevated) was, I believe, a sky deity, associated with lightning and fire (Villacorta 1962, pp. 20–22; Edmonson 1965, p. 121). Like K'ucumatz, Tepew was dualistic, his sky aspect symbolically uniting with an earth aspect when lightning rays meet the earth (especially on mountains). Though primarily masculine, the association of lightning with rain and water gave this deity a feminine aspect as well. Perhaps Tepew functioned like K'ucumatz as a symbolic mediator between great deity forces, such as the sky (as Tojil) and earth (as Jakawitz). Whatever its symbolic function, the Tepew temple was probably paired in some spatial way with the K'ucumatz temple.

The most important deities of Utatlán and some of their cosmological relationships are summarized in Table 7.1.

Another question to ponder about the gods at Utatlán arises from a statement by Zorita (1941) that outside peoples had temples at Utatlán, the principal one belonging to the people of Chiquimula. Where were these "foreign" temples? What symbolic roles, if any, did they play? Chiquimula was a Tamub town, and possibly a Tamub temple was placed near the guardhouse (resguardo), which is reported to have been defended by warriors from Chiquimula.

Our information on the Tamubs of Pismachi is too sketchy to work out the detailed cosmological integration of their gods. The moiety political organization of the Tamubs may have overshadowed any preeminence Tojil might have had in that town. Tojil, as patron of the Kakoj moiety, appears to have been symbolically balanced by Awilix, a deity of the Ekoamak' moiety (Recinos 1957, pp. 50, 54). There were other Tamub deity pairs, but they do not form a simple, symbolic framework. The following pairings between the male and female patron deities of the four major Tamub lineages seem likely: (1) Julajuj (Ten, male) of the C'ochojlan lineage, with Tunala (Water Trumpet, female) of the C'opichoch lineage; (2) Julajuj (Ten, male) of the C'ok'anawil lineage, with Yacola (Water Servant, female) of the Majquinalo lineage; (3) the two remaining deities of the C'ok'anawil lineage, Yatas (Bundle, male?) and Yacola (Water Servant, female), were perhaps paired internally. The complex set of relationships makes it difficult to associate Tamub big houses and palaces with their temples at Pismachi. For the Ilocabs of Mukwitz we have too little information in the chronicles to make possible even a tentative reconstruction of such cosmological relationships (but see chapter 8).

A drawing accompanying the *Título Totonicapán* (n.d.) provides us with a dramatic reminder of the extent to which political considerations could modify the ideal cosmological relationships described above. A brief analysis of its contents will illustrate the problem.

The figures in the drawing (Fig. 7.3), that are said to be "buildings" (*tz'ak*)

Table 7.1. **The Deities of Utatlán**

```
                    Nic'aj Tak'aj (North)              +
                            |
              −             |
 Tojil (East) ──────────── Kucumatz ──────────────── Awilix (West)
                          (Center)
      +              Tepew        |
                  ╲               | −
                     ╲   Jakawitz (South)
```

Tojil (east)

    Young Man
    Sun
    Cawek major lineage
    Sky
      Day
      Storm
      Lightning
      Venus (morning)
    Junajpu
      Hunter
      Warrior
      Ball game
      Human Sacrifice
    20th calendar day
      May (20-year unit)
      Quej (year-bearer)
    Temple
      Faces east
      Elevated
      Tzompantli altar
      Situated southward

Awilix (west)

    Maiden
    Moon
    Nijaib major lineage
    Underworld
      Night

      Venus (evening)
    Xbalanque

      Ball game
      Sickness
    15th calendar day
      Ik' (year-bearer)
    Temple
      Faces west
      Unelevated
      Front altar
      Situated northward

Jakawitz (south)
    Male
      Mountain
      Phallic
    Sun (zenith)
    Ajaw Quiché major lineage
    Sky
    Noj (year-bearer)
    Temple
      Elevated
      Faces southward

Nic'aj Tak'aj (north)
    Female
      Plains
      Mammary
    Sun (nadir), moon
    Tzutuja Sakic major lineage
    Underworld (sacred stone)
    E (year-bearer)
    Temple
      Unelevated
      Faces northward

      K'ucumatz (center)
      Male–Female
        Rain and wind
        Serpent and feathers
      Cawek sublineage
      Binds sun and moon
      Temple
        Round
        Faces east and west

      Tepew (center)
      Male–Female
        Lightning

      Cawek sublineage
      Binds rising and zenith suns
      Temple
        Faces north and south (?)
        Southward

at Utatlán have already been identified as four big houses and gladiatorial and skull-rack altars. It is possible that the drawing is a native map and that the spatial relationships between the figures give an idea of how the buildings were arranged at Utatlán. If that is the case, then we are shown a large plaza with four big houses placed at the corners and two altar platforms standing near the center. From the reconstruction of cosmological relationships above, it follows that the Ajpop Big House would have stood near the Tojil temple, somewhere west of the Nijaib Big House. Such an arrangement would place the Nijaib buildings eastward in the direction of the Ajaw Quichés, though north of that group. The gladiatorial and skull-rack altars would be southeast of the Ajpop buildings. This arrangement is consistent with the above reconstruction, and informs us of the general location of these two important altars (for further identifications, see chapter 8).

The map challenges the previously worked out cosmological scheme, however, by listing the Nima Rajpop Achij as the fourth big house, rather than the expected Tzutuja Sakic big house. As already explained in "Social Structure" above, Nima Rajpop Achij was a high Cawek political office at Utatlán, with an impressive minimal lineage house (equipped with court and double canopies). That explains its prominence on the map. The Sakic building was presumably deleted from the map for reasons of political expediency, though its sacred position as a northern low point in Utatlán cosmology may have been preserved in some fashion. The location of the Nima Rajpop Achij building, west and south of the Ajpop Big House, may be an indication of the direction in which the administrative buildings associated with the Tojil temple were placed. It may have had some cosmological significance as well, perhaps through association with the green quetzal bird, the nagual of Tecum, the contact-period holder of the *nima rajpop achij* title. Without more information, however, we cannot reconstruct the system in its complete form, and we are left with a complex of political and cosmological relations that conform to no simple structural scheme.

Town and Country Ties

The cosmological patterns symbolized by the temples and other buildings of Utatlán must have been meaningful to the vassals as well as the lords of the rural areas. The sun, moon, sky, and earth, as well as the cardinal directions, were of fundamental importance to the rural peasants, as they are today (Bunzel 1952; Falla 1975; Carmack n.d.; Shaw 1971). No doubt the Quiché peasants distorted the meanings of town symbols. Ancestral and kinship personifications probably pushed aside the astral associations of the lords; for example, for the peasants the moon was (and is) emphatically Katit (Our Grandmother) rather than Awilix. The gods and temples most closely associated with the earth would have found special favor with the rural peoples, particularly Jakawitz, the mountain deity, and Nic'aj Takaj, the deity of the lower parts of the earth. Despite such differences between town and country the interpretation of cosmological forces at Utatlán by lords and vassals probably overlapped enough to provide a loose symbolic integration of the two groups.

Much more inviting to the rural people of the Utatlán community were the actual ceremonies held in town. As the Catholic priests were to discover later, Quiché peasants were highly attracted to the outward forms of ritual (see chapter 9). The processions, dances, dramas, and singing and drinking festivals that took place periodically at Utatlán must have involved the active participation of rural peoples, though we are not told about the specific roles they played (Las Casas 1909, p. 630). If modern survivals of the old dances are an indication, the townspeople organized the events and financed the most expensive paraphernalia, while the rural peoples provide the special dancers, musicians, and natural resources (pine branches, flowers, fermented drinks, animals, and so on). They may also have engaged in some of the revelry seen today during town celebrations, such as heavy drinking, dancing, and buying and selling (though within the context of the rather spartan military society at Utatlán such activities were probably more closely controlled then than they are today.) At any rate, it is inconceivable that the Quiché peasants did not come in vast numbers to Utatlán to attend the frequent festive occasions mentioned in the documents. As a respite from their agricultural activities they no doubt greatly enjoyed the colorful festivities and in this way found solidarity with their lords.

Our sources indicate that dance dramas emphasizing military and sacrificial themes were given priority in the celebrations at Utatlán (Carmack 1973, p. 295). This priority came from the lords, who, as the leaders of a military society, were constrained to keep warfare always before their vassal warriors. Nevertheless, myths and dances surviving into modern times suggest that the dances and dramas with lighter, more nature-oriented themes were the ones most enjoyed and internalized by the rural peoples (Carmack 1973, pp. 168–71). I would hypothesize that the dramas expressing the hero-twin stories (Junajpu, Xbalanque, Xmucane, and so on) were their favorites. We are informed that they were frequently performed at Utatlán (Carmack 1973, p. 295; *Título Totonicapán* n.d.), especially the episodes having to do with the Macaw (Cakix) family and the brothers who turned into monkeys (Jun Batz, Jun Chowen) (Villacorta 1962, pp. 47–85, 129–36). They must have been of intense interest and amusement to the rural peoples, just as similar dances (such as the jesters and monkey pole climbing) are for the Quiché peasants of the twentieth century.

The lords may have played to these rural interests, especially with respect to the master story, the descent of Junajpu and Xbalanque into the underworld. Was an attempt made to interpret the town of Utatlán, with its buildings, complexes, and plazas, as a microcosm of that great myth? It has already been noted that the ball court represented the underworld and that there the players re-created the fight between the hero-twins and the lords of death. The temples of Tojil and Awilix may also have symbolized the hero-twins. The symbolism may have been expanded into an elaborate mythic pattern for the entire ceremonial center at Utatlán, though that is never explicitly stated in the sources. I would speculate, for example, that the *tzumpan* ("skull-rack altar") symbolized the tree upon which the skull of Junjunajpu was hung. Could some altar in the central plaza have symbolized the patio (*cul nic'aj ja*) of the house of the Old Grandmother (Xmucane)? We are told that canes (*aj*) were planted there, which shriveled up when her grandsons were harmed and flourished when they were well. The canes became a household altar, because she burned copal before them (Villacorta 1962, pp. 211ff.). If such an altar of old reeds existed at Utatlán, and if it was equated with Old Grandmother's house, that might explain the strange name given to the town: K'umarcaaj (Old House or Old Reeds), an idea first suggested by Brasseur in 1861.

It is possible to think of ways in which the myth might have been used to bind the lords of town symbolically with the wider Utatlán community. The artisans are represented in the story as frivolous kinsmen of the hero-twins. They are turned into monkeys and thus remain in the forest on the margins of society. The hero-twins are sent to work the agricultural fields, but they are not allowed to perform any labor. The rural area is, instead, the domain of the tools and of the animals: lions, jaguars, deer, rabbits, mountain cats, coyotes, peccary, *pisotes*, and birds. The rural peoples of the Utatlán community must have identified with those animals, some of whom were the totem animals of their lineages. So the hero-twins, who stood for the lords, performed neither artisan nor agricultural labors. They were ballplayers and hunters, men who conquered dangerous outsiders, whether evil lords of the dead or powerful beasts of the forest. It would have been clear to all members of the Utatlán community that the function of lords was to make war and to conquer. That was a noble calling and one in which, like Junajpu and Xbalanque, they were destined to be successful. On the other hand, agriculture would be seen as the domain of mountain people, the vassals, who were closely associated with animals of the forest.

This mythic symbolization of the Utatlán community, if it really existed, potentially provided the basis for a common set of religious values for town and rural peoples. Closely related to these possibly shared understandings was a calendric system to which the Junajpú myths were tied. Our sources indicate that the same solar and "sacred" calendars used by the lords to schedule wars, public works, marriages, and rituals were used by the vassals to perform agricultural labor and conduct lineage affairs (see chapter 4). Apparently for both lord and peasant the solar calendar began during early spring (late February to early March), had the same year-bearers (Noj, Ik', Quej, E), marked off the same eighteen twenty-day periods, and ended on the same five unlucky days. Most of the 20-day units were identified with agricultural periods, but some were defined in military and ritual terms. This suggests that a single solar calendar was in use, controlled by the lords but adapted to the particular needs of the rural vassals. This process may have led the lords to correlate major town rituals with periods of time already ritually significant to the peasants. For example, there is evidence that the first two twenty-day periods fixed the time when the patrons of the year (today called Mam, Year-bearers) took their seats at the cardinal points. The peasants were careful to note which year-bearer was in place, whether Noj, Ik', Quej, or E, for each had a different effect on the weather and agricultural productivity (Carmack n.d.). By equating the principal Utatlán deities and their rituals with the year-bearers, it would have been possible for the lords to exercise symbolic control over the agricultural cycle of their vassals. I believe it possible that the Utatlán lords did just that and that Tojil was equated with the good year-bearer Quej (Deer); and Awilix, with the bad year-bearer Ik' (Wind, Moon). Unfortunately, our sources do not allow us to elaborate on these relationships.

Both the town and the rural peoples of the Utatlán community also followed the sacred, or 260-day, calendar. Surviving calendars of this kind suggest that the two groups probably used the same names and numbers and were in sequence with one another (Miles 1952). It has already been noted that there were many similarities between ritual and custom in the rural and town contexts, and this must have led to a partial convergence of their 260-day calendars. At least that occurred under Spanish rule, Quiché peasants syncretizing Christian and native ritual dates (Bunzel 1952; see also chapter 9). But syncretisms of this kind are partial, and since the lineage rituals of the rural peoples of Utatlán must have been of great antiquity, their original correlations with the 260-day calendar were probably retained despite contrary interpretations in town. That is suggested by the variations found today among Quiché municipalities and even lineages and hamlets within the same community with respect to the relative fates of the days, the scheduling of ritual and customary practices (such as marriage), and the strength of calendric influence on social life.

Like the ritual and mythic modes of symbolic integration described above, calendrics helped bind together the Utatlán community. As with the other modes, the lords attempted to control calendrics for their own advantage. They shared symbolic systems with the vassals, but their superiority was always expressed clearly in each system. The integrational success the Quichés achieved in this way must have been partly a result of the basic sociocultural roots that were shared by the two groups. Nevertheless, town and rural symbols, or at least the interpretations of those symbols, were never identical.

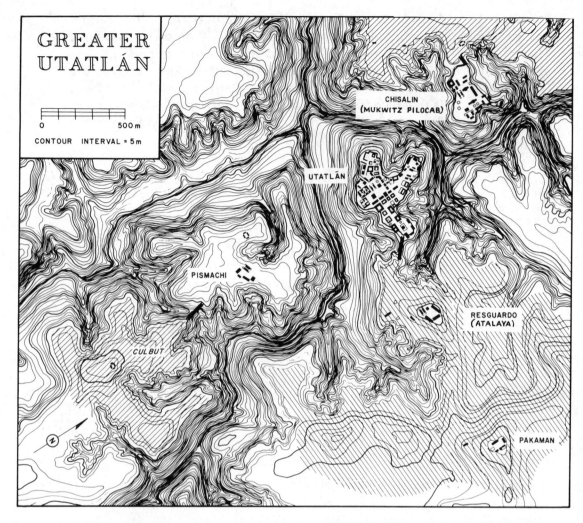

Fig. 8.1. Greater Utatlán (outer occupation areas hatched). From Wallace 1977.

8
SETTLEMENT PATTERNS

WE NOW TURN FROM THE QUICHÉS' own view of their community to the actual physical layout of their towns, hamlets, and other settlements. By "settlement pattern" I mean simply the physical and symbolic relations among sites and buildings within sites. Obviously I must rely heavily on archaeological research, though an attempt will be made to integrate documentary information where relevant. As the reader will discover, the archaelogy and the ethnohistory are generally in close conformity. Nevertheless, there will be occasion to point out apparent contradictions between the archaeological and ethnohistoric views. That is to be expected. The documentary sources present us with an ideal view of the Utatlán settlements—what the peoples who wrote the chronicles ideally wanted their community to be. The archaelogy, in contrast, provides us with a rather objective, "statistical" view of the material conditions—what the settlements were actually like. Therefore, in some cases the differences between the two reconstructions of Utatlán reflect differences between ideal (largely ethnohistorical) and actual (archaeological) models of the same community. It is important to study these differences, for they reveal some of the underlying contradictions at Utatlán. The Quichés, like all other peoples, struggled to make their actual social life conform to their ideal view of the world. Material conditions necessarily influenced that view, continually introducing changes into it. Such a "dialectical" approach to the Utatlán settlements is well served by a combined ethnohistorical and archaelogical approach.

Very limited archaeological research has been carried out in the central Quiché area. Of the nuclear Utatlán sites only Utatlán itself has been the most excavated, and that excavation has been limited to a few exploratory pits and trenches to follow out building forms.

Robert Wauchope (1949; 1970), the first modern-day archaeologist to excavate at Utatlán, sank nine test pits at various points in the site in the 1940s. His data consisted of a good sample of stratified sherds and a few features of major buildings near the main plaza. In 1956 the late Swiss archaeologist Jorge Guillemin cleared the Utatlán site and prepared a map of the structures there and at Pismachi, Atalaya, and Chisalin (Mukwitz Pilocab).

SUNY at Albany work at Utatlán began in 1971, when a team of students and I gathered surface sherds and mapped the site. In the summer of 1972, Dwight Wallace and a small team uncovered the compound that Wauchope had suggested was residential, as well as a long structure situated along the western side of the main plaza. This team also prepared an improved map of the site, based on ground measurements and air photos taken in 1957, after the site was cleared of trees and brush. Chisalin was trenched at that time to obtain a ceramic sample. In 1973, John Weeks, of SUNY at Albany, dug test pits just outside the Atalaya and Pakaman sites. In 1974, under Wallace's direction, a SUNY at Albany team again trenched Utatlán, this time in the palace area and four long structures closely associated with the palace. The architectural and ceramic reports and maps from the three seasons of SUNY at Albany excavations at Utatlán are still in preparation. However, many of the data are summarized in a monograph published in the fall of 1977 by the SUNY at Albany Institute for Mesoamerican Studies (Wallace and Carmack 1977).

A brief survey of rural sites in the central Quiché area was carried out by Russell Stewart, of SUNY at Albany, in 1973. The survey was conducted especially to determine the kinds of settlements associated with ancient *calpul* territories. Recently Gruhn and Bryan (1976) also briefly surveyed sites in the Chichicastenango area. A more thorough survey of the Quiché basin is now in progress, under the direction of Kenneth Brown, of the University of Houston.

Many other archaeologists and antiquarians have visited Quiché and made observations about surface features, mostly of Utatlán itself. The researchers include Miguel Rivera y Maestre, commissioned by Mariano Glávez (1832); John Lloyd Stephens (1839); César Daly (1857); Alfred P. Maudslay (1887); Karl Sapper (1894); Antonio Villacorta and Flavio Rodas (1928); Samuel K. Lothrop (1932); Edwin Shook (1940s); and William Sanders and Joseph Michels (1972). The most important descriptions by colonial writers are those of Martín Alfonso Tovilla (ca. 1630), Francisco Antonio Fuentes y Guzmán (ca. 1690); Fray Francisco Ximénez (ca. 1700), and the anonymous author of the *Isagoge historica* (1711).

In the account that follows, first I discuss the general features of greater Utatlán, the composite center made up of several nuclear sites. Next I describe the individual nuclear sites themselves. Finally I discuss the rural settlement patterns of the entire central basin. My procedure throughout is to describe settlement features revealed by archaeological research and then to integrate the ethnohistoric information taken either from prior reconstructions in this book or from the primary sources themselves.

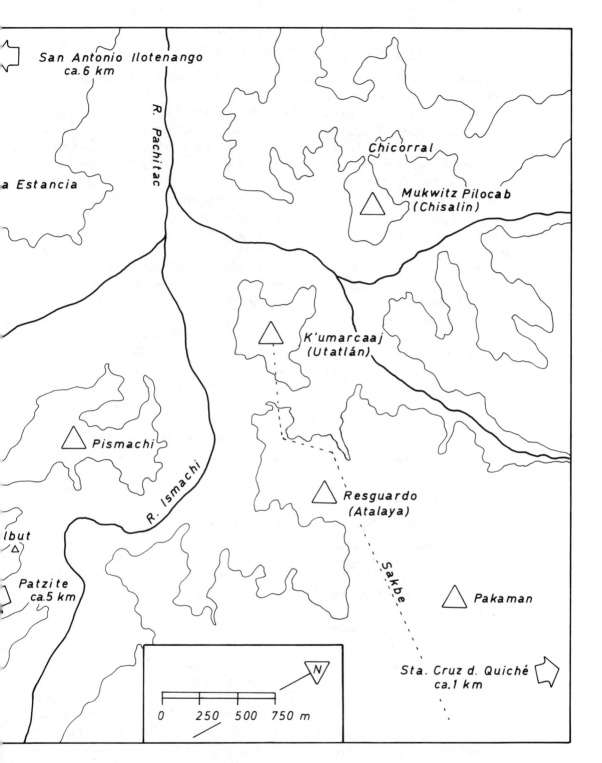

Fig. 8.2. Utatlán and its satellite sites, Pismachi, Chisalin, and Resguardo
(Atalaya). Modified from Fox 1975.

215

THE GREATER UTATLÁN SETTLEMENT

The dominant feature of the Utatlán settlement pattern is the large, nucle-ated site, which I shall refer to as nuclear, or greater, Utatlán. This large site is composed of four major nuclei, or subsites, on the closely adjacent plateaus Pismachi, Utatlán, Resguardo (Atalaya), and Chisalin (Mukwitz Pilocab) (Fig. 8.1). When our archaeological survey team discovered the Chisalin site and found that it was located at the approximate northern cardinal point from Utatlán, we began to realize that Pismachi (south), Resguardo or Atalaya (east), and Chisalin (north) must have been satellite sites of Utatlán. When we searched for a corresponding western satellite, we found a small plaza site in the proper location, but it appears to date from a pre-Quiché phase.

We also discovered that the major subsites—Pismachi, Utatlán, and Chisalin—were associated with smaller "auxiliary" sites near narrow cause-ways connecting the major centers with large expanses of land. The Res-guardo (Atalaya) site appears to have been an auxiliary of Utatlán that was later elevated in category. The Pakaman site apparently also functioned as an auxiliary to Utatlán. The Pismachi auxiliary site is known as Culbut, while a badly ruined site in Chicorral is probably the auxiliary site of Chisalin (Fig. 8.2). Together the major and auxiliary sites form a nuclear settlement of large proportions. The remains of 150 to 200 buildings have been detected by archaeologists from surface remains at these nuclear sites.

More than a century ago Daly (1865) noted ruins on three separate plateaus at Utatlán, but Guillemin (1956) was perhaps the first archaeologist to recog-nize the significance of greater Utatlán as a single, late center. He noted the defensive nature of each subsite and called attention to the existence of a ball court at each one, observing that four ball courts situated close together are an unusual feature. That is an important observation, because Resguardo's ball court suggests a higher category for the site than merely an auxiliary settlement. Guillemin also commented on the "aristocratic and priestly residential character" of the Pismachi and Chisalin subsites, suggesting that they were inhabited by overflow members of the twenty-four expanding lineages.

Several settlement features become evident when greater Utatlán sites are compared with early Quiché sites in Chujuyup (Fox 1975; see chapter 2 above). The Utatlán subsites are much closer together than the early sites. Whereas the Utatlán sites are separated by 300 to 600 meters, the early sites are two to three kilometers apart. The buildings of the Utatlán subsites, both residential and civic buildings, are much larger and more numerous than those of the early phase. Construction is different, too, the finely cut pumice and limestone blocks of Utatlán contrasting with the schistose slabs of the early sites.

The Utatlán pattern—two temples facing each other across a single plaza—contrasts with the early sites, in which separate plazas with single temples were placed back to back. This difference may also be correlated with directional contrasts, for, compared with the consistent east-west–facing temples of nuclear Utatlán, the temples of the early sites face in varying directions (for example, at Chitinamit the temples face south; at Cruz Che, east and west). It might be postulated that the construction of two or more temples in one plaza at nuclear Utatlán replaced the early pattern of situating temples or altars of major deities in mountain shrines above the more secular centers. There is no evidence of this early pattern at nuclear Utatlán. Fox (1975) suggests that the Utatlán temple pattern may have evolved from the early arrangement through the combining into one plaza of separate sites with their respective temples. The flanking structures of the nuclear Utatlán temples are not found at the early sites, though Fox thinks that the short, rectangular buildings placed perpendicular to the temples at the early sites might be their forerunners.

Important differences in the subsites of greater Utatlán reveal additional settlement features of the nuclear complex. One obvious difference is size. Utatlán proper is by far the largest of the nuclear sites, both in the number of structures (seventy to eighty) and in the size of the structures. Chisalin is next in size, with over forty structures, but they are smaller than the buildings at Utatlán. Pismachi has only about ten structures, which again are smaller than those at Utatlán. As Fox notes (1975), however, a second small plaza may have existed northwest of the Pismachi ruins. The Resguardo (Atalaya) site is the smallest of the nuclear sites, having only seven visible structures. The buildings there are about the same size as those of Pismachi and Chisalin, but they are smaller than those of Utatlán.

Fox (1975) has pointed to differences among the plazas of the greater Utatlán sites with respect to directional orientation of buildings. The Utatlán buildings are close to the cardinal points, deviating at most by five degrees. Chisalin is neatly aligned to the cardinal points. The Resguardo plaza buildings are oriented to the cardinal points but diverge from them by ten degrees. Pakaman, best considered an auxiliary site, is perfectly aligned to the cardinal points. Pismachi, however, in contrast to the other nuclear sites, shows only a very approximate alignment with the cardinal directions (forty degrees off). Pismachi also contrasts to the other sites in the position of its ball court—northwest rather than southwest of the plaza—and the existence of two slightly varying directional axes within the main plaza.

The growth of a large political and religious center at Utatlán, as revealed by the archaeology, is also clearly indicated in the documents, which tie its development to the emergence of the Quiché state. The highly defensive nature of the greater Utatlán settlements, surrounded by deep canyons and entered by narrow causeways guarded by elevated forts, is also consistent with the documented militaristic nature of the Utatlán community. What is more, the existence of a single center with three or four component nuclei correlates well with the documentary view of a political confederacy among the Nima Quichés, the Tamubs, the Ilocabs, and later the Nijaibs. These units of the confederacy can be identified with the respective nuclear settlements K'umarcaaj (Utatlán), Pismachi, Mukwitz Pilocab (Chisalin), and the Nijaib town (Resguardo). The integration of the different confederate units into a central administrative apparatus, documented in the chronicles, is confirmed by the locations of these large sites, close to each other in the same canyon system. Their nucleation dramatically illustrates the political unity of the new state as contrasted to the loose, segmentary alliance of the original Quiché confederacy, isolated in the scattered mountain sites of Chujuyup (see chapter 3).

The superiority of the Nima Quichés in the confederacy and the growing centralization of the state, documented in our sources, are seen in the larger size of Utatlán compared with the sizes of the other subsites of nuclear Utatlán. In fact, the other sites seem to be satellites around Utatlán, further attesting to the control that the Nima Quichés exercised over their political partners.

With respect to the satellite settlements, it might be asked why there was no site west of Utatlán (at least the archaeology to date has failed to turn up one). The documents indicate that the ideal political system of the Quichés was quadripartite and that the emergence of the Nijaibs as the fourth unit in the confederacy completed the system. Evidence was cited in chapter 6 that the Nijaibs and the Tamubs were closely allied while the Caweks and the Ilocabs formed a separate but similar alliance (in marriage, descent, ritual, and so on). These alliances resulted in a northern-southern division within the confederated settlement, which contrasted and overlapped with the satellite arrangement I have been discussing. Nevertheless, the locations of the three sites approximately at the cardinal points from Utatlán argue that the satellite arrangement, and thus centralized political structure, was the more important principle of the two operating in the greater Utatlán community.

The satellite settlements also raise the question why they varied in their directional orientations. Utatlán and Resguardo were about equal in their degree of cardinal-point orientation, which is consistent with the interpretation that the two settlements were occupied by lineages from the same Nima Quiché unit. The archaeology of Mukwitz Pilocab (Chisalin) suggests that the Ilocabs were strongly oriented to the cardinal directions, a point not made clear in the documentary sources (see the section "Mukwitz Pilocab" below). At first glance it is surprising to discover that the Tamub settlement deviated so far from the cardinal points. That confederate unit was strongly organized along traditional lines, with moiety and quadripartite lineage divisions and presumably cardinal-point directions. The sources indicate, however, that Pismachi was the first of the nuclear Utatlán sites to be occupied and that the early occupants were Nima Quichés rather than Tamubs. K'umarcaaj and probably the Resguardo and Pilocab centers were planned settlements colonized from the Pismachi plateau. Archaeology suggests that the orientation of Quiché towns to the cardinal points was developmental and that Pismachi, as the first town, lacked precise orientation. By this reasoning, Mukwitz Pilocab must have been the last settlement formed (along with Pakaman, an auxiliary site), which explains its perfect alignment with the cardinal directions.

The existence of auxiliary settlements in connection with nuclear Utatlán is not clearly seen from the documentary sources. Nevertheless, the town Panpetak of the chronicles seems to fit well the characteristics of these sites. Panpetak was probably a military garrison (as were, no doubt, the other auxiliary settlements). Ethnohistory documents the rise of a military "class" (*achij*) in late Quiché society (see chapter 6), and its leaders must have been closely associated with the auxiliary settlements. The documents also tell us that the administrative apparatus of the Quiché state became more complex through time and that a third level of militarized officials was created. Since the auxiliary settlements served as mediators between the lords inside the towns and the vassals of the rural area, they would have been appropriate locations for these officials. In this regard the ethnohistorical description of the confederate units as administrators of territorial units (*calpules*) outside the political centers fits the pattern being described. The Utatlán causeway and auxiliary settlements (first Resguardo and later Pakaman) lead eastward in the general direction of the major Nima Quiché *calpules*. The narrow Tamub road and the auxiliary site Culbut are southwest, in the general direction of their most important *calpules*. And the causeway leading from the Ilocab center of Mukwitz Pilocab to its Chicorral auxiliary site and from there on northwest, is consistent with the direction of the Ilocab *calpules*. If Resguardo was a Nijaib town, then we would expect its special entryway or auxiliary settlement (if any) to be southwest of the towns where the documents indicate that the main Nijaib *calpules* were placed.

Guillemin's suggestion that the sites surrounding Utatlán functioned as residential centers for the overflow from the center is valid in a general rather than a literal sense. The ethnohistory identifies the sites with separate groups, as has been mentioned. Historically Utatlán was populated by an overflow from Pismachi, though superior topographic conditions at Utatlán rather than overcrowding at Pismachi were probably the reason behind the move. The promotion of the Resguardo settlement to major-town status may represent just the kind of spillover that Guillemin had in mind. If the site was inhabited by the Nijaibs, they may have moved there primarily because there was no room in Utatlán for a second powerful lineage alongside the Caweks. Nevertheless, the Nijaibs probably continued to occupy buildings inside Utatlán, at least in the central plaza.

In terms of its relation to greater Utatlán, the Ilocab settlement Mukwitz Pilocab (Chisalin) is the most difficult to interpret. Quiché history tells us that the Ilocabs were militarily humbled by the Nima Quichés and placed under tight administrative control. In view of the elaborate colonial program the Quichés maintained among conquered peoples outside the Utatlán area, it seems likely that the Caweks settled military representatives among the Ilocabs in the town. If so, that would constitute another, special form of spillover from Utatlán.

When the features at late Utatlán sites are contrasted with those of early Quiché sites, they reveal an increase in settlement complexity not made sufficiently clear in our documentary sources. The native authors of the chronicles associated the founding of the Utatlán towns with the use of mortar, stone, and stucco, and mentioned the construction of multiterraced, staired buildings. But the tremendous increase in the size, number, and quality of the buildings revealed by the archaeology is not adequately described. Nor do we gain a clear picture of the complex resettling of lineage, priestly, military, and confederate groups into new composite plazas, towns, and town divisions.

INDIVIDUAL NUCLEAR SETTLEMENTS

The review of internal settlement patterns for the nuclear sites to follow is based mainly on the excavations of Wauchope and the archaeologists of SUNY at Albany. Since the sites have deteriorated through time and some of the earlier visitors observed features that are no longer visible, their documentary reports will also be used to describe the sites.

Utatlán

Dwight T. Wallace (1977) prepared a highly detailed map of the structures of Utatlán based on aerial photographs, surface-feature measurements, and limited excavations (Fig. 8.3). The elevation, form, and architectural characteristics permitted him to distinguish building types, and the positions and associations of the structures made it possible to him to assign functions to them. In his highly simplified scheme only three fundamental building types constitute most of the structures at Utatlán: long structures associated with council activities; high, square structures that were temple bases; and low, multichambered residential or palace units. He argued that, with only six possible exceptions, all the structures at the site can be assigned to one of

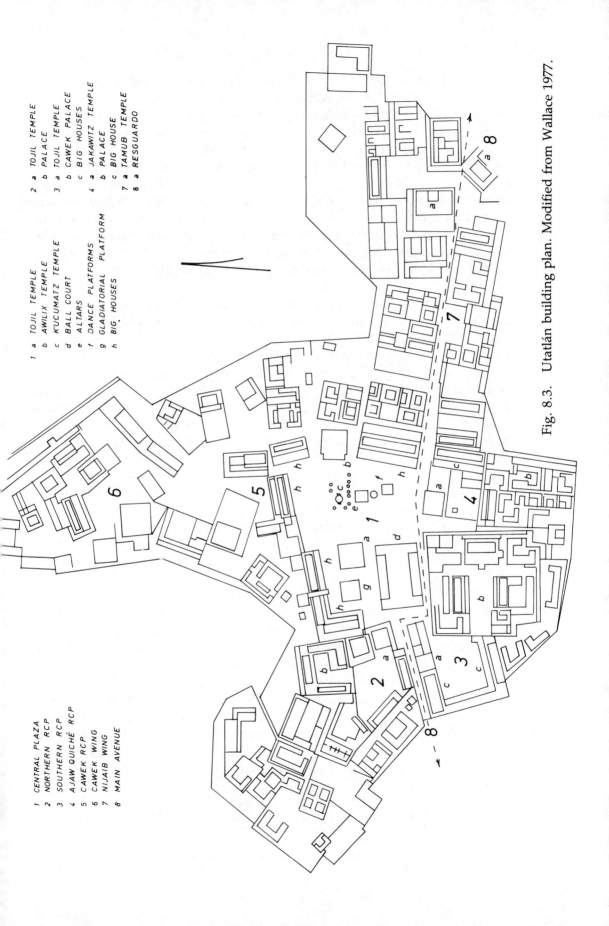

1 CENTRAL PLAZA
2 NORTHERN RCP
3 SOUTHERN RCP
4 AJAW QUICHÉ RCP
5 CAWEK RCP
6 CAWEK WING
7 NIJAIB WING
8 MAIN AVENUE

1 a TOJIL TEMPLE
   b AWILIX TEMPLE
   c K'UCUMATZ TEMPLE
   d BALL COURT
   e ALTARS
   f DANCE PLATFORMS
   g GLADIATORIAL PLATFORM
   h BIG. HOUSES

2 a TOJIL TEMPLE
   b PALACE
3 a TOJIL TEMPLE
   b CAWEK PALACE
   c BIG HOUSES
4 a JAKAWITZ TEMPLE
   b PALACE
   c BIG HOUSE
7 a TAMUB TEMPLE
8 a RESGUARDO

Fig. 8.3.   Utatlán building plan. Modified from Wallace 1977.

those three functions. As he noted, however, these are only primary functions, for buildings at Utatlán actually served several functions. Of the approximately eighty structures that he identified with these three functions, about thirty are said to be residential, thirty council, and twelve ritual (temple) buildings. Of the six unassigned buildings only one is thought to have a distinct function—that of fortifying the causeway entrance to the site.

Wallace went on to suggest that the three basic building types were combined into consistent patterns or arrangements. The basic pattern consists of an open space (court), enclosed by council and temple buildings, adjacent to a palace (residential building). This ritual-council-palace complex (RCP) occurs in varying sizes throughout the site. He defines twelve RCPs for the entire site, though he admits that not all of them are equally well delimited.

A second important building pattern detected by Wallace is a moiety division of the site into northwestern and southeastern halves. His proposed dividing line (Figure 8.4) follows the old causeway, which leads from the western staired canyon, splits the ball court into equal sides, juts northward as it crosses the main plaza, and separates the northern and eastern wings, ending at the northern canyon wall. The proposed moietal line has the effect of placing the following buildings and complexes in opposite northern and southern halves: the sidewalls of the ball court, the facing temples of the main court, the council houses of the main plaza, two subplazas associated with the main plaza, the two major RCPs, and the buildings of the northern and eastern wings. The division would place six RCPs on the northern side and six on the southern. Wallace finds an interesting difference between the buildings of the two halves with respect to directional orientation, the southeastern moietal buildings being much more closely oriented to the cardinal points than are those of the northwest.

Wallace sees in the over-all patterning of the site a complex interplay between centralization and segmentation. The main plaza, with its two associated large palace complexes, represents the center of the site and the locus of high rank, authority, and sacredness. Yet the site is also segmented into equal, opposite halves and further divided into replicating complexes of ritual, council, and residence (the RCPs). Other lesser principles enter in, such as defensibility and directional orientation, but the "segmentative centralism" is the fundamental locational pattern.

How well does Wallace's analysis of Utatlán correlate with the ethnohistory of the town? In general it correlates well, though there are significant differences. Some of the incongruities are as interesting as the correspondences. Since Wallace has also looked at the ethnohistoric data on Utatlán, his comments will be discussed along with my own observations in the account to follow.

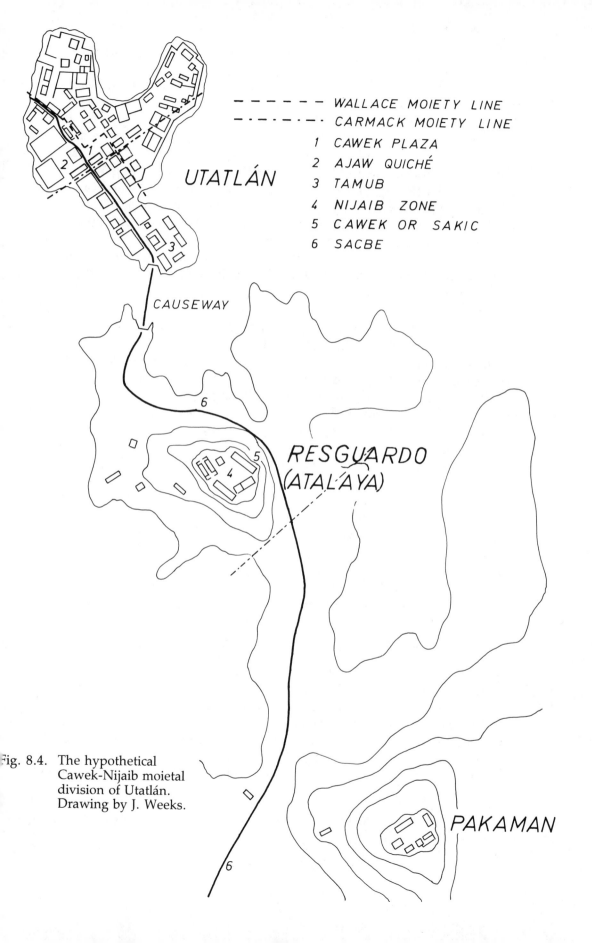

--- --- --- WALLACE MOIETY LINE
-·- -·- -·- CARMACK MOIETY LINE

1 CAWEK PLAZA
2 AJAW QUICHÉ
3 TAMUB
4 NIJAIB ZONE
5 CAWEK OR SAKIC
6 SACBE

UTATLÁN

CAUSEWAY

RESGUARDO
(ATALAYA)

PAKAMAN

Fig. 8.4. The hypothetical
Cawek-Nijaib moietal
division of Utatlán.
Drawing by J. Weeks.

The reconstruction of Quiché society from the documents reveals a broad spectrum of functional social units. There are references to council houses (big houses), temples, and residences (palaces), but we also read about altars, military quarters, armories, storage houses, craft shops, servants' houses, courthouses, rulers' courts, gardens, schools, religious auxiliary buildings, fortifications, and others. Thus the ethnohistory suggests a functionally much richer social life than could be inferred from Wallace's analysis of building types alone. The documentary sources agree with him that many functions were carried out in a limited number of building types. For example, the temples and big houses are sometimes called by the same term as residences, *ochoch*. Another term, *tz'ak*, is also used for both big houses and temples, and it may well have been applied to the palaces also. This supports Wallace's argument that the Utatlán buildings were multifunctional. Significantly, recent excavations by the SUNY at Albany group at the southwest major palace revealed that one long building there, a primarily residential structure, also functioned as a council house.

The segmentary-lineage system at Utatlán (reconstructed in chapter 6) correlates well with the proposed replicating RCP complexes of Utatlán. Four major lineages and twenty-four principal lineages, as well as other minimal lineages, resided at Utatlán. As discussed earlier, the principal lineages were called "big houses" (*nim ja*) after the large buildings they occupied. Since the principal lineages fulfilled administrative responsibilities for the Quiché state at Utatlán, their big houses might well be called council houses. The lineages were also ritual units, for each had its patron deity and, presumably, associated temple. Residence and domestic affairs, such as marriage arrangements, were also closely linked to lineage organization. Thus there is ample ethnohistoric basis for the RCP complex within the lineage organization of Utatlán.

If there is a difference in emphasis between the lineage organization of the documents and the RCP complexes revealed by archaeology, it would be in the greater emphasis the documents give to political considerations. Thus, for example, though ritual and residential activities are mentioned in connection with the big houses, they are subordinated to the political and administrative functions of these groups. Hierarchically ranked offices and political superiority characterize relations among the principal lineages, rather than the dual, or quadripartite, lineage organization suggested by Wallace. On the other hand, in talking about the over-all pattern of the site as a complex interplay between segmentative and centralizing tendencies, Wallace's description is very close to that of the documents. My discussion of centralization and decentralization in the Utatlán community, which is based on documentary references (see chapter 6) details a situation very similar to the locational structure of Utatlán as outlined by Wallace on archaelogical grounds.

It is in connection with Wallace's proposed moiety division at Utatlán that the archaeology comes into strongest conflict with the ethnohistory. The documents refer to a moietal division only indirectly, if at all. They stress instead a hierarchical ranking, in which four principal lineages (Ajpop, Ajpop C'amja, K'alel, and Atzij Wanak) are placed above the other lineages, one of the four (Ajpop) being clearly superior to the other three. How do we account for the discrepancy between the two views—the moietal suggested by archaeology and the hierarchical suggested by ethnohistory?

A return to the documents provides some evidence that the hierarchical model presented to us by the chronicles may have been a partly idealized view and that the political situation resulted in the pattern revealed by archaeology. For example, some of the documents suggest that the dominant Cawek lineage at Utatlán was being challenged by the second-ranked Nijaib lineage. Since the other lineages were clearly subordinate in rank to those two, a conflict between them over power at Utatlán would result in a bifactional, or "moietal," division similar to that described by Wallace. The Caweks, as the authors of the major chronicles, would attempt to hide the sharing of power with the Nijaibs in presenting their idealized (i.e., hierarchical) view of community organization. The Nijaibs, on the other hand, as challengers would probably idealize society along quadripartite or moiety lines, since that arrangement would tend to support their struggle for equality with the Caweks. Significantly, the Tamubs, who were close allies of the Nijaibs, tended to stress a moiety organization in their chronicles. In this regard Wallace observes that perhaps the southeastern moiety at Utatlán oriented its buildings to the cardinal directions rather than to the northwestern half because of "stronger feelings about carrying out the ideal model for its buildings." This would suggest that the Nijaibs might be associated with the southeastern moiety (as Wallace argues on other grounds), for they were interested in maintaining the "ideal model" (that is, quadripartite and moiety organization), with its cardinal-point directions.

Despite this potential harmonizing of the archaeology and the ethnohistory, other problems arise in Wallace's proposed moiety division. They are best seen in the identification of specific buildings with particular sociopolitical groups.

Wallace has suggested that the west and east temples of the main plaza can be identified with Tojil and Awilix. This identification is consistent with ethnohistorically-worked-out symbolic associations between Tojil and Awilix and the west and east, light and dark, male and female (see chapter 7). The documents also suggest that Tojil was placed south of Awilix and at a higher elevation. Archaeology reveals that the western temple, which we have identified with Tojil, is indeed slightly south of the eastern temple. Though poor preservation prevents us from determining whether or not the western temple was higher than its eastern counterpart, early descriptions of these structures prove that this was the case. Wallace's assignment of half the ball court to one temple and the other half to the second temple is also consistent with the historically defined symbolic role of Tojil and Awilix as male and female patrons of the ball game.

While the documents link the temple of Tojil to that of Awilix, they nevertheless also ascribe to it a central place within the community, seeming to support Wallace's suggestion that the Tojil temple may have had stairways facing all four directions. A nineteenth-century drawing of the Tojil temple indicates that it had stairways on only three of its four sides, the western side consisting of a long, sloping, flat surface, but an even earlier description of the temple by Ximénez seems to state that there were stairways on all four sides. In view of such conflicting reports, we cannot be certain of the original form of the Tojil temple, though the careful observations upon which the nineteenth-century drawing was based would support the statement that there were three rather than four stairways.

It can be argued that the three (or four) stairways were functionally related to the central position of the Tojil temple and that it provided ritual patronage for the main plaza. If there was no stairway on the west, then the area northwest of the Tojil temple must have been a special part of the main plaza, for there was no entry to the temple from there. Perhaps that section of the plaza was a somewhat more secular zone. The documents, in fact (*Título Totonicapán* n.d.), indicate that this section was a continuous part of the main precinct and was occupied by one of the Cawek military sublineages, the Nima Rajpop Achij (Fig. 7.3). Viewed from the ethnohistoric perspective, then, the main plaza seems more like a Cawek political center than a ritually shared moiety complex.

A similar problem arises when we examine Wallace's identification of the occupants of the large northern and southern palaces. He assigns the northern palace to the Caweks because of its propinquity with the Tojil temple. The southern palace is assigned to the Nijaibs, despite its distance from their temple (Awilix) on the main plaza. His suggested association between the Nijaibs and the southern sidewall of the ball court constitutes only a weak basis for the proposed identification. In contrast to this interpretation there is evidence that both palaces should be assigned to Cawek lineages. The nearness of the Tojil temple and the northwest-plaza location of other Cawek lineages would suggest that the Caweks lived in the northwestern palace, as Wallace has argued. On the other hand, the displacement of the temple of Tojil south of that of Awilix and the general association of Tojil with the south would be arguments for also assigning the southwestern palace to the Caweks. Fuentes y Guzmán (1932–33, 7:415–22), using the native map in his possession, refers to a central street leading southwest from the ceremonial precinct to the "castle" of the Quiché king. This would seem to support a Cawek identification for the southwestern palace. According to this interpretation the main plaza was Cawek-dominated, and both major western palaces were occupied by the Caweks. Possibly the Ajpop lineage of the Caweks occupied the southern palace, and another Cawek lineage, perhaps the Ajpop C'amja, resided in the northern one.

Wallace has suggested that the temples of the special courts associated with the two major palaces were dedicated to subsidiary priestly deities, K'ucumatz for the Caweks and Yacolatam for the Nijaibs. If both palaces were occupied by Cawek lineages, Yacolatam would necessarily be ruled out. It is also unlikely that K'ucumatz had a temple in either court. K'ucumatz was a creator deity for all the Quiché lineages, as well as patron of the Cawek priests. An enclosed location in a court away from the ceremonial center would seem to be inappropriate. Perhaps the round structure in the main plaza, situated between the Tojil and Awilix temples, was dedicated to K'ucumatz. That was the approximate location of the Aztec round temple at Tenochtitlán, dedicated to Quetzalcoatl, the cognate deity of K'ucumatz (both names mean Feathered Serpent). This central plaza location would be consistent with K'ucumatz's association with the wind and with round structures, his possible mediating role between the masculine Tojil and the feminine Awilix, and his notable role as patron of priests (see chapter 8).

Presumably Tojil was the patron deity of all the Cawek lineages, though they may have had additional subpatrons. In view of the Quichés' tendency to replicate structures, it is probable that the court temples near the two major palaces were dedicated to Tojil in his various aspects. In this regard we should consider the possibility that the temple in the northern court had stairways on its eastern as well as its archaeologically documented western side. The remains of what may have been an altar can be seen on the eastern side of the temple mound. This is a question that excavation could probably resolve. Why the temple of the southwestern court should face south when Tojil's primary direction was east has an explanation in the interpretation being given here. Since Tojil had several aspects and could face all the directions, his temple might have had stairways on different sides depending on the context.

The discussion of these two special court temples, which are actually components of the two major RCPs of Utatlán, raises the question of the third major RCP of the site. It is situated just south of the main plaza, and Wallace has identified it with the Ajaw Quiché lineage. This identification accords well with the ethnohistory. The *Título Totonicapán* map (see chapter 7 and Fig.

7.3) places the Ajaw Quiché big house southeast of the Cawek big house. Jakawitz, the patron of the Ajaw Quichés, was a mountain deity with a high temple like that of Tojil and faced south. Consistent with this, the temple of this RCP was apparently very high, like the Tojil temple of the main plaza, and faced south. Wallace's claim that the temple faced south and was not directly a part of the main plaza is confirmed by the Rivera y Maestre map of the site, which shows a wall in front of the structure on the side of the main plaza.

It would be appropriate that, as close allies of the Caweks, the Ajaw Quichés would occupy the only other large RCP near the main plaza. Its location adjacent to the southwestern Cawek palace is also consistent with the close alliance between the two lineages. Wallace's argument that this court functioned as a moiety subplaza is seriously weakened by these Cawek relationships. Besides, we would expect to find the Ajaw Quichés, as allies of the Caweks, in the same moiety with that lineage, and not with the Nijaibs, where Wallace places them.

I have ended by assigning most of the main plaza and the area around it to the Caweks and their allies. We may add the northern wing to this unit on the assumption that the other principal and several minimal lineages of the Caweks would have been situated close to their leaders. Wallace attempted to identify the first RCP north of the main plaza, suggesting that it may have been occupied by the Tzutuja Sakic lineage. That is a possibility, given that lineage's association with the north direction (see chapter 7). Nevertheless, the Sakics were the close allies of the Nijaibs and would more likely be situated in the Nijaib, rather than the Cawek, section of town. The northern RCP referred to by Wallace, therefore, might correspond to one of the other Cawek principal lineages—Nim Chocoj, Ajtojil, Ajk'ucumatz, Popol Winak Chituy, Lolmet Quejnay, Popol Winak Pajom, Tepew Yaqui—or perhaps one or both of the two important military minimal lineages of the Caweks (Nima and Ch'uti Rajpop Achij).

The ethnohistory also requires that some structures must have been occupied by the Caweks' slaves and serfs. The various habitation buildings that Wallace identifies around the periphery of the northern, western, and southern wings would seem to fit that requirement.

The question then arises where the Nijaibs were located. It was argued above that they were moving upward in the politics of Utatlán. Yet our interpretation of the Utatlán buildings has filled the entire central and western section with the Caweks and their Ajaw Quiché allies. Were the Nijaibs relegated to the solitary eastern wing? That would seem to be at least the right direction, for, as we have seen, the temple of Awilix, the Nijaib patron deity, was on the eastern side of the main plaza. Wallace has also argued that some of the Nijaib principal lineages may have occupied the large residential structures behind the eastern side of the main plaza. That is a reasonable suggestion since the documents indicate that related lineages tended to locate contiguously.

Wallace observes that the eastern wing is different in building arrangement from the other sections of the site. For example, there are several council houses without the usual associated temples. Furthermore, the wing is closely oriented to the cardinal directions, more so than other large sections of the site. Perhaps the eastern wing was a Nijaib zone, and these differences express a Nijaib pattern. Some indirect support for this interpretation comes from the documents, which tell us that Chiquimula warriors were stationed in the area. References to Chiquimula in the documents invariably identify Tamub groups, and since the Tamubs were close allies of the Nijaibs, their presence in the eastern wing would further associate that zone with the Nijaibs. Perhaps the unusual temple complex near the eastern end of that wing was built by Tamub warriors.

The Nijaibs still seem to come up second-best when we compare the Cawek main plaza and large residential zones with the rather small eastern wing. An interesting possibility is that the Nijaibs had extended beyond the eastern wing, across the causeway to the eastern site we have called Resguardo or Atalaya (Fig. 8.4). The Resguardo site has a plaza not unlike that of the main plaza of Utatlán: east-west facing temples, north-south big houses, and, most important, a southwestern ball court. I think it likely that the temples and big houses at the Resguardo site were occupied by the Nijaibs and the allied Tzutuja Sakic lineages in similar fashion to the main plaza of Utatlán (see below). In that case the Nijaibs would be the dominant group, and the plaza their precinct. The Nijaib division, according to this interpretation, would include the Resguardo plaza and at least part of the eastern wing at Utatlán. As with the Caweks', the Nijaibs' residences would be west of the ceremonial precinct (that is, the Resguardo plaza), either between the plaza and the causeway or on the eastern wing within Utatlán. The Tzutuja Sakic residences would also be nearby, probably at some lower position near the Resguardo plaza.

Unfortunately there is no direct ethnohistoric evidence to support the proposed identification of the Nijaibs with the eastern part of Utatlán and the associated Resguardo site. Even though Resguardo was obviously an important town, its identity was lost to outsiders after the Conquest. In the 1930s aged native informants from Santa Cruz del Quiché told Juan de León (n.d.) that the Resguardo site was formerly called Caj Ja. That is reminiscent of the name of the Tzutuja Sakic temple, Cajbaja, which our sources seem to place outside Utatlán itself (Villacorta 1962, p. 354). Brasseur (1857, 2:493–94) claimed that this temple had a sacred black stone that attracted pilgrims from far away. The patrons of the shrine were the Sakics, allies of the Nijaibs.

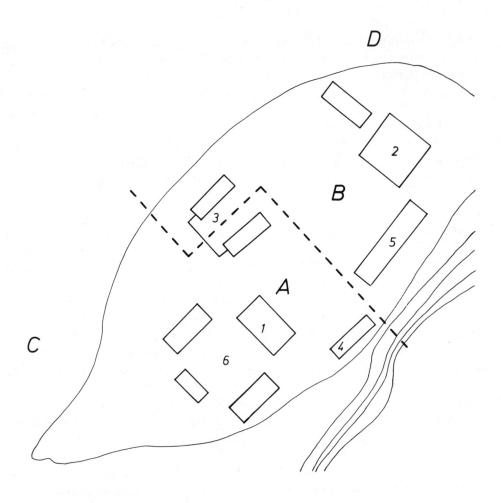

1	TOJIL TEMPLE OF CAWEK	A	KAKOJ MOIETY
2	AWILIX TEMPLE OF NIJAIB	B	EKOAMAK' MOIETY
3	BALL COURT	C	KAKOJ BIG HOUSES
4	CAWEK BIG HOUSE	D	EKOAMAK' BIG HOUSES
5	NIJAIB BIG HOUSE		
6	AJAW QUICHÉ COURT		

Fig. 8.5. Pismachi building plan. From Fox 1975.

230

Unfortunately, the term *caja* is applied to other ruins in the central Quiché, and thus its application to the Resguardo site does not constitute proof of its identification with the Sakics and Nijaibs.

In conclusion, the ethnohistory supports Wallace's claim that Utatlán was made up of ritual-council-palace complexes, and they have been identified with the principal lineage units. Wallace's proposed moiety division is not supported by the documents, which indicate instead hierarchical dominance of the settlement by the Caweks. That is expressed in the Caweks' control of the main plaza and adjacent buildings on all but the east side. Wallace's warning that changes were taking place through time and that building patterns were a complex interplay between segmentation and centralization could account for the discrepancy. The eastern division of the site is seen to have quasi-moietal characteristics, if it is extended beyond the causeway to include the Resguardo site, just east of Utatlán. This "half" of the site has been tentatively assigned to the Nijaibs, a rising lineage competing with the Caweks for power at Utatlán. This view of building patterns and their occupants suggests that Utatlán may have been more closely tied to its satellite settlements than our first look at the archaeology would lead us to believe.

Pismachi

Our best archaeological information on Pismachi comes from a surface survey of the plateau by John W. Fox in 1972. He has provided us with a map and a brief description of the ruins in his dissertation (1975, pp. 30–33). Guillemin mapped the site in 1956, and I visited and mapped it in 1971.

According to our preliminary studies the Pismachi mounds form a plaza located on a small rise in the central part of the southern side of the plateau (Fig. 8.5). The plaza has southwest and northeast temples, the former wider than the latter. Both of these temples are smaller than their counterparts in the main plaza of Utatlán, and are much less closely oriented to the cardinal directions. Aligned with the northeastern temple is a flanking structure on its western side, which is today only a flattened mound. There is a long structure on the eastern side of this temple. Both the flanking and the long structures are about two-thirds the size of their counterparts in the Utatlán plaza. Aligned with the southwestern temple is a ball court on the west and a small, long structure on the east. Since the alignments of the buildings associated with the two temples are different, it is apparent that the plaza consists of two separate plazas combined into one. This conclusion is supported by the unusual construction of the ball court, for its sidewalls are oriented in slightly different directions to conform to the two alignments. The southern sidewall aligns with the southwest side of the plaza, and the northern sidewall with the northeast side. There are many plaster fragments in the plaza, indicating that it was once coated with white plaster.

The remains of other constructions are barely visible around the margins of the plaza. A slight rise along the western side of the northeast half of the plaza may be the remains of another structure. There was also a building of some kind behind the northeastern temple, but a modern house stands there today, making its description impossible without excavations. The remains of a terraced wall can be seen along the canyon edge in that direction. In the other direction behind the southwestern temple, are low mounds that may have once formed a small court or plaza. Fragments of plaster have been found in that area also.

Fox (1975) discovered heavy concentrations of sherds and obsidian points over a large section of the plateau northeast of the main plaza. These artifacts appear to be generally similar to those described for other nuclear Utatlán sites. Most of the points that Fox found are the typical late side-notched or indented-base types, though he found one lance-type point. In a narrow northern extension of this section is a large, elevated platform joined to a wall that extends to the canyon edge. This construction undoubtedly was for defensive purposes. Another zone of heavy sherd and point concentration has been found southeast of the main plaza. Behind that, on a narrow finger of land extending toward the northern canyon, are the remains of a badly destroyed court. All that remains today is a small rectangular structure, facing southwest across a court onto a severely eroded mound, perhaps also rectangular in construction. Fox thinks that additional structures may have stood there, part of a small court complex. It is clear then that the entire Pismachi plateau was occupied, first, by the main complex of buildings and, second, by living zones adjacent to the plaza.

The only other construction of note associated with the Pismachi site is a single small pyramidal mound in the Culbut hamlet near the narrow southern entryway onto the Pismachi plateau. The mound was built on the side of a hill. Just west of and below the mound Fox found a heavy concentration of late sherds. The Culbut site has been identified above as an auxiliary settlement to the Pismachi town.

The ethnohistoric interpretation of the Pismachi ruins is complicated because the Nima Quichés were the original primary occupants of the site, while the Tamubs became the sole occupants after the founding of K'umarcaaj. The Tamubs took over around 1400 (see chapter 5), and during the approximately 125 years of their occupation they must have modified the original Nima Quiché pattern.

During the Nima Quiché domination of the site only three lineages were represented with their temples, lineage houses, and residences: the Caweks, the Nijaibs, and the Ajaw Quichés. Perhaps the southwest temple, with its associated buildings, was occupied by the Caweks while the northeast complex belonged to the Nijaibs. The Cawek temple faced northeast, in a direction roughly similar to its position in the original Cawek settlement, Patojil (Carmack, Fox, and Stewart 1975, p. 117). The Awilix temple of the Nijaibs faced southwest. Possibly the Tojil temple had stairways on both northeast and southwest sides, for there is a small court just behind it. The Awilix temple had a flanking structure on its northwest side, like the Awilix temple in the main plaza of Utatlán.

Whereas the Caweks and Nijaibs had previously shared a big house, the two long structures along the eastern side of the plaza support the documentary claim that they had separate big houses at Pismachi. Interestingly, the Nijaib Big House appears to have been larger than the Cawek. Also in contrast to the early situation in which the Nima Quiché ball court was most closely associated with the Ajaw Quiché lineage, at Pismachi it was associated with the Cawek and Nijaib lineages. Control over it must have been exercised by the Caweks, for it is nearest the temple and side of the plaza belonging to that lineage. The orientation of the ball court was changed from its east-west direction at Jakawitz to an intermediate northeast-southwest direction. The ball court was later built along its traditional east-west orientation in the main plaza of Utatlán.

The above proposed identifications fail to include the temple and big house of the Ajaw Quiché lineage. These structures apparently disappeared owing to Tamub rebuilding or post-Hispanic ravages of the site. Possibly the Ajaw Quiché buildings were part of the "court" behind the Cawek side of the plaza, which would be consistent with their positioning at Utatlán. We would expect the Jakawitz temple to face south, and its big house to be placed east of it. Excavations in this area might produce enough remains of foundations to test this suggestion. Excavations might also turn up evidence for the location of residential structures in the zone surrounding the plaza.

It is evident from the small size of the plaza, where there is barely room for the three Nima Quiché lineages, that any early occupation of Pismachi by the Tamubs or Ilocabs was very limited. They apparently had no large buildings of their own, though the documents make it clear that they were represented at the settlement. It is also clear that the Cawek and Nijaib lineages had already eclipsed the Ajaw Quiché lineage in importance, also a point the documents make. The chronicles indicate that the Caweks at this time were having internal lineage problems (see chapter 5 on the founding of Pismachi), and their dominance at Pismachi was far from complete. That is perhaps reflected in the small size of their big house and the apparently equal sharing of the main plaza with the Nijaibs. The over-all view, nevertheless, is as portrayed in the chronicles: Pismachi was much larger than any settlement that had existed previously in Quiché history, and it had prominent multi-terraced, staired buildings of stone and mortar.

When the Tamubs took over the site, they apparently retained much of the construction. The two divisions of the main plaza, with their different directional orientations, may have become the loci for the moietal division that characterized Tamub social organization. From the chronicles we learn that Tojil was a patron deity of the Kakoj moiety, and Awilix a patroness of the Ekoamak' moiety. Each moiety must have had its respective big house on the eastern side of the plaza and its half of the ball court. According to this interpretation the somewhat more politically powerful Kakoj moiety, with its twelve big houses, would be situated at the western side of the site. The more ritually prominent Ekoamak' moiety, with ten big houses, would occupy the eastern side. This would make the Tamub situation roughly similar to that at Utatlán, where the secularized, military Caweks occupied the western side of the main plaza and site while the more ritual, weaker Nijaibs were in the eastern wing. The ethnohistoric evidence indicates, however, that the relative rank of the two moietal divisions was more nearly equal in the case of the Tamubs at Pismachi.

Since an imaginary line between the two divisions of the main plaza roughly bisects the Pismachi plateau into similarly shaped eastern and western wings (see Fig. 8.1), the two moieties probably occupied territorial halves of the entire plateau. Possibly the two leading lineages of the Kakojs, the K'alels and the Atzij Winaks, occupied adjacent chambers of the long structure next to the southwest (Tojil) temple and so participated in the public life of the plaza. The most powerful principal lineages of the Ekoamak' moiety, Atzij Winak Tam and K'alel Tam, would have inhabited the long structure next to the northeast (Awilix) temple. The other eighteen big houses would have been scattered throughout the large territorial extensions making up the two halves of the plateau. As noted above, the archaeology has revealed evidence of heavy occupation in these two zones but limited evidence of large buildings. Perhaps the Tamub big houses outside the main Pismachi plaza were smaller than their counterparts at Utatlán and were more closely related to domestic affairs. The documentary sources support such an interpretation, but excavations within these territories will be necessary to prove it.

Chisalin (Mukwitz Pilocab)

The following description is based on my own mapping of the site, Fox's report of it (1975), and a partial map made by Guillemin in 1956. The site has been excavated by John Weeks, of SUNY at Albany, and the artifacts are being analyzed at the time of this writing.

The central plaza at Chisalin, the Ilocabs' town, is about half the size of the main plaza at Utatlán (Fig. 8.6). The buildings are also much smaller, except for the large long structure on the north end of the plaza. As noted earlier, the buildings of the main plaza at Chisalin are more closely oriented to the

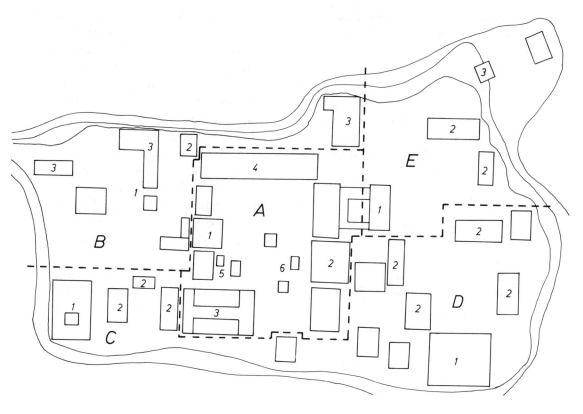

A	CENTRAL PLAZA		C	4 AJ ZONE
1	TOJIL TEMPLE		1	PALACE
2	ROKCHE TEMPLE		2	BIG HOUSES
3	BALL COURT		D	ROKCHE ZONE
4	4 AJ BIG HOUSE		1	PALACE
5	SKULL RACK		2	BIG HOUSES
6	ALTARS		E	SIC'A ZONE
B	WUKMIL ZONE		1	PALACE
1	STAIRED ENTRY		2	BIG HOUSES
2	TEMPLE		3	TEMPLE
3	BIG HOUSES			

Fig. 8.6.   Pilocab (Chisalin) building plan. From Fox 1975.

cardinal points than are those at Pismachi. Like Utatlán's, the temples face each other on the west and east sides, the temple on the east being wider than the one on the west. Unlike the west temple at Utatlán, however, the west temple at Chisalin has flanking structures and stands north of its counterpart across the plaza. The temple on the east, with its two flanking structures, is considerably larger than the west temple complex. And, like its counterpart at Utatlán, it appears to have been constructed on two terraces.

The northern long structure at Chisalin is smaller than the one at Utatlán, though it too encloses the entire northern side of the plaza. It was tiered and appears to have had two chambers. At its east and west ends it joins the flanking structures of the two temples. While the ball court is placed in the southwest part of the plaza as at Utatlán, it extends farther eastward into the plaza itself. It is about two-thirds the size of the Utatlán ball court. It had stairways at the east and west sides of the end zones. A terraced wall encloses the southern end of the main plaza.

The small platforms, which are only impressions on the plaza floor at Utatlán, are elevated mounds at Chisalin. As at Utatlán there is a row of tiny round and square "altar" platforms in the northern section of the plaza, and there are two larger platforms in the southeastern half of the plaza. The platform once seen at the southeast corner of the Tojil temple at Utatlán is a visible mound (about three by five meters) at Chisalin. A second, larger platform (about six by seven meters) is just southeast of it. There is a small platform (about four by five meters) directly in front of the west-facing temple, with two tiny altars in front of it.

The area outside the main plaza at Chisalin is divided into four zones, separated by stone walls and buildings (Fig. 8.6). Except for the northwestern zone (B), each zone is made up of small palaces, temples, long structures, and courtyards. The northwestern zone is rather open on its western side, though several low mounds can be detected there. Two of the low mounds toward the eastern side appear to have formed a terraced stairway, which leads directly to a small temple mound behind it. Beyond the temple, on the east, is a narrow corridor formed by the northern canyon and the long structure of the main plaza. This leads to a two-tiered long structure, which blocks the eastern end of the zone. The southern section of this zone provides an open path into the southwestern corner of the main plaza alongside the ball court.

We find the zones surrounding the main plaza of Chisalin to be occupied with RCPs, though on a smaller scale than the Utatlán model. The pattern of the northwestern zone, in contrast, suggests that it functioned primarily for receiving visitors to the town and for defending the main plaza and residential areas.

The causeway that entered the Chisalin site consisted of a narrow road built above the steep canyon at the point where it came together on the northwestern corner of the Chisalin plateau. The part of the causeway leading to the plateau itself was a narrow opening carved out of stone. The canyon on the southern side of the causeway had been cut away in the form of a moat or sloping channel ending at the elevated causeway. A terraced wall built at the point where the channel drops off steeply into the canyon protected the entry into the channel. There are signs of fortified walls above the channel on the western side of the Chisalin site. A few meters northwest of the causeway are the remains of four or five badly damaged mounds, the auxiliary site.

Unfortunately, there is little ethnohistory to help us interpret the settlement pattern of Chisalin. Probably the most significant social aspect of the Ilocabs was their extremely close and subordinate relationship with the Cawek rulers of Utatlán. The two groups were allied through marriage and ritual, the Caweks being the dominant partner of the alliance. That probably explains the similarity between the main plazas at Chisalin and Utatlán, as well as the much smaller size of the former. Perhaps the Ilocabs provided more ritual functions in the alliance, especially after their unsuccessful revolt, while the Caweks were the more militarized, secular partners. This special ritual function might be expressed by the more precise cardinal-point symmetry of the Chisalin plaza (compared with the plaza of Utatlán), the elaborate altar arrangement in the Chisalin plaza, the presence of two flanking structures for both temples in the main plaza at Chisalin (presumably to accommodate priestly functions), and the unusual reception zone at the entry of the Chisalin site. The presence of ritual-council-palace complexes at Chisalin is a further sign of its close ties with the Caweks at Utatlán.

With respect to the Ilocab deities, we know only that, like the Nima Quichés and the Tamubs, the Ilocabs worshiped Tojil. This one fact allows us to postulate that the east-facing temple at Chisalin was dedicated to Tojil. Tojil was probably the patron deity of the Cajib Aj (four reed) major lineage, the second-ranked political lineage of the Ilocabs.

Accordingly, the Cajib Aj lineage must have occupied the northern long house and been closely associated with the ball court. Analogy with the Tojil temple at Utatlán suggests that one of the two altar platforms southeast of the Tojil temple at Chisalin was the skull-rack altar. The relatively good condition of these two platforms makes it likely that their excavation would permit us to determine this identification for certain.

The west-facing temple of the main plaza may have been dedicated to Awilix or, more likely, to some other, exclusively Ilocab deity. In construction it is similar to the Awilix temple at Utatlán, but there are significant differences. Chisalin's west-facing temple is part of a much larger complex than its east-facing (Tojil) temple and is farther south. The altar arrangement in front of the Chisalin temple is unlike that of the temple at Utatlán. Taken together, these differences have led me to postulate that the west-facing temple at Chisalin housed some native Ilocab deity, probably female and associated with the western underworld. The leading political lineage of the Ilocabs, the Rokche (Wood House) lineage, was probably the "owner" of the temple. As the "marriage partner" of the Caweks, whose patron deity was Tojil, the female nature of Rokche's deity would be symbolically appropriate.

The chronicles state that there were eighteen big houses at Pilocab, divided among five major lineages: Rokche, Cajib Aj, Sic'a, Xuwanija, and Wukmil. Only four of the major lineages were prominent (Xuwanija is usually mentioned along with the Sic'a lineage), and three of the four controlled the important political offices (see chapter 6). It can be postulated that the four zones surrounding the main plaza at Chisalin correspond to the four major lineages of the Pilocab town in the chronicles. The southwestern zone (C) must have been occupied by the Cajib Aj lineage, for it seems to be connected to the Tojil temple and ball court. At least three big houses (long structures) and a substantial palace and court are found in this section, which supports the suggestion in the chronicles that the Cajib Aj was an important lineage. The southeastern zone (D) was tied to the west-facing temple and, therefore, the Rokche lineage. This zone has at least five big houses and several residential buildings, including a substantial palace. The large size of this zone and its temple supports the thesis that the Rokche lineage held the highest rank.

The northeastern zone (E) of Chisalin was probably occupied by the only other politically prominent Ilocab lineage, the Sic'a (and the Xuwanija). There were perhaps three big houses in the zone and one large palace unit. The small temple in the northeast corner of the zone may have been the ritual site for the Sic'a lineage, which may not have had representation in the main plaza.

The northwestern zone would be left to the politically weak Wukmil lineage. There are two or three structures in this zone that may have been big houses, but no obvious residential unit. As we have seen, the lineage occupying this zone must have functioned primarily as both military and administrative guardians of the site.

It will be noted that the total number of big houses listed for the four zones at Chisalin does not equal the eighteen the chronicles say were built at Pilocab. This should not surprise us, for, as we saw in the Utatlán analysis, some of the big houses may have been constructed outside the main center (for example, at the auxiliary site). Furthermore, until we know more about the buildings excavated at Chisalin, we cannot determine the number of long structures actually found in each zone. At any rate, the above identifications of buildings as big houses or palaces are only tentative.

The documentary sources cast no light on the occupants of Chisalin's auxiliary site. It is similar to the Pakaman site in having no defensive character, though presumably, like Pakaman, it was a defensive center, because military personnel were stationed there. Excavations within the poorly preserved plaza of Chisalin's auxiliary site might confirm its presumed military character, as well as humbler rank vis à vis Chisalin.

Resguardo (Atalaya)

Most of the vistors to Utatlán through the years have mentioned the Resguardo site. The only known excavations at the site were carried out by John Weeks of SUNY at Albany in 1973. He excavated a low structure just south of the center and gathered many artifact samples. I have drawn on his master's thesis, which is a full report on his work there, for my account. The central plaza of Resguardo was also surveyed by the SUNY at Albany archaeologists in 1973, and I have personal notes and maps of the plaza made in 1971.

The plaza of the Resguardo site stands on a hill that has been terraced into at least three levels (Fig. 8.7). The top terrace is steep, measuring five meters in height in some places. The buildings along the sides of the plaza form still another terrace, giving the complex a highly fortified appearance. However, as Maudslay noted (1899) when he visited the site, the plaza itself does not have the appearance of a fort. There is today no readily visible entryway into the plaza.

According to the surface survey of Resguardo, the plaza is similar to the main plaza at Utatlán, except that it is about half the size. It has east-west–facing temples, which are also smaller than their counterparts at Utatlán, though they are separated from each other by about the same distance (about fifty meters). The west-facing temple is slightly south of the east-facing temple, the reverse of the Utatlán locations.

The Resguardo plaza has long structures on its north and south sides, and a ball court at the southwest corner. The northern long structure is much shorter than the one at Utatlán, but a flanking structure on the northern side of the west-facing temple is about the same size as that of its counterpart at Utatlán. The southern long structure at Resguardo is not well preserved, and its original construction is not clear. Apparently it was about the same size as the northern long structure, but because its eastern end was placed alongside the temple, it has the appearance of being another flanking structure. Maudslay's map of the site confirms that there was a single, southern long structure, perpendicular to and in contact with the west-facing temple. The ball court is slightly smaller than the one at Utatlán and is situated eastward, partly within the plaza itself.

On the terrace just below the plaza level west of the east-facing temple is what appears to be a small, square platform. It overlooks a small mound

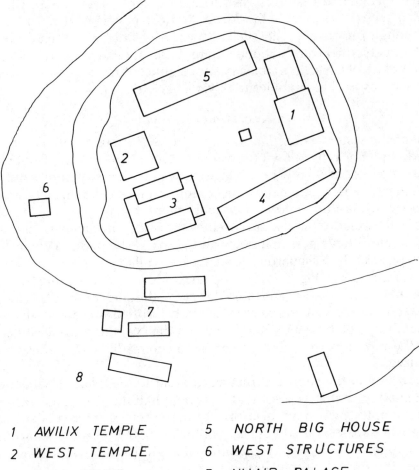

1   AWILIX TEMPLE   5   NORTH BIG HOUSE

2   WEST TEMPLE   6   WEST STRUCTURES

3   BALL COURT   7   NIJAIB PALACE

4   NIJAIB BIG HOUSE   8   EXCAVATION AREA

Fig. 8.7.   Resguardo (Atalaya) building plan. From Fox 1975.

situated on the broad terrace below. The platform and small mound are on a rough westerly line with the Utatlán site.

There are signs of many low mounds on the southwest side of the elevated plaza. Weeks excavated one of the mounds, 75 meters southwest of the plaza. He uncovered a platform, probably residential in function, measuring about 23 by 18 meters, with a central patio 11 by 10 meters. There were two construction levels, each of pumice and mud mortar, covered with plaster coating. The building had recessed interior stairways leading to the patio and exterior stairs flanked by *talud y tablero* balustrades. There is evidence of drainage ducts and, on the south side of the structure, a water trough. The interior and exterior walls of the first level had painted frescos in green, red, yellow, blue, and black. One of the paintings was a geometric pattern of black-outlined squares of red and yellow. Weeks thinks that it may have represented the woven mat (*pop*). A second motif consisted of two eye-shaped objects, painted yellow and outlined in black. Both paintings were bordered on top with a yellow band and above that a field of blue.

The ceramics uncovered by Weeks suggest that domestic activities were carried on at the building (Fig. 8.8). Ninety percent of the vessels were jars, bowls, and griddles used for carrying and storing water and for cooking. Most of the ceramics (85 percent) were the typical red ware of Utatlán, but there was also a small number of bichrome (9 percent) and polychrome (2 percent) ceramics. Except for a few waste flakes, there is no indication that stone tools were of much importance to the inhabitants of the building. The excavation did, however, yield twenty-seven clay fragments that laboratory analysis has shown were used for molding copper ingots (but not for smelting or alloying). Nearby Weeks also found a white-on-red jar with an attached effigy in the form of a seated figure with a tail. The figure is holding a thick tube to his mouth. Weeks interprets the figure to be a monkey, the patron of craftsmen, using a blowtube used for processing metals. From the evidence of the molds and the simian vessel Weeks concluded that middle-status metalworkers resided in the building.

From the observations of visitors to the Resguardo site we can add a few details to the description provided us by recent archaeological studies. Maudslay observed that the plaza was built on a natural mound that had been terraced along the sides. He made a map of the plaza and left this description:

Within this space are several mounds surrounding a level plaza. A reference to the plan will show that two of the mounds are nearly square at the base, and these probably supported small "cues" or temples; the other two mounds are longer, and may have supported long houses. If these houses were built of stone with stone roofs they probably contained two parallel corridors or rooms not more than 9 feet wide and 200 feet long, divided off by transverse partitions into smaller chambers. If the lower part only were built of stone and the upper part of the walls and the roof were of wood and thatch, then the breadth of the houses may have been 20 to 25 feet, as no longitudinal partition wall would have been needed. [Maudslay 1899, pp. 67–68]

Maudslay's account confirms that the two big houses were about the same length. His map also shows a large platform below the plaza floor on the

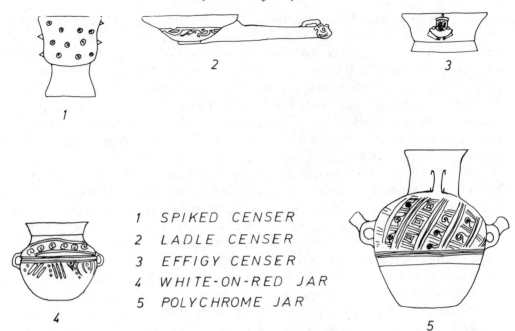

1 SPIKED CENSER
2 LADLE CENSER
3 EFFIGY CENSER
4 WHITE-ON-RED JAR
5 POLYCHROME JAR

Fig. 8.8.   Quiché ceramic wares from greater Utatlán sites. Drawing by J. Weeks.

southwest. It is slightly north of the area excavated by Weeks, suggesting that the building described by Weeks was an outlying section of a much larger structure.

John Lloyd Stephens apparently took the old road that passed by Pakaman and led to Utatlán by way of the Resguardo site. He described the site in these words (1841, p. 171):

Within this line was an elevation, which grew more imposing as we approached, square, with terraces, and having in the centre a tower, in all one hundred and twenty feet high. We ascended by steps to three ranges of terraces, and on the top entered an area enclosed by stone walls, and covered with hard cement, in many places still perfect. Thence we ascended by stone steps to the top of the tower, the whole of which was formerly covered with stucco, and stood as a fortress at the entrance of the great city of Utatlán.

Stephens seems to have referred to the whole complex as a tower, which he says was 120 feet high. Apparently this height included the eastern temple, which could be ascended by stairs. There were also stairs on the (eastern) side of the terraces, by which Stephens climbed up to the plaza. The stone

Fig. 8.9.   Resguardo (Atalaya) from the south side. Drawing by M. Rivera y Maestre, 1834. From Atlas Guatemalteco n.d.

buildings were still partly intact, as was much of the plaster covering the
plaza floor and buildings.

The drawings made in 1834 by Miguel Rivera y Maestre (Villacorta and
Villacorta 1927) include four different views of the Resguardo site and measurements of the plaza buildings. In one of the drawings (Fig. 8.9) he
portrays the three major terraces, showing the eastern terraces to have been
much steeper than those of the western side. The eastern temple is also
shown much higher than the western temple, and its second terrace, placed
toward the rear of the base terrace, was still intact. The eastern temple was
also wider than its western counterpart. In one of the drawings a small slope
can be seen at the base of the eastern temple. The ball court is depicted as a

simple square enclosure, and the long structures are portrayed as nothing more than thick walls surrounding the plaza.

Of the colonial writers only Fuentes y Guzmán mentions the Resguardo site. His account, based entirely on the native map in his possession, has already been summarized in chapter 7.

The archaeology of Resguardo finds some correlation with ethnohistoric reconstructions. It has been tentatively suggested that Nijaib lords were dominant at the Resguardo settlement and that they were using it as a base for their competitive politics with the Caweks of Utatlán (see the section "Utatlán" above). The site looks very much like what we would expect of an important Utatlán plaza that had been constructed outside the town itself. It is built up high and fortified with terraces and has a building plan similar to that of the main plaza in Utatlán.

In contrast to the Utatlán plaza, however, the west-facing temple of the Resguardo plaza was considerably larger than its opposite temple, and was placed slightly south of it. That is what we would expect of a Nijaib-dominated plaza, whose patroness, Awilix, would have been the principal deity of the plaza. This temple was constructed of two major terraces, the second recessed on top of the first, in similar fashion to the Awilix temple of the main plaza at Utatlán. The Nijaib dominance can also be seen in the northern flanking structure of the eastern temple, as well as the southern long structure alongside the temple. Though the ball court had to be in the western part of the site for cosmological balance, it extended into the plaza, possibly in order to be closer to the Nijaib side of the precinct.

The smaller temple on the west side of the site was possibly the Tzutuja Sakic temple of Cajbaja (House of Sacrifice). As a temple to an earth deity, Nic'aj Tak'aj (Middle of the Plains), it was necessarily lower than that of the moon goddess, Awilix. There was a sacred stone (*abaj*) at the Sakic temple that was much visited by the lords of Utatlán and outsiders. The position of the Sakic temple north of Awilix would be dictated by the higher rank accorded the southern over the the northern side. The north also appears to have been the cardinal direction of the Sakic patron deity in the larger Utatlán cosmology, which included Tojil, Awilix, and Jakawitz (see chapter 7). That would also associate the northern big house with the Sakic lineage. We are told in the chronicles that the Sakics had only one big house but two lords. Perhaps the northern long structure at the Resguardo settlement had two chambers. In connection with the Sakics I would also suggest that the platform and small mound just behind the western temple were associated with that lineage. Perhaps the Sakics had a small ritual-council-palace complex there similar to the Cawek RCPs west of the main plaza at Utatlán.

The Nijaib residences were presumably on the southern side of the Resguardo plaza. The building excavated by Weeks was elaborate, with *talud y tablero* balustrades, patio, painted walls, water system, and decorated pottery. I think it likely that the building was a small section of the Nijaib palace, whose main sections were on the north in the area where Maudslay's map shows a large platform. This interpretation would also argue that the metallurgy Weeks found was a craft of Nijaib lords rather than of the middle class. It is possible that the Nijaibs were more involved in crafts than the Caweks were, but we have no direct evidence for that in the chronicles. The issue whether or not there is a palace in this area could probably be settled by extending northward the excavations initiated by Weeks.

Pakaman

This site has received little attention from visitors to Utatlán. SUNY at Albany archaeologists have surveyed and mapped it, and Weeks dug in a single structure southwest of the plaza. I have visited the site several times and draw on my own notes for part of the following account.

The Pakaman site is situated on top of a leveled and terraced hill. Since the terraces are not large and the slope of the hill is gradual, Pakaman is less naturally defensive than Resguardo. Just across the valley floor on the southwest is a second hill with evidence of two mounds on top of it. The two sites together give the appearance of being outposts, the first major ones on the old road leading west toward Utatlán (Fig. 8.10).

The small plaza at the Pakaman site is badly preserved, and the building forms are uncertain. Nevertheless, the SUNY at Albany archaeologists describe a small temple facing due west, flanked on the northern side by a large, square platform. It is faced on the eastern side by a long structure. There were structures on the south and north sides of the plaza, but without excavation it is impossible to determine their exact forms. There is no evidence of a ball court at the site. The central plaza measures about fifty meters at its north-south axis, and twenty-five meters along its east-west axis. The many plaster fragments scattered throughout the plaza indicate that the entire site was once coated with plaster.

Fox (1977) argues that the building arrangement at Pakaman is similar to plazas found at several Cakchiquel-dominated sites: a temple on the east side; a long structure spanning the west side; short, rectangular structures on the south side; and a multiroom platform on the north side. These plazas are said to be military "garrisons," which functioned to guard some larger, more elite community (as at Iximché) or the community of a conquered people (as at Jilotepeque Viejo). Fox also notes the similarity between this type of plaza and the ritual-council-palace units at Utatlán.

Test excavations by Weeks (1975) in the zone surrounding the Pakaman plaza revealed small residential structures. His excavations of one of them, fifty meters southwest of the plaza, turned up a platform measuring about twelve by fifteen meters. The construction and design were simple, stone and adobe without mortar serving as the main building material. At least part of the building was covered with plaster. At one end of the platform Weeks found evidence of a hearth, and an urn burial was uncovered nearby. The burial was simple, a single greenstone offering placed with the flexed body inside an ordinary water jar. The remains, an individual thirteen to seventeen years old, had incisors that had been filed into two narrow grooves.

The ceramics Weeks found in association with the building were similar to those of the Resguardo residential building: about 90 percent jars, bowls, and griddles; of the wares 92 percent were Utatlán red, with a few bichromes (5 percent) and polychromes (1 percent). Thus the building was primarily domestic in function, though it was less elaborate than the one near the Atalaya plaza. The building also yielded many obsidian stone tools (twenty-three blades, three scrapers, and one drill), four points, and fourteen working cores. Weeks interprets this as indicating that the occupants of the building were craftsmen of stone tools and weapons and that the settlement was a military outpost.

The only prior visitors to Utatlán who mentioned the Pakaman site were Cesar Daly and John Lloyd Stephens. Daly (1867, p. 156) referred to "fortresses" and the vestiges of a great road east of Utatlán and reported finding many obsidian points. Pakaman was probably one of these fortresses. Stephens's brief comment is as follows:

> At about a mile from the village [Santa Cruz] we came to a range of elevations, extending to a great distance, and connected by a ditch, which had evidently formed the line of fortifications for the ruined city. They consisted of the remains of stone buildings, probably towers, the stones well cut and laid together, and the mass of rubbish around abounded in flint arrowheads. [1841, p. 171]

The ditch mentioned by Stephens, alongside which was a line of fortifications, is probably the ridge connecting the Pakaman and Resguardo sites. The cut stone at Pakaman (and probably at the other outpost just south) was apparently still in place at the time he wrote. Significantly, the site was littered with stone points.

The limited archaeology available on Pakaman is consistent with the suggestion above that it was the Panpetak settlement mentioned in the *Annals* (Villacorta 1934, p. 230). Our native source describes Panpetak as, like Pakaman, an elevated, defensive settlement where the Quiché ruler could be protected. Pakaman's outpost location correlates with the etymology of Panpetak (Arrival Place). It would have been the first major section of greater Utatlán reached by incoming groups. As further required by our documentary reference, Pakaman was a "town," which is to say, a center with plaza

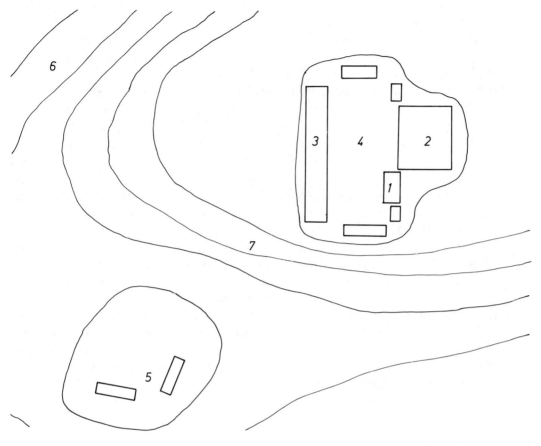

1   TEMPLE
2   RESIDENCE
3   BIG HOUSE
4   PLAZA
5   OUTPOST
6   OBSIDIAN - POINT DEPOSIT
7   EXCAVATION AREA

Fig. 8.10.   Pakaman building plan. From Fox 1975.

and buildings. The king (*ajpop*) had a residence at Panpetak, and Pakaman's large northern residential (?) platform is consistent with that fact.

It has already been noted that the building arrangement of the Pakaman plaza is similar to a Cakchiquel pattern found at Iximché and other Cakchiquel-dominated sites (Fox 1977). Fox has called the complex a "garrison," noting that one such complex at Iximché is situated in a similar position to Pakaman relative to the main center. Could Pakaman have been a settlement occupied by Cakchiquel warriors? There is convincing ethnohistoric support for this suggestion, if the identification of the site with Panpetak can be verified. *The Annals of the Cakchiquels* is the only document we have that mentions Panpetak—which raises another question: Why is Panpetak mentioned only in a Cakchiquel source? The answer may be that the Cakchiquels resided there. That would explain why Panpetak is referred to twice in the *Annals* and why settlement details are given—that it was placed high and that it contained the king's house. We are also told that the king was defended at Panpetak by "the warriors of the *Xajil Ajpop* [Cakchiquel chief]."

The circumstantial evidence is strong, therefore, that Panpetak was inhabited by Cakchiquel warriors and that they formed part of the personal staff of the ruler who maintained a residence there. At least some of the Cakchiquel warriors were killed in the revolt against Q'uik'ab, and from then on the Cakchiquels appear to have withdrawn entirely from the Utatlán towns. It is likely that the settlement at Pakaman was thereafter occupied by the new stratum of local military nobles (the *achij*). It may have been quickly rebuilt in order to erase the memory of the Cakchiquels, who became bitter enemies of the Quichés.

The outpost position of the Pakaman settlement relative to Utatlán and Resguardo, as well as the many arrow points found in and around the site, support its proposed identification with the Panpetak garrison. It is also evident from the simple artifacts and architecture of the building excavated by Weeks just outside the Pakaman plaza that nonelite groups resided close by. Some of them made stone weapons, at least part time. Perhaps these people were part of the rising military class of commoners who had begun settling near the elite centers of Utatlán. They provided protection for the lords, who lived safely within their elite centers; served as intermediate officials between the rulers and the vassal commoners; and apparently manufactured weapons. Our evidence indicates that most of them lived close to the elite plazas but not in them, they were craftsmen as well as warriors, they used the same red pottery that was used inside Utatlán, including the painted wares, they buried the dead in jars without elaborate offerings and did not cremate their dead, and they had houses that were crude compared with the palaces of the lords but even so were made of stone and had some plaster coating.

RURAL SETTLEMENTS

Russell E. Stewart (1977) has observed that the early settlements of the Quiché rural area were largely abandoned during the period of occupation of greater Utatlán. Peoples were concentrated into the nuclear sites at Utatlán, giving an overall appearance of settlement loss in the Quiché basin. Some of the rural inhabitants became craft specialists who provided sumptuous goods for the growing aristocracy in the Utatlán towns. Others became virtually full-time warriors and were constantly engaged in conquest outside the Quiché basin. Stewart suggests that some peasants became specialized farmers, fewer in number than the earlier generalized peasantry but sufficient to provide the immediate or emergency subsistence needs of the lords and retainers.

The rural zone surrounding nuclear Utatlán may have been partly replaced as a sustaining area by the colonization of faraway regions. Fox (1975; 1977) has documented this outward expansion of the Utatlán Quichés into first the lowland valleys of the Río Negro and Río Motagua and later highland basins ecologically similar to the Quiché basin. Finally they reached the Pacific piedmont, with its lowland ecology.

Fox has gone on to investigage the different kinds of Quiché influence at colonial settlements and concluded that the Utatlán Quichés were far from monolithic in their control of outside settlements. The documents suggest that they usually won tributary rights by sending military colonists to guard provincial regions. In addition, they employed flexible social techniques to ensure control: wife exchanges between Utatlán rulers and local lords, joint participation in rituals, ceremonial authorization by Utatlán rulers of local political succession, elaborate gift exchanges, support of rebellious local factions, and trading alliances. Presumably the various degrees of Quiché influence that Fox has documented at Quiché colonial sites reflect these differing modes of control.

The situation described by Fox for the Quiché colonies is roughly similar to what is found archaeologically in the rural zones surrounding nuclear Utatlán. The archaeology reveals no single type of settlement, and there is evidence that some pre-Quiché patterns continued. The Utatlán-period ceramics recovered in the rural area are generally like nuclear Utatlán wares, as far as is known. Further, in very few cases are the pre-Quiché wares mixed with the diagnostic sherds of the Utatlán period (that is, red wares, white-on-red bichromes, Chinautla polychromes, and thin, micaceous wares). For that reason the Utatlán-phase sites can usually be easily distinguished from sites occupied before that period.

One sign of continuity is the evidence that many Utatlán-period settlements were established near pre-Quiché settlements, though most of the pre-Quiché sites are on hills in the midst of plains, while the Quiché sites are in slightly more defensive positions—at canyon edges, on narrow spurs of land, on steep hills, and so on. There is, moreover, considerable variation in settlement patterns in the rural sites that have been identified with the Utatlán period. That is significant, considering the limited sample of sites with which we have to work (about twenty) and the lack of excavation work at any of them. I have tentatively classified the sites into three settlement types: plaza, canyon edge, and hilltop shrine. Descriptions of these types will characterize most of the settlement patterns known for the rural area of the Utatlán period.

There are nine known plaza sites in the central Quiché (excluding the nuclear Utatlán sites): Los Cimientos, Pacaja-Chioculjib, Uwila (?), Las Rosas, Tzakibala, Pugertinamit Tz'oloche, Chitinamit, Oquin, and Cruz Che (see Fig. 8.11). All these sites have enclosed plazas on defensive ridges, hills, and narrow spurs of land. The plazas are much smaller than that at Utatlán both in over-all size and in number and size of buildings. With the possible exception of Pacaja-Chioculjib, the arrangement of the buildings differs greatly from that of Utatlán. Los Cimientos, for example, seems to have a large, staired entryway dominating the center of the plaza. Chitinamit, which was the first Quiché center in Chujuyup and continued to be occupied after the founding of the nuclear Utatlán settlement, has two linearly arranged plazas.

The buildings forming the Pacaja plaza site are badly deteriorated, but they apparently included a long structure on the west side and a temple mound on the north side. There are signs of other structures along the east side of the plaza, but they are in such a state of ruin that their forms cannot be determined. Chioculjib is connected to this plaza by a narrow neck of land, about 250 meters south. The small plaza of Chioculjib is enclosed on three sides by a long structure on the north side and two temples on the east and west. The open south side is terraced down to the point where it reaches a steep canyon. The location of the Pacaja settlement, its building arrangement, and its relationship with Chioculjib make it the rural site most similar to Utatlán and its associated early auxiliary settlement, Resguardo.

The canyon-edge sites are not easily delimited, but at least five of them have been defined by the archaeologists: Ilotenango, Panajxit, La Estancia, Santa Cruz del Quiché, and Chicabracan. These sites consist of small platforms, isolated mounds, terraces, and walls along the edges of large plateaus. None of them is particularly distinct, and each can be identified as Utatlán phase only because of its associated ceramics. Fox (1975), who surveyed the immediate zone surrounding nuclear Utatlán, found evidence for a heavy concentration of Utatlán-phase sherds and points along the edges of all the surrounding plateaus, even in places where there was no construction. The Utatlán-phase sites along the southern Chicabracan

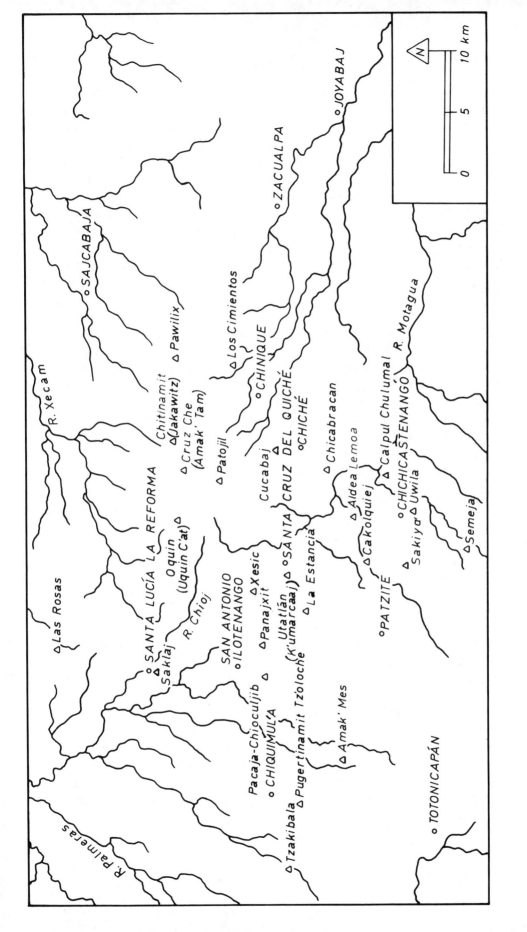

Fig. 8.11.   Utatlán-phase rural archaeological sites. Modified from Carmack, Fox, and Stewart 1975.

plateau show that this type of settlement also existed outside the nuclear Utatlán zone. One Chicabracan canyon-edge site, for example, is situated in the middle of a 100-meter-long spur of land, surrounded on all sides by 80-meter-high cliffs. It consists of a single small mound constructed of cut stone. Utatlán-phase sherds are littered on the ground near the mound (Fox 1975).

Six hilltop-shrine sites have been identified: Cakolquiej, Xesic, Cucabaj, Calpul-Chulumal, Semeja, Patojil. These sites consist of temple mounds placed on relatively isolated hilltops, associated with few if any other buildings. This type of site is hard to find, and there must have been many more of them in the Quiché basin. Most of the hills on which these sites stand are steep, and any gradually sloping sides were terraced for protection. Any structures in addition to the pyramidal mound are in linear relation to the main shrine.

Hilltop-shrine buildings were at least partly constructed of cut stone, but there is no evidence of the use of plaster. The Cakolquiej site, for example, is on a bluff 40 meters above the valley on the north and 120 meters above it on the south and west. The site consists of a single mound made of cut pumice stone, 6 meters along the sides and 4 meters high. Next to it are the remains of a platform, now leveled. There are Utatlán-phase sherds and side-notched arrow points on the ground near the buildings (Fox 1975). Another site, Patojil, is included within the hilltop-shrine type, since it continued to be occupied from the early Jakawitz phase to the Utatlán phase. The small temple of this site was surrounded by several low, rectangular buildings (Carmack, Fox, and Stewart 1975, p. 117). Obviously the hilltop shrines were varied in their settlement patterns.

In general the later settlements were more defensive than the pre-Quiché settlements were. There were few attempts to occupy the old settlements; instead new sites were built at more defensible locations nearby. That is shown most clearly at the canyon-edge sites, which were obviously marginal settlements established to protect the strategic interests of the occupants of Utatlán. The Quichés did not usually replace the old settlements with large rural ones. Nevertheless, the plaza settlements described above were perhaps more tightly organized and better constructed than their pre-Quiché equivalents. Significantly, plaza-type settlements were established in the basin in all four directions from nuclear Utatlán.

It has been noted that the plaza settlements differed considerably one from another and from Utatlán. In this they reflect the same tendency to be differentially influenced by Utatlán as described by Fox for the provincial centers. Some of the plaza settlements appear to have retained indigenous patterns, much like the situation Fox found for some Quiché colonies. The hilltop-shrine settlements show the same tendency. They are similar to

Table 8.1. **Settlement Features of Rural Sites in the Quiché Basin**

Type	Name	Chronology	Settlement Pattern	Social Structure	Functions
Town	Utatlán Pismachi Chisalin Resguardo	Middle to late Quiché	Plaza complexes and associated residences; auxiliary sites; more than 10 buildings	Ruling major lineages	Central administration and ritual; central defense; residential
Plaza	Los Cimientos Pacaja-Chioculjip Uwila Las Rosas Pugertinamit Tz'olojche Chitinamit Oquin Cruz Che	Early through late Quiché	Small hilltop plazas; fewer than 10 buildings	*Calpules*	Political administration, ritual, border defense
Hilltop shrine	Cakolquiej Xesic Cucubaj Calpul-Chulumal Semeja Patojil	Early through late Quiché	Central mound, with or without other buildings; fewer than 5 buildings	*Calpules* or lineages	Ritual
Canyon-edge	Santa Cruz Panajxit La Estancia Chicabracan Ilotenango	Late Quiché	Continuous walls and low buildings	Estates (*chinamit*)	Perimeter defense, political administration
Pre-Utatlán	Amak' Mes Sakiya Saklaj Aldea Lemoa	Pre-Quiché through late Quiché	2 to 3 linear plazas; about 10 buildings	*Calpules*	Ritual, residential

many pre-Quiché sites, except that they are more defensive and better constructed. They certainly differ from the contemporaneous plaza sites and, thus reflect the flexible control exercised by Utatlán over the rural populations. The settlement features of the rural sites are summarized in Table 8.1.

Ethnohistoric sources have little to say about the rural settlements of the Utatlán community, and the archaeology has provided substantial new insights into their patterns. For example, as Stewart has emphasized (1977), many of the sites within territories specifically identified with *calpules* in the documents (see chapters 4 and 6) turn out to have only pre-Quiché shrine settlements; at least that is the view provided by our survey data. Examples of *calpul* sites without Utatlán-phase ceramics or settlements would be Amak' Mes, Sakiya', K'ak'alaj (Saklaj), and Chobolo (Aldea Lemoa) (see Fig. 8.11). At still other *calpul* sites, the Utatlán phase settlements turn out to be smaller and less differentiated than expected. These are the canyon-edge and hilltop-shrine sites described above, such as at Panajxit, Chicabracan, Cakolquiej, and Xesic.

From the evidence available from the above sources (and I have warned that the data are limited), it must be concluded that the Quichés from Utatlán did not introduce major changes in rural *civic* patterns of some *calpules* (we do not have solid data on rural *residential* patterns). In some places apparently the old shrine settlements either continued to function in the traditional way or were abandoned and not replaced. In other places defensive but small hilltop shrines or canyon-edge settlements replaced the large, monumental settlements of the past. In either case the changes do not seem to have been the large-scale social mobilization of the rural population that the documents indicate was taking place. One is left to conclude with Stewart that much administration of the rural peoples of the basin took place at nuclear Utatlán itself rather than in the rural zones. The threat of indigenous leaders was removed by forcing them to abandon their large settlements and taking them to nuclear Utatlán as adopted kinsmen or slaves. The relatively small defensive sites found near the pre-Quiché settlements perhaps attest to the minimal threat represented by these idigenous leaders during the Utatlán phase. On the other hand, the variety of settlements from the Utatlán period confirms hints in the documents that local traditions and social patterns continued to exercise an influence on the emerging rural *calpul* organization.

The centralization of control over rural populations must have given added importance to the military retainers of Utatlán. They mediated between the lords and the rural peoples from auxiliary settlements near which they resided. The lineage and hamlet organizations (*alaxic, amak'*) described for the rural populations of Utatlán (see chapter 6) accommodated to a pattern in which the major civic centers were away from the *calpules*, in the Utatlán towns. This pattern still prevails in some of the more traditional areas of modern Quiché (such as Cruz Che and Lemoa of Santa Cruz del Quiché and many cantons of San Pedro Jocopilas and Chichicastenango).

We have seen that some of the *calpules* did have substantial civic centers—the so-called plaza settlements. The documents provide an explanation for the developed character of these settlements, though they do not specifically identify all the *calpules* that had plazas. Most *calpules* with plazas occupied positions near the frontiers of the central Quiché area (Paq'uiche), where the threat to nuclear Utatlán was still serious. Apparently the settlements of these *calpules* took on many of the town characteristics of provincial colonies. Specifically, Chinique, the plaza site of Los Cimientos, was at the eastern border of the central Quiché area. Beyond this *calpul* were the hostile Sajcabaja and Joyabaj peoples, who eventually were subjected to provincial towns built in their territories. Similarly, Uwila was a *calpul* on the border with the Cakchiquels; Las Rosas was probably the northernmost Tamub *calpul*, bordering with the Ak'aab peoples of Comitancillo; Tzakibala' was at the border of the Tz'olojche *calpul* adjacent to the Mam-influenced Momostenango peoples.

The plaza settlements at Chitinamit, Pugertinamit Tz'olojche, and Pacaja-Chioculjib receive a slightly different interpretation in the documents. Chitinamit, the first Quiché capital of Jakawitz, early developed into a town. Presumably the Quichés continued to occupy it as a historical "monument," though it would also have been a strategic, defensive town, situated at the northern border of central Quiché hegemony.

The documents make it clear that Pacaja-Chioculjib was in Ilocab territory. In view of the location of the settlement in the heart of Ilocab lands, it must have functioned as a control center over the Ilocab *calpules*. Further, the historically documented conflict between the Nima Quichés of Utatlán and the Ilocabs suggests that the Pacaja town might also have been built to protect the Ilocabs against their Quiché rivals. Possibly the nuclear Utatlán town Chisalin was built as a safe place in which to resettle the Ilocab lords of Pacaja (Fox 1975). Excavations at the Pacaja site might indicate whether or not it was, in fact, substantially abandoned late in Quiché history (ca. 1400).

Pugertinamit Tz'olojche was the major settlement of the Tz'olojche *calpul*. It was a Tamub *calpul*, and Pugertinamit must have been an important secondary town (besides Pismachi) for that confederate group. It was strategically placed for exercising control over the Tamubs' most distant *calpules*, such as Amak' Mes, Pach'alib, Warabal K'alel, and Tz'olojche. Further, settlement features, along with certain references in the documentary sources, suggest that, like the Ilocabs, the Tamubs at one time were more independent of the Nima Quichés. The Tamubs probably moved their political center from the Tz'olojche area to Pismachi late in Quiché history (after 1400). Though the move may not have been forced (as with the Ilocabs), the

Nima Quichés of Utatlán may have applied pressure to the Tamubs to make the change.

The archaeologists' discovery of the canyon-edge sites, with their walled constructions on the plateaus surrounding nuclear Utatlán, brings to mind the estate organization of the Quiché social structure. The estates (*chinamit*) were walled territories of vassals and serfs, providing military and other services for the lords of the Utatlán towns. It is unlikely that the walls extended very far into the countryside; perhaps they were confined largely to the large plateaus surrounding the nuclear Utatlán settlements. The canyon-edge sites may be the remains of the defensive walls, armories, and residences assigned to the estate vassals. The chronicles indicate that there were twenty-four walled divisions guarding Utatlán, twenty-two guarding Pismachi, and eighteen guarding Pilocab. Presumably, the Nima Quiché walls were mainly east of town and would generally correspond to the canyon-edge settlement Santa Cruz; the Tamub walls would be on the west, at the sites of La Estancia and Panajxit; and the Ilocab walls would be on the north, at San Antonio Ilotenango and along the borders of the Chicorral plateau. It might be possible to verify the existence of walls and fortified structures through exploratory excavations in these canyon-edge zones.

Aerial photograph of Utatlán
in which the major mounds
are clearly visible. Note the
road leading onto the site from
the east. *Photograph courtesy of
the National Geographic Institute
of Guatemala.*

The Tojil temple facing east onto the main plaza at Utatlán. Impressions left in the
cement floor reveal the location of the ancient square "dance platforms" and the
round K'ucumatz temple. *Photograph by Dwight T. Wallace.*

The Awilix temple facing west onto the main plaza at Utatlán. The small square and round "altars" and the K'ucumatz temple are visible from impressions in the plaza floor. *Photograph by Dwight T. Wallace.*

Mounds of the Utatlán site seen from the western section. The remains of the ball court and the Tojil temple are visible in the center. *Photograph by Dwight T. Wallace.*

A mound cleared of brush in the northern wing of Utatlán. *Photograph by Dwight T. Wallace.*

The eastern wing of Utatlán, heavily overgrown with trees. The depression on the right side is thought to be the remains of the ancient causeway.

The "water-tank" feature revealed by excavations in the main palace at Utatlán. A small drainage canal can be seen running along the left side of the tank. *Photograph by Dwight T. Wallace.*

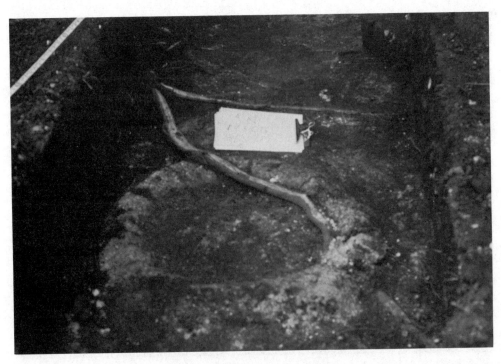

An ancient hearth excavated in one of the big houses at Utatlán. *Photograph by Dwight T. Wallace.*

The remains of the monkey mural uncovered in the Cawek palace at Utatlán. The skirt and legs of the figure are barely visible. *Photograph by Dwight T. Wallace.*

Partial clearing by excavation of walls and patios of a structure flanking a temple near the main palace at Utatlán. *Photograph by Dwight T. Wallace.*

Skeletal remains of a burial excavated from the bench of the flanking structure shown in the previous photograph. *Photograph by Dwight T. Wallace.*

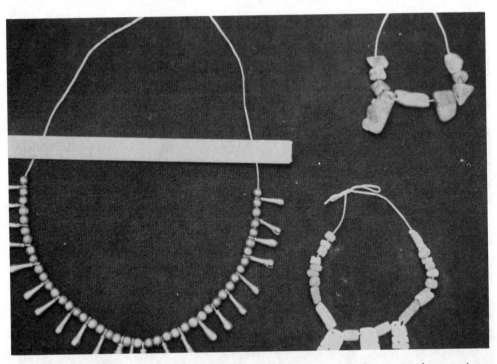

A gold-piece and two jade-piece necklaces from the burial shown in the previous photograph. An amber lip plug was also found among the remains. *Photograph by Dwight T. Wallace.*

The main plaza of the Chisalin site. The small mounds protruding from the plaza floor are the remains of altar platforms.

Aerial photograph of the Pismachi plateau. Ruins of the Pismachi site can be seen in the center. *Photograph courtesy of the National Geographic Institute of Guatemala.*

9
THE BUILDINGS
OF UTATLÁN

WE NOW MOVE FROM A STUDY of the relationships among buildings and settlements at Utatlán to a consideration of the individual buildings. For each building, features found through archaeology will be correlated with information from the documentary sources. Nothing better illustrates the exceptional nature of Utatlán than our ability to describe in some detail the main buildings of that great settlement. Only for Tenochtitlán, Mayapán, and a few other sites in ancient Mesoamerica is it possible to reconstruct in such detail the physical buildings and associated meanings of a native community. As will be seen, the documentary sources allow us to tie specific social groups and symbols to the stone and dirt forms still standing at Utatlán.

The buildings selected for discussion in this chapter are those that are the most important according to our sources and for which we have the best archaeological information. The order of presentation generally follows that used in earlier chapters: the temples of Tojil, Awilix, K'ucumatz, and Jakawitz; the ball court; the plaza platforms; the big houses; the main palace; and the main street (see Fig. 9.1, Wallace and Weeks's reconstructed site drawing for the locations of these buildings).

THE TOJIL TEMPLE

The mound on the main Utatlán plaza that has been identified as the temple of Tojil is today nothing but a shell. All of the outer stone has been removed through local vandalism, and even plaster layers of substructures have disappeared. Less than 150 years ago this temple was in better condition, as shown in the following description by John Lloyd Stephens (1841, p. 184):

El Sacrificatorio, or the place of sacrifice . . . is a quadrangular stone structure, 66 feet on each side at the base, and rising in a pyramidal form to the height, in its present condition, of 33 feet. On three sides there is a range of steps in the middle, each step 17 inches high, and but 8 inches on the upper surface, which makes the range so

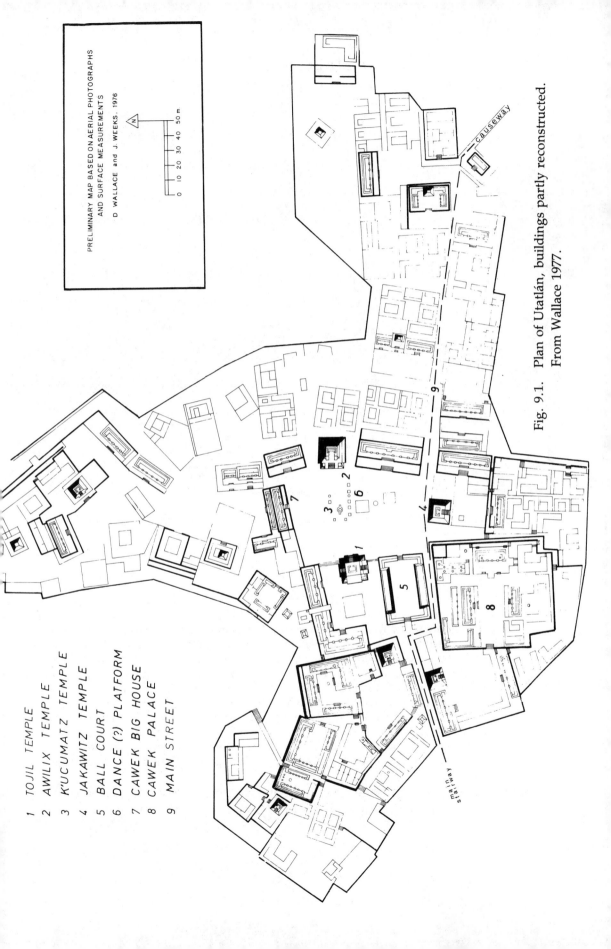

PRELIMINARY MAP BASED ON AERIAL PHOTOGRAPHS
AND SURFACE MEASUREMENTS
D WALLACE and J. WEEKS. 1976

0 10 20 30 40 50 m

1 TOJIL TEMPLE
2 AWILIX TEMPLE
3 K'UCUMATZ TEMPLE
4 JAKAWITZ TEMPLE
5 BALL COURT
6 DANCE (?) PLATFORM
7 CAWEK BIG HOUSE
8 CAWEK PALACE
9 MAIN STREET

causeway

main stairway

Fig. 9.1. Plan of Utatlán, buildings partly reconstructed.
From Wallace 1977.

Fig. 9.2. The Tojil temple. Drawing by Rivera y Maestre, 1834. From Atlas Guatemalteco n.d.

steep that in descending some caution is necessary. At the corners are 4 buttresses of
cut stone, diminishing in size from the line of the square, and apparently intended to
support the structure. On the side facing the west there are no steps, but the surface
is smooth and covered with stucco, gray from long exposure. By breaking a little at
the corners we saw that there were different layers of stucco, doubtless put on at
different times, and all had been ornamented with painted figures. In one place we
made out part of the body of a leopard, well drawn and coloured. The top of the
Sacrificatorio is broken and ruined, but there is no doubt that it once supported an
altar for those sacrifices of human victims which struck even the Spaniards with
horror. It was barely large enough for the altar and officiating priests, and the idol to
whom the sacrifice was offered. The whole was in full view of the people at the foot.

The Catherwood drawing accompanying Stephens' description is a copy of
the more accurate drawing by Rivera y Maestre. It depicts the pyramid with

Fig. 9.3.   Utatlán from a distance. Drawing by Rivera y Maestre, 1834. From Atlas
Guatemalteco n.d.

nineteen steps on each of three sides and at least four terraces, each of which
had a panel and inset base. The remains of the actual temple or shrine on top
were in two tiers. Stephens confirms the view that there were stairways on
only three sides, describing the west side as a flat slope covered with stucco.

The Rivera y Maestre drawing of the Tojil temple (Fig. 9.2, Villacorta and
Villacorta 1927) shows twenty-four stairway steps and six terrace levels, each
with a narrow upper panel and a broad lower batter. The two balustrades
that flanked the stairway facing east are shown with most of their stucco
surface still intact. The batter of these balustrades became vertical about
halfway up the pyramid. A similar form is shown in side view for the
balustrades on the north and south stairways. The west side of the temple is
portrayed as a single sloping wall without stairs. Another Rivera y Maestre

drawing of Utatlán (Fig. 9.3) portrays the site from a distant point which appears to have been the Pismachi plateau. By visiting various points outside Utatlán, I verified that only from Pismachi do the mountains behind the site match those shown in the background of the drawing. Thus the drawing provides us with a southern view of the site. It shows that the Tojil temple towered over all other buildings at Utatlán and that it had a long, single stairway on the south side, flanked by two large balustrades.

Around the turn of the seventeenth century Ximénez described the Tojil temple as follows (1929, pp. 74–75):

In the middle of these little plazas rises a massive square tower in the form of a pyramid, with stairways on each of its sides, and fortifying supports or bastions at the corners also diminishing in size toward the top. The stairs were narrow and low, so that climbing them was frightening. Each stairway had 30 to 40 stairs. All this mass is made of stone and mud, and put together with a mixture of fine lime and sand, which today preserves its strength. At the top was placed the idol called Tojil, above which was a straw roof, sustained by pillars of the same stone and mud construction. To the left side, next to this tower, there rose a large wall, about two yards [*varas*] wide and one yard and a half high. At the end of this wall there is another wall about three-fourths of a yard in width, and the same two yards wide (which is the thickness of the foundation) and three yards high. This [wall] is full of holes made in it, indicating that in this place the victim who was to be sacrificed was tied up firmly by putting ropes through those holes. Tied in this way with his face toward the direction of the idol, the chest of [the victim] was opened up cruelly, which is what their histories say: "they gave the peoples their chests and armpits." They opened [their chests] and took out the heart, which is what they offered to the idol, preserving its natural heat since it was so close that they could offer the blood before it became cold. This tower dominates all the patios and plazas formed by the houses, and so the idol was seen from all parts. [My translation]

It is noteworthy that the identity of the building was known in Ximénez's time. Further, it appears that more than thirty stairs of each stairway were still visible. He also saw the remains of pillars supporting the temple roof. The thick wall with holes at the left of the temple may have been the remains of another room of the temple complex. The great height of the building was commented on by Ximénez.

Finally we have the description of Fuentes y Guzmán (1933–34, 7:422):

. . . the *sacrificadero* today remains almost intact toward the western part. . . . This melancholy theater is raised from the ground by a thing that one climbs by certain elevations, the number of which we cannot give for certain, though from the map of the Quiché that forms a part of my papers for this history we learn that there were perhaps four of those elevations. From the height of these elevations it seems to me that there were perhaps four or five stairs [each] and no more. The pavement [of the elevation] is 4 yards [*varas*] long, leaving out the floor that receives the second grade. Toward the third and fourth [grades] there is a flat place with a smooth stone that is about 2¾ yards long, and from side to side 6 feet [*de a tercia*] wide. On this sad and burned. This bloody, melancholy theater had as its headpiece a stone coming from below, or taken from a lower section, all worked into the form of a plow. [The victim] was placed on his back on this lower stone, with an incline on one end where the feet were, and another on the other end where the head fell, so that the chest was elevated very high. [The victim's] locks of hair were put into openings of the headpiece and fastened with a wooden piece used just for this sacrifice. They gave [the victim] a strong, cruel blow to knock him out, and then with a wide obsidian stone knife they opened his chest, took out the palpitating heart, and offered it to the idol. [My translation]

Fuentes y Guzmán does not mention the name Tojil, but obviously he is describing that temple building. His account is not as detailed as Ximénez's, as seen in his failure to count the stairs. He does note, however, four or five terraces of the pyramid and a central stairway on each side. For the temple itself he describes a sacrificial stone shaped like a "plow." He associates with it perforations used to tie up the sacrificial victims and details the manner in which the hair was tied to the holes. The part about striking the victim and then extracting the heart with an obsidian knife came from the chronicles in his possession rather than from the ruins that he visited.

Tovilla (1960) had seen the famous sacrificial stone several years before Fuentes y Guzmán saw it. His only comment was that it was a great stone and that it had been broken.

The details of the Tojil temple preserved for us in the several archaeological accounts suggest that it was the most impressive building at Utatlán. Its great height, elegant panel-and-base terraces, three stairways, *talud y tablero* balustrades, painted stucco exterior, pillared shrine, and elaborate sacrificial stone together seem worthy of Tojil, the patron god of Utatlán. All these features are reminiscent of the main temples at Mayapán and Chichén Itzá and so must have had strong association with the Toltec heritage so highly prized by the Quichés (Fig. 9.4).

The three stairways and sloping western side, facing the cardinal points, probably symbolized Tojil's elevation to universal patronage at Utatlán. As a sky deity Tojil needed a southern side to symbolize the upward direction (*xucut caj*). Being phallic, Tojil also symbolized mountains; hence the northern side and its earthly direction (*xucut ulew*). Tojil's association with the east side was even clearer, since it expressed the ascent of the sun in its daily trajectory. Guillemin has argued (1958) that the west side of the Tojil temple was flat so that sacrificial victims could be brought up the stairs during the morning ascent of the sun, sacrificed at the zenith point, and then slid down the west side during the afternoon descent of the sun. Though this is a possible explanation for the temple's unusual stairway pattern, it is more likely that sacrificial victims were hurled down the front stairs, where their heads were removed and impaled on the skull-rack altar standing there. Guillemin's argument was based in part on a supposedly similar temple with

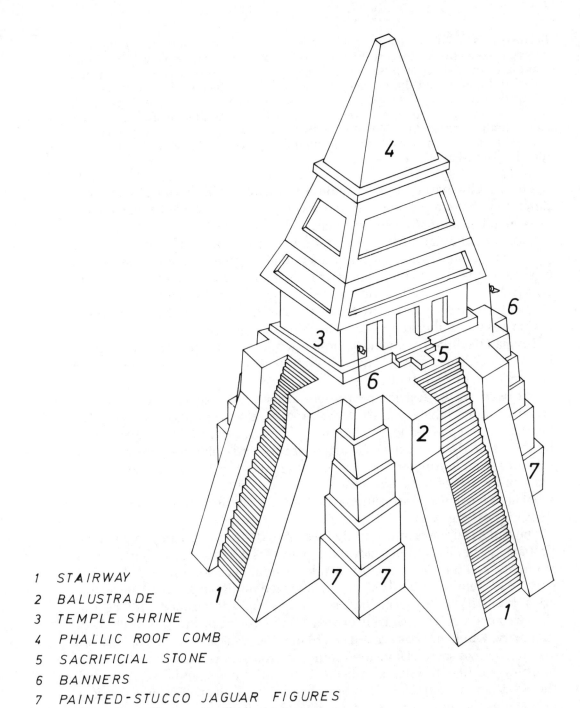

1 STAIRWAY
2 BALUSTRADE
3 TEMPLE SHRINE
4 PHALLIC ROOF COMB
5 SACRIFICIAL STONE
6 BANNERS
7 PAINTED-STUCCO JAGUAR FIGURES

Fig. 9.4. Reconstruction of the Tojil temple. Drawing by J. Weeks.

three stairways at Jilotepeque Viejo (Mixco Viejo), but, as Guillemin has since concluded (personal communication), the reconstruction of that building with three stairways and a sloping west side is probably inaccurate. It is more likely that the sloping western side was related to two other elements: (1) the descent of the sun each day under the care of Awilix, whose temple stairway *was* on the western side, and (2) the secular nature of the northwest section of the main plaza, which required (or allowed?) no entrance to the Tojil temple.

The painted jaguar on the stucco surface of the Tojil temple reminds us that the jaguar (*balam*) was one of the naguals of the Cawek ruling lineage and of their patron deity, Tojil. The founding father of this lineage was Balam Quitze (Forest Jaguar), whose nagual, according to the *Popol Vuh*, was the jaguar. Painted and carved jaguars are also associated with the major Toltec temples at Tula and Chichén Itzá dedicated to Quetzalcoatl, one of the aspects of Tojil. Presumably the characteristics of the jaguar having to do with power, majesty, and leadership made it an appropriate totem for the Cawek temple dedicated to Tojil.

The elaborate sacrificial "altar," or stone and shrine, defined from the early archaeology of the Tojil temple, corresponds with the view in the documents that most human sacrifices at Utatlán were dedicated to Tojil. The documents state that the Quichés used a stone knife ("the hand of the god") to cut out the hearts of victims, but they do not describe the sacrificial altar or shrine with its perforations. Nevertheless, the importance of human sacrifice at Utatlán makes the rather complex construction of the sacrificial alter and shrine understandable. Apparently Quiche craftsmen made special wooden objects to fasten the victims' hair to the shrine wall.

Our information on the numbers of terraces and stairs is not accurate enough to determine whether or not it correlates with esoteric Quiché symbolism. Thompson (1970) argued that four terraces on one side and another four on the opposite side of a temple might correspond to the levels of heaven in Maya culture. There is no direct evidence that the Quichés of Utatlán makes the rather complex construction of the sacrificial altar and there may have been six terraces on each side of the Tojil temple. They might correspond to the presumed thirteen levels of the underworld, although that is unlikely since Tojil was a sky god. As for the stairs, they seem to have been more than twenty, the sacred number, but fewer than fifty-two, the number of years in a Mesoamerican "century." Perhaps political as well as cosmological factors were symbolized in the numerical counts of features of the Tojil temple at Utatlán.

The pillars of the Tojil shrine suggest that it had a more substantial roof than the straw roof described by Ximénez. Pillars could have supported a masonry roof and elaborate decoration. As noted in chapter 7, there is evidence that some Utatlán buildings had symbolic roof adornments. Since Tojil was specifically said to symbolize the male organ, a large phallic roof adornment seems likely (Carmack 1973, p. 290).

THE AWILIX TEMPLE

This temple has retained some of its architectural form through time, though all of the stone facing has been removed. Fox (1975, p. 27) observed that it is composed of two major terraces, a broad lower terrace and a second one set back on top of it. There was a single, broad stairway on the west side that spanned both levels and was flanked by large, sloping balustrades. The limited space on top of the second level indicates that the shrine there must have been small. Photographs taken of the building in 1932 by Lothrop (1936) indicate these features and further indicate that the western side of the bottom terrace consisted of two huge *talud y tablero* panels on each side of the stairway and balustrades. The construction of the west-facing temple mound of the first plaza at Iximché is similar to that of the Awilix temple (Fox 1975, p. 193).

Lothrop also observed six layers of plaster on the north corner of the mound, which he interpreted as building resurfacing. Wauchope (1970) dug a test pit into the flanking structure just north of the temple and determined a construction stratigraphy that he claims also held for the temple mound. He found four main building stages and six plaster floors. Four of the floors were at the bottom of the last building phase. The plaster floor below the third building stage was painted dark green. At the base of the earliest building phase he found a pavement of cut stone. This flanking building was shown to have had at least two tiers. In another test pit behind the pyramid Wauchope found the same four building stages, though the only two plaster floors he encountered were under the first stage. In the same pit Wauchope found ladle-censer sherds.

Except for Rivera y Maestre's drawings of Utatlán, none of the sources contains references to the Awilix temple. Apparently the tradition of its identification was lost early. Rivera y Maestre's view of Utatlán from the south (Fig. 9.3; Villacorta and Villacorta 1927) clearly portrays the Awilix temple east of Tojil. Later observations agree with the drawing that the second-level terrace was placed toward the back of the first-level terrace. It also shows that the lower terrace was wide from west to east and had an inset panel at the back side. The elevation of the Awilix temple is substantially lower than that of the Tojil temple in the drawing.

The Awilix temple was an impressive building, though not as eleborate as its Tojil counterpart (Fig. 9.5). That is consistent with the rank of the Nijaib lineage, which was just below that of the Cawek lineage. The lower, wider

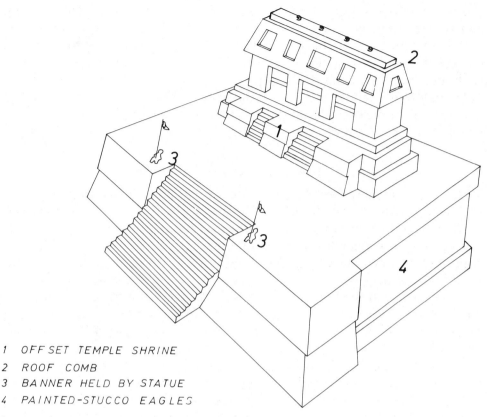

1 OFFSET TEMPLE SHRINE
2 ROOF COMB
3 BANNER HELD BY STATUE
4 PAINTED-STUCCO EAGLES

Fig. 9.5. Reconstruction of the Awilix temple. Drawing by John Weeks.

construction of the building also correlates with the contrast between the feminine Awilix and the masculine Tojil. Perhaps that explains why the temple's structure is so similar to that of the main temple of the Cakchiquels at Iximché, whose patron, Nic'aj Tak'aj, was also female. The dark-green plaster floor of one stage of the Awilix temple probably represented water, another characteristic associated with the female principle in Quiché culture. Since the green plaster floor lies forty centimeters below the surface, it seems possible that this early building stage might be in relatively good condition. If the outer construction were peeled down to this level, the green floor might reveal not only the architectural form of an earlier temple but also painted symbols associated with Awilix.

The chronicles suggest that the eagle was the totem of the Nijaibs. Presumably the eagle was somehow associated with the moon aspect of Awilix. Unfortunately, in the archaeology of the Awilix temple nothing found as yet correlates with those symbols. The Awilix temple was probably connected with the building behind it, suggesting that the Nijaibs occupied the palacelike buildings behind the mound and perhaps the entire east wing. Excavations in the east part of the temple complex would probably provide proof of this connection.

THE K'UCUMATZ TEMPLE

Today the K'ucumatz temple is nothing more than a circular impression on the main plaza floor. It is almost exactly midway between the Tojil and Awilix temples, slightly north of the Tojil center line and slightly south of the Awilix center line. It is clear from the impression that at one time the building consisted of a cylindrical stone wall, about four meters in diameter, surrounding a solid-stone core, with a narrow, one-meter-wide circular passageway between the two walls. On both the west and the east sides were small stone platforms about the width of the passageway. Photographs taken in 1932 by Lothrop (1936) reveal that the platforms, cylindrical wall, and internal core were all made of uncut stone joined with mortar.

Evidently the cylindrical wall and the central core were originally built up taller than a man's height and were enclosed at the top with some kind of roof structure. The small platforms on the east and west apparently supported stairways, which gave access to the narrow internal circular chamber. Since the plaster floor of this chamber is even with the plaza-floor level, it can be assumed that the stairways led up to a small terrace and then down to the chamber floor below. Thus the functionary entering the temple would not have been visible to persons outside.

This building must have been dismantled shortly after the Conquest, for none of the early visitors mention it despite its unique construction. Rivera y Maestre's drawing of 1834 (Fig. 9.2, Villacorta and Villacorta 1927) includes a section of the main plaza in front of the Tojil temple, but it was overgrown with grass, and there is no sign of the round temple.

Other Quiché sites of the Late Postclassic cultures of highland Guatemala have round structures (Smith 1955). Guillemin (1958) noted the similarity between the Tojil temple, with its associated round structure, and a small round structure thirteen meters northeast of pyramid B6 at Jilotepeque Viejo. Guillemin (1959) later found a small round structure in the second plaza of Iximché, similarly aligned with the east-facing temple there. He suggested the possibility of Quiché influence to account for the similarity in building arrangements between the two sites and Utatlán. He also tied the unusual round structure at Utatlán to the tradition that K'ucumatz, the feathered-serpent deity, helped the sun (Tojil) in his daily ascent to the zenith.

The De León tradition seems to offer a satisfactory explanation for the building alignment between the Tojil and round temples and also links them to the Awilix temple. The full tradition is as follows (De León n.d., pp. 45–46):

K'ij, the Sun, [was] the splendid god, husband of the Moon. Physically considered, it is the astral body that gives the idea of time. Theosophically, it is the God of the gods. In the morning it is called Teojil, Divinity. At noon it is Cawach (Cakwitz), God of the Two Faces. In the afternoon it is named Ajwilitz, for permitting night to come with its maleficent spirits. They considered him a young traveler, and, since he could not walk in space, they supposed that the immense, ineluctable snake, K'uk' Cumatz, took him up to the sky between its jaws. Upon descending, it took him over the waters of the ocean, safe from all harm. [My translation]

Unfortunately, De León did not cite his source (presumably aged informants in the Santa Cruz del Quiché area). He was also inclined to give exaggerated astronomic interpretations of Quiché symbols. Nevertheless, the tradition is compatible with what we know from the chronicles about Quiché deities. As we have seen (chapter 7), Tojil symbolized the sun and light, Awilix the moon and darkness. Jakawitz (erroneously given by De León as Cawach or Cakwitz—see also De León n.d., p. 62—who was a mountain deity associated with the south direction), might well have represented the sun at its zenith. The chronicles portray K'ucumatz as a deity associated with sky and water, as well as with the clouds that link the two. Hence De León's version, in which K'ucumatz carried the sky god Tojil up to the zenith and then carried the water goddess Awilix down to the ocean, is consistent with Quiché symbolism.

Though it is not known for certain why round buildings were used to house the feathered-serpent deity, the two are an ancient association in Mesoamerica (Pollock 1936). It is thought that the round form had something to do with the deity's cloud-and-wind aspect, though it is possible that the cylindrical shape of the coiled serpent was the tangible basis for the form. Similarly, the mediating role of K'ucumatz between male and female principles was perhaps symbolized by its composite nature: the serpent, in its phallic aspect, was masculine, while the feathers, as a symbol of water, were feminine.

The small round temple (or "shrine," as some would call it) at Utatlán was in all likelihood dedicated to K'ucumatz. Situated between the Tojil and Awilix temples, it was ideally placed for carrying out its great cosmogonical act of transporting the sun in its daily orbit. No doubt the stairways on both sides of the temple facilitated some ritual enactment of seizing the sun in the

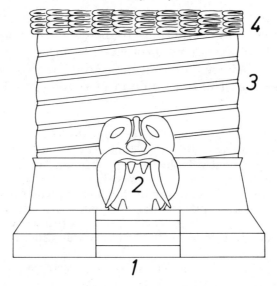

1 ENTRY STAIRWAY
2 SERPENT - HEAD DOOR
3 TEMPLE CYLINDER (SERPENT BODY)
4 GREEN FEATHERS

Fig. 9.6.   Reconstruction of the K'ucumatz temple. Drawing by John Weeks.

east and releasing it in the west. It can be assumed that painted and sculptured serpent and green-feather symbols richly adorned the building (Fig. 9.6).

The priests in charge of the K'ucumatz temple at Utatlán formed a principal lineage of the Caweks. Control over the rites associated with this great creator deity, who was also active in the daily solar drama, must have given the Caweks considerable power and prestige. It is another indication of that group's domination of the main plaza. It can be speculated that the easternmost section of the northern big house bordering on the main plaza was occupied by the K'ucumatz lineage. This section of the long structure was directly north of the K'ucumatz temple. A central location for the K'ucumatz big house is consistent with the fact that members of this principal lineage also served as stewards in the Utatlán political system.

Discussion of K'ucumatz calls to mind Tepew, for the two deities are usually mentioned together in the chronicles. The ethnohistory suggests that the Tepew temple would be near that of K'ucumatz (see chapter 7). Indeed, since the Tepew priestly lineage was part of the Cawek group, we would expect its temple to be somewhere within the main plaza. Since Tepew was possibly a mediator between Tojil (sky) and Jakawitz (earth), the Tepew temple may have stood southeast of the Tojil temple. There are impressions of various small structures in that area of the plaza, including one small, altarlike platform with nine outer layers of stucco. Since this structure is larger than the tiny ones next to it, it may have functioned as a small temple or shrine, perhaps dedicated to Tepew. That is only speculation, however.

THE JAKAWITZ TEMPLE

A large mound on the south side of the main plaza has been identified as the Jakawitz temple. All of its outside stone facing has been removed, and its original form has been almost totally lost, owing to the depredations of looters. Today it is merely a high mound of mud-and-stone rubble. Nevertheless, Wallace (1977) identifies it as a temple mound and associates it with a palace-and-court complex. The court is enclosed by the temple on the north, a long structure on the east, and a palace on the south. An unusual feature of the palace is that a long structure stands along its north side facing onto the court. The Jakawitz complex has never been excavated.

The only early visitor to Utatlán to provide information on the Jakawitz temple was Rivera y Maestre. His "aerial-view" drawing of Utatlán (Fig. 9.7; "Atlas Guatemalteco" n.d.) depicts the temple as a pyramidal mount in the south part of the main plaza. The structure is the southernmost building numbered 2 on the map, labeled *sacrificatorio* ("place of sacrifice"). The drawing shows clearly that there was a wall just north of the structure, forming a passageway that connected with the street leading into the main plaza. This proves that the temple faced south onto its own court rather than north onto the main plaza.

Rivera y Maestre's drawing of Utatlán from the south (Fig. 9.3; Villacorta and Villacorta 1927) portrays the Jakawitz temple as a small pyramid in front and just east of the much larger Tojil temple. From this view the Jakawitz temple is a narrow structure with four or five terraces. This view also shows the remains of a wall-like construction along the canyon edge south of the Jakawitz complex.

I believe that Rivera y Maestre's close-up drawing of a second temple at Utatlán (Fig. 9.8; Villacorta and Villacorta 1927) is a representation of the Jakawitz temple. From what I have been able to determine from personal inspection, the drawing of the Jakawitz temple was made from a spot south of the palace platform. From this vantage point it is possible to correlate the following buildings with features in the drawing: the low mound with trees in front of the temple is the palace structure; the high masonry structure at

Fig. 9.7. Schematic aerial drawing of Utatlán by Rivera y Maestre, 1834.
From Atlas Guatemalteco n.d.

PLANO DEL TERRE
N QUE SE HALLAN SITUADOS LOS VEST
E LOS EDIFICIOS ANTIGUOS DEL K
LEVANTÓ DE ORDEN DEL GEFE DEL ES
. DR MARIANO GALV
Año de 1834.

Sacrificatorio principal
Sacrificatorios
Edificios arruinados
Fuerte que defiende la entrada de los edifici

N.° 1.

1   Tojil temple

2   (east) Awilix temple

2   (west) Cawek palace temple

2   (south) Jakawitz temple

3   (north) Cawek big house

3   (east) Nijaib big house

3   (south) Cawek palace

4   Resguardo (Atalaya)

Fig. 9.8.   Drawing of the Jakawitz temple by Rivera y Maestre, 1834. From Atlas
Guatemalteco n.d.

the left of the temple is the east side of the Cawek palace; the corner of the
high rectangular structure on the right side of the temple is the edge of the
long structure on the north side of the main plaza; the steep mound overgrown with shrubs at the right of the temple is the front of the Awilix temple;
the stone pile in the right foreground is part of the eastern long structure of
the Jakawitz complex. There is no longer a road in the location shown in the
drawing, but there has been considerable erosion of the plateau south of the
Jakawitz complex where we would expect to find the road. All these correlations support the conclusion that the drawing represents the Jakawitz temple, to which must be added the observation that it does not seem to match
any other temple at Utatlán.

From the drawing of the temple it is clear that the structure was in much better condition in 1834 than it is now. The outer facing of cut stone was still in place, and large sections still had the outer plaster coating. On the right-hand (east) side of the mound three terraces could be seen, suggesting that there were originally five or six terraces. The terraces on the east side were recessed with respect to a ramp that extended up the central part of that side of the temple. Apparently there was a single narrow stairway in the center of the south side of the temple. There are no signs that the stairway was flanked by balustrades.

Jakawitz was a mountain deity and, as patron of the first Quiché rulers in the mountains of Chujuyup, was probably their most prominent deity. A Jakawitz temple built in the first Quiché capital had the following features: (1) it was situated in the south plaza, (2) it faced south, and (3) it was attached to the ball court (Carmack, Fox, and Stewart 1975, p. 116). As seen from the archaeology reviewed above, the Jakawitz temple at Utatlán stood in the same position south of the main plaza, also faced south, and also was situated close to the ball court (though not attached to it). Nevertheless, Jakawitz's position at Utatlán represented a radical drop in the rank of the deity, for it was definitely outside the main plaza. That is consistent with the transfer of Quiché power from the mountains to the plains and the drop in rank of the Ajaw Quiché lineage described in the documents.

As noted in chapter 7, Jakawitz continued to function at Utatlán as a phallic, mountain deity. The steep, narrow temple revealed by the archaeology is consistent with those aspects of the god. The roof shape of the Jakawitz temple shrine was probably also phallic. At Utatlán, however, Jakawitz possibly became more closely associated with the great solar drama of each day. He was the companion of Tojil, the Sun, whom he met at the zenith point from his lofty mountaintop. Accordingly, the temple of Jakawitz was placed in the direction of the sky (*xucut caj*) from Tojil, on the south. Closely linked to the sun, the temple of Jakawitz was probably the scene of human sacrifices similar to those carried out at the Tojil temple. Correspondingly, the Ajaw Quiché lineage was companion to the Cawek lineage in ritual and war, and their respective palaces were adjacent.

THE BALL COURT

The sunken ball court has retained its I shape, though the stone facing and plaster cover have been removed by looters. It is no longer possible to make out the slope of the sidewalls or determine the exact position of the stairways, which no doubt gave entrance to the court from both ends. Nor are there traces of the stone markers that must have been attached to the sidewalls. Archaeological excavations might turn up the stairways and perhaps fragments of the markers. Most of the architectural detail, however, is irretrievably lost.

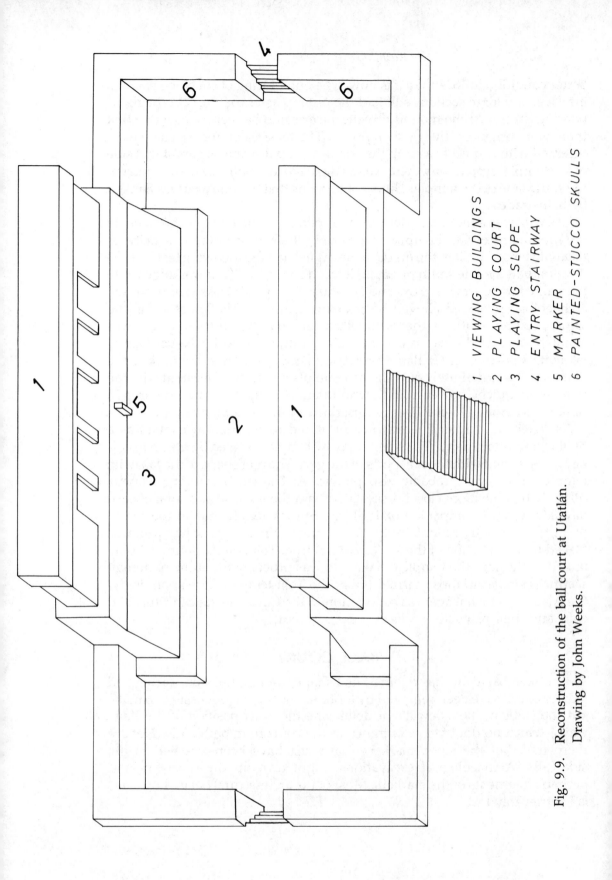

1 VIEWING BUILDINGS
2 PLAYING COURT
3 PLAYING SLOPE
4 ENTRY STAIRWAY
5 MARKER
6 PAINTED-STUCCO SKULLS

Fig. 9.9. Reconstruction of the ball court at Utatlán.
Drawing by John Weeks.

Although modern archaeologists such as Guillemin, Wauchope, and Lo-throp identified this complex as the ancient Quiché ball court, most earlier visitors to the site did not. Villacorta and Rodas (1926) referred to it as the "king's residence." Maudslay and Stephens did not mention it, presumably because they did not know what it was. It is shown in Rivera y Maestre's drawing ("Atlas Guatemalteco" n.d.) as a large rectangle in the southwest part of the main plaza. A corner of the northern sidewall was apparently portrayed in the same artist's drawing of the Tojil temple (Fig. 9.2). Though the sidewall was much higher then than it is today, it appears that as early as 1834 the stone facing had been removed. The same artist's view of Utatlán from the south shows the sidewall of the ball court as a high, rectangular masonry structure (Fig. 9.3). In the drawing are signs of plaster on the back of the wall.

Ximénez (1929, p. 75) described the ball court as it appeared when it was in better condition:

. . . next to this tower [temple of Tojil] there was a [construction] like a great tank, with very large edges of stone and mud and with crowns or pyramids that enclosed it. They are quite wide, so that many people could fit there to watch the ball games that were played to entertain the kings and other lords.

It would appear that the stone facing still existed in Ximénez's time.

Though Fuentes y Guzmán had a reference to the ball court on a native map in his possession, he apparently did not identify it with any of the ruins he saw. Tovilla (1960), on the other hand, recognized the ball court but stated only that "it remains a very good hall which served them for their ball games."

The Quichés called the ball court *jom tzalatz* ("sunken court with narrow walls"). The archaeology reveals that it was fittingly named (Fig. 9.9). The I shape, with its mirror-image end zones, also seems to correlate with the organization of the game into two sides (*cabichal*) of opposing players. Possibly the directional associations of the different lineages were maintained, for example, the Caweks always defending the western side and the Nijaibs the eastern side of the court. Perhaps major lineages needed their own ball courts to retain the "home-court advantage." The "home team" of the Utatlán court must have been the Caweks, since one of their lineages, the Popol Winak, was assigned to administer it. Our sources indicate that the lords of opposing lineages observed the contests from seats atop the two sidewalls. The directional scheme that I have worked out for the Utatlán lineages would place the Cawek lords on the south sidewall and the Nijaib lineage—or visitors—on the north sidewall. From the documents we also learn that icons of the patron deities of the lineages were placed next to the lords on the sidewalls.

Beyond the sunken construction of the ball court, the archaeology has not yet revealed any of the extensive underworld symbolism that must have been expressed there in painting, carving, and architecture. Excavations of the building complex might provide some of those details.

THE PLAZA PLATFORMS

The central section of the main plaza bears the impressions of thirteen small structures that once rose above the floor. All of them appear to have been constructed in a similar manner: mounds of stone and mud were built up, and then faced with stone-and-mortar walls, which were plastered on the outside. There were three tiny structures of this kind (about 2½ meters wide) north of the K'ucumatz temple. Photographs taken in 1932 by Lothrop (1936) reveal another row of small structures just south of the K'ucumatz temple. There were five alternating round and square platforms in the row, plus another small square platform joined to a larger square on the south side. This latter structure (the Tepew temple?) had nine layers of plaster on its smaller section. It has been reported that the plaza floor had three plaster layers, but I have observed six layers in some parts of the plaza.

South of the row of small structures are the impressions of two larger square platforms, about ten and eight square meters, respectively. They are separated by an oval-shaped impression that must have been a different kind of platform. Rivera y Maestre's 1834 drawing of the Tojil temple (Fig. 9.2) shows in the main plaza still another large platform at the southeast corner of the temple. It appears to have been constructed of cut stone and elevated more than a meter above the ground. Finally, there is a large, square platform in the northwest section of the plaza, just behind the Tojil temple. It measures about eighteen meters on each side and is about two meters in elevation. Though the outer stone is missing, the remains of six plaster floors can be made out at the top of the structure.

For the most part these several platforms of the main plaza have been neglected by archaeologists in favor of the more impressive buildings at the site. They are important, nevertheless, and the whole plaza floor should be carefully cleared and studied to determine the complete pattern of platforms.

The smaller platforms have generally been identified as altars. Lothrop (1933, p. 109) specifically identified them with the *quemaduras* ("burning altars") widely used in modern times by priest-shamans of the Quiché area. Significantly, some of the modern altars are situated in front of colonial-period churches, and copal and other incense are burned there in honor of the saints, ancestors, and gods associated with these post-Hispanic temples. An altar of this kind at San Pedro Jocopilas has four stone "horns," suggesting one form that the superstructures of the ancient altars may have had. Probably even more similar, however, are the altars of the rural area described in chapter 7. Both square "earth's table" and round "communal" altars are used by lineage heads and other shamans to make contact with the great powers of the earth and sky. Perhaps the tiny altars of Utatlán, also round and square, served as sacred places where lineages from the rural zone could make contact with their ancestors and, through them, with the temple deities of the town. If that was the case, offerings were probably placed on the altars according to the good and bad fates dictated by the 260-day calendar. That is the practice today at the rural altars of Quiché.

The larger platforms of the main plaza at Utatlán may also have been altars auxiliary to the main temples, but their larger size suggests that they were more prominent locations. One of them must have been the skull-rack platform (*tzumpan*) mentioned in the sources. The Totonicapán map places this building in the main plaza southeast of the Cawek big house. The skull-rack platform Guillemin found at Iximché in 1959 is at the southeast corner of the east-facing temple in the first plaza. It would correspond to the platform next to the Tojil temple shown in Rivera y Maestre's drawing (Fig. 9.2). It would have been an appropriate place to display the sacrificial offerings to Tojil. The plaza floor in this area is now covered with overfill from the Tojil temple. Excavations there would probably reveal remnants of the structure and might turn up skulls (as Guillemin found behind the skull-rack altar at Iximché) and even painted or carved representations of skull and crossbones (also found at Iximché).

Another platform described in our sources is the gladiatorial structure (*soquibal*). In the Totonicapán map it is drawn larger than the skull-rack platform and has cube adornments along the sides. (Fig. 7.3). It is placed near the big house of the Nima Rajpop Achij lineage, which can be identified with the northwestern section of the main plaza. Therefore, it seems likely that the large platform behind the Tojil temple is the gladiatorial platform. Even though this is the back part of the plaza, the northern sidewall of the ball court and the Cawek big houses would have provided strategic vantage points from which important people could view the spectacles. Excavations of this platform might confirm the proposed identification. There may still be vestiges of the circular stone to which the prisoners were fastened along one side of the platform and fragments of the cube adornments may exist just beyond the platform within the overfill.

It seems clear that these two important platforms, the skull-rack and the gladiatorial, were under Cawek control. The skull rack was very close to the Cawek Tojil temple, and the grim ritual associated with it was probably carried out by the priests of the Tojil lineage. The gladiatorial platform may have been closely tied to Cawek military lineages, such as the Nima Rajpop Achij. Ritual associated with it was perhaps a secularized form suitable to this northwest section of the plaza.

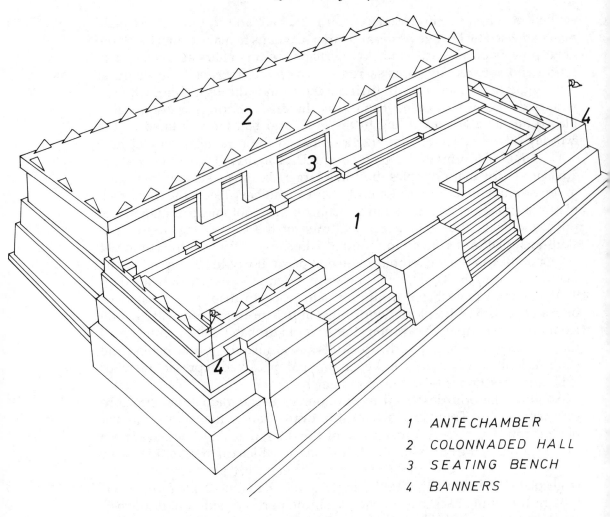

Fig. 9.10. Reconstruction of a big house at Utatlán. Drawing by John Weeks.

1 ANTECHAMBER
2 COLONNADED HALL
3 SEATING BENCH
4 BANNERS

This leaves still unidentified the two large platforms in the southeast part of the main plaza. Ritual dances, especially the "Junajpu C'oy" ("One Blowgunner Monkey") and "Wukub Cakix" ("Seven Macaw"), were prominent at Utatlán (see chapter 7). They were apparently dramatizations of Quiché myths, some of which are recorded in the first part of the *Popol Vuh*. Perhaps two platforms were required so that the Cawek and Nijaib lineages could participate jointly in the dances. The positions of these platforms in the Awilix (east) side of the main plaza might suggest that the Nijaibs were preeminent in the ritual dances, at least in comparison to the highly militarized Caweks. Guillemin (1959) found similar platforms in roughly the same positions in the first plaza at Iximché. The Xajil "(Dancer) lineage at Iximché, whose members must have been preeminent in dance, probably occupied the east side of the first plaza near the "dance" platforms there.

THE BIG HOUSES

These are the council houses described by Wallace in his study of Utatlán (1977). Though in every case badly deteriorated, and with surface stone and plaster gone, the houses can nevertheless be distinguished by their long, rectangular form. They stand along the sides of the plazas, elevated on terraces about one meter above the plaza floor. The superstructures themselves appear to be two-tiered, the lower tier forming porchlike sections in front of the chambers. In some long structures there remains evidence of multiple stairway entries in the lower sections and pillars or multiple doorways on the chamber floors.

The southeast long structure of the main plaza was excavated by the SUNY at Albany archaeologists in 1972. Its superstructure consisted of a single chamber with a back bench and central altar. Near the altar an urn burial was uncovered, one of six found inside this long structure. It contained rich offerings, including a necklace of gold pieces. There were signs of concave hearths at the ends of the main chamber. Some of the other long structures may have been multichambered, as Guillemin (1959) has shown for similar buildings at Iximché. That is patently true of the long structure along the north side of the main plaza at Utatlán. It appears to have had four chambers, or separate long structures, the westernmost of which turns southward in the shape of an L. Recent excavations by the SUNY at Albany archaeologists inside the southwest palace complex have demonstrated that there were at least three long structures there, similar in design and construction to those along the sides of the main plaza.

Most visitors to Utatlán have noted the long structures but have not described them. Maudslay (1899, p. 69) left this account:

> The sides of the long mounds, which are just indicated in my plan, are perpendicular, and these foundations may have supported stone-roofed buildings, in which case we know that the chambers could not have been more than nine feet wide, and even on the larger mounds there would not have been room for more than two of such chambers side by side. The small fragment of a stone-vaulted roof in the remains of a half-buried chamber shows that the Quichés understood the art of building stone roofs.

The evidence of pillars associated with the construction of long structures does not prove Maudslay's contention that they had stone roofs, since they could also have supported timber-and-thatch roofs. Our evidence indicates that the long structures contained only one chamber from front to back, probably measuring the 9-foot width estimated by Maudslay.

Rivera y Maestre's aerial view (Fig. 9.7; "Atlas Guatemalteco" n.d.) clearly depicts the southeast and north long structures of the main plaza. The drawing indicates that the north long structure was a single unit and was L-shaped at the northwest corner.

It appears that in one passage of Ximénez's description of Utatlán he was referring to the long structures. He wrote (1929, p. 73):

> At the high point [of the Utatlán site] there are some buildings along the edges, forming little plazalike arrangements, which were the twenty-four big houses mentioned in connection with the lords. Each one is like a large room, elevated about two yards [varas] like a terrace above the flat part of the floor. This room made a corridor, and all this was covered with straw roofs, because they did not gain the use of tile until the Spaniards came. [My translation]

This is an accurate description of the long structures as revealed by recent archaeological work. Apparently in Ximénez's day the terraces on which the chambers rested were two *varas* above the plaza floor. Though he correctly noted that the Quichés lacked tile, he evidently failed to realize that they could have built roofs of stone.

The long structures revealed by the archaeology are clearly the "big houses" of the documentary sources (Fig. 9.10). Apparently their "bigness" referred to their horizontal size rather than to their height. The multiple stairways and entrances of these structures were functionally related to the long benches against the back walls, where the ruling lords met to set public policy. It would have been important to have both visual and physical access to all those sitting in council. The burials underneath the bench, especially the impressive one near the central "altar"—or perhaps "throne"—reminds us of López Medel's claim that just rulers were buried underneath the place where they sat in judgment.

According to the documents there were cube adornments and pendants at the base of the big houses. Excavations might uncover some of these. Indeed, a plaster-covered conical stone found at Utatlán by the SUNY at Albany archaeologists might well be one of those decorations. The Totonicapán map suggests that the big houses had stone roofs capped with light, simple adornments. The hearths at the ends of the long structures surely correspond to the lineage fires, which the documents indicate symbolized the independence of each lineage unit.

Without additional archaeological work at the long structures it is fruitless to attempt to identify the twenty-four individual big houses mentioned in the sources. Besides, some of the lineages may have spilled out of Utatlán

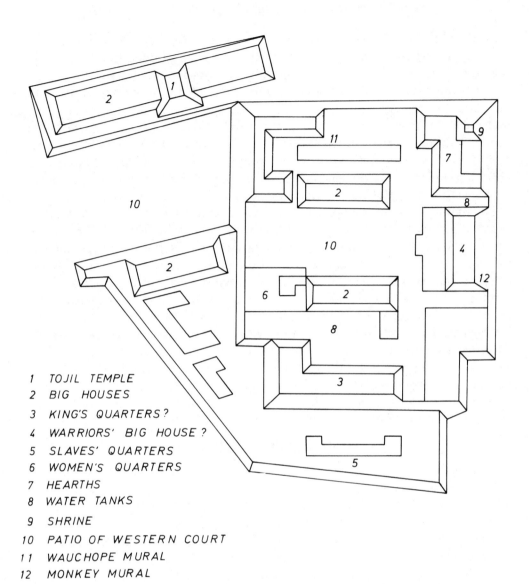

1 TOJIL TEMPLE
2 BIG HOUSES
3 KING'S QUARTERS?
4 WARRIORS' BIG HOUSE?
5 SLAVES' QUARTERS
6 WOMEN'S QUARTERS
7 HEARTHS
8 WATER TANKS
9 SHRINE
10 PATIO OF WESTERN COURT
11 WAUCHOPE MURAL
12 MONKEY MURAL

Fig. 9.11. The Cawek palace complex. Schematic drawing by John Weeks.

into adjacent sites. To complicate the identification further, some of the long structures were multichambered, notably the long L-shaped building along the north side of the main plaza. Probably this was a major-lineage building, perhaps the Caweks', whose separate chambers were occupied by representatives of the principal lineages of that political unit. The chronicles suggest just such an arrangement and specifically mention that one of the four Cawek sublineages (the Nima Rajpop Achij) had a big house adjacent to the main Cawek lineage in the northwestern part of the main plaza. I have also speculated that the two easternmost chambers of this composite big house were occupied by the Tepew and K'ucumatz lineages (see chapter 7).

The main-plaza big houses are not directly connected to residential buildings, which supports the argument that they were primarily administrative centers for the major lineages. In this regard it must be remembered that the principal and minimal lineages were the residential units while the major lineages had political, ritual, and social functions only. Nevertheless, it is possible that the residential-type buildings behind the main plaza long structures could have functioned in conjunction with those buildings. Where the big houses formed integral components of the palace complexes, as in the southwest compound, we see concrete evidence for the close association between the big houses and residential activity mentioned in the documents. Controlled excavations designed to compare the long structures with other buildings within the palaces would probably turn up significant differences in the structural types with respect to domestic activities.

THE MAIN PALACE

The large, flat compound in the southwest corner of Utatlán can be identified with the main Cawek palace (see chapter 8). Wauchope (1970) sank two test pits in the structure and cleared a small portion of the architecture revealed by his pits. He also dug one pit in the court just west of this compound. Under Wallace's direction SUNY at Albany archaeologists trenched the central area of the compound and uncovered architectural features in the north, south, and west sections. They also excavated the flanking structure of the temple facing the court west of the compound. In addition, a small group of archaeologists from the University of Nevada excavated an amorphous structure in the south part of the same court. Later, SUNY at Albany archaeologists excavated a small southeast section of the other major palace compound, north of the one under discussion.

The palace compound was formed by a huge platform about ninety meters long, eighty meters wide, and between four and five meters high (Fig. 9.11). Though all the surface stone and plaster have disappeared, some gross features of the compound's internal structure can still be made out from surface observations. A small mound at the northeast corner of the compound is clearly the remains of a shrine of some kind. A large sunken area in the center of the compound, about forty-five meters wide and twenty meters long, was once a patio. The patio may have extended into the southeast corner of the compound. The various ditches left when the cut stone was removed by looters indicate that many chambers once lined the compound surrounding the large central patio.

Excavations have uncovered many additional features. Wauchope found that the northern section of the compound consisted of small rooms divided by walls made of adobelike clay. The rooms had white-plaster floors. Wauchope found four main building levels; the first two were filled in and plastered over to provide the base for the two more recent, closely adjoining levels. The rooms of at least the uppermost levels had clay hearths, each about fifty centimeters in diameter and eight centimeters deep. On one of the walls of a fourth-level room Wauchope found traces of a painted mural. The red, green, yellow, and blue colors were applied to a fine clay veneer covering the wall. The mural tended to detach from the wall when it was uncovered, and, though it appeared to extend the whole length of the room, Wauchope did not attempt to uncover the entire scene. What he saw of it portrayed "a blue lake with yellow shells, covered by an ornamented canopy, with a much-plumed green snake winding above it" (Wauchope 1965, p. 67).

Wallace dug in the same section of the compound where Wauchope had uncovered the painted murals and uncovered what appears to be a continuation of the mural. The same red, green, yellow, and blue colors are in evidence, as well as brown paint used to represent flesh color. Wallace's reconstruction of the scene shows an individual richly adorned with beads, feathers, and necklace, holding a shield in one hand and what appears to be a rattle in the other. The figure is standing over a band of maize and other objects. The wall containing the mural was retained, covered with plastic, and reburied by Wallace.

Other paintings were discovered by the SUNY at Albany archaeologists while they were excavating at the compound. On a wall along the back of the southeast corner of the compound was found a mural portraying the figure of a monkey. The monkey, depicted in bent-over position, has pronounced fingernails and a long penis. Wallace has reconstructed the scene from photographs and drawings of the original wall.

The SUNY at Albany excavations revealed several additional features of the palace. A room in the northeastern section of the compound was found to contain several hearths placed close together, all of them similar to the concave clay constructions found by Wauchope in another room. In an open patio just south of this "kitchen" was revealed a large round water "tank," constructed of stone and mortar and covered with plaster. There is a convenient step on the north side of the tank and a small drainage canal on the south side. The drainage canal joined with a larger canal coming from the structure just south of the tank. Wallace believes (personal communication) that this northeastern section was domestic in function and that it was used for communal cooking.

Excavations of the structure just south of this section indicate that it was similar in construction to the big houses of the main plaza. The building is narrow and rectangular, standing on top of an elevated terrace. It was entered from the west side through multiple doorways and probably had a bench spanning the back side of the chamber. It had hearths at both ends of the chamber. Two other long buildings of similar construction have been identified inside the palace compound. One of these is in the northern part of the compound and faces south onto the central patio. The other is on the south and apparently faces south, away from the main patio. Behind this latter building the archaeologists uncovered a second water tank. It is about the same size and construction as the one next to the "kitchen" and is also situated in a small patio. Next to the tank, attached to the cement floor, are the remains of a plaster adornment in the shape of what may be a bird's head.

Wallace interprets the location of the big houses, in direct association with residential activities, as clear evidence of the multifunctionality of the buildings. In this Cawek compound they appear to have functioned at least in part as elaborate living quarters.

A test pit dug by Wauchope into the court just west of the palace compound revealed the same four construction levels that he found at the palace itself. As with the palace, true construction levels consisted of plaster floors and subfloors of earth, clay, or stone. Plaster floors were often placed on top of one another (for example, on the second and fourth levels of the court), but Wauchope does not believe that they represent true building construction. Excavations of the flanking structure on the temple in the western court (Fig. 9.11, no. 10) and buildings across that court from the temple revealed that both buildings had typical long-house features: two tiers, portaled doorways, and back benches. They faced onto the court from opposite directions.

Excavations by the SUNY at Albany archaeologists in a small section of the northern palace compound showed that it was similar in construction to the southern palace. In one of the small rooms of this section the remains of a fine Mixteca-Puebla polychrome vessel and an "antique" plumbate vessel were recovered. A round stone structure was uncovered in the center of the patio nearest this section.

The identity of the main Cawek palace was apparently lost during the nineteenth century. Maudslay did not know where it was. Villacorta and Rodas early in the twentieth century described the palace compound but could not identify it. They reported (1926) that it was 4½ meters in elevation and that it had a temple in the northeast corner. Apparently the small mound now standing in that position was much larger at the time.

Early in the nineteenth century the parish priest of Santa Cruz had used old manuscripts to identify the palace. He showed it to Stephens, who described it in these words (1841, p. 183):

The palace, as the cura told us, with its courts and corridors, once covering the whole diameter, is completely destroyed, and the materials have been carried away to build the present village. In part, however, the floor remains entire, with fragments of the partition walls, so that the plan of the apartments can be distinctly made out. This floor is of a hard cement, which, though year after year washed by the floods of the rainy season, is hard and durable as stone. The inner walls were covered with plaster of a finer description, and in corners where there had been less exposure were the remains of colours; no doubt the whole interior had been ornamented with paintings. It gave a strange sensation to walk the floor of that roofless palace.

So in Stephens's day some of the plaster floors of the compound were still intact, and parts of the walls of the rooms surrounding the patio were still standing. His observation about the painted inner walls suggests that the murals recently found by the archaeologists represent but a fraction of the paintings that once adorned this structure.

Rivera y Maestre's map (Fig. 9.7; Villacorta and Villacorta 1927) portrays the palace compound as a simple rectangle next to the ball court. This at least confirms its unity as a single compound. Another view of Utatlán from the south by the same artist (Fig. 9.3) appears to depict the Cawek palace as a high, square terrace west of the ball court and the prominent Tojil temple. Behind this structure are two mounds, probably the remains of the temples associated with the two main palace courts. The drawing makes it clear that the Cawek palace had high masonry terrace walls separating it from other buildings of the site.

Fuentes y Guzmán had a reference to the main palace in the native map in his possession, and at the time he visited the site some of the construction was still intact. However, as explained earlier (see chapter 7), he confused the whole western section of the site with the palace. The ruins that he thought were the "seminary" were probably those of the palace. He described them as follows (1933–34, 7:417):

This college was, without doubt, one of the most elegant constructions of those times, considering the large territory that was occupied by its ruins. It is not easy to delineate perfectly its design and original arrangement, though its great foundation and large square pavement can be seen. But it is indistinct and confused, because in the center part its order has been altered, as well as the lines of its compartments. Nevertheless, there is evidence that it was of great distinction, and had a variety of habitations. We have not been able to investigate whether or not there was just one level, or four floors. [My translation]

293

Fuentes y Guzmán's reference to "compartments," a "variety of habitations," and a large, paved square area all suggest that he was talking about the palace compound. Apparently he was confused by the maze of rooms. Though much of the stone had already been carried off, as he tells us, there was still evidence that the building at one time had been elaborately decorated. He obviously found no sign that it had more than one level, for he would have used even the slightest evidence of such a condition to support his contention that the Quichés had multistoried buildings.

The archaeology of the Cawek palace reveals a building complex grander than the rather modest description of the "houses" (*cochoch*) of the lords given by the native chroniclers, but more modest than the grandiose account provided by the Spaniards (especially Fuentes y Guzmán). In the chronicles we are told that these houses were built by the vassals through the estate organization (*chinamit*). That is, the peasants living within the territory controlled by a given elite lineage provided the labor and materials to build the palace of their patron lords. As the buildings were elaborated through time, serfs no doubt also contributed their labor. Materials for construction may have come from tribute collection; we are specifically informed that cut stone was an important tribute item received by the Caweks of Utatlán. Since in form and elaborateness the palaces became quite distinct from the residences in earlier Quiché towns (such as Pismachi and Jakawitz), most of the design and construction in Utatlán must have been directed by the ruling lords. They had their own sculptors, painters, and master craftsmen, who probably were responsible for most of the elaborate decoration of the buildings.

The many rooms and divisions revealed by the archaeology are consistent with the complex social arrangement in the Cawek palace described in the documents. The section where the militia was quartered is said to have been near special kitchens used to provide food for many people, and next to them, according to the sources, were the rooms of the young male lords who were also soldiers. It can be tentatively suggested that the kitchen area in the northeast section of the compound and the long structure south of it—that is to say, the east side of the compound—were the ones occupied by the militiamen and princely soldiers. The young princesses were in another section near a "secret" passageway to one of the temples. The wives of the lords were no doubt close by. Possibly the women of the palace occupied the west side of the compound, near the court and temple that adjoin the palace on the west. It should be possible to find archaeological evidence of communal cooking and the sweathouse mentioned in the documents.

The king (*ajpop*) had his court (*k'alibal*) in another section of the palace with an elevated throne and a four-tiered canopy. The structure on the north side facing the main patio of the compound best corresponds with the king's court. The elaborate murals discovered in rooms of this section support the view that this was the area of maximum prestige in the palace. The living quarters of the ruler were perhaps either the rooms behind the court or the buildings on the south side of the main patio. Next to the water tank is the plastered bird's head in the private patio of the south side, suggesting that that may have been the section where the ruler resided. The living quarters of the palace slaves who served the Cawek lords are probably the rather simple structures the archaeologists have found below the compound on the south and southwest sides.

There is little hope of finding evidence in the archaeology of the vertical construction employed in certain sections of the palace. We are told that the wives' quarters were two-storied, that upper levels of the palace had windows for astronomical observations, and that ancestral shrines up to "eight persons tall" were attached to the house walls. What these features were like can only be vaguely perceived from the native drawings that have come down to us. In contrast, documentary references to rewhitening the house of a deceased lord and the whole town when the king died might have correspondence in the stratified remains. We have noted the consistent pattern of four building phases both inside the palace and at other Utatlán buildings. The number of plaster floors usually exceeds the number of building phases, often two or more floors resting directly on top of one another. Perhaps the building phases are related to the deaths of Cawek rulers, while the new plaster floors were laid down in honor of lesser lords closely associated with a particular building or plaza. This interpretation would suggest that the four building phases correlate with the deaths of four Cawek rulers at Utatlán. That is consistent with the genealogy and chronology worked out for Utatlán from information in the native chronicles (see chapter 5). The number of plaster floors would have to be worked out independently for each building or room, and the numbers of floors would vary with the fortunes of different important individuals.

The murals of the Cawek palace offer perhaps the richest field for correlating the documentary accounts with archaeological findings. The documents inform us that the palace walls were elaborately adorned with painted frescoes. The paintings are said to have portrayed important events in the lives of past lords. When a lord died, new frescoes were painted over the old ones to honor him. Not all the paintings were historical; the archaeologists found patches of murals with geometric designs, not to mention the painting of the monkey figure in the eastern section of the compound. The monkey was the patron of master craftsmen and probably also of promiscuity. This latter aspect is suggested by the very long penis. As noted, this section of the compound may have been inhabited by young lords. Our sources indicate that they were trained in warfare, but many of them also practiced the master crafts. More important, in Quiché society the youth of noble caste married late (after age thirty) and so, living together, engaged in frivolous homosexual as well as heterosexual activity. In the rather open symbolism characteristic of Quiché culture, the monkey might well have been an expression of this aspect of life in the young men's quarters.

The mural section uncovered by Wauchope may have portrayed a historical scene. The blue lake with shells and the feathered serpent above it are strongly reminiscent of the legendary place of origin in Quiché history. The documentary accounts tell of the coming of the forefathers to the Quiché area from a land of lakes and water, which I have identified as the Gulf Coast area (see chapter 2). As shown by Roys, Thompson, and others, this was the land of the Putuns, whose patron deity was the feathered serpent. Thus Wauchope may have stumbled on a painting in which the Caweks attempted to record their glorious migration from the east. The canopy portrayed in the scene was probably similar to the one offering shade to the Cawek king in his court, which was four-tiered and made of feathers. Apparently the canopy's tiers and feathers symbolized K'ucumatz, the feathered-serpent deity. This canopy pattern no doubt came from their Gulf Coast homeland, an association possibly suggested by the mural. It should be noted that the painting showing the canopy was in a part of the building complex that has been tentatively identified with the Cawek ruler's court, where, perhaps, the feathered canopy was actually placed.

The painted figure found by Wallace can be more fully interpreted through the ethnohistoric sources (Fig. 9.12). The following analysis of the figure is based on Wallace's painstaking reconstruction of the details, which he saw personally and which were recorded in photographs. First an attempt will be made to identify the key symbolic elements in the mural. This will permit me to suggest the meaning of the scene and, finally, to say something about the main purpose for which it may have been painted.

The round shield in the figure's left hand was called *pocob* in Quiché. It was directly associated with the Quichés' Toltec heritage and was also known by the Nahua term *chimal*. It was made of twisted vines or string and symbolized the essence of warfare for the Quichés: *Pocob* had the ancillary meaning "fortification."

The sacred object in the right hand of the figure was probably the *sochoj* ("rattle"), always associated with precious metals and stones (jade, turquoise, gold, and silver). It was often taken as spoils after a military conquest. The name derives from the rattlesnake, one of the totems of the Utatlán plateaus.

The figure appears to have a tobacco-pouch pendant, called *c'uz buz* by the Quichés. Recinos (1953) identified the word as Yucatecan, and translated it as "small gourd with ground tobacco." Thompson (1970) noted that the

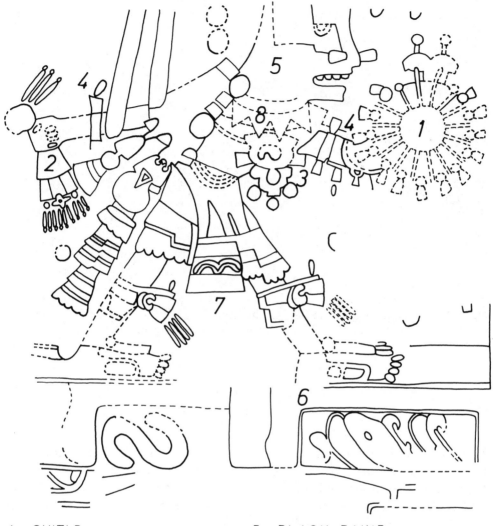

1	SHIELD	5	BLACK PAINT
2	RATTLE	6	MOUNTAINS AND PLAINS
3	TOBACCO PENDANT	7	LOINCLOTH
4	WRISTBANDS	8	SOLAR DISK

Fig. 9.12. Reconstruction of painted mural from Cawek palace. Drawing by
K. Kurbjuhn and Dwight T. Wallace.

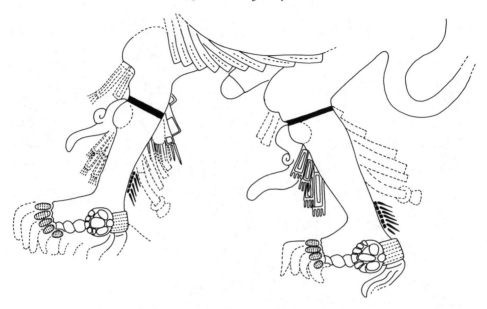

Fig. 9.13. Monkey figure painted on the mural wall at the Cawek palace. Reconstruction by Dwight T. Wallace; drawing by John Weeks.

Mexicas used the tobacco gourd as a priestly insignia. It was also, however, used in time of warfare and at investitures, a use possibly close to the one depicted in the Utatlán mural. In Quiché the term for "tobacco" (*c'us*) may have been a homonym for "heart" (*c'ux*), suggesting a possible association between its position on the chest and its psychotropic effects.

The figure's wristbands were called *macutax*, a term taken directly from the Nahua word *macuetlaxtli* (Edmonson 1971). It implied the possession of "power."

The striking blue (or black?) face of the painted figure may have been associated with the Quiché *titil abaj* ("black stone"). *Titil*, a Nahua-derived term, was an ointment made from black mineral rocks and used to paint the lords during ritual events, including accession to political office. Yellow and red ointments were also used on ceremonial occasions.

We can surmise that the earth band on which the warrior figure stands was expressed by the Quiché term for the earth, *juyup tak'aj* ("mountains and plains"). The mural seems to portray the earth's surface and ears of corn. Perhaps the meaning corresponds to one often found in the chronicles: the earth as territory that Quiché warriors subdued through conquest with the "arrow and shield."

The entire scene appears to portray a ritual dance. This is indicated by the rattle in the figure's hand in place of the atlatl or hatchet so often seen in Mexican military scenes. The feathered leg bands also indicate a dance theme. The warrior's dance was an important ritual in Quiché culture. In the best-known Quiché dance, the "Xajoj Tun," or "Rabinal Achi," a Quiché military lord stamped his feet, moving back and forth to and from the four corners of the court to the rhythm of flute and drums (Brasseur 1862). Most of the ornaments found in the Utatlán mural are mentioned in the written version of the "Rabinal" dance: the round shield and the arrows (in the left hand with the shield), the sacred armbands, the metal-gilded rattle (*sochi pwak*), the sandals, and the loincloth.

Another Quiché document, the *Título C'oyoi* (Carmack 1973, pp. 292, 295), mentions several pre-Hispanic dances performed at Utatlán, including the "Monkey" and "Macaw" dances described in the *Popol Vuh*. Of special interest with regard to the palace mural is still another dance, referred to in the C'oyoi document as the "War Dance" ("Tzala Tun"). It was performed at Utatlán by military heroes on their return from conquest. These great war-lords danced to the flute and drum, roaring like fierce animals (the open mouth of the mural figure could express this howling). The Mexica origin of the dance is indicated by an esoteric Nahua phrase chanted along with the dance.

It would thus seem that the Utatlán mural portrays a scene that corresponds in considerable detail to the war dance frequently mentioned in the Quiché documentary sources. The figure's solar disk ties him to the sun and hence to Tojil, the Quiché sky and war god. As patron of the Caweks, Tojil would properly be symbolized in this important painting at the main Cawek palace.

THE MAIN STREET

Recent maps of Utatlán made from surface features reveal what appears to be a long, narrow street traversing the entire east-west length of the site (see Fig. 9.1). It is the only major street visible from present-day surface features. The causeway that once connected the Utatlán plateau with the broad plains to the east has now all but disappeared. The only remains are some stone-and-mud structures near the modern road, about thirty meters below the east end of the Utatlán plateau. An earth-slide area along the southeast side of the eastern tip of the plateau may mark the place where the old causeway once joined Utatlán. On the north side of this entry point is a high platform. On the south side Wallace found in air photos taken in 1957 evidence of a similar structure that has now too fallen away.

The narrow, channellike street separates the buildings of the entire eastern wing into north and south divisions. The street appears to be a continuation of the causeway and leads directly into the southeastern corner of the main plaza. The street was probably made of stone and plaster, but until excavations are carried out, that is only supposition. It appears to pass along the Jakawitz temple, and then to head westward between the ball court and the Cawek palace. Beyond the ball court the street turns and runs north for about ten meters, then forms a cross as streets head east into the ball court, north into the main plaza and west behind the temple of the Cawek-palace court. In this western section a low wall appears to separate the street from the northern-palace court. The street continues to the western edge of the canyon, where it ends. There is no sign of any substantial building construction at the point where the street enters the western canyon.

The point at the eastern tip of the Utatlán plateau where the causeway entered the site has been known since the Conquest. Juan de León (n.d.) showed it clearly in his map of the 1930s and indicates that it entered the plateau at a point between two large constructions. His map traces the rest of the street as it courses westward through the site to the western canyon. Earlier Villacorta and Rodas (1926) portrayed a building at the point where the causeway once connected Utatlán with the eastern end of the plateau. They accurately placed the "avenue" that traverses the eastern wing, showing how it divided buildings into north and south sections. They were unable to trace the street once it reached the main plaza, however.

Maudslay (1899) had depicted the causeway connecting the eastern Resguardo area with the Utatlán plateau and described it as though it were present in his day, though it was not. His map gives no indication that he was aware of the main street inside Utatlán. Stephens (1841, p. 170), fifty years earlier, had made no mention of the causeway or main street, though his map clearly shows that the causeway no longer connected the Utatlán site with the eastern plains. Nevertheless, the road shown on his map follows the correct course of the main street until it reaches the main plaza.

Rivera y Maestre's aerial view of Utatlán (Fig. 9.1; "Atlas Guatemalteco" n.d.) graphically portrays the old causeway up to a point where it breaks off into the canyon just before reaching the Utatlán plateau. However, it shows the connecting point and the road entering the main plaza far south of where it actually is. The path of the street along the southern edge of the main plaza is shown, and we see clearly that a wall behind the Jakawitz temple separated the street from the main plaza. In Rivera y Maestre's view of the site from the south (Fig. 9.3; Villacorta and Villacorta 1927), the causeway is not shown at all, but the main street entering the central plaza from the east is marked by a row of trees.

Ximénez mentioned only that there was a narrow neck of land connecting

Utatlán with the outside, and Fuentes y Guzmán based his account on documentary sources rather than on his own observations. In 1711 the anonymous author of the *Isogoge histórica* described the street as follows (1935, pp. 188–89):

> In particular, the site of Utatlán, where the Quiché kings had their court, is encircled by a very deep canyon, which, beginning with the southern part, encircles all the western part, turns to the north and east, and then to the eastern and southern parts, where nature left some space for it to join the rest of the plains. Here they cut the plains with a very wide and deep excavation, leaving a very narrow battlement along which only one man could pass on foot, and with great danger, because on the left side was the precipice of the canyon and on the right side the precipice of the excavation, or ditch, also very deep. In front of this battlement, which served as an entrance, was a castle, part of which can be seen today, made of cut stone. Its walls ran for more than 150 steps, and along all those [steps] there was a narrow road going toward the west, so that to the left was the precipice of the very deep canyon, and to the right was the wall of the castle. From the wall it was easy to use lances, darts, or stones to kill or knock into the canyon those who passed under it. This little narrow road in front led to another castle, so that upon entering this path one had to resist the blows from the lances that were thrown from the wall on the right side toward the canyon, and also at the same time withstand the shots from the frontal castle without having space to impede them because it was such a narrow road. Upon passing through this path, on the right side one entered a plaza covered with plaster, where one discovers certain very high towers and other great buildings and walls of flat stones, with short streets so narrow that two men could barely go down them side by side. [My translation]

The two "castles" mentioned by the anonymous author apparently refer to the Resguardo complex east of Utatlán and a defensive building positioned just at the entrance to the site. A narrow causeway ran for 150 steps between the two buildings alongside the southern canyon. A deep trench and fortifications along its northern side provided a location from which Quiché warriors could defend the entry into Utatlán. At the end of the causeway was a fortified building, apparently divided in two sections so as to give entry to the site. Once on the Utatlán plateau, according to our author, plazas and narrow streets were encountered.

The causeway, northern trench and fortifications have all disappeared, largely because of a modern road built right at the point where the causeway joined with the plateau. Much of the "castle" at the end of the causeway has disappeared also, apparently falling into the southern canyon. The northern section of that building remains today as a large mound, and excavations might confirm its hypothesized defensive function.

Our sources refer to a major causeway and street entering Utatlán from the outside. Down this street triumphant military lords and their vassal warriors were escorted into town with pomp and ceremony. Since the returning soldiers were met some distance outside town, we must conclude that the street started well out on the plains east of the Utatlán plateau. Remains of its presumed stone and plaster construction are probably buried in that zone.

Fuentes y Guzmán confirms that the causeway by which the street entered the Utatlán plateau was well defended. At its narrowest part it consisted of a removable bridge. The Spaniards believed that the causeway had been cut away in preparation for their coming, but the archaeology suggests that it had been a permanent feature. Our source also mentions the fortification (*resguardo*, "guardhouse") at the point where the causeway joins the plateau, as well as a stone door opening into it. Most of the guardhouse (and certainly the stone door) has disappeared, though, as has been noted, early visitors to Utatlán saw much of the structure intact. The large platform at the south side of the eastern tip of Utatlán is probably all that remains of the guardhouse itself.

The documents ascribe a highly defensive character to the main street as it coursed westward through the eastern wing. There are references in the documents to fortified "turrets," probably examples of the palisaded (*tz'alam*) stone (*coxtun*) walls the Quichés built to defend their town. Excavations should turn up remains of the wall in this area, which was where the fierce Tamub warriors were stationed; possibly the low-lying structures south of the main street are the remains of their quarters. The limited archaeology known for the eastern wing suggests that its settlement pattern may have been different from that of the rest of Utatlán. Presumably that is a reflection of the special defenses built alongside the main street in this area.

The route of the street through the east wing and into the main plaza indicates that it was used at least in part for ceremonial purposes. Military heroes were led into the sacred precinct, as the chronicles state, to pay homage to the gods and rulers. Processions in which deity icons were brought into Utatlán must also have gone down this street. The arrival of the priests and their retinues from sacred shrines and caves in the rural zone and from satellite towns was usually in accordance with calendric schedules. On special occasions priests also came from provincial towns and towns of independent kingdoms. Our sources indicate that invariably they went to the center of Utatlán, the main plaza.

These religious processions may explain in part why the section of the main street was built along the south side of the main plaza. The deity icons were taken on ceremonial pilgrimages alongside the important buildings of Utatlán. This street would have been one of the many narrow, winding streets the documents describe at the center of the city. Thorough clearing of the rubble at the site might reveal the remains of other streets of this kind.

The street along the southern border of the main plaza also provided direct connection between the main street and the Cawek palaces. The street continues westward between the ball court and the front terrace of the southwestern Cawek palace and then divides, one branch continuing straight into the court of the Cawek palace and the other heading north toward the eastern side of the main plaza. That the main street leads directly to the private palace of the leading Cawek lineage dramatizes the preeminence of that lineage at Utatlán. It also shows that a great deal of the "business" coming to Utatlán from the outside must have been conducted within the palaces themselves. Both these conclusions, based on the archaeology of the main street, are confirmed by the ethnohistory.

The cross formed by the main street in the western section of the site must have been a sacred place. The documents inform us that the Quichés considered road junctions highly sacred, apparently because they symbolized the four directions of the cosmos. Shrines were built at those places, and a thorough clearing of the area where the main street branches might uncover remains of such a shrine.

The fortification the Spanish chroniclers mention in connection with the western entryway to Utatlán has not been found archaeologically, but the stone steps have been identified. Fox and Wallace (personal communication) found a stairway leading from the plateau down to a landing, where it connects with a ramp running northwest down to the river below. Wallace believes that a similar ramp might run down from the landing in the southwest direction, toward Pismachi.

The western street, it may be noted, seems to lead directly to the two major palaces. It also leads to the main plaza and so may have had ceremonial uses similar to those of the eastern main street. However, its short length, and its rather inaccessible steep steps suggest that it was used primarily by the servant classes. Serfs and slaves perhaps traveled this route to the palaces where they worked and to bring firewood, water, maize, pots, and other supplies to their masters.

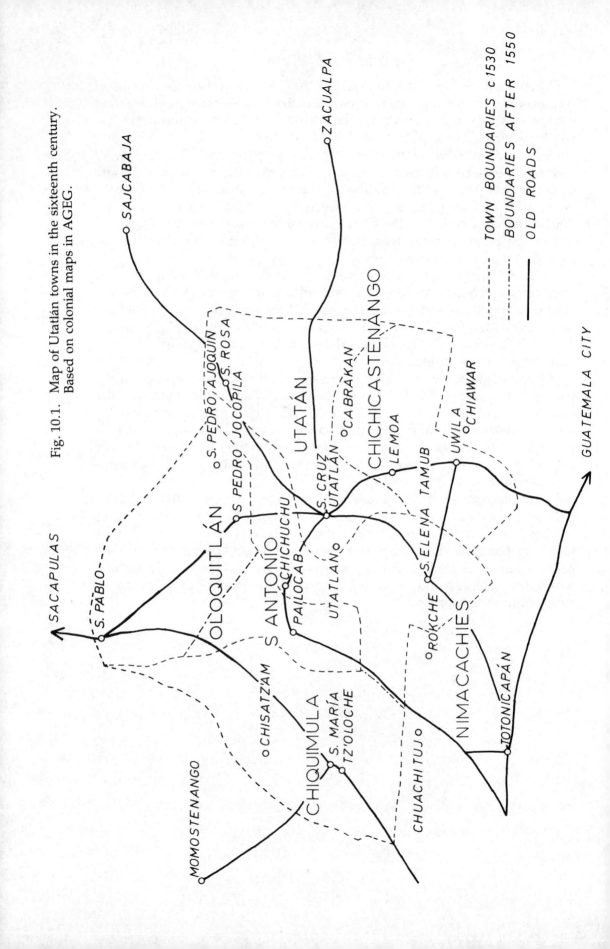

Fig. 10.1. Map of Utatlán towns in the sixteenth century. Based on colonial maps in AGEG.

TOWN BOUNDARIES c 1530
BOUNDARIES AFTER 1550
OLD ROADS

10
AFTER THE FALL

ONE OF THE TESTS OF A COMMUNITY is its capacity to survive in the face of strong pressures to change or be eliminated altogether. A community well adapted to its ecological setting, with an integrated social structure and consistent symbolic system, can both resist and adapt to severe pressures brought to bear on it. Utatlán was that kind of community. It rebounded from the "revolution" of the warriors and commoners during the days of Q'uik'ab and the subsequent secession from the kingdom by the Cakchiquels and other former allies. When the Spaniards arrived about fifty years later, Utatlán was strong and culturally flourishing.

The Spanish conquest, of course, had a devastating effect on the Utatlán community. Nevertheless, as will be shown in this chapter, the Quichés of Utatlán rebounded somewhat even from that blow. They worked out an accommodation with their Spanish overlords and restored a surprisingly large part of their political structure and belief system. Through time, however, the weight of the colonial apparatus took its toll on Quiché culture, as explained in the second part of the chapter. It slowly eroded the old aristocracy, pushed the people into a servile, peasant condition, divided them into ethnically distinct communities, and gradually infused more and more Christian elements into their "Christo-pagan" religion. It will be shown, however, that the rural communities became pockets of resistance, egalitarianized and syncretized, but nevertheless fundamentally Quiché in culture.

CENTURY OF CONQUEST

The military victory of the Spaniards at Utatlán (see chapter 5) was only the beginning of the conquest of the Quiché community. The much more difficult task of transforming Utatlán society into a unit of the Spanish colonial system remained, as did the even more difficult job of changing Quiché belief. As we shall see, the Utatlán community proved to be highly refractory in resisting the Spaniards' goals. The sixteenth century was especially difficult for the Spaniards, because there were few of them and the Quichés tenaciously held to as much of their old social life as they could.

The techniques the Spaniards used to colonize Utatlán were similar to those they used in other parts of Mesoamerica. Fray Betanzos, one of the first priests to labor in Guatemala, has left us a summary of colonization at Utatlán during the first years after contact. He wrote in 1559 (Carrasco 1967a, p. 255):

. . . forty years ago the Spaniards won this land . . . .and the town became subject to tribute payment to Your Majesty. . . . this land became subject to the Royal Crown and its king, Don Philip our Lord, . . . and was provided with presidents, judges, and governors to rule and govern these towns in justice, and sustain the preaching of the Gospel. . . . And Your Majesty has the land divided and allocated into towns of *encomiendas*, and each town or town chief goes to his *encomendero* with his tributes. . . . each chief has an account with the town or towns subject to him, which he governs, and has no communication or jurisdiction with other neighboring chiefdoms; rather, each one governs and rules his town according to the laws and ordinances, which the King and his Royal Court give him. And it has happened many times that they have wanted to rebel, seeing that the Spaniards are few compared to them, but because the chiefs and chiefdoms are all subject to the Royal Crown, divided and allocated to each chief alone without recognizing any one chiefdom, thus they have never been able to agree on any one [chief] in order to carry out their intention [to rebel]. . . . For any opening which the Court might give them, because of compelling them to doctrine, or for any other thing, they are accustomed to rise up and try to put into effect their bad purpose and intention, because they are new people, very changeable, and great friends of novelties. . . . they will believe more the words [of some native chief] than what the priests tell them; and as [a given chief] is new in the faith and a son of idolatrous fathers, it would be easy for him to return to the old rites, and take with him the people who were with him before. [My translation]

It is clear from Betanzos's account that the Spaniards operated according to the principle of divide and conquer. They divided the Utatlán community into towns, and assigned them to the conquistadors as tribute-paying *encomiendas*. The *encomenderos* forced the native rulers in the Utatlán community to administer the collection of tribute and other affairs of the towns and *encomiendas*. The Spanish priests were assigned the task of organizing the natives into the new towns and indoctrinating them in the Catholic religion. For these "pacification" services they were supported by *encomienda* tributes.

Utatlán itself was organized into a town called Santa Cruz Utatán by the Dominican priests sent to administer the province (Fig. 10.1). We are told (Remesal 1932, 1:178) that the major pre-Hispanic lineage groups were brought together at the town's formation: "Zaguaquib [Sakic], Niab [Nijaib], Achauil [Ajaw Quiché], Quiché Tamub, and many others." It appears that during the first years following the Conquest the town center remained at

Utatlán. In 1539, when Bishop Francisco Marroquín gave the town its official name, Santa Cruz, "he was in that court, and blessed the place, and raised and fixed the standard of faith there, the sign of our Redeemer; it was in the same place where for so many years the Prince of Darkness, that idol Tojil, had reigned; thus it was a sign of triumph and trophy" (Ximénez 1929, p. 115). The *Popol Vuh* (1962, p. 335) confirms that Utatlán itself was "blessed" by the bishop. These are our only references to the early Spanish occupation of the site, which must have been partly restored after Alvarado burned it.

Two other towns formed very early out of the Utatlán community were Chiquimula and Oloquitlán (Las Casas 1909, p. 616). The name Chiquimula was from the Nahua name for Tz'oloche, formerly a Tamub *calpul*. It became the Tamub town and extended southwest from Pismachi to present-day Chiquimula. Oloquitlán was apparently from the Nahua name given to the Ilocab town organized northwest of Pilocab. These two towns, along with Utatán, must have been very large, covering almost all the territory of the central Quiché area. There is evidence that Chichicastenango was also organized as a separate town sometime during the early years of colonization (CDI 1925, p. 157).

Santa Cruz Utatán was apparently made the *encomienda* of one of Pedro de Alvarado's captains or lieutenants (Carrasco 1967a, p. 252; cf. Sherman 1969). Tribute rights over the Tamub and Ilocab towns apparently also fell to Alvarado's captains. Alvarado himself carried off a large number of Utatán inhabitants as his personal slaves (Lutz 1976, pp. 122ff.). He settled them on milpa lands in the valley of Jocotenango, just north of the new Santiago Guatemala (near present-day Antigua). Slaves from other towns besides Utatán resided there, but the settlement became known as Santiago Utatleca. After Alvarado's death and the emancipation of his slaves, the settlement was further augmented by native peoples from other towns, including Cakchiquels. By 1580 there were 156 tributaries in Santiago Utatleca, but we do not know the number of slaves originally brought there from Santa Cruz Utatán.

The first Quiché lords to be made chiefs in the Utatán *encomienda* were Tecum and Tepepul. They were the sons of the *ajpop* and *ajpop c'amja* burned to death by Alvarado during the fall of Utatlán. While they may have served their Spanish masters at first, the limited information we have from the post-Conquest period suggests that they eventually rebelled against Spanish rule. There is much confusion on this point, for the sources appear to give contradictory information (Contreras 1965, pp. 42ff.). The Cakchiquel revolt against the Spaniards occurred shortly after the occupation of Iximché in 1524, and under the leadership of Sinacan, the Ajpop Sotzil, they formed a government-in-exile that lasted for some six years. Sinacan was aided by another rebel leader named Sequechul, or Sachil, whom Fuentes y Guzmán

(1933–34, 7:390) believed was a Quiché ruler. As pointed out by Contreras (1965), however, Sachil was a Cakchiquel lord, probably Xajil Ajpop. Far from fighting alongside the rebellious Cakchiquel, the Quiché chiefs aided the Spaniards against the rebels. The treason of the Cakchiquels, in inviting the Spaniards to Guatemala and then aiding them in the conquest of Utatlán was still very fresh at this time in the minds of the Quichés.

But native uprisings continued in Guatemala after the subjugation of the Cakchiquels in 1530. According to Vázquez's summary of the missing second Cabildo book (1937–44, 1:39), between 1531 and 1535 native uprisings were continuous. It is likely that during this time the chiefs at Santa Cruz Utatán led their followers in revolt. Fuentes y Guzmán (1932–33, 8:48) learned from one of his native sources that a Quiché leader from Utatán named Chignaui Ucelut (Nahua for Nine Tiger) had revolted against the Spaniards. He was later captured in Chiquimula, where he was sentenced and hanged. Fuentes y Guzmán identifies this leader as "the son of the king Tecum, put in possession of the government at Utatlán by Don Pedro de Alvarado on the death of his father." Fuentes y Guzmán notwithstanding, this rebel must have been Tecum himself. It was Tecum whom Alvarado put in the Utatlán king's place. Further, if he had been the son of Tecum, he would have been called by his baptized name, Juan de Rojas. Instead the successor is called by his native name, 9 Tiger (Belejeb Balam in Quiché), which I interpret to be the calendar name of Tecum.

It would appear that Alvarado's other chief, Tepepul, also got into trouble with the Spaniards. He is referred to by the Nahua name Chicuey Quiaguit (8 Rain) in an early colonial document (Carrasco 1967, p. 253). This name also appears to be calendric, Wajxak Caok in Quiché. We are told that 8 Rain was driven from Utatán—"almost from the entire province"—by the holder of the Santa Cruz *encomienda*. Though this event supposedly took place after Alvarado's death in 1541, other evidence suggests that it had happened sometime earlier. In 1540, according to the *Annals* (Villacorta 1934, p. 272), Quivawit Caok (8 Rain, Tepepul) was hanged by Alvarado along with Sinacan, the *ajpop sotzil* of the Cakchiquels. At the time both were in prison for rebelling against Spanish rule. Rather than risk their escaping and again leading their peoples in an uprising, the Spaniards executed them.

It would appear then that the first native chiefs of Utatán attempted to perpetuate Quiché rule in exile rather than serve the new Spanish lords. The *Popol Vuh* (1962, p. 364) states that the *ajpop* and *ajpop c'amja* ruling when the Spaniards came to Utatlán were hanged, though the authors knew very well that Alvarado had burned them. Apparently they meant to say that their successors, Tecum and Tepepul, were hanged. It might be added that the ruler of the Tamub town Chiquimula may have suffered a similar fate, for the rebellion led by Tecum apparently had its focal point there. That may account for the reputation Chiquimula gained shortly after the Conquest as a powerful, militant town (Zorita 1941, p. 205). We have no information on whether or not the Ilocabs of Oloquitlán participated in these early uprisings against Spanish rule.

The hostility of the first Quiché chiefs against the Spaniards' rule is understandable. Alvarado and his men stripped them of their privileges and ruled with a strong military hand. Alonzo de Zorita (1941, p. 204), an early Spanish judge in Guatemala, commented that "the lords of the town called Utatlán . . . were as poor and miserable as the poorest Indian in town. Their wives made tortillas to eat, because they had no servants or goods for their maintenance, and they carried water and wood for their houses." Another early source (Carrasco 1967a, p. 253) reported that the *encomenderos* spurned the claims of legitimate native rulers at Utatlán, putting in their place chiefs "who could be most easily taken advantage of."

The native priests under Spanish rule were even greater losers than the Quiché rulers, especially after the Dominicans arrived and began teaching Christianity in the native language. It is not surprising therefore, to find that the early rebellions at Utatán were linked to nativistic religious beliefs. Ximénez (1929, p. 57) provided the following account from an ancient unidentified source:

It happened in this kingdom a little after being conquered that, hearing the lives of Christ and Our Lady, John the Baptist, and Saint Peter and others which the friars taught them, that a Mexican Indian came forth, a pseudo-prophet. He taught them that Huhapu [Junajpu] was God and that Hununapu [Junjunajpu] was the son of God; Xuchinquezal, which is Mexican, or Aquiexquic [Xquic'] was Saint Mary, Vaxaquicab [Wajxakib Q'uik'ab?] was Saint John the Baptist, and Huntihax [Junlibatz?] was Saint Paul. This caused so much commotion among the Indians that the kingdom was almost lost over it, for they came to imagine that our Holy Gospel told them nothing new. [My translation]

Ximénez explained that the first Catholic missionaries taught the simple stories of the Bible in Quiché and that the stories reminded the natives of their own myths. Their priests no doubt encouraged the Quiché rebellion at Utatán, for they had everything to lose from Spanish-Christian rule. They used the old myths to prove that native religion was as powerful as that taught by the Spaniards: like Christ, Junajpu had conquered the underworld; Xquic' had been "impregnated" by Junjunajpu with mere spittle; the decapitation of John the Baptist and the hanging of Saint Paul also had their parallels in Quiché mythology—perhaps the story of Paul reminded them of the hanging of the monkey twins from a tree by their breechcloths.

Much mythic parallelism of this kind was doubtless worked out by the Quiché priests and leaders, for the Spaniards claimed that the natives were

1   CATHEDRAL AT SANTA CRUZ DEL QUICHÉ
2   CATHEDRAL AT SAN ANTONIO PAILOCAB (ILOTENANGO)
3   CATHEDRAL AT SANTIAGO CHUWA TZ'AK (MOMOSTENANGO)
4   LAKE PAILOCAB
5   RÍO JOCOL
6   SIERRA MADRE

Fig. 10.2.   Quiché churches, ca. 1550, in a pictorial found in Santiago Momostenango. Drawing by John Weeks.

carried away by every new doctrine taught by one of their own leaders but
had a "total aversion" to anything taught by the Spanish priests (see the
Betanzos excerpt quoted above). Some of the strength of the native priests
came from painted codices in their possession, which contained the old
myths and rituals. Las Casas (1909, p. 618) reported that the Dominicans
"saw some of those books, and even I saw some, and they have been burned
because it seemed to the friars that since they had to do with religion at a time
in the beginning of their conversion, perhaps they would do them harm."
This extreme act of destruction illustrates the severity of the conflict that
raged over religious belief during the early colonial period. The first years
were a time of insecurity on both sides and little understanding between the
two peoples.

By midcentury the situation at Quiché had begun to change. Alvarado had died, and new, more enlightened officials had arrived to administer the Guatemalan kingdom. They passed laws against slavery, lightened tribute burdens, controlled the excesses of *encomenderos*, and listened to the claims of the legitimate heirs of pre-Hispanic rulers. Under the influence of Las Casas the Dominicans began taking more interest in Quiché culture and history and championing the cause of Quiché chiefs before the Spanish government. Priests of considerable linguistic talent, such as Friars Juan de Torre and Domingo de Vico, prepared Quiché vocabularies and grammars. A sign of the times was the careful attention the Dominicans gave to the Quiché term for God: they finally decided to gloss the word as C'abawil (see chapter 7 for the pre-Hispanic use of this word).

The Spaniards also made important changes in town jurisdictions to facilitate administration. From the *Popol Vuh* (Villacorta 1962, p. 335) we learn that by the time that great book was written (about 1560) the original Utatlán had been abandoned. The new settlement had been established on the flat plains on the east, where Santa Cruz del Quiché stands today. A pictorial (Fig. 10.2) drawn about 1550 that I found in the possession of Indians living in Santiago Momostenango (Carmack 1973, pp. 12, 62) shows a tall, handsome Catholic cathedral that had been built at Santa Cruz. It had a high tower and two large bells in the belfry.

There is evidence that by midcentury Santa Cruz Utatán had been severely depopulated. Besides the huge losses to disease, which became virtually universal among the native peoples in Guatemala upon contact with the Spaniards, large numbers of people were carried off as slaves. Others fled to escape the ruthless exploitation of Alvarado and his men—there are traditions that places like Chichicastenango, Santa Lucía Utatlán, and Santa Catarina Ixtahuacán received immigrants from Santa Cruz in that manner. By 1553 few tributaries were left in the town, and rights over them had been transferred from Alvarado's men to the crown. A tribute record from that year (AGC, A3:1797–40, 466) reveals that Utatán was required to pay each year only 100 cotton cloths, 50 chickens, and 30 *jiquipiles* of cacao (1 *jiquipil* equals a load of 8,000 cacao beans). Just how small this tribute obligation was can be seen by comparing it with the payment of 800 chickens and 600 *jiquipiles* of cacao required of Santiago Atitlán the same year.

By 1574 (AGC, A3:2713–38, 916) tributes had been converted from cotton cloths to money, the town paying 210 *tostones* each year (2 *tostones* equal 1 peso). The number of chickens was increased to 70, but the same *jiquipiles* of cacao were paid. We also learn that 13 *tostones* of the tribute went to support the Dominican priest who administered the sacraments in town. As will be described below, still other tributes were paid at this time to native chiefs rather than to the Spaniards. The complex tributary situation at Santa Cruz makes it difficult to estimate accurately the population of the town at that early period (see chapter 4), but clearly it was not large.

Before midcentury the town of Chichicastenango had definitely been formed, in part from territory that previously had belonged to Santa Cruz Utatán. It may have been established partly as compensation to a chief from Chichicastenango, Don Miguel, who in 1541 aided the Dominicans in the pacification of Verapaz (Remesal 1932, 2:228). Among the settlements brought together to form the town Remesal (1932, 1:178) mentions Carrabarracan (Cabrakan), Chulimal, Huyla (Uwila'), and Zizicastenango. The Dominicans made Saint Thomas the patron of the new town. It is noteworthy that the town was formed out of several pre-Hispanic Quiché *calpules*, as well as the province of Uwila'.

During this same period Oloquitlán was apparently divided into the two Ilocab towns San Pedro Ajoquín (Jocopilas) and San Antonio Pailocab (Ilotenango) (Remesal 1932, 1:178; *Diccionario geográfico* 1961–62, vol. 2). The pictorial mentioned above shows a cathedral at San Antonio Pailocab as large as the one at Santa Cruz, but with its tower positioned to one side. It is likely, too, that at midcentury eastern and western sections of the Tamub town Chiquimula were recognized. The western section was called Santa Elena de la Cruz Tamub, and was centered in the area of present-day Patzite. Like other central Quiché towns it was administered by Dominican priests. By this time tribute rights over the natives of Chiquimula were equally divided between the Spanish crown and the *encomenderos* (AGC, A1:5939–51,962).

Second-generation native chiefs were much more cooperative with Spanish officials and *encomenderos* than their fathers had been. They had good reason to be—they were more thoroughly indoctrinated by the priests, received better treatment from their superiors, and were given important perquisites befitting their status as descendants of native rulers. Some of them learned to write in Quiché, using Latin characters. The first to do so was Diego Reynoso (Ximénez 1929, p. 115), a descendant of the old Popol Winak lineage at Utatlán. He was taken to the Spanish capital by the first bishop of Guatemala and taught to write in Quiché. When in midcentury the Spaniards began granting substantial privileges to native lords who could prove their genealogical lines from pre-Hispanic rulers, Reynoso and others transcribed the histories contained in the native codices (which either had been destroyed by the Spaniards or were unintelligible to them). These new chronicles became prime evidence for chiefly status, and many of them were written between 1550 and 1560 (Carmack 1973, pp. 19–22). Apparently the Dominicans taught several native chiefs to write in Quiché at that time.

A fairly large number of natives gained the status of chiefs at Utatán at midcentury. They included descendants from all four major lineages of pre-Hispanic Utatlán (Recinos 1950, p. 244; Recinos 1957, pp. 93, 115–16, 180;

Gall 1963). From the Cawek lineage the Spaniards recognized Juan de Rojas (Ajpop), Juan Cortés (Ajpop C'amja), Diego García (Chituy), Gabriel de Vigo (Ajk'ucumatz), Cristobal Velasco (Nim Chocoj), Juan Lucas (Ajtojil), Diego Reynoso (Popol Winak), and Pedro Xiquitzal (Tepew Yaqui). The Nijaib chiefs were Don Jorge and Cristobal Fernández (K'alel), while those of the Ajaw Quichés were Diego Pérez (Atzij Winak) and Don Martín. The lone Sakic chief was Pedro de Salazar. Similar chief status was given to descendants of Tamub and Ilocab rulers from Santa Elena (Chitamub), Chiquimula, and San Antonio Ilotenango. Around midcentury important chiefs from these towns included Juan de Torres (Atzij Winak, Tamub), Juan Gómez (Rokche, Ilocab), and Alonzo Gómez (Us, Chiquimula).

The various chiefs were town leaders indispensable to the Spanish officials and *encomenderos*. They collected tribute from their respective lineages, carried out censuses, organized work obligations (*tequios*), enforced church attendance and instruction, and adjudicated disputes of a traditional nature. They also filled the positions of governors (*gobernadores*) and *alcaldes* in local government, thus meeting the requirement of Spanish law that such officials must exist, even if in name only. For their valuable services the chiefs were freed of tribute and work obligations. They were treated with respect and were called by the prestigious title "don," and they were allowed to take on Spanish ways: they could dress in European clothing and ride horses. These privileges applied to their immediate family members provided the chiefs could demonstrate through proper documentation direct ancestry from pre-Hispanic rulers. The privileged status of the native chiefs was rationalized by Spanish officials as a way to show proper respect for the "natural" aristocratic order of native society.

Fortified by chiefly status, the Quiché rulers retained a surprisingly large part of Utatlán's pre-Hispanic political organization. Juan de Rojas and Juan Cortés, the sons of Tecum and Tepepul, according to the *Popol Vuh* (Villacorta 1962, p. 364), continued to be recognized as "kings." They had to be consulted on all matters pertaining to Santa Cruz Utatán, and even tribute payments to the Spaniards were considered to belong first to them and secondarily to the Spaniards. More significantly, they continued to exercise authority in towns and provinces outside Utatán itself. We find them in these towns authorizing accessions to office, settling land disputes, putting histories into writing, testifying to chiefly status, carrying out censuses, and performing other important tasks.

In 1554, when the *Título Totonicapán* (Recinos 1950, pp. 211–42) was composed, the two Utatán "kings" signed the document. For that important event they used the title *q'uik'ab*, an eponym of the famous Quiché ruler of the past. As witnesses to the Totonicapán document they assembled the descendants of eleven of the twenty-four officials who had ruled at Utatlán in pre-Hispanic times, including eight of the nine original Cawek officers. On a similar occasion, when the *Título Santa Clara* was written (Recinos 1957, pp. 172ff.), they turned out representatives from all four major pre-Hispanic lineages of Utatlán.

Another remarkable event was the accession ceremony for the chief of Momostenango. Juan Cortés, as "Rey," and two Ajaw Quiché assistants directed the proceedings. They assembled as authorizing witnesses the native chiefs of Quezaltenango, Chichicastenango, Sajcabaja, Ilotenango, Chiquimula, Totonicapán, Ixtahuacán, Mazatenango, San Felipe, Zapotitlán, San Luis, Cuyotenango, Samayac, and six unidentified towns. The document written in conjunction with the ceremony recorded that the office and authority given to the Momostenango chief had not come from any bishop, president, judge, king's magistrate, governor, or alcalde. Rather, "I give it, I Don Juan Cortés, king and gentleman, in the presence of all these [lords]" (Recinos 1957, p. 102). The ceremony had the markings of a pre-Hispanic Quiché rite, except that after the chief had been elevated to office the participants entered the hermitage and participated in the Catholic mass.

Ximénez tells us (1929, p. 79) that Juan de Rojas sought and obtained a special receiving room at the Royal Palace of Guatemala, next to that of the president himself. From there he administered native affairs for the Spanish government, though it is doubtful that he had much actual authority. Nevertheless, the spectacle of the Quiché "king" officiating from the Spanish capital must have been a powerful symbol for the natives of the Quiché area. Juan de Rojas and Juan Cortés, perhaps encouraged by the Dominicans, importuned the Spanish government to give them most of the rights and powers the Utatlán kings had held before the Conquest. Cortés, for example, traveled all the way to Spain with a Dominican priest to make his claim before the crown (Carrasco 1967a, pp. 253–54). He took with him extensive documentation to prove his descent from Quiché kings, but on the way his papers were seized by French pirates. Despite the setback, he gained audiences at the highest courts, who sent the case back to the colonial court for consideration.

At Santiago de Guatemala two of the most enlightened Spanish officials, Judge Alonzo de Zorita and President Francisco Briceño, often sided with the Utatán chiefs and decided in their favor on many requests. Rojas and Cortés, it seems, were seeking nothing less than a restoration of the Utatlán kingdom, though now to be subject to the higher authority of the crown. They attempted to regain tributary rights and political jurisdiction over twenty to thirty of the towns that had formerly been provinces of the pre-Hispanic Utatlán state (Carrasco 1967a, p. 255). The idea of disrupting the authority of local native chiefs in each town and of having to work through Utatán each time an order was issued to the Indians was too much for Spanish officials.

Not surprisingly, the Franciscan priests were also opposed to increased power for the Utatán chiefs, because it enhanced the position of the Dominicans who administered in the Quiché area. The request was rejected, though the degree to which these Quiché "kings" had achieved favor with Spanish officials may be seen in the fact that the request was considered at all.

Restoration of another ancient right was also sought by Rojas and Cortés: the services of the descendants of a group of serfs (*nimak achi*) belonging to their forefathers. As they explained to the Spanish officials, these people were "slaves" who had been captured in war and had settled on their fathers' lands (Carmack 1973, pp. 285–89). Close to one hundred families, descendants of the *nimacachi* serfs still lived in the southwest corner of Utatán territory. Though technically the families had been freed from slavery, Rojas and Cortés asked for the privilege of retaining them on their lands as tributaries and servants. The request was granted, and these families were thereafter excluded from the crown's tribute list for Santa Cruz Utatán.

In similar fashion some of the retainers who had served the Quiché kings in the Utatlán palace were resettled on lands adjacent to those occupied by the *nimacachis* (Carmack 1973, pp. 363–66). Among them were Juan Bautista and Cristobal Soc, originally from the Chiquimula area, who had been barbers (*soc*) of the Utatlán king. Like the *nimacachis*, these serfs were excluded from Utatán tribute lists, but they were expected to provide tribute and services to the descendants of the Quiché kings.

The serfs provided a critical economic basis for the power exercised by Rojas and Cortés. Besides paying tribute, they were made to work extra milpa land for their masters, repair their houses, and take care of small horse ranches that Rojas and Cortés had begun. They were also used in commercial ventures. The Quiché chiefs would send them to the coast to collect tribute from dependent settlements. They loaded the serfs with cloths and other goods to be sold on the coast and had them return with cotton to be woven into more cloth by their wives (Carmack 1973, p. 386). The arrangement was highly beneficial to the Utatán chiefs, and, as we shall see below, they tenaciously held on to their rights over the *nimacachis*.

The Quiché chiefs, including Rojas and Cortés, also received services from commoners (*maceguales*) living in their jurisdictions. As seen in the records of complaints registered with Spanish officials, the Utatán kings tended to treat commoners like serfs. They demanded more milpa work than they had rights to, and they attempted to force them to become carriers of commercial goods. As tribute collectors for the crown the chiefs apparently collected more tribute than was due, keeping part of it for themselves.

Relations between the Utatán kings and the commoners are illustrated by a dispute that broke out in 1550 (Lutz 1976, pp. 152ff.). Under the direction of Rojas, a group of commoners from Utatán moved to Santiago de Guatemala and formed a colony of merchants. It seems likely that Rojas hoped to benefit commercially from the venture, for he and his lineage purchased the land on which they settled. The land, near the Franciscan monastery, was purchased from a Spaniard for one hundred pesos. Once the merchants had settled on the land, they refused to recognize Rojas as their chief and tried to buy the land for themselves. Rojas complained to the crown that they were his subjects, that they had paid tribute in Santa Cruz, and that they had moved to the land only to escape tribute and work obligations. The merchants responded that Rojas had mistreated them, ordering them to esteem him as their "lord," and to pay him tribute. This was one dispute that Rojas lost, for the crown allowed the merchants to remain on the land and freed them of obligations to Rojas, though they were required to pay him the original land purchase price in full. Later this settlement of merchants became known as Barrio Santa Cruz.

The sociopolitical accommodation between the Spanish government and the native chiefs had its religious parallel. The Quichés were allowed to retain much of their native religion as long as they supported the church and outwardly accepted Christian tenets. There was some compromising on both sides: the Dominican priests began acknowledging elements similar to Christianity in the Quiché religion, and the religious leaders of the Quichés found similarities between their native religion and Christianity. A syncretized religion developed among the Quichés of Utatán.

The Dominicans studied Quiché religion and concluded that it ultimately derived from biblical sources. Fray Domingo de Vico, for example, argued that "these Indians descend from the ten tribes who separated from the Jews, not returning to their land; so they preserved as traditions all the events which the sacred text relates, though the devil mixed in [with these traditions] many errors" (Ximénez 1967, p. 5). Las Casas specified some of the beliefs in Quiché religion that were similar to those found in Christianity: the creation of the earth before the appearance of sun, moon, and stars; a "common, superior god," called Cavovil; a hell, where the dead were tormented, called *chixibalba*; "spirits or angels, good and bad"; an ancient flood, called *butic*, from which one man escaped whom they referred to as "the great father and great mother" (Las Casas 1909, pp. 618–20). Las Casas also pointed out the many demonic "errors" in Quiché religion, but even in them he saw evidence of an impressive religiosity. Human sacrifice he partly rationalized, saying that the Quichés practiced it for religious rather than "vicious" reasons (Las Casas 1909, p. 469).

The descendants of the rulers and priests of Utatlán responded to this Dominican liberalism by developing a sophisticated Christian syncretism from their old religion. The first attempt at this of which we have record is found in the *Título Totonicapán* (n.d.). The first section of that document contains a brief summary of the biblical stories from the creation to the departure of the ten tribes of Israel from Babylon. The account appears to follow closely the version of the stories the Spanish priests told the Quichés and ends by stating that "we are the sons and grandsons of Israel and Saint Moisés, within the tribe of Israel." Nevertheless, the native authors tried to harmonize the account with their old religion, as the following examples illustrate.

In the Totonicapán creation story the celestial bodies as well as the graded angels are said to be nine in number, thus conforming to the sacred numerology of the Quichés. The Quichés substitute their old dualistic creator deity, Tz'akol Bitol, for God, and later allude to Adam and Eve as the creator mother and father (Xmucane, Xpiyacok). When man is created, it is only partly out of the earth, for his body is formed from a *masa* ("mass"), which includes earth, maize, fire, water, and wind. The changing of the languages at Babylon is said to involve "thirteen groups of languages," an allusion to the thirteen groups who came into the Quiché area. The wanderings of the Israelites in the wilderness reminds the Quichés of their own peregrinations, and some of the places in the Old World receive Quiché names: Canaan becomes Mountain (Juyup), and the names of some places in Palestine are rendered in Quiché names, such as Chimoab. The tribal organization of the Israelites is equated with the traditional Quiché lineage-estate structure (*chinamital*). Three groups of peoples are distinguished in Palestine: Israelites, Hebrews, and Canaanites—to conform to the original tripartite Quiché confederacy (Nima Quiché, Tamub, and Ilocab). Finally, the place of captivity of the ten tribes in Babylon is equated with the Toltec homeland, Ciwan Tulan, from which the Quiché forefathers migrated to the Guatemalan highlands.

The cautious syncretism of the *Título Totonicapán* suggests close supervision by Spanish priests. In contrast, the *Popol Vuh* reveals an overwhelmingly native religion subtly syncretized with a few major Christian elements. Since Don Cristóbal, a Nijaib chief from Utatán, signed the *Título Totonicapán* in 1554 but died before the *Popol Vuh* was written (Recinos 1950, p. 241; Villacorta 1962, p. 368), it is apparent that the *Popol Vuh* was written after the Totonicapán account. Apparently the Utatán chiefs attempted in the *Popol Vuh* to transcribe as authentically as possible their aboriginal religious beliefs and traditions. Though the Dominicans may have encouraged them to do so, it nevertheless is testimony to the audacity with which the Utatán chiefs preserved their old beliefs.

The Christian elements the Utatán chiefs syncretized with native religion in reproducing their old "Book of the Council" (*Popol Vuh*) are so subtle as to indicate that the process may have been largely unconscious. The syncretism may not have been detected by the Spanish priests, though the authors admit that they wrote the book after becoming Christians. Nevertheless, the Christian elements are there to attest to the accommodation between the two cultures that was being achieved at midcentury. Some of the more significant Christian syncretic elements in the *Popol Vuh* will now be briefly summarized.

The beautiful creation account in the *Popol Vuh* may be one of the most deeply Christian-influenced parts of the book. The absolute power of the gods, who create living beings rapidly, *de novo*, and by command, seems strongly Christian in origin. Many elements of the account are native, of course, most obviously the many deities involved in the act of creation. Even with respect to the deities, however, there is an attempt to identify them as merely different aspects of the same god. In the end a Dominican idea is used to equate them all: "And these are the names of God [C'abawil], as they say" (Villacorta 1962, p. 20).

The multiple creations that follow the initial one are peculiarly indigenous. Consistent with this, an active role is played in them by the old couple Xmucane and Xpiyacok, who "create" by procreation and magical transformation. The story of a downpour of a resin that destroys the wooden people is also indigenous, though the subsequent sending of rains by Jurakan is probably a Christian addition. As Las Casas noted (see above), the authors of the *Popol Vuh* refer to the flood as *butic* ("heavy rain").

The *Popol Vuh* story of Wukub Cakix (Seven Parrot) and his family is primarily indigenous, though the initial setting is made to correspond with the biblical story of Lucifer. Like Lucifer, Wukub Cakix is proud and boastful, and his rebellious acts are said to have taken place at a time before the sun, moon, and stars appeared. The rest of the narrative is native.

The long, involved tales in which the lords from the earth descend to the underworld (Xibalba) and fight the lords and messengers of death and sickness are entirely indigenous. Since the Spanish priests had already drawn a parallel between Xibalba and hell, the authors of the *Popol Vuh* must have been aware of that connection. Yet nowhere in the tale is biblical syncretism evident, except for an episode involving Xquic', the daughter of one of the underworld lords. Xquic' is tempted to partake of the fruit of a tree upon which hangs the decapitated head of Junjunajpu, a lord from the earth. The language in this section was clearly made to conform to the biblical Garden of Eden story about the forbidden fruit: "No one is to partake of the fruit." "Why can I not see the tree, for in truth its fruit is good?" "I will not die if I take one." "Do you want it? Extend your hands over here." The subsequent "virgin" birth involving Xquic' might have been syncretized with the Christian story of the Virgin Mary, but the authors refrained from drawing the parallel. Xquic' conceives because of the spittle Junjunajpu places on her hand. The elaborate adventures of her twin sons, Junajpu and Xbalanque, appear to be totally devoid of Christian influence.

The last section of the *Popol Vuh*, beginning with the creation of the Quiché people, contains more syncretized Christian elements than any other part of the book. In that section also the Quiché chiefs syncretized native mythology with the history of their forefathers who came from the Gulf Coast to the highlands. The creation of the forefathers, Balam Quitze, Balam Ak'ab, Majucutaj, and Iq'ui Balam, is largely an indigenous account, for they are created out of maize. Nevertheless, biblical elements can be seen in the absolute power of Tz'akol Bitol, who creates men, and in the derivation of women from their sleeping husbands. Further, the coastal area from which the forefathers came (Panpaxil, Panc'ayala) is equated with the Garden of Eden as paradise. It is described as fruitful and beautiful and filled with delightful foods—cacao, mataxte, zapotes, jocotés, anonas, and nances.

The coastal area is also associated with Babylon of the Bible, though that is never directly stated. The area is repeatedly referred to as the "east" (*relibal k'ij*). It is the place where different peoples ("black and white peoples") lived and where the languages (*ch'abal*) were changed. When the authors state that in the east the forefathers did not worship stone or wood (*che, abaj*), they employ the same biblical language used to describe the precaptivity condition of the Israelites. Finally the forefathers cross a body of water somewhere in the Gulf Coast area, and that event is likened to the Israelites' crossing of the Red Sea. The Quichés cross on sand, with the aid of stones (See chapter 3 for my interpretation of the historical elements found in the Quiché origin story).

The content of the *Popol Vuh* demonstrates that by midcentury the Quichés had been able to preserve much of their old religion while achieving a "respectable" accommodation with Catholic Christianity. That was largely the work of the descendants of the Cawek rulers of Utatlán.

The major native chronicle prepared by Tamub chiefs, written in the 1560s, lacks the elaborate mythology found in the *Popol Vuh* (Recinos 1957, pp. 24ff.; Carmack 1975). Its only detectable syncretic Christian element consists of a statement that the Tamub forefathers came from "the east, across the sea, there at Babylon," and that they crossed the sea on rocks placed in the sand. Ilocab chiefs apparently wrote their own chronicles at this time, though only one short document from 1592 has come down to us (Carmack 1975). It contains a brief summary of biblical stories similar to those found in the *Título Totonicapán* and ends by claiming that the Ilocab forefathers were from the family (*ralc'wal*) of Jacob and Moisés who came from Tulan, "across the sea . . . at Babylon." Obviously the chiefs of Santa Cruz Utatán continued to be leaders in religious belief and tradition in the Quiché area, just as their fathers had been at the pre-Hispanic Utatlán.

The political and religious accommodation reached at midcentury by the natives of the Quiché area and Spanish officials and priests generally held through the remainder of the sixteenth century. At least, there is no evidence that any major changes took place. Toward the end of the century tensions began appearing, but for a time the problems were kept in check. One source of tension, for example, was the special privileges held by descendants of the Utatlán kings (Carmack 1973, pp. 388–89). In 1593, Spanish officials tried to collect tribute from members of the Cortés family. Juan Cortés petitioned their exemption, reminding the colonial judges that "the sons and grandsons of nobles are nobles, even though they may not be firstborn or chiefs." And in 1595 the *nimacachi* serfs subject to the Utatán chiefs disputed with their masters over the onerous obligations with which they were burdened. Some of the Spanish officials were sympathetic to their cause, one even arguing that such tributes were "vestiges of barbarous servitude." Nevertheless, the old rights were sustained after all of the documentation had been examined.

Another source of tension came from the town and ethnic territorial boundaries the Spaniards had imposed on the natives. For example, in 1592, the territorial rights of the palace serfs (especially the Socs, the barbers), who had been settled in an isolated area southwest of Utatlán, were contested by their neighbors. At about this time, too, certain descendants of the Caweks living in Chiquimula territory were having similar problems. Both disputes were temporarily settled through the authority and testimony of the Rojas and Cortés chiefs (Carmack 1973, pp. 363–68). Similarly, in 1601, when the Ilocabs of San Pedro Jocopilas crossed over into Chichuchu, which was claimed by the Tamubs of Chiquimula, the testimony of Juan de Rojas and other leaders from Santa Cruz "Otlatlán" won the case for the Tamubs.

THE COLONIAL AND EARLY-REPUBLICAN CENTURIES

By the end of the sixteenth century the Spaniards had implemented a colonial system that was to endure at least in part for the next two centuries. And even independence from Spain did not radically alter the social situation of the natives of the Quiché area. They continued to be subject to authorities above them, first Latin and creole officials of the new Republic of Central America and later those of Guatemala. Therefore, in describing below the fate of the Utatlán community after the century of conquest, I combine the Spanish colonial and early republican periods in a single discussion.

Sociopolitical Continuity and Change

Students of the Quichés have discovered with surprise that the special chiefly status held by the descendants of Utatlán rulers survived practically the entire colonial period (Contreras 1965; Carrasco 1967a). The Rojas and Cortés lines retained tribute rights over the *nimacachi* serfs, even when the crown systematically withdrew similar rights from Spaniards. Undoubtedly the fact that Santa Cruz chiefs were descendants of the Utatlán kings had much to do with this remarkable perpetuation of native privilege.

Our sources do not permit us to reconstruct the complete Rojas and Cortés lines. For the Cortés line we know only that Juan Cortés was succeeded by Joseph Cortés, who exercised rights during the first part of the seventeenth century (Tovilla 1960; Carmack 1973:368). The office of chief was passed down to successors during the rest of the seventeenth and into the middle of the eighteenth century. Death records from Santa Cruz (AEQ, 1757–90) reveal that a Juan Cortés was living in that town at midcentury; however, the tribute census of 1768 has no listing for a Cortés chief. In 1788, we are informed by elders of Santa Cruz, "there are no longer any descendants of the chief Don Juan Cortés in this town" (AGC, A1:202–4090). Down to the present day no natives named Cortés have lived in the municipality of Santa Cruz del Quiché.

Juan de Rojas, the sixteenth-century chief, was succeeded by another Juan Rojas around the turn of the century (Carmack 1973, pp. 364–65). There followed a line of Rojas chiefs during the seventeenth century, our sources finally referring to a Juan Rojas serving as "the privileged chief of this town" in the early part of the eighteenth century (AGC, A1:202–4090). This chief had two sons and two daughters, all of whom were exempt from paying tribute or providing services to the crown. The oldest son, Francisco, inherited the office of chief (AGC, A3:501–10,262). Though Francisco had two sons of his own (Francisco Cuzal and Sebastián Reynoso), the chiefly line passed through his sister Isabel Rojas to her son Juan Pérez Rojas. Perhaps the female link was used because Isabel had married into another chiefly line (Pérez), while Francisco's sons married commoners. At any rate, Juan Pérez Rojas became chief, and his older son, Juan Rojas, was in line to succeed him (AGC, A1:202–4090). Later, when Juan Pérez Rojas died (sometime before 1797), the tributary rights to the *nimacachi* serfs were eliminated, and Rojas was no longer an important name in the colonial records. As we shall see in chapter 11, the Rojas line has continued into modern times, but without privilege.

The Rojas and Cortés chiefs retained their special rights in the colonial era only with great effort. Spanish officials continually revoked those rights, forcing each generation of chiefs to appear before them to justify their preservation. Ximénez wrote that in the seventeenth century "the ministers took little care [in preserving these rights], because tyranny is what prevailed; so much so, that they even wanted to take away a portion of their slaves, and they (the native chiefs) contested it and won in a contradictory judgement against the King" (1929, pp. 79–80). At one point in the seventeenth century all privileges were withdrawn from the Santa Cruz chiefs, and they were commanded "to pay tribute and provide labor [*tequios*] like the most common of people." Around midcentury one of the Rojas chiefs patiently waited until the official who had revoked his privileges was replaced and then took his papers to the new official at Sololá. Ximénez (1929, p. 80) relates that the official put the papers under his bed and forgot about them. Each night when he retired, he could not sleep for noises he kept hearing under his bed. In this miraculous fashion he discovered the papers, acted to restore the rights to the Santa Cruz chiefs, and was again able to sleep in peace.

Spanish harassment of the Santa Cruz chiefs intensified in the eighteenth century. In 1721 the crown decreed the termination of *encomienda* rights, to be revoked as each holder died. Juan Rojas was forced to obtain a special royal provision in 1730 to retain his *nimacachi* serfs. In 1762, Spanish officials began counting the *nimacachis* as crown tributaries, though in 1768 the Rojas family again won the right to their tributes. The year 1773 found the Rojas chief in Santiago de Guatemala, litigating with the old papers. An earthquake struck the city, and half the papers were lost to the dust and water that accompanied the collapse of crown buildings. Other papers were stolen, and, strangely, those that were recovered were found in the house of the *coheteros* ("firecracker makers").

Finally, in 1774, Spanish officials again stopped tribute payment by the *nimacachi* families, now numbering only twenty. The officials complained that "it was not reasonable that some Indians should pay tribute to others . . . or that the Indian chiefs should be better off than the Spaniards from whom their slaves had been taken" (AGC, *A*1:202–4090). Juan Pérez Rojas petitioned for the ancient rights that had come through his family and called for witnesses from Santa Cruz to prove that he was the legitimate heir to "the privilege of [having] tributaries." But the colony had changed too much to allow the old *encomienda* privileges of the Santa Cruz chiefs to continue, and in 1801 the royal court took them away once and for all (Contreras 1965, pp. 40–41).

Other chiefs in the Quiché area also eventually lost their limited privileges, such as freedom from tribute payments and work obligations. Some of them retained special chiefly status throughout much of the seventeenth century (AGC, *A*1:1559–10,203), though by the middle of the eighteenth century only the Rojas chiefs of Santa Cruz and the Carlos chiefs of Chichicastenango were still recognized as chiefs by the crown. The Carlos chiefs (AGC, *A*3:2831–41,163) had intermarried with Spaniards, introducing a mestizo element into Chichicastenango.

The authority and power of Quiché chiefs during the colonial period was greatly reduced in all aspects of social life. Local Spanish priests and officials usurped the roles the Quiché chiefs had played during the sixteenth century. Ximénez (1929, p. 104) tells us that the natives took their disputes before

Spanish officials rather than their chiefs, even though those officials "processed them for long periods of time, taking their money and leaving them to die in jail." We shall see too how the Spaniards intervened in territorial matters, a practice that was copied and intensified by republican officials after independence. In addition to crown officials, *encomenderos* interceded in the affairs of the natives. Santa Cruz paid tribute to and was governed solely by crown officials, but all the other Quiché towns were at least partly subject to *encomiendas*. Chichicastenango had the misfortune of being subdivided into five or six *encomiendas* (AGC, A1:5794–48,802). By the end of the eighteenth century *encomienda* rights had been terminated, though creole ranchers and departmental officials in the republican period continued to function much like the *encomenderos*.

The Dominican priests had dominant leadership roles among the natives to an even greater extent. They were held in highest esteem, and considerable wealth was turned over to them for their support and for the adornment of the churches. This exaggerated respect for the priests persisted after independence. The natives continued the colonial practice of piling maize, chickens, eggs, and firewood in the convent for the priests (Scherzer 1967, p. 30, note 1). Stephens was told by the priest at Santa Cruz that the natives there held the priests "almost as saints" (1841, p. 187).

At the same time the authority and respect of native chiefs was being usurped by Spanish (and republican) officials, within the indigenous communities more egalitarian social forms were replacing the aristocratic structure of the past. Ximénez, who observed the system firsthand as it functioned at Chichicastenango about 1700, described the native government as follows:

Although [the Indians] have Alcaldes and Governors in many places, [named] by your Majesty, when they have a complaint against anyone who has been delinquent, they call for the heads of the *chinamitales*. In front of them they continue the trial against the culprit, all verbally. When the decision is made, they proceed to the execution of the punishment, without written records or legal documents. . . . Nor are the *alcaldes* absolute in other matters and works for which the people of the towns come together. Rather, they call for the elders [*principales*], who together confer on the matter, and they are not so rustic that they do not know what is convenient for them. Once the decision is reached, they determine the necessary means for carrying it out, and what task is to be given to each person in town. Each *calpul* head takes what is his obligation [*cargo*], giving to the first person his task, and the same to the alcaldes. Thus, everyone is measured equally, unless there are some who are very poor, and they take this into account. . . . The offices of alcalde and all the others, down to the lowest, go by turns to all the *calpules*, loading everyone equally with honor or work, excusing no one. Before the new year, all these heads along with their officials meet together, naming all [the replacements] so that no one is overburdened. They even assign those who are to carry water and firewood for the public table and those who sweep the plaza. It is done with such order and unanimity that it is marvelous [to see]. One *calpul* is not assigned more than its share, because its leader is there to defend it. [Ximénez 1929,pp. 104–105; my translation]

This penetrating account reveals that the authority of the individual chiefs had been largely replaced by a collective authority. The chiefs had originally served as the alcaldes and governors, but that practice was discontinued as men from commoner families attained those offices. Even more important, these officials no longer exercised primary authority. That resided with the elders and lineage and canton (*chinamital, calpul*) heads. Authority had become both an honor and an obligation, and it was to be shared by everyone in turn. Implicit in this rotating system of authority was a hierarchy of tasks, a ladder to be climbed by men in the community. Starting with such menial tasks as gathering firewood, it led to the highest political and religious offices in the community [alcalde, *cofradia* heads] and above those to the decision-making status of elder [*principal*].

The canton heads may have constituted a remnant of the old aristocracy during the colonial period, at least in the case of descendants of chiefly lineages. Ximénez (1967, pp. 8, 9) said that they were "the heads of their *calpules* and clans [*parcialidades*]" and that "there scarcely was an Indian among them who did not obey the head of the *calpul* in the task given him; and if there were such a case, everyone would turn against him to see that he was punished." In contrast with the past, however, these leaders now shared authority with the elders and chosen officials, the alcaldes and others, and were dependent on the collective will for their decisions. Furthermore, leaders from commoner lineages seem to have had nearly equal authority with those from the chiefly lineages.

It is clear that by the middle of the colonial era the Quichés had developed a civil-religious hierarchy similar to the organizations found in modern times by anthropologists (see chapter 11; see also Nash 1958; Tax and Hinshaw 1969). It signaled the replacement of the native aristocracy with a more egalitarian and collective form of leadership, as surely as did the elimination of the chiefly rights. The descendants of Utatlán could no longer support the luxury of a native aristocracy, dividing their limited resources and political power. The civil-religious hierarchy leveled their differences in wealth and permitted the natives of each community to present a common front to their colonial exploiters.

The egalitarian structure described by Ximénez further suggests that the Quichés had become thoroughly peasantized. The population was dispersed widely over the land, "rarely forming towns; rather [the people lived] in hamlets [*parajes*], where the land was good, generally in low places and canyons; there the family or clan [*chinamital*] lived, not together, but each one in his milpa" (Ximénez 1967, p. 12). As shown in Bishop Cortés y Larraz's

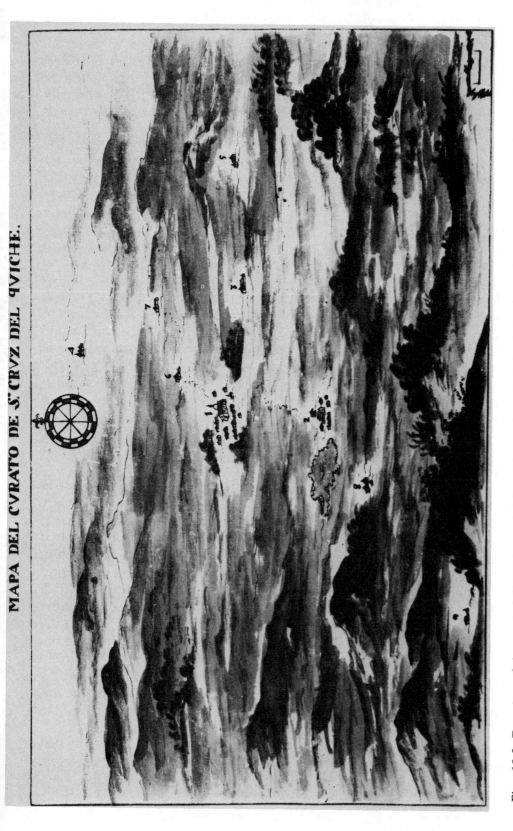

MAPA DEL CVRATO DE S.ᵗ CRVZ DEL QVICHE.

Fig. 10.3. Drawing of the central Quiché area in the eighteenth century by P. Cortés y Larraz. From Archivo General de Indias. (1) Santa Cruz, (2) Lemoa, (3) Chiché, (4) Chinique.

drawings from about 1770, the town centers consisted of only the church, a municipal building, and a few houses (Fig. 10.3; Cortés y Larraz 1958). Santa Cruz, the largest town of the area, had a population of fewer than five hundred late in the eighteenth century. The settlements were rural, and visitors to the Quiché area in the seventeenth, eighteenth, and nineteenth centuries reported that its economy was almost exclusively agricultural. The natives grew maize, wheat, and beans in large quantities, supplying food for the Spanish haciendas and towns—as late as 1830 Antigua Guatemala was receiving food from Quiché. Some of the native communities that were unable to produce sufficient food, such as Momostenango, received maize from Quiché (AMQ 1831).

Cattle and sheep raising was an important economic activity in the area too, but all large-scale husbandry was in the hands of the Spaniards and mestizos (and later the Latins). The Quiché peasants provided food to such cattle haciendas as Chinic' and Patzite. The haciendas gave little in return to the peasants, and their cattle often broke into the natives' fields. The haciendas also had the reputation of being havens for mestizo thieves, who carried off the few sheep the native peasants owned. The Chiquimultecos were somewhat unusual in the Quiché area, for they were said to have many sheep and to be wealthier than other peasants in the area. This probably accounts in part for the favored treatment they so often received from Spanish and republican officials—they had funds to pay special rents and tributes (AGC, *A*1:6052–53,491). The natives from Ilotenango also raised sheep (Falla 1975), though apparently not as many as the Chiquimultecos raised.

It is a remarkable fact that few native craftsmen or merchants were able to survive within colonial society in Quiché. One early-seventeenth-century official stated that the inhabitants of Chichicastenango were "all rich Indians, half-merchants and great workers—I will say *par excellence*, for they have more than 3,000 mules for their work" (Tovilla 1960, p. 223). He went on to say that they traded bread and cloth for coastal cacao and cotton. Later visitors to the town mentioned only its agricultural production, which suggests that trading was curtailed as the colonial economy was more fully implanted. Chiquimultecos also became involved in trade, but their long struggles with other Quiché communities over lands (see below) indicate that agriculture was the dominant economic activity among them as well. Pottery making and selling are mentioned for San Pedro Jocopilas (Cortés y Larraz 1958, 1:52), but it was clearly secondary to the production of "maize and beans." By 1740 (Anonymous 1935, pp. 27–28) the few "artisans" said to reside in Santa Cruz were all mestizos.

Census data from the end of the nineteenth century show that even by that late date the inhabitants of the Quiché area were overwhelmingly peasants.

Of a population of more than 50,000 people, only about 400 were classified as craftsmen and some 300 as merchants. Many of these were probably Latins, and the natives most likely were also part-time farmers. For example, in the late nineteenth century 60 percent of the peasant farmers of Ilotenango were part-time wool spinners (Falla 1972, p. 445). The elimination of economic specialists and the creation of a universal peasant condition among the descendants of the Utatlán community had a devastating effect on the old native social structures, especially the elite authority system. It also helped transform ties to the land and religious beliefs, as we shall see below.

Territorial Continuity and Change

Falla (1971) has argued that native communities of the Department of Totonicapán recovered from the population losses of the Conquest period more quickly than the Quiché communities in the Department of Sololá. Conflicts over land arose, especially between Chiquimula (Totonicapán) and San Antonio Ilotenango (Sololá), as natives from the former community sought territory into which their population overflow could expand. And, as we shall see, the situation was more complicated than that, for territorial conflicts similar to those between Chiquimula and Ilotenango flared up *within* the Quiché area as well. Furthermore, the demographic "recovery" of the Totonicapán communities was probably more rapid because they lost fewer inhabitants than the Quiché towns did (cf. Veblen 1975). As shown above, Quiché was heavily depleted of its indigenous population through slave raids and out-migrations, as well as losses from Spanish diseases.

While demographic changes certainly must have influenced the territorial disputes in the Quiché area (to be described below), it should also be emphasized that historically based claims provided the spark that made these land disputes so emotional. Many of the claims extended all the way back to pre-Hispanic Utatlán, and that is the aspect of the territorial changes that will be emphasized. Each alteration of old boundaries and territorial rights represented an agonizing step in the dismantling of the original Utatlán community.

The territorial arrangements laid down during the sixteenth century remained relatively unchanged during the seventeenth century. At the beginning of the century adjustments were made in the boundaries of some of the more controversial and sensitive territories, especially those that had belonged to the Tamubs before the Conquest. Thus Chichuchu, a wedge of territory that the Tamubs had driven between Ilocab lands, was infiltrated by the natives of San Pedro Jocopilas (Ilocab) in 1601. The Chiquimultecos, as post-Hispanic heirs of the Tamubs, protested the intrusion and gained the support of native leaders from Santa Cruz. In the settlement that followed, Santa Cruz acquired jurisdiction over the lands. The natives of San Pedro were permitted to use the lands, but they were required to pay rent to the Utatecos (AGC, *A*1:5939–51,962; 6019–53,061). In that same year, 1601, the territory of Santa Elena Tamub, situated in the area of present-day Patzite, was claimed for the jurisdiction of Santa Cruz rather than Chiquimula (AGC, *A*1:6021–53,078). Also in that year boundaries between Chiquimula and Ilotenango (Pailocab) were restudied by crown officials (AGC, *A*1:1,574– 10,218), and as a result the Tamubs of Chiquimula gained some land at the expense of the Ilocabs.

A few land disputes arose in the second half of the seventeenth century— for example, Santa Cruz had to defend its rights to Chinic' against a claim by the Cabracanos of Chichicastenango—and in general, old territorial lines held. There must have been only negligible pressure for land at that time; the total population during the century apparently dropped to fewer than 5,000 persons in the Quiché area (Santa Cruz Utatán, San Pedro Jocopilas, San Antonio Ilotenango, Santo Tomás Chichicastenango, and Santa María Chiquimula). The three major pre-Hispanic groups were approximately equal in numbers at that time: about 1,000 Quichés, 800 Ilocabs, and 1,000 Tamubs. The Quichés of Chichicastenango were a fourth territorial and demographic unit, with about 1,500 inhabitants. Thus the three major political groups of the pre-Hispanic Utatlán community continued to control large territories of land. The Quichés had lost the entire Chichicastenango area, but they still held land all the way east to Chinic', and they gained former Tamub lands on the west. The Ilocabs controlled the extensive lands of both San Pedro and San Antonio, including some Tamub lands in the former. The Tamubs lost lands to both the Quichés and the Ilocabs and controlled only the relatively poor lands of Chiquimula. Still they were able to expand their holdings a bit at the expense of the Ilocabs of San Antonio.

Our demographic data indicate that the population of Quiché continued to drop during the first half of the eighteenth century. By 1770, however, the native population had begun to grow rapidly; by 1800 it was triple the seventh-century levels, and there were about 13,000 native inhabitants in all. The population of the area was then divided rather unevenly among the four groups: about 3,000 Quichés, 3,000 Chichicastecos, 1,000 Ilocabs of San Pedro and San Antonio, and 6,000 Tamubs (Chiquimultecos). As we shall see, the prodigious growth of population at Chiquimula and the relatively slow growth at San Pedro Jocopilas and San Antonio Ilotenango created pressures to change the traditionally based boundaries.

The growth of native populations, associated with the loss of *encomienda* rights during the first half of the eighteenth century, led to large-scale Spanish encroachment into native lands. Lands long left unoccupied by the natives were acquired and converted into cattle and farming ranches (haciendas). Santa Cruz lost all of its eastern lands in this fashion. By the eighteenth century the Dominicans already owned the Chiché territory, where they ran a hacienda called San Juan Bauptista Chiché. In 1717, Captain Juan de la Zavala was allowed to purchase the rest of the eastern territory of Santa Cruz, including the Chujuyup and Chinic' areas (AGC, A1, 6019–53,061). A Spanish official rationalized the sale with the statement that the natives "have large territories of land which they do not work." Later, in 1755, that huge territory was purchased by the Dominicans, who added it to their Chiché hacienda. Chinic' became a cattle ranch, and Chujuyup a huge maize farm.

The Spaniards acquired other haciendas in Santa Cruz territory: the Urisars had a hacienda near Chitatul north of Lemoa (AML 1752), and the Dominicans ran small haciendas in the Chichuchu and Santa Elena areas (AMP, 1833). By 1750 the community of Santa Elena Tamub had become so disorganized that it was abandoned. Its lands were measured and were purchased by a wealthy Indian who gave them to the Dominicans. The Dominicans converted the territory into a vast cattle hacienda known as Patzite (AMQ 1831). In all, Santa Cruz may have lost half its best lands to the Spaniards during that crucial period. Traditional native social relations must have also been severely interrupted at this time by the labor practices of the haciendas.

Spanish haciendas were not established in the other Quiché towns, whose lands were not suitable for either cattle raising or large-scale agriculture. Around midcentury only about sixteen families of *ladinos* lived in the Quiché area, all of them in Santa Cruz territory (Cortés y Larraz 1958, 1:301). One hacienda was owned by natives of San Pedro, who purchased the land on the plains of Comitancillo in the eighteenth century. They converted the territory into a cattle ranch called Santa María, dedicated to the *cofradía* of Our Lady of the Rosary. Later a Spaniard named Argüeta entered the territory and grazed his cattle there. He attempted to purchase the land, apparently without success (AGEG, Sololá, 1820). In this exceptional case natives in the Quiché area gained lands beyond what they had held before the Conquest.

Pressures for land were strong by the middle of the eighteenth century, especially in Chiquimula. A chronic dispute over the boundary between Chiquimula and Ilotenango had developed from land gained early in the century by Chiquimultecos at the expense of the Ilotecos. Both sides illegally removed boundary markers, and fighting erupted from time to time (Falla 1971). Apparently a vague boundary line between the pre-Hispanic Ilocab territory and Tamub *calpul* of Tz'oloche (Chiquimula) provided the Chiquimultecos with a point of entry into these San Antonio lands.

Another dispute arose over the territory around Patzité and Chituj, which was under the jurisdiction of Santa Cruz. Chiquimultecos had been given permission to settle there, in return for which they paid "rent" to the

Quichés in the form of maize, sheep, eggs, chickens, and personal services. Ilotecos also moved into a northern section of this territory, planting and grazing sheep there. In 1770 they claimed the land as their own and, like the Quichés, began renting part of it to Chiquimultecos (AGC, A1:6021–53,078). The Chiquimultecos soon agitated for ownership of the lands, since they constituted the vast majority of its inhabitants. By the turn of the century a three-way fight for the territory was in full swing (AGC, A1:1801–24,615). The dispute was partly the result of the complex territorial rights that had existed there in pre-Hispanic times: the lands had originally belonged to the Ilocabs; later they became part of the Tamub territories; and finally the ruling Quichés claimed the now-isolated lands as a place to settle their serfs.

The land-seeking Chiquimultecos also settled in the vicinity of present-day Santa Lucía la Reforma, at that time under the jurisdiction of San Pedro Jocopilas. The lands had once been part of Tamub territory, so it was logical that the Chiquimultecos, as Tamub heirs, should seek additional lands there. They paid rent to the San Pedro natives in money, roofing tiles, and personal services. Conflict arose when the Chiquimultecos began infiltrating lands beyond and agitating for jurisdiction over the area (Falla 1971; AGEC, Totonicapán, 1895). Around 1790, Chiquimultecos gained control of an area south of Santa Lucía called Sica. Sica had previously been the link between the Ilocabs of San Pedro and those of San Antonio (Fig. 10.4), and this encroachment aroused the Ilocabs against the Chiquimultecos.

The turbulent events of the independence movement in Guatemala during the first quarter of the nineteenth century opened the door to major changes in the territorial arrangements of the Quiché area. Spanish authority had been severely weakened a decade before independence was actually won in 1821, and raw power dominated political relations in the area for a while. Even after the republican government was established, its officials necessarily bent to the forces that had been unleashed in the years leading up to independence. As we shall see, some of the territorial boundaries based on traditional claims were pushed aside.

Contreras (1951) has shown that the natives of Totonicapán took advantage of the confusion associated with independence to rebel against local Spanish rule. Under the leadership of Atanasio Tzul they established in 1820 a nativistic Quiché "kingdom," though it lasted only twenty-nine days. The Chiquimultecos, who had revolted against tribute payments in 1818, joined that movement, refusing to pay tribute to local Spanish officials and sending soldiers to fight with Tzul (Martínez 1973, p. 15). Their action is understandable in view of their desire for more lands and the restraints on expansion the Spanish officials had imposed.

The Quiché communities did not join the Tzul movement. As Falla (1971) pointed out, Santa Cruz, San Antonio, and San Pedro were in sharp conflict

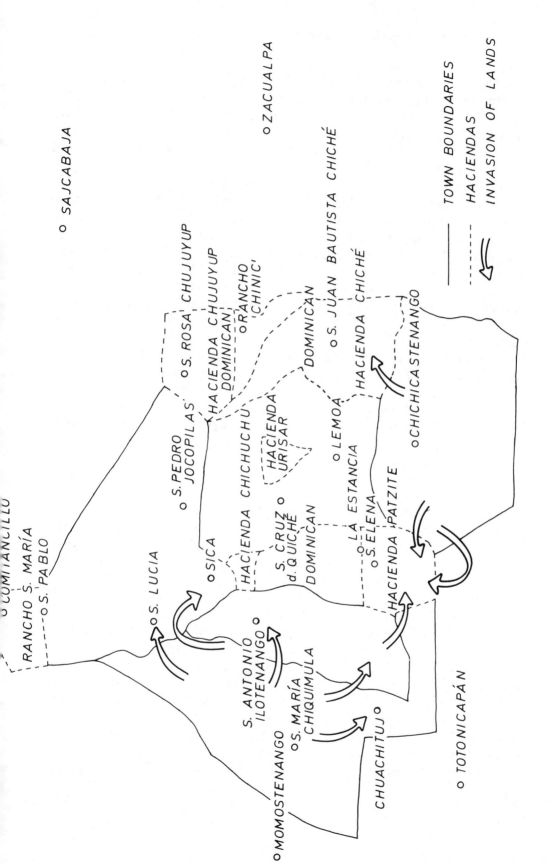

Fig. 10.4. Map of Utatlán towns, ca. 1800. Based on colonial maps in AGEG.

with Chiquimula over territorial rights, and this blocked any alliance that might have been formed between the Totonicapán and Quiché natives. Falla documents a hapless seven-year attempt by the Ilotecos to obtain rents from Chiquimultecos for use of their lands. The Spanish officials were too preoccupied with native revolts to minister to their needs, while the Ilotecos were too concerned with preserving their lands against Chiquimultec incursions to participate in the revolts.

That was not the case with the more powerful Quichés and Chichicastecos. A nativistic movement similar to Tzul's emerged in Quiché, as the natives took advantage of weakened Spanish authority to revolt. In 1811, Chichicastenango, whose population like Chiquimula's was increasing at an alarming rate, seized the opportunity to invade and regain control over the Chiché lands held by the Dominicans (AGC, *A*1:6052–53,491). They used arms to defend their claim against Spanish officials. Led by two local leaders named Sucuqui and Tebalam, both from commoner lineages, the Chichicastecos defied Spanish authority. They obtained guns and vowed that they would kill the priest or alcalde mayor if either tried to remove them from the land. The Chichicastecos are reported to have threatened "a bloody fight here if you do not leave at once." One reason for their anger was the Dominicans' attempt to rent the Chiché lands to Chiquimultecos. The lands had belonged to Chichicastenango until the Dominicans obtained them, and that growing town was not disposed to see them turned over to the Tamub-derived Chiquimultecos.

In 1813 the Chichicastecos again took up arms against Spanish officials, this time to prevent them from turning over Mactzul lands to the Totonicapán natives of Chimenté (Contreras 1951, pp. 29ff.). Originally these lands had belonged to the Tamub town Santa Elena.

The natives of Santa Cruz were equally rebellious against the Spanish masters around the time of independence. We are informed that "a few years before the expulsion [of the Dominican priests] the natives of Quiché began to lose respect for them; they took possession of the Chujuyup mountain, where they cut down the forest and covered it with maize and wheat" (AMQ, 1831). This act against the church may have been partly brought on by church prohibitions against native rituals on sacred mountains at Chujuyup imposed shortly after independence (De León n.d., p. 150). As early as 1812, however, Luis Reyes, "risking all the dangers and receiving the hate of those religious leaders," invaded Chujuyup lands. Other natives quickly followed his example, and the land transfer soon became a *fait accompli*. It is important to remember that Chujuyup was the original homeland of the Quiché forefathers, and its restoration to native hands was thus of symbolic as well as economic significance.

The natives of Quiché also opposed the reinstitution of tribute payments, the same issue that sparked the Tzul revolt in Totonicapán. A leader emerged who united the natives of the several old Utatlán towns—Quiché, Lemoa, San Pedro, and San Antonio. His name was Mariano Aguilar, but he became known as "Casaca." In 1818, Casaca told the natives not to pay tribute, and he traveled to Guatemala to demand exemptions for them. The cry went up to do away with the Spanish *alcalde mayor* and put an "Indian" in his place. As in Totonicapán, the Quiché movement took on a nativistic character, though we lack details on the specific events of the movement or its outcome (AGC, *A3*:2844–49,416). As in native revolts elsewhere in the highlands, the real issue was "independence" from local Spanish exploitation rather than from the Spanish crown.

The major territorial changes and the worst violence were still to come. In 1827 the new republic initiated an "agrarian reform," designed to take lands away from those communities with surplus and give to those who needed them. This policy greatly intensified the power struggle that had begun during the independence period and brought further changes in the native communities. As might be expected, the Chiquimultecos were the main beneficiaries of the land-reform policy, while the relatively less populous towns, San Pedro and San Antonio, were the main losers.

General C. Rivas, an official of the state, remeasured all the Quiché lands (AGEG, Quiché, 1830). A huge imbalance was detected between Chiquimula's large population (said to be 15,000 persons) and small territory as compared with the small populations and large territories of San Antonio and San Pedro (said to have 487 and 1,998 inhabitants, respectively). By government decree the Chituj lands of San Antonio and the Santa Lucía lands of San Pedro, already occupied for several years by Chiquimultecos, became Chiquimula lands. The decree was a violation of rights that had existed for perhaps two hundred years, and both towns refused to accept it. In resisting government authority they were joined by the Quichés of Santa Cruz. Rivas led the Chiquimultecos *en masse* to the town hall (*cabildo*) at San Pedro to force acceptance of the new territorial arrangement (Falla 1971). The Chiquimultecos also invaded the town square at San Antonio, where they killed or injured six Ilotecos (AGEG, Quiché, 1830). In this fashion the natives of San Pedro and San Antonio were bludgeoned into submission to the new "social reality." The priest of San Antonio informs us that Rivas became virtually "king" of the Chiquimultecos.

The conflict over the transfer of land from San Pedro and San Antonio to Chiquimula continued to smoulder and periodically flare up during subsequent years. The situation was exacerbated by further incursions of Chiquimultecos into the territory of these two towns—as into Chacalté and Sacxac in San Antonio and Sica in San Pedro. At times the conflict broke into open combat, as in 1851, when Chiquimultecos and Ilotecos fought each

333

other with knives, slings, and stones. Falla (1971) says that on that occasion San Antonio succeeded in pushing out many of the Chiquimultecos who had infiltrated their lands after the Rivas "reform." According to oral tradition the men of San Pedro also fought the Chiquimultecos over Sica, successfully defending their rights to that territory. Later, in 1880, they sold the Sica lands to San Antonio (AGEG, Totonicapán, 1895).

At first it appeared that the agrarian reform would benefit Santa Cruz. The Dominicans were forced out, and in 1825 the town moved to recover the lands of Patzité and Chujuyup. But the Chiquimultecos living in Patzité refused to pay rent, appealing to General Rivas for support. Once again Rivas backed the Chiquimultecos, and jurisdiction of the territory was turned over to Chiquimula. The Quichés rose up in arms and, led by a native chief named K'alel, fought the Chiquimultecos in open war. The major battle took place in about 1830 on the plains of La Estancia at Xolch'oj (Where The Battle [was]). This place became the boundary between Patzité and Quiché, which meant that most of La Estancia and all of Panajxit were retained as Quiché lands as a result of the fighting (AMP, 1833).

In the 1830s attempts were also made by Latins to take the Chujuyup lands from Santa Cruz. The Latin *jefe político* of the new Department of Quiché, aided by priests, petitioned the government to add the Chujuyup lands to the Chinique hacienda. That was contrary to the agrarian reform, and the request was denied (AMQ, 1831). During subsequent years Latins kept pressing to regain the Chujuyup lands and finally succeeded in part (see below).

In summary, dramatic changes in territorial boundaries were made during the years following independence. Because of land decisions favoring the needy Chiquimultecos, Chiquimula, a town of the Department of Totonicapán, was given control over territories in the southern (Chituj, Patzité) and northern (Santa Lucía) zones of the Department of Quiché. A study of the *ejido* measurements made between 1831 and 1835 (AGEG) reveals that to a surprising degree the territorial divisions of the pre-Hispanic groups had been restored and balanced. Chiquimula, the administrative heir of the Tamubs, finally had sufficient lands. Significantly, the new Chiquimula territories, Chituj, Patzite, and Santa Lucía, had all been Tamub lands at one time. Thus the Chiquimultecos restored the old Tamub hegemony without ever mentioning it or perhaps even being aware that they were doing so. The Quichés regained jurisdiction over most of their major pre-Conquest holdings, except for the Chichicastenango territory, which had long been independent. These two towns sometimes joined together against outsiders, whether Spaniards, Latins, or native peoples from other towns. Their lands together were greater than the territory controlled by the pre-Hispanic Nima Quichés in the central area. The descendants of the Ilocabs retained most of their old territory, divided between San Antonio and San Pedro. The other Ilocab lands lost as part of the agrarian reform had been acquired by the Ilocabs from the Tamubs shortly after the Conquest.

While the territorial continuities from the old Utatlán community cannot be mere coincidence, neither were they the result of some hidden native plan; as we have seen, the Quiché "kings" had lost their economic and social power. Rather, the descendants of the old pre-Hispanic groups continued to occupy roughly similar ecological zones and therefore had similar territorial requisites. But ancient ties to the land were not forgotten either, so that wherever possible they were retained or, when lost, were later restored.

The population of the Quiché area increased about fivefold during the nineteenth century. According to the national census of 1893 it had over 50,000 inhabitants. Almost 20,000 of them lived in former Quiché territories, 16,000 lived in Chichicastenango, 12,000 lived in Tamub territory (Chiquimula), and about 5,000 resided in former Ilocab territory (San Pedro and San Antonio). After the 1830s population expansion generally occurred within territorial boundaries established soon after independence, and disputes were infrequent and relatively nonviolent.

The reforms of Justo Rufino Barrios in the 1870s again brought land changes. Chinique and Chiché were made independent of Santa Cruz, and Patzité became separate from Chiquimula. In the case of Chinique at least, independence was probably granted as a reward to Latins who had helped Barrios gain national power. Barrios expropriated other lands in the Quiché area and allocated them to his militiamen. Chujuyup in Santa Cruz and Sica in San Pedro were among the lands that changed hands during the Barrios period (AGEG, Totonicapán, 1895). Santa Cruz militiamen, perhaps confident of support from the Guatemalan capital, fought for lands against the natives of Canton Lemoa, and Lemoa apparently separated from Santa Cruz as an independent town because of the fighting (De León n.d., p. 139).

By the beginning of the twentieth century, then, the lands of pre-Hispanic Utatlán had been subdivided into nine towns: Santa Cruz del Quiché, San Sebastián Lemoa, Chichicastenango, San Pedro Jocopilas, San Antonio Ilotenango, Patzité, Chinique, Chiché, and Santa María Chiquimula. A little later Santa Lucía la Reforma was also established as a separate town. Despite the incredible persistence of old territorial divisions described above, the resemblances between Quiché territory in 1900 and what it had been in 1524 were becoming remote.

Religious Beliefs and Practices

The scanty information available on native religion during the colonial and early republican periods indicates that it was thoroughly "Christo-pagan"—Catholic in outward form but Quiché in basic structure. It had become more particularistic too, adapted to the family, clan, canton, and community divisions of the peasantry. The elaborate historical and doctrinal syncretism worked out by the native chiefs in the sixteenth century was no longer consulted or understood. "Theology" had been replaced by more populist ritual forms—dances, saint worship, and curing ceremonies. The folk religion that survived the period was different in detail and organization from the sacerdotal religion of pre-Hispanic Utatlán, though much of its fundamental symbolism remained the same.

The church became thoroughly entrenched in the Quiché communities during the colonial period. The Dominicans who administered them, subject to the convent of Sacapulas in the early years (Remesal 1932, 1:487), established new headquarters at Santa Cruz during the seventeenth century. The ecclesiastical district had four priests at midcentury (AGC, *A*3: 825–1507), but that number had doubled by 1700 (Ximénez 1931, p. 412). Eight priests were stationed at Santa Cruz alone in 1770, even though they were "not always there" (Cortés y Larraz 1958, 1:58). Around the middle of the seventeenth century construction was begun on a convent at Santa Cruz under the direction of Fray Francisco de Guerra. We are told that "he made it out of the stones of the palaces of the kings of that land, the ruins of which may still be seen" (Molina 1943, p. 113). That the natives would permit their ancient town to be dismantled in this fashion and would personally carry the stones to build a Christian convent shows the extent to which the Dominican priests had replaced the native chiefs and priests as religious leaders. A visitor to the convent in the nineteenth century described it as made of stone, with "massive walls, and corridors, pavements, and courtyard strong enough for a fortress" (Stephens 1841, p. 170).

The church was well established economically. It has already been noted that the Dominicans maintained several haciendas in the area. Ximénez (1967, p. 8) lamented that in his day (about 1700) the priests were more interested in founding haciendas than preaching to the natives. He also informs us that the natives were generous in their donations to the church, so generous, in fact, that the impressive cathedrals in the towns were more lavishly adorned with statuary than those in Spanish towns. Payments also came to the church from the sacraments and from a certain percentage of tribute paid by each town (AGC, *A*1:5794–48,802). In 1770 over eight hundred pesos were collected a year from these payments at Santa Cruz, and another five hundred pesos from San Pedro and San Antonio (Cortés y Larraz 1958, 1:51, 56).

The Dominican priests considered their work to be primarily administering the sacraments rather than converting the natives—who were all baptized members anyway. It was a notable occurrence when in 1664 an aged, unbaptized native woman was found living between Chichicastenango and

Lemoa (Molina 1943, p. 115). The woman's father had hidden her in a milpa field when the priests first came to the area. She was baptized forthwith— and died shortly thereafter. It was also unusual for the priests to speak Quiché or to use a catechism written in that language. Ximénez (1967, p. 7) complained that the priests preached and taught in Spanish, though in the few instances where the natives were taught to read Quiché they greatly benefited from it. The truth was, there were few catechisms in Quiché, and in no town did the priests teach the natives to read either Spanish or Quiché (Cortés y Larraz 1958, 1:55–64).

As might be expected under these circumstances, the natives took on the external features of Christianity, but their basic values and beliefs continued to be those of their ancestors. Thoughtful priests living among them soon came to recognize this. In 1700, Ximénez (1929; 1967, p. 6) observed that the natives of Chichicastenango taught the traditional beliefs to their children "like the milk with which they are nursed." He mused that, with respect to the Catholic faith, "they are in the same errors and blunders, and even though it appears that it is no more than a flicker [of incredulity], it is actually a great fire." Seventy years later, in the same town, another Dominican priest was so disturbed by the unconverted condition of the natives that he lost his own faith in the church. He came to doubt that the Indians were really "sons of the Church" and found it impossible to administer the sacraments to them (Cortés y Larraz 1958, 1:60–64). Seventy years after that the Dominican priest of Santa Cruz admitted that the Indians "in their hearts were still full of superstitions and still idolaters. . . . [But he] was compelled to wink at this" (Stephens 1841, p. 191).

The same priests reported that the natives had both altered public Catholic rituals to conform to the old religion and in secrecy continued to practice ancient rites in a purer form. Some of the native practices they detected and recorded were as follows: the old grandmother and grandfather deities (Xmucane, Xpiyacok) were revered as the guardians of milpa (Ximénez n.d.); men called *naguals* were said to be able to transform themselves into animals which, if injured, brought injury to these men in their human forms (Ximénez 1929:75); the mountains were believed to be alive and capable of enclosing men inside them (AESP, 1757–90); stone idols were worshiped in canyons and on mountaintops (Stephens 1841, p. 191); astrologic observations were made at mountain shrines (De León n.d., p. 150); at the birth of children diviners were consulted to determine their fates; the same diviners forbade parents to let the house fires go out (to prevent newborns from becoming arsonists later on), or to take the infants out of the houses (so that later they would not become transients) (Ximénez 1967, p. 10); the 260-day sacred calendar was used for all manner of divinations and was articulated with the 365-day calendar (Ximénez 1929, pp. 101–102); the sweathouse was used as a curing place by shamans (Cortés y Larraz 1958, p. 62); and tools, jars, grinding stones, and other useful implements were buried with the dead, and the living were painted yellow to indicate the survivors' mourning (Ximénez 1967, p. 35). This short list suggests that ancient belief and ritual were associated with every aspect of native life and that within the confines of the family, clan, canton, and even community they constituted the essence of the Quiché peasants' religion.

The priests who were aware of the clandestine practices mentioned above considered them to be part of a religion separate from the church. For the natives, however, the two formed a single system of belief and ritual. The saints either were assimilated with the native deities or were added to the pantheon. They were to be worshiped like the stone idols in the hills and canyons through procession, music, dance, and offering (of copal, flowers, liquor, and so on). The *cofradías*, originally set up by the Catholic priests as voluntary organizations for celebrating rituals devoted to the saints, were assimilated with traditional Quiché social forms. Ritual for the saints became the right of particular cantons and clans, and membership in the *cofradías* was assigned accordingly by the elders and canton heads.

To a large extent, then, the natives of Quiché used the colonial Catholic church for their own purposes. Most of the priests disliked this, but there was little they could do about it, as was dramatically illustrated for the archbishop during his visit to Chichicastenango late in the eighteenth century (Cortés y Larraz 1958, 1:63). Upon discovering a girl whose parents had married her off when she was very young, in conformance with traditional Quiché practice, he summoned the parents and separated the young couple. To his surprise this action angered the natives, and no one, not even the "principals or cofrades," would attend mass with him. Similarly, though the priests abhorred the manner in which the *cofradía* members celebrated the ritual of the saints, they could not stop it. The natives would accompany their processions of the saints with "drums, trumpets, and the noise of bells, because they are very inclined to commotions" (Ximénez 1967, p. 6). The processions were followed by dances (*zarabandas*), in which much drinking and "sexual corruption" occurred (Cortés y Larraz 1958, 1:60).

Many other alterations of Christian ritual provided constant reminders to the priests that their charges were far from "normal" Christians. Ximénez (1967, p. 6) mentioned that the natives "were careful to attend church more on the days that they celebrate [that is, according to the native calendar] than on the days prescribed [by the church]." Cortés y Larraz (1958, 1:51) complained that they used the holy oil as medicine rather than as part of a sacrament. In 1839 the priest of Santa Cruz observed that each day upon entering the church the natives would bow to the west, "in reverence to the setting sun" (Stephens 1841, p. 191). Toward the close of the century

Maudslay (1899, pp. 72–73) found the natives using the Catholic cathedral like an ancient Quiché shrine. At Chichicastenango they celebrated Candelaria (February 2) with a giant cross made of flowers placed on pine leaves along the entire length of the cathedral floor. The people began the ceremony by burning copal before the open door and then moving forward on their knees the whole length of the cross. They would stop to light candles, placing them along the edge of the cross, and to pray in Quiché. This remarkably syncretic rite was performed entirely without intervention by the Catholic priests.

Ritual dances were among the most powerful symbols of native resistance to Spanish religion and colonial rule. The people danced on the holiest of Christian days but celebrated native themes. Ximénez (1967, p. 8) perceptively observed that the dances originated in stories of the saints translated for the Indians by the first priests but that over time the natives had altered them to conform to "pretty memories of their gentile condition." He went on to remark that the Indians, "as very rustic people, do not reflect upon the good that has come to them from entering into the association of Our Holy Mother Church, but instead remember only the bad treatment they have received." Indeed, one of the major functions of the colonial dances appears to have been as a means of expressing animosity toward their Spanish overlords and of testifying to their continued adherence to ancient Quiché tradition. Since the dance steps and the accompanying drum music and spoken words were indigenous, the dancers and other performers must have truly felt united as a community of Quiché people. The heavy drinking and exhaustion from prolonged dancing no doubt facilitated the euphoric state.

We have little information on the actual dances performed in the Quiché area during the colonial and early republican periods. Ximénez (1929, p. 78; 1967, p. 17) claimed that in his day "in their fiestas they dance only the 'Quiché Winak.' " That dance appears to have been a native production and an overt symbol of surviving Quiché culture. It was a dance (*tun*), which also included singing and a story. The text sung with the dance was in Quiché. It included the phrase, "We came from there where the sun is born" (Ximénez 1929, p. 72), a reference to the coming of the Utatlán forefathers from the Gulf Coast. The dancing and singing were carried out to the rhythm of the hollow-log drum (*k'ojom*) and the music of the trumpet (*tun*), for which the musicians "have a pact with the devil."

The text tells the story of a Cakchiquel warrior who visits Utatlán and that night insults the Quiché king, calling him an "old sourpuss" (*mama c'aixon*). The king sends a powerful shaman after the warrior, and they leap from hill to hill in the chase that follows. Finally the stranger is brought back to Utatlán and placed before the rulers. They dance around him, transforming themselves into "eagles, lions, and tigers." Before they sacrifice him, he asks to speak. He delivers a speech in which he warns that calamities are about to befall them. "And this old sourpuss will also die, for know you, that men [will come] who will be dressed, not naked like you, and armed from head to feet. They will be terrible men, and cruel, the sons of tile." He goes on to say that the men will destroy their buildings and that Utatlán will become "the habitation of owls and wildcats, and all the greatness of that court [will] cease" (Ximénez 1967, p. 17).

It is clear from the story that the natives of the Quiché area still remembered the greatness of pre-Hispanic Utatlán. But just as owls and wildcats now lived at the site, so that kingdom had come to an end. The disrespect the Cakchiquel warrior showed for the Utatlán king could be emphasized by Quiché peasants, because their largely egalitarian society no longer maintained the old aristocracy. The tale shows the continuing native belief in animal transformations and suggests that the dances themselves were transforming media. It also reveals something of the natives' view of the Spaniards. The natives seem to have recognized that the Spaniards had brought them some superior cultural items (arms, clothing, and tiles), but "they were terrible men and cruel."

It is informative to contemplate the natives' desire to dance only this dance at their fiestas and the aversion the priests felt toward it. The "Quiché Winak" gives its own explanation of why the Quiché peasants had rejected Spanish Catholicism and at the same time is a concrete expression of those aspects of Quiché religion they had retained.

Despite Ximénez's claim that the "Quiché Winak" was the only dance performed by the colonial Quichés, it was probably the preferred dance among several that were performed. Shortly after the Conquest, Spanish missionaries introduced the natives to a number of dance dramas to facilitate their conversion to Christianity and adoption of Spanish culture (Carmack 1973, pp. 168–71). These dances must have persisted through the colonial period, though they may have been pushed into the background in favor of native dances.

When the "Quiché Winak" was eliminated along with other dances at the time of independence (De León n.d., p. 168), there may have been something of a revival of the Conquest dances. Late in the nineteenth century, perhaps stimulated by the liberal reforms of that period, many of the Spanish-inspired dances were performed (Bode 1961).

One of these dance dramas, telling the story of the Spanish conquest, was promoted in Quiché during the 1880s. Known as the "Conquest of Utatlán" (Silva L. n.d.), it tells the story of the Conquest as it supposedly took place at Utatlán and then on the plains of Pinal, where Tecum was killed. The anxiety of the king of Utatlán is portrayed, as well as Tecum's valor and political ambition. The original text must have been written in the sixteenth century by Spaniards, for the Quiché participants act and speak like medieval lords. Nevertheless, the conquistadors come off as bloodthirsty and greedy, suggesting that some Las Casas–influenced Dominican missionary wrote it.

The presentation of the "Conquest of Utatlán" at Quiché may have produced considerable local native pride. In it Tojil is glorified as an omniscient god similar to the Christian God. The Quiché warriors are said to have defended the "nation," and Tecum dies a genuine hero. These are symbols around which the Quichés could rally. Utatlán is glorified, as are its gods, buildings, and fortifications. Only the pre-Hispanic king comes off badly. He is portrayed as fearful and maudlin. Clearly the prestige of the descendants of the Utatlán kings was very low by the end of the nineteenth century. There was no room for such elite concepts in the egalitarian culture of the Quiché peasants.

The town center of Santa María Chiquimula (Tz'oloche), the ancient Tamub settlement. *Photograph by Duncan Earle.*

Aerial view of Chiché, a few kilometers east of Santa Cruz del Quiché. Historically Chiché was part of a Dominican hacienda.

A Quiché shaman (*chuchkajaw*) burns copal incense at an old altar in front of the Catholic Cathedral of San Pedro Jocopilas. *Photograph by Duncan Earle.*

A Quiché shaman offers gifts to the earth deity at a shrine on top of Mount Patojil. *Photograph by Duncan Earle.*

A ritual procession in honor of Saint Thomas along the highway outside Chichicastenango. The small figure of a man on a horse being carried at the head of the procession represents Tz'ijolaj, thought to be the ancient Quiché fire god. *Photograph by Duncan Earle.*

Principales of Chichicastenango, dressed in traditional costume and holding the sacred *cofradía* staffs, take part in a funeral rite. The penetration of modernizing influences is evident in the cigarette advertisements displayed on store fronts. *Photograph by Duncan Earle.*

344

A masked dancer holds a small serpent in a rendition of the Snake Dance at Santa Rosa Chujuyup, a canton of Santa Cruz del Quiché. *Photograph by Duncan Earle.*

A traditional Quiché family lives isolated in a tile-roofed house surrounded by cornstalks. The area is between Chiché and Chiniqué. *Photograph by Duncan Earle.*

Native converts to the Catholic Action movement celebrate Holy Week in front of a chapel in a hamlet of Santa Cruz del Quiché. *Photograph by Duncan Earle.*

The paved streets and park benches visible in this scene from the town center of Santa Cruz del Quiché are indicative of its Latin character. The Juan de León Normal School is in the background.

11
SURVIVALS

THE GENERAL PICTURE in the twentieth century has been one of change away from traditional Quiché community patterns. Yet some of those patterns have survived, and much can be learned by studying them. Acculturation has not occurred evenly, either in time or in space. Until the 1940s, for example, the natives of the Quiché area maintained a social life very similar to what it had been during the colonial and early republican periods. Some of the cultural features of that time have been studied in elaborate detail by ethnographers, especially at Chichicastenango. Their accounts tell us about changes and continuities from the Utatlán community but also provide valuable insight into the nature of the original pre-Hispanic condition. The studies by Bunzel, Schultze-Jena, Tax, and Rodas on Chichicastenango in the 1930s permit us to reconstruct traditional Quiché community life before it was drastically changed by the forces of modernization associated with the revolution of 1944 and subsequent events.

My summary of present-day community life in the Quiché will be brief. The effects of modernization are too complex to discuss briefly and are largely irrelevant to the main subject of this book. Suffice it to say that, to a large extent, social life in the Quiché communities is now controlled by the Latins who live in the town centers, and the natives are being integrated into national Guatemalan life. Many natives have acculturated to that way of life, taking on Latin language, dress, and economic modes. These "bourgeois indigenes," as they might be called (Carmack 1976b), have lost interest in Quiché culture, except as symbols either to be admired or to be ashamed of. Still most natives remain peasants, tied to the land and their ancient crafts. In traditional zones, as in some rural sections of Chichicastenango, they continue ancient Quiché practices. In most places, however, the Quiché peasants have suffered a drastic "deculturation" as they have been forced into labor and commercial activities to survive (Guzman Böckler and Herbert 1970). These peasants share with natives of other areas a common alienation and a hope for better living conditions, and in that sense they belong more to a class than to a culture. It is still unclear whether or not they will eventually be able to create a meaningful culture of their own.

EARLY-TWENTIETH-CENTURY SURVIVALS

The liberal reforms of the latter part of the nineteenth century led to significant changes in the Quiché communities during the first third of the twentieth. The liberals strongly promoted (1) capitalism, especially in the form of plantation agriculture; (2) Latinization—the transformation of Indians to *ladino* ways (Martinez 1970); and (3) modern culture expressed through programs of education and public health and the separation of church and state. The acculturation forces affecting Quiché communities as a result of these "liberal" policies came mainly from forced migration to the coastal plantations, growing numbers of Latins resident in the town centers, and increasing population pressure on subsistence farmers.

Population in the central Quiché area grew by about 40 percent during the first third of the twentieth century, reaching a total of 78,000 inhabitants by 1940. This probably represented close to the maximum population that could be supported by peasant subsistence economy, and pressures for land were beginning to be felt. This pressure was tied to work on the plantations, since that was a source of income for the peasant who could not produce enough to meet his family's needs. In the 1930s natives were migrating to the coasts from Quiché towns such as Chiché and Chichicastenango (Termer 1957, p. 43; Bunzel 1952, pp. 9–12). Tax (1947) claimed that in 1935 almost half of Chichicastenango's inhabitants were living on the coast and that others migrated there for short periods of labor. Nevertheless, in most of the Quiché towns pressures to work on the plantations still were not very strong. These pressures were to intensify greatly in the following decades, as were acculturation influences on natives as a result of the increased work on the plantations.

Perhaps more influential for change was the presence of increasing numbers of Latins in the towns. By 1940 they made up most of the town-center populations and more than one-tenth of the total municipal populations. They were especially concentrated in Santa Cruz and Chinique, where they totaled about one-fifth and one-third of the populations, respectively. In Chichicastenango the Latins were only a small fraction of the total population (less than 3 percent), and the percentage was even smaller in such towns as San Pedro, San Antonio, and Chiquimula. Bunzel (1952, p. 12) minimized their influence on native culture at Chichicastenango in the 1930s, correctly noting that Latins did not own large land estates there as they did in other areas of Guatemala. She referred to them as "a group of underprivileged, debt-ridden shopkeepers , depending for their existence on patronage from above. They squeeze where they can. The Indians pay their tribute, as the price of peace and exemptions." This statement fails to take into account "neocolonial" ties the Latins had been able to build up in the years preceding her visit and the accumulation of considerable wealth by some of the Latin shopkeepers. Tax (1947) found that the Indians had a deep hatred for the Latins, doubtless produced by years of exploitation.

In some of the towns, notably Santa Cruz and Chinique, Latins did own rather large tracts of lands, though they were smaller than the great *latifundias* of the coast. Nor should we ignore the Latin influence that resulted from bringing literacy to perhaps 4 percent of the indigenous Quiché population (as of about 1945). Many literate natives became skeptical about Quiché culture, and some of them were leaders in later movements for the adoption of modern institutions.

Termer (1957) visited the Quiché area in the late 1920s and discovered remnants of traditional Quiché culture in every town. He particularly mentioned the native dances, though he claimed that only the Snake Dance was recited in the Quiché language. He also noted the use of the 260-day calendar to determine the fates of each day and observed special altars for burning copal in front of old churches and on hilltops near the towns.

Termer found Chichicastenango the most traditional of the communities. Besides the universal use of the Quiché language and traditional dress, he observed that the natives of Chichicastenango worshiped a large stone idol on a hill near town. The idol was called Pascual Abaj, a combined Christian and Quiché name. The hill on which it stood had the Quiché name Turc'aj (Rodas and Rodas 1938, p. 18). The idol stood on a small altar, surrounded by stone artifacts, crosses, freshly cut pine branches, flowers, and copal. Day and night the shamans (*chuchkajaw*) prayed there on behalf of their clients:

Oh thou, Heart of Heaven. What did Sakic [a blind supplicant] do so that thou didst take away his sight? He is honorable, a worker, he fulfills his duty to the town, as a son of the town, and he fulfills his duty to thee as a faithful believer. He is a good husband, a magnificent father who cares for his children, and when he was a son, he was respectful toward his forefathers. . . . What sin dost thou hide from Sakic? Why didst thou take away from him that wonderful gift of seeing, of seeing thee here, of seeing thee in the mountain, in the sky, in the tree; of admiring thee in the light, the sun, the river? Make his eyes whole again. [Rodas and Rodas 1938, pp. 18–19; my translation]

Termer (1957, p. 174) thought that the shrine of Pascual Abaj was the most impressive survival of native culture he had seen in Guatemala.

Termer (1957, pp. 231–39) also described the fiesta in honor of Chichicastenango's patron saint, Santo Tomás, claiming that it was an "ancient cult, though externally the acts were related with the form of the Christian religion." The fiesta, held in association with a huge market, attracted several thousand natives to town. Each of the four days of celebration was given over to masked dances, incense burning and prayers both outside and inside the church and on the Calvarium, processions of saints carried on litters to the sound of drums and flute music and exploding firecrackers, and, as the climax, the "dance" of a tiny figure of a man on a horse (*tzijolaj*). The figure was moved up and down a rope that extended from the top of a tall tree trunk to the belfry of the church. Termer noted that the December celebration corresponded in time to the harvest season (he erroneously thought that it also corresponded to the end of the Quiché year). The dancing figure was identified with the old fire deity, whose ritual supposedly was held in connection with the end of the year.

Ethnography of Chichicastenango

Termer's brief notes scarcely portray the extent to which native culture had been preserved at Chichicastenango. For that we must turn to the work of two ethnographers, Bunzel and Schultze-Jena, who made detailed studies of the community. Bunzel's account (1952) is based mainly on interviews with a key native informant and her own astute observations. She was especially interested in viewing Chichicastenango as a community. Schultze-Jena (1933, 1947) studied the community indirectly, largely through native texts he obtained from informants. He was more interested than Bunzel in continuities in traditional Quiché culture. Additional information on the community was provided by Sol Tax (1947), who lived in the community for a few months in the years 1934 to 1936, and by Flavio Rodas, a local *ladino* well versed in native culture (Rodas and Rodas 1938). Much of the description that follows is drawn from the accounts of these ethnographers.

In the 1930s, Chichicastenango formed a self-contained native community in which religious and political administration was united. The town was a ceremonial center, the leaders and masses alike living almost wholly in the rural area. The Latins resided in town the year round, but the natives' houses were mostly occupied only on ritual or market occasions. The native officials collaborated with the national government, which was represented in town by the Latins, though they were largely independent of it.

The rural area was organized into sixty-four cantons, each with its own leader (*tzanabe*) and messengers (*samajel*) (Rodas and Rodas). These were service and taxpaying as well as territorial divisions. Each canton was composed of exogamous patrilineal clans. The clans were the landholding units of the canton, inheritance residing exclusively in the male line (Tax 1947; Rodas and Rodas 1938). The cantons were grouped into four larger territorial divisions, each associated with a cardinal point and having its own chief (*calpul*). The four chiefs were ranked, the one in the west apparently being first in rank, the one in the south second (Rodas and Rodas 1938). By 1935 the number of chiefs had grown to six (Tax 1947). The community was further divided into east and west moieties, territorial units that sometimes competed with one another in political (and perhaps ritual) matters (Bunzel 1952).

The leaders of the cantons and the *calpul* chiefs together chose the many officials who served (*patan*) the community. These officials, both religious and civil, consisted of (1) 6 to 8 *mayordomos* for each of the 14 saint cults (*cofradías*) and (2) 2 alcaldes, 8 *regidores*, and many lesser officials, *mayores*, *alguaciles*, and *chajales*, of the civil administration (*alcaldía*). The various offices were arranged in a pyramid-shaped ladder, the men of the community moving up the rungs as they served and grew older. They began serving as lesser officials (*alguaciles* and *chajales*), of which there were about 230. They moved up to the lower cult offices (*mayordomos*), which had 48 positions. The next step up was the *regidor* office of the civil government, 8 positions in all. From there they could be named to the two alcalde positions in the civil administration or to the first two *mayordomo* offices of the *cofradías* (also referred to as alcaldes), theoretically 28 in number but actually fewer, because many officials served in more than one position at the same time. The alcalde positions, whether religious or civil, were the highest rank in the hierarchy, and carried with them the right to bear silver staffs or standards (*varas*) (Bunzel 1952).

In the government of Chichicastenango there was a clear division between the policy makers (*principales*) and the executors, the civil-religious officials. The leading *principales* were the *calpul* chiefs who had successfully climbed the ladder and who could also claim high status on other grounds. The first *calpul* chief, bearing the lineage name Ajanel, claimed descent from the Quiché kings. He was too powerful to officiate in public. The second *calpul* chief was similarly descended from a royal line of Utatlán (the Sakic), but he was active in public, where he usually represented the first *calpul* chief (Bunzel 1952; Tax 1947). All the *calpul* chiefs were powerful shamans (*chuchkajaw*), and they were sometimes in political conflict with each other (Rodas and Rodas 1938; Tax 1947). Others who climbed the ladder invariably came from wealthy families who owned houses in town. They too became *principales*, policy makers. Thus the *principales* actually formed something of a ruling "aristocracy" (Bunzel 1952), though that was denied by community members. The "sunburst" embroidery on the jackets of the *principales* may once have been an insignia exclusive to that aristocracy (Rodas and Rodas 1938).

In the 1930s there was no more important function for the *principales* and civil-religious officials than the proper administration of the major Christo-pagan ceremonies of the community. The church was like a "state temple in which the rulers and their surrogates discharge their religious obligations to the commonwealth" (Bunzel 1952). Though the rituals invariably involved the saints of the Catholic church, their purpose was not Christian. They were meant to commemorate the ancestors and to perpetuate the community and its traditional life begun by the ancestors long before:

It is not for us to abandon him [a saint] but rather to fulfill the rites and customs which have been laid down and marked out for us by the first ancestors. . . . We have received and humbly accepted the second coat, the garment of service in the *cofradías*, and we have received the sanctified staff of the first ancestors . . . and now the time has come for us to kneel down and bow our heads within the cold house, as we did when we received the second coat and the sanctified staff, and to leave it and return it again to the ancestors. [Bunzel 1952]

The ritual of the saints, then, was presented in honor of the ancestors and the aboriginal powers with which they were associated. The essence of the ancestors was thought to live on as "the great moral force of the universe" (Bunzel 1952). Bones were the "seed" of a person and had latent life. Thus the cemetery was an important site for rituals to the ancestors. Even more important than the bones, however, was the heart of the dead, which lived on in the form of an insect, a tiny fly (*us, natub, amelo*) that moved about in the clouds and air (Schultze-Jena 1933, 1947). These deceased nomads would return to the sacred shrines where they had worshiped and exercised authority in life: inside the church building, especially toward the front and in the nave; at sacred clan and canton altars; and at family houses. The dead were thought to have emotions and to be involved in the lives of the natives. The people could placate them by conforming to the traditions of the past and by ritually "feeding" them with aromatics from candles, incense, copal, and flowers (Bunzel 1952).

The great power paralleling the ancestors was Earth (Juyup Tak'aj). The ancestors often interceded with Earth on behalf of the living, but Earth was considered to have its own powers for good or ill. It provided maize and other food to the native peasants and was closely associated with rain—as when rain clouds congregated around high peaks. It was also the "owner" of wild animals. Earth guarded the animals inside itself and sent them to man as messengers bearing portents. Earth could take anthropomorphic forms, such as a giant white man (*rajaw juyup*) who buried people inside the mountain forever or revealed hidden treasures to them (Bunzel 1952). Earth could also take the form of a tiny, red-faced, golden-haired man (Sakixol) who punished adulterers (Tax 1948). Ritual devoted to Earth was carried out on mountain- and hilltops, to the cardinal directions, in the cemetery (where the dead returned to Earth), and in the church (which was perhaps a miniature version of Earth). At Chichicastenango, Mount Pocojil was the most frequented Earth altar, but at least twenty other hills, including Turc'aj (the altar of Pascual Abaj), also had important earth altars (Schultze-Jena 1933, 1947; Tax 1948).

In the 1930s the days were thought of as lords and represented still another complex set of powers closely associated with the ancestors at Chichicastenango (Schultze-Jena 1933, 1947). The ancestors had respected and conformed to the fates of the days, and the living were expected to do the same. The fate of each day was determined by both its name and its number. There were twenty names and thirteen numbers (see chapter 4). Each day name was associated with some aspect of life: Quiej with the dead, Ik' with the earth, K'anel with milpa, Batz with the calendar itself. The lower numbers (one to three) made a day's fate gentle, and the higher numbers (eleven to thirteen) made it violent, while the middle numbers (seven to nine) were more or less neutral. The days affected all aspects of life. The day on which a person was born influenced the kind of person he would be; for example, a person born on Tz'i (Dog) would be sexually "loose" unless efforts were made to counteract the fate. Some days were good for buying and selling, getting married, or planting crops, while others were bad for the same actitivies. Many middle-numbered days were ceremonial days on which special offerings were required. Bunzel lists sixty-nine ceremonial days.

The fate of individuals was also tied up with alter-ego animals, called *alxic*. Animals not easily caught, such as snakes, coyotes, tigers, dogs, and birds, were typical *alxic*. They had the same propensities as their companion persons, so that, for example, thieves had coyotes as *alxic*, and men who chased women had dogs. If the animal was killed or hurt, the person suffered the same fate. The *alxic* might also help, however, as in the case of a woman who was attacked by a man but saved herself by turning into her vulture *alxic* and flying away (Tax 1948).

Many other powers inhabited the universe: the sun ("our father"), the moon ("our grandmother"), the stars, clouds and mist, the cold wind, the cardinal points, the great and small idols, the lords of sickness and pain, and others. The Catholic saints gave new dimensions to these native powers (Bunzel 1952) and became the tangible symbols for elaborate rites in their honor. Some of the symbolic associations between the saints and the native powers have been clarified: the Holy Cross, an expression of Earth; Santo Tomás, San José, and San Sebastián, the patrons of the community; Christ, the "source of tradition"; San Juan, "the moon and stars"; San Pedro, the patron of shamans; Santiago, the destructive winds; Tzijolaj, fire (Bunzel 1952).

In general the native powers were neither friendly nor hostile. They could bring either good or ill, and so had to be bribed, cajoled, and convinced that the ritual participants were worthy of blessings. Much of the drinking, eating, and dancing connected with native ritual was designed to please the saints and associated powers. These activities made the participants happy, and that in turn pleased the powers. In that state of mind they were more likely to bring good to the people of the community (Bunzel 1952).

An ancient ritual cycle could be detected in the major Christo-pagan ceremonies at Chichicastenango in the 1930s. The cycle included major celebrations for Holy Week in March, the saints and the dead in November, Santo Tomás in December, and lesser celebrations for the other thirteen saint cults. Ostensibly determined by the Christian ceremonial calendar, the most important dates were equated with the Quiché ceremonial calendar: the Exaltation of the Cross in May was equivalent to eight Ik', the day of Earth; Corpus Christi in May was tied with Eight K'anel and the coming of rains to make the milpa grow; All Souls' Day in November was equated with Eight Quiej, the Day of the Ancestors (Bunzel 1952).

These major Christo-pagan ceremonies shared a basic ritual pattern that, like the dates on which they were held, was ostensibly Christian but fundamentally Quiché. The pattern consisted of building symbols and ritual performers through a cumulative process. The ceremony would begin with a minimum of participants and symbols. At first participants carried empty litters, only a few dancers performed, drinking was limited, and a few firecrackers were set off. Gradually more participants joined in, until at the climax all the saints were carried in the procession, several dance groups performed, the town was filled with marketers and visitors, and huge amounts of liquor were consumed. The celebrants then gradually formed into smaller groups and returned to their ritual houses to bring the fiesta to an end. The focus of the ritual was always the church, the "elevated building where the temporal power of the community is enthroned" (Bunzel 1952).

A second ritual pattern described by the ethnographers for Chichicastenango appears to have been thoroughly indigenous and closely associated with more particularistic elements of the rural community. This pattern consisted of clients consulting with shamans (*chuchkajaw*) over specific problems that plagued them. The shamans divined the causes of the problems, using a combination of *tzité* beans placed in rows, calendar days recited in order, and "twitches" in the blood. Once the shaman had divined the cause of the problem, he and his client visited sacred altars of Earth, especially mountain shrines. The shaman approached the power with formal speeches, which included an announcement ("Hail, Earth, . . ."), a request for help ("Earth, . . . cure me forever of this grievous sickness which has touched me"), and a farewell ("Hail, Earth, I have finished"). Along with the speech, which was itself a kind of offering, the shaman presented the power with candles, copal incense, flowers, and liquor. These rites were carried out according to the fates of the days and repeated several times on appropriate days (Bunzel 1952; Tax 1948; Schultze-Jena 1933, 1947).

From this summary of traditional culture in Chichicastenango in the 1930s it is clear that the Quiché peasants had structured their community and their beliefs after the culture that had been handed down to them by their forefathers. To be sure, the resulting patterns were highly provincial and distorted versions of that ancient culture. They were more rural and egalitarian, with leadership given largely to the collectivity. The supernatural power was more egalitarian too, the ancestors, Earth, and the days of the calendar all but resolved into a single pantheistic deity. Ritual was less well integrated, reflecting several layers of accretion through time; it was also at least superficially Christian in symbolism. Yet it is not difficult to find continuities in pattern from the Utatlán culture. In the political sphere we recognize the old rural quadripartite, moietal, and calpul divisions, the remnants of a central hierarchy of four rulers (the supreme ruler's assistant taking the active role in public affairs), the articulation between lineages and territorial groups, and the provision of services and "tributes" by the peasants. In the ritual sphere a temple cult was still in operation, with its elaborate dances, processions, deity icons (now saints), drinking, feasting, and fire making. The concept of the patron deity still existed, as did the belief in the dual nature of the gods (good and ill, male and female, and so on). The concept of companion animals had also persisted. The elaborate public ceremonies contrasted with simpler shamanic rites at mountain shrines. The latter rites perhaps provide us with a new appreciation of ritual life as it must have flourished in pre-Hispanic days in the rural areas outside Utatlán.

It is unlikely that any other twentieth-century community in the Quiché retained traditional culture to the degree or on the scale of Chichicastenango's. Termer described a celebration at Chiquimula in the late 1920s that suggests that culture there was also fundamentally Quiché in structure (Termer 1957, p. 181). The ceremony was held in the plaza underneath a large ceiba tree on Nine E, a ritually important calendar day. The natives, seated as "family" (probably clan) groups around the plaza, from time to time burned copal and offered prayers facing toward the church. In a nearby house the *mayordomos* worshiped the saints, drinking and dancing in their honor. The men and women danced alone rather than with each other. Though much smaller and less dramatic than the celebrations at Chichicastenango, the rites at Chiquimula were similar.

Falla (1975) painted a similar picture in his reconstruction of social life at Ilotenango before the revolutionary period. He documented the importance of patrilineal clans, which he related to property rights, patrilocal residence, elaborate marriage exchanges, and leadership by ritual specialists

355

(*chuchkajaw*). As at Chichicastenango, the fundamental community divisions were rural cantons, which alternated in providing civil and religious officials to conduct the ceremonial life of the town. The ten Ilotenango cantons were associated with the cardinal directions and performed their services in a cycle moving from north to west to south to east. The same calendric system found at Chichicastenango was followed at Ilotenango, including four days (Noj, Ik', Quiej, and E) as year-bearers. The beginning of the traditional solar year was March 9 to 13, five days being added in each twenty-year period to keep the count in accord with the seasons (see Ximénez's statement about 1700 that the Quiché year began on February 21).

Traditional Culture at Santa Cruz

There is evidence that Santa Cruz had lost many of its traditional cultural features by the 1930s, though the natives had preserved them throughout most of the nineteenth century. Apparently toward the end of the century there was an erosion of traditional culture at Santa Cruz as a result of the liberal reforms. Juan de León (n.d.), a schoolteacher in Santa Cruz, questioned informants who remembered how things had been a few decades before the 1930s. He was able to record the following traditional cultural elements: (1) the names of the days in the 260-day calendar, as well as the complete solar calendar with its eighteen month names; (2) a set of kinship terms, including the ancient terms for "uncle" and "aunt" (*wican achi*, *wican ixok*); (3) many names of pre-Hispanic deities, such as Tojil, K'ucumatz, Tepew, Jurakan, and many more; (4) astronomical beliefs, including the association of the sun with Tojil; the moon with Awilix; the two sides of the Milky Way with summer (*sak be*) and winter (*xibalba*); the summer and winter solstices with the silkworm (*cacchaj*) and the butterfly (*pepel*), respectively; the dry season with the serpent (*cumatz*) and the wet season with the quetzal bird (*k'uk'*); Venus with the male quetzal (*mamk'uk'*); the constellation Orion with Jurakan; and (5) several dance dramas, a war hymn, and a song in honor of the moon.

The war hymn is a surprising Quiché survival; according to De León it was reported by Quiché "priests" who lived near the ruins of Utatlán. In 1885 native Santa Cruz militiamen had climbed the mounds at Utatlán and recited it before going into battle against the people of nearby Lemoa. The song has imagery similar to that found in the *Popol Vuh*, as well as mention of such deities as Cabrakan, Jurakan, Tojil, Tepew, and K'ucumatz. The earth and sky (*cajulew*), the underworld (Xibalba), lightning (*cakulja'*), and destructive fire (*nimalaj k'ak'*) are other features found in both the *Popol Vuh* and the hymn. The language of the song makes it clear that copal (*pom*) was burned on an ancient altar (*tanabal*) and that the log drum (*k'ojom*) was played in preparation for the fighting. As in ancient times the warriors left with bows and arrows (*ch'ap*) and lances (*kakabal*). They sang:

> Oh, warriors of Quiché, let us go to the battle with courage.
> Tojil will go before us on the land and in the underworld.

The survivals of Quiché culture that De León recovered from old informants at Santa Cruz reveal that, in contrast to traditions in other communities in the Quiché area, those in Santa Cruz were highly esoteric. They appear to have derived from an elite group who once lived at Utatlán, as indicated by the many names of Quiché deities, as well as the songs, astronomic correlations, and calendrics remembered at Santa Cruz but lost to the other communities. Their disappearance from Santa Cruz during the first part of the century is an incalculable loss to the student interested in reconstructing Utatlán's cultural tradition.

Termer found in the late 1920s that Santa Cruz rituals were already acculturated (1957, pp. 215ff.). For example, though the Snake Dance (Patztaj) was still being performed, it had been significantly modified from the version danced in other communities. In Santa Cruz the dancers dressed in the clothing of different Quiché communities and did not wear animal skins. The theme of the dance was the same as elsewhere: native men trying to protect a native woman (actually a man dressed as a woman) from the Spaniards, meanwhile struggling with snakes that were wrapping themselves around their bodies. But the mock coitus between the woman and the natives that concluded the dance in other areas had been eliminated at Santa Cruz.

It is likely that the Latins were responsible for the elimination of such "indecent" elements from native rituals. In the case of the Palo Volador Dance ("Flying Tree"), Latin interference can be documented. During a performance of the dance at Chiquimula in 1917, two natives were killed in a fall, and the dance was suspended by Latin officials. We are told that the dance was not performed at Chichicastenango in 1929 "because of conflicts with the *ladinos*" (Termer 1957, p. 228). It was not performed at Santa Cruz during those years, but in 1938 it was reinstated at the command of the *jefe político* (departmental chief) as a tourist attraction (Carmack n.d.; De León n.d., p. 168).

Cultural changes in Santa Cruz were coming from the natives too, some of whom during the first third of the twentieth century were already highly acculturated. Old Santa Cruz informants recall that the "chief" of the natives for many years was Guillermo Morales, who spoke on their behalf before municipal, departmental, and national authorities (Carmack n.d.). Significantly, Morales was an acculturated native who had worked as a department official. Though he paid homage to the town's patron saint, he was not a shaman. Nor was he a descendant of one of the ancient Utatlán families; in fact, he was born in another town far to the west. Bunzel (1952) mentions another native "chief" from Santa Cruz who claimed to be descended from Quiché kings, but he too was highly acculturated to Latin ways. He tried to sell her artifacts and an old book with dance texts. He claimed to have worked in the past for "archaeologists." Perhaps he was the same man who claimed that he was told in a dream to go to the cave next to the ruins of Utatlán. He entered the cave late one night with an ocote torch and walked all the way to the end of it. There he saw, "in person and all decked out, Tecum, Quiché, and other princes, and he talked with them." He told everyone this story, gained fame as a representative of the ancient kings, and became one of the leading *principales* of Santa Cruz (Tax 1947, p. 471).

It is clear, then, that by the 1930s the traditional native community at Santa Cruz had been disrupted by influence from Latins and acculturated natives. According to informants, there was already a partial separation between the civil and religious hierarchies—*mayordomos*, called *alpares*, were named within the *cofradías* rather than by the *principales*. An ancient altar for burning copal had been removed from in front of the church, though the natives continued to burn candles on the floor inside the church. Many natives had ceased to practice shamanistic rituals at the rural altars.

Despite the many changes, Santa Cruz informants remember those times as traditional compared with the present day. We have seen that Tecum legends were very much alive and that an active public ceremonial cycle centered around the saints. In the rural area shamans still performed traditional rituals. There were eight saint cults (*cofradías*), each with five *mayordomos* (called alcalde, *ucab achi, rox achi*, . . .) and their wives (*xokajaw, ucab ixok, rox ixok*, . . .). Though the civil-religious ladder had been disrupted, the civil alcalde was still expected to become head of the Saint Cecilia cult after his service in the municipality.

The saints were celebrated in elaborate ceremonies: processions similar to those at Chichicastenango in which the adorned saints were carried on litters, dances, fireworks, eating and drinking, and drum and flute music. The most important celebration was in November in honor of Saint Cecilia. There was a myth that this saint had been found in Panajxit and that when she was taken to the town church she would disappear and reappear miraculously at Panajxit. Finally, a great celebration was performed for her, and she remained in the central church. The highlight of the Saint Cecilia ceremony was a duck race. The night before the race the ducks were taken from house to house, where they were given liquor to make them drunk. The next day the ducks were tied up, and the *mayordomos* grabbed at their necks while riding by them on horseback. The "sacrificial" ducks were later eaten by the cult members in a ceremonial meal. Though the race derives from

Spanish sources, it apparently had been syncretized with native symbols and beliefs.

The other major celebration was held in August in honor of Saint Elena, the old Tamub saint and now patroness of Santa Cruz. This female saint was paired with the male saint, Child of the Cross, whose celebration was in May. Together these saints were associated with the coming of rain. Saint Elena, dressed as a native, was believed to be the most "miraculous" of the saints. According to local myth, one time she was taken out in procession in hopes that she would intervene to end a long dry spell. Three Huehuetecos arrived in town on horseback and made fun of the town "superstition." Soon after the procession great rain clouds formed, and lightning rays struck and killed the three strangers' horses. According to another myth, Saint Elena appeared on a battlefield in San Salvador. Her appearance so stunned the soldiers that they stopped fighting. The ceremonies in her honor were similar to those of the other saints at Santa Cruz, except that there was more Latin participation, and the Snake Dance was performed in her honor.

Shamanic ritual in the rural area of Santa Cruz was similar to what has been described for Chichicastenango and other Quiché communities. The shamans (*chuchkajaw*) performed rituals at several sacred places in the area: the ruins of Utatlán, a hill in Xatinap, the ruins at Panajxit, a cross near Mount Patojil, Mounts Sakajaw and Ixwabaj overlooking San Andrés, and Mount Mamaj. The shamans celebrated the beginning of each solar year, apparently around the beginning of March, by "seating" the year-bearers. Shamans also officiated on behalf of clans, called *palaxic* (also called *jomay*, *chekamay*), making offerings at clan altars (*warabal ja*). These were primarily agricultural rituals associated with the clan members' maize farms.

The Rojas clan, descendants of the Quiché "king" of Utatlán, were participants in the traditional rural social life of Santa Cruz (Carmack n.d.). Leadership had passed from them to the Latins and the acculturated natives in the town center. The Rojas clan lived humbly in the Patz'ak canton, which included the ruins of Utatlán and Resguardo (Atalaya). The lands were planted in milpa, and the Rojas clan members were peasant farmers like their neighbors. The patriarch of the clan, Juan Rojas, was their shamanic leader (*chuchkajaw*), and his wife, Herlinda, was also a powerful shaman. The altar (*warabal ja*) at which Juan gave offerings to Earth, the ancestors, and other powers on behalf of the clan was in front of the western mound at the Resguardo site. The site was referred to by clan members as *mumus* ("platform") and was believed to be enchanted, peopled by tiny spirit beings called *tzitzimit*. The *tzitzimit* were linked in some fashion with the ancestors. Perhaps the Rojas clan members were somewhat more traditional than other natives living around them, but there is no evidence that their ritual or social forms were exceptional in any significant way.

It is clear that Santa Cruz lacked the integrated traditional culture found at Chichicastenango during the first third of the twentieth century, though much of its public celebrations and its rural rituals reveal patterns ultimately derived from Utatlán. Chinique was far more Latin than Santa Cruz at the time, and presumably even fewer traditional patterns were followed there. Other towns, such as San Pedro and Chiquimula, were highly traditional, much like Chichicastenango.

THE SITUATION TODAY

The revolutionary movement of 1944 brought powerful changes to the Quiché communities. Among the most important directed changes were the elimination of forced labor, the introduction of free elections, and the formation of peasant groups. The removal of unpaid labor obligations freed the natives of the area to engage in a wider variety of economic activities. Much of the artisanry and commerce now practiced by the natives had their beginnings at that time. The introduction of local elections cut into the power of the shamans and *principales*. Whereas formerly the *principales* had named civil officials in conjunction with service in the *cofradías*, now alcaldes and other officials were elected by popular vote. The Latins and the natives engaged in commerce began exercising decisive voting power and eventually chose candidates who supported their interests rather than those of the traditional community. In Santa Cruz, for example, the *principales* fought hard to keep the native alcalde off the ballot, since that official traditionally had succeeded to the head of the Saint Cecilia *cofradía* and so had to be a traditionalist (Carmack n.d.). In Ilotenango, where the alcalde had the right to name *cofradía* officials and later to become head of the San Antonio *cofradía*, a similar struggle developed over his election. In 1966 a nontraditionalist was elected alcalde in San Antonio, and he began blocking the activities of the *cofradías* (Falla 1972, pp. 443–44).

The peasant leagues and committees organized by the revolutionary government apparently were ineffective in the Quiché area. Nevertheless, the government created a favorable climate for the introduction of the Catholic Action (Reformed Catholic) movement. That movement was as much social as religious, the priests assisting their peasant converts in agricultural methods, credit cooperatives, hygiene, Christian Democratic politics, and education. Through Catholic Action chemical fertilizers were introduced to the Quiché farmers, with the result that agricultural production doubled (Carmack 1974; Falla 1972; Stearns n.d.), and population growth was greatly stimulated. In Santa Cruz, Catholic Action also became the vehicle for organizing the Peasant League (Stearns n.d.; Carmack n.d.). Through the league the natives learned about agrarian politics and began to understand their shared condition of poverty with peasants of adjacent communities.

The league was opposed by local Latins, conservative officials, and priests, and did not last long. Nevertheless, it was a socializing force whose effects have continued to this day.

In the hands of the Spanish priests who administered in the Quiché area, Catholic Action launched a direct assault on traditional Quiché religion. Every community experienced a holy war of sorts between the *"catequistas"* (progressives) and the *"costumbristas"* (traditionalists). Violence erupted often, especially in the 1950s. At Santa Cruz the priests managed to eradicate the burning of candles to the ancestors in the church, but when they tried to take the Buried Jesus saint from the control of the *cofradías*, a struggle ensued. Several converts to Catholic Action were thrown in jail, and the traditionalists tried unsuccessfully to have the priest removed from his post (Carmack n.d.). An even more violent struggle took place in Chichicastenango in 1957 (Gruhn 1973, pp. 247–48). There one night the Catholics invaded the shrine of Pascual Abaj and cast the idol down the canyon. Later the priest tried to abolish the *cofradía* ritual and other "customs" practiced in the church. The traditionalists rose up in arms and attacked the convent. The priest barely escaped with his life and returned later with an armed guard. The traditionalists were too powerful to be blocked in Chichicastenango, and to the present day the priests do not interfere with them. Nevertheless, even in communities like Chichicastenango, where traditional rituals are carried out openly, Catholic Action has led many of the natives away from the old religion.

The changes begun by the revolutionary government have drastically eroded traditional life in the Quiché communities. The erosion process continues today, mainly as a consequence of socioeconomic factors affecting every Quiché community: severe overpopulation; heavy involvement in external economic exchanges; the presence of an important class of commercialized indigenes; sharply competitive factions of reformed Catholics, Protestants, and traditionalists; development programs sponsored by national and international agencies; and politically influential Latins residing in the town centers. The description that follows briefly summarizes the specific sociocultural conditions of the central Quiché communities (Fig. 11.1), especially as they relate to traditional Quiché patterns.

Santa Cruz del Quiché

The population has more than doubled in the last thirty years and now numbers about 35,000 persons (as of the 1974 census). About 8,000 of its inhabitants (around 23 percent) live in the town center. The land can support only about one-third of the population (Mantz n.d.), and large numbers of natives now work on the coast a few months each year. Many others have left the community permanently. The manufacture of hats from woven palm fronds has become a major local industry; the hats are sold widely in Guatemala and throughout Central America. About half of the townspeople are indigenous, but they are strongly acculturated. Many of them own stores, trucks, or craft shops or are traveling merchants. The community is deeply divided into religiopolitical factions. The Catholic Action movement has divided the natives in half—those who have joined the movement and taken on more modern ways and those who continue traditional lifeways. Several large, powerful Protestant sects also compete for the natives' allegiance. Among the most significant outside agencies operating in Santa Cruz are a Catholic and a national cooperative and development programs provided by CARE, Guatemalan Community Development, and Catholic Relief (Stearns n.d.). The Latins still control the most lucrative stores and businesses and the municipal government. Hostility between the Latins and the natives remains deep, though usually below the surface.

Traditional Quiché patterns have been all but eliminated from public town ritual. The ritual of the saints is now largely confined to "purified" processions geared to the major church holidays. The *cofradías* barely hold on, now largely as quaint vestiges of the past. The same natives fill the positions year after year. The *principales* no longer unite as a decision-making body, and the Indian alcalde is powerless, subject to the orders of the municipal alcalde.

Much of the traditional culture persists in the rural area, but it is no longer integrated by the fundamental social groups there. Clans, hamlets, and cantons are divided by class and religious differences and do not support "customs" in a united way. Nevertheless, there are some practicing shamans, the Quiché language is widely spoken, the sacred altars are remembered and sporadically used, and many traditional domestic activities prevail. The traditional lifeway is still a possible option in the rural areas, albeit a marginal one.

The Rojas clan perhaps typifies what has happened in Santa Cruz. The lineage descended from Juan, the patriarch of the prerevolutionary period, has continued to occupy lands near the ruins. But two closely related Rojas lineages sold their lands and moved into town. Within Juan's own lineage one son became a merchant and at the time of this writing lives in Guatemala City. Another son and a daughter have moved to town. When Catholic Action propaganda reached the clan in 1955, members of the younger generation (Juan's grandchildren) joined the movement, while the older generation rejected it. This division led to sharp conflict, the elders criticizing their younger kin for abandoning the ancestors. Albert, of the older generation, continues to serve as priest-shaman for the lineage, but he does so on his own without support from the reformed Catholics among the clan members.

Typical of the younger generation is Juan Rojas, the grandson of the patriarch Juan. He owns 7 *cuerdas* of land (about 0.8 acre) next to the Res-

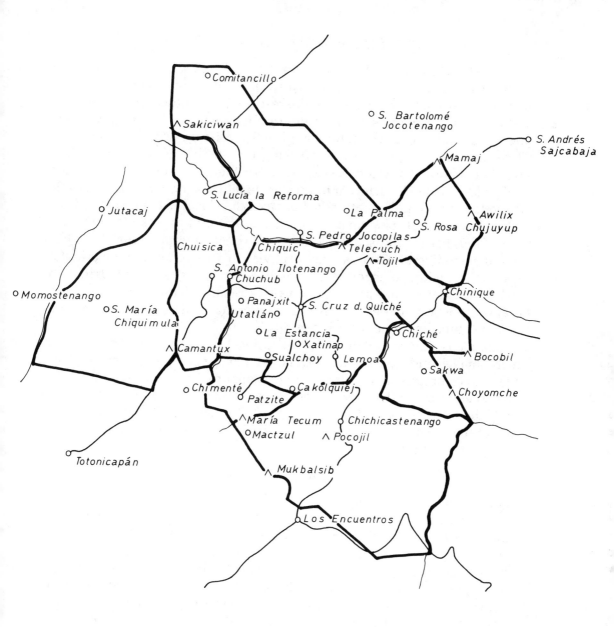

Fig. 11.1. Map of present-day Quiché *municipios*. Based on IGN maps, 1:50,000.

guardo site, and another 4 *cuerdas* in canton La Estancia. He farms the land each year, but the maize crop provides only about one-half his family's needs. To earn money to purchase the rest, as well as other foods, clothing, and medicine, Juan sews woven palm fronds into hats. He can make up to one dollar a day, though he cannot work at the task regularly. His oldest son, Cleto, has taken a job in town working on small construction projects. Together Juan and Cleto barely scratch out the two hundred dollars the family of seven needs each year to survive. Juan finds comfort in his Catholic Action faith and regularly attends mass and catechism. He has rejected the world view of the old shamans, favoring instead the "Protestant" ethic: faith in one God, hard work, self-discipline, and constant improvement. He has no understanding of his royal ancestry, viewing the ruins as the work of a mysterious, unknown people. The archaeologists have recruited him to work on the excavations at Utatlán. He is extremely pleased about that, not because he is learning about his Quiché heritage but because it provides work and thus betterment for his family.

Chinique is similar to Santa Cruz in sociocultural condition, though it is much smaller and has a relatively larger Latin population. Few natives engage in commerce, and peasant life is similar to that in rural Santa Cruz. External economic influences are very weak, and change is occurring more slowly there than in Santa Cruz (Earle n.d.). Pockets of traditional culture in some of the isolated cantons of Chinique may persist longer than those in similar areas of Santa Cruz.

Chichicastenango

Population in this community has about doubled in the past thirty years, mushrooming to 45,000 persons (1974), all but about 5 percent of them living in the rural zone. The lands cannot support such numbers of people, and many natives now depend on weaving, woodcarving, and other crafts, as well as long-distance trading. Tourism has become a major industry at Chichicastenango, and most of the craft goods are sold to the thousands of foreigners who visit the town each year. These various economic developments in the community have fostered the emergence of a class of commercialized *indigenes*. Some of them have become wealthy: owners of tourist-goods stores, trucks and buses, small bars and hotels, and stores of various kinds in Guatemala City and other large towns and cities. Other acculturated natives have modest earnings from practicing crafts, serving as guides and waiters, and hawking goods around the country. In Chichicastenango a powerful symbol of the emergence of this indigenous class was the election in the mid-1970s for the first time of an indigenous municipal alcalde. True to his background, he proved to be more interested in promoting business than in perpetuating traditional native culture.

The traditionalists remain dominant in the rural area, despite Catholic Action's success in winning over 25 to 30 percent of the peasantry. Traditional ritual and political processes of the 1930s continue much as they were. The *principales* and *calpules*, the latter still numbering six, continue to govern the sixty-four cantons of the rural community. The native alcalde administers under their direction, along with the traditional civil-religious hierarchy. The *cofradías* still carry out elaborate ceremonies in honor of the saints, though fewer of them now. Shamanistic ritual at mountain altar shrines on behalf of both clan members and individual clients persists unabated. The extensive traditionalism of Chichicastenango is not a false creation for tourist consumption, but it is nevertheless strengthened by tourists' interest in it. As Gruhn has remarked (1973), though Chichicastenango "has been exposed to powerful outside influences in recent years, nevertheless traditional culture persists in its basic elements."

Chiché, San Antonio Ilotenango, and San Pedro Jocopilas are similar to Chichicastenango in their traditional community structure. They lack the tourist industry, and their Latin and acculturated indigenous sectors are small compared with those of Chichicastenango. Small-scale commerce and work on the coastal plantations provide the external economic opportunities needed to counter overpopulation of the land. As in Chichicastenango, Catholic Action has won over only about 25 to 30 percent of the population. Today commercial influences probably represent a stronger threat to traditional culture than Catholicism. In general, however, traditional town and rural ritual and political processes continue.

In San Antonio, despite some loss of power by the *principales* and the shamans, a combined hierarchy of eight *cofradías* and many civil officials still functions, as does a rural organization made up of clans and cantons (Falla 1972; 1975; Carmack n.d.). Many priest-shamans (*chuchkajaw*) operate in the rural zones, and one of them performs rituals on behalf of the entire community at sacred mountains at the cardinal points. These traditional practices continue despite an active Catholic Action membership (about one-third of the population), a demographic increase of almost 3 percent a year, the massive annual migration of almost one thousand workers to the coast, and the activities of about two hundred long-distance merchants (Falla 1972, p. 442).

Santa María Chiquimula

In the past thirty-five years the population of this community has increased by about 50 percent (in 1974 it totaled more than fifteen thousand persons). This has created intolerable pressures on the land, forcing perhaps half the male adults into either long-distance commerce or artisanry, especially tailoring (Herbert 1971). Many native workers migrate to the coasts each year. The numbers of commercial natives are particularly large, though their "petit mercantile capitalism" has brought less wealth to them than to their counterparts in either Santa Cruz or Chichicastenango. These "petit bourgeoisie" have been attracted to Protestant sects, and today more than half the population may be Protestants. The other half is roughly divided between the Reformed Catholics and the traditionalists. Strong sectarian opposition exists between the Catholics and Protestants. There are virtually no Latins in the community, and the town center has remained small (about 1,500 persons) and undeveloped.

As might be supposed, traditional public ritual has been drastically curtailed. Shamanic ritual in the rural zone remains, but it is highly fragmented. A secular, syncretized form of government exists in which town and rural administrations are combined, officials being named by consensus. These officials are invariably natives who are more or less unacculturated; presumably the merchants are too preoccupied with business matters outside the community to serve.

Patzité and Santa Lucía la Reforma are similar to Chiquimula, though on a much smaller scale. More land seems to be available in these communities, and there are fewer merchants and artisans. Catholic Action has had greater success there vis à vis the Protestant sects, and traditional culture is somewhat stronger.

Today the old site of Utatlán languishes in ruin and neglect. Its glorious past has been forgotten, even by the direct descendants of its kings (notably the Rojas clan). The growing numbers of acculturated natives still have not championed Utatlán culture as their own, and the Latins continue to view it either as a source of profit (through tourism or looting) or as a symbol of their domination of the natives. Even the progressive peasants, those who have been socialized by the Catholic Action movement, do not identify with the culture of their ancestors. Instead they find hope in the social-reform programs, partly religious and partly secular, that are sweeping Guatemala. Only the shamans and other traditional peasants find meaning in ancient Quiché forms, as expressed in the rituals they perform at the ruins and sacred shrines and in other customary practices: use of the old calendar, ancestor worship, supplication of Earth, and *cofradía* service. Nevertheless, by present standards they are representatives of a marginal culture lacking the substance and integration that characterized the Quiché community in the past.

In general it can be said that Utatlán culture has been lost in such communities as Santa Cruz and Chinique, as well as in important native sectors of the other communities. In more traditional communities like Chichicastenango the old Quiché traditions have become a "culture of refuge." They now provide the forms around which conservative peasants coalesce in their struggle to retain their corporate community against the onslaught of modern forces. But it is a struggle of attrition, as each year ancient patterns are neglected and new recruits are gained by the agents of modernization. The day will come when even this peasantized version of Quiché survivals will be altered beyond recognition. Utatlán culture as an unconscious way of life, will have passed irreversibly into the realm of history. We can be certain, however, that in some new, revitalized guise, this dynamic culture will yet inspire the native peoples of Quiché in years to come.

12
CONCLUSIONS

In the conclusions to a large work it is always tempting to repeat too much of what has already been said or to introduce new information. Yet another temptation is to try to conclude more than the data and analyses warrant. In the discussion to follow, I try to resist such temptations by returning to problems raised in the first chapter of the book. In particular I attempt to draw conclusions about the *development* of the Utatlán community.

I begin by discussing developmental factors suggested specifically by the Quiché case. That is, I look at the Utatlán Quichés as an instance of "specific evolution." Next I examine the Quichés from a comparative perspective to determine their commonalities with and contrasts to other Mesoamerican peoples. The first set of comparisons is with Maya communities very similar to Utatlán. Conclusions about Quiché development obtained by this procedure take us beyond the specific case but remain controlled and relatively reliable. Next I make broader comparisons with Mesoamerican peoples— especially the Mexicas—who provide greater historical, ecological, and structural contrasts to the Utatlán Quichés. Conclusions derived from this second approach must be considered more speculative and less reliable. Nevertheless, they lead to the discovery of certain broad features in Quiché development that can be referred to as "general evolution."

THE SPECIFIC UTATLÁN CASE

In simple terms Quiché development would appear to be a classic case of evolution from chiefdom to state (Service 1962; 1975). The early Quiché chiefdom of Chujuyup consisted of a group of lineages confederated for purposes of war and common defense. The lineages were unstratified and were multifunctional. Lineage heads were both political and religious leaders, as well as warriors. Success in war brought goods, subjects, wives, and lands, all of which were redistributed among the lineages. With these developments came lineage specialization and stratification. One lineage, the Ajaw Quiché, gained leadership authority, and its town, Jakawitz, became the political center of the chiefdom. Development from that chiefly nucleus to the emergence of the Quiché state was in a straight line. The Quichés themselves recognized the change in their society and explained that it had required special symbols brought from Toltec country and transfer to new, more impressive towns, Pismachi and Utatlán.

In the discussion to follow, I examine the factors that seem to have been most important in the evolution of the Quichés from the Chujuyup chiefdom to the Utatlán state. These are the factors suggested by the specific data of the Quiché case. I refer to them as the frontier, ecological, urban, political, and ideological factors. For the present they can be considered the specific characteristics of Quiché evolution. In the two subsequent sections, where these factors are examined in the context of other Mesoamerican cultures, I draw some conclusions about the relative importance of these factors in Quiché development and their general applicability to Mesoamerica as a whole.

The Frontier Factor

It has been shown that the Quiché forefathers came to Utatlán from a frontier zone (the Gulf Coast), bringing with them cultural patterns containing elements of both Mexica and Maya traditions. While we cannot know for certain the extent to which the resulting Quiché state was based on models the warlords brought with them from the coast, it seems clear that they were a crucial factor. The frontier patterns gave the Quichés definite advantages in highland Guatemala. Principal among these advantages was a superior war-making capacity. The superiority appears to have consisted of effective over-all military organization rather than any special technological capability. The Quichés combined the best weapons available—bows and arrows, lances, hatchets, spear-throwers, swords—with fearless daring (one example being that they fought at night) and rigid lineage discipline (the Toltec "code" of honor). Also behind their military success was a religious ideology adapted to conquest warfare: gods who demanded human sacrifice and tribute goods; priest-leaders who it was believed could transform themselves into those gods and fierce beasts; chiefs convinced that they were successors to mighty Toltec conquerors of the past and hence destined to rule those around them and to live in pomp and splendor.

Quiché military ideology was integrated through artistic symbols of great power. These master symbols were also key elements of their frontier culture. Monumental architecture in Toltec style (with skull-rack altars and *talud y tablero* temples); dramatic sacrificial dances, typified by the

"Rabinal-Achi"; and accession ceremonies with their Toltec insignia and body painting must have been awe-inspiring to the indigenous peoples. Such symbols surely facilitated the acceptance of Quiché authority on a basis more stable than raw military superiority.

In contrast to the Quiché warlords, the native peoples of the Quiché area appear to have been steeped in an ancient, specialized culture. They were perhaps stronger in ritual than in warfare. Politically they were fragmented into weak chiefdoms and lived in tiny, undefended settlements. They relied heavily on the ritualism of warfare rather than on military preparedness. After many centuries of isolation they were vulnerable to the Quiché bands that suddenly invaded their territory in the early part of the thirteenth century. In the military competition that ensued, the Quichés were resoundingly victorious. The evidence now available indicates that the Quichés used their military success to destroy most of the native elite culture, assimilate its rural elements, and greatly expand their own cultural patterns.

The Ecological Factor

Local ecological conditions of the Quiché area can be viewed as a second major factor in the rise of the state at Utatlán. The Chujuyup area, for example, where the Quiché chiefdom was first implanted, was an ideal base of operations for the early stage of development. Its mountain peaks and ridges afforded impregnable defenses for the small lineage groups of immigrant warlords. The native population of the area was sparse and at a simple level of social integration even by standards of the provincial central Quiché area. The natives of the Chujuyup Mountains lived scattered in deerskin tents, hunting and gathering much of their subsistence. Both the social and the material conditions of the area provided a setting in which the Quichés could develop their political system, at first on a small scale. Later, after gaining control of the mountainous region surrounding the Jakawitz capital, Quiché political development demanded an ecological zone of far greater potential. The Utatlán plains provided the needed setting.

Any evaluation of the ecological conditions of the central plains in terms of their influence on the emerging Quiché state at Utatlán is deceptive, for no single feature stands out. The zone of Quiché activities was not one of great river valleys or basins, as was the case with some of the other Mesoamerican states. Nor was it the site of a highly intensive form of agriculture, such as irrigation, *chinampa* farming, or complex terracing. No strategic resource blessed the area—there were no deposits of obsidian, jade, salt, or metals. Nevertheless, the central Quiché area was characterized by a combination of ecological factors that provided favorable conditions for cultural development. The topography permitted defense but did not prevent relatively good communication in all directions. Weather and altitude combined to provide a healthy environment for the people and a stable setting for agriculture. Soils were deep and rich, and, as long as they were not overused or left open to erosion, they could support very productive highland dry farming. Though agriculture was not intensive, the people produced maize, beans, and squash in surplus quantities. Natural resources included basic materials for buildings and for utilitarian ceramic and fiber wares. These factors combined to produce a large, dense local population, well above the minimum density levels needed to support advanced cultural systems.

It would appear, then, that an ecological basis can be found for the Quiché state on the central plains, despite the absence of a single dominant ecological feature. Nevertheless, it is also apparent that the Utatlán state could not have functioned without its provinces. They supplied resources and information needed to maintain some of Utatlán's more cosmopolitan features: metallurgy, crafts, markets, Mexica *haute culture*. Significantly, Quiché conquests outside the central basin gave them control over the gamut of Mesoamerican ecologies: high *tierra fria* basins rich in maize (such as Quezaltenango); intermediate *tierra templada* zones with precious-stone and metal resources (such as the Joyabaj area); and *tierra caliente* lowlands where exotic goods—cacao and feathers—could be obtained (Sajcabaja and the Pacific Coast). Control of these various zones integrated the Quichés with a complex series of regional symbioses, the result of which was to make virtually every known Mesoamerican resource available to them. So, even though the Utatlán community was primarily formed in the central area and continued to the end to draw on that region for its essential sustenance, it was also dependent upon the much wider ecological niche made available by the vast conquests of the Utatlán armies.

The Urban Factor

A third major factor in the rise of the Quiché state was the emergence of a nucleated center at Utatlán. While the center may have been both a cause and a consequence of the Quiché state, its causal role is of primary interest here. Archaelogical research has been more useful than the documentary sources in clarifying this factor.

The political center of the Quiché chiefdom at Jakawitz represented an advance in nucleation over earlier settlements in the Quiché area. At least twelve major buildings were constructed in a small, confined zone, making it more nucleated and perhaps twice as large as any of the native centers of the area. Adjacent house platforms and walls added still further to the Jakawitz complex. The center was designed to serve as a town (*tinamit*), a central place where elites resided, ritual was performed, markets were held, chiefs met in council, enemies were fought off, and the sacredness of the chiefdom was symbolized. These were the same functions performed later at Utatlán, showing that Jakawitz was the prototype for the later urban center. In other ways, however, Jakawitz lacked "urban" character. The residents were probably restricted to members of chiefly families, who could not have numbered more than a few hundred. Other chiefs of the confederacy lived in towns a few kilometers away. Much ritual was performed at shrines some distance from the town, even rituals significant to the chiefdom as a whole. There is no evidence that craft and marketing activities at Jakawitz were superior to the same activities at other centers in the chiefdom.

Utatlán retained all the urban features of Jakawitz and added many new ones. It was the place of residence of the highest officials of the state. At Utatlán leaders from different lineages came together within the same settlements, with their own living quarters, lineage houses, and temples. The result was the development of towns with up to one hundred major buildings, almost ten times the number at Jakawitz. While some officials of different confederate units (the Nima Quichés, Nijaibs, Tamubs, and Ilocabs) may have resided at different towns, the towns were within a few hundred meters of each other. In effect they formed a single, nucleated town connected by causeways and paths. The total number of buildings at this giant nuclear center reached two to three hundred. Similarly, the number of residents of nuclear Utatlán (Utatlán, Pismachi, Pilocab, and Resguardo) greatly increased. If we count the suburbs, perhaps ten to twenty thousand people lived there.

Ritual formerly performed on mountaintops outside town came to be performed publicly within a single center. This not only brought the officiants into town to live but also stimulated the integration of ritual buildings, symbols, and ceremonies. Our evidence indicates that many of the symbolic orientations holding *between* centers during the chiefdom period were combined *within* Utatlán. The formation of these new composite court, temple, and shrine complexes led to major developments in Quiché ritual. Similarly, the dispersed crafts and markets of the Jakawitz period came under the control of nuclear Utatlán. This brought artisans and merchants to the urban center, particularly the suburban zones. The presence of these "classes" in town must have significantly affected Quiché social life, though our sources do not permit us to specify the precise nature of their influence.

Like Jakawitz before it, nuclear Utatlán provided protection against the Quichés' enemies. In contrast to events of the Jakawitz period, however, there is no evidence that the Utatlán center was ever attacked until the arrival of the Spaniards in 1524. This indicates that Utatlán's defenses were militarily superior to those of Jakawitz. Compared with Jakawitz, the Utatlán towns had deeper canyon sides, larger walls, and many more defenders. Beyond that, the main political center was protected by the three large satellite centers surrounding it. They in turn had outer defensive garrisons, the auxiliary settlements. Finally, contingents of commoner warriors (*chinamital*) in walled fortifications manned the canyon edges surrounding the nuclear complex, and other armed commoner units (*calpules*) were strategically stationed throughout the Quiché basin. The Quichés of Utatlán considered themselves invulnerable to outside attack, and they probably were to all but the Spaniards with their European military technology. The military security provided by nuclear Utatlán must have had an important influence on sociocultural development. It surely was linked to such cultural trends as external military conquest and expansion, internal political competition (see below), and the elaborate organizing of rural peoples.

We should not overlook the symbolic impact the urban character of Utatlán had on the peoples in highland Guatemala. Utatlán's thousands of inhabitants, monumental buildings, impregnable fortifications, dramatic ceremonies, sophisticated goods, painted artworks, and priestly sages were grandly impressive. Visitors to the town were humbled; even its conquerors the Spaniards praised its grandeur. The native sources indicate that Utatlán was famed as the place of power and majesty (*k'ak'al, tepewal*) and for its sacred aura (*awas*). The native settlements encountered by the Quiché forefathers when they first came to the area, or even Jakawitz, their first political center, could not compare in splendor with nuclear Utatlán. In setting apart the Quichés from other peoples and making them sacred, urban Utatlán played an important role in the development of the Quiché state.

The Political Factor

Our sources suggest that political competition was another major factor in the evolution of the Quiché state. Rivalry among the competing lineages, confederacies, social strata, and states characterized Quiché history from beginning to end. It had the effect of propelling victorious groups upward, each lift bringing with it more complex and powerful political forms. The developmental movement was not all upward, however. There were valleys along with the peaks, for some conflicts eroded Quiché sociocultural integration, though never below the state level after the founding of Utatlán.

During the early phase of Quiché history in the Chujuyup region the competition was between indigenous and Quiché confederacies. The struggle was so intense, so difficult, that Quiché lineages united internally in an all-out effort to prevail. Even distant lineages, such as those of the Rabinals, the Cakchiquels, and the Tzutujils, were allied in those early days. The Nima Quichés, somewhat favorably situated in the Chujuyup Valley, gained leadership authority over the other lineages, the Tamubs, the Ilocabs, and the Cakchiquels. The political relations forged during that crucial period of struggle were never really broken. They provided the basic infrastructure of the Quiché state that later crystallized at Utatlán.

Once the Quiché basin had been secured, political competition shifted to the lineages within the incipient Quiché state. Our sources indicate that there was considerable maneuvering for control by the Nima Quiché lineages. Strategies of all kinds were employed to gain advantage: casting aspersions on the legitimacy of the line of another lineage, acquiring Toltec icons from the east, establishing marital alliances with powerful outside groups, extolling the power of patron deities, and so on. In the final analysis, the ability of a lineage to make war was probably decisive, and competition for military success must have been intense. Its military prowess appears to have thrust the Cawek lineage from a secondary position to the forefront in the Quiché political system. The Caweks credited their political success to magical leaders (C'otuja, K'ucumatz, Q'uik'ab), and indeed charismatic military leaders may have been a factor. But it can also be demonstrated that material advantage came from the Caweks' control over the best lands, the largest numbers of peoples, and the richest resources.

Important to the Caweks' rise to power was the military challenge raised at Pismachi by the Ilocabs during the days of King C'otuja. Not only did the Caweks' victory prove their military superiority—indeed, it may have given them the kingship—but, by adding the resources of the defeated Ilocabs, in effect it doubled their already considerable holdings. It must have also secured the Caweks' ties with other lineages, including the Tamubs, who were forced to take sides. The Caweks' successes of this kind laid the power base from which K'ucumatz and Q'uik'ab were later able to undertake the vast conquests for which the Quichés became famous.

The political competition that erupted at Utatlán in the days of Q'uik'ab is more difficult to evaluate in developmental terms. The protagonists came from competing social strata, though on the surface elite lineages carried forward the action. Vassal warriors competed with the lords and their serfs. The conflict greatly strengthened the commoner sector at Utatlán while diminishing the power and authority of the ruling aristocracy. It is clear that this weakened the Quiché kingdom as a whole, as shown by the immediate secession of their Cakchiquel subjects. Utatlán and its rural peoples (the Utatlán community), on the other hand, experienced only a loosening of the stratification system. If, as seems to have been the case, Utatlán society moved to a degree from a status to a class structure, then the change was in the direction of greater social complexity. That might well be viewed as evolutionary development.

During the final phase of Quiché history political competition appears to have shifted to rival kingdoms of the Quichés. The Utatlán Quichés were almost continually at war with the Cakchiquels, the Tzutujils, the Mexicas, and finally the Spaniards. The wars provided strong incentive for the Quichés to maintain internal harmony and hold onto their subject provinces.

Our sources for this period are limited, but they indicate that political unity was restored at Utatlán. Significantly, however, the Nijaibs emerged as a power alongside the Caweks, sharing authority with them. Competition between the two lineages may have led to important political developments at Utatlán, but that was at least partly subordinated to the need for unity in the face of common outside enemies.

Other competitive struggles at Utatlán could be mentioned. For example, Utatlán "princes" competed with each other for the highest offices of state. As shown by Gluckman (1963) in the case of the native African kingdoms, conflicts of this kind tend to promote the values of high office and help create and support them. In the Utatlán case elite minimal lineages appear to have been the main participants in this competitive conflict. Our sources also indicate that the provinces of the Quiché state rebelled from time to time and even participated in revolts at Utatlán itself. The creation of the *calpul* organization in the rural area of Utatlán may have been partly a response to provincial problems, for its organizational principles were exported to the provinces as a form of colonial rule. The active role of Quiché priests in resisting Spanish Catholicism after the Conquest suggests that the priests may have been a further competitive power within Utatlán society. There are hints in the documents that they competed with the warriors for influence, a situation which may have led them to organize internally beyond what was needed for performance of ritual.

The Ideological Factor

A fifth possible major factor in the rise of the Quiché state was an elaborate cosmological scheme that the sources suggest was created by the Quichés of Utatlán. Fragmentary information points to the synthesis by the Quiché elite of a well-integrated, adaptively successful world view centered on the Tojil cult. There is some evidence that this symbolic scheme provided both goals for the development of a statelike community and an ideological basis for integrating the disparate elements that went into its formation.

The first Spanish missionaries claimed that the Quiché religion had monotheistic features. While that observation was undoubtedly in part the result of Christian bias, it had some basis in fact. While there is much evidence that Quiché religion was polytheistic, nevertheless, the patron god of Utatlán, Tojil, became the supreme god of the Quichés and the means of unifying most symbolism related to the other deities. For example, Junajpu was apparently made an aspect of Tojil, and the hallowed myths of the hero-twins were integrated into Quiché cosmology. Similarly, K'ucumatz and Jurakan became additional aspects of Tojil, who was thereby linked to the great creation myths. Tojil's association with the jaguar, the lord of beasts, provided a symbolic link with the powerful totemic belief system (nagualism). Nagualism in turn was intimately tied to the earth-deity complex, Juyup Tak'aj. Tojil was also the sun and the rain (and thunder) and hence the ruler of the natural forces most important in agriculture. Tojil's procreative powers extended to human as well as vegetal spheres, for he symbolized the phallic principle. Thus all the important sacred, deified forces of the Quiché universe found unification and personification in Tojil.

Time and space, conceptual domains of fundamental importance to the Quichés, also were unified in the Tojil concept. Tojil was associated with the most important calendric units: the first month of the year (Tequexepual), the twentieth day (Junajpu), a year-bearer (Quej), the daily appearance of Venus (Ikok'ij), and the daylight hours in general (*K'ij*, "sun"). The all-important east direction, "where the sun goes up," was symbolically linked to Tojil. That directional symbolism in turn gave Tojil the key position in the scheme of cosmological directions, with their four associated colors, roads, year-bearers, and fates.

Tojil was the patron of the ruling Cawek lineage of the Quichés. This link provided an association not only of authority but also of conquest and human sacrifice. Hence Tojil was the patron of rulers of all the Quiché groups, whether Nima Quiché, Tamub, or Ilocab. He was also patron of all warriors and all sacrificial priests. Through his ties with sun and rain Tojil provided patronage for Quiché milpa farmers. It is even possible that the artisans at Utatlán were Tojil clients, since their patron deity the monkey had definite ties with the sun in Maya cosmology (Thompson 1960, p. 143).

It has been emphasized that the symbolism associated with Tojil played a directing role in the settlement patterning of Utatlán (see chapter 7). We find his political prominence expressed in the large size, the central location, and the elaborate architectural design of the Tojil temple. The military patronage of Tojil was expressed by positioning close to his temple the skull-rack altar, the gladiatorial platform, and the council houses of military lineages (the Rajpop Achij). Tojil's close relationship with the major cosmological forces of the universe found locational expression in the positioning nearby of temples dedicated to the creator deities (K'ucumatz, Tepew), the deity of night and the female principle (Awilix), and the underworld (the ball court, representing Xibalba). There are also hints in our sources that key elements of the master myth about the hero-twins found locational expression in Tojil and his temple. Junajpu, an aspect of Tojil, perhaps provided the orienting point for this association between myth and settlement pattern.

The temple of Tojil too was the focal point for definite time and directional orientations at Utatlán. The fundamental pattern was the cardinal-point arrangement that linked together the western Tojil temple with the temples of Awilix (east), Jakawitz (south), and K'ucumatz (north). The year-bearer pattern apparently followed directional lines, Tojil as Quej, Awilix as Ik', and

Jakawitz and K'ucumatz as Noj and E. Many other settlement features at Utatlán may well have received their locational patterns from Tojil, for example, palace courts with Tojil subtemples, streets leading to and from Tojil temple plazas, and warrior sections linked to Tojil buildings.

In summary, the symbols associated with the Tojil concept gave coherence to the powerful natural forces, supernatural deities, social units, and spatiotemporal principles of the Quiché universe. It appears to have provided an essential "rationalization" (in the Weberian sense) of the state: it made its actualization a goal, it harmonized the disparate beliefs of its diverse components, it promoted awe and respect for its authority, and it allowed some congruity between its social and symbolic domains. It would be easy to see more form to Quiché "religion" than it actually had, but at the same time the powerful integrational role played by that religion in the development of the Utatlán state must not be overlooked.

Unfortunately, the process by which Utatlán priests and lords synthesized the Tojil religion will probably never be known. The Spanish conquerors dealt ruthlessly with Quiché priests and erased much of the elite religion before it could be recorded. But that is true also of the formation of the Quiché state in general, and the discussion above of major factors in its development is based on highly fragmentary information. The archaeological materials have been most helpful in preserving insights into the process, and we can expect a better understanding of it in years to come as the archaeological work goes forward.

CONTROLLED COMPARISON

Developmental features of the Utatlán community can be further elucidated by comparison with other Maya communities. I have chosen to compare cases similar to Utatlán in historical origins, time period, political status, and general level of development. I also limit myself to those cases for which relatively detailed archaeological and ethnohistoric studies are available. These limitations are designed to eliminate highly extraneous variables affecting development. In this way it is hoped that some of the less obvious but nonetheless significant features of Utatlán development will be cast into relief.

Iximché

The first comparative case is Iximché, the Cakchiquel capital. The ruins of the site have been investigated by Guillemin (1965; 1967; 1969), and Fox (1975, pp. 185ff.) has summarized its settlement features. The ethnohistoric sources, principal among which is *The Annals of the Cakchiquels*, have yet to receive a thorough analysis (Carmack 1973). Iximché was very similar to

Utatlán, being a direct offshoot of that settlement. Nevertheless, some fine differences between the communities are suggestive of different lines of development.

The similarities between the Cakchiquels of Iximché and the Quichés of Utatlán were numerous and fundamental: leaders claimed origins from the Toltecs; the economy was based on highland-basin dry farming, to which control over lowland products was later added; history was mainly dynastic and military, culminating in an internal military revolt; society was divided into three fundamental strata: lords, vassals, and slaves; patrilineal segmentation prevailed and was strengthened by control over territorial estates; authority was vested in confederated lineages whose heads (*ajpop, ajpop c'amaja, k'alel,* and so on) formed the administrative hierarchy of state; elite symbolism centered upon deities who were both the patrons of social groups and Mexicanized personifications of the forces of nature.

The settlement patterns of Iximché are also similar to those of Utatlán. The Iximché settlement was highly nucleated and densely populated. It was strongly defensive, surrounded by deep canyons on all sides and a strategic fortification at the entrance. Buildings were arranged in repetitive ritual-council-palace complexes. Main-plaza temples, long structures, and ball courts show partial orientation to the cardinal directions. Architectural styles follow the Epi-Toltec pattern, and painted murals are in the Mixteca-Puebla art style (Marqusee n.d.). Multiple levels of construction and plaster layers are found throughout the site.

Although the Cakchiquels initially welcomed the Spaniards into their town, they later resisted conquest in a manner much like the Quichés'. Also like the Quichés, they syncretized traditional and Spanish culture and eventually fell into a retreating culture of refuge.

The differences between Utatlán and Iximché are harder to define, but important cultural variations can be detected. For example, the Cakchiquels admitted that their Toltec affiliation was indirect, through Quiché lords who were their superiors. They acknowledged the debt to Utatlán in forming the Iximché community but also claimed that they were militarily superior to the Quichés. Iximché was situated at an elevation almost a thousand feet higher than Utatlán, subjecting the inhabitants to frost and less stable agricultural conditions than those in the Quiché basin. Cakchiquel history was more secular than that recorded for the Quichés, showing more interest in such events as natural disasters and absolute dates (the Cakchiquels using a long-count dating system). Stratification at Iximché was less rigid than at Utatlán, with a very close relationship between lords and warriors. Serfs were less important also, since lineages maintained greater corporate integrity. Consequently, the great Tukuchee revolt at Iximché involved lineages and their warriors rather than representatives of social classes. The hierarchy of officials at Iximché was somewhat shallow and was shared vertically by confederated lineages (especially the Xajil and Sotzil lineages). Ritual was somewhat "nonecclesiastical" compared with that at Utatlán. The highly integrated sun cult of the Quichés was only weakly developed by the Cakchiquels, who instead emphasized earth deities, such as the Cakix family (mountains, earthquakes) and the serpent (the plains).

The archaeology of the Utatlán and Iximché sites provides further interesting contrasts. Iximché lacked the satellite sites that made greater Utatlán the large nucleated center that it was. A commoner section at Iximché was more discrete (separated by a wall and a moat) but closer to the main center than comparable sections at Utatlán. Only three or four ritual-council-palace complexes are visible at Iximché, and in the absence of one central plaza they form the pluralized main plazas of the settlement. There is evidence that the divisions between these building complexes were accentuated by separating walls, presumably because of the widespread interlineage conflict in the community. The presence of two separate ball courts at Iximché shows this same pluralism relative to Utatlán, which has only one ball court. Similarly, no central temple like Tojil's stands out. Most buildings in the main plazas of Iximché are less closely oriented to the cardinal points than are those at Utatlán; instead they follow the natural contours of the land. The big houses at Iximché are confined to the northern side of the site, and none of them flank the temples as at Utatlán. The painted murals at Iximché are more Mexican than Utatlán examples, though that may only reflect the limited nature of our sample.

The colonial history of the Cakchiquels has not been worked out in detail, but it is my impression that once the native rulers of Iximché capitulated they and their followers were less rebellious than the Quichés in the centuries that followed. Nativistic movements have been less notable, and traditional culture has deteriorated in Tecpan Guatemala (Iximché) far more than it has in Quiché. It must be realized, however, that relative closeness to the colonial capital of Santiago (now Antigua) may have affected the process of culture destruction among the Cakchiquels.

What does Iximché teach us about the development of Utatlán? To begin with, we note the rapidity with which the Cakchiquels in the time of Q'uik'ab were able to convert their provincial organization into a political unit nearly the equal of Utatlán. Indeed, the defeat of the Quiché armies at Iximché by the Cakchiquels soon after their secession (see chapter 5) dramatized this fact. Obviously, the Quichés at Utatlán held only minimal advantage over political units elsewhere in the highlands, including the various provincial divisions of the kingdom. Through time the degree of Quiché political superiority decreased, as their patterns became transportable or replicable in other areas.

Much like the manner in which early Quiché culture represented a simplified frontier version of the complex Mexican and Mayan civilizations around them, so too the Cakchiquels may have represented a simplification of later Quiché community patterns. At any rate, compared with Iximché, Utatlán was culturally complex. The Quiché urban center consisted of aggregates of towns and rings of sub-urban zones, while Iximché formed a single town. Bureaucratizing offices with a definite centralized hierarchy at Utatlán contrasted with the simpler Cakchiquel rule by lineage confederation. And the relative simplicity of power through military prowess seen at Iximché was complicated at Utatlán by the development of power derived from sacred traditions and religious symbols. The complexity of the Quiché community is probably reflected too in the greater difficulty with which they reached accommodation with their Spanish overlords. Other relatively complex features of Utatlán already mentioned would be the more fully developed middle "classes," the more elaborate priesthood, and the more extensively "rationalized" mythology (for example, evolution of the Tojil cult).

Iximché provides a useful perspective for viewing the secularization that has been noted for Utatlán. The intensified military nature of Iximché seems to represent a step beyond Utatlán in secularization. That was perhaps expressed at Iximché by the haphazard use of cardinal-point directions for building orientation, the considerable dissociation of political and priestly functions (as suggested, for example, by the placement of council houses away from temples), the recording of chronologically exact history, and the close ties between lords and commoners (as shown by, among other things, the propinquity of the two groups at the Iximché center). Fox (1977) has also called attention to the Cakchiquels' use of what appear to have been military garrisons at their provincial centers, whereas the Quichés tended to adapt their colonial units to the old ceremonial centers of provincial peoples. I suspect that there are many other secular features in Cakchiquel culture not found at Utatlán, but a more thorough reconstruction of the Iximché community will be required before they can be defined.

Mayapán

Mayapán, the large settlement in Yucatán, is an ideal case to compare with the Utatlán community. The documentary sources regarding Mayapán have been admirably summarized by Roys (1943; 1957; 1962; 1964), and the archaeology of the site was exhaustively studied by the Carnegie Institution (Pollock et al. 1962; Smith 1971; Thompson 1957). In addition, nearly all general statements about Maya culture since the Carnegie studies have taken Mayapán into account (Haviland 1968; 1969; Willey and Bullard 1965; Pollock 1965; Proskouriakoff 1965; Weaver 1972).

In a previous study I pointed out some of the more obvious similarities between the Quiché and the Mayapán communities (1968, pp. 85–86). I noted that both had traditions of Mexican origin that could probably be traced to the Gulf Coast of the thirteenth century. The settlements were similar in that they were both fortified (Mayapán was surrounded by a wall) and urbanized (Mayapán had about eleven to twelve thousand inhabitants). Architectural similarities consisted of the rather crude construction of both, such as the use of uncut stones covered with stucco and Toltec stylistic features (*talud y tablero* at the base of buildings, slanting balustrades ending vertically, colonnaded long structures, and so on). At both Utatlán and Mayapán the main town was said to have been established by the Maya equivalent of the Toltec ruler Quetzalcoatl. Each suffered a severe schism around mid-fifteenth century. Like Utatlán, Mayapán was characterized by militaristic political rule, joint authority of elite lineages, and management of tributary collection. Ritual similarities consisted of prominent Quetzalcoatl cults (the god's temple was central at both places) and of human sacrifice, of both the "arrow" (shooting the victim with arrows while tied to a tree) and the "heart" types. Even the pottery of the two places showed some basic similarities, such as its break with past ceramic traditions, the dominance of red ware, the popularity of censers with attached effigy gods, and the correspondence between the distribution of diagnostic ceramic wares and general political boundaries. The syncretic Mexican and Mayan patterns seen in Yucatán and highland Guatemala, I argued, were to be interpreted as the heritage of Gulf Coast people rather than a reassertion of Mayan over Mexican patterns. Thus the striking parallels between the two areas can be explained in terms of the similar direction, duration, and nature of the Toltec influence reaching these areas (Carmack 1968, p. 86).

It is now possible to compare Utatlán and Mayapán more closely in hopes of shedding additional light on their respective developmental processes. Let us begin with the origin question. The Mayapán origin story as analyzed by Roys (1962; 1964) is more complex than the Quiché tradition. It apparently includes references to the early Postclassic Toltecs who occupied Chichén Itzá around 900 to 1200. The original ancestors of the Mayapán dynasty are referred to as Itzás. They are said to have come from Champotón, in the Campeche area. Around 1200 these Itzá founding fathers began a series of long migrations that took them to the Petén and the eastern part of Yucatán. Like their Quiché counterparts, they were warlords and strangers (*dzul*), conquering native peoples wherever they went. Their first important settlement in Yucatán was Chichén Itzá, which had been abandoned by that time (ca. 1224–44). The Chichén Itzá period is similar to though shorter than the Jakawitz phase in Quiché history. Events were ritualized: the Itzá political alliance was subdivided into four groups corresponding to the cardinal points and a dawn ritual dedicated to Venus was prominent, as was a miraculous rain cult at the sacred cenote. From Chichén the Itzás began exercising great influence on the native people of Yucatán and soon founded Mayapán (ca. 1263–83).

It is clear in the Itzá origin tradition that the forefathers were Nahuatized Chontal speakers. The Quiché forefathers appear to have come from farther west in the Gulf Coast area and had closer Mexican affiliation. Unlike the Quiché lords the Itzá fathers seem to have been purely military and not as strongly associated with the magical powers of animal transformation (nagualism). In the central highlands the Quiché forefathers found no settlement to match the importance of Chichén Itzá, even if that town had been largely abandoned by the time the Itzás arrived there. The traditions of Chichén Itzá and its material remains had a detectable influence on the Itzás' development when they later built Mayapán. Parallels between Itzá and Quiché origins confirm the suggestion made above that both were part of a major diaspora of hybrid Mexican-Mayan military groups moving out of the Gulf Coast area around the beginning of the thirteenth century.

The drastically different ecological settings of Mayapán and Utatlán should be recognized in comparing the development of the two cultures. Mayapán was situated in a semiarid lowland zone of relatively low agricultural and resource potential. Most of the typical lowland crops, such as cotton and cacao, did not grow well in the area, and milpa cultivation was necessarily slash-and-burn. The considerable population of Mayapán— about twelve thousand people, at a density of about three thousand persons per square kilometer—must have been brought in from a large surrounding territory. Mayapán required a wide horticultural zone to sustain it. An ecological fact of primary significance for Mayapán development was its strategic location near well-established trade routes connecting lowland and highland zones. Much trade of that kind was carried out by Gulf Coast Putun merchants traveling by water (Thompson 1970).

In comparison with ecological conditions at Mayapán, those in the Quiché involved fewer centrifugal forces. There was more basis for community development within the Quiché basin itself, and greater focus on local culture was possible. Such "parochialism" relative to Mayapán can be seen in the elaboration of local population control, town-settlement patterning, and craft development. The lesser importance of merchants at Utatlán compared with those at Mayapán is consistent with the differences in trading opportunities between the two areas.

The original cultural patterns of the Mayapán community were somewhat obscured by the disruption that came with the abandonment of the site, but their reconstruction by Roys (1943; 1957) for Yucatán as a whole at the time of the Spanish conquest should apply with some adjustments. Mayapán stratification closely parallels that of the Quichés, though interesting differences appear. The three fundamental divisions in Quiché society—nobles, commoners, and slaves—existed at Mayapán. However, that lords and ladies were called by terms which in Quiché were used for commoners (al, mehen; ixik) may indicate that in Yucatán rank started at a lower level and became sharper downward. For example, Yucatecan traveling merchants were of noble rather than middle rank. There are suggestions in the sources that slaves played a larger social role in Mayapán than they did at Utatlán. Middle "classes" were important at Mayapán too, especially petty merchants, artisans, and stewards. Military mercenaries possibly formed part of the middle sector, though they may have been somewhat lower in rank. Serfs, it would appear, were less important at Mayapán than among the Quichés. That was probably related to the greater importance of slaves in Yucatecan society.

Patrilineal descent groups were a fundamental component of Mayapán social structure, just as they were at Utatlán. Our evidence indicates, however, that lineages at Mayapán were less segmentary than they were in Utatlán. Large nonlocalized clans internally stratified provided important social functions in Yucatán, while such functions were more generally handled by localized communities in the Quiché area. The ward or territorial estate was known in Yucatán but was much less well developed than at Quiché. Thus the term china, equivalent to Quiché chinamit ("estate"), was known but not widely used. The even wider canton divisions of the Quichés (calpules) were apparently unknown or less well developed in Yucatán.

Political authority at Mayapán seems to have paralleled closely that of Utatlán. It was purportedly under the joint control of Mexican-derived aristocratic lineages but tended to become centralized within the most powerful lineage, the Cocom. As with the Quichés, lords of Mayapán's ruling lineages were sent to subject provinces to reside and rule. But Mayapán's centralizing procedures went beyond Utatlán's in forcing provincial chiefs to reside at the capital. Except for the priests, second-level officials at Mayapán appear to have been organized much like their counterparts at Utatlán and even bore some of the same titles: kulel, ajcuchcab, jolpop (compare the Quiché k'alel, ajuchan, ajpop). Yucatecan priests had more power and were more highly esteemed than were Quiché priests. Their hereditary line was kept pure, partly through the administration of tests of esoteric knowledge. They controlled more complex divinatory ritual than their Quiché counterparts did, and that gave them a more prominent role in Mayapán society.

While symbolism at Mayapán may have manifested many of the same tendencies noted for the Quichés, there were significant differences. Like the Tojil cult of the Quichés, rituals associated with Kukulcan, the feathered-serpent deity, were elaborated at Mayapán. There is indirect evidence that

Kukulcan became the patron of the Mayapán "kingdom" and that lords from all over Yucatán attended celebrations for him. But the Kukulcan cult was not as fully integrated with other Yucatecan gods as Tojil was with highland deities. The old sky god (Itzamna), the rain god (Chac), the moon goddess (Ix Chel), and various wind and corner gods retained their independent importance at Mayapán and probably defied successful assimilation into the Kukulcan cult. The merchant god Ekchuuah was prominent at Mayapán, certainly far more so than he was at Utatlán. The proliferation of "idols," both wood and ceramic, at Mayapán suggests that there were patron deities for many different groups and individuals. That too attests to symbolic pluralism at the Mayapán community.

The highly elaborate Maya calendar competed with Mexican patron-god cults as an integrating symbolic system at Mayapán. Mayapán's calendrical knowledge and ritual were more highly esoteric and complex than Utatlán's. Ritual associated with the 260- and 365-day calendars was more extensive in Yucatán, and beyond those two calendars 256-year units (*katúns*) also received ritual celebration. The *katúns* provided an ancient form of recording history in which events repeated themselves. Cyclic *katún* counts (repeating events every 256 years) must have competed with the more linear history introduced by the Mexican-oriented rulers. Maya hieroglyphic writing was another complicated symbolic system found at Mayapán but absent from Quiché. It was surely foreign to the Mexicanized political rulers, at least initially.

Community differences between Mayapán and Utatlán suggest that the Quichés did not have to assimilate as much native culture as the Itzás did in Yucatán. The Quichés apparently were faced with less powerful social and symbolic forms (lineages, calendrics, rituals) and so were able to impose their own patterns. This resulted in a better-integrated and more stable community than Mayapán. Presumably also the Quichés kept intact more of the cultural forms brought from the original homeland than did the Itzás.

Some major archaeological differences between Utatlán and Mayapán underlay the broad similarities described above for the two sites. To begin with, the unitary nature of the Mayapán site (surrounded by a single wall) contrasts with the composite settlement arrangement of Utatlán. The nucleated area of each site was about four square kilometers, but whereas Utatlán was divided among four separate nuclear centers, Mayapán was a single, continuous center. The approximately 140 major civic buildings at Mayapán corresponds reasonably well with the total number of buildings at the Utatlán sites, but again they are subdivided into four separate central plazas in Utatlán. A second major distinction between the settlement patterns of the two sites concerns their zoning features. Mayapán consists of a circumscribed, unzoned and randomly compressed mass of structures. There are no major causeways or roads to provide a zoned pattern. Its main organization consists of the central position of the civic buildings, grading off to lesser constructions in the zone surrounding the central precinct. Haviland (1969) likens this pattern to Tikal's and contrasts it with the gridded pattern of Mexican centers. Utatlán clearly follows the Mexican pattern. Gridded zones lined off by walls, causeways, roads, and canyons subdivide the Utatlán sites. Zonal divisions of many kinds have been distinguished, including moietal, quadripartite, commoner-elite, and military-ceremonial-administrative divisions.

Building assemblages were not as discrete or consistently organized at Mayapán as they were at Utatlán. The two main temples of the central precinct at Mayapán, the Castillo and Caracol, seem to lack the integrated orientation found at the Utatlán centers (compare the Tojil and Awilix temples). Mayapán's "temple assemblage" (Proskouriakoff 1962, p. 91) consists of a temple at right angles with a colonnaded hall and "oratory" and a shrine at the foot of the stairway. The assemblage is similar to building arrangements at Utatlán, though the residential units added to the complex are not found at Mayapán. The thirty most elaborate residential structures at Mayapán are adjacent to the central zone, but they do not appear to have formed units within building assemblages as at Utatlán. Furthermore, while these structures might well be referred to as palaces, there is a grading into simpler residential structures that is much more gradual at Mayapán than at Utatlán (a conclusion based on preliminary evidence at the latter site).

The most prevalent complex of buildings at Mayapán is the colonnaded hall, shrine, and oratory. This complex occurs frequently at Mayapán and is partly responsible for the atomistic, zoneless pattern of the site vis à vis Utatlán. The colonnaded halls are probably lineage houses like their equivalents at Utatlán, though the Carnegie archaeologists tentatively identified them as "men's houses." The thirteen independent colonnaded halls at Mayapán would be equivalent to the twenty-four big houses at Utatlán, corresponding to the number of ruling lineages living at the center. Oratories in both public and residential structures are more common at Mayapán than at Utatlán, probably because of the proliferation of cult groups at Mayapán.

Mayapán architecture and artifacts share more features with Chichén Itzá than is the case for Utatlán. Proskouriakoff (1962, pp. 133ff.) mentions such Chichén features at Mayapán as Atlantean and serpent columns, burial shafts, colonnaded halls, the round Caracol and the four-sided Castillo, and the "dance platform" at the foot of the Castillo. Utatlán lacks some of these features, though it does have colonnaded halls (nongalleried, as at Mayapán), and the Tojil temple is similar to the Castillo in its central position and in having more than one stairway. Further, Utatlán has the sweathouse, ball-court, and *tzompantli* (skull-rack) structures found at Chichén Itzá but missing from Mayapán. Mayapán and Utatlán share the contrast with Chichén Itzá in the use of crude stone and stucco rather than veneer masonry and high-relief stucco figures rather than low-relief stone carvings.

The conspicuous stratum of classic Maya patterns underlying Mayapán forms is absent from Utatlán. This contrast may be seen most prominently in the carved stelae at Mayapán, some with hieroglyphic inscriptions, and in Maya art styles and icons (shown in details of dress). On the other hand, the so-called East Coast features at Mayapán generally occur at Utatlán also: crude masonry, lavish use of stucco, figure censers. The tiny shrines characteristic of both the East Coast and Mayapán are less numerous at Utatlán, though some have been found by the archaeologists, and they were reportedly common along the roadside. Some Mexican influence is reported for Mayapán, probably by way of the Gulf Coast. The skull and squatting-figure motifs reported by Proskouriakoff (1962, p. 137) at Mayapán are also found at Utatlán. The many additional Mexican motifs found at Utatlán suggest that it experienced stronger Mexican influence than did Mayapán.

Both Mayapán and Utatlán were associated with ceramic complexes that made their appearance during the Late Postclassic Period (about 1200 to 1500), though the Utatlán complex has been only preliminarily defined (Wauchope 1970). In both cases a slipped red or brown ware is diagnostic. Effigy censers are another diagnostic marker of the two complexes, and they increase in importance through time—at least at Mayapán (Smith 1971, p. 255). The effigies seem to depict deities, many of which (about half the figures at Mayapán) are of Mexican derivation (Thompson 1957). For neither complex do we know the places of manufacture, though they were probably close to the two political centers. Wares from both complexes are scattered throughout the territories of the two "kingdoms," although there appears to be a more regional distribution in Guatemala. In Yucatán an early ware of the complex (Peto Cream, also called Coarse Slateware) seems to correspond with the arrival of the Itzá forefathers. Furthermore, Fine Orange wares from the Gulf Coast area occur at Mayapán from beginning to end. In contrast, neither early transitional wares nor Gulf Coast Fine Orange wares have been identified for the Quiché area.

These archaeological contrasts between Mayapán and Utatlán provide the basis for some important conclusions about Quiché development. Settlement data suggest, for example, that urbanizing trends at Utatlán were stronger than might be supposed from population figures alone. In terms of zoning and standardizing of units, Utatlán had developed beyond towns like Mayapán. In this and in features of art and architecture mentioned above, Utatlán reveals a relatively strong "Mexican" (so-called Toltec) pattern. Despite the segmentive nature of Utatlán social structure and building arrangements, when compared with those of Mayapán, Utatlán seems to have been more like an organized community of integrated components, Mayapán a collection of loosely allied units. Once again we find evidence that Quiché culture represents a drastic break with past cultural traditions (examples are the Maya substratum and Chichén Itzá features at Mayapán that do not occur at Quiché). The Quichés were cut off from their original homeland, too, a factor that perhaps correlated with the conclusion above that, unlike Utatlán, Mayapán was enmeshed in a continuous trading network including the Gulf Coast.

For comparisons of the destruction of the Mayapán and of the Utatlán communities we must start with events that occurred at Mayapán before the Conquest. Sometime between 1441 and 1461 the Xiu lineage at Mayapán led a revolt against the town's Cocom rulers. We are told that the revolt occurred when the Cocom ruler brought in mercenaries from the Gulf Coast and tyrannized the "poorer people" (Roys 1964, p. 170). The Cocom lords were slain, and their lands and riches were taken. Mayapán was abandoned, the Xius establishing a new center at Maní, just south of the old site. The remnants of the Cocom rulers recouped and formed a rival center at Sotutá," northwest of the Mayapán district.

The revolt of the Xius is strongly reminiscent of the conflict that broke out at Utatlán during the reign of Q'uik'ab (see chapter 5). The same issues were involved, except that in Utatlán the hated supporters of the ruler were foreign serfs rather than Gulf Coast mercenaries. The fact that the rival Xiu and Cocom groups at Mayapán had diverse ethnic origins contrasts with the Quiché case too and helps explain why the revolt was shattering at Mayapán. Nevertheless, the secession of the Cakchiquels shortly after the Quiché revolt and the establishment of a rival state at Iximché parallel closely events at Mayapán. The Cakchiquels, unlike the Xius, had sided with the Quiché rulers, and their departure did not cause the abandonment of Utatlán.

The fragmentation of the Mayapán kingdom into several independent warring states not long before the arrival of the Spaniards reveals the fragile nature of community there. Besides Maní and Sotutá, other states modeled after Mayapán were formed in the east at Izamal and Cochuah. On the west the Mexican mercenaries became leaders of independent towns. When the Spaniards arrived, the state of Sotutá, heir to the Mayapán kingdom, led the fight against them. Some of the eastern states rallied around Sotutá in the ensuing confrontation. The western towns, in contrast, remained independent, failing to unite even among themselves. The Xius at Maní chose to join the Spaniards rather than aid the Cocoms of Sotutá. The situation at Utatlán was different, for Utatlán was able to enlist the cooperation of most highland peoples in the struggle against the Spaniards. Only the initial Cakchiquel collaboration with the conquistadors reminds us of the Yucatán situation, and it did not last long.

Roys (1943, pp. 129–71) has reconstructed the process by which states like Maní and Sotutá were broken down under Spanish rule into dependent pueblos and *encomiendas*, and native rulers converted into colonial administrators (*caciques*). The process was generally like the one described for the Quichés (see chapter 9), though some contrasts are detectable. Yucatecan native chiefs, like their Quiché counterparts (especially the chiefs of Sotutá and Maní), agitated for retention of old jurisdictions (Roys 1943, pp. 175ff.). Nevertheless, their claims reflected the highly fragmented situation of Yucatán at the time of conquest and usually pertained to land rights rather than to political organization. Compared with the Quiché area, large political jurisdictions quickly became simple towns, and chiefly status was reduced to limited headmanships over the towns. Nativistic movements certainly took place in Yucatán (notably the Caste War of the nineteenth century), but the early examples seem local compared with those in the Quiché area; later ones were almost nationalistic. Modern-day Maya communities in Yucatán are far more acculturated than are those in the Quiché area. Unilineal descent groups, ancient crafts, and native gods have largely disappeared (Villa Rojas 1971), though ancient milpa rites continue in isolated rural zones (Press 1975). This contrasts sharply with the lively traditional culture still found in Quiché towns, such as Chichicastenango and San Antonio Ilotenango (see chapter 11).

The over-all history of the destruction of Mayapán leads to the view that the town was only superficially integrated. Its disintegration went further and at a faster rate than Utatlán's. Nevertheless, we find a surprising cultural unity in Yucatán as a whole, expressed in widespread retention of the Maya language and isolated elements of culture. A similar phenomenon can be detected from the nineteenth century in the symbols and wide scale of the Caste War. It surpasses the Quiché area in extension but lacks the degree of specificity of cultural survival found in Quiché. Some degree of pre-Mayapán political unity, as well as broadly similar ecological factors in Yucatán, probably explains the contrast with the Quichés.

Petén Itzá

The final Maya community to be compared with Utatlán is that of the Petén Itzás. The documentary information on the Petén Itzás was summarized by Thompson (1951) and has been supplemented by Hellmuth (1971). Unfortunately, Tayasal, the Petén Itzá capital, is buried under the town of Flores, Guatemala, and few remains have been uncovered there (Borhegyi 1963; Cowgill 1963). The archaeological site of Topoxté, however, on a series of islands in Lake Yaxhá east of Lake Petén, appears to have been contemporaneous with the Petén Itzás. It is likely that Topoxté was occupied either by the Petén Itzás themselves or by a people under their control. The site, therefore, can be used as an archaeological manifestation of Petén Itzá culture, though it must be remembered that the proposed historical connection is not certain. Bullard (1970) briefly excavated the site and has left us a full report of his findings.

Chase (1976) has recently argued that Topoxté was, in fact, Tayasal. That is highly unlikely. The identification of so important a natural feature as Lake Petén but are impossibly large for the tiny Lake Yaxhá, the site of Topoxté. century. All the early accounts, including that of Cortés (1961, pp. 309ff.), refer to Petén Itzá Lake as the largest in the area. Further, the large dimensions given by Fray Avendaño (1696) for the lake closely match those of Lake Petén but are impossibly large for the tiny Lake Yaxha, the site of Topoxté. Besides, there are historical statements that Lake Yaxhá was uninhabited during the seventeenth century.

Bullard dated the Topoxté site at about 1200 to 1400, basing the calculation on ties in pottery with that at Mayapán. But the site may well have been occupied by Itzá-controlled people during the sixteenth century, a possibility that Bullard recognized. At any rate, it is clear that the Yaxhá area in general was under Itzá control during the seventeenth century and probably bordered with the Tipú Mayas on the northeast (Thompson 1938; 1977; Avendaño 1696, pp. 106ff.).

The Petén Itzás stood to Mayapán much the way the Cakchiquels of Iximché stood to Utatlán: they were a political breakoff. According to the reconstruction of Roys (1926, p. 47), the Itzás were forced to leave Chichén Itzá when one of their chiefs captured the bride of the Izamal ruler. He had been charmed into the act by Hunac Ceel, a lord from Mayapán. In the resulting turmoil the Itzás left for Tanxulicmul, a site near Lake Petén. This story is similar to the one told by the Quichés to account for their wars with the Tzutujils (see chapter 5). The Itzás' migration to the Petén took place in Katún Ahau, which Roys dated at 1441 to 1461. This date would place the Itzás in the Petén area only one hundred years before the conquest of Yucatán, which is precisely what Fray Avendaño was told during his visit to the Petén Itzá capital in 1696. Nevertheless, there is both documentary and archaeological evidence that Itzá peoples came to the Petén from the Champotón area around 1200. Thus the Petén Itzá case would be similar to the Quiché, except that in the former a second major migration from Yucatán occurred 250 years after the arrival of the forefathers.

Ecological contrasts between the Petén Itzás and the Quichés are striking. The center of Petén Itzá habitation was on five or more islands in the lake, though they also controlled large territories in the surrounding jungle lowlands. The lowland-and-lake setting was entirely different from the Quiché basin, but the division of the central Petén Itzá community into several small, nucleated towns was similar to the Utatlán pattern. The subsistence base of the Petén Itzás included maize, beans, and squash, two or three harvests a year being possible in that area. But chile, pineapple, cacao, and root crops were also produced, as were cotton, tobacco, and vanilla. When we add the many tropical birds and animals available as food, the great variety of products that characterized Petén Itzá subsistence as compared with the Quichés becomes clear.

Population density at Petén Itzá appears to have been on the same order as that of Utatlán. The main island alone had about two hundred houses, and a total of 2,000 people. The figure 10 persons a household suggested by these numbers is generally confirmed for the central lowlands by the ethnohistoric sources (Hellmuth 1971, p. 23). Avendaño estimated the total population of the islands and mainland around the lake at approximately 24,000 to 25,000 people. That is about half the population estimated for the central Quiché but is equivalent in size considering the smaller territory involved (roughly half that of central Quiché, or about 750 square kilometers).

In general terms Petén Itzá social structure seems to have been similar to that of the Utatlán Quichés. Lords (*ahau*), commoners, and slaves made up the basic social strata. Perhaps the break between commoners and lords was less sharp than that among the Quichés, for the two strata lived and associated together rather freely at Tayasal. Slaves may have been less numerous and important in the Petén, commoners providing most of the services for nobility. There is no mention of serfs. Warriors and artisans from the middle sector were important at the Petén Itzá centers, but merchants may have been few and relatively insignificant. Tayasal appears to have been more of a stop in a long-distance trading route than an active trading center per se. Utatlán apparently was not a major trading center either, though it was probably more active than Tayasal in commerce.

Our information on Petén Itzá descent groups is very limited. As with the Quichés, there were noble lineages with claims to Mexican ancestry, but hints in our sources suggest that affinal and matrilineal principles were pushing them in the direction of cognatic descent. In a relationship similar to the Quiché estate system (*chinamit*) districts of people were subject to and took the names of noble chiefs. There were twenty-two districts clustered in the central Petén area. They were not provinces but were probably similar to the *calpules* of the Quichés.

The Canek lineage ruled at Tayasal, much as the Cawek lineage ruled at Utatlán. From that lineage came the "king" and also the high priest. The two shared supreme authority. In the late seventeenth century the king's cousin was the high priest, suggesting a situation like that of the *ajpop* and *ajpop c'amja* rulers at Utatlán: the two officers came from sublineages of the same ruling lineage. In contrast to the structure among the Petén Itzás, the *ajpop c'amja* at Utatlán was definitely lower in rank than the *ajpop* and was not a ritual specialist. The quadripartite principle was a secondary feature of Petén Itzá government, much as it was at Utatlán. Three chiefs (*batab*) joined with the king and the high priest to form a ruling body fictionalized as "four kings" (in fact there were five).

District chiefs and their military assistants (*nacon*) formed a council under the four rulers. Events associated with the conquest of the Petén reveal that there was considerable political infighting among the council members. Especially was there conflict between the Canek rulers and the Covoh chiefs of the Chakan district. The Canek rulers were far from having absolute authority, and district chiefs were always poised to act independently if they felt militarily strong enough. The situation was a close parallel to the Quichés', especially the competitive relations among the Nima Quichés, Tamubs, and Ilocabs.

Petén Itzá religion and symbolics were very similar to what has been described for Mayapán. Patron deities were numerous and not unified around a single important cult (there is no evidence of the Kululchan cult among the Petén Itzás). As among the Quichés war deities were especially important. Deity icons could talk, and they gave instructions to the priests. They had to be fed sacrificed human beings. There were many individual or family shrines among the Petén Itzás. Esoteric calendrical ritual was prevalent, and *katún* counts, kept on bark-cloth codices, provided a prophetic or cyclic form of history. Like the Quichés, the Petén Itzás believed that men and animals were mystically connected and that the one could be transformed into the other (nagualism). But the practice was not wholly approved; it is said that, out of fear that older men would transform themselves into dangerous naguals, the Petén Itzás killed men over fifty years of age who were not priests.

Comparisons between Petén Itzá and Utatlán settlement patterns must take into account that Topoxté, the only late Petén site known to us, was only a district or provincial center. The number of main structures described by Bullard for the main Topoxté site, eleven or so, falls far short of the many buildings crowded together in the capital. Our sources mention about twenty temples at Tayasal and many other ritual, administrative, and residential buildings.

Topoxté features that Bullard (1970, pp. 273–76) relates to Late Postclassic patterns in Yucatán apply also to Utatlán. The site was highly defensive, situated on a series of islands within Lake Yaxhá. Settlements were nucleated, with perhaps two hundred houses concentrated on three of the tiny islands. Building arrangements included a central plaza surrounded by temples and facing long structures. Small altars were placed in front of temples. I detected what was possibly a palace-temple-long structure (RCP) complex at the site. Architecture featured beam-and-mortar roofs (versus the

Classic Maya vaults); colonnaded doorways; long, open buildings; balustrades with vertical upper zones; and inset moldings similar to the *talud* y *tablero* style. Diagnostic Topoxté ceramic wares included figure censers very similar to those of Mayapán and cream slipped polychrome and monochrome red wares generically similar to wares found in Yucatán and at Utatlán.

Settlement contrasts between Topoxté and Utatlán are also evident. For example, small stucco-covered stelae and tiny shrines were found at Topoxté but not at Utatlán. Unlike Utatlán, the Topoxté settlement was not zoned or gridded, though some simple building arrangements are common to the two sites. Details of pottery decoration and manufacture differ, the Topoxté wares showing definite ties with earlier Petén traditions. In these and other features Topoxté reveals its closer affinity with Mayapán than with Utatlán. Still, as noted above, Topoxté and Utatlán share broadly similar community patterns and development.

The manner of the destruction of the Petén Itzá community was drastically different from that of Utatlán. The location of the Petén Itzás in the jungle lowlands made them an unattractive target for the Spaniards. They were far removed from the sea or other easy trade routes. They were not major producers of goods in which the Spaniards were interested, such as gold or cacao. The Petén climate was distasteful to Europeans, and, though food was grown in surplus, the dispersed residential pattern of farmers outside the lake area would have made it difficult to control a large peasantry.

The conquest of the Petén Itzás begun by the Spaniards in the seventeenth century proved far more difficult than that of the Quichés. Lake Petén provided defenses that were superior even to the Utatlán canyons and were overcome only by sophisticated Spanish ship-making technology. The stresses of the Conquest revealed divisions in Petén Itzá society that were possibly more serious than those that surfaced during the conquest of Utatlán. It was factionalism in the central community (as the Covohs versus the Caneks) that weakened the Petén Itzás' resistance to the Spaniards. This contrasts with the Quiché divisions, which came from peoples well outside the central community (the Cakchiquels and the Tzutujils).

The story of the breakdown of Petén Itzá culture in colonial times is not yet known in detail. Preliminary information (Hellmuth 1971) suggests that the Petén community quickly fragmented into a large number of "tribes" and villages after the conquest of Tayasal. The Canek rulers tried to hold onto their privileges, but other lineages came forward with competing claims. It should be remembered, however, that, while the Petén Itzás seem to have been weaker than the Quichés in the face of Spanish colonization, many special factors complicate the comparison. These include such major considerations as lowland versus highland ecology, the more experienced Spanish colonial system of the seventeenth century, and the involvement of peoples other than the conquistadors in the Petén conquest.

In summary, the Petén Itzás were generally similar to the Quichés of Utatlán and specifically like the people of Mayapán. This similarity strongly confirms the theory that Utatlán was part of a large cultural movement from the Gulf Coast, the people bringing with them such features as warrior rulers, patron war deities demanding human sacrifice, nucleated towns, and Mexican building arrangements and architectural styles. In contrast to the Petén Itzás manifestation of this cultural movement, the Utatlán community seems to have been more urbanized (in terms of population size, zoning, and nucleation), more complexly stratified (especially in the middle and lower sectors), more centralized in authority (as seen, for example, in the subordinate position of the high priest to the king at Utatlán), less indebted to local indigenous beliefs and patterns (hence more "Mexican"), and more deeply integrated from top to bottom (and so better able to resist the Hispanization of their culture). The lowland ecology and isolation of the Petén Itzás no doubt limited their sociocultural integration relative to that of the Quichés. The Petén area allowed only a limited population density, had no precious stones or metals, was difficult to traverse, had little communication of ideas with major Mesoamerican centers, and had shifting settlements. However slightly, these factors operated to repress sociocultural development, while, in a positive sense, their presence in the Utatlán area stimulated community development.

THE GENERAL MESOAMERICAN CASE

It has been repeatedly argued in this book that the Utatlán community shared both substantive and developmental features with other communities in Mesoamerica. A comparison between the development at Utatlán and broader Mesoamerican developments should provide additional insight into the specific Quiché case. I am particularly interested in the *general* features of Quiché development—those shared by other communities of Mesoamerica.

Communities at different levels of development were found in pre-Hispanic Mesoamerica, though the "civilization" level usually defines the area as a cultural unit. The features of the typical Mesoamerican community that are widely used to define it as a civilization are (1) monumental public architecture; (2) a "great" art style expressed in several media; (3) complex writing, calendrical, and counting systems; (4) large, dense populations; (5) social differentiation of the population into hierarchically stratified "classes"; (6) exploitation of natural and human resources for large-scale public enterprises; (7) extensive trade; and (8) formally organized political and religious systems (Willey et al. 1964). The Utatlán community shared these general features, as has been emphasized throughout the book and in the sections above. The Utatlán community was "civilized."

General Processes

Within Mesoamerican civilization two developmental types have been distinguished (Coe 1961*b*; Sanders and Price 1968; Willey et al. 1964, pp. 490ff.; Webb 1975). The first type, widely referred to in the literature as the "chiefdom," is said to have developed mainly in the lowlands. The second type, usually referred to as the "state," developed in the highlands, especially in central Mexico. In simple developmental terms the two contrast as follows: chiefdoms have ceremonial centers surrounded by dispersed populations; states have nucleated, urban centers. Chiefdoms have theocratic leaders backed by powerful religious symbols; states are ruled by military officials holding a monopoly on force. Chiefdom stratification is a simple lord-commoner castelike division; state stratification is made complex by middle-sector "classes." Chiefdoms have corporate unilineal kin groups with land holdings; state kin groups lose political and property rights to territorially based units. Chiefdom trade consists of long-distance exchanges of exotic goods; state trade consists of politically controlled long-distance exchanges and extensive local marketing.

Before an examination of the Quiché case within the chiefdom-state contrast some clarifications are necessary. To begin with, we should understand that the chiefdom and state types are ideal and can be used to define communities only in the broadest terms. They are not necessarily stages in a developmental line but are adaptations to different physical and social conditions. Nor is there any clearly demarcated characteristic whose development qualitatively transforms a people from chiefdom to state. Rather we find "a continuum of directional change" (Service 1975, p. 305), even for the feature of monopolized authority, which can be cumulatively acquired. Instances of development known only from archaeology, such as that of the Olmecs or the lowland Classic Mayas, are not readily amenable to the chiefdom-state distinction (Service 1975, pp. 304ff.). Even where documentary information is available, as in the Quiché case, the models are far from easy to apply.

Many students of development argue that the chiefdom-state distinction is too rigid, preferring to use some broader concept to cover a wide variety of sociopolitical forms. Coe (1961*b*), for example, notes the contrast between lowland ("unilateral") and highland ("organic") civilizations. While lowland civilizations, such as the Khmer and the Maya, had chiefdomlike characteristics, he argues that nevertheless they were organized at a state level of development. Similarly, Gluckman (1965, pp. 123–68) refers to a wide spectrum of African sociopolitical "states" that manifest both chiefdom and state characteristics. He finds no easy dividing line between them and so loosely classifies them as greater- or lesser-developed states (albeit "tribal states" in some cases). For these students the essential state characteristic is the development of a central authority, "ensuring security internally and at its frontiers, . . . and the execution of basic decisions in the whole country under its jurisdiction" (Balandier 1970, p. 149). Nevertheless, traditional states have difficulty controlling at the margins of their territory, where dissident units tend to segment off. This somewhat flexible use of the state concepts is desirable, leaving the chiefdom concept to be applied to simple tribal confederations (Webb 1975, pp. 166ff.). It frees us from unseemly references to communities with great cultural traditions, such as the classic lowland Mayas, as chiefdoms.

Another distinction often made is that between "pristine states," which supposedly develop independently, and "secondary states," which evolve under the stimulus of other extant states (Fried 1967). This distinction, for example, is used by Sanders and Price (1968) to explain the transformation of the lowland Mayan "chiefdom" at Tikal to a state (the primary state in this case being Teotihuacán from central Mexico). I believe the pristine-secondary distinction to be largely misleading, a means too often used to explain away cases that do not happen to fit preconceived notions. More likely, the evolution of the indigenous state is a unitary process, similar in its *broader* features regardless of when it appears on the historical scene. Thus, while the Utatlán Quiché state would probably be considered by some students a secondary state and relatively uninformative and unproblematic in its development, I consider it as good a case as any for understanding the general features of the evolution of a state.

The Mesoamerican continuum of more or less developed states can be used as a framework for clarifying additional features of Quiché development. It will be argued that the Utatlán community represents the organic or highland type of state. In the discussion to follow, the Quichés will be compared with the Mexicas (Aztecs) of central Mexico. The Mexica case was selected because its central community is generally thought to express advanced features of highland-state development.

Tenochtitlán, the Mexica capital, was perhaps the largest of all Mesoamerican urban centers. The island nuclear area covered at least 7.5 square kilometers and had a total population of well over 100,000 people, giving it a density of more than 10,000 persons per square kilometer (Sanders 1971, pp. 24ff.). Tenochtitlán was zoned and gridded and had axial roads, central squares, multiple-plaza arrangements, measured residential zones, and suburbs (Calnek 1976).

Utatlán too was more an urban than a ceremonial center. The tentative figures that have been presented suggest that Utatlán's total nuclear population reached 10,000 to 20,000, concentrated in an area of slightly less than 4 square kilometers. This makes the Utatlán nuclear area fall under Sanders's "city" type of settlement (1971, pp. 23–24). Still, Tenochtitlán was at least twice as large as nuclear Utatlán and five times more densely populated. The zonal pattern of streets, courts, plazas, and suburbs at Utatlán was less systematized than the pattern at Tenochtitlán but was similar in form. Our evidence suggests, then, that Utatlán is best classed as a highland, urbanizing type of Mesoamerican state. The Mayapán and Petén Itzá settlements demonstrate that urban patterns can be found in lowland settings too, though the greater urbanization of Utatlán perhaps reflects the importance of a highland setting for urban development.

Authority was secular at Tenochtitlán (Carrasco 1971, pp. 349ff.), where rulers came primarily from the military sector. The king (*tlatoani*) was assisted by a vice-ruler (*ciuacoatl*) and lower-ranking military chiefs who formed a ladder leading to the two top positions. Military success elevated Tenochtitlán rulers above Texcoco and Tlacopán officials in the Mexica triple alliance (Gibson 1971, pp. 383–89). Commoners could achieve noble status through success in warfare, and rulers sometimes gained office through military achievement rather than inheritance. Despite the emphasis on militarism, priests were very influential at Tenochtitlán (Nicholson 1971, pp. 436ff.), partly because they educated the noble children at special schools (*calmecac*). The high priest was highly respected—"to the same degree as Moctezuma." Secular officials participated in important ritual ceremonies, and in some towns of central Mexico, such as Cholula, the rulers were priests. Nicholson says that while Tenochitlán was not a theocracy, "the power and influence of the priesthood was truly remarkable" (1971, p. 444).

As indicated above, Utatlán too was ruled by military rather than priestly leaders. The king (*ajpop*) and his three assistants came from the military ranks, and a ladder from the military sector led up to these positions. The king's assistant (*ajpop c'amja*) appears to have been a vice-ruler similar to the equivalent Mexica official. Military capability pushed the Nima Quichés of Utatlán to the top of their alliances with the Tamubs and the Ilocabs, much like the superiority of the Tenochca rulers at Tenochtitlán. As with the Mexicas, the priests were highly respected by the Utatlán Quichés and occupied important positions in state administration (including the stewardship of tribute goods). Like their Mexica counterparts Quiché rulers participated in public ceremonies at Utatlán. The Quichés and the peoples of central Mexico appear to have reached similar stages of development with respect to state authority, and in both cases military rule was strongly influenced by religion. The even greater priestly influence on authority in lowland Maya cultures, seen at Mayapán and Petén Itzá, would appear to represent no greater variation than that in central Mexico itself (as in the Cholula case).

The complexity of central Mexican stratification, with its middle "classes," is well documented (Carrasco 1971, pp. 349ff.; Carrasco and Broda 1976b; Katz 1966; Soustelle 1962). The lines between the basic castelike divisions—nobles (*pipiltin*), commoners (*macehualtin*), and slaves (*tlacotin*)—were permeable. Warfare, trade, and the priesthood provided means by which commoners moved up to noble status (Carrasco 1961). Continuous movement down from commoner to slave status resulted from poverty, crime, or marriage with slaves. At least two groups of commoners, the merchants (*pochteca*) and the artisans, were differentiated as middle "classes." They were exempt from corvee labor, lived together in special wards, had their own patron gods and rituals, and used their wealth to obtain special favors from the lords. Other groups, such as successful warriors, specialized priests, and ward heads, might also be considered part of the middle sector. Vassal commoners included both local peasants (*calpuleque*) and serfs brought in from the outside (*mayeque*). There is evidence (Hicks 1976) that the serfs were no worse off than the free peasants and were a growing, dynamic class at Tenochtitlán.

Stratification of the Utatlán Quichés seems similar in structure to that of the Mexicas. It reveals the same castelike divisions, prominent merchant and artisan classes, and dynamic class of serfs (*nimak achi*). Perhaps there was less mobility in Quiché society, warfare providing the only avenue for moving from commoner to noble status (and instituted only with a major revolt). Our sources also indicate that the merchants were less well organized at Utatlán and certainly were not as prominent in state affairs as the Pochtecas were. The growing influence of the serfs vis à vis the free peasants (*al, c'ajol*) in Quiché society closely parallels the situation at Tenochtitlán. In both places, too, the serfs appear to have been overshadowing the slaves in economic significance; slaves are said to have been like "pawns" at Tenochititlán (Carrasco 1971, p. 356). The generally simpler social stratification at the lowland Maya centers Mayapán and Petén Itzá contrasts with that at Utatlán and Tenochtitlán. In Mayapán the merchants became a more important component of the social structure and formed an integral constituent of the ruling status.

The transformation of the early Aztec *calpulli* (clans) into territorial units has been documented by ethnohistorians (Monzon 1949; Carrasco 1971). The *calpulli* were landholding groups of varying size, made up of such divisions as migrating ethnic groups ("tribes"), whole towns, and town and rural wards. As wards the *calpulli* had property, military, ritual, and tribute functions. Only rarely were they also descent groups, though endogamy and a recognition of common kin ties of all kinds (ambilateral) gave the rural wards a certain kinship identity. Carrasco (1976*a*) has recently documented the existence of small noble lineages (*tlacamecayotl*) at Tenochititlán. These lineages were cognatic, for, even though they had a patrilineal orientation, maternal links were also used. They were not exogamous, and marriage often occurred between close relatives. Mexica noble lineages administered estates (*teccalli*), consisting of lands occupied by their noble and commoner descendants and attached serfs and commoners (*calpulque, mayeque*). The *calpulli* and their heads were subject to the estate chiefs (*teuctli*) of the noble lineages. Thus the territorial, cognatic, stratified bias of the *calpulli* structure, which some authors consider an important developmental feature of Mexica society (Sanders and Price 1968, pp. 153ff.; Kirchhoff 1955), would apply even more strongly to the estate (*teccalli*) organization.

Exogamous landholding patrilineal-descent groups, called "big houses" (*nim ja*, the Quiché gloss for *calpulli*), characterized both noble and vassal social organization at Utatlán and contrast it with the social structure at Tenochtitlán. There is no evidence that noble lineages of Utatlán dropped exogamy rules or traced descent cognatically. The estate (*chinamit*) organization of the Quichés was similar to the Mexica *teccalli*, however. Like the Mexica estates, the *chinamit* were landholding units controlled by noble lineages (patrilineal among the Quichés), which administered both commoners and serfs. The further division of the rural Quiché peoples into *calpul* units suggests that the estate system was being extended far into the countryside to include territorial units of varying sizes, as in the Mexica case. The continuation of patrilineal-descent principles and exogamous lineages at Utatlán indicates that the process of replacing kinship with territorial forms had gone further in central Mexico than it had at Utatlán. The lowland Maya groups (at Mayapán and Petén Itzá), with their less well developed territorial units and more pronounced unilineal descent groups, were lower than the Quichés on the social-development line.

The extreme complexity of trade and marketing activities in central Mexico is cited as an important index of over-all cultural development there (Sanders and Price 1968, pp. 159ff.; Parsons and Price 1971). The market at Tenochtitlán operated daily and attracted tens of thousands of people. Every conceivable kind of goods, both raw and manufactured, could be bought there. Standard mediums of exchange, the most important of which were cacao beans, feathers, jade, gold, cotton cloths, and copper disks, were also used in buying and selling. Government officials regulated the market, setting tariffs and schedules and settling disputes. Extensive long-distance trade was carried out also with the goal of obtaining luxury and exotic goods from distant regions (Chapman 1957). Such trade was conducted by specialized guilds (*pochteca*), who traveled along established routes. They traded through contracts entered into with foreign peoples at politically neutral ports of trade, such as Xicalango. As with local marketing, long-distance trade was subject to the Mexican government; for example the *pochteca* performed military functions for the state. Both local and long-distance trade was essential to the survival of the urban inhabitants of Tenochtitlán.

Local markets have a long history in the central Quiché area, especially the one at Chichicastenango (anciently known as Chuwila'). Today they are held weekly and deal in many manufactured and natural products. That they were important at Utatlán seems certain, though the more strategically located Chichicastenango may have had the largest market of the central area. There is evidence of some government intervention in the Utatlán market, but details are lacking. Utatlán Quichés also engaged in long-distance trade, and special merchants (*ajbeyom*) traveled far to bring luxury goods to the capital. Like the Mexican merchants, they paid tribute and performed tasks for the government. Trade at Quiché was on a much smaller scale than that in central Mexico, but it was similar in characteristics. Lowland Maya trade was less well developed, except for the extensive long-distance trading to and from Mayapán. Local markets were relatively unimportant both in Yucatán and in the Petén, while long-distance trading was limited in the latter area.

A note should be added about the development of a "rationalized" state religion in central Mexico (Nicholson 1971; Soustelle 1962, pp. 95–119; Caso 1958). It is well known that the Mexicas did not force their gods on other peoples and even adopted the gods of conquered peoples into their own pantheon. Priests in Tenochtitlán exercised little if any control over cults in other towns. Nor did they establish a mummy cult to deceased rulers in Tenochtitlán. The many Mexican gods, rituals, and symbols were not worked into a single coherent theology. Soustelle (1962, p. 117) claims that the Aztecs had an "imperial religion of a great state . . . in the process of formation, but that [it was] . . . still no more than a confederation of many little highly individual states (and cults)." Nevertheless, the Mexicas elevated the sacrificial cult of the sun to first position at Tenochtitlán, and all the symbols associated with that cult became preeminent. Huitzilopochtli, the patron of the Aztec founders and of warfare, became a solar deity. Tezcatlipoca, the young warrior-transformer god, was given expanded powers and importance. Creator and solar deities were conceptualized as aspects of this deity, and he became the "supreme god." Despite such rationalizing tendencies, the rain god (Tlaloc) retained a position alongside the solar deity, while Quetzalcoatl, Xipe Totec, and other deities also held prominent positions in the Tenochtitlán pantheon.

Similar incipient trends toward rationalizing culture can be seen in other spheres. The Mexicas standardized their calendar and dated events annually or in fifty-two-year cycles by the year-bearers (Caso 1971). They did not force other peoples of the central area to follow their standard, and they did not develop an absolute chronology. The Mexicas had a strong historical sense, and in their codices myth was slighted in favor of secular events (Nicholson 1969). But their writing system remained largely pictographic, except for the use of the rebus principle for recording names and places. Some students have argued that Mexica priests conceptualized an incipient philosophy and "attempted to discover the meaning of life on an intellectual plane" (León-Portilla 1963, p. 177). They found that truth and meaning could come from "flower and song," poetry and art. The concept of a single, self-existent, invisible divine omnipresence (*ometeotl*) emerged from their poetry and speculation. This kind of thinking was limited to a few sages (*tlamatinime*) and was part of an ancient Toltec tradition passed down in the priestly schools (*calmecac*).

The remarkable interviews of Spanish missionaries with Mexica priests, preserved for us by Sahagún, have no parallel in the Quiché case. Nevertheless, the *Popol Vuh* appears to express some of the religious thinking of the Quiché priesthood. It and other sources indicate that the Quichés of Utatlán had the same developmental religious tendencies as the Mexicas, but did not carry them as far. The preeminence of the Quiché solar sacrificial cult has been pointed out. It may have dominated religion at Utatlán even more than its counterpart did at Tenochtitlán. At Utatlán the cult was centered on Tojil, whose aspects, as we have seen, were expanded to include most of the other important deities in the Quiché pantheon (somewhat like Tezcatlipoca of the Mexicas). It could be argued that the Quichés developed the concept of a single divine principle that unified all the deities, called *c'abawil*. The first Spanish priests claimed that the Quichés held the concept, though Christian influence is suspected in this case.

The extensive mythology of the *Popol Vuh* suggests that philosophical speculation was very limited. It was not absent, however, as the *c'abawil* concept and the following passage from the *Popol Vuh* indicate:

This is my head; it has nothing on it; it is pure bone; it has no flesh. So too are the skulls of the great lords. The flesh is what gives them a good appearance. But when they die, the people are afraid of their bones. But the son of a lord is in the spittle and saliva [of his father], even though he be the son of a wise man or orator. When the lord, the warrior, the wise man, the orator disappear, go away, they are not extinguished, for they stay on through the daughters and sons who are created." [Villacorta 1962, pp. 109–10; my translation]

There is speculative thought here about the transitory nature of fame and appearances and of the conquest of death through biological descent.

Quiché calendrics and writing were similar to their Mexica equivalents, to judge from what we know about both. There is no evidence that the Quichés dated events by the year-bearers, although that is a possibility. The same historical interest noted for the Mexicas appears in the Quiché chronicles (Carmack 1973). A similar historical bent has been claimed for the lowland Maya groups at Mayapán and Petén Itzá; in those cases, however, dating was cyclic (*katún* counts), and the narrated events were expressed in more esoteric terms. There is some indication that the Mayas of Yucatán speculated about a supreme incorporeal god, Hunabku (Only God) (Roys 1943, 73), and developed a state cult in honor of Kukulchán. In general, however, lowland Maya religion remained highly polytheistic and relatively unrationalized.

Adaptive Pressures

The features we have been examining relate Quiché development to the evolution of the state in central Mexico and elsewhere in Mesoamerica. These features are specific instances of well-known evolutionary processes, such as specialization, centralization, and integration (Carneiro 1973). It was pointed out in chapter 1 of this book that we should examine not only those processes but also the pressures and forces to which they were adaptive responses. Many students of development have argued that particular adaptive pressures are "prime movers," universal "causes" of the evolutionary processes we have been discussing. In contrast, I follow Flannery (1972) and others who view adaptive pressures as variables that may act together in feedback systems and may be specific to the particular regions and cultures under study. It is simplistic to speak of prime movers when we are dealing with community development. Development in particular cases appears to be the result of interacting pressures, though the resulting processes may be general. I made no a priori judgment about which pressures and combinations of pressures may have been most important in the Quiché case.

Let us now analyze the Utatlán case in terms of the pressures or variables that have been considered most important in Mesoamerican evolution. I make no attempt at a critical evaluation of these "theories," since it can be assumed that none of them alone is sufficient cause for development of the state or necessarily relevant to the Quiché casé (for critiques see Service 1975, pp. 266ff.; Flannery 1972, pp. 404–407; Webb 1975; Willey 1971; Sanders and Price 1968). The variables most often suggested are population growth, irrigation, trade and symbiosis, warfare, religious integration, and frontier hybridization.

Students of Mesoamerica have noted the correlation between increasing population densities and the development of civilization and the state. Sanders and Price (1968, pp. 74–79) argue that advanced states require a population of at least ten thousand people, either locally dense (one hundred persons per square kilometer) or distributed in dense clusters. Demographic increases of that magnitude set off a chain of reactions, such as the creation of new agricultural technology, competition for resources, and specialization, which lead to more complex cultural systems. It has been further suggested that population increase within a circumscribed area, in terms of both physical and social barriers—that is, competing groups—is necessary for the evolution of the state (Carneiro 1970). The development of authoritative structures needed to control large numbers of people can be a direct response to circumscribed demographic increase.

The total population in the central Quiché area was several times the ten thousand minimum that Sanders believes necessary for the development of the state. Its over-all density of between thirty and forty persons per square kilometer would be considered low for urban development, though considerably higher than the density of classic Maya populations in the Petén lowlands, which supposedly was not conducive to the development of a state. There was also some clustering of population in the flat zones of the Quiché area, though this pattern was not pronounced until the establishment of the Utatlán towns. The comparatively open topography of the Quiché basin would seem to deny physical circumscription as a factor in Quiché development. Politically, however, the Quichés were hemmed in first by the indigenous chiefdoms of the central area (the Wukamaks) and later by powerful states surrounding the area, such as the Cakchiquels, the Tzutujils, the Rabinals, and the Mams. Thus there is evidence for fairly strong population pressure on the Quichés, though far less than that experienced by other Mesoamerican peoples (especially in central Mexico). Significantly, the Quichés themselves mentioned in their chronicles the pressures of population increase and conflict resulting from it.

One result of population increase can be the intensification of agricultural technology. Many students of Mesoamerican development have argued that irrigation is the specific agricultural intensification most closely linked to the origins of urban and state society. The argument is based on Wittfogel's thesis that control over large waterworks leads to centralization of authority, which is then used in other state endeavors, such as warfare, adjudication, and tribute collection. A large hydraulic system has been documented for the Mexica state (Palerm 1955; cf. Calnek 1977), and tentative evidence has been presented to show such a system in Classic Teotihuacán (Sanders 1965). Some argue that irrigation played "an exceptionally critical role in the evolution of the largest Mesoamerican states" (Sanders and Price 1968, p. 187), especially in central Mexico and Oaxaca. Others, however, caution that irrigation was not involved in state development in every case and that in some instances where it was involved it appeared after the state had already been established (Adams 1966). Consequently, even the most ardent advocates of the hydraulic theory admit that irrigation is effective only in conjunction with other closely related factors, such as increased production, specialization, and conflict.

There is no evidence whatever of irrigation in the central Quiché basin, nor was it practiced in the Quiché provinces except in the cacao groves of the Pacific Coast. The small lagoons and lakes of the Quiché area were not amenable to *chinampa* farming (hand-watered kitchen gardens), and even terracing was not widespread. Thus the considerable development of state features at Utatlán could not have been related to the pressures of hydraulic control. Nor are other forms of agricultural intensification evident in the Quiché. The only feature that can be pointed to was the dry farming in the fertile flat basin lands, which required little if any fallowing. Obviously this practice did not tend to create pressures for control by a central authority.

Irrigation and other intensified forms of agriculture are part of the technological specialization that often characterizes regions of ecological diversity. Mesoamerica, especially the highlands, is an area of extreme ecological diversity. This diversity has resulted in "a corresponding diversity and highly localized distribution of raw materials," according to Sanders and Price (1968, p. 188). Product diversity in turn brings powerful pressures to make exchanges between specialized zones—to create symbiotic relations. Local and long-distance trade is one mechanism by which these exchanges are made. Like irrigation, trade is said to be more effective if it is controlled by central authority. From such control adaptive pressures arise for the development of the state. In addition, trade wealth accruing to central authority can be used to finance the development of a state bureaucracy (Webb 1975, pp. 179ff.). Well-developed trade has been linked to the rise of the urban state in central Mexico (Parsons and Price 1971; Sanders and Price 1968, pp. 188ff.) and lowland civilizations such as the Olmecs and the Mayas (Rathje 1971; Coe 1961b). Lowland trade, however, is said to result from a lack of essential raw materials rather than from product specialization. Trade in such cases is primarily with distant highland peoples, is tied closely to a religious cult (Adams 1966, p. 125), and is relatively depoliticized in order to meet the requirements of neutral ports of trade. In contrast, the more centrally controlled trade of highly symbiotic regions—especially central Mexico—is politicized, long-distance trade and may be used to colonize lowland zones (Parsons and Price 1971).

Information on trade at Utatlán is scarce, which would seem to argue against its having provided powerful pressure for development. Utatlán was outside the extensive trading network of the Putuns from the Gulf Coast, despite the origin of the Quiché forefathers in the general area. The Quiché highlands present a diversified ecology, and a traditional marketing system in the area has provided regional symbiosis in modern times. These markets, however, have not been firmly tied to political authority, though there is evidence of some control before the Conquest. Our sources affirm that the primary basis for regional symbiosis in pre-Hispanic times was tribute collection rather than trade. In the Utatlán case long-distance trade may have been a somewhat stronger adaptive stimulus for development than were local markets. Specialized traders traveled from the central Quiché area to at least the Pacific coastal and Río Negro regions, and they were closely watched by Utatlán rulers. Nevertheless, such merchants have continued to function in post-Hispanic times, with only extremely tenuous ties to political authorities. Trade in the Quiché highlands seems to function almost as an alternative to political integration, and markets flourish along the margins of political boundaries.

Warfare has often been correlated with the development of complex state societies in Mesoamerica, since the peoples encountered by the Spaniards were highly militarized. In particular, the role of the military in the development of the state has been documented for the Aztecs (Katz 1966, pp. 151–79). In addition, Mesoamerican archaeology has revealed "a considerable increase in warfare in the stages immediately preceding the emergence of the state," though it is said to have occurred relatively late in history (Webb 1975, p. 186). Most students relate warfare to other adaptive pressures, such as population circumscription, control of hydraulic works, competition for special resources, and struggles for rights to trade. Warfare stimulates political development by (1) favoring those groups who can coordinate their military action through central authority, (2) producing an inequality of conquerors and subjects in whom authority can be vested, and (3) providing "free" wealth with which military leaders can establish an independent bureaucracy (Webb 1975, pp. 186ff.; Adams 1966, pp. 133–51). Warfare is an explanation for state formation sometimes given by the natives themselves, in those Postclassic Mesoamerican societies for which we have documentary information. Webb (1975, p. 157) argues that the natives are more realistic than are many students of development and that this realism "consists of a deep appreciation of the full potentiality—if not actuality—of factionalism, force, conflict, and domination in the process of state formation and maintenance."

Quiché development took place in an atmosphere of continual warfare and conflict. As shown earlier, military success propelled the Nima Quiché group in general and the Cawek lineage in particular into the central position of authority at Utatlán. The Quiché forefathers entered the highlands with certain military advantages, but those advantages were tremendously expanded in the conflicts with the indigenous enemies of the Quiché basin and surrounding regions. The growth of a ruling hierarchy of military officials among the Quichés has been documented, as has the creation of a militarized state cult. Conquest in the Quiché area provided the crucial local vassal supporters of the Utatlán rulers and later led to the additional incorporation of the serfs and slaves, who also functioned to maintain state institutions. Conquest brought wealth, initially as spoils and later as tribute, which the Quichés used to support an expanding bureaucracy of officials (both at Utatlán and in the colonized provinces). The stress of warfare, while perhaps self-induced by the Quichés, nevertheless was a powerful stimulus to development of a state at Utatlán.

Strong roles for religion and other symbolic systems in the development of Mesoamerican civilization have been advanced by some students. They have argued that the early civilizations were theocratic and laid the foundation for the development of later advanced states (Covarrubias 1957; Wolf 1959; Coe 1961*b*). In particular, the Olmecs, who have been called the "mother culture" of Mesoamerica, are thought to have created a rain-god cult and art system that provided the "compulsive force which held together these first civilized societies" (Coe 1961*b*, p. 82). Willey (1962; 1971, p. 108) argues that a well-integrated religious ideology can provide intercommunication between "discrete social segments" and so bind them together into a complex unity. Furthermore, some ideologies may be better than others, better adapted to the particular conditions—an example being the way the Olmec religion combined social inequality and tropical natural forces into an integrating were-jaguar rain cult. Religion, then, can be a stimulus to state development by (1) providing coherence, "an intelligible moral framework of organization for society" (Adams 1966, p. 121), (2) promoting authority through ascribing to leaders control over powerful forces (such as rainfall and warfare), and (3) promoting the accumulation of wealth through "sacrificial" offerings to deities, which can be used to support a (priestly) bureaucracy. Mesoamerica shows that even where state rulers become differentiated from priestly officials religious ideology continues to play a political role, emphasis merely shifting from control over nature to social forces (Adams 1966, p. 135). This process can be viewed as a response to the need for additional modes of symbolic communication. Along with writing, calendrics, and philosophy, state religious cults help process the increased information coming into the more complex system (Flannery 1972, p. 411).

The integrational function of the Tojil cult in Quiché culture was discussed above. There must have been strong pressures for its development, for it brought some symbolic unity to such widely disparate social elements as military leaders, priests, subject vassals, and political confederates and allies. The cult was undoubtedly a powerful support base for the ruling lords, since Tojil was associated with the sun in its daily-cycle, rain-and-thunder, warfare, lifeblood, and male-virility aspects. While great wealth may not have accumulated at the Tojil temple itself, tribute goods delivered to Utatlán stewards were likened to the offerings made to Tojil and other deities. The role of religion was even greater in early Quiché development at Jakawitz, before the founding of Utatlán and the creation of the state cult. Quiché chiefs at that time were also priests, and the presentation of dramatic rituals (offering blood sacrifices, receiving the morning star) were apparently essential to their authority. The same rituals provided communication among the confederate units in those early days; for example we are informed that allies attended each other's dawning ceremonies. The Quichés claimed that the sharing of a common patron deity, Tojil, was the basis of social unity.

Despite fragmentary data, it is evident that the Quichés greatly elaborated their modes of symbolic communication as the state developed at Utatlán. Besides the Tojil state cult, the modes of communication elaborated by the Quichés consisted of a literary tradition, with maps and a book of council (*Popol Vuh*); a systematized art style that was a variant of the Mixteca-Puebla style; calendric permutations that permitted year-bearer annual counts (and possibly fifty-two-year cycles) and perhaps absolute dates; a highly zoned urban center; and incipient *linguae francae* of the Quiché and Nahua languages. Finally, as noted above, the first halting steps in the direction of philosophical speculation may have been taken at Utatlán.

The replacement of theocratic with more militaristic society in Mesoamerica has been related to frontier hybridization by a number of students (Wolf 1959; Adams 1966, pp. 59–63; Service 1975, pp. 311–22). The argument is made that peoples along the borders of some powerful civilization or state will be unspecialized and therefore better able to adapt to changing conditions. These frontier societies assimilate cultural elements from both the dominant civilization and the uncivilized peoples beyond. In Mesoamerica this has resulted in hybrid frontier cultures relatively free of the pervasive influence of the religious symbols of the dominant civilization but strongly imbued with militaristic patterns derived from the independent tribes. Eventually the frontier people with "a less committed, less cumbersome government rose to dominance . . . by successfully initiating some bureaucratic methods, weapons, tactics, or whatever, that the original government was too complexly structured, too involuted, to adopt" (Service 1975, p. 320). Peoples in Mesoamerica said to have developed under such conditions are the Toltecs and the Aztecs along the northern borders of central Mexico, the Xochicalcos on the southern borders of the same area, and the Putuns along the western borders of the lowland Maya area (Wolf 1959, p. 109; Thompson 1970, pp. 3–47). While the frontier factor is usually associated with "secondary"-state formation, there is no reason to believe that it has not also played a key role in the origin of "pristine" states; that is, frontier people of a chiefdom might develop hybrid patterns that are more statelike than those of the dominant chiefdom.

The importance to the Quichés of frontier hybridization has already been stressed. The initiators of the Quiché state apparently came from the Gulf Coast area, perhaps from a marginal zone of the former Toltec state. The area may be considered frontier with respect to the Toltec centers both at Tula in central Mexico and at Chichén Itzá in Yucatán. A Postclassic frontier condition for the Gulf Coast area is confirmed by the absence of any major Toltec center and the relatively few specific Toltec artifacts found there (Coe 1965, pp. 710–12). Some of the characteristics of the Quiché forefathers that appear to be modified, late-frontier versions of Toltec culture from the heartland would be use of the Nahua language, though they were linguistically "stutterers," probably Chontal speakers who knew only limited Nahua; militarism, the Quichés having settled the Toltec conflict between military and ritual tendencies in favor of the former; astral cosmology, giving priority to astral deities though balancing them off with chthonic forces; administrative tetrarchy, but only when politically feasible; Toltec arts, the Quichés constructing buildings in Epi-Toltec architectural style and producing craft goods that were rather poor imitations of the excellent Toltec works; descent-group infrastructure, providing military "orders" through lineage structure; military mobility, emphasizing the bow and arrow and spear-thrower in warfare; and urbanized centers, orienting towns at least in part according to sacred directions and in part for defensive purposes (for the Toltecs and Epi-Toltecs see Carrasco 1971, pp. 463ff.; Wolf 1959; Weaver 1972, pp. 202ff.).

From the Gulf Coast peoples around them the Quiché forefathers presumably assimilated such features as a Maya language, long-distance trade and travel, ethnic confederation, erotic symbols and practices, cacao exploitation and consumption, sky-dragon (K'ucumatz) and moon (Awilix) deities, and the system of counting by units of 400 (see Scholes and Roys 1968; Thompson 1970). The hybrid "vigor" resulting from the combined Toltec and Gulf Coast patterns seems to have been a major factor in the Quichés' rapid subordination of the more specialized peoples of the central Quiché area and the subsequent development of the Utatlán state.

In summary, the development of the state at Utatlán shares many general features with such development in Mesoamerica as a whole, especially central Mexico. The general evolutionary processes of centralization, specialization, and integration can be detected in the development at Utatlán of an urban center, a central-authority hierarchy, new middle and servile classes, territorial rather than kin groupings, special markets and trade, and a rationalized cult of the state. No single prime mover would seem to explain those developments. Most adaptive pressures that have been considered important elsewhere in Mesoamerican evolution were also present to some degree in the Quiché case. The importance of these "variables" for the specific Quiché case would appear to be as follows, in decreasing order:

frontier hybridization, warfare, religious integration, trade and symbiosis, population growth, and irrigation. The pressures for development represented by these variables impinged on the Quichés at different strengths, together and in sequence, and in feedback relationship with one another. It was the unique combination of these variables in the Quiché case that stimulated the general development of the state at Utatlán and gave it a specific character.

In 1524, when the Spaniards launched an all-out attack on the Utatlán community, the Quichés began a long war of cultural resistance. Despite substantial losses, they have managed to retain important fragments of their traditional patterns. In modern times, when even these fragments seem to be on the verge of succumbing to powerful modernizing forces, educated Quiché indigenes have begun looking back to their pre-Hispanic heritage. It is likely that Quiché culture will flourish again, this time as an ethnic symbol for political and social coalition. Perhaps such conscious revitalizing of a cultural tradition actually represents the end of that tradition and the beginning of a new one. Even should this prove to be the case, study of the Utatlán Quichés will undoubtedly go on, and not just to provide material for a revitalized culture. The Utatlán Quichés have much to teach us about cultural evolution in general and the specifics of one highly interesting manifestation of Maya civilization.

REFERENCES

Adams, R. M.
 1966 *The evolution of urban society: early Mesopotamia and Prehispanic Mexico*. Chicago: Aldine.
AE *Archivo Eclesiástico*. Documents cited by *municipio*, as Q *(Quiché)* and SP (San Pedro), and by year.
AGC Archivo General de Centroamérica, Guatemala. *A* refers to colonial documents, followed by *legajo* and *expediente* numbers.
AGEG Archivo General de la Escribanía del Gobierno, Guatemala. Documents cited by department and year.
AGI Archivo General de Indias, Seville, Spain. Documents cited by Audiencia de Guatemala number.
Alvarado, P. de
 1946 *Relación hecha por Pedro de Alvarado a Hernando Cortés (1524)*. Biblioteca de Autores Españoles, vol. 22. Madrid.
AM Archivo Municipal. Documents cited by *municipio*, as Q (Quiché), P (Patzite), and L (Lemoa), and by year.
Andrews, E. W.
 1943 *Archaeology of southwestern Campeche*. Carnegie Institution of Washington Contributions to American Anthropology and History, no. 40.
Annals See *The Annals of the Cakchiquels*.
Annals of the Cakchiquels
 1934 *Memorial de Tecpán-Atitlán*. Trans. J. Antonio Villacorta C. Guatemala.
Anonymous
 1934 *Libro Viejo de la fundación de Guatemala, y papeles relativos a don Pedro de Alvarado*. Biblioteca Goathemala, vol. 12.
 1935 *Isagoge histórica apologética de las indias occidentales*. Biblioteca Goathemala, vol. 8.
 1963 *La muerte de Tecún Umán: estudio crítico de la conquista del Altiplano Occidental de la República*. Guatemala: Editorial del Ejército.
Atlas Guatemalteco
 N.d. Maps commissioned by Jefe del Estado, C. Doctor Mariano Gálvez, and produced by M. Rivera Maestre, 1834. MS. Bibliothèque Nationale, Paris.

Avendaño y Loyola, A.
  1696   *Relation of two trips to Petén*. Trans. C. P. Bowditch. MS. Peabody Museum Library, Harvard University, Cambridge, Mass.
Balandier, G.
  1970   *Political anthropology*. Trans. A. M. Sheridan Smith. New York: Penguin Press.
Bancroft, H. H.
  1886   *History of Central America*. History of the Pacific States of North America, vol. 1 (1501–30). San Francisco.
Basseta, D. de
  N.d.   Vocabulario de lengua Quiché. Copy of MS. Tulane University Library, New Orleans.
Berendt, C. H.
  N.d.   Calendario de los Indios de Guatemala Kiché (1722). Copy of MS. University of Pennsylvania Museum Library, Philadelphia.
Berlin, H.
  1935   *Archaeological reconnaissance in Tabasco*. Carnegie Institution of Washington Current Reports, vol. 1.
Betanzos, P. de
  1967   Letter to the king in 1559. In P. Carrasco. Don Juan Cortés, cacique de Santa Cruz Quiché. *Estudios de cultura Maya* 6:251–66.
Bode, B. O.
  1961   *The dance of the conquest of Guatemala*. Middle American Research Institute Publication no. 30, pp. 205–93. New Orleans: Tulane University.
Borhegyi, S. F. de
  1963   Exploration in Lake Petén Itzá. *Archaeology* 16:14–24.
  1967   Archaeological synthesis of the Guatemalan highlands. In G. R. Willey, ed. *Handbook of Middle American Indians*, 2:3–58. Austin: University of Texas Press.
Brasseur de Bourbourg, C. E.
  1857   *Histoire des nations civilisées du Mexique et de l'Amérique Centrale*. 4 vols. Paris.
  1861   *Popol Vuh: le Livre Sacré et les mythes de l'antiquité americaine*. Paris.
  1862   *Grammaire de la langue Quichée et Rabinal-Achi*. Paris.
  1972   *Popol Vuh: el Libro Sagrado*. Trans. J. L. Arriola. Guatemala: Ministerio de Educación Pública.
Brinton, D. G.
  1881   *The names of the gods in the Kiché myths, Central America*. Philadelphia.
  1885   *The annals of the Cakchiquels*. Brinton's Library of Aboriginal American Literature. Philadelphia.
  1891   *American race*. Philadelphia.
  1893   *The native calendar of Central America and Mexico*. Philadelphia.
  1896   *The myths of the New World*. Philadelphia.
Brunius, S. G., and Whitehead, P. G.
  N.d.   Santa Rosa Chujuyup: a peasant society in highland Guatemala. MS. SUNY Albany, N.Y.
Bullard, W. R.
  1970   *Topoxté: A Postclassic Maya site in Petén, Guatemala*. Monographs and Papers in Maya Archaeology, Papers of the Peabody Museum of Ar-

chaeology and Ethnology, 61:245–308. Cambridge, Mass.: Harvard University.

Bunzel, R.
1952   *Chichicastenango*. American Ethnological Society Publication no. 22. New York: J. J. Augustin.

Calnek, E. E.
1976   The internal structure of Tenochtitlán. In E. R. Wolf, ed. *The Valley of Mexico: studies in pre-Hispanic ecology and society*. Albuquerque: University of New Mexico Press.

1977   Irrigation and the Aztec state [paraphrased title]. Paper read at American Anthropological Association Meeting, Houston, Texas.

Campbell, L. R.
1970   Nahua loan words in Quichean languages. *Chicago Linguistics Society* 6:3–11.

1976   Quichean prehistory: Linguistic considerations. MS. SUNY Albany, N.Y.

1977   *Quichean linguistic prehistory*. University of California Publications in Linguistics, vol. 81.

Carmack, R. M.
1965   The documentary sources, ecology, and culture history of pre-Hispanic Quiché-Maya of highland Guatemala. Ph.D. dissertation, University of California, Los Angeles.

1966   El Ajpop Quiché, K'uk'cumatz: un problema de la sociología historica. *Antropología e historia de Guatemala* 18:43–50.

1968   Toltec influence on the Postclassic culture history of highland Guatemala. *Archaeological Studies of Middle America*, Middle American Research Institute Publication no. 26, pp. 42–92. New Orleans: Tulane University.

1973   *Quichean civilization: the ethnohistoric, ethnographic, and archaeological source*. Berkeley: University of California Press.

1974   Agriculture in the Guatemalan western highlands. Report for Basic Village Education Program. MS. Guatemala.

1975   New Quichean chronicles from highland Guatemala. Paper read at Society for American Archaeology Meeting, Austin, Texas.

1976a   *La estratificación quicheana prehispánica: estratificación social en la Mesoamérica prehispánica*. Mexico City: Instituto Nacional de Antropología e Historia de México, pp. 245–77.

1976b   Estratificación y cambio social en las tierras altas occidentales de Guatemela: el caso de Tecpanaco. *América Indígena* 36:253–301.

N.d.   Ethnographic field notes from the central Quiché and Totonicapán areas, 1966–76. MS.

———; Fox, J. W.; and Stewart, R. E.
1975   *La formacion del reino quiche*. Instituto de Antropología e Historia de Guatemala Special Publication no. 7.

Carneiro, R. L.
1970   A theory of the origin of the state. *Science* 169:733–38.

1973   The four faces of evolution: unilinear, universal, multilinear, and differential. In J. J. Honigmann, ed. *Handbook of social and cultural anthropology*. Chicago: Rand, McNally.

References

1965   Archaeological synthesis of southern Veracruz and Tabasco. In G. R. Willey, ed. *Handbook of Middle American Indians*, 3:679–714. Austin: University of Texas Press.

1967   *The Maya*. New York: Frederick A. Praeger.

Conte, C.

N.d.   Traditional craft production in two Quichean *municipios* of highland Guatemala. MS. SUNY Albany, N.Y.

Contreras, R., J. D.

1951   *Una rebelión indígena en el partido de Totonicapán en 1820: el indio y la independencia*. Guatemala.

1965   El último cacique de la casa de Cavec. *Cuadernos de Antropología* 5:37–48.

Cortés, H.

1961   *Cartas de relación de la conquista de Mexico*. Mexico City; Espasa-Calpe Mexicana.

Cortés y Larraz, P.

1968   *Descripción geográfico-moral de la diócesis de Goathemala*. 2 vols. Biblioteca Goathemala, vol. 22.

Coto, T.

N.d.   Vocabulario de la lengua cakchiquel y guatemalteca (ca. 1690). Original MS. American Philosophical Society, Philadelphia.

Covarrubias, M.

1957   *Indian art of Mexico and Central America*. New York: Alfred A. Knopf.

Cowgill, G. L.

1963   Postclassic period cultures in the vicinity of Flores, Petén, Guatemala. 2 vols. Ph.D. dissertation, Harvard University.

Daly, C.

1865   Note: pouvant servir a l'exploration de anciens monuments du Mexique. *Archives de la Commission Scientifique du Mexique* 1:146–61.

Díaz del Castillo, B.

1933   Historia verdadera de la conquista de la Nueva España. Madrid: Espasa-Calpe.

Diccionario geográfico

1961–62   Diccionario geográfico de Guatemala. 2 vols. Guatemala: Dirección General de Cartografía.

Dutton, B. P., and Hobbs, H. R.

1943   *Excavations at Tajumulco, Guatemala*. School of American Research Monographs, no. 9. Albuquerque: University of New Mexico Press.

Earle, D. M.

N.d.   Ethnographic notes on Chinique. MS. SUNY Albany, N.Y.

Edmonson, M.

1964   Historia de las tierras altas mayas según los documentos indígenas. In E. Z. Vogt and A. L. Ruz, eds. *Desarrollo cultural de los Mayas*, pp. 255–78. Mexico City.

1965   *Quiché-English dictionary*. Middle American Research Institute publication no. 30. New Orleans: Tulane University.

1971   *The Book of Counsel: the Popol Vuh of the Quiché Maya of Guatemala*. Middle American Research Institute publication no. 35. New Orleans: Tulane University.

1976   Anthropology of the Quiché [paraphrased title]. Paper read at Quichean Conference, Institute for Mesoamerican Studies, Albany, N.Y.

Estrada, J. de
1955   Descripción de la provincia de Zapotitlán y Suchitepéquez. *Anales de la Sociedad de Geografía e Historia de Guatemala* 28:68–84.

Falla, R.
1970   La conversión religiosa como fenómeno sociológico. *Estudios sociales*, no. 2, pp. 8–32.
1971   Actitud de los indígenas de Guatemala en la época de la independencia, 1800–1850: el problema de los limites entre las comunidades indígenas de Santa María Chiquimula y San Antonio Ilotenango. *Estudios Centroamericános*, pp. 702–18.
1972   Hacia la revolución verde: adopción y dependencia del fertilizante químico en un municipio del Quiché, Guatemala. *América Indígena* 32:437–80.
1975   La conversión religiosa: estudio sobre un movimiento rebelde a las creencias tradicionales en San Antonio Ilotenango, Quiché, Guatemala. Ph.D. dissertation, University of Texas.

Flannery, K. V.
1972   The cultural evolution of civilizations. *Annual Review of Ecology and Systematics* 3:399–426.

Foshag, W. F.
1957   *Mineralogical studies of Guatemalan jade*. Smithsonian Institution Miscellaneous Collection, no. 135. Washington, D.C.

Fox, J. W.
1975   Centralism and regionalism: Quiché acculturation processes in settlement patterning. Ph.D. dissertation, SUNY Albany.
1977   Quiché expansion processes: differential ecological growth bases within an archaic state. in R. M. Carmack and D. T. Wallace, eds. *Archaeology and ethnohistory of the Central Quiché*. Institute for Mesoamerican Studies Publication no. 1, pp. 82–97. Albany, N.Y.

Fried, M. H.
1967   *The evolution of political society*. New York: Random House.

Fuentes y Guzmán, F. A. de
1932–33 Recordación Florida: discurso historial y demonstración natural, material, militar, y politica del reino de Guatemala. Biblioteca Goathemala, vols. 6–8.

Gall, F.
1963   *Título del Ajpop Huitzitzil Tzunún: probanza de méritos de los de León y Cardona*. Guatemala: Ministerio de Educación Pública.

Gibson, C.
1971   Structure of the Aztec Empire. In G. F. Eckholm and I. Bernal, eds. *Handbook of Middle American Indians*, 10:376–94. Austin: University of Texas Press.

Girard, R.
1952   *El Popol-Vuh: fuente histórica*. Guatemala: Ministerio de Educación Pública.
1966   *Los Mayas: su civilización, su historia, sus vinculaciones continentales*. Mexico City: Libro México.

Gluckman, M.
1963   *Custom and conflict in Africa*. Glencoe, Ill.: Free Press.
1965   *Politics, law, and ritual in tribal society*. Oxford: Basil Blackwell.

Goubaud Carrera, A.
  1949   Problemas etnológicos del Popol Vuh. *Antropología e Historia de Guatemala*, vol. 1.
Gruhn, R.
  1973   Observations in Chichicastenango in 1969. *Estudios de Cultura Maya* 9:231–56.
———, and Bryan, A. L.
  1976   An archaeological survey of the Chichicastenango area of highland Guatemala. *Cerámica de cultura Maya* 9:75–119.
Guillemin, J. F.
  1956   El Quiché y Gumarkaaj. *El Imparcial* (Guatemala), November 9, 1956.
  1958   La pirámide B-6 de Mixco Viejo y el sacrificatorio de Utatlán. *Antropología e Historia de Guatemala* 10:21–27.
  1959   Iximché. *Antropológia e historia de Guatemala* 11:22–64.
  1965   *Iximché: capital del Antiguo Reino Cakchiquel*. Publicaciones del Instituto de Antropológia e Historia de Guatemala.
  1967   The ancient Cakchiquel capital of Iximché. *Expedition* 9:22–35.
  1969   Exploración du Groupe C d'Iximché (Guatemala). *Bulletin de la Société Suisse des Americanistes* 33:23–33.
Harris, M.
  1965   *The rise of anthropological theory*. New York: Thomas Y. Crowell.
Haviland, W. A.
  1968   Ancient lowland Maya social organization. *Archaeological Studies in Middle America*, Middle American Research Institute Publication no. 26, pp. 93–118. New Orleans: Tulane University.
  1969   A new population estimate for Tikal, Guatemala. *American Antiquity* 34:429–33.
Hellmuth, N. M.
  1970   Progress report and notes on research on ethnohistory of the 16th–19th century southern lowland Maya. MS. Guatemala.
Herbert, J. L.
  1971   Una comunidad frente al capitalismo de una estructura colonial. *Revista Alero* 4:1. Guatemala: Universidad de San Carlos.
———, and Guzmán Bockler, C.
  1970   *Guatemala: una interpretación historico-social*. Mexico City.
Hicks, F.
  1976   Mayeque y calpuleque en el sistema de clases de México. In P. Carrasco, J. Broda, et al. *Estratificación social en la Mesoamerica prehispanica*. Mexico City: Centro de Investigaciones Superiores, Instituto Nacional de Antropología e Historia.
Ichon, A.
  1975   *Organización de un centro quiché protohistórico: Pueblo Viejo Chichaj*. Instituto de Antropología e Historia de Guatemala Special Publication no. 9.
IGN   Instituto Geográfico Nacional. 1:250,000 and 1:50,000 maps, published by year. Guatemala.
INAFOR   Instituto Nacional Forrestal. Unpublished maps on file at institute, Guatemala.
Jiménez Moreno, W.
  1942   El enigma de los Olmecas. *Cuadernos Americanos* 1:113–45.

Katz, F.
1966   *Situación social y económica de los Aztecas durante los siglos XV y XVI.* Mexico City: Instituto de Investigaciones Históricas, Universidad Nacional Autónoma de México.

Kaufman, T.
1964   Materiales lingüísticos para el estudio de las relaciones internas y externas de la familia de idiomas mayanos. In E. Z. Vogt and A. Ruz, eds. *Desarrollo cultural de los Mayas*, pp. 81–136. Mexico City: Universidad Nacional Autónoma de México.
1974   *Idiomas de Mesoamérica.* Seminario de Integración Social Guatemalteca Publication no. 33.
1976   New Mayan languages in Guatemala: Sacapultec, Sipacapa, and others. *Maya Linguistics* 1:67–89.

Kirchhoff, P.
1952   *Mesoamerica: heritage of conquest,* ed. S. Tax. Glencoe, Ill.: Free Press.
1955   The principles of clanship in human society. *Davidson Journal of Anthropology* (Seattle, Wash.).

Kuhn, T. S.
1962   *The structure of scientific revolutions.* Chicago: University of Chicago Press.

Las Cases, B. de
1909   *Apologética historia de las Indias.* 2 vols. Nueva Biblioteca de Autores Expañoles, vol. 13. Madrid.

Lehmann, W.
1911   Der Kalender der Quiché Indianer Guatemalas. *Anthropos* 6:403–10.

León, Juan de
N.d.   *El mundo Quiché.* Guatemala.

León-Portilla, M.
1963   *Aztec thought and culture: a study of the ancient Nahuatl mind.* Norman: University of Oklahoma Press.

Lopez Medel, T.
N.d.   Tratado cuyo título es de los tres elementos, aire, agua, y tierra . . . acerca de los occidentales Indios [ca. 1560]. Muños Collection of Documents, Real Academia de la Historia de Madrid, vol. 42.

Lothrop, S. K.
1933   *Atitlán: an archaeological study of ancient remains on the borders of Lake Atitlán, Guatemala.* Carnegie Institution of Washington Publication no. 44. Washington, D.C.
1936   *Zacualpa: a study of ancient Quiché artifacts.* Carnegie Institution of Washington Publication no. 472. Washington, D.C.

Lutz, C. H.
1976   Santiago de Guatemala, 1541–1773: the socio-demographic history of a Spanish American colonial city. Ph.D. dissertation, University of Wisconsin.

McBryde, F. W.
1947   *Cultural and historical geography of southwest Guatemala.* Smithsonian Institution, Institute of Social Anthropology, Publication no. 4. Washington, D.C.

MacLeod, M. J.
1973   *Spanish Central America: a socioeconomic history, 1520–1720.* Berkeley: University of California Press.

Mantz, B.
    N.d.   Investigación etnográfica de Santa Cruz del Quiché. MS, SUNY Albany, N.Y.

Marqusee, S. J.
    N.d.   Mixteca-Puebla trade and styles in Guatemala. Paper read at the 41st International Congress of Americanists Meeting, Mexico City, 1974.

Martínez P., S.
    1970   *La patria del Criollo: ensayo de interpretación de la realidad colonial Guatemalteca*. Guatemala: Editorial Universitaria.
    1973   Los motines de indios en el periodo colonial Guatemalteco. Paper read at Primer Congreso Centroamericano de Historia Demográfica, Económica, y Social, Costa Rica.

Maudslay, A. P.
    1899   *A glimpse at Guatemala and some notes on the ancient monuments of Central America*. London.

Miles, S. W.
    1952   An analysis of modern Middle American calendars: a study in conservation. In S. Tax, ed. *Acculturation in the Americas*. Proceedings and Selected Papers of the 29th International Congress of Americanists. Chicago: University of Chicago Press.
    1957   The sixteenth-century Pokom-Maya: a documentary analysis of social structure and archaeological setting. *Transactions of the American Philosophical Society* 47:731–81.
    1965   Summary of pre-Conquest ethnology of the Guatemala-Chiapas highlands and Pacific slopes. In G. R. Willey, ed. *Handbook of Middle American Indians*, 2:276–87.

Milla, J. (Salomé Jil)
    1937   *Historia de la América Central*. Vol. 1. Guatemala.

Molina, A. de
    1943   Vocabulario en lengua castellana y mexicana (1571). Mexico City: Editorial Porrúa.

Monzon, A.
    1949   *El calpulli en la organización social de los tenochca*. Mexico City: Instituto de Historia, Universidad Nacional Autónoma de México.

Motul
    1929   *Diccionario de Motul, maya-español, atribuida a Fray Antonio de Ciudad Real y arte de la lengua maya* [16th century]. Ed. J. Martínez Hernández. Mérida.

Nash, M.
    1958   Political relations in Guatemala. *Social and Economic Studies* 7:65–75.

Nicholson, H. B.
    1957   Topiltzin Quetzalcoatl of Tollan: a problem in Meosamerican ethnohistory. Ph.D. dissertation, Harvard University.
    1969   Pre-Hispanic central Mexican historiography. Paper read at Mesa Redonda Meetings, Oaxtepec, Mexico.
    1971   Religion in Pre-Hispanic Central Mexico. In G. F. Eckholm and I. Bernal, eds. *Handbook of Middle American Indians*, 10:395–446. Austin: University of Texas Press.
    1976   The Quiché and Aztecs compared [paraphrased title]. Paper read at Quichean Conference, Albany, N.Y.

Paez Betancour, A. P., and Arboleda, P. de
    1965   Descripción de San Bartolomé, del partido de Atitlán (1585). *Anales de la*

Sociedad de Geografía e Historia de Guatemala 38:262–76.

Palerm, A.
1955   The agricultural basis of urban civilization in Mesoamerica. In J. H. Steward, ed. *Irrigation civilizations: a comparative study*. Pan American Union, Social Science Monographs, no. 1, pp. 28–42. Washington, D.C.

Parson, L. A., and Price, B. J.
1971   Mesoamerican trade and its role in the emergence of civilization. In R. F. Heizer and J. A. Graham, eds. *Observations on the emergence of civilization in Mesoamerica*. Department of Anthropology Publication no. 11, pp. 169–95. Berkeley: University of California.

Pollock, H. E. D.
1936   *Round structures of aboriginal Middle America*. Carnegie Institution of Washington Publication no. 471. Washington, D.C.
1965   Architecture of the Maya lowlands. In G. R. Willey, ed. *Handbook of Middle American Indians*, 2:378–440. Austin: University of Texas Press.

———; Roys, R. L.; Proskouriakoff, T.; and Smith, A. L.
1962   Mayapán, Yucatán, Mexico. Carnegie Institution of Washington Publication no. 619. Washington, D.C.

Popol Vuh
1861   *Popol Vuh: le Livre Sacré et les mythes de l'antiquité américaine*. Trans. C. E. Brasseur de Bourbourg. Paris.
1950   *Popol Vuh: the Sacred Book of the ancient Quiché Maya*. Trans. A. Recinos, D. Goetz, and S. G. Morley. Norman: University of Oklahoma Press.
1962   *Popol Vuh de Diego Reinoso*. Trans. J. Antonio Villacorta C. Guatemala: Ministerio de Educación Pública.
1971   *The Book of Counsel: The Popol Vuh of the Quiché Maya of Guatemala*. Trans. M. S. Edmonson. Middle American Research Institute Publication no. 35. New Orleans: Tulane University.

Press, I.
1975   *Tradition and adaptation: life in a modern Yucatan Maya village*. Westport, Conn.: Greenwood Press.

Proskouriakoff, T.
1962   Civic and religious structures of Mayapan. In H. E. D. Pollock, R. L. Roys, T. Proskouriakoff, and A. L. Smith. *Mayapán, Yucatán, Mexico*. Carnegie Institution of Washington Publication no. 619. Washington, D.C.
1965   Sculpture and major arts of the Maya lowlands. In G. R. Willey, ed. *Handbook of Middle American Indians*, 2:469–97. Austin: University of Texas Press.

Rabinal Achi
1955   *Teatro indígena prehispánico: Rabinal Achi*. Trans. F. Monterde. Mexico City: Universidad Nacional Autónoma.

Rands, R. L., and Smith, R. E.
1965   Pottery of the Guatemalan highlands. In G. R. Willey, ed. *Handbook of Middle American Indians*, 2:95–114. Austin: University of Texas Press.

Rathje, W. L.
1971   The origin and development of lowland Classic Maya civilization. *American Antiquity* 36:275–85.

———, and Sabloff, J. A.
1975a   The rise of a Maya merchant class. *Scientific American* 233:73–82.

1975b   *Changing Pre-Columbian commercial systems: the 1972–1973 seasons at Cozumel, Mexico.* Monographs of the Peabody Museum, no. 3. Cambridge, Mass.: Harvard University.

Recinos, A.
1950   *Popol Vuh: the Sacred Book of the ancient Quiché Maya.* Trans. D. Goetz and S. G. Morley. Norman: University of Oklahoma Press.
1953   *The Annals of the Cakchiquels.* Trans. D. Goetz and S. G. Morley. Norman: University of Oklahoma Press.
1957   *Crónicas indígenas de Guatemala.* Guatemala: Editorial Universitaria.
1958   *Doña Leonor de Alvarado y otros estudios.* Guatemala: Editorial Universitaria.

Remesal, A. de
1932   *Historia general de las indias occidentales, y particular de la gobernación de Chiapa y Guatemala.* 2 vols. Biblioteca Goathemala, vols. 4, 5.

Rivera y Maestre, M.
1834   *Atlas guatemalteco en ocho cartas formadas y grabadas en Guatemala.* Guatemala.

Rodas N., F., and Rodas C., O.
1938   Simbolismos (maya-quichés) de Guatemala. Guatemala.

Roys, R. L.
1943   *The Indian background of colonial Yucatán.* Carnegie Institution of Washington Publication no. 548. Washington, D.C. New ed. Norman: University of Oklahoma Press, 1972.
1957   *The political geography of the Yucatán Maya.* Carnegie Institution of Washington Publication no. 613. Washington, D.C.
1962   Literary sources for the history of Mayapan. In H. E. D. Pollock, R. L. Roys, T. Proskouriakoff, and A. L. Smith. *Mayapán Yucatán, Mexico.* Carnegie Institution of Washington Publication no. 619, pp. 23–86. Washington, D.C.
1966   Native empires in Yucatán. *Revista mexicana de estudios antropológicos* 20:153–75.

Saenz de Santa María, C.
1940   *Diccionario Cakchiquel-Español.* Guatemala: Tipografía Nacional.

Sahagún, B. de
1959–63   *Florentine Codex: general history of the things of New Spain.* Trans. C. E. Dibble and A. J. O. Anderson. Monographs of the School of American Research and the Museum of New Mexico. 13 vols. Albuquerque, N. Mex.

Sahlins, M. D.
1961   The segmentary lineage: an organization of predatory expansion. *American Anthropologist* 63:332–45.
———, and Service, E. R.
1960   *Evolution and culture.* Ann Arbor: University of Michigan Press.

Sanders, W. T.
1965   *The cultural ecology of the Teotihuacán Valley: a preliminary report of the results of the Teotihuacán Valley project.* University Park: Pennsylvania State University.
1971   Settlement patterns in central Mexico. In G. F. Eckholm and I. Bernal, eds. *Handbook of Middle American Indians*, 10:3–44. Austin: University of Texas Press.

————, and Price, B. J.
1968 *Mesoamerica: the evolution of a civilization*. New York: Random House.
Scherzer, K.
1856 *Die Indianer von Santa Catalina Istlavacan*. Vienna.
1857 *Las historias del origen de los indios de esta provincia de Guatemala: traducidas de la lengua quiché al castellano por F. Ximénez*. London: Trubner and Co.
1967 *Notes on Escolios a las historias del origen de los indios (F. Ximénez)*. Sociedad de Geografía e Historia de Guatemala Special Publication no. 13. Guatemala.
Scholes, F. V., and Roys, R. L.
1968 *The Maya Chontal Indians of Acalán-Tixchel: a contribution to the history and ethnography of the Yucatán Peninsula*. Norman: University of Oklahoma Press.
Schultze-Jena, L.
1933 *Leban, Glaube, und Sprache der Quiché von Guatemala*. Jena: Gustav Fischer.
1944 *Popol Vuh: Das heilige Buch der Quiché Indianer von Guatemala*. Stuttgart.
1947 *La vida y las creencias de los indígenas Quichés de Guatemala*. Guatemala: Ministerio de Educación Pública.
Seler, E.
1960 *Gesammelte Abhandlungen zur americanischen Sprach- und Alterumskunde*. Vols. 1–5. Graz.
Service, E. R.
1962 *Primitive social organization*. New York: Random House.
1975 *Origins of the state and civilization*. New York: Norton.
Shaw, M., ed.
1971 *According to our ancestors: folklore texts from Guatemala and Honduras*. Guatemala: Summer Institute of Linguistics.
Sherman, W. L.
1969 A conqueror's wealth: notes on the estate of don Pedro de Alvarado. *Americas* 26:199–213.
Silva L., S.
N.d. *La conquista de Utatlán: drama histórica, escrito bajo el plan de un antiguo manuscrito de cuyo original se conservan los nombres y locuciones indígenas, y se refiere al año de 1524*. Guatemala [ca. 1887].
Simmons, C. S.; Tarano T., J. M.; and Pinto Z., J. H.
1959 *Clasificación de reconocimiento de los suelos de la República de Guatemala*. Guatemala: Ministerio de Agricultura.
Smith, A. L.
1955 *Archaeological reconnaissance in central Guatemala*. Carnegie Institution of Washington Publication no. 608. Washington, D.C.
Smith, R. E.
1971 *The pottery of Mayapán*. Papers of the Peabody Museum of Archaeology and Ethnology, vol. 61. Cambridge, Mass.: Harvard University.
Soustelle, J.
1962 *The daily life of the Aztecs on the eve of the Spanish conquest*. New York: Macmillan.
Spence, L.
1908 *The mythic and heroic sagas of the Kichés of Central America*. London: David Nutt.

Stearns, S.
N.d.   Summary of agricultural information, *municipio* of Santa Cruz del Quiché, Guatemala. MS, SUNY Albany, N.Y.

Stephens, J. L.
1841   *Incidents of travel in Central America, Chiapas, and Yucatán.* 2 vols. New York: Harper. New ed. *Incidents of Travel in Yucatán.* Norman University of Oklahoma Press, 1962.

Stewart, R. E.
1975   The cultural history of the early Quiché kingdom in the Santa Cruz del Quiché Basin. Master's thesis, SUNY Albany, N.Y.
1977   Classic to Postclassic period settlement trends in the region of Santa Cruz del Quiché. In R. M. Carmack and D. T. Wallace, eds. *Archaeology and ethnohistory of the central Quiché.* Institute for Mesoamerican Studies Publication no. 1, pp. 68–81. Albany, N.Y.

Stoll, O.
1886   *Guatemala: Reisen und Schilderungen aud den Jahren 1878–1883.* Leipzig.
1889   *Die Etnologie der Indianerstamme von Guatemala.* Leyden: P. W. M. Trap.

Tax, S.
1947   Notes on Santo Tomás Chichicastenango. Microfilm Collection of Manuscripts in Middle American Cultural Anthropology, no. 16. University of Chicago Library, Chicago.

———, and Hinshaw, R.
1969   The Maya of the midwestern highlands. In E. Z. Vogt, ed. *Handbook of Middle American Indians*, 7:69–100. Austin: University of Texas Press.

Termer, F.
1957   *Etnología y etnografía de Guatemala.* Seminario de Integración Social Guatemalteca Publication no. 5.

Thompson, Sir J. E. S.
1938   Sixteenth- and seventeenth-century reports on the Chol Mayas. *American Anthropologist* 40:584–604.
1943   A trial survey of the southern Maya area. *American Antiquity* 9:106–34.
1954   *The rise and fall of Maya civilization.* Norman: University of Oklahoma Press.
1957   *Deities portrayed on censers at Mayapán.* Carnegie Institution of Washington Current Reports, no. 40.
1960   *Maya hieroglyphic writing: an introduction.* Norman: University of Oklahoma Press.
1966   Merchant gods of Middle America. *Summa Antropológica*, pp. 159–72.
1970   *Maya history and religion.* Norman: University of Oklahoma Press.
1977   A proposal for constituting a Maya subgroup, cultural and linguistic, in the Petén and adjacent regions. In G. D. Jones, ed. *Anthropology and history in Yucatán.* Austin: University of Texas Press.

Título C'oyoi
1973   A case study: Título C'oyoi (ca. 1550–1570). Trans. R. M. Carmack. In R. M. Carmack. *Quichean civilization: the ethnohistoric ethnographic, and archaeological sources*, pp. 265–345. Berkeley: University of California Press.

Título Nijaib
1957a   Título de la casa Izquín Nehaib, señora del territorio de Otzoya (ca. 1550–60). Trans. A. Recinos. In A. Recinos. *Crónicas indígenas de*

Guatemala, pp. 71–96. Guatemala: Editorial Universitaria.
1957b   Título real de don Francisco Izquín Nehaib (1558). Trans. A. Recinos. In A. Recinos. *Crónicas indígenas de Guatemala*, pp. 97–120. Guatemala: Editorial Universitaria.
Título Santa Clara
1957   Título del pueblo de Santa Clara la Laguna (1583). Trans. A. Recinos. In A. Recinos. *Crónicas indígenas de Guatemala*, pp. 171–81. Guatemala: Editorial Universitaria.
Título Tamub
1957   Historia Quiché de don Juan de Torres (1580). Trans. A. Recinos. In A. Recinos. *Crónicas indígenas de Guatemala*, pp. 25–70. Guatemala: Editorial Universitaria.
Título Totonicapán
1953   Title of the Lords of Totonicapán. Trans. D. J. Chonay and D. Goetz. In *The Annals of the Cakchiquels* (trans. A. Recinos and D. Goetz) [and] *Title of the Lords of Totonicapán*. Norman: University of Oklahoma Press.
N.d.   Original Quiché of the Título de los Señores de Totonicapán. 31 fols. Copy of MS, R. M. Carmack, SUNY Albany, N.Y.
Título Xpantzay
1957a   Guerras comunes de Quichés y Cakchiqueles (ca. 1550–60). Trans. A. Recinos. In A. Recinos. *Crónicas indígenas de Guatemala*, pp. 132–49. Guatemala: Editorial Universitaria.
1957b   Historia de los Xpantzay de Tecpán (ca. 1550–60). Trans. A. Recinos. In A. Recinos. *Crónicas indígenas de Guatemala*, pp. 120–29. Guatemala: Editorial Universitaria.
1957c   Testamento de los Xpantzay (1554). Trans. by A. Recinos. In A. Recinos. *Crónicas indígenas de Guatemala*, pp. 152–69. Guatemala: Editorial Universitaria.
Título Zapotitlán
1950   Paper concerning the origin of the Lords. In *Popol Vuh: the Sacred Book of the ancient Quiché Maya*. Trans. A. Recinos. Norman: University of Oklahoma Press.
Torquemada, J. de
1943   *Monarquía indiana*. 3 vols. Mexico City.
Tovilla, M. A.
1960   *Relación histórica descriptiva de las provincias de la Verapaz y de la del Manche (1635)*. Guatemala: Editorial Universitaria.
Vázquez, F.
1937–44   *Crónica de la provincia del Santísimo Nombre de Jesús de Guatemala de la Orden de Nuestra Seráfico Padre San Francisco (1714–1717)*. Biblioteca Goathemala, vols. 14–17.
Veblen, T. T.
1975   The ecological, cultural, and historical bases of forest preservation in Totonicapán, Guatemala. Ph.D. dissertation, University of California, Berkeley.
Vico, D. de
N.d.   Vocabulario de la lengua cakchiquel y quiché (ca. 1555). MS. copy in Newberry Library, Chicago.
Villacorta, J. A.
1934   *Memorial de Tecpán Atitlán (Anales de los Cakchiqueles)*. Guatemala:

References

Sociedad de Geografía e Historia de Guatemala.
1962   *Popol Vuh*. Guatemala: Ministerio de Educación Pública.

———, and Rodas N., F.
1927   *Arqueología guatemalteca*. Guatemala.

Villa Rojas, A.
1964   Patrones culturales Mayas antiguos y modernos en las comunidades contemporaneas de Yucatán. In E. Z. Vogt and A. Ruz L. *Desarrollo cultural de los Mayas*, pp. 354–85. Mexico City: Universidad Nacional Autónoma de México.

Wallace, D. T.
1977   An intra-site locational analysis of Utatlán: the structure of an urban site. In R. M. Carmack and D. T. Wallace, eds. *Archaeology and ethnohistory of the central Quiché*. Institute for Mesoamerican Studies Publication no. 1, pp. 20–54. SUNY Albany, N.Y.

———, and Carmack, R. M., eds.
1977   *Archaeology and ethnohistory of the central Quiche*. Institute for Mesoamerican Studies Publication no. 1. Albany, N.Y.

Wauchope, R.
1947   An approach to the Maya correlation problem through Guatemala highland archaeology and native annals. *American Antiquity* 13:59–66.

1948   *Excavations at Zacualpa, Guatemala*. Middle American Research Institute Publication no. 14. New Orleans: Tulane University.

1949   Las edades de Utatlán e Iximché. *Antropología e Historia de Guatemala* 1:10–22.

1965   *They found the buried cities*. Chicago: University of Chicago Press.

1970   *Protohistoric pottery of the Guatemala highlands*. Monographs and Papers in Maya Archaeology, Papers of the Peabody Museum of Archaeology and Ethnology, 61:89–245. Cambridge, Mass.: Harvard University.

1975   *Zacualpa, El Quiché, Guatemala: an ancient provincial center of the highland Maya*. Middle American Research Institution Publication no. 39. New Orleans: Tulane University.

Weaver, M. P.
1972   *The Aztecs, Maya, and their predecessors: archaeology of Mesoamerica*. New York: Seminar Press.

Webb, M. C.
1975   The flag follows trade: an essay on the necessary interaction of military and commercial factors in state formation. In J. A. Sabloff and C. C. Lamberg-Karlovsky, eds. *Ancient civilization and trade*. Albuquerque: University of New Mexico Press.

Weeks, J. M.
1975   *The archaeology of greater Utatlán: El Resguardo and Pakaman excavations*. Master's thesis, SUNY Albany.

White, L. A.
1945   History, evolutionism, and functionalism: three types of interpretation of culture. *Southwestern Journal of Anthropology* 1:221–48.

Willey, G. R.
1962   The early great styles and the rise of the pre-Columbian civilizations. *American Anthropologist* 44:1–14.

1971   Commentary on the emergence of civilization in the Maya lowlands. In R. F. Heizer and J. A. Graham, eds. *Observations on the emergence of civilization in Mesoamerica*. Department of Anthropology Publication no. 11, pp. 97–111. Berkeley: University of California.

———, and Bullard, W. R.

1965   Prehistoric settlement patterns in the Maya lowlands. In G. R. Willey, ed. *Handbook of Middle American Indians*, 2:360–77.

———; Eckholm, G. F.; and Millon, R. F.

1964   The patterns of farming life and civilization. In Robert Wauchope, ed. *Handbook of Middle American Indians*, 1:446–500.

Wolf, E. R.

1959   *Sons of the shaking earth*. Chicago: University of Chicago Press.

Woodbury, R. B., and Trik, A. S.

1953   *The ruins of Zaculeu, Guatemala*. 2 vols. Richmond, Va.: William Byrd Press.

Ximénez, F.

1929   *Historia de la provincia de San Vincente de Chiapa y Guatemala*. Vol. 1. Biblioteca Goathemala, vol. 1.

1931   *Historia de la provincia de San Vincente de Chiapa y Guatemala*. Vol. 3. Biblioteca Goathemala, vol. 3.

1967   *Escolios a las historias de origen de los indios*. Sociedad de Geografía e Historia de Guatemala Special Publication no. 13.

N.d.   Primera parte de el tesoro de las lenguas K'ak'chiquel, Quiché, y Tz'utujil. MS. Bancroft Library, Berkeley, Calif.

Zorita, A. de

1941   *Breve y sumaria relación de los señores . . . en la Nueva Espana*. Mexico City: Editorial Salvador Chávez Hayhoe.

Index